LEAVING CERTIFICATE POLITICS AND SOCIETY

POWER AND PEOPLE

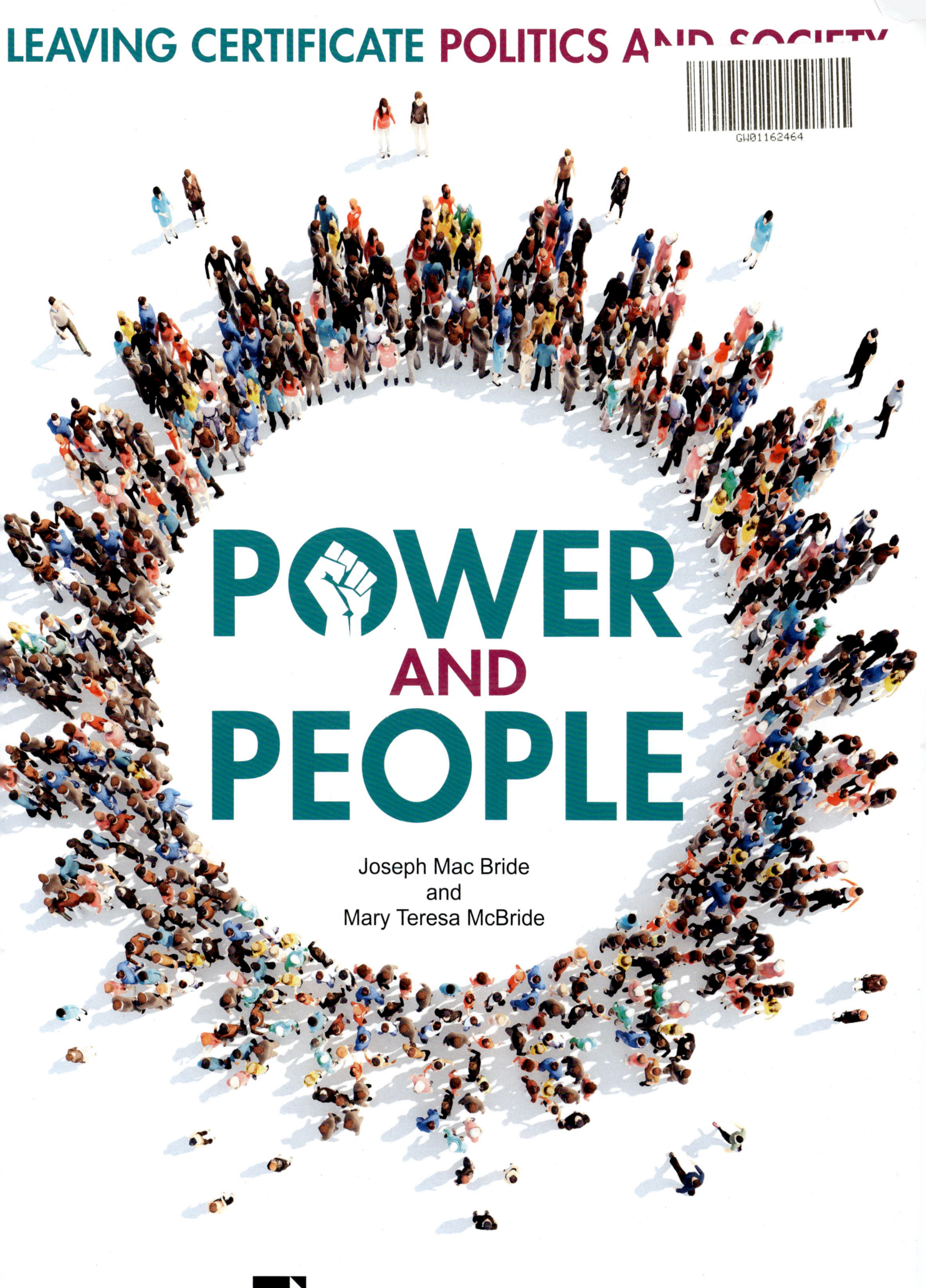

Joseph Mac Bride
and
Mary Teresa McBride

educate.ie

educate.ie

PUBLISHED BY:
Educate.ie
Walsh Educational Books Ltd
Castleisland, Co. Kerry, Ireland
www.educate.ie

PRINTED AND BOUND BY:
Walsh Colour Print, Castleisland

Copyright © Joseph Mac Bride and Mary Teresa McBride 2018

Without limiting the rights under copyright, this book is sold subject to the condition that it shall not, by way of trade or otherwise, be reproduced, stored in or introduced into a retrieval system, or transmitted, in any form or by any means (electronic, mechanical, photocopying, recording or otherwise), or otherwise circulated, without the publisher's prior consent, in any form other than that in which it is published and without a similar condition, including this condition, being imposed on the subsequent publisher. The author and publisher have made every effort to trace all copyright holders, but if some have been inadvertently overlooked, we would be happy to make the necessary arrangements at the first opportunity.

Web links were active and contained relevant information at the time of going to press. URLs and content may change beyond our control. Educate.ie does not accept responsibility for the views or opinions contained on third-party websites. Students should be supervised when visiting third-party websites.

ISBN: 978-1-910936-91-7

ACKNOWLEDGEMENTS

This textbook would not have been completed without the invaluable contributions of our many collaborators, who have expertise across a range of disciplines: politics, sociology, economics, human rights, social justice, women's rights and gender equality, media studies, environment and sustainable development, and development education. In particular, we would like to thank the following.

ActionAid Ireland
An Taisce
Barnardos
Central Statistics Office
Mr Filip Czuk
Dublin City University
Debt and Development Coalition Ireland
Department of Housing, Planning and Local Government
DevelopmentEducation.ie
Dr Nat O'Connor (Ulster University)
ECO-UNESCO
Educate Together
Economic and Social Research Institute
Europa Teachers' Corner
Fairtrade Ireland
Father Sean McDonagh (SCC)
Houses of the Oireachtas Service
Immigrant Council of Ireland
Irish Aid
Irish Second-Level Students' Union
Mr Peadar Kirby (Cloughjordan Ecovillage)
Professor Gail McElroy (TCD)
Northern Ireland Assembly Education Service
Ms Elham Osman
The Political Studies Association
Professor Kevin Rafter (DCU)
Think-tank for Action on Social Change
Trinity College Dublin (Department of Political Science)
Trócaire
Mr Senan Turnbull (TASC)
UPLIFT.ie
Youth Work Ireland
Mr Hans Zomer (Áras an Uachtaráin)

Contents

Chapter 1 **Framing Our Ideas about Politics and Society**
Introduction 1
What is Politics? 2
Political Spectrum: Left or Right? 4
Political Ideologies 4
What is Society? 11
Key Political and Social Thinkers: Past and Present 14
The Politics and Society Course 27

Chapter 2 **Power and Decision-Making in School**
Introduction 37
The Need for Rules in Schools 39
The Role of Education in Society 41
Where Do School Rules Come From? 48
The Power to Make Rules 49
Participation and Power in Decision-Making in Schools 52
How are Rules Enforced? 60
Do All Rules Affect Everyone Equally? 62
Discrimination 64

Chapter 3 **Political Representation**
Introduction 69
Types of Government 71
Political Representation and the Right to Participate
   in a Democracy 74
Groups in Society 77
Social Stratification in Ireland 80
Representation Through Civil Society Bodies 85
Representation Through Political Parties 87
Voting Patterns 89
Voting Patterns in Ireland 90

Chapter 4 — Selecting Our Representatives

Introduction 94
Political Representation Through Government
    Institutions 97
The Oireachtas 102
The Executive: Taoiseach and Government 113
The Courts 116
Government in Northern Ireland 117
The Northern Ireland Assembly 118
The Northern Ireland Executive 119
European Union 124
European Parliament: The Voice of the People 125
Council of the European Union: The Ministers of the
    Member States 128
European Commission: Executive Body of the EU 130
Electoral Systems and Issues of Representation 132

Chapter 5 — Policy-making

Introduction 141
Policies: The 'Fruits of Government Decision-Making' 143
Decision-Makers and Influencers:
    Who Makes Our Policies and Laws? 150
Decision-Makers 151
Influencers 155
The Policy-Making Process 161
The Law-Making Process 162
Primary Legislation 162
Secondary Legislation 171
Citizen Participation in Decision-Making 173
Citizen Voice in Irish Policy-Making 175

Chapter 6: The Role of the Media

Introduction	185
What is the Media?	187
Media Consumption Patterns	189
Media Consumption: Social Media and the News	191
The Role of the Media in Society	194
The Power and Influence of the Media	197
Media Stereotyping	205
The Rights and Responsibilities of the Media in a Democracy	208
Social Responsibility and Accountability	210
Ownership and Control of the Media	213
Who Controls Media Content?	215
Modern Trends and Debates on Media Ownership and Control	224
Growing Concentration of Media Ownership	224
The Rise of Social Media and Citizen Journalism	227

Chapter 7: Human Rights and Responsibilities in Ireland

Introduction	234
What are Human Rights?	236
Types of Human Rights	241
Human Rights Principles	242
Rights Holders and Duty Bearers	246
The Nature of Duty Bearer Obligations	247
Human Right in Focus: The Right to Education in Ireland	249
The Right to Education: Equality and Non-discrimination	254
Discrimination in Education: Ireland and Northern Ireland	258
How are Human Rights Monitored and Protected?	259
Reporting to the United Nations	261

Chapter 8	**Human Rights and Responsibilities in Europe and Beyond**	
	Introduction	269
	The Rights of the Child Around the World	271
	Global Implementation of the UNCRC	273
	The Right to Survival and Development: Article 6	275
	The Right to Freedom of Thought, Conscience and Religion: Article 14	281
	The Right to Protection from Abuse and Neglect: Article 19	284
	The Right to Rest, Leisure and Play: Article 31	288
	Human Rights in Europe	292
	Human Rights Debates in the Wider World	295
	Human Rights in the Wider World	298
	Global Poverty and Development	300
	A Matter of Human Rights: The Right to Development	302
	UN Declaration on the Right to Development	303
	International Cooperation	305

Chapter 9	**Identity in a Global Age**	
	Introduction	312
	Identity and Culture	314
	National Identities on the Island of Ireland	320
	Diversity and Cultural Change	338
	Diversity in the European Union: United in Diversity	347
	Ethnic Identity: A Source of Community or Conflict?	355
	Identity and Culture in a Global Age: Key Debates	359
	Globalisation of Politics and Decision-making	363

Chapter 10	**Global Development**	
	Introduction	371
	What is Development?	372
	Unsustainable Development	376
	Unequal Development	383
	Theories of Development	386
	Corruption	402

Chapter 11 — Sustainable Development

- Introduction 409
- What is Sustainable Development? 411
- Solutions to our Environmental Problems 415
- Taking Action for a Sustainable Future 440
- Fairtrade 449
- Tax Justice: Debt and Development Coalition Ireland (DDCI) 451

Appendix — Additional Information on Political and Social Thinkers 458

Index 466

Icons Used in this Textbook

	The **Learning Intentions** box appears at the start of each chapter and states clearly what you will have learned by the end of the chapter, and how you will be able to demonstrate this.
	This icon indicates a **Key Term**. The Key Terms boxes provide clear definitions of all the key terms and ideas in the Politics and Society course.
	This icon indicates a **Key Thinkers** box. The Key Thinkers boxes explain the ideas and views of important political and social thinkers on the issues arising in the textbook.
	This icon indicates a **Cross-reference** to another part of this book.
	This icon indicates that you will take part in a **Think–Pair–Share** exercise with a partner.
	This icon indicates that you will take part in a **Group Work** activity.
	This icon indicates that you will engage in **Jigsaw Learning** with other groups in your class.
	This icon indicates that you will take part in a **Moving Debate** or a **Traditional Debate**.
	This icon indicates a **Research Assignment** in which you will conduct your own research into a set topic or issue.
	This icon indicates **Exercise Questions** and **Revision Questions** which assess your knowledge and understanding of content. This will help prepare you for the short-answer questions in Section A of the Leaving Certificate examination.
	This icon is included at the end of each chapter and indicates that you should complete the end of chapter **Fill in the blanks** revision exercise in the Skills Book.
	This icon is included at the end of each chapter and indicates that you should complete the end of chapter **Crossword** exercise in the Skills Book.
	This icon appears beside important pieces of **Research Data** in each chapter. You will be expected to examine and critically evaluate various extracts of qualitative and quantitative research data in each chapter. It also appears at the end of each chapter to indicate when to complete each Data-Based Question in the Skills Book. This will prepare you for Section B of the Leaving Certificate examination.
	This icon appears beside sample **Discursive Essay Topics** that could be asked in Section C of the Leaving Certificate.
	This icon appears beside questions that have been designed to prepare students for Sections A, B or C of the Leaving Certificate exam.
	This icon indicates that you should use the Skills Book to help you complete a **Reflective Journal** entry. Your Reflective Journal will help you to think about what you are learning, and to reflect on how you can relate this learning to your own life experiences and opinions.
	This icon indicates that you should use the Skills Book to help you develop your personal **Learning Portfolio**. This will help you to self-assess the extent to which you have achieved the learning intentions for each chapter, and assist you in identifying the areas where you can improve.
	This icon indicates an end-of-chapter **Summary**. The Summary boxes provide concise summaries of the most important points learned in each chapter.

CHAPTER 1
Framing Our Ideas about Politics and Society

'If I have seen further than others, it is by standing upon the shoulders of giants.' Isaac Newton

KEY TERMS

- Politics
- Political spectrum
- Ideology
- Left
- Right
- Capitalism
- Socialism
- Liberalism
- Conservatism
- Communism
- Marxism
- Neo-Marxism
- Laissez-faire
- Fascism
- Xenophobia
- Libertarianism
- Feminism
- Social stratification
- Social class
- Structural functionalism
- Social conflict theory
- Symbolic interactionism
- Democracy
- Enlightenment
- Deliberative democracy
- Dialogue
- Debate
- Active listening
- Qualitative data
- Quantitative data

Introduction

The Politics and Society course is about equipping us with the skills and knowledge to engage in critical reflection, research and analysis, and to make informed opinions and arguments on social and political issues that affect our national, European and global societies. As Greek philosopher Aristotle famously said: 'Man is by nature a political animal.' We live, breathe and experience politics in our everyday lives, whether that is in our schools, our families or our communities. We all have views, ideas and opinions on our society. However, what does it mean to have an informed opinion, to make evidence-based arguments, and to frame our ideas with political and sociological concepts and theories? Why is that important? Chapter 1 will introduce us to important tools we will use throughout the course when we look at different political and social issues (e.g. power, human rights, globalisation, multiculturalism) and institutions (e.g. Dáil, Seanad, EU). We will look at the concept of the **political spectrum** and the different **ideologies** of 'the **left**' and 'the **right**'. We will engage with the ideas and arguments of some of the 'big thinkers' of politics and sociology – past and present. These theorists have done much thinking and research in relation to big issues concerning politics and society. We may agree with some, and not with others, but making use of these concepts and ideas helps us to organise and present our own ideas and arguments in a considered way. In Chapter 1 we will also explore the five key skills that are central to learning at Senior Cycle and are integral to the learning intentions for Politics and Society. We will see how the skills-based active learning activities in this book develop the five key skills.

KEY TERMS

Political spectrum is the term used to describe a system for classifying one's political position. Traditionally, the political spectrum runs between the **left** and **right**.

An **ideology** is a set of common ideas and beliefs. It can be religious, social, political, economic or cultural and it often details a particular view or understanding of something (e.g. society) and a desired future plan for how it should be.

By the end of this chapter you will be able to:
- Define politics.
- Explain the political spectrum and identify the main ideologies that constitute left and right.
- Outline the main characteristics of left-wing and right-wing political views.
- Summarise the main beliefs of key political ideologies, such as: communism, socialism, Marxism, neo-Marxism, liberalism, libertarianism, conservatism, feminism and religious fundamentalism.
- Define society, and explain the different ways in which society can be viewed and classified.
- Explain social stratification and describe the three main theories on it.
- Explain the main ideas of key thinkers (e.g. Hobbes, Locke, Rousseau, Mill) on the purpose of government and the balance between individual freedom and liberty, and security and order.
- Outline the main beliefs of Karl Marx and Kathleen Lynch.
- List and describe the five key skills that you will learn and develop in the Politics and Society course.
- Understand the different types of student-centred, active learning activities used frequently in this textbook (e.g. Think–Pair–Share, Group Work, Jigsaw Learning, Moving Debate).
- List examples of actions that could be undertaken as part of an Active Citizenship project.

What is Politics?

Writers, thinkers and scholars have debated the meaning of the term 'politics' for centuries. What is politics? Is it something only a few select people do – or is everyone involved? Does politics take place only in particular settings (e.g. government buildings) or does it happen everywhere? As we will see, the concept of politics has been defined in many different ways.

Fig. 1.1 *Prime Time* leaders' debate before the 2016 General Election

Definitions of Politics

The term 'politics' can be understood in a variety of ways.

'The Art of Government'
Politics is what governments and states 'do'. Politics concerns everything involved in running the government, such as making decisions, laws and policies for the good of society. Politics is practised by people directly active in government.

'The Interaction of Citizens in the Public Sphere'
Political scientist Hannah Arendt defined politics as 'the interaction of free and equal citizens in society'. Politics is about more than government. It involves all interactions within the public sphere, outside our private lives. Politics can be practised by government, business, school, culture, work and art. Politics involves *everyone*.

'A Process of Conflict Resolution'

Politics involves the use of tools such as negotiation and compromise to solve society's problems peacefully and without violence. Through dialogue and diplomacy, states use politics instead of war to resolve their conflicts.

'The Power Struggle for Limited Resources'

In society, our resources (e.g. land, money) are scarce. Politics is about deciding how our limited resources are distributed among people in society – who gets what. Politics is the struggle for power as everyone tries to get their share of these resources. Every day, politics takes place in government, in the community and in our homes.

'Politics Always Involves Conflict'

People will always have different views, opinions and ideas because of their different backgrounds and circumstances. When people interact in discussions, this leads to conflict. For example, when deciding what to do with public land, some people might argue that it should be protected to preserve wildlife, while others may believe it should be developed industrially to produce benefits for the economy.

QUESTIONS

1. Would you agree that politics in Ireland is 'the art of government' and is restricted to those who actively participate in government? Why/why not?
2. Hannah Arendt claims that politics is 'the interaction of free and equal citizens in society'. Give examples of political interactions that are not related to official government.
3. Which of the definitions of politics most accurately reflects the development of politics in Northern Ireland over the past twenty years?
4. Which of the definitions of politics do you most agree with? Why?

ACTIVITY 1.1

1. Think individually for a moment about the word 'politics'. Reflect on what you have learned so far in this chapter. What is politics about? *(Think)*
2. With your partner, agree on a definition of politics. Take into account the definitions in the box, but use your own words and find consensus. *(Pair)*
3. Share your definition with the rest of the class. *(Share)*

See page 30 for more information on Think–Pair–Share activities.

FRAMING OUR IDEAS ABOUT POLITICS AND SOCIETY

Political Spectrum: Left or Right?

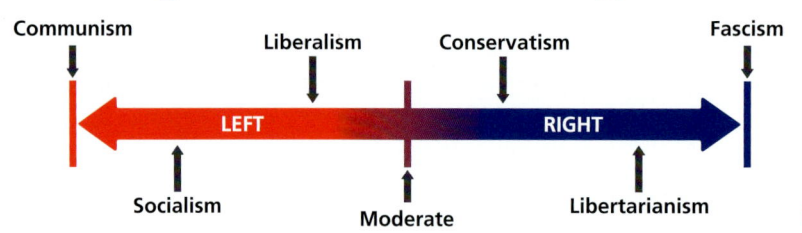

Fig. 1.2 The political spectrum

Every day we read news about the so-called 'left' and 'right' in politics, but what do these terms mean? 'The political spectrum' is a term used to explain and present the range of differences in political ideologies. The term has its origins in the seating arrangements that were put in place in the French parliament following the French Revolution. Traditional supporters of the king sat on the right, and supporters of a fully democratic form of governance sat on the left. The spectrum has evolved over time. Some critics now question the usefulness of the concept in modern politics, with its ever-growing diversity of views. However, at its simplest form, ideas to the left are *liberal*, to the right are *conservative*, and in the centre are *moderate*.

IN THE MEDIA

Fig. 1.3 Left and right

Differences Between Left and Right

Left	Right
Prioritises social equality and social welfare	Prioritises economic freedom and individual liberty
Progressive	Traditional
Greater government regulation of the economy	Less government regulation of the economy
Less government regulation of individual behaviour (usually in favour of gay rights, reproductive rights, freedom of speech, etc.)	Greater government regulation of individual behaviour (usually pro-life, not in favour of gay rights, etc.)
Not in favour of globalisation and free trade	In favour of globalisation and free trade

Political Ideologies

Political ideologies initially developed in response to the nineteenth-century transition from feudalism and an agrarian society (landlord and peasant) to industrialisation and **capitalism** (merchant capitalists and workers). Societies struggled to make sense of the changes taking place and wanted to influence their direction. The classic ideologies –

> **KEY TERM**
>
> **Capitalism** is an economic system that features private ownership of the means of production (e.g. factories, offices, shipping enterprises) and in which market forces determine which goods are produced and how income and profit are distributed.

socialism, liberalism and conservatism – were born. As societies developed throughout the twentieth century and new challenges emerged (such as war and social, political, economic and environmental issues), new ideologies developed in response. The political spectrum continues to evolve. Today we have a diverse range of issue-based and moral-based ideologies from left to right.

The Left

At the extreme end of the left is **communism**. Communism is based on the idea that private property and a capitalist (profit-making) economy should be replaced by public ownership and control of property and natural resources. The aim is to establish a classless society. Political philosophers Karl Marx and Friedrich Engels are considered the founding fathers of communism as an ideology (See key terms: **Marxism** and **neo-Marxism**.). In communist theory, a truly communist society lacks hierarchy and has no currency and no private property. The production of goods and services is based on the simple principle of contribution according to one's ability and benefit based on one's need. Socialism is considered a kind of stepping stone towards communism. In the words of Lenin, founder of the Russian Communist Party and head of the first Soviet State: 'The goal of socialism is communism.'

The terms 'communism' and 'socialism' are often used interchangeably, but they are different. Under socialism, the people indirectly control property and resources through representatives (the state). The distribution of goods and services is centrally managed by government until such time as true communism has been achieved.

The world's first experiment with 'far left' ideologies came about in Russia in 1917, and resulted in the Union of Soviet Socialist Republics (USSR) in 1922 – after expansion into the former territories of the Russian Empire. The USSR was based on a single-party system of governance. All forms of social,

Fig. 1.4 Political ideologies

KEY TERMS

Socialism is a political and economic system in which most forms of economically valuable property and resources are owned or controlled by the public or the state. Most socialist systems provide citizens with significant social benefits: guaranteed employment (or unemployment insurance), and free or heavily subsidised healthcare, childcare and education. Socialism is the major alternative to capitalism.

Liberalism is a political ideology based on belief in progress, the essential goodness of human beings, the protection of political and civil liberties, and using government to address social inequalities (e.g. class, race).

Conservatism is a political ideology based on tradition and social stability, respect for established institutions, and a preference for gradual development rather than rapid change. Conservatives normally support lower taxes, limited government regulation of business and the economy, and a strong system of national defence (military).

Communism is a theory that believes in a society without different social classes. It advocates for the elimination of private property and for all property to be owned by the community. Within the community, each person contributes and receives according to their ability and needs.

Marxism is the term used to describe the nineteenth-century ideas and writings of Karl Marx and Friedrich Engels. Marxism formed the philosophical basis for the rise of communism in the late twentieth century.

Neo-Marxism (*neo* means 'new') refers to theories or ideas that attempt to address issues that some people believed were not addressed by classic Marxism. Neo-Marxism uses elements of classic Marxist teachings and combines them with other approaches, such as psychology. The most influential ideas within neo-Marxism came from the Frankfurt School, which founded the Institute for Social Research in 1923. The Frankfurt School is critical of capitalism and of Soviet state communism.

See page 22 for more information on Karl Marx.

FRAMING OUR IDEAS ABOUT POLITICS AND SOCIETY 5

political and cultural organisation (e.g. sports, schools, cultural groups) were state-controlled. In 1989 the USSR collapsed following prolonged peaceful resistance within the Soviet states. Many thinkers highlight this as evidence of the 'failure of communism'. However, other thinkers state that the USSR had not yet achieved true communism. Today, five countries declare themselves as communist: China, Cuba, Laos, North Korea and Vietnam.

Fig. 1.5 The global economic crash of 2007 saw a resurgence in socialism

Since the collapse of the USSR, the terms 'communism' and 'socialism' are often used to distinguish between those who support the radical USSR style of socialism (communists) and those who support a more evolutionary form of socialism which places greater emphasis on civil liberties and democratic freedoms, and works through electoral and legislative processes (socialists).

Fig. 1.6 United Against Austerity movement, Spain

'Social democrats' sit between socialism and liberalism. They reject communism and socialism in their purest forms and accept capitalism as a reality in our societies. Social democrats advocate for government regulation to make capitalism as democratic as possible. The global economic crash of 2007 saw a resurgence in socialism: many political and economic thinkers pointed to the crash as evidence of the inherent flaws of capitalism.

Just left of centre on the spectrum is liberalism. Liberalism initially developed in reaction to the absolutism of monarchy and feudalism in the late eighteenth century. This classic liberalism is quite different from liberalism as we know it today. Individual freedom, liberty and equality before the law are paramount in liberalism. Classic liberalism was quite suspicious of government intervention, particularly in relation to economic affairs, given the importance that classic liberalism assigned to the economic freedom of the individual. By the late nineteenth century, however, it became apparent that unregulated capitalism had led to deepening inequality and injustices. Modern liberalism began to develop the idea of state intervention as a way to ensure freedom and equality.

Fig. 1.7 Syriza: a left-wing political party in Greece

Fig. 1.8 Margaret Thatcher implemented neo-liberal policies such as social welfare cuts and privatisation of certain industries during her time as Prime Minister of the United Kingdom in the 1980s

Modern liberalism (sometimes referred to as *welfare state liberalism*) should not be confused with neo-liberalism, which developed following the economic crisis in the west in the late 1970s. Neo-liberals such as Margaret Thatcher in the UK and Ronald Reagan in the US supported a return to **laissez-faire**

> **KEY TERM**
>
> **Laissez-faire** ('allow to do' in French) is the policy of minimal government interference in the economic affairs of individuals and society.

POWER AND PEOPLE

Fig. 1.9 Senator David Norris: a vocal advocate for liberalism and gay and civil rights

economic policies based on reduced government control or regulation of the economy. Neo-liberalism is about increased privatisation, free trade and reduced government spending on public services.

Modern liberals, on the other hand, are often associated with greater government action to adopt progressive policies and positions, including: wealth distribution through taxation, social welfare schemes, and the rights of migrants, women and the LGBTQ+ community.

The Right

Fascism is an ideology of the far right. It is based on an extreme form of militaristic nationalism, hierarchical order based on rule by elites, and a rejection of many aspects of liberalism (e.g. civil liberties, participatory democracy). Fascists believe that liberal ideals weaken social and political order. Fascism arose during World War I in Italy. Between 1919 and 1945, fascism spread to several European countries, including Germany. Fascism is associated with a dictatorship-style leadership, such as that of Benito Mussolini (Fascist Italy) and Adolf Hitler (Nazi Germany). However, with the end of World War II, fascism as a dominant political ideology disappeared. Today, few political parties would openly describe themselves as fascist. The term 'fascism' is now often used to describe extreme-right groups such as neo-Nazis and anti-democratic or **xenophobic** political positions and actions.

> ### KEY TERMS
>
> **Fascism** is a political system based on a very powerful leader, state control, and an extreme pride in one's country and race, and in which political opposition is not allowed.
>
> **Xenophobia** is the extreme fear of, or hatred for, foreigners and strangers.

Fig. 1.10 Adolf Hitler

IN THE MEDIA

Fig. 1.11 The term 'fascist' is commonly used to describe right-wing political leaders or actions

FRAMING OUR IDEAS ABOUT POLITICS AND SOCIETY

Libertarianism is an ideology that believes that the main purpose of political and legal order is to ensure the freedom of the individual, and thus it supports limited government intervention. Although it can be positioned either left or right on the political spectrum, it is often considered a right-wing ideology because of its conservative position on economics. On social and political issues, such as the protection of civil liberties and individual freedom, libertarianism would be more closely aligned to liberalism – on the left. On economic issues, libertarianism would share some of the views of the conservative right: supporting the economic freedom of the individual (free market economics) over government intervention.

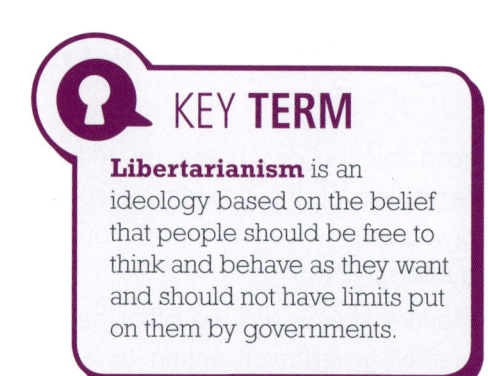

> **KEY TERM**
>
> **Libertarianism** is an ideology based on the belief that people should be free to think and behave as they want and should not have limits put on them by governments.

Fig. 1.12 Logos of conservative organisations: Conservative Party (UK), European People's Party (EU) and Republican Party (US)

Conservatism is the dominant right-wing ideology in modern-day politics. Conservatism is based on the belief that society should respect past traditions, authority, customs and habits. Conservatives prefer a slow and gradual approach to political reform: they believe that this ensures continuity and stability in society. The term 'conservative' developed to describe supporters of the restored monarchy in early nineteenth-century France. In modern-day politics, conservatives include the UK Conservative Party (Tories), the US Republican Party, and the European People's Party (formerly the Christian Democrat Group) within the European Parliament, of which Fine Gael is a member. Conservatives are normally in favour of minimal government regulation of the economy. They tend to take a pro-life position in the abortion debate. They take a strong stance on security and crime. They usually support stricter immigration controls.

The Centre

In the middle of the spectrum, we find people who are termed 'moderates'. Moderates tend not to have extreme views from either leaning (left or right), as their positions often include elements from both sides.

The Importance of Context

Whether we consider an individual to be left or right, liberal, socialist or conservative, in our modern and complex world it helps to look at specific issues when discussing the political spectrum. An individual or a political party may lean to the left on some issues (e.g. social) and may lean to the right on other issues (e.g. economic). Equally, the political spectrum can differ between countries. What might be considered a liberal position in the US, for example, might be moderate in Europe (e.g. heavily subsidised healthcare).

Modern Political Ideologies

Green Politics

Developed in the 1970s, green politics is an ideology that advocates for an environmentally sustainable and socially just world. Political parties based on green politics have developed in most modern western democracies (e.g. the Green Party in Ireland). The main aspirations of green politics include: the environmental protection of natural resources (e.g. land, sea, air), and the building of an economy based on sustainable development without environmental damage.

Fig. 1.13 Green Party logo

Feminism

Feminism is an ideology that advocates for equal rights for women. Since the nineteenth century, feminist movements have campaigned for a variety of women's rights, including the right to vote, the right to work, the right to equal wages and the right to own property. More recently, feminists have focused attention on issues related to women's bodily rights (including abortion), and protection from domestic violence, rape and sexual harassment.

Fig. 1.14 Rosie the Riveter

> **KEY TERM**
>
> **Feminism** is the belief that women should be allowed the same rights, power and opportunities as men, and should be treated in the same way. The ideology advocates for the end to a system of society or government in which men hold the power and women are excluded (**patriarchy**).

Religious Fundamentalism

Religious fundamentalism calls for strict adherence to rules based on sacred texts (e.g. the Bible or the Koran). The term 'religious fundamentalism' became more common following the September 11, 2001 attacks on the US, when the term was used to refer to al-Qaeda, the terrorist group behind the attacks. The term is commonly associated with extreme Islamic groups such as ISIS/ISIL (the Islamic State of Iraq and Syria/the Islamic State of Iraq and the Levant). However, many major world religions have fundamentalist movements. Members of the 'Christian Right' in the Republican Party in the US often make reference to the Bible when they express conservative views on issues such as abortion and LGBTQ+ rights. Zionism in the Jewish nationalist movement seeks the creation of a Jewish national state in Palestine.

Fig. 1.15 Fundamentalist demonstrator

FRAMING OUR IDEAS ABOUT POLITICS AND SOCIETY

QUESTIONS

1. What does the term 'political spectrum' refer to?
2. Explain **three** basic differences between left and right political positions.
3. Which of the political ideologies would agree with the following statements?
   (a) 'A country should ensure most of its energy needs are met through renewable sources, regardless of cost.'
   (b) 'The fact that in many professional sectors today women earn less than men is evidence that we still live in a gender-unequal society.'
   (c) 'A wealth tax is required to address widening inequality in society.'
   (d) 'Private companies – not governments – are best placed to develop the world economy.'
4. True or false?
   (a) 'From each according to their abilities, to each according to their needs' is a conservative slogan.
   (b) Liberals believe that it is the state's primary duty to protect the rights of individuals and to promote liberty and equality.
   (c) Socialists are influenced by the teachings of Karl Marx and argue for public ownership of a country's natural resources and critical industries.
   (d) Those on the right of the political spectrum believe in imposing more laws and regulations to control the economy so that it brings benefit to all members of society.
5. Explain the key differences between capitalism and socialism.
6. What is neo-Marxism?
7. What is the difference between *social welfare liberalism* and *neo-liberalism*?
8. Explain any **two** of the following ideologies: fascism, libertarianism, conservatism.
9. Identify whether the following modern political ideologies sit on the left or the right of the political spectrum:
   (a) Green politics
   (b) Feminism
   (c) Religious fundamentalism
   (d) Ultra-nationalism
   (e) Liberalism.

ACTIVITY 1.2

Your teacher will read out various political views. You will take part in a 'moving debate'. Decide where on the political spectrum (left–right) each statement belongs.

SKILLS BOOK LINK 1.1

Go to pages 1–2 of your Skills Book to complete Skill Task 1.1 on the political spectrum.

SKILLS BOOK LINK 1.2

Go to pages 2–4 of your Skills Book to complete Skill Task 1.2 on political party policies.

Complete your next Reflective Journal entry (pages 1–2)

What is Society?

Humans tend not to live alone or in isolation. Instead, we live in groups. A group of people who share a common lifestyle and organisation is known as a society. Human societies can be defined in different ways.

Different ways of Viewing Society

The term 'society' comes from the Latin word *socius*, which means association or companionship. There are three main approaches to classifying society. While each approach looks at a specific aspect of group lifestyle and organisation, it is possible to make use of all three approaches to understand society.

Fig. 1.16 Grafton Street, Dublin

Anthropology

Anthropology is the study of human societies and cultures. Traditionally, anthropologists look at the methods a group uses for its subsistence (survival) as the basis for classifying society. For example, groups who survive by hunting animals and gathering plants to eat are classified as 'hunter-gatherer societies'. Groups who raise animals for meat or milk are considered 'pastoralist' societies. Communities who grow crops are termed 'agrarian' or 'agriculturalist' societies. Communities who base their survival on industrial activities are called 'industrial societies'. One of the newest classifications is the 'knowledge' or 'information' society' – a society that is based on the creation and dissemination of scientific and technological knowledge, and the internet.

Political Science

Political scientists look at the leadership and decision-making structures of societies. A tribal society is organised by kinship relationships: family, blood or ancestral connections between people. A chiefdom is a more complex version of a tribal society: it involves a community of different families under the leadership of one leader (chief). The most complex political organisation of society is the state: a political community living under one system of government.

> See Chapter 3 (pages 69–93) for more information on the state and political representation.

Sociology

Sociology is the study of human relationships and institutions. Sociology often looks at a group's relation to the Industrial Revolution, which is considered to have brought about the most significant social, political and economic change to the world in modern times. Under this approach, a society can be classified as pre-industrial, industrial or post-industrial. The term 'pre-industrial society' describes most societies up to the eighteenth century. These societies had several common characteristics: they were agriculture-based, small, and had limited contact with other societies. Beginning in the late eighteenth century, industrial societies began to emerge in Europe and the US, with the spread of mass production. During this period, more people began to move from rural to new urban centres, farmers became factory workers, and the industrial society began. Post-industrial societies are societies that have moved from manual labour to knowledge- and technology-based professions.

Differences exist not only *between* societies but also *within* them. Each society is organised and ordered in a particular way. In society, we often rank different categories or groups of people in a hierarchy. Society then rewards these groups differently based on their position in the hierarchy. Some groups have greater status, power and wealth than other groups. This is known as **social stratification**. It is universal: it happens all around the world. But it is variable: it takes different forms in different societies. Modern stratification systems include the **class** system present in almost all societies and the caste system in countries such as India. Additional bases for social stratification include age, gender, ethnicity, race, etc. Social stratification can persist across generations. In sociology, there are three main perspectives on social stratification.

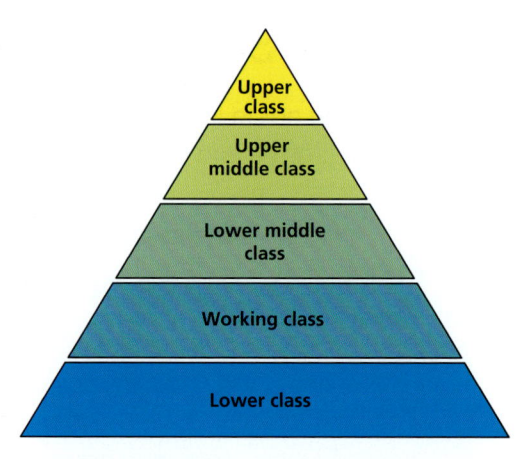

Fig. 1.17 Pyramid of social stratification: a five-class model

KEY TERMS

Social stratification is the system by which a society groups and ranks categories of people in a hierarchy.

Social class is the division of a society based on the social and economic status assigned to members of that society.

Structural functionalism is a sociological theory that attempts to explain how and why society functions as it does. The theory explores the relationships between the different social institutions that make up society (e.g. government, law, family, education, religion). Émile Durkheim is considered the 'father' of structural functionalism.

Social conflict theory is a theory in sociology that views society as a place of inequality that generates conflict and social change. Society is structured in ways that benefit a few at the expense of the majority, and factors such as race, sex, class and age are linked to social inequality. Karl Marx is considered the 'father' of social conflict theory.

Symbolic interactionism is a theory about social behaviour which explores how people interact with one another based on the meanings they assign to things such as language, actions and statuses.

Fig. 1.18 Social stratification

KEY THINKERS

SOCIAL STRATIFICATION

The three dominant theories of stratification are: **structural functionalism**, **social conflict** and **symbolic interactionism**.

Structural Functionalism

Sociologists Kingsley Davis and Wilbert E. Moore believed that stratification is necessary for society to function properly. In society, we have many different tasks that need to be completed. These tasks have a hierarchy in terms of their level of difficulty: from cleaning our streets to performing live-saving surgeries. If people are to be encouraged to invest the time necessary to develop the knowledge and skills required for society's more complex tasks, we need to provide them with greater rewards. Social stratification ensures society is constantly progressing and improving by providing a system of rewards (e.g. prestige, status, wealth) and sanctions (e.g. punishment).

POWER AND PEOPLE

KEY THINKERS

Social Conflict Theory

Social conflict theorists disagree that social stratification is necessary for society to function. They argue instead that social stratification benefits some individuals and groups at the expense of others, which causes social conflict. Karl Marx and Max Weber are two of the main thinkers within this perspective. For Marx, society is based on the existence of two main classes: the *bourgeoisie* and the *proletariat*. The system of capitalism requires this class-based social stratification. It needs workers (proletariat) to perform the labour in the factories and companies, which creates profits for the owners (bourgeoisie). The proletariat are exploited by the bourgeoisie. The proletariat are provided with just enough money and resources to survive. The class system benefits the bourgeoisie only.

For Max Weber, the process is a little more complex. The hierarchy of groups in society is based on multiple factors: economic, social and political. Like Marx, Weber acknowledged the importance of economic position as a basis for social stratification. This hierarchy is called 'class'. However, Weber pointed to two additional factors. The hierarchy of groups in society is also based on social status (prestige). Society assigns higher social status to certain groups, based on education or occupation. This hierarchy is based on 'status groups'. For example, an artist may have a low economic position in society but a high social status. Also, according to Weber, society is ordered on the basis of political power – the ability to influence decisions and actions in society. A person can be a member of a lower class but obtain higher political status, if they are a member of a political group/party.

Symbolic Interactionism

Symbolic interactionism is a theory that looks at the everyday interactions between individuals to explain society as a whole. According to the theory, people mainly interact with others who share the same social standing. We tend to live, work and associate with others who share the same income level, educational background or ethnicity – and even the same tastes in food, music and clothing. Our appearance and lifestyle choices reflect how we perceive ourselves in society. Housing, clothing, hairstyles, the food we eat, the music we listen to, and the hobbies or leisure activities we choose are all symbolic of the social position we consider ourselves to have, and the groups in society to which we believe we belong. The term 'conspicuous consumption' refers to buying certain products to make a social statement about status. A car that costs €10,000 provides transportation in much the same way as a car that costs €100,000, but the luxury car makes a social statement about our perceived status.

QUESTIONS

1. Explain the term 'social stratification'. Provide **two** examples of social stratification in your answer: one from your school and one from your community.
2. According to structural functionalists, why is social stratification necessary?
3. What does social stratification cause, according to social conflict theory?
4. Name and describe the two classes that are in conflict with each other, according to Karl Marx.
5. According to Max Weber, what other factors determine one's position in society, other than economic/class position?
6. In your opinion, what is the most important factor that determines one's social standing in your local area? Why?
7. Explain the theory of symbolic interactionism.
8. What does the term 'conspicuous consumption' mean?
9. Which of the three theories best explains the type of social stratification that exists in Ireland today? Give reasons for your answer.

Complete your next Reflective Journal entry (pages 1–2)

FRAMING OUR IDEAS ABOUT POLITICS AND SOCIETY

Key Political and Social Thinkers: Past and Present

When trying to understand politics and society, it can be useful to look at the ideas and arguments of key thinkers who studied and wrote about these issues. Many writers and scholars, past and present, have made important contributions to the study of politics and society. When developing our own ideas, opinions and arguments, it is important to learn about these key thinkers – what they argued and the time and context within which they developed their arguments. We can strengthen our own arguments on different topics by referring to these key thinkers.

Thomas Hobbes (1588–1679)

Thomas Hobbes was born in London in 1588. He was a graduate of Oxford University, where he studied Classics. He was very interested in different forms of government and travelled many times to different European countries. Hobbes was especially interested in understanding why we allow ourselves to be ruled, and what would be the best type of government for his own country – England. Heavily influenced by the violence of the English Civil War (1642–51), Hobbes believed that humans are naturally unruly and need a strong external ruler to ensure we do not go to war with one another. He believed that humans cannot be trusted to govern themselves. He was in support of an *absolute monarchy*: all power entrusted to a king or queen.

Hobbes believed that humans are primarily selfish and put their own interests above all else. They are willing to do anything (including using violence or even starting a war) to further or protect these interests. The natural state of society is, therefore, a 'state of war' in which humans live in perpetual fear of one another. If left to make their own decisions, people will always act selfishly and impulsively. Hobbes understood nations in the same way. In Hobbes's view, all countries are in constant conflict for power and resources. In 1651, Hobbes described his theory in a book entitled *Leviathan* (named after a powerful sea monster referenced in the Old Testament of the Bible).

When you see growing conflict around the world, do you think Hobbes was right?

According to Hobbes, fear of war leads humans to come together to develop a 'social contract', whereby the people agree to being ruled and governed by one supreme authority. Governments are needed to protect people from their own selfish and evil impulses. Hobbes believed that a monarchy is the best option because it provides the necessary authority figure and leadership. Hobbes was not a fan of **democracy**. In his view, because people are mainly selfish and

'The condition of man ... is a condition of war of everyone against everyone.'

Thomas Hobbes

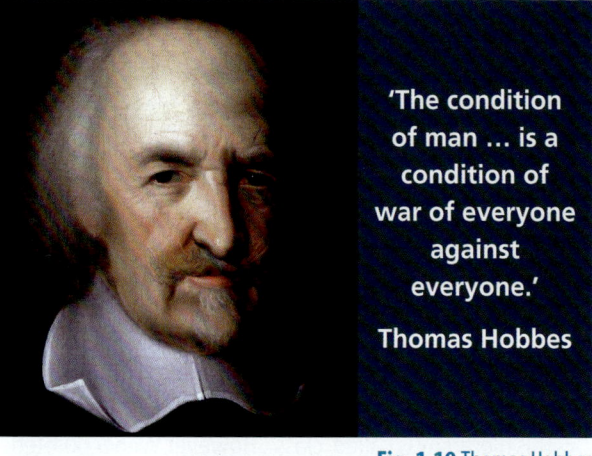

Fig. 1.19 Thomas Hobbes

> **KEY TERM**
>
> The word **democracy** literally means 'rule by the people.' It is derived from a Greek word coined from the words *demos* (people) and *kratos* (rule) in the middle of the fifth century BCE, as a name for the political system that existed at the time in some of the cities of Greece – notably Athens. As a form of government, democracy contrasts with monarchy (rule by a king, queen or emperor), oligarchy (rule by a few persons), aristocracy (rule by a privileged class) and despotism (absolute rule by a single person – the modern term for which is 'dictatorship').

See Chapter 3 (pages 69–93) for more information on the different forms of government.

self-interested, they cannot be given power, as it will result in war. Hobbes stated that democracy would lead to a situation of 'war of every man against every man' and make life 'solitary, poor, nasty, brutish and short'. We need strong rules to protect us from others and from ourselves.

Hobbes did, however, recognise the need for a group of representatives and he coined the famous phrase 'voice of the people'. He believed that such representatives could raise the concerns and problems of the people to the monarch. This would provide some protection from a cruel and unfair ruler. However, final decisions should be made by the king or queen, and he or she does not have to accept the views of the people.

The Main Theories of Thomas Hobbes

- Human beings are naturally selfish and wicked, and pursue self-interest relentlessly. Nations and countries are the same.
- The state of nature is a state of war.
- Fear of war leads humans to come together to develop a 'social contract', whereby people consent to being ruled and governed by one supreme authority.
- Monarchy is the best form of government.
- Democracy will lead to a situation of 'war of every man against every man' and make life 'solitary, poor, nasty, brutish and short.'

QUESTIONS

1. Did Thomas Hobbes have an optimistic or a pessimistic view of human nature? Give reasons for your answer.
2. What event had a major influence on Hobbes's ideas?
3. What form of government did Hobbes support?
4. How does Hobbes describe the natural state of society? What events in the world today appear to provide evidence to support this view?
5. Name the famous book in which Hobbes outlined his theory.
6. Explain what Hobbes meant by a 'social contract'.
7. Give **two** reasons why Hobbes opposed democracy.
8. What did Hobbes suggest as a potential safeguard against a cruel or unfair ruler?

John Locke (1632–1704)

John Locke was born in 1632 in Wrington, Somerset, England. He was a student of Logic, Metaphysics and Classics, and later Medicine, at Christ Church Oxford, where he eventually became a lecturer. Locke is widely known as the 'father of liberalism' and made a ground-breaking contribution to the **Enlightenment**. Locke's main ideas on politics and government are contained in his *Two Treatises of Government* (1680–90). Contrary to Hobbes, Locke believed that government should be formed with the consent of citizens (the governed) and he rejected the concept of the divine right of kings. Locke was writing during a time of great political upheaval between royalists and parliamentarians in England. He supported 'majority rule' as the best form of government. The principal aim of government in Locke's theory is to protect 'life, liberty and estate', an idea that heavily influenced the founding Constitution of the United States.

'The only task of the government is the protection of private property.'

John Locke

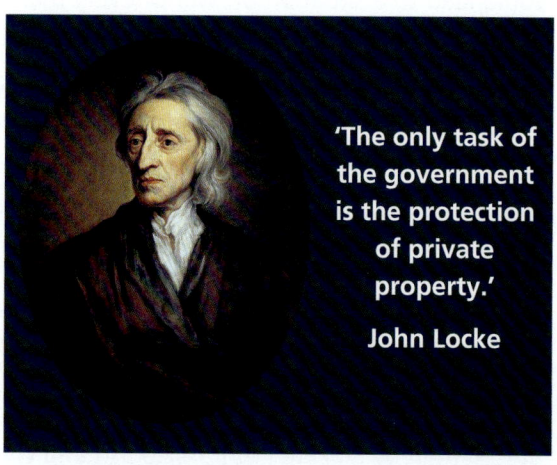

Fig. 1.20 John Locke

> **KEY TERM**
>
> The **Enlightenment** was a period of great cultural and political change in Europe during the eighteenth century. It was marked by a rejection of traditional sources of authority, such as religion, and a move towards science, rational thought, human rights and new forms of government, such as the democratic republic.

According to Locke, in their natural state, humans are equal and free to do as they wish, as long as they maintain peace and do not harm humankind. Unlike Hobbes, Locke believed that humans are rational and have a natural ability to reason. However, given the high risk of chaos and violence in the competing interests among humans – particularly in relation to the ownership of land and property – people willingly (consent) and consciously enter into a 'social contract' with a higher authority (government). In exchange for order and peace, people give up certain freedoms. They do this because government can protect rights and freedoms for the common good, better than any one individual could. In this sense, government can be considered a type of 'referee' in, for example, a game of football, with the 'common good' and the protection of private property as the ultimate goals.

Unlike Hobbes, Locke believed that the power of government should be limited. Government should not take a citizen's property, for example. Locke supported revolt and rebellion under certain conditions. If government acts against the common good, it can be justifiably removed by the people, since the 'social contract' has been broken. Indeed, Locke believed that people have an obligation to remove a government that acts against the common good.

How do you think Locke would have viewed the Arab Spring phenomenon?

In addition to private property, another key area in which Locke believed government should not intervene was religion. He believed in religious tolerance and the protection of diverse views, and his writings (*Letters Concerning Toleration*) provided one of the earliest arguments for the separation of church and state. According to Locke, governments should respect and protect freedom of religion, and intervene only if there is a threat to public order and the preservation of society.

Fig. 1.21 Majority rule

POWER AND PEOPLE

Locke identified three necessary components of government:
- Common agreed rules for society (legislature)
- A formal and independent body to provide judgement (judiciary)
- Power to enforce these concepts (executive).

This idea is at the core of many western systems of government, including Ireland today.

The Main Theories of John Locke
- Human beings are naturally rational with the ability to reason.
- The laws of nature include an obligation to preserve humankind.
- Logic and reason lead to the development of a 'social contract', whereby humans consent to forming a government that can best protect the common good.
- Majority rule is the best form of government.
- Government power should be limited and should not intervene in all areas of life.
- Freedom of religion and diversity of opinion should be protected by government.
- Government has three main components: legislature, judiciary and executive.

QUESTIONS

1. John Locke is known as the father of which ideology?
2. Name the document that contains Locke's main ideas on politics and government.
3. How should a government be formed, according to Locke?
4. What concept did Locke reject?
5. Name a famous document that was heavily influenced by Locke's ideas.
6. Locke had a more positive view of human nature than Hobbes. Provide evidence to support this statement. Which key thinker do you agree with more: Hobbes or Locke?
7. Explain Locke's interpretation of the 'social contract'.
8. Identify **two** ways in which the power of government should be limited, according to Locke.
9. Describe the **three** components of government proposed by Locke.

Jean-Jacques Rousseau (1712–1778)

Jean-Jacques Rousseau was born in Geneva, Switzerland, in 1712. He moved to Paris in his thirties but was forced to flee because of controversy caused by his writings published in 1762. For his remaining years, he lived a somewhat fugitive life in different countries, including Switzerland, Germany, France and Scotland. After his death, he was eventually recognised as a national hero in 1794 by the French Revolutionary government. He made significant contributions to the French Revolution, the growth of nationalism, and the development of modern social

'Man is born free, and everywhere he is in chains.'

Jean-Jacques Rousseau

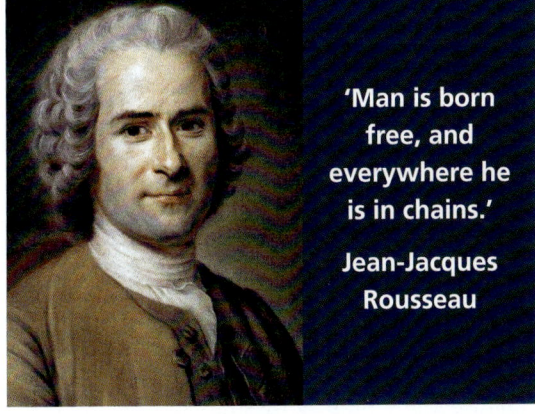

Fig. 1.22 Jean-Jacques Rousseau

FRAMING OUR IDEAS ABOUT POLITICS AND SOCIETY

and political theory. His writings have shaped modern democracies (*The Social Contract*, 1762) and approaches to education (*Emile, or On Education*, 1762). The first of Rousseau's prominent works was entitled *First Discourse on the Arts and Sciences* (1752). With it, he won the Academy of Dijon award. Here Rousseau laid out his core ideas on humankind and civilisation, which would inform his later political writings. He viewed civilisation in a negative light. He believed that civilisation ultimately acts to take humans, who are naturally good and moral, and corrupt them.

Rousseau discussed the concepts of his predecessors, such as Locke and Hobbes. Freedom was the dominant theme in Rousseau's writings. He uses the Hobbesian 'state of nature' as his starting point, but his view is more aligned to that of Locke's: humans are naturally free and equal. Rousseau's natural freedom has two forms – physical and psychological. Humans are physically free to do as they please; and they are psychologically free, as they are concerned only with their natural desires and needs (e.g. food, sleep). With the onset of civilisation and the division of labour, humans lose this psychological freedom as they start to develop 'unnatural' needs (e.g. luxury items, entertainment, status) based on a desire to compare and compete with other people. People become slaves to these new desires. This is what Rousseau meant when he said: 'Man is born free, and everywhere he is in chains' (*The Social Contract*, 1762).

Freedom and inequality are linked in Rousseau's political ideas. Inequalities arise with civilisation, since some people are forced to perform tasks (work) to fulfil the new unnatural needs of other people. This produces relationships of domination and subordination. Eventually, the subordinated (i.e. the poor, workers) will revolt with war to challenge their unequal state. A modern example of Rousseau's thoughts on freedom and inequality can be observed in the dominant force of consumerism in our western culture today, with popular phrases such as 'slave to fashion'.

For Rousseau, the primary purpose of government is to ensure freedoms and equality. Adopting Locke's social contract approach, Rousseau states that humans consent to be governed in the interest of their own preservation and the preservation of others. Although Rousseau uses the term 'sovereign' to describe his proposed government, it is very different from that proposed by Hobbes. For Rousseau, the sovereign is not a monarch: it is the 'general will' of the people. This collective will is different from the individual interests, opinions and desires of each person: it is the shared desire for the 'common good' of all. Many of our public services today (e.g. safety, health, traffic lights) are based on this idea of 'common good'.

Unlike Hobbes, Rousseau does not believe that man gives up any freedom other than 'natural freedom' when governed. Instead, in exchange, government will ensure civil freedoms (pursuing one's interests where the law is silent) and moral freedoms (living one's life on the basis of one's values and beliefs), as long as these individual freedoms do not conflict with the freedoms of other people.

According to Rousseau, the laws of a country should be an expression of this general will, and should also protect freedoms and ensure equality. Some form of government will be needed to ensure the laws are implemented. However, to avoid government going against the will of the people, government should call regular assemblies, modelled on the ancient Roman *comitia*, where people would vote on issues related to the common good. In this sense, Rousseau supported some form of direct democracy.

Rousseau warned against the dangers of individual interests and disliked the idea of political parties. According to Rousseau, political parties can damage the common good if they push their own cause or agenda. Rousseau was aware that conflicts could arise in his proposed form of government and therefore a court (tribunate) capable of providing independent adjudication (like a referee) would be required. His

Fig. 1.23 Direct democracy in Ancient Greece

POWER AND PEOPLE

passion for freedom, equality, general will and common good, and his proposal for a separation of the powers of government – legislative, executive and judicial – influenced the great revolutions and the models of government in many of our modern western democracies.

Rousseau concludes *The Social Contract* with a discussion of religion. A self-professed Christian, he found the moral teachings of most religions as having the potential to produce positive benefits for society and, therefore, he supported religious freedom. However, he strongly opposed dogmatic religions that set out well-defined and rigorous rules, such as Catholicism: obedience to these can result in a conflict with what Rousseau termed 'civil religion'. Civil religion is based on the citizen's loyalty to the laws established for the common good and this, above all else, is what needs to be followed.

Fig. 1.24 Direct democracy in action in a Swiss canton

See page 72 for more information on direct democracy.

The Main Theories of Jean-Jacques Rousseau

- Civilisation takes people, who are naturally good and moral, and corrupts them.
- Humans become slaves to unnatural desires produced by civilisation: 'Man is born free, and everywhere he is in chains' (*The Social Contract*, 1762).
- Inequalities arise with civilisation: some people are forced to perform tasks (work) to fulfil the new unnatural needs of other people. This produces relationships of domination and subordination.
- The primary purpose of government is to ensure freedoms and equality.
- The sovereign is the 'general will' of the people for the common good.
- Government power should be separated: legislative, executive and judicial.

QUESTIONS

1. The ideas of Jean-Jacques Rousseau contributed to which historical event?
2. Name **two** famous works published by Rousseau in 1762.
3. Did Rousseau have a positive or negative view of civilisation? Explain.
4. 'Man is born free, and everywhere he is in chains.' Explain this Rousseau quote. In your opinion, does it apply to modern Irish society?
5. What is the primary purpose of government, according to Rousseau?
6. Explain what Rousseau means by the 'general will' of the people.
7. According to Rousseau, what types of freedoms must the government protect?
8. What did Rousseau propose to ensure that the government would not go against the general will of the people?
9. Why was Rousseau opposed to the idea of political parties? In your opinion, do the political parties in Ireland today prove Rousseau's view to be correct?
10. In your opinion, why did Rousseau call for a complete separation of the three branches of government?

FRAMING OUR IDEAS ABOUT POLITICS AND SOCIETY

John Stuart Mill (1806–1873)

John Stuart Mill was born in London in 1806. He was a prominent political thinker, writer, activist, and eventually parliamentarian in England. In his early adulthood, Mill was heavily influenced by the writings of Jeremy Bentham (1748–1832) the so-called 'father of utilitarianism' – the theory that actions, policies and laws are good or bad based on the effects or results they produce and how many people they benefit or hurt. Put simply, utilitarianism is the belief that 'the end justifies the means'.

Despite being a utilitarian, Mill was a social and political activist concerned with protecting the rights of the individual, particularly women. In his later writings, he advocated socialist views on labour unions and other issues. Mill's writings have contributed to many fields of philosophy (e.g. metaphysics, history of ideas, language, science).

'The only purpose for which power can be rightfully exercised over any member of a civilised community against his will is to prevent harm to other members.'

John Stuart Mill

Fig. 1.25 John Stuart Mill

Mill's greatest contribution to political, social and economic philosophy came in three of his major texts: *Principles of Political Economy* (1871), *On Liberty* (1859) and *The Subjection of Women* (1869). In these works, Mill outlined his approach to utilitarianism, the 'no harm' principle, his theories of liberty and justice, and women's rights.

Hobbes, Locke, Rousseau and others looked at humans in the 'state of nature' versus humans entering civilised society. For Mill, these were not to be viewed separately. Mill was interested in defining the best model of government that would ensure that both the individual and society could flourish. Indeed, Mill viewed the progress of the individual and the progress of society as interrelated. For Mill, the key aim is to find balance between individual liberty and social justice.

Mill was a classic liberal. According to Mill, government power over the individual should be limited to that which is necessary (e.g. security and taxation), and people should be free to do as they wish (individual liberty) unless there is a good reason why they should not. Each person's individual self-interest does not necessarily conflict with the common good. Therefore, excessive rules and regulations are not required, nor are they morally acceptable.

Mill's *On Liberty* (1859) sets out what he considers to be the legitimate use of authority of government or society over the individual, and what the limits of this should be. Mill establishes two general principles. First, an individual can freely act as he or she wishes, once doing so concerns only their own interests and does not negatively affect another. Second, government can intervene when an individual's action affects the interests of others. In cases where an action negatively impacts the interests or freedoms of another, punishment on the basis of established social or legal rules may need to be applied. To view Mill's principles in action, we can think about how we regulate the use of alcohol through our laws in modern western democracies, such as Ireland. While adult citizens can freely purchase and consume alcohol, they are not allowed to drink and drive, or to act in a disorderly way in public.

According to utilitarianism, to determine whether an action is good or bad, we must look at the end result of that action: what results in 'the greatest good for the greatest number' (principle of utility). Actions are not inherently good or bad, but they produce a greater or lesser amount of pleasure or pain. Moral rules should be established on what would produce the greatest level of wellbeing in a society. An action is deemed positive or acceptable if it follows these rules, given that the rules themselves have been established to produce the most positive effect in relation to the issue. Some individual freedom will be compromised. For example, while rules of the road and traffic regulations restrict our freedom of movement (to drive as we wish), they produce greater safety for a greater number of people. In Mill's view, the positives will outweigh the negatives in this case.

Mill supports representative democracy as the best form of government. However, he warns against the dangers of the so-called 'tyranny of the majority', where individual liberty can be threatened by the interests of the majority. Mill was one of the earliest supporters of the Proportional Representation by Single Transferable Vote (PR-STV) system of election. This is the model we use for electing members of both the Dáil and Seanad in Ireland. Mill has also heavily influenced how we approach the issue of minority rights in the sphere of human rights. Mill recognised the importance of **deliberative democracy** and the representation of a diversity of opinions as the way to ensure the best possible outcome in decision-making. It could be said that Mill takes the approach: 'Two heads are better than one.'

Mill was writing during a time of political reform in England. New legislation in 1832 marked the beginning of a gradual extension of voting rights (franchise), starting with the granting of voting rights to small farmers and landowners. However, Mill was not a supporter of full universal suffrage (the right to vote for all citizens). He proposed some form of restrictions to safeguard against risks he associated with permitting 'uneducated workers' to vote. He was a vocal advocate for women's right to vote. He also actively supported other women's rights issues, including employment equality and reproductive rights. He was famously arrested for distributing information on contraception to London's poor women. With his wife, Harriet Taylor Mill, he co-authored an essay entitled *The Subjection of Women* (1869). The essay argues against a type of slavery faced by women in Victorian society, and calls for the education of women and equality between the sexes as a positive contribution to the progress of society.

John Stuart Mill's ideas have had a lasting impact on western models of representative democracy, civil liberties and women's rights.

> See page 72 for more information on representative democracy.

KEY TERM

Deliberative democracy is a system of government whereby decisions are made and laws are passed following in-depth discussion, debate and eventual consensus among citizens. Supporters of this system argue that better-quality deliberation leads to better-quality decisions and laws.

In many representative democracies around the world, deliberative democracy is practised when political representatives and citizens discuss and debate important issues or new laws and policies as part of the decision-making process.

> See page 108 for more information on Proportional Representation by Single Transferable Vote (PR-STV). See Chapter 7 (pages 234–68) and Chapter 8 (pages 269–311) for more information on human rights.

Fig. 1.26 Women's suffrage movement

The Main Theories of John Stuart Mill

- Ensuring the liberty of the individual is of critical importance: government intervention should be limited.
- An individual should be allowed to freely act as he or she wishes, once this does not negatively affect others (first principle of liberty).
- Government should intervene only when an individual's action affects the interests of others (second principle of liberty).
- Punishment and regulation should be based on established social or legal rules, which are designed to ensure the greatest good for society (rule of utilitarianism).
- Representative democracy is the best form of government.
- Society will progress if we ensure individual liberties, including those of women.

ACTIVITY 1.3

Work with your partner to complete the following activity.

1. Think individually for a moment about school rules and national laws that Mill might view as impacting unnecessarily on the freedom of individuals. Could any of these rules/laws be removed without impacting negatively on the rights of others and society? *(Think)*
2. With your partner, agree a list of these rules/laws. *(Pair)*
3. Share your conclusions with the rest of the class. *(Share)*

QUESTIONS

1. Who influenced John Stuart Mill in his early years?
2. What is 'utilitarianism'?
3. Name any **two** of Mill's famous texts.
4. What is the key aim of politics and government, according to Mill? Do you agree with him?
5. According to Mill, under what circumstances should the government **(a)** be allowed and **(b)** not be allowed to exercise its power and authority over an individual?
6. Explain 'the greatest good for the greatest number' principle.
7. Describe the system of government proposed by Mill.
8. What danger of democracy did Mill identify? Can you think of examples of this in the world, either today or in the past?
9. What does the term 'universal suffrage' mean? Why did Mill not support it?
10. For what social issues did Mill advocate?

Karl Marx (1818–1883)

Karl Marx was born in 1818 in Prussia (modern-day Germany). He studied Law at the University of Bonn, and later Philosophy in Berlin. On moving to France in his thirties, Marx met fellow German immigrant and social scientist Friedrich Engels, who would greatly influence the development of Marx's thinking on economics and class struggle. Marx and Engels co-authored important works, such as *The German Ideology* (1846) and *The Communist Manifesto* (1848). Marx's greatest work was *Capital* (1867). It is often viewed as presenting his main contribution to political theory: a theory of capitalism and its effects on society and humans.

'The proletarians have nothing to lose but their chains.'

Karl Marx

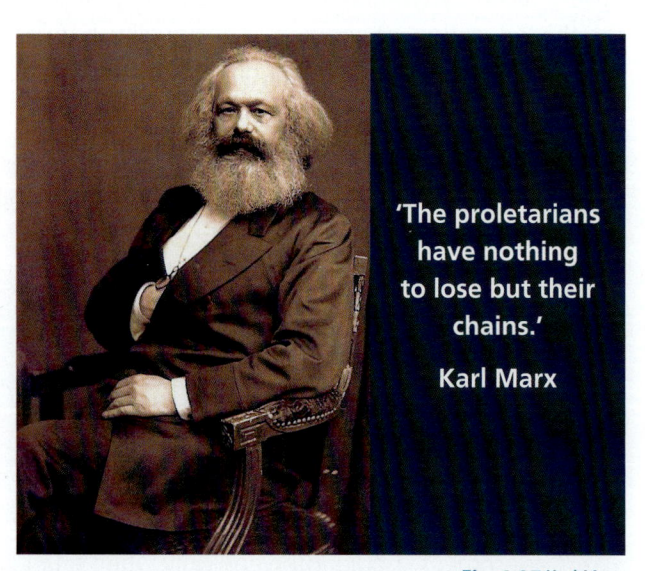

Fig. 1.27 Karl Marx

Considering that Marx witnessed the major social changes brought about by the Industrial Revolution, he was particularly interested in industrialisation and capitalism and their impacts on society. Society was divided along class lines. Although he built on ideas from predecessors such as Rousseau, Marx was one of the first great theorists to look at social class as a key determining factor in relation to one's opportunities and life in general. The Industrial Revolution was taking place at the time and a new upper class emerged, alongside the traditional aristocrats and church leadership. At its simplest, in Marx's view, the upper classes (bourgeoisie) were 'owners' and would enjoy a life of wealth and leisure, while the lower classes (proletariat) were 'workers' and would live a life of poverty and hardship in service to the bourgeoisie. What mattered most in Marx's theory was *who* controlled and owned resources (e.g. land) and what he called the 'means of production' (e.g. factories, businesses). In Marx's world, the bourgeoisie controlled all aspects of society, and the proletariat would become poorer in the unjust capitalist system.

Fig. 1.28 The 'proletariat' of Marxist theory

Marx's theory was prophetic. He identified three main stages. In his view, capitalism (the first stage) will inevitably come to an end when the proletariat (workers) eventually rise up (revolution) against the unjust system after they have experienced what he called 'alienation': a sense of distance or disconnect with their work life (means of production). The proletariat will take over the state (government) and replace capitalism with a socialist system (the second stage), which will challenge and collapse the class structure and make everyone equal. In Marx's theory, socialism will ensure the needs of everyone are met equally. In the capitalist model, business (private enterprise) operates freely and, therefore, dictates the economic, social and political aspects of a society. This causes competition and creates social divide and conflict. By contrast, in the socialist system, the state (public) is the owner of most property and all resources (with some exceptions, such as an individual's house). Given that the state is 'the people', the use of and distribution of benefits will be more equal.

Fig. 1.29 Pyramid of the capitalist system

It is important to distinguish between socialism and communism. While socialism supports public ownership of property and resources, and state regulation to ensure a more equal distribution of resources and services, communism goes further. Communism includes full state control over goods and services (i.e. what gets produced and who produces it) and the removal of all private ownership. Communism was the 'end stage' of Marx's theory. Many political analysts point to the fall of the Soviet Union in the 1990s as evidence of the failure of the communist project.

FRAMING OUR IDEAS ABOUT POLITICS AND SOCIETY

The Main Theories of Karl Marx

- Society is constructed on *who* owns and controls the means of producing the goods and services to meet the needs of the population.
- Capitalism (first stage) is a model based on profit-making. It creates an unjust divide between the ownership class (bourgeoisie) and the workers (proletariat).
- Capitalism will end when the workers become disconnected and disgruntled (alienation) and revolt, bringing in a socialist system (second stage).
- Socialism supports public ownership of property and resources, and state regulation to ensure equal distribution of resources and benefits.
- Communism (final stage) involves full state control over property, the means of production, goods and services.

Fig. 1.30 Representations of capitalism and communism

ACTIVITY 1.4

Work with your partner to complete the following activity.

1. Examine Fig. 1.30 above. Think individually for a moment about:
   - The message of the cartoon
   - The pros and cons of capitalism
   - The pros and cons of Marxism. *(Think)*
2. With your partner, agree the answers to the questions. *(Pair)*
3. Share your conclusions with the rest of the class. *(Share)*

POWER AND PEOPLE

QUESTIONS

1. Who was Karl Marx's co-author on *The Communist Manifesto*?
2. In what famous work did Marx present his theory on capitalism and its effects on society?
3. What is the single key factor that determines one's opportunities in life, according to Marx?
4. Who are the bourgeoisie and the proletariat?
5. What are the 'means of production' and who controls them, according to Marx?
6. In Marx's theory, what happens at the second stage?
7. In the socialist system, who owns most of the property and all the resources? What benefit will this bring, according to Marx? Do you agree with this view? Why/why not?
8. What is the final end stage, according to Marx? How does it differ from the second stage?
9. Do you believe that the Irish government, on behalf of the Irish people, should take direct control and ownership of any resources in Ireland today? If so, what resources and why? If not, why not?

Kathleen Lynch (1951–)

Kathleen Lynch was born in 1951 in Co. Clare. She undertook a degree in social sciences, specialising in sociology in her Master's and PhD. She is now an academic with international standing in the field of equality studies. She played a leading role in establishing the Equality Studies Centre in 1990. In 2005 she also played a central role in establishing the UCD School of Social Justice. Lynch is an academic activist and uses research as a tool to advocate for equality and social justice, both internationally and in Ireland.

In her first book *The Hidden Curriculum* (1989) Lynch examined how inequality operates, often invisibly, through the hidden curriculum, namely through unspoken curricular and pedagogical practices, selection and stratification in the organisation of school life. In her study with Anne Lodge, *Equality and Power in Schools* (2002), she attempted to understand and explain how social class, gender, sexual orientation, ethnicity and religion affect access to education. She also examined power relations among students, and between students and teachers. It was found that education can act to reinforce the existing inequalities within Irish society. With respect to gender, for example, the research showed that subject scheduling in some schools prevented students from taking subjects that were traditionally considered 'female' (e.g. Home Economics) or 'male' (e.g. Woodwork). This reinforces gender stereotypes associated with subjects. The practice of entrance exams and subsequent streaming (grouping students on academic ability/results) was found to reinforce inequalities based on social class and background. Students from working-class and lower socio-economic backgrounds, and those from certain ethnic minorities (e.g. the Traveller community), are more likely to be allocated to the lower bands or streams. In her most recent book (co-authored with Bernie Grummell and Dympna Devine), *New Managerialism in Education: Commercialization, Carelessness and Gender* (2012), Lynch likens the education system to a market where schools are businesses and parents are customers. Her research finds that this approach acts to reinforce inequality.

Fig. 1.31 Kathleen Lynch

'Why are we passive in the face of persistent inequality?'

Kathleen Lynch

Fig. 1.32 Inequality in the Irish education system

In collaboration with colleagues at UCD (Baker, Cantillon and Walsh), Lynch presented a framework for understanding equality in *Equality: From Theory to Action* (2004, 2009). A core idea in this work is the concept of *equality of condition*. Traditional liberal theories on equality aim to 'reduce' inequalities that are viewed as inevitable outcomes of our capitalist and liberal democratic societies. However, Lynch's model challenges this by arguing for equality that not only challenges the unequal position of the individual *in* the system, but also challenges the system *itself*. Society is this system, and its values and attitudes are deeply unequal. For example, to achieve equality of condition in relation to education, Lynch argues that a simple increase in learning support or resources to help students compete in the existing system may not be enough to address the inequalities in education. Instead, we may need to look at changing key aspects of the education system itself, such as the curriculum and assessment. We need to ensure that the education system is more inclusive of different types of human intelligences, presented across gender, class and ethnicity.

Lynch is a passionate advocate for equality. In her view, equality contributes to successful societies. Lynch's research points to social and economic data from around the world, which shows that some of the most equal countries (e.g. Norway) are also performing well economically. Lynch's research and writings have made significant contributions to the thinking and government policies on equality in many different sectors, such as education, health and disability. Lynch has heavily influenced how we talk about inequality in Ireland.

Recently, Lynch has focused attention on the relationship between care and social justice in her co-authored book *Affective Equality: Love, Care and Injustice* (2009). She has developed a critique of what she terms the 'careless state', namely the ways in which there have been cutbacks to all types of public services across several European countries. There is a shift to the right in Ireland, towards a profit-making approach to rights and public services, where citizens have become 'customers'. In recent years, she has been a strong critic of the funding cuts which forced the closure of equality agencies in Ireland, such as Combat Poverty Agency (closed in 2008), People With Disabilities in Ireland (closed in 2011), the National Council on Ageing and Older People (closed in 2009) and the Women's Health Council (closed in 2009).

The Main Theories of Kathleen Lynch

- The education system can act to reinforce the existing inequalities within society.
- We need to focus on achieving *equality of condition* rather than equal opportunities, as one's conditions will influence one's opportunities.
- Equality of condition refers to the main life conditions of people being as equal as possible.
- Affective equality matters; that is to say, social justice is not only about economic, political and cultural equality, it is also about institutionalising ways to promote love, care and solidarity in society, and it is about ensuring that love and care work are undertaken equally by men and women.

Complete your next Reflective Journal entry (pages 1–2)

QUESTIONS

1. What did Kathleen Lynch investigate in *Equality and Power in Schools*?
2. What did Lynch's research reveal in terms of (a) gender inequality and (b) socio-economic inequality?
3. Do you agree with Lynch that the Irish education system reinforces inequalities? Explain why/why not, with reference to your own experience at school.
4. Explain Lynch's concept of 'equality of condition'.
5. According to Lynch, what changes are needed in the Irish education system to make it more fair and equitable? Do you agree with Lynch on these changes?
6. Does Lynch believe that there is a correlation between the extent of equality in a country and its level of economic success?
7. What does the 'careless state' refer to?

The Politics and Society Course

This chapter has introduced us to the concepts of politics and society. We have looked at several major political and social thinkers who have made significant contributions to many of the topics and issues we will cover in the Politics and Society course. These thinkers have used their research, writings and ideas to influence thinking and action in their societies and beyond. Throughout this book, we will use these concepts and ideas to help us to analyse and discuss many topics: power and decision-making, political representation, human rights and equality, and globalisation and multiculturalism. When developing our own ideas and arguments on any issue, it is important to understand where our arguments may sit on the political spectrum, or how they stand in relation to contributions made by important social and political thinkers.

Developing Key Skills

A vital aim of the Politics and Society course is that students learn how to use and develop key skills. Politics and Society is one of the first subjects at Senior Cycle to move away from the traditional focus on learning content towards the development of key skills. It is hoped that this shift towards developing skills will enable you, as a learner, to better fulfil your potential – not just during your time in school, but in the future as an active citizen and independent learner. After all, education does not end when we leave school. Learning is a continual process and a life-long journey. To equip you for this educational journey, the Politics and Society course promotes the development of the following five key skills which have been identified as essential to teaching and learning at Senior Cycle.

Key Skill 1: Information Processing

Developing the skills of sourcing, analysing and interpreting data is an important objective of the Politics and Society course. Every chapter in this book contains research assignments that will enable you to

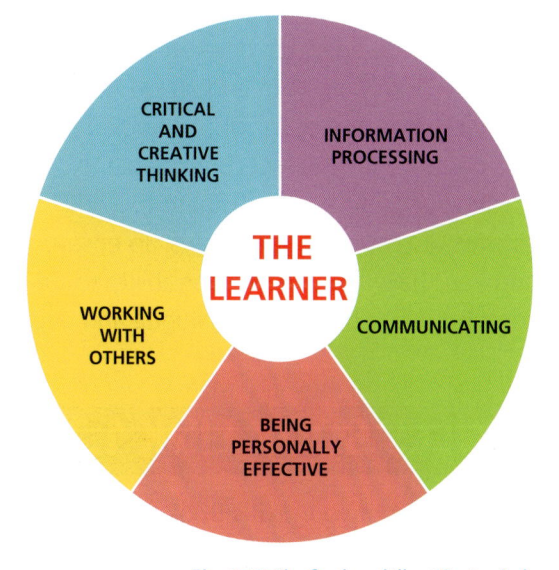

Fig. 1.33 The five key skills at Senior Cycle

FRAMING OUR IDEAS ABOUT POLITICS AND SOCIETY

develop these information processing skills. With the support of your teacher, you will learn how to conduct independent research on various concepts and issues related to politics and society. You will discover how to:

- Access and gather reliable information from reputable sources – available both online and offline.
- Evaluate the validity and usefulness of different sources of information, such as newspaper articles, academic research papers, official reports and websites.
- Browse through large extracts of text to locate and record the key points of information by using speed-reading techniques such as scanning and skimming.
- Note-take, summarise and organise information using concept maps, mind maps, Venn diagrams and other visual/graphic organisers.

Key Skill 2: Communicating

The ability to communicate effectively is an essential skill in the Politics and Society course. Many of the activities in this textbook require that you actively engage in group discussions, presentations, **dialogue** and **debate**. It is through your participation in such activities that you will develop important communication skills. This book will challenge you to move beyond simply stating your opinion on an issue, towards explaining your point of view by using evidence-based arguments. You will learn to construct and deliver clear arguments based on sound reasoning and backed up by relevant evidence and reliable data (Key Skill 1). At the same time, you will learn to listen and respond empathetically to alternative points of view voiced by other students in your classroom. The ability to listen to others is vital to effective communication and you will be encouraged to develop **active listening** skills as you engage in the activities in each chapter of this book. It is important that you feel comfortable to speak your mind and participate fully in all class discussions and debates. To ensure this, all the students in your class, as well as your teacher and you, have a shared responsibility to promote an atmosphere of mutual trust and respect for all contributors to discussion, dialogue and debate.

> **KEY TERMS**
>
> **Dialogue** is a conversation between two or more people with the objective of airing and considering different viewpoints. In the Politics and Society course, dialogue may be used to verify the veracity (i.e. accuracy, truth, legitimacy) of an argument, to resolve a problem or to reach consensus (general agreement). Dialogue will allow you to gain a greater understanding of an issue and open your mind to alternative views. Dialogue is most effective when participants are open to having their assumptions and ideas challenged (and even changed as a result).
>
> **Debate** is a formal discussion on a particular issue, in which opposing arguments are put forward by the participants. While most debates usually end in a vote for a 'winner', in the Politics and Society course the primary focus is on the quality of the debate itself. The process, rather than the outcome, is the important element.
>
> **Active listening** is an important communication technique used in dialogue, debate, negotiation and conflict resolution. In the Politics and Society course, active listening requires that you listen carefully to others and fully concentrate on the exact meaning of what they say. Active listening involves asking questions to seek clarification and verify that you understand exactly what is being said.

SKILLS BOOK LINK 1.3

Go to page 4 of your Skills Book to complete Skill Task 1.3 on classroom communication rules.

Key Skill 3: Being Personally Effective

Being personally effective is an important skill to develop – not just in the Politics and Society course, but in life in general. It involves becoming an independent, self-aware and self-directed learner. In being personally effective, you will take responsibility for your own learning by regularly evaluating your own progress in this subject. This will require planning, goal-setting and reviewing the progress you make throughout the year. To help you develop these skills, page iv of your Reflective Journal and Learning Portfolio provides detailed guidelines on maintaining a Reflective Journal and Learning Portfolio. These will help you to plan, reflect on and evaluate your own learning as you progress through each chapter of the textbook. This reflective practice will be particularly helpful to you when planning and evaluating your learning as part of the Citizenship Action Project (worth 20 per cent of your Leaving Certificate Grade).

Key Skill 4: Working with Others

Like Communicating (Key Skill 2), the ability to work effectively with others is essential in the Politics and Society classroom. Many of the activities in this textbook are centred on group work and collaborative learning strategies. You will learn how to contribute positively to various group tasks. With the guidance and support of your teacher, you will develop key skills that are of vital importance to the successful functioning of a group. The different group activities in this book will encourage important teamwork skills, such as active listening, motivating, timekeeping, leading, recording, summarising, critiquing and negotiating differences of opinion.

> **SKILLS BOOK LINK 1.4**
>
> Go to page 5 of your Skills Book to complete Skill Task 1.4 on rules for effective group work.

Key Skill 5: Critical and Creative Thinking

As part of the Politics and Society course, you will move beyond a basic understanding of information and facts. You will develop the ability to think critically and creatively. Critical thinking means objectively analysing and evaluating an issue or evidence to form a reasoned judgement (i.e. an opinion that has some evidence to back it up). Many questions and activities in this book are designed to help you develop critical thinking skills, such as: critically questioning the accuracy of data/information, evaluating different arguments, exploring complexities and connections, and examining causes and relationships. Each chapter contains several pieces of research data which you will examine and from which you will draw conclusions. In addition, in line with the Politics and Society Exam Specification, the Skills Book contains data-based questions (DBQ) exercises based on the main topic examined in each chapter of the textbook. The DBQ is worth 30 per cent of the Leaving Certificate grade at both Higher and Ordinary levels. In each DBQ exercise, you will analyse and evaluate both a **qualitative** and a

> **KEY TERM**
>
> **Qualitative data** is data that is descriptive. This type of data is used to gain an understanding of underlying reasons, opinions and motivations. It provides deeper insights into a problem or issue. For example, when researching the extent of poverty in a region, a researcher might select a sample of five individuals from the region to conduct detailed interviews to gain a deeper understanding of the people's experiences of poverty. Qualitative data collection methods include individual interviews, observation in communities or groups, and focus groups (group discussions).

quantitative piece of research data on a set topic that was discussed in the relevant chapter. By completing these exercises in the Skills Book, you will learn to assess the strengths, weaknesses, overall usefulness and limitations of different types of research data. You will also develop the ability to think creatively by discussing and proposing possible solutions to the many problems in modern society.

Learning Methodologies

You will encounter several different learning methodologies throughout this book. The active learning activities have been designed to help you develop the five key skills. The following is an explanation of the activities that will appear frequently throughout the chapters. Become familiar with these activities, the icons that represent them, and the instructions on how to successfully complete them.

> **KEY TERM**
>
> **Quantitative data** is data that can be quantified and verified: it can be measured and written in numerical or statistical format. This data is then used to formulate facts and to highlight patterns in research, such as causes and effects.
>
> Quantitative data is often used to quantify attitudes, opinions, behaviours or the extent to which a problem exists. For example, to investigate the extent of poverty in a region, a researcher might gather statistics on income levels, the unemployment rate, levels of education and the health status of local inhabitants, before making a reasoned judgement on the extent to which poverty exists in the region. Quantitative data collection methods include surveys, questionnaires and online polls.

Learning Methodology 1: Think–Pair–Share

This icon prompts you to engage in either brainstorming or higher-order thinking on a specified topic with the help of your partner. When you see this icon, complete the following steps.

Step 1: *Think:* Take some time to think quietly and carefully to yourself about the topic and the possible answer(s) to the question posed.

Step 2: *Pair:* Pair up with a nearby partner to share your ideas with him or her and to listen carefully to his or her ideas.

Step 3: *Share:* Reach consensus and write down an agreed solution or answer to the question posed. Together, share your answer with the rest of the class.

Think about the question

Pair with your partner

Share your ideas with others

Fig. 1.34 Think–Pair–Share

Learning Methodology 2: Group Work

This icon means that an activity involves working together as part of a group to solve a problem or to complete a specific group task. In group activities, you will use your communication skills and the skill of working effectively with others. In group work, it is important that all members of the group engage productively in the assigned task and share responsibility for successfully completing the task. The two tips below will ensure that your group works well together.

1. Your group should operate according to agreed procedures and ground rules (see Skill Task 1.4).

2. Assign a specific role to each member of the group. Depending on the task, these roles may include:
   - **Facilitator:** Chairs and moderates the team discussion, keeps the group on task and ensures that all members of the team are heard and that all contribute equally.

- **Recorder:** Takes notes summarising all team discussions and decisions made, and keeps all the necessary records.
- **Reporter:** Serves as the group spokesperson to the rest of the class. Provides feedback and communicates the main ideas or conclusions arrived at by the group.
- **Timekeeper:** Keeps the group aware of time constraints and provides support to any members requiring extra help.
- **Checker:** Checks to ensure that all group members understand the task, the concepts being discussed and the group's conclusions.

Fig. 1.35 Group work

Learning Methodology 3: Jigsaw Learning

This icon indicates that your group will engage in jigsaw learning. Your teacher divides your class into groups. Each group will be given (a) a certain sub-topic within a larger, more general topic or (b) an extract of research material to be read. In jigsaw learning, your group members become experts on your sub-topic. Your group works together to examine the sub-topic carefully and summarise the main points. Once every member of your group is confident that he or she can teach the sub-topic to another group, the first part of the process is complete: the jigsaw pieces are ready, and now you need to put them together. Your original group breaks up to form new groups: each new group will contain different people who are experts on different sub-topics: the jigsaw pieces are put together. In the new groups that are formed, each member is an expert on one aspect, and he or she teaches the other members in the group.

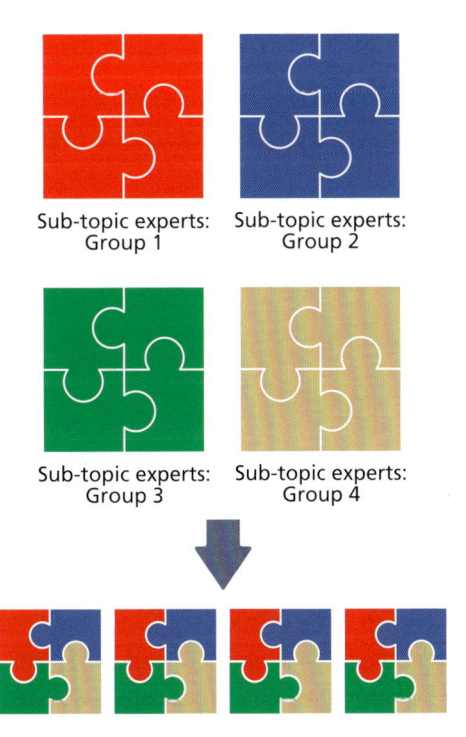

Sub-topic experts: Group 1
Sub-topic experts: Group 2
Sub-topic experts: Group 3
Sub-topic experts: Group 4

Step 1:
Each expert group studies its assigned topic.

Step 2:
The original expert groups break up to form new groups. Each new group will contain different people who are experts on different sub-topics.

Fig. 1.36 Jigsaw learning

FRAMING OUR IDEAS ABOUT POLITICS AND SOCIETY

Learning Methodology 4: Debate

This icon indicates that you will take part in either a moving debate or a traditional debate. In a moving debate, your teacher calls out several statements for discussion and debate. You listen carefully to each statement and then position yourself on a moving spectrum: from 'strongly agree' on one side of the classroom, to 'strongly disagree' on the other side of the classroom. You can move from one side of the classroom to the other, depending on your opinion on each statement. Be prepared to justify your opinion on each of the statements by using appropriate evidence where possible. Remember that it is okay to change your opinion and reposition yourself in moving debates, if you are persuaded by any of the alternative views put forward by other students in your class. In fact, this is a sign that you are an active listener and a critical and creative thinker!

Fig. 1.37 Debate

In a traditional debate, you will prepare written debate notes and take part in a team debate on a specific motion (a disputed idea or statement). You will be either proposing (in favour of) the motion or opposing (against) the motion. You will research and prepare evidence-based arguments that back up your reasoned judgements on the motion. Below is a typical structure of an evidence-based argument:

- State your thesis (argument) clearly.
- Explain the reason(s) why your argument is correct.
- Provide evidence (e.g. statistics, research data) to back up your reasons/argument.
- Conclude your argument by referring to the motion, and show how the argument justifies your stance on the motion.

Your teacher will provide you with more information on how to prepare for, and successfully participate in, a debate. You will learn tips on important debating skills such as developing appropriate body language, eye contact, hand gesturing, posture, tone of voice, pace and pitch.

Remember: in the Politics and Society course, the objective of debates is not for one side to win and the other to lose. Your debating skill will be assessed on how you listen to others, critique and respond to arguments, and use reasoned opinion and evidence to back up your arguments. The end goal is that you move towards a more reflective and informed conclusion on the motion – even if that means altering your views during the debate.

Learning Methodology 5: Research Activities

This logo in the textbook indicates that the students will have to examine a specific extract of research data. This will involve reading, analysing and critically evaluating pieces of quantitative or qualitative research data in either the textbook or the Skills Book. These have been designed to prepare you for the 'Data-Based Questions' in Section B of the Leaving Certificate written examination.

This logo/icon is used to indicate research assignments. In research assignments students will have to conduct their own research to investigate a specific issue or topic (either individually or collectively as part of a group). Many of these assignments have been designed so that you can supplement the research data in the textbook with the most up-to-date research on discursive essay topics that may appear in Section C of the Leaving Certificate written examination.

Research Tips

Where Can I Find Suitable Sources of Information?

In the Politics and Society course, you need to cite hard evidence and data from credible sources to back up your opinions. This means that you need to be careful when conducting your research, and to use only the most reliable sources when extracting data. Reliable statistics can be sourced from official government records, parliamentary debates, EU and UN publications, CSO data and ESRI reports. Newspapers are an excellent source for topical issues and events. Reputable broadsheet newspapers – national and international – are now available to view for free through the Irish Newspaper Archives – accessible through your school broadband network. This provides access to a national database of 69 newspapers spanning a 300-year period. Academic periodicals can be sourced via Google Scholar and are useful when looking for an academic perspective. For local data, the county library, government offices and local newspaper archives are valuable sources of information.

Fig. 1.38 Research

How Do I Cite Sources in My Research?

While conducting research, it is important to keep a record of the sources of your information so that you can cite them properly in your written assignment. Make sure that you take note of the name of the author(s), title of the publication, year of publication, publisher, place of publication and web address (if online).

How Do I Evaluate a Source?

Depending on your topic, some sources will be more useful than others. To save time, you need to quickly identify whether or not a source is useful to your research. The following tips will help you to evaluate each source.

- Always read the introduction/preface/executive summary first. This will tell you what the author will focus on in the rest of the document, which will help you decide whether this piece is worth reading for your assignment.
- Use the table of contents or index to help you locate the sections that are most relevant to your research topic.
- Check the bibliography, footnotes and list of references to see if they contain any other valuable sources of information that you could read.
- Consider the purpose of the publication. Why did the author write it? What did he or she want to achieve? Could there be a hidden agenda? Could it be a biased publication? Could it be considered a piece of propaganda?

FRAMING OUR IDEAS ABOUT POLITICS AND SOCIETY

- Assess the objectivity of the source. How objective is it? Does it contain many facts or is it full of opinions that lack evidence to back them up? Is it one-sided in its treatment of the topic? Does it cover all aspects of the issue equally?

- Assess the validity of the research. How valid are the facts? Is it clear where the facts came from? Are they cited properly? Are there any weaknesses in the research method adopted by the author? How representative is the research sample (e.g. how many respondents to a survey)? Consider the appropriateness of the 'types' of respondents. For example: surveying men only on a topic entitled 'Women's Experiences of Workplace Discrimination' would be inappropriate, whereas this sample *would* be appropriate for a topic entitled 'Men's Opinions on Women's Experiences of Workplace Discrimination'.

- Examine the relevance of the source. Does the source contain up-to-date information? How old is the source? Is it outdated? Is more contemporary data available elsewhere?

ACTIVE CITIZENSHIP: Ideas for Action

The development of Active Citizenship skills is an integral part of the Politics and Society course. To prepare you for the Active Citizenship project (worth 20 per cent of the grade), this book contains several suggestions for citizenship actions that can be taken by your class.

Ideas for action include:

- Launching an awareness-raising campaign using different types of media: designing posters, writing letters/articles for publication in newspapers or magazines, and using broadcast and social media to highlight your issue
- Undertaking fundraising for an organisation that is actively involved in advocating for your issue
- Lobbying public representatives and local politicians to take action on an issue by writing letters/emails and arranging meetings at constituency clinics or other locations
- Conducting a community-wide campaign through door-to-door campaigning, leaflet drops, arranging community meetings and inviting a guest speaker to address the community on a social issue
- Creating and submitting a petition to elected representatives
- Lobbying for new laws or changes to existing laws that are of particular concern
- Volunteering for a community or charitable project
- Participating in a political discussion
- Wearing a badge or putting a sticker with a social/political message on your car
- Demonstrating by organising marches, boycotts, sit-ins or other forms of protest.

Before deciding on the appropriate course of action to take, it is important that your class chooses a suitable issue to campaign for in the first place. This can only be achieved by first gathering qualitative and quantitative evidence, using surveys, questionnaires, interviews and research data to highlight the problem and the need to take action. More details on the Citizenship Project, and the precise topics for assessment each year, can be found on Curriculum Online at: https://educateplus.ie/go/curriculum

Key Thinkers

Throughout this book, you will see the Key Thinkers icon. This draws your attention to how a specific issue (e.g. power and decision-making in school) would be viewed 'through the eyes' of important political and social thinkers.

SUMMARY

- Politics involves more than just the decision-making processes of government. It includes all the interactions by people in the public sphere (including schools and workplaces) concerning the distribution of power and resources.
- The terms 'left-wing', 'centre' and 'right-wing' are used to describe where a person's beliefs can be placed on the political spectrum of ideologies.
- 'The left' generally refers to people who are socially liberal, who value political and civil rights, and who want greater government control or regulation of the economy to ensure a more equal distribution of wealth among all citizens.
- 'The right' generally refers to people who are socially conservative, who want to maintain traditional morals and values, and who support liberal economic policies such as free trade and low taxation.
- Capitalism is an economic system that features private ownership of the means of production (e.g. factories, offices, shipping enterprises) and in which market forces determine which goods are produced and how income and profit are distributed.
- Communism lies on the extreme left of the political spectrum and is based on the idea that private property and a capitalist (profit-making) economy should be replaced by complete public ownership and control of all property and natural resources.
- Karl Marx and Friedrich Engels are considered the founding fathers of communist ideology.
- Socialism is a political and economic system in which most forms of economically valuable property and resources are owned or controlled by the public or the state.
- Socialists advocate for a strong social welfare system with free or subsidised healthcare and education for all – usually to be paid by imposing higher taxes on the wealthy.
- Fascism is an extreme right-wing ideology that supports giving all power to an elite group or strong leader (usually a dictator) and does not allow any political opposition.
- Fascism is characterised by anti-democratic, anti-socialist, anti-liberal and sometimes racist or xenophobic policies.
- Fascists are extreme nationalists who value tradition and order in society and usually view their own country or race as superior to others.
- Libertarianism is an ideology based on the belief that people should be free to think and behave as they want and should not have limits put on them by governments.
- Conservatism is the dominant right-wing ideology today.
- Green politics, feminism and religious fundamentalism are political ideologies that have emerged in more recent times.
- Feminism is the belief that women should be allowed the same rights, power and opportunities as men, and that men and women should be treated equally.
- 'Society' refers to a group of people who share a common lifestyle in an organised community.
- People in society are often divided into different groups in a hierarchical structure according to their status, power and wealth. This is known as social stratification.
- In sociology, structural functionalism, social conflict theory and symbolic interactionism are the three main theories that attempt to explain social stratification.

- Thomas Hobbes, John Locke, Jean-Jacques Rousseau, John Stuart Mill, Karl Marx and Kathleen Lynch are key thinkers who have provided influential insights into important political and social issues.
- Information processing, communicating, being personally effective, working with others and critical and creative thinking are the five key skills that will be developed through the various active learning methodologies, activities and exercises in this book.

Fig. 1.39 Key Word cloud

REVISION EXERCISES

Complete the revision exercises on pages 6–8 of your Skills Book.

EXAM FOCUS: Section A of LC Exam

Reflective Practice

Ensure that you have completed all the Reflective Journal entries for this chapter (pages 1–2 of your Reflective Journal and Learning Portfolio) before moving on to the next chapter.

Complete the Learning Portfolio activities on pages 2–4 of your Reflective Journal and Learning Portfolio. This will help you to self-assess the extent to which you have achieved the learning intentions for this chapter, and will help you to monitor your progress.

CHAPTER 2

Power and Decision-Making in School

KEY TERMS

- Power
- Autonomy
- Rules
- Norms
- Myth of meritocracy
- Meritocracy
- Zero tolerance
- Stakeholder
- Representation
- Coercive power
- Authority

Introduction

Politics is about decision-making, and decision-making is about **power**! We make decisions every day of our lives on topics great and small: what we eat for breakfast, who we spend our lunch-break with, what we do in the evenings, etc. However, not all decisions are made solely by ourselves. To varying degrees, and in different areas of our lives and in society, we do not have absolute freedom to make decisions **autonomously** or independently, free from outside control.

Sometimes the choices available to us are restricted or limited by external influences in our society. For example, under Irish law all children under the age of 16 must receive a basic standard of education. The choice open to us in this regard is restricted to two options: enrolment in a standard school or home-schooling. Sometimes the decisions we take will be influenced by others (e.g. attending a particular school because our friends/neighbours go there). Sometimes other people make the decisions for us (e.g. the amount of time we spend at school each day).

KEY TERMS

Power is the ability to influence the thoughts, behaviours or actions of others.

Autonomy in decision-making means being able to make decisions independently, without external control.

Fig. 2.1 How we behave at school is not only determined by school rules but also by social norms

Power in decision-making is about *who* decides. The power to decide who gets what, when and how, or what we can and cannot do in our societies, is often dictated by sets of **rules** and **norms**. The enforcement of rules in school and wider society is also about power, and there are different ways to exercise power in order to make people act and behave in certain ways.

As students, much of our time is spent at school. Schools can be considered as mini-societies. Life in school is organised and managed by a set of established rules that govern many areas of our conduct and behaviour. Many decisions are made for us: what clothing we may or may not wear, how we spend our time, and how we behave inside and outside the classroom. But why do we have rules in the first place? What would happen if we did not have rules? Who establishes the rules? Who participates? Who benefits? Do the rules affect some individuals or groups more than others? How are rules enforced? Are there winners and losers? These are all central questions to understanding power and decision-making in school. A wealth of interesting ideas, research and case studies from Ireland and beyond have made important contributions to this debate.

KEY TERMS

Rules are about what we 'can' and 'cannot' do. We have rules in many different spheres of our lives and society: how we play sports, how we behave at the cinema, how we dress and act in school, etc. Rules can be formal or informal, written or unwritten. If rules are broken, there may or may not be consequences.

Norms are about what we 'should' and 'should not' do. 'Norms' refers to the ways we are expected to think and act. These expectations are influenced by culture, society, religion and other types of organising principles. Norms are often used as the basis to form rules. However, in the absence of rules, we will often act according to socially accepted norms and values. Can you identify any norms that influence your thoughts and actions?

By the end of this chapter you will be able to:

- List arguments for and against the need for school rules.
- Summarise the views of key social and political thinkers regarding the need for rules in society, and explain how these views can be applied to a debate on school rules.
- Describe and explain Marxist, feminist and functionalist perspectives on the purpose and role of education in society.
- Define the term 'stakeholder' and list all the stakeholders in your school.
- Explain the roles of the various stakeholders in the decision-making process at your school, with specific reference to the roles played by the Department of Education, board of management, principal, patron, teachers, parents and students.
- Explain how students can use the student council to have their voices heard and to be represented in the decision-making process at school.
- Describe in detail the steps that were involved in the decision-making process that led to the creation of two rules at your school.
- Describe the hierarchy of power at your school by identifying the people/groups with the most power and those with the least influence in making decisions.
- Summarise research evidence on the extent to which some groups are under-represented in decision-making processes in schools.
- Describe the different methods that can be used to implement and enforce school rules.
- Summarise the views of key thinkers on the issue of how power and order is maintained in society, and explain how the views of these key thinkers can be applied to the maintenance of order at school.
- Identify the groups who benefit the most and least from the decision-making structures, policies and rules that exist in Irish schools.
- Evaluate the extent to which decision-making processes in schools are appropriate, with reference to different viewpoints, specific research and evidence.
- Suggest actions that can be taken to improve the power structures and decision-making processes in Irish schools.

By the end of this chapter you will have developed the following skills:
- Better communication skills, by taking part in various class discussions, debates and short presentations.
- Improved interpersonal skills and the ability to work effectively with other students as a member of a group on shared tasks.
- Research skills, by searching for and locating relevant research on the role of education and on the concepts of power and decision-making in Irish schools.
- Information processing and critical thinking skills, by examining the strengths, weaknesses and limitations of key pieces of research and viewpoints concerning power and decision-making in schools.

ACTIVITY 2.1

Norms are different from rules. One example of a norm is that we should greet people with a handshake in order to show respect. An example of a rule is that we must stop at a red traffic light. Work with your partner to complete the following activity.

1. Think individually for a moment about some of the norms that you experience in everyday Irish life. *(Think)*
2. With your partner, agree a list of three norms. Make sure that they are not rules! *(Pair)*
3. Share your list with the rest of the class. *(Share)*

SKILLS BOOK LINK 2.1

Go to page 9 of your Skills Book to complete Skill Task 2.1 on remote island rules.

The Need for Rules in Schools

A wide range of different views and positions exists with regard to the need for rules in schools in the first place. Some of these arguments are summarised in Table 2.1 (page 41). As you can see, there are differences in opinion on what the rules should and should not cover with respect to school and student life. Should rules be concerned with student safety only, or promoting an orderly environment that supports learning? Should rules be extended so that they cultivate in students certain social values and norms, such as respect, equality and tolerance? Do we need rules prohibiting absence from class and restricting freedom of movement of students during class (e.g. forbidding toilet breaks)? Do schools need rigid rules about student conduct and communication during lessons (e.g. putting one's hand up to ask a question or speak)? Or do we simply need rules that prohibit intolerant or disrespectful treatment of students and teachers? The ideas of many prominent political and social thinkers in relation to government can be applied to the debate on school rules. We can think of schools as small societies, where school management is the government and students are the citizens. We can examine the ideas of political thinkers so that we can understand the different sides and start to develop our own position in the debate.

KEY THINKERS

Thomas Hobbes
People are naturally selfish and unruly and so must give control to a powerful authority to rule them in order to ensure the preservation of all.

John Locke
Government must respect and protect the rights and freedoms of the individual.

John Stuart Mill
Government should intervene only if the actions of an individual will negatively impact the interests or freedom of another.

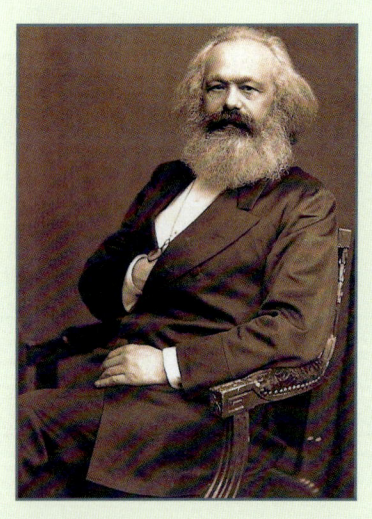

Karl Marx
In a capitalist society, rules exist to protect and perpetuate the position of powerful groups.

Émile Durkheim
We are all interdependent and order is achieved through shared and internalised norms and values rather than external enforcement of rules.

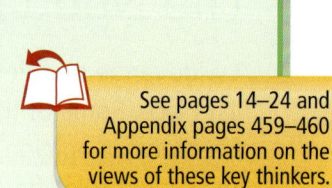

See pages 14–24 and Appendix pages 459–460 for more information on the views of these key thinkers.

SKILLS BOOK LINK 2.2

Go to pages 10–11 of your Skills Book to complete Skill Task 2.2 on key thinkers.

POWER AND PEOPLE

For	Against
Rules promote good behaviour and punish bad behaviour, creating a positive school environment for all.	Excessive rules limit personal freedom and liberty.
Rules provide order, which is necessary for a good learning environment and the health and safety of all.	Rules stifle student creativity and self-expression.
Rules ensure that we respect important customs and traditions in our schools.	Certain rules can act to maintain existing inequalities in society, such as class, gender and ethnicity.
Rules promote predictable behaviour, making it easier to govern the student body.	Too many rules result in excessive time spent on rule enforcement and disciplinary action, rather than teaching.
Certain rules are needed to ensure equality of treatment and opportunity for students disadvantaged by class, ethnicity or disability.	Some rules are unnecessary and counter-productive; they cause resentment and often lead to heightened tension and needless conflict.

Table 2.1 Arguments for and against the need for rules in school

QUESTIONS

1. Which **two** of the *for* arguments in Table 2.1 do you most agree with? Give reasons to support your choice, making specific reference to your own school context.

2. Which **two** of the *against* arguments in Table 2.1 do you most agree with? Give reasons to support your choice, making specific reference to your own school context.

3. Can you list any other arguments for and against school rules?

4. What is the difference between norms and rules?

ACTIVITY 2.2

Your teacher will call out several arguments/statements concerning rules at school. You will take part in a moving debate and express your opinion on each statement.

SKILLS BOOK LINK 2.3

After the debate in Activity 2.2, go to pages 11–12 of your Skills Book to complete Skill Task 2.3 on school rules.

The Role of Education in Society

Sociological theory has contributed much to our understanding of schools and education systems in societies. A person's opinion on the types of rules we should have in school can be influenced by his or her view on the overall role of education in society.

KEY THINKERS: THE ROLE OF EDUCATION IN SOCIETY

Some sociologists have studied how education is used as a tool in society. The concept of the hidden curriculum refers to lessons that are taught informally, and usually unintentionally, in a school system. These lessons include behaviours, views and attitudes that students learn to adopt while they are at school. There are three dominant perspectives: Marxist, functionalist and feminist.

Complete your next Reflective Journal entry (pages 5–6)

KEY THINKERS

MARXIST PERSPECTIVE

Paulo Freire

Paulo Freire was a Brazilian educator and social activist who developed important and influential ideas on the role of education in liberation. Freire's main argument was that education is never 'neutral' or objective. Instead, it involves the active selection (and exclusion) of the types of knowledge that are imparted in society. Freire believed that traditional teaching approaches acted to maintain the status quo in society. In this model, the student is a passive actor receiving information and knowledge from the teacher. Freire termed this 'banking education', whereby the teacher makes deposits of knowledge in the mind (bank) of the passive student. This banking approach dehumanises the student and leads to what Freire calls a 'culture of silence'.

Freire shared Marx's understanding of societal divisions and class conflict and Freire considered traditional approaches to education as serving the interests of the dominant class. However, he believed that just as education could play a role in maintaining oppressive relations in a society, it could also liberate it. Freire offered an alternative to the traditional banking approach, which he termed 'problem-posing education'. Critical inquiry, active dialogue and mutually respectful learning between students and teachers are central to his model. The classroom becomes a democratic space where the voices of students and teachers are equal.

Freire's model was based on a cycle whereby we critically reflect on an issue or subject, take action in relation to the issue, and critically reflect once more. Freire termed this process 'praxis'. Through praxis, Freire believed that students would develop a critical consciousness ('conscientisation') and have the skills and capacity to become better citizens who are able to contribute to society and address injustices.

KEY TERMS

Myth of meritocracy is the idea that a false competition based on 'fairness' is created between individuals in a system (e.g. education) in order to maintain or reproduce the status quo (e.g. class system or capitalism).

Sam Bowles

Herb Gintis

In the 1970s, American economists and social theorists Sam Bowles and Herb Gintis developed a theory on the relationship between social inequality and education. Their theory detailed how the US schooling system reproduced the class inequalities of US society. They argued that the school system prepared students for the workforce in a capitalist system in two main ways: reinforcing a hierarchy of social relations; and cultivating desirable characteristics and behaviours (i.e. respecting authority and being obedient). This is known as the correspondence principle. In the school system, the relationships between administrators and teachers, teachers and students, students and students, and students and their work are designed to mirror the hierarchical divisions of labour of the capitalist model (e.g. manager and worker).

The second element of Bowles and Gintis's theory is the **myth of meritocracy**. Making use of Marx's concept of alienation, the theory states that students become alienated from their learning and from each other through the system of external rewards (grades) which acts to create competition between students and a work ethic that is suitable for the capitalist model of production. According to Bowles and Gintis, we do not challenge the system, since it appears to be objective and fair. The education system exerts control over students through more rigid rules during earlier stages (i.e. elementary and high school) than the later stages (i.e. third-level colleges and universities). The system allows students to have more freedom once they have accepted and adopted the appropriate behaviour from each stage.

Bowles and Gintis argued that school systems differ on the basis of social class. Working-class schools tend to emphasise behavioural control and respect for clear rules, while schools in middle- or upper-class neighbourhoods employ relatively open systems that permit student participation, with less direct supervision, and rely on the internalisation of values and norms of how to behave, rather than strict rules. The dominant class in society ensures that the education system operates in this way to maintain the existing capitalist model that privileges its position.

FUNCTIONALIST PERSPECTIVE

Émile Durkheim

Émile Durkheim was born in France in 1858. He was a functional sociologist, which means that he looked at different institutions in society (e.g. family, religion, education) and their role in keeping society working properly. Durkheim viewed the school as a mini-society. Education provides two main functions in society: it promotes social unity and solidarity, and it creates specialist skills.

The first function involves creating a sense of common shared history and belonging between students. This is achieved through teaching the main norms and values of our society (fairness, respect, work ethic, etc.). Solidarity, which can be understood as the bonds between individuals in society, is essential to the functioning and order of society.

The second function of education is to create the skills necessary for individuals to be functional members of society. As with the human body, society has different *parts* which make up the *whole*. The different parts of society require skills from different people, such as doctors, lawyers, farmers and teachers. Education creates these skills.

Talcott Parsons

American sociologist Talcott Parsons further developed Durkheim's ideas in the 1950s and 1960s. Parsons argued that education is one of the main 'socialising' agents in society: it ensures that we act in ways that are 'acceptable' to society. The family unit is involved in the first stages of socialisation ('primary socialisation'). Children are judged by rules that apply only to them or their family ('particularistic rules'). Parents design unique rules or adapt rules on the basis of their child's unique traits and abilities. However, society operates on the basis of universal standards and rules (e.g. laws) that are generic and apply to everyone. Schools play a role in preparing children and young people to engage with societal rules (accepted norms and values). In addition, through the curriculum and exam standards, schools play a role in distributing future roles (i.e. professions) and introducing individuals to the concept of **meritocracy**.

> ### KEY TERMS
>
> **Meritocracy** refers to a system whereby people succeed or are rewarded on the basis of their skills and ability (merit).

FEMINIST PERSPECTIVE

Feminist sociologists look at how education and the education system is designed to support patriarchy in society. Education reproduces gender stereotypes and relations. Where *class* is the determining factor for Marxists, *gender* is the focus in the feminist perspective. In the feminist perspective, children begin to learn gender-differentiated social roles in the family. Girls and boys are given different roles in the household, and parents have different expectations of their children's behaviour based on their gender. Examples include: parents may be more likely to disapprove if a girl fights with another child than if a boy fights with another child; girls may be given household cleaning tasks, while

POWER AND DECISION-MAKING IN SCHOOL

KEY THINKERS

boys are given gardening tasks. From the feminist perspective, before children start school, they have already undergone a significant amount of gender learning (primary socialisation).

Feminists argue that education is an agent of secondary socialisation, since it takes over from the family in the teaching of gender roles. Feminists argue that the 'hidden curriculum' is used to teach gender-based roles, i.e. the 'accepted' roles and behaviours of girls and boys. Subjects and sports are aimed at different groups based on gender (e.g. Home Economics and hockey may be targeted at girls, while Woodwork and rugby may be targeted at boys).

Feminist sociologists have pointed out that the literature studied in school often portrays women in a particular way on the basis of gender stereotypes, i.e. women are the 'weaker sex' or 'dependent' on men. Feminists have also pointed out that some teachers may hold sexist views that result in gender discrimination, i.e. asking boys to move furniture and girls to perform cleaning tasks. Sociologists writing about feminist perspectives on education include: **Ann Oakley**, **Eileen Byrne**, **Sue Sharpe**, **Lesley Best** and **Sylvia Walby**.

Fig. 2.2 According to feminists, gender stereotypes and roles are learned at school

QUESTIONS

1. Do you agree with Paulo Freire that education is not neutral or objective but deliberately tailored to maintain the status quo of society? Can you think of any aspects of the curriculum or subjects at school that show a biased focus on knowledge that maintains the status quo? Do you learn anything at school that challenges the status quo?

2. Is Bowles and Gintis's analysis of education and their 'correspondence principle' applicable to the Irish education system today? What rules and practices at your school reinforce the capitalist hierarchy of social relations? In what ways are you being prepared for life as a worker in a capitalist economy?

3. To what extent can your school be viewed from a functionalist perspective? Do you think certain rules are in place in your school to prepare you to contribute to society as a whole?

4. Do you agree with feminists such as Sylvia Walby that the education system reinforces gender stereotypes and promotes patriarchy? Refer to specific rules or practices at your school that support your argument.

ACTIVITY 2.3

Identify any two rules or practices in your school. Discuss and explain how these rules could be viewed through the three main sociological perspectives:

(a) Marxist   (b) Functionalist   (c) Feminist.

Complete your next Reflective Journal entry (pages 5–6)

The Political Spectrum

The political spectrum can be a useful tool when looking at the debate surrounding school rules. Conservatives, liberals, socialists, environmentalists and feminists all have arguments for and against the need for rules in schools. The arguments of each group are based on their particular beliefs about the primary purpose of school rules – the reason a rule is needed in the first place. For example, a conservative argument for rules might be based on the desire to respect custom and tradition or to ensure order. A liberal may wish to see rules that protect the rights and freedoms of individuals and particular groups, such as students with disabilities or students who are LGBTQ+. A socialist may argue that we need certain rules in schools to promote equal learning and education opportunities for those students who are disadvantaged based on class. An environmentalist may argue that we need rules on recycling and the promotion of environmentally friendly modes of transportation to and from school (e.g. walking, cycling). A feminist may argue that schools need special rules to address discrimination that female students face (e.g. in relation to subject choices). Whatever position we take in the debate surrounding school rules, it is important to always back up our argument with facts and figures. There is a wealth of research and data to support the different sides of the debate.

See page 4 for more information on the political spectrum.

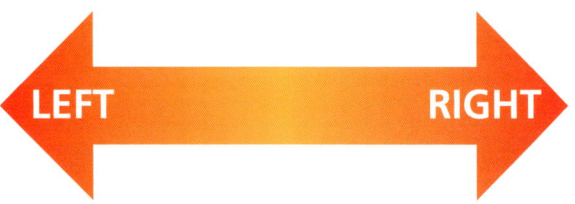

Fig. 2.3 The political spectrum

SKILLS BOOK LINK 2.4

Go to pages 13–14 of your Skills Book to complete Skill Task 2.4 on the orientation of school rules.

WHAT THE RESEARCH SAYS!

THE CASE *FOR* RULES IN SCHOOLS

Ban on Mobile Phones in School Leads to Improved Academic Performance

A study published in May 2015 by the Centre for Economic Performance at the London School of Economics (LSE) claims that banning mobile phones from school premises adds up to the equivalent of an extra week's schooling over a student's academic year. The research, carried out at secondary schools in Birmingham, Leicester, London and Manchester, assessed the academic performance of students aged 16 before and after mobile phone bans were introduced. Academic performance was found to have increased by an average of 6.4 per cent. The research factored in student characteristics of gender, special educational needs, prior educational attainment, and eligibility for free school meals. In doing so, the research also found that low-income and low-achieving students benefited the most. Little or no change was recorded for high-achieving students.

Fig. 2.4 Mobile phones in the classroom

Student Anti-Bullying Contracts – KiVa Programme, Finland

KiVa (from the Finnish words *kiusaamista vastaan*, meaning 'against bullying') is a national anti-bullying programme in Finland developed by the University of Turku and funded by the Ministry of Education and Culture. The programme provides teachers, students and parents with tools to prevent and address bullying in primary and secondary schools. KiVa is based on the idea that bystanders are just as influential as the perpetrator in providing the conditions for bullying to take place and continue. One important aspect of the KiVa programme is the participatory establishment of anti-bullying rules by the teacher and students. The programme consists of a series of themed lessons and a rule is associated with each of these themes. Following each lesson, the class agrees to adopt the rule and by the end of the year a contract containing all the agreed rules is developed and all students sign it. Statistics show that 98 per cent of students whose cases of bullying were handled by the KiVa approach have stated that their situation improved. Over 80 per cent of schools in Finland now implement KiVa, and the programme has also been adopted in several European countries, New Zealand and Chile. In 2009 the programme received first prize in the European Crime Prevention Awards (ECPA) and is widely acknowledged around the world as anti-bullying best practice.

Fig. 2.5 Bullying at school

WHAT THE **RESEARCH** SAYS!

THE CASE *AGAINST* RULES IN SCHOOLS

A 'Zero Tolerance' Approach to Discipline is Ineffective in Preventing ESL

The Education Disadvantage Centre (EDC) at Dublin City University (DCU) is at the forefront of research on the prevention of Early School Leaving (ESL) in European countries. Multi-country research conducted by EDC has found that a **zero tolerance** approach to school discipline, and in particular the procedure

Fig. 2.6 Discipline in school

KEY TERM

Zero tolerance is a term used to describe an approach to the enforcement of a rule or policy by imposing strict punishment for any breaches, however small.

POWER AND PEOPLE

of suspension, is highly ineffective in preventing ESL. Suspension is not always an effective response for students who are already at risk of dropping out of school. Students at higher risk of non-attendance and ESL experience a range of social and educational difficulties that cannot be effectively addressed by traditional and strict approaches to discipline. The EDC recommends alternatives to suspension and expulsion, especially in schools with higher rates of student disengagement, behavioural issues, discipline problems and ESL. Some of the alternatives proposed include: the use of a 'time out' room, changes in class management policies, and the use of multidisciplinary teams made up of social workers, school psychologists, family support workers and mentors.

Stand Up for Better Learning!

A 2014 study by the Texas A&M Health Science Center (published in the *International Journal of Environmental Research and Public Health*) found that allowing students to stand during class produced health benefits and increased cognitive function. The two-year study covered a group of 374 elementary school students in Texas. Half of these students were provided with standing desks. Each of the 374 students wore a biometric monitor that measured his or her heart rate, movement and calorie burn. A group of educational psychologists observed the level of engagement of these 374 students in learning. The study found that children who were overweight or obese burned more calories at the standing desks, and that all students using standing desks were more engaged in their learning than the group in traditional seated environments.

Fig. 2.7 Stand up for better learning

QUESTIONS

1. Which of the **four** research pieces contains the strongest evidence to support its argument? Make reference to the precise evidence used in the chosen research piece and explain why the evidence is stronger than that presented in the other research pieces.

2. Are there any limitations to the evidence used in the research piece you chose for Question 1?

3. Which of the **four** research pieces contains the weakest evidence to support its argument? Explain why you think the evidence is weak and suggest alternative types of research that could have been conducted to improve the argument in the research piece.

4. With reference to your own experience of school, do you agree or disagree with the arguments presented in the first two research pieces? Give reasons for your answer.

POWER AND DECISION-MAKING IN SCHOOL

ACTIVITY 2.4

Your teacher will call out several of the rules at your school. You will take part in a 'moving debate' where you express your opinion on each of the rules.

ACTIVITY 2.5

Imagine that you are the new board of management of your school. Work together as a group to agree on:

- **Two** school rules that should be abolished
- **Two** rules that should be maintained
- **Two** new school rules to be adopted.

Explain your reasons for each decision.

SKILLS BOOK LINK 2.5

Go to pages 14–15 of your Skills Book to complete Skill Task 2.5 on school rules and policies.

See **RESEARCH TIPS** on page 33.

Where Do School Rules Come From?

Schools in Ireland have a lot of autonomy when it comes to certain aspects of school management, such as deciding on school ethos and values. Schools in Ireland have less autonomy in relation to other aspects that are regulated by national policies set by the government through the Department of Education and Skills (e.g. curriculum and assessment, and health and safety). The school management body (patron, board of management, principal, etc.) establishes the rules; however, these rules must be in line with national laws and policies.

Each school has several policy documents showing the rules that are in place for issues such as enrolment, school uniform, child protection, anti-bullying, and health and safety. Usually, the majority of rules that directly affect students will be gathered together in a document called the *code of behaviour*. The code of behaviour is a policy document that outlines the practices and procedures a school adopts to promote and ensure good student behaviour and a healthy and safe learning environment. Irish law includes the Education (Welfare) Act, 2000. Under this Act, the board of management of a school is responsible for preparing the code of behaviour, which must comply with guidelines set by the National Educational Welfare Board (NEWB).

According to NEWB guidelines, the code of behaviour should be developed using an inclusive, whole-school approach that involves all the major **stakeholders** in the school community (e.g. parents, students, teaching staff). The code must also comply with national and international legislation, including:

- Education Act, 1998
- European Convention on Human Rights (1950)
- UN Convention on the Rights of the Child (1989).

KEY TERM

A **stakeholder** is anyone with a particular interest or concern in relation to an issue or an organisation and is considered as having a legitimate right to be involved in related decision-making processes.

See page 293 for more information on the European Convention on Human Rights.

POWER AND PEOPLE

This legislation limits what the board of management can include in the code of behaviour, and protects students from excessive use of power by school management. Students give up certain freedoms in exchange for certain benefits in a type of *social contract* with school management. As such, the code of behaviour is not unlike the constitution of a democratic country, which protects the rights of citizens and places limits on the powers of government.

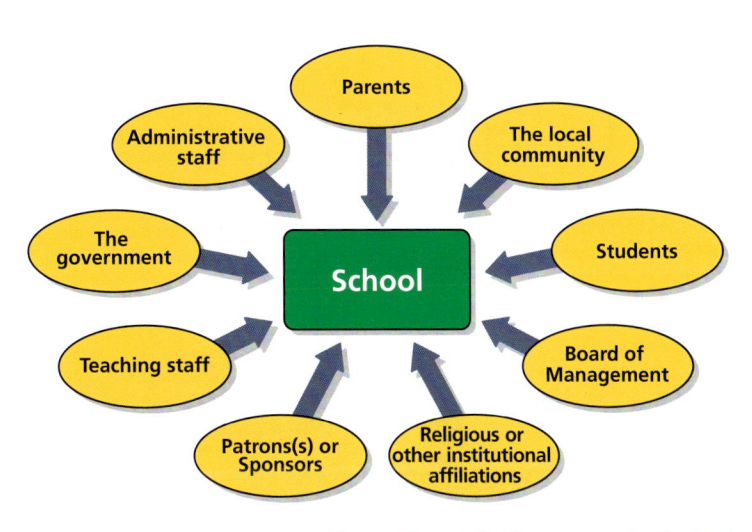

Fig. 2.8 The stakeholders in a typical Irish school

See page 272 for more information on the UN Convention on the Rights of the Child.

ACTIVITY 2.6

In 2005 Tony Benn, a British political activist and Labour MP, posed five 'essential questions of democracy' which he claimed must always be protected and used to make accountable any people who are in power. Benn's essential questions of democracy are:

1. What power have you got?
2. Where did you get it from?
3. In whose interests do you exercise it?
4. To whom are you accountable?
5. How can we get rid of you?

Why not ask your teacher or principal if they can answer these questions?

Work with your partner to complete the following activity.

1. Think individually for a moment about how either your teacher or the principal of your school might answer Benn's five questions. (*Think*)
2. With your partner, write down possible answers that your teacher or principal might give to each of the five questions. (*Pair*)
3. Share your answers with the rest of the class. (*Share*)

The Power to Make Rules

Whether in school or wider society, the decision-making processes behind the establishment of rules is at the heart of politics. If decision-making is about power, then the decision-making process is a political issue. How rules are made, who is involved and who is not involved, are political questions. What is the basis for being involved in decision-making? Where does decision-making power come from? In Ireland, the post-primary education sector includes different types of schools: vocational schools and community colleges, voluntary schools that are privately owned and managed (e.g. religious communities), and community and comprehensive schools. Vocational schools and community colleges are established by government and are managed by Education and Training Boards (ETBs). All other school types are managed by boards of management that vary in composition, but normally include **representation** from parents, teachers and patrons (owners) who are considered stakeholders.

> ## KEY TERM
>
> **Representation** in decision-making refers to the way in which individuals act on behalf of the entire population (e.g. citizens of a country) or a specific section of the population (e.g. women and/or people with disabilities) in decision-making processes. The rationale is that it is not possible for everyone to directly participate in the decision-making process. In the school context, on the board of management we often have representatives for groups such as parents and teachers.

KEY THINKERS

SOURCES OF POWER

Max Weber

German sociologist Max Weber provided one of the first sociological explanations of power in the early nineteenth century. For Weber, power could be either 'coercive' or 'legitimate'. **Coercive power** is based on forcing people to act as you want, on the basis of a threat of punishment or force. Legitimate power is known as '**authority**'. It is power that is institutionalised and recognised by the people over whom it is exercised.

Weber defined three types of legitimate power.

- *Charismatic authority* is a type of power based on an individual's personality and charisma. These leaders inspire others to act in a certain way. Famous charismatic leaders have included Gandhi in India and Adolf Hitler in Germany.
- *Traditional authority* is based on traditional beliefs or customs: authority is passed down in a hereditary manner. Examples of traditional authority include religious leaders or monarchs (kings or queens).
- *Rational-legal authority* is what we associate with many of our modern democracies. In this type of power, leaders get their authority on the basis of a system of rules (e.g. laws). Once they leave their office or position, they lose the authority. Examples include leaders in government, organisations and businesses.

> ## KEY TERMS
>
> **Coercive power** is authority that is dependent on fear, suppression of free will and the use or threat of punishment.
>
> **Authority** is when an individual or group in society has a legitimate right to use power. In western democracies, authority comes from established rules, laws, policies and regulations.

Robert A. Dahl and C. Wright Mills

In the late 1950s and early 1960s, American political theorists Robert A. Dahl and C. Wright Mills were involved in an academic battle over their competing theories of power. For Dahl, political power in the US was not concentrated but was distributed among a variety of different actors in society (e.g. business groups, unions, media organisations). This theory is known as a 'pluralist' theory.

In contrast, the opposing theory of C. Wright Mills was the 'power elite' theory. It states that power is in fact monopolised (under exclusive control) by a few elite individuals or institutions of society (e.g. wealthy people, business, the military).

Karl Marx

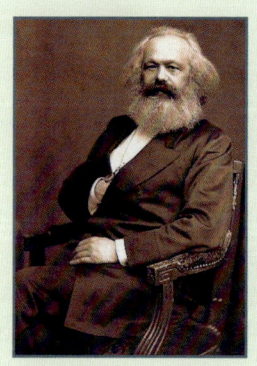

Marx's understanding of power is tied to his theory of social class. The division of power follows the division of labour. The ownership class (bourgeoisie) exercise power over the working class (proletariat).

QUESTIONS

1. According to Max Weber there are three types of authority. Which type(s) is most reflective of the power structure in your school?
2. Which of the ideas of the key thinkers (on page 50) best applies to power at school? Which of the ideas least applies to power at school?

ACTIVITY 2.7

Work with your partner to complete the following activity. In each case below, which theory best applies: pluralist theory or power elite theory?

(a) Power in your school
(b) Economic power in Ireland
(c) Political power in Ireland.

1. Think individually for a moment about the question. *(Think)*
2. With your partner, agree an answer for each part of the question. *(Pair)*
3. Share your answer with the rest of the class. *(Share)*

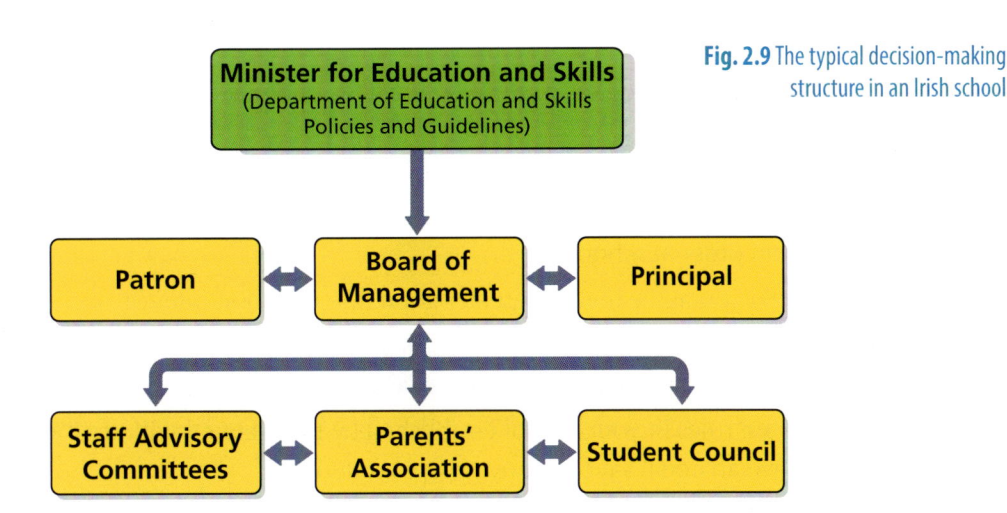

Fig. 2.9 The typical decision-making structure in an Irish school

QUESTIONS

1. The three stakeholders at the bottom of Fig. 2.9 play a primarily consultative role in the decision-making process. Is this fair? Should they have more power?
2. Find out what stakeholders have a seat on your own school's board of management. Is it composed in a balanced and representative manner?

POWER AND DECISION-MAKING IN SCHOOL

KEY THINKERS

SOCIAL CONTRACT

Thomas Hobbes
People will compete on the basis of their own selfish interests and therefore need to enter into a social contract whereby they exchange their liberty to gain security.

John Locke
The social contract involves the surrender of the individual right to maintain general order but it should have as few rules as possible so that it does not affect important rights, such as life, liberty and personal property. 'Make but a few laws but see they be well observed, when once made.'

Jean-Jacques Rousseau
The social contract is made up of rules established by the 'general will' of all.

QUESTIONS

1. Do schools operate according to a 'social contract' as outlined by Hobbes? Give reasons to support your answer.
2. Make a list of the individual rights that you 'surrender' at school (according to your school rules) in order to 'maintain general order'. Do you think it is necessary to surrender all these rights to maintain order at school?
3. In general, would you agree that the greater good (the common interest) should supersede (be treated as more important than) the rights of the individual? Explain your answer.
4. Do you agree with Locke that rules should be 'as few as possible'?
5. To what extent are rules in your school established by the 'general will of all'? Do all stakeholders have an equal say? Are any groups excluded?
6. Can your code of behaviour be considered a type of constitution? What specific aspects of the code of behaviour in your school protect your rights as a student? In what ways does the code of behaviour in your school limit the power of school management?

Participation and Power in Decision-Making in Schools

In the context of school rules, a variety of actors can participate in decision-making. But what does it mean to participate? Participation in decision-making can take a variety of forms, each with its own degree of 'power' (see Fig. 2.10). While the board of management of a school is the primary decision-maker in relation to establishing school rules, it must consult with the main stakeholders of the school community – teachers, parents, educational welfare officers, etc. The inclusion of these groups in decision-making is based on important democratic principles of representation and participation.

Ladder of participation and levels of power in decision-making

Decision-making: Having a direct say or vote on the final decision (high level of power)

Consultation: Having your views or opinions considered in the decision-making process (medium level of power)

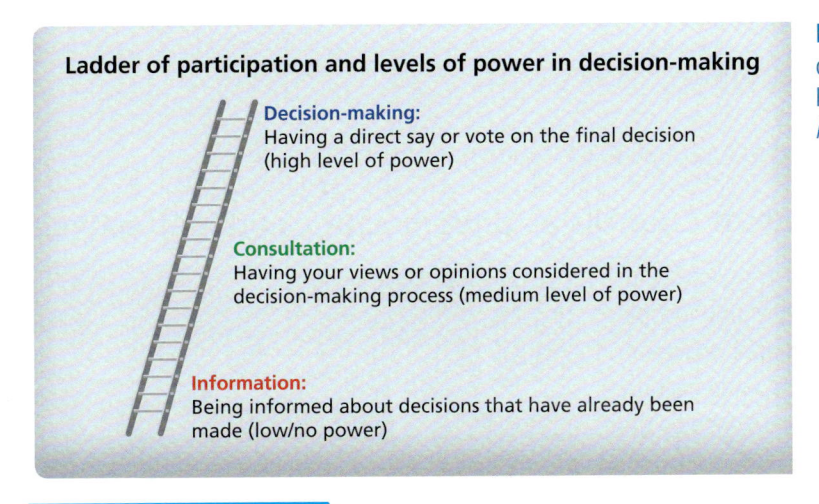

Information: Being informed about decisions that have already been made (low/no power)

Fig. 2.10 Ladder of participation and levels of power in decision-making. (Note: The ladder metaphor is borrowed from Sherry Arnstein, 1969.)

QUESTIONS

1. Give examples of any instances in which you were involved in (a) decision-making or (b) consultation.
2. At what stage of the ladder are you as a student at your school?
3. At what stage of the ladder is your student council? Should it be higher or lower? Give reasons to support your answer.

Student Participation in Decision-Making

Since the 1990s there has been a growing focus on the need for participation by children and young people in the global rights movement. It is now recommended as best practice in Ireland to include consultation with students in the decision-making processes within the school system. A student council (see below) is the most common formal mechanism used by students in Ireland to engage with school management in an attempt to have students' views heard and their interests represented in school decision-making processes. The effectiveness of student councils in influencing decision-making processes in schools has been the focus of much research in Ireland and beyond.

See page 56 for more information on the right to participate.

Student Council

A student council is a representative structure through which students in a post-primary school can become involved in the affairs of the school, working in partnership with school management and staff and parents for the benefit of the school and its students.

The Education Act, 1998 recognises that student councils are an increasingly common feature in post-primary schools and have worked to the benefit of many schools. Students have a valuable contribution to make to the effective running of schools. The involvement of students in the operation of their school is in itself a valuable part of the education process for the students. Research indicates that student councils can improve academic standards and reduce dropout rates in schools. Student councils can create a sense of ownership of the school and its activities among the student population. The contribution made by a student council to the development of school policy in a number of areas can have significant benefits for students and the school. School policies are far more likely to be successful where they are clearly understood and accepted by all partners within the school community.

Fig. 2.11 Student councils

POWER AND DECISION-MAKING IN SCHOOL

WHAT THE RESEARCH SAYS!

STUDENT COUNCILS

Irish Students View Student Councils as Undemocratic and Ineffective

A 2015 study on the views and experiences of participation of Irish children and young people found that they generally view formal spaces in schools for student participation as undemocratic and ineffective. The study was commissioned by the Department of Children and Youth Affairs (DCYA) and involved interviews with 74 children and young people by a team of researchers from University College Cork. Students stated that they had very little influence over school management and rules, or how teaching and education is conducted. Students felt that student councils did not have influence over important decisions, did not offer a real opportunity to give students a voice, were not representative of the diversity of students, and did not always properly communicate decisions made by the council. The two most important issues identified by study participants were teaching methods and subject choice. Students suggested having a specific class or time set aside to discuss issues of concern to them in a structured and regular manner.

Fig. 2.12 Students have a valuable contribution to make to the effective running of schools

Second-Level Students in Ireland Enjoy Comparatively Lower Participation in School Life

In 2009 the International Civic and Citizenship Education Study (ICCS) found that students in Ireland had lower perceived influence in decision-making compared to the other 37 countries covered by the study. In comparison with average results, a smaller percentage of students in Ireland felt that their opinions were taken into account to a moderate/large extent in:

- Decision-making about school rules – 34 per cent versus 51 per cent
- How classes are taught – 29 per cent versus 56 per cent
- Teaching and learning materials – 33 per cent versus 50 per cent.

A subsequent analysis of Ireland's ICCS results found that the legal provisions of the Education Act, 1998 are weak in relation to the establishment and functioning of student councils. The establishment of student councils is not mandatory in Ireland, and student councils have little or no input in relation to decision-making on issues such as teaching and subject content.

School Councils in England and the Need for Greater Representation of Students with Diverse Interests

According to a 2010 study conducted in England by the Children's Rights Alliance for England, the overwhelming majority of children and young people interviewed felt that they do not have a sufficient level of influence in decision-making processes in school. The study involved focus group interviews with 44 boys and 42 girls aged between 3 and 20 years. It noted that members of school councils were perceived to be the more 'clever, popular, well-behaved children'. The study recommended that student councils diversify members to include under-represented groups such as children from refugee or migrant backgrounds and those with disabilities.

QUESTIONS

1. Do you agree with the first research piece that student councils are 'undemocratic and ineffective'? Give evidence from your own school context to support your answer.
2. Does your student council adequately represent the diverse interests of the entire student body? Give reasons for your answer.
3. According to the second research piece, Irish students have little or no input in relation to the decision-making on issues such as teaching and subject content. On which school issues should student councils have a direct role in decision-making? Explain why.
4. Are there any school-related decisions in which the role of the student council should be limited or minimal?
5. In your opinion, what actions could be taken to enhance the role of student councils in decision-making processes in Irish schools?

Students can have different levels of participation in decision-making processes at school. As shown in Fig. 2.10, student participation can range from sharing views on problems and offering ideas for solutions, to collaborating directly with school management in designing strategies to resolve these problems, to proactively seeking change and setting the agenda on an issue or rule. In practice, the level of student influence often depends on the space or mechanisms available to students, as well as the actual issue being addressed. In many ways, the limits that are placed on student participation reflect the debate between liberals and conservatives. Supporters of a liberal approach call for increased student voice in more areas of school management and rules. Meanwhile, conservatives call for 'reasonable' limits on student participation in decision-making so that health and safety issues are taken into consideration and order is preserved.

Pyramid of Student Voice

Student participation happens at different levels.

- **Being heard:** This is the most common and basic level of student voice. It involves school management or staff listening to the views of students in relation to a problem.
- **Collaborating with adults:** This is the next level of student voice and it is less common. It involves students working with school management or staff to address problems and find solutions.
- **Building capacity for leadership:** This is the highest level and it has the fewest examples in practice. It involves students taking the lead on seeking change within schools.

Fig. 2.13 Pyramid of student voice (Dana Mitra)

ACTIVITY 2.8

Your group will be given a section of Dana Mitra's article 'Increasing Student Voice and Moving Toward Youth Leadership' to examine. As a group, write a summary report on the main findings in the article. Make sure that you understand the summary before you split up and teach it to a new group using the **jigsaw method** (see page 31).

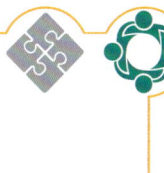

> ### SKILLS BOOK LINK 2.6
> Go to page 16 of your Skills Book to complete Skill Task 2.6 on decision-making in your school.
>
> See **RESEARCH TIPS** on page 33.

Right to Participate

The right of the child to have her or his voice heard does not mean that the child has the right to make decisions, but it does mean that their views must be considered. A number of important laws and policies exist at international, European and national level in relation to child and youth participation in decision-making in Ireland.

United Nations Convention of the Rights of the Child (UNCRC)

Article 12(1) of the UNCRC relates to the Child's Opinion. This article requires that governments ensure meaningful opportunities for children and young people to express an opinion, and to have that opinion taken into account, in any matter or procedure affecting the child, in accordance with his or her age and maturity. This right is established in many different areas of child and youth life, including the school environment.

EU Charter of Fundamental Rights

Similar to the UNCRC, the EU Charter of Fundamental Rights, Article 24(1), states that children should have the opportunity to have their views heard in relation to situations that concern them, depending on their age and maturity.

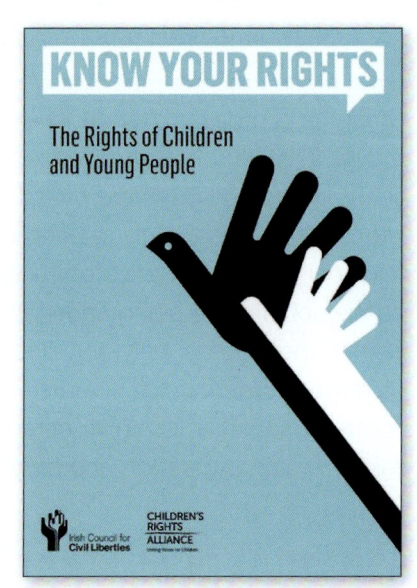

Fig. 2.14 Children's rights

Education Act, 1998

In Ireland, Section 27 of the Education Act, 1998 establishes the rights of children to be involved in educational matters. Section 27(2) of the Act states that schools 'shall facilitate the involvement of students in the operation of the school, having regard to the age and experience of the students, in association with their parents and teachers'. Section 27(3) of the Act states that under the direction of school management, students of post-primary schools 'may establish a student council'. Schools must facilitate the involvement of students in the school; however, schools have no obligation to include students in the setting of the objectives of the school.

National Strategy on Children and Young People's Participation in Decision-Making 2015–2020

The Irish government has developed the National Strategy on Children and Young People's Participation in Decision-Making 2015–2020. This strategy outlines government plans to address child and youth participation in many areas: local and community initiatives, health and social services, and the court system and legal services. Objective 2 of the strategy relates to decision-making in school and it 'strongly promotes the importance of children and young people's involvement in decision-making in education policy, in the running of schools and services, in school inspections, in schools' self-evaluations, in the curriculum, in behaviour and bullying policies, in support services and other areas'. The strategy recognises the need to improve the effectiveness of student councils in secondary schools and calls for the establishment of councils at primary level also.

Different Levels of Student Voice

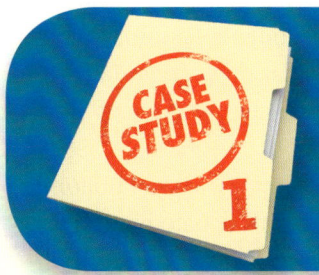

CASE STUDY 1: Summerhill, UK: A School Managed by Students and Teachers

Summerhill School is an independent boarding school in the UK in which no rules are formally set by school management. It was founded in 1921 by libertarian educator Alexander Sutherland Neill, who believed that children should learn and develop in a liberal and democratic school environment, free from adult interference unless a student is in some way causing harm to others. The school is run by

Fig. 2.15 Alexander Sutherland Neill's Summerhill School in Suffolk, England – the original alternative 'free' school and 'oldest children's democracy' in the world

both staff and pupils: they make joint decisions through community meetings and agree on rules and principles. Students and teachers have equal voting rights. Students decide whether or not they wish to attend class and what subjects they wish to take. The principal and teachers intervene only if a student's action is causing harm to another. Previous attempts by the UK government to close the controversial school have failed, and in 2011 Summerhill received a positive report from an official school inspection which praised: 'outstanding pupils' spiritual, moral, social and cultural development', teaching that was 'never less than good, with some outstanding features' and 'learning ... closely tailored to match pupils' individual needs'. Academic results have been 'satisfactory': 46 per cent of students gained a C grade or higher at five or more subjects, including English and Maths, against a national average of 58.6 per cent.

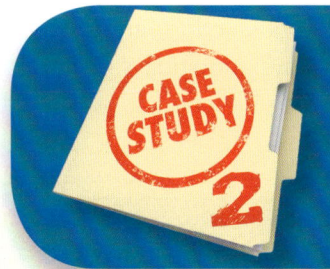

CASE STUDY 2: Educate Together, Ireland: Shared Decision-Making

In 2014 Educate Together opened its first second-level schools. These schools build on the network of Educate Together schools at primary level. Each school has its own model and method for electing students to the council. In some schools, students are also represented on the board of management of the school. In Educate Together second-level schools, students participate in decision-making before they even start First Year. For example, students are asked to nominate the subjects they would like to study. This has a direct impact on the teachers who will be employed in the school. In new schools, students vote on whether or not personal IT devices will be used in the schools. As a result, some Educate Together schools use textbooks, while others use digital learning platforms. Educate Together second-level schools

Fig. 2.16 Educate Together logo

POWER AND DECISION-MAKING IN SCHOOL 57

Different Levels of Student Voice

begin without an official uniform. Like other school policies, decisions about the dress code are made in consultation with students. Because of this, different Educate Together schools take different approaches to uniforms. In some schools, students wear their own clothes but agree to a particular dress code. In other schools, students wear a school 'hoody' along with their own clothes, and in other schools, students wear full uniforms. Educate Together schools acknowledge that coming to an agreement that everyone is happy with is not always an easy task, particularly when it comes to a dress code and uniform. Tracksuit bottoms and leggings are two items of clothing that cause a lot of debate. In some schools, this debate has not yet been settled; however, negotiation between school management and the student councils continues!

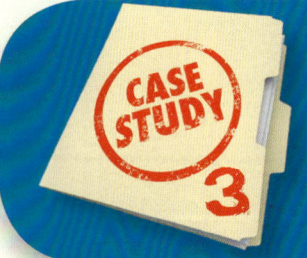

CASE STUDY 3: St Louis High School, Dublin: Student Council Influences New School Rules

The student council can provide an important channel for students to have their voices heard in school management decision-making processes. The student council at St Louis High School in Rathmines, Dublin has a strong record of engaging in school decision-making and has produced a number of changes to school rules over the years. The council has supported school management in accessing funding to improve various facilities in the school, and it has also influenced a number of school policies. The council played a role in developing a school policy regarding mobile phone usage. Students who do not abide by the school's phone usage policy must hand over their phones at the beginning of a school day, with the phone being returned to them at the end of the day. This disciplinary procedure happens for three consecutive school days, during which students must also do a detention. Students agreed that this option was preferable to the complete confiscation of a phone for a three-day period, which sometimes resulted in a student being without her phone over a weekend. Through the council, students also voted to change the school timetable. St Louis High School voted for an earlier start five days a week in exchange for an earlier finish on Wednesdays, Thursdays and Fridays. A key to the success of the council has been the high level of mutual respect between the council, school management, teachers, parents and students.

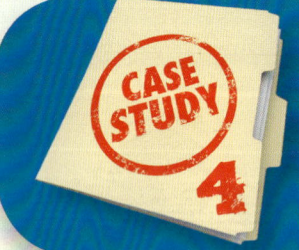

Fig. 2.17 St Louis High School, Dublin

CASE STUDY 4: Four Dwellings Academy, UK: Student Voice in Teaching and Learning Practices

Four Dwellings is an Academy in Quinton, Birmingham, which is committed to student participation. Student participation is facilitated through three mechanisms: teaching and learning discussion groups (TLDGs), school councils, and youth marshals. The TLDGs are made up of representatives chosen by a teacher from each year group on the basis of gender, ethnicity and ability. TLDGs meet once every term to discuss issues related to teaching and learning. Together with the school, the TLDGs conducted research to review the impact of participation on students. One of the key findings from their research

> **CASE STUDY**
>
> **Different Levels of Student Voice**

was a positive relationship between student involvement in decision-making and academic achievement: students who were permitted to develop their own learning resources achieved better results. The TLDGs and participating teachers used the research to influence other teachers, students and school management to increase student involvement in the decision-making around teaching and learning practices.

CASE STUDY 5: St Joseph's Academy, South Tyneside, UK: Students Influence Change in Homework and 'Banding' Policies

St Joseph's is a large academy school in South Tyneside, UK, with about 1,500 students. The school ensures that students have a say on school policies through opinion surveys. Students have successfully influenced reform of the school's homework policy and its approach to organising class groups on the basis of academic ability (banding). Questionnaires on student experiences and opinions of homework practices were developed by the student council and distributed to students. Some of the key findings included the view that homework was not always relevant to the work being covered during lessons, that it took too much time to complete and that marking was sometimes late. The findings were shared with school management and directly fed into the revised homework policy. Similarly, research conducted by a teacher on the students' views of the school's 'banding system' found that students felt demotivated by being 'grouped' on the basis of ability. Following negotiation, the school management adopted a policy of 'mixed-ability classes'.

QUESTIONS

1. What might be the positive and negative potential consequences for your learning if your school decided to adopt the system used at Summerhill School?
2. Do you think the rules at your school would change much if students had a direct input into rule-making and decision-making? Would this change be for the better or for the worse?
3. Look at Case Studies 2, 3, 4 and 5. Do you believe that student involvement in these kinds of issues is a good idea? Why/why not?
4. Look at Dana Mitra's pyramid of student voice (Fig. 2.13 on page 55). In which segment of the pyramid are the students in each of the case studies? Explain your answers.
5. Are there limits to which students should be involved in school-related decisions? If so, what school issues should students have more of a say in? What should students have less of a say in?

Schools can adopt different approaches to decision-making processes, with varying levels of participation of different actors. The case studies above demonstrate that active participation in a decision-making process can result in power to influence the final outcomes (e.g. rules, policies and decisions).

SKILLS BOOK LINK 2.7

Go to page 17 of your Skills Book to complete Skill Task 2.7 on researching the process of decision-making in your school.

Complete your next Reflective Journal entry (pages 5–6)

POWER AND DECISION-MAKING IN SCHOOL

How are Rules Enforced?

Once rules are established, how do we ensure that everyone follows them? Why do we follow rules? There are many ways in which society can enforce rules, encourage certain behaviours and ensure order. Similarly, in our schools we have different systems of reward and punishment. Some of the systems are visible and explicit. There can be clear consequences for breaking the rules (e.g. detention, suspension, expulsion) and clear rewards for good behaviour (e.g. student awards, positive letters being sent home). However, rules are not always visible. Sometimes rules are enforced in invisible ways. Sometimes we act in certain ways and avoid certain actions or behaviours not out of fear of a resulting punishment, but because we have 'internalised the rule'.

KEY THINKERS: POWER TO ENFORCE RULES

Many theories have been offered about how power is exercised. We can apply many of these ideas to an analysis of how rules are enforced in our schools.

Émile Durkheim

Durkheim viewed society as a body with all parts dependent on one another (interdependence). Order is maintained, not by enforcement of rules by government, but by shared cultural and social norms and values, through a process termed 'socialisation'. We act in the ways we believe we are supposed to act. This is known as 'conformity'. From an early age, beginning in our family context, we are taught certain values and norms, about how we should act, and what we should do and not do. Schools continue this socialisation process, using the hidden curriculum.

See pages 41 and 44 for more information on the hidden curriculum.

Václav Havel

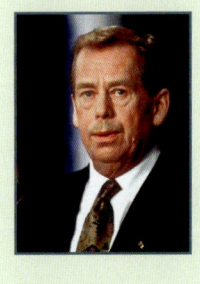

Václav Havel was born in Prague (Czech Republic) in 1936. He was an anti-communist activist and subsequent head of state. He shared his ideas on the communist regime and people power in a famous essay entitled 'The Power of the Powerless'. Havel described the communist regime as based on a system of false principles and rituals. People living within this system had to live a lie and hide what they truly believed. Communism was dependent on this compliance of the people. The ability to reject the system was what gave people power. There is no power if no one submits to it.

Steven Lukes

American sociologist Steven Lukes was born in 1941. He is a professor at New York University. In his book *Power: A Radical View* (1974), he considers power as having three dimensions. The first type of power is winning an argument or a decision on an issue. The second relates to deciding on what will be argued or discussed in the first place (setting the agenda). These first two types of power are obvious, in so far as we can clearly see them taking place in a given situation, e.g. a parent winning an argument with his or her child (first type), a management committee setting the agenda and deciding what issues will/will not be discussed during a meeting (second type). The third type of power is a covert (hidden) power based, for example, on ideology or values (capitalism, patriarchy, religion, etc.). It involves making people think, desire or act in a certain way, even if this might actually go against their self-interests. For example, some would argue that the power of consumerism makes us buy things we do not need and cannot afford.

POWER AND PEOPLE

Michel Foucault

Philosopher Michel Foucault was born in France in 1926. Foucault looked at power as enforcement through coercion and control. His ideas on coercive power and discipline have been used to analyse many of our modern state institutions, such as prisons and schools. Mass control is achieved through organising the space and time of an individual (e.g. timetables).

QUESTIONS

1. In your opinion, does school life operate according to Émile Durkheim's analysis of power (i.e. that order is maintained not by enforcement of rules but by shared cultural and social norms and values)?
   (a) Give **two** examples from your experience at school that support this view.
   (b) Give **two** examples from your experience at school that contradict this view.

2. 'There is no power if no one submits to it.' In relation to the power structures and the levels of obedience to rules at your school, to what extent would you agree with the viewpoint of Václav Havel?

3. Can you think of any examples of Steven Lukes's three types of power in your own life? Give at least **one** example of each.

4. 'Mass control is achieved through organising the space and time of an individual.' Would you agree with this claim by Michel Foucault in relation to:
   (a) Your experience at school
   (b) Your experience outside school?

5. (a) Which of the ideas of the four key thinkers best applies to power at school?
   (b) Which of the ideas least applies?

ACTIVITY 2.9

Your school's board of management is drawing up a new code of behaviour for the school. The board has requested that the student council create proposals specifically related to the enforcement of school rules and the disciplinary procedure.

In groups, create a detailed proposal on how school rules should be enforced and describe the disciplinary procedure. Include the following:

- Areas where the teaching of 'norms and values' (hidden curriculum) can replace the need for rules and disciplinary action
- Rules that require punishment when broken
- A list of repercussions for breaches of rules
- A rationale for your proposals, based on the key thinkers of your choice.

Complete your next Reflective Journal entry (pages 5–6)

POWER AND DECISION-MAKING IN SCHOOL

Do All Rules Affect Everyone Equally?

Whether we are thinking about school rules or the laws and policies of a country, it is important to analyse how these things are experienced by different individuals and groups. School rules are said to apply to all students, but do they affect everyone equally? Who benefits most from the rules? Are there winners and losers? Much research has been conducted on whether school rules produce different impacts on different students, e.g. students of particular gender, ethnicity or disability. The evidence suggests that rules can impact on different groups in different ways.

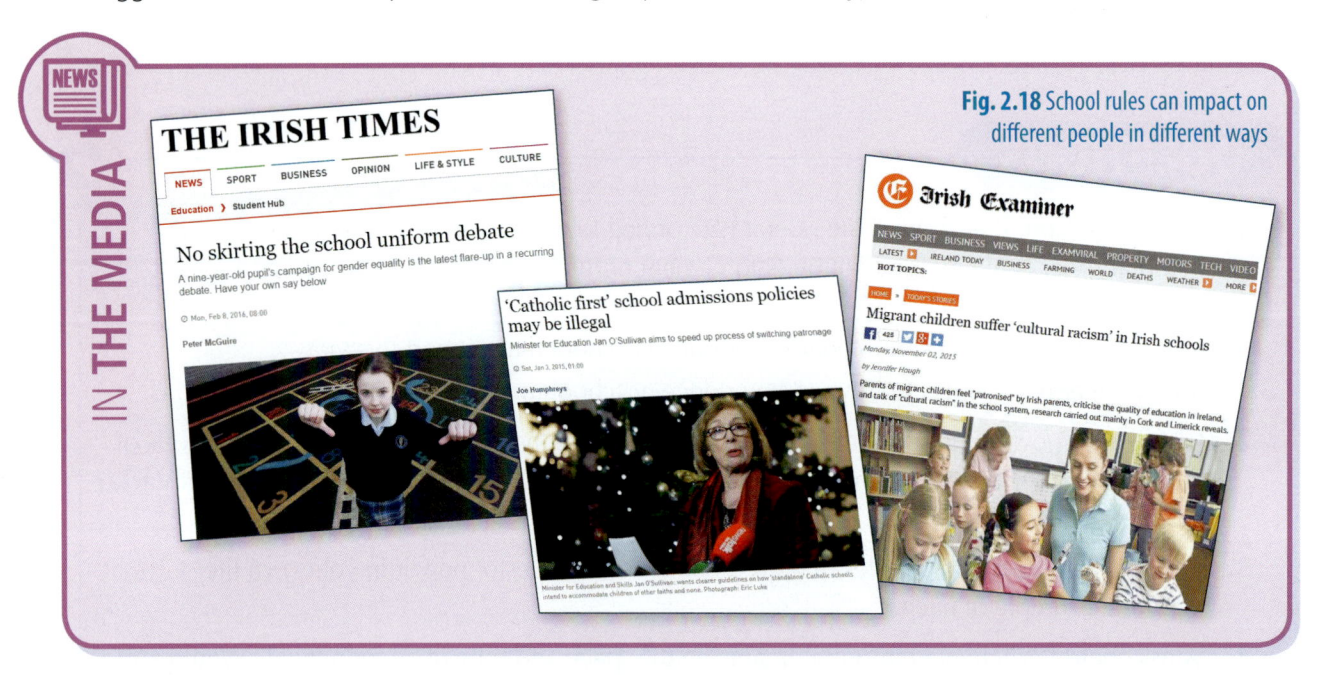

IN THE MEDIA

Fig. 2.18 School rules can impact on different people in different ways

WHAT THE RESEARCH SAYS!

SCHOOL POLICIES AND SOCIAL INEQUALITY

How School Policies Create and Reinforce Social Inequality

The under-representation and under-achievement of people from lower socio-economic backgrounds in the Irish education system has been the focus of much research and debate. The cost of secondary education is one obvious problem area: it deprives students from poorer backgrounds of the same chances as their middle-class peers. According to an extensive survey carried out in 2015 by Barnardos, Ireland's largest children's charity, the average cost of sending a child to secondary school has climbed by more than five times the rate of inflation and is now just under €800 per year. A significant portion of this cost is determined by school rules regarding book rental schemes and school uniform policies. Among the most expensive school items are crested school

Fig. 2.19 School uniform costs are high

uniforms, which in 2015 had an average price of €258 per child (secondary school). This comes at a time when income inequality is at an all-time high in Ireland: a succession of austerity budgets have disproportionately hit the bottom 30 per cent of households.

A survey carried out by the Irish Second-Level Students' Union (2014) found that one of the biggest concerns of Transition Year students was the increasing cost of contributions requested for mandatory trips away and Transition Year courses. The survey found that the average contribution per student for such extra-curricular activities was €300, with some schools requesting as much as €900.

Examination costs are another major financial burden on poorer households, especially if more than one child is sitting a state exam in the same year. The fee for the Leaving Certificate is €116, while the Junior Certificate costs €109. In addition, an *Irish Independent* survey (2016) has found that one in five schools charge parents over €100 per child for mock examinations.

As a result of such policies, students from lower socio-economic backgrounds are less likely to participate in extra-curricular trips, school tours, Transition Year and mock exams. Kathleen Lynch has highlighted the 'banding' of students into separate streams based on ability as one of the main reasons for underachievement and early school-leaving of working-class students. She argues that due to the lack of resources and supports at home, working-class students are less likely to excel in linguistic and mathematical tests; and these tests are most commonly used to decide what stream a student is placed into. This system reinforces social inequality: those in the lowest stream often face limited curricular choice, restricted choice of level, and poor-quality lessons because of low expectations from teachers. This in turn leads to disillusionment and early school-leaving.

Discriminatory School Admission Policies in Ireland

Many people consider school rules to be legitimate because they apply equally to all students. But what happens when certain rules appear to disproportionately affect some groups over others? In 2006 Mary Hanafin (the then Minister for Education in Ireland) called attention to the 'subtle' admission policies of schools (e.g. parental and sibling preferences) which were believed to exclude children from certain disadvantaged groups. An audit of school enrolment policies was then ordered by the Department of Education and Skills.

Fig. 2.20 School enrolment: open to all?

The audit found that the approach to applicant selection adopted by certain schools resulted in children with disabilities, children of migrants and Traveller children being concentrated in particular schools, mainly vocational and community schools (Department of Education and Skills, 2007). As a result of the audit, the Department published a document outlining its concerns and recommendations in relation to enrolment policy in 2011. An Education (Admission to Schools) Bill was drafted in 2014 to 'make the process of enrolling in schools more open, equitable and consistent'. The Bill is expected to be passed in the near future. In 2015 Mary Stokes, a member of the Traveller community, lost her court case against a secondary school in Co. Tipperary after the Supreme Court ruled that evidence presented to both the Circuit Court and Equality Tribunal was insufficient to prove that her son, John, who was refused enrolment, had been particularly disadvantaged because of the fact that neither his father nor siblings had attended the school.

For more discussion of discrimination in school admission policies, see page 258.

Some key thinkers argue that school rules uphold the status quo of society, i.e. society's existing power relations and order. The argument is that if certain inequalities already exist in society, these will be reflected in the rules of schools, which are part of that society.

KEY THINKERS: RULES AND SOCIAL INEQUALITY

Kathleen Lynch

Kathleen Lynch has stated that the education system can act to reinforce existing inequalities within society, such as social class, gender, sexual orientation, ethnicity and religion.

Karl Marx

Although Marx never wrote anything directly on education, his views on capitalism and class struggle have been used to analyse school rules and education systems. In the Marxist analysis, the education system is yet another institution of society which reproduces the class system.

Sylvia Walby

Walby shows that gender relations in education are less unequal than in many other parts of society. Gender regimes are uneven.

QUESTIONS

1. In what ways are people from lower socio-economic groups disadvantaged by the Irish education system?
2. Would you agree that traditional school rules and policies give an unfair advantage to certain cultures and socio-economic groups over others?
3. Can you think of any rules or practices in your school that treat females unequally to males, or vice versa?

Discrimination

When a rule has a disproportionate and unequal impact on someone, it may be considered a form of discrimination. Discrimination can be positive or negative: producing an unfair advantage or disadvantage. In Ireland, we legally recognise nine grounds on the basis of which it is unlawful to discriminate against someone.

The Nine Grounds of Unlawful Discrimination in Ireland

1. **Gender:** a man, a woman or a transsexual person
2. **Marital status:** single, married, separated, divorced or widowed
3. **Family status:** having responsibility either as a parent or legal guardian for someone below 18 years of age, or as a parent or resident primary carer for someone 18 years or over with a disability who requires a high degree of support and attention
4. **Age:** people in employment between the ages of 18 and 65, and people in vocational training between the ages of 15 and 65
5. **Disability:** people with physical, intellectual, learning, cognitive or emotional disabilities and a range of medical conditions
6. **Race:** includes race, colour, nationality, ethnic or national origin
7. **Sexual orientation:** gay, lesbian, bisexual or heterosexual
8. **Religious belief:** includes religious background/outlook or lack of religious belief
9. **Membership of the Traveller community:** people who are commonly called Travellers, who are identified both by Travellers and others as people with a shared history, culture and traditions, identified historically as people with a nomadic way of life on the island of Ireland.

Discrimination
The prejudicial treatment or consideration of a person, racial group, minority, etc. based on category rather than individual, excluding or restricting members of ... on the grounds of race, sex, or age ...

Fig. 2.21 Unlawful discrimination

ACTIVITY 2.10

Your group will be assigned a specific group identity (e.g. students from the Traveller community, students with disabilities, migrant students). Identify **three** rules that you think might disproportionately affect your assigned group.

Fig. 2.22 Key Word cloud

POWER AND DECISION-MAKING IN SCHOOL 65

SUMMARY

- There is a wide variety of views on the debate concerning the need for rules in schools.
- The school rules debate can be viewed through the lens of the left wing–right wing spectrum.
- Conservatives argue that school rules are needed to ensure respect for custom and tradition and to uphold social order.
- Liberals believe that rules should focus primarily on protecting the rights and freedoms of individuals and particular groups.
- Sociology looks at the role of education in the socialisation process. The three main sociological perspectives on education are Marxist, functionalist and feminist.
- Marxism and feminism are 'conflict theories'. Marxism views the education system as recreating and reinforcing society's class-based divisions and the dominant ideology of the elite class. Feminists argue that education reinforces patriarchy in society through the teaching of gender roles, behaviours and stereotypes.
- People may act according to norms and values, which are internalised rules.
- There are many stakeholders involved in the decision-making process at school, e.g. the Department of Education and Skills, patrons, principal, board of management and parents' association.
- Decision-making processes in schools can take a variety of forms with different levels of student participation.
- There are different levels of participation and power: information, consultation and decision-making.
- Research shows that students can positively impact on the decision-making process in schools when afforded the opportunity to do so.
- Rules can be enforced in different ways. Power can be coercive or legitimate.
- Some groups are under-represented in the decision-making process and some groups can suffer unequal treatment as a result of the rules imposed.

REVISION QUESTIONS

1. Explain clearly the difference between norms and rules, with reference to examples.
2. Give **two** arguments in favour of school rules and **two** arguments against school rules.
3. Explain in your own words what the following key thinkers think about rules:
   - Hobbes
   - Mill
   - Durkheim.
4. What is the 'hidden curriculum'? What types of norms and values are promoted through the hidden curriculum at your school?
5. Describe the Marxist view of the education system, with reference to the ideas of at least **two** named Marxist thinkers.
6. Describe the functionalist view of the education system, with reference to the ideas of at least **two** named functionalist thinkers.
7. How do feminists view the education system?
8. Which of the **three** perspectives (Marxist, functionalist or feminist) best applies to your own experience of school? Give reasons to support your answer.
9. Name **one** school rule or policy that you think should be abolished or changed and explain the reasons why.
10. With the aid of a diagram, describe the hierarchical structure of decision-making in your school.
11. Define the following terms: *autonomy, stakeholder, coercive power*.
12. Explain Max Weber's **three** types of 'legitimate authority'.

13. Compare and contrast the theories of power proposed by Robert A. Dahl and C. Wright Mills.
14. What is the 'social contract'? Explain the views of any **two** key thinkers on the social contract.
15. Explain how your school operates according to a social contract.
16. What is the 'ladder of participation'? How does it apply to the decision-making process at your school?
17. **(a)** What is a student council? **(b)** What are the functions of a student council? **(c)** Why is it important that every school has a student council? **(d)** Give **one** common criticism of student councils in Ireland. **(e)** Give **two** examples where a student council has influenced decisions at a school.
18. Name **two** international agreements and **one** Irish law that protect the right of students to participate in the decision-making process.
19. Explain the 'socialisation process' according to Émile Durkheim. How does school contribute to the socialisation process?
20. What is the 'power of the powerless', according to Václav Havel? Would you agree that order at your school is heavily dependent on the compliance of students?
21. Explain Steven Lukes' three dimensions of power.
22. According to Michel Foucault, how are control and power maintained?
23. Explain how certain school rules can act to reinforce social inequality.
24. How do the admissions policies of certain schools discriminate against **(a)** non-Catholics and **(b)** members of the Traveller community?
25. Explain Sylvia Walby's views on the education system.
26. List the **nine** grounds of unlawful discrimination recognised in Irish law. Can you think of any additional grounds that should be added to the list?

DATA-BASED QUESTIONS

Complete the qualitative and quantitative research data-based questions exercise on pages 19–22 of your Skills Book.

EXAM FOCUS: Section B of LC Exam

REVISION EXERCISES

Complete the revision exercises on pages 23–25 of your Skills Book.

EXAM FOCUS: Section A of LC Exam

DISCURSIVE ESSAY TOPICS

1. Compare and contrast what **two** or more thinkers have to say about the exercise of power. Explain how the ideas of each key thinker relate to the decision-making process and rules at school.
2. Consider the **three** sociological perspectives on education. Which of them, do you think, best explains the Irish school system today? Use research to back up your argument.
3. 'The education system can act to reinforce existing inequalities within Irish society, such as social class, gender, sexual orientation, ethnicity and religion.' To what extent do you agree with this statement? Back up your answer with reference to the ideas of **two** or more key thinkers, along with relevant research data.

EXAM FOCUS: Section C of LC Exam

4. 'Schools operate on the basis of a "social contract".' Discuss.

5. How useful are the ideas of Thomas Hobbes or John Locke for organising the rules and workings of a school? Identify a political or social theorist that would most influence or inspire the way you would wish to organise your school and explain why.

6. 'Education either functions as an instrument which is used to facilitate integration of the younger generation into the logic of the present system and bring about conformity, or it becomes the practice of freedom, the means by which men and women deal critically and creatively with reality, and discover how to participate in the transformation of their world.'
Paulo Freire

Looking at contemporary Ireland and/or another country, to what extent can Freire's view be backed up by evidence? Your answer should refer to relevant qualitative or quantitative data.

ACTIVE CITIZENSHIP: Ideas for Action

Action 1: Increase Student Participation in the Decision-Making Processes

Task: As a class, identify a specific area(s) where the student body is not adequately represented in the decision-making process at your school. Create an action plan to achieve greater student participation in the area(s) identified.

Action 2: Introduce a New Rule or Change an Existing Rule

Task: As a class, identify one rule that you would like to see introduced to your school. Alternatively, identify an existing rule that you think should be amended or abolished. This might be a rule that affects all the student body or particular groups based on age, gender, disability, ethnicity, etc. Create an action plan to have a new rule introduced or an existing one amended/abolished.

Guidelines:

- Devise an action plan outlining your goals and specifying the steps and actions that need to be taken in order to achieve them.
- Assign roles to committees and individual tasks to students who will be responsible for carrying out your planned actions.
- On completion, evaluate how successful your campaign/action was.

Reflective Practice

Ensure that you have completed all the Reflective Journal entries for this chapter (pages 5–6 of your Reflective Journal and Learning Portfolio) before moving on to the next chapter.

Complete the Learning Portfolio activities on pages 7–9 of your Reflective Journal and Learning Portfolio. This will help you to self-assess the extent to which you have achieved the learning intentions for this chapter, and will help you to monitor your progress.

CHAPTER 3
Political Representation

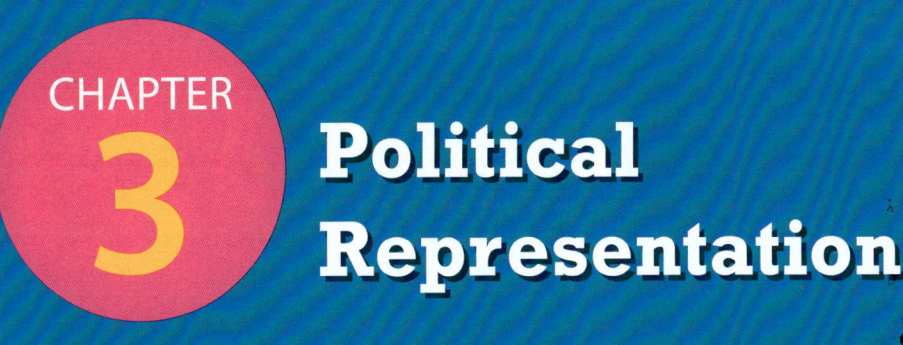

'Democracy is the worst form of government except all those other forms that have been tried from time to time.' Winston Churchill

KEY TERMS
- Citizen
- Political representation
- Civil society
- Political party
- Direct democracy
- Representative democracy
- Floating voter
- Dealignment

Introduction

Just as decision-making is organised in school, we have a variety of structures inside and outside our country to shape the many decisions that affect our lives. In a democracy, such as Ireland, **citizens** are represented in the structures that make the political decisions that affect their lives. This is known as **political representation**. The need for such representation is based on the democratic principle of ensuring that the opinions, views and voices of citizens are present in political decision-making processes. In democracies, citizens are the 'represented'. Each individual citizen has the right to be represented. However, society is quite diverse. Citizens often organise themselves, or are organised by others, into different social groups. These groups share common interests or characteristics. We can look at groups on the basis of gender, social class, ethnicity and many other categories. Each group will have different interests, concerns and priorities based on its members' experiences of life in society.

I am a citizen.
I am a woman.
I am a member of the Irish Traveller community.
I am a member of the National Youth Council.
I am a member of Party ABC.

Fig. 3.1 Politics is about representing various interests

Groups and their interests can be represented in a variety of ways. **Civil society** bodies (such as charities, community groups, unions and associations) play an important role in representing different

KEY TERMS

A **citizen** is a person who is legally recognised as a member of a particular country and is entitled to certain rights as a result.

Political representation is about making sure that the voices, opinions and views of citizens are included in political decision-making processes. Political representatives speak and act on behalf of citizens in the political institutions of government.

Civil society is a term used to describe groups or organisations that work for and/or represent the interests of citizens or specific groups in society (e.g. homeless people, immigrants, Traveller community, women, and so on). Civil society bodies are not part of the government and they are usually not-for-profit.

Fig. 3.2 Students stage a protest on third-level fees in order to have their voices heard by political representatives

groups. Political representation in most western democracies, including Ireland, is organised through **political parties**. Political parties are groups of people who share common interests or a common vision for society and who come together in the hope of having their vision represented in decision-making institutions. Citizens in Ireland, north and south, are represented by institutions at local, national and European levels: the Government of Ireland, the Northern Ireland Executive and the institutions of the European Union. Before looking at how representatives to these institutions are selected and their different roles in making decisions and policies, it is important to understand what we mean by representation and who is being represented.

> **KEY TERM**
>
> A **political party** is a group of people who organise to win power in government. Political parties often share a common vision or ideology of how society should be. They usually share positions on specific issues (e.g. health, education, justice, economy).

See Chapter 4 (pages 94–140) for more information on how representatives are selected. See Chapter 5 (page 141–184) for more information on policy-making.

By the end of this chapter you will be able to:

- Explain the term 'political representation'.
- List and describe the main forms of government: monarchy, dictatorship, oligarchy, theocracy, direct democracy and representative democracy.
- Assess the strengths and weaknesses of the different forms of government.
- Explain the differences between direct democracy and representative democracy, and evaluate the limitations of both these systems of government.
- Outline and evaluate the views of at least three key thinkers on the issue of political representation.
- Define the term 'social class'.
- Use research-based evidence to illustrate and critically evaluate the view that social class is an important way of categorising who does/does not have power in capitalist societies.
- Define the term 'patriarchy'.
- Use research-based evidence to illustrate and critically evaluate the view that modern Irish society is a patriarchy.
- Describe and explain the different ways in which civil society bodies represent the interests of Irish citizens.
- List the main political parties in Ireland and evaluate the extent to which their respective manifestos/policies reflect the interests of all social groups in Ireland.
- Evaluate the strengths and weaknesses of the Irish political party system.
- Explain how gender and social class impact on voting patterns.

POWER AND PEOPLE

By the end of this chapter you will have developed the following skills:

- Communication skills and the ability to present information and ideas verbally.
- Interpersonal skills and the ability to work effectively with small and large groups to reach agreed conclusions and achieve consensus.
- Research skills and information processing on a variety of issues related to political representation.
- Critical and creative thinking skills in relation to the strengths, weaknesses and limitations of key pieces of research and important viewpoints on political representation.

Types of Government

If you compared all the different systems of government in the world today, you would find that they all have one thing in common: they are designed to make and enforce rules for the society and the people they govern. How these systems of government differ revolves around two important questions: *Who is in charge? How do they represent citizens?* Some systems place all power and control in the hands of one leader. Others give power to the people. What follows is a discussion of some forms of government that exist (or have existed) in the world.

Autocracy: Rule by One

An autocracy is a government in which one person has all the power. There are two main types of autocracy: monarchy and dictatorship.

Monarchy

In a monarchy, a king or queen rules the country. The king or queen is known as a *monarch*. Monarchs usually come to power through their family line (e.g. the current monarch's eldest child becomes the next king or queen). There are two types of monarchy: *absolute monarchy* and *constitutional monarchy*.

Fig. 3.3 Queen Elizabeth II

The first monarchies to emerge before the modern era were known as absolute monarchies. In an absolute monarchy, the monarch holds all the power and has the absolute authority to rule as he/she sees fit. Absolute monarchy often resulted in the abuse of power by tyrannical monarchs. As a result, the powers of monarchs were gradually reduced and diminished over the centuries. For example, in 1215 disgruntled nobles rebelled in England, forcing King John to pass a charter, the Magna Carta, which curtailed his absolute powers and made the monarchy subject to the same laws that were applied to the rest of society. The French went one step further when, in 1789, the French Revolution resulted in the complete abolition of monarchy, the formation of a Republic and the beheading of Louis XVI.

Today, most monarchies are constitutional monarchies, as is the case in the UK and Norway. A constitutional monarchy is one in which the monarch is bound by a *constitution.* This usually involves sharing power with other parts of government and allowing an elected parliament to run the country. For example, in the UK, Queen Elizabeth II is the head of state but has a mainly ceremonial role. Real power lies with the parliament at Westminster.

Dictatorship

A dictatorship is a form of government where one leader has absolute control over citizens' lives. If a parliament exists, the dictator has full powers to veto any decisions it takes, rendering parliament powerless. If there is a constitution, the dictator has control over it too. Although other parts of the government may exist (e.g. courts or a law-making body), these branches always follow the orders of the dictator: they do not represent citizens. Many dictators are democratically elected at first, but then proceed to pass laws to replace the democratic system with a dictatorship. Examples of dictatorships in history include Hitler's Nazi Germany and Mussolini's Fascist regime in Italy. There are approximately 50 dictatorships in the world today, including North Korea.

Fig. 3.4 Kim Jong-un, Dictator of North Korea, inspecting the troops

Oligarchy: Rule by a Few

In an oligarchy, government is contolled by a few people. *Oligarchy* is a Greek word that means 'rule by a few'. Sometimes this means that only a certain group has political rights (e.g. members of one political party, social class or race). The former Soviet Union was ruled by a communist oligarchy. A modern example of an oligarchy is China. In an oligarchy, government is controlled by a few people. A *junta* is a small group of people – usually military officers – who rule a country after taking it over by force. A junta often operates much like a dictatorship, except that several people share power. Several military juntas emerged in Latin America during the Cold War (1947–91).

Fig. 3.5 Members of the military junta that seized power in Chile on 11 September 1973

Democracy: Rule by All

A democracy is a system of government in which power is vested in the people and exercised by all eligible citizens of the state. The people rule either directly themselves – **direct democracy** – or through freely elected representatives – **representative democracy**.

Fig. 3.6 Abraham Lincoln, President of the US (1861–5) famously summed up democracy as 'government of the people, by the people, for the people'

KEY TERMS

In a **direct democracy**, there are no representatives: all citizens are directly involved in the day-to-day work of governing their country. Citizens might be required to participate in law-making or act as judges, for example. The most popular form of direct democracy is via a *referendum:* when all citizens are given the opportunity to vote on a proposed law. Switzerland is one of the best-known modern examples of a direct democracy. In Switzerland, citizens can demand a referendum on any federal law once they obtain 50,000 petition signatures. Approximately a dozen referendums take place each year in Switzerland.

In a **representative democracy**, citizens elect leaders to represent their rights and interests in government. The elected leaders – the representatives – do the day-to-day work of governing the country. The representatives consider the issues, work to find solutions and pass laws in a parliament. However, citizens hold the ultimate power, as they can vote for new representatives at election time if they are not satisfied with the current representatives.

Today the majority of countries in the world, including Ireland, are democracies. Decision-making in democracies can follow different models.

Theocracy: Rule by God

A theocracy is a government that recognises God or a divine being as the ultimate authority (*theos* is a Greek word that means 'god'). In a theocracy, religious law is used to settle disputes and rule the people. A theocracy can also be a democracy, dictatorship, monarchy, or just about any other kind of government. For example, the Republic of Iran recognises Islamic law, but Iran's citizens vote to elect their leaders.

Anarchy: No Rule

Anarchy is the absence of government, similar to Thomas Hobbes's idea of the 'state of nature'. Sometimes the word *anarchy* is used to refer to an out-of-control mob. Today, people who call themselves anarchists usually believe that people should be allowed to live in absolute freedom without being subject to any form of institutional control, such as laws enforced by governments. No country in the world has anarchy as its formal form of government.

Fig. 3.7 Anarchist symbol

See page 14 for more information on the Thomas Hobbes's idea of the 'state of nature'.

WHO RULES?

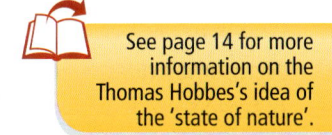

- NONE — Anarchy
- ONE — Monarchy, Dictatorship
- FEW — Oligarchy, Junta
- ALL — Democracy (Direct, Representative)

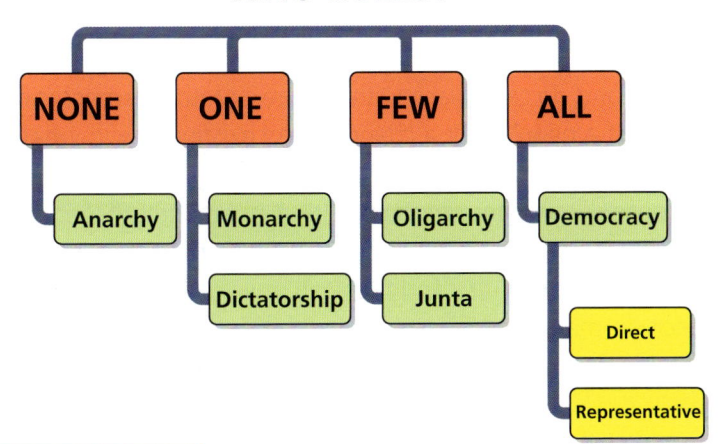

Fig. 3.8 Who rules?

QUESTIONS

1. What does the term 'political representation' mean?
2. In your opinion, why do citizens form political parties?
3. Explain the difference between an absolute monarchy and a constitutional monarchy.
4. What are the similarities and differences between a dictatorship and an oligarchy?
5. Compare and contrast direct democracy with representative democracy.
6. List **one** strength and **one** weakness of both types of democracy.
7. In your opinion, under which system of government is political representation strongest? Give reasons for your answer.

SKILLS BOOK LINK 3.1

Go to pages 26–27 of your Skills Book to complete Skill Task 3.1 on forms of government.

Complete your next Reflective Journal entry (page 10)

POLITICAL REPRESENTATION

Political Representation and the Right to Participate in a Democracy

The term 'democracy' originated in ancient Greece and means 'rule of the people' (*demos* meaning 'people' and *kratos* meaning 'power' or 'rule'). Citizens in ancient cities such as Athens voiced their concerns and shared their opinions directly with their rulers. During these meetings, citizens voted on the new rules and laws for their cities. This was direct democracy: citizens participated in political discussions and decision-making. As the centuries passed, however, this form of direct democracy began to disappear. As attractive as it may sound, a pure direct democracy is seldom a viable option in the modern era because of the larger populations that make up the countries of the world today. Most modern democracies are representative. In a representative democracy, citizens do not directly vote or decide on laws (e.g. speed limits) or policies (e.g. how the education system should address the special learning needs of students). We select representatives to do this on our behalf.

Fig. 3.9 Democracy in Ancient Greece

However, acts of direct democracy can and do take place within representative democracies. Citizens sometimes directly vote on a proposal of a new law or a change to an existing law in what is called a *referendum*. In Ireland, we have had referendums on a variety of issues: divorce, proposals to give more power to the institutions of the European Union and, most recently, same-sex marriage. However, for the majority of the political decisions and law-making in our country, we participate indirectly through our representatives. As you can see, direct democracy and representative democracy involve different types of citizen participation in decision-making. Key thinkers have offered many different views on this issue.

See page 76 for more information on the views of key thinkers on direct democracy and representative democracy.

SKILLS BOOK LINK 3.2

Go to pages 28–29 of your Skills Book to complete Skill Task 3.2 on different types of democracy.

KEY THINKERS

POLITICAL REPRESENTATIVES: DELEGATES OR TRUSTEES?

In a representative democracy, we select our leaders to represent our interests. However, there are different views on the exact manner in which our representatives should perform their role. Should our representatives act as *delegates* or *trustees*?

James Madison

James Madison, 'father of the US Constitution', supported the idea that political representatives should act as *delegates* for their local constituents. The US system of government is based on a federal structure, whereby each state is represented in government. For Madison and other supporters of the delegate model of representation, political representatives should, first and foremost, act in the interests of their local area or group. The delegates' decisions should be based on the preferences of their constituents.

Edmund Burke

In contrast, eighteenth-century Irish MP and political philosopher Edmund Burke believed that political representatives should represent the nation as a whole, and not specific constituencies. Parliament is 'not a congress of ambassadors from different and hostile interests [but a] deliberative assembly of one nation, with one interest, that of the whole'. In Burke's *trustee* model of representation, our representatives have been given the power to act in the interest of the common good. In this sense, sometimes they may need to go against the specific interests of their local constituencies in order to serve the nation as a whole.

QUESTIONS

1. According to Madison, what is a delegate's main function?
2. How does the role of a trustee differ from that of a delegate?
3. On the role of political representatives, with which key thinker do you agree: Madison or Burke? Give reasons to support your answer.
4. In your opinion, do elected representatives in Ireland act more like trustees or delegates? Give examples to support your answer.

KEY THINKERS

POLITICAL REPRESENTATION

Thomas Hobbes
The sovereign *is* the people: 'a multitude of men are made one person, when they are by one man, or one person, represented'.

Jean-Jacques Rousseau
Politics requires the direct participation of the individual. The general will 'does not admit of being represented'. Direct democracy will ensure the general will of all is followed.

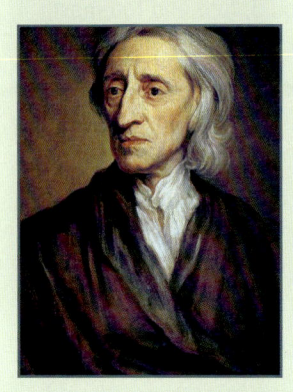

John Locke
No person has natural authority over another. However, government is the best form of providing safety and protecting one's possessions. Everyone has the right to be represented in government. A representative is 'acted by the will of the society […] thus he has no will, no power, but that of the law'.

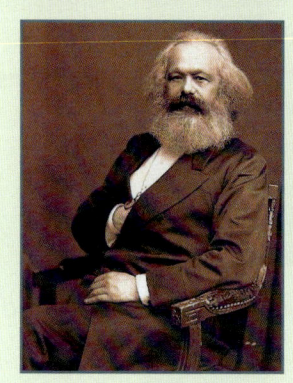

Karl Marx
Marx did not explicitly support direct democracy, but he did believe that everyone must participate in the executive and legislative power of the political society.

Montesquieu
'As, in a free state, every man, considered to have a free soul, should be governed by himself, the people as a body should have legislative power; but, as this is impossible in large states and is subject to many drawbacks in small ones, the people must have their representatives do all that they themselves cannot do.' Direct democracy is the ideal but it is not realistic or possible in modern states. Therefore, representative democracy is the solution.

QUESTIONS

1. Which **one** of the above key thinkers displays views that could justify an autocracy? Explain your answer.
2. Name **three** of the above key thinkers who support the notion of a representative democracy.
3. Name the key thinker who supports the idea of direct democracy.
4. (a) What does Locke mean when he claims that representatives are acting by 'the will of society'? Revise Locke's ideas on pages 16–17 to help you answer this question.
   (b) How can Irish citizens ensure that politicians are held to account in representing the general 'will of society'?
5. Do you agree with Montesquieu that direct democracy is 'impossible in large states and is subject to many drawbacks in smaller ones'? Give reasons to support your answer.

POWER AND PEOPLE

RESEARCH ASSIGNMENT 3.1

Using the internet and national newspapers, find evidence of and compile a report on the following:

(a) An occasion when a TD put the national interest ahead of the interests of his or her own constituents

(b) An occasion when a TD placed their constituents' interests ahead of the national interest

(c) **Two** recent examples when Irish citizens actively participated in direct democracy.

See **RESEARCH TIPS** on page 33.

Whether through direct democracy or representative democracy, citizen participation in decision-making is a right. The *right to participate* is based on the idea that an individual has the right to be involved in decision-making that affects his or her interests. Everyone in society should be able to defend their interests and contribute to ensuring that society protects all their other rights (education, health, freedom from violence, etc.). There are different aspects to the right to participate, such as the right to vote, the right to stand for elections, and the right to establish and be part of a representative association or group that makes one's voice heard in the decision-making processes (e.g. Irish Farmers' Association or a student union).

The Right to Participate in Public Affairs

The International Covenant on Civil and Political Rights (ICCPR) is an international agreement and human rights law signed by countries, including Ireland, that are members of the United Nations. The ICCPR obligates countries to protect and preserve basic human rights, including: the right to life and human dignity; to be treated equally before the law; freedom of speech, assembly, and association; religious freedom and privacy; and freedom from torture. Article 25 of the ICCPR details the right to participate in public affairs:

> *Every citizen shall have the right and the opportunity:*
>
> *(a) To take part in the conduct of public affairs, directly or through freely chosen representatives;*
>
> *(b) To vote and to be elected at genuine periodic elections which shall be by universal and equal suffrage and shall be held by secret ballot, guaranteeing the free expression of the will of the electors;*
>
> *(c) To have access, on general terms of equality, to public service in his country.*

The Constitution of Ireland, which is the main or 'mother' law of our country, also protects these rights.

Groups in Society

As we have seen in previous chapters, there are many different groups in society. Individuals will experience society differently because of their membership of a particular group (men/women, poor/rich, etc.).

In Chapter 2 we looked at decision-making in schools and how the views of different groups – teachers, parents and students – are represented in decision-making on school

Fig. 3.10 Groups in society

Complete your next Reflective Journal entry (page 10)

POLITICAL REPRESENTATION

rules and management, and how school rules can affect groups differently (e.g. admission policies and members of the Traveller community). Societal rules work in much the same way.

In Chapter 1 we looked at social stratification and how society can be ordered. It is not always helpful to think of citizens as one mass group. Different people have different identities. Different groups may have special interests and concerns based on their unique experience of society. In ancient Greece, not all citizens participated in the forums for direct democracy. Slaves, women, children and people who did not own land did not have the right to participate. A healthy and truly democratic society, on the other hand, will ensure that *all* groups will be represented: women, men, youth, elderly, people living in poverty, people with disabilities, members of the Traveller, immigrant or LGBTQ+ communities, etc. In later chapters, we will look at how different groups in Ireland are represented – or not – in terms of how we select our leaders and decision-makers and make our laws and policies.

SKILLS BOOK LINK 3.3

Go to pages 29–30 of your Skills Book to complete Skill Task 3.3 on interest groups.

See **RESEARCH TIPS** on page 33.

KEY THINKERS

SOCIAL STRATIFICATION: SUMMARY

In society, we rank different categories or groups of people in a hierarchy. Society rewards groups differently. Some groups have greater status, power and wealth than other groups. This is known as *social stratification*. An example of a historical stratification system is slavery. Modern stratification systems include the class system present in all societies and the caste system in countries such as India. Additional bases of social stratification include age, sex and ethnicity. As we learned in Chapter 1, there are three dominant perspectives on social stratification: structural functionalism, social conflict theory and symbolic interactionism.

Structural functionalism attempts to explain how and why society functions as it does. Émile Durkheim is considered the 'father' of structural functionalism. Sociologists Kingsley Davis and Wilbert E. Moore argued that stratification is necessary for society to function properly. For them, social stratification ensures that society is constantly progressing and improving, since it provides a system of rewards (e.g. wealth) and sanctions (e.g. punishment).

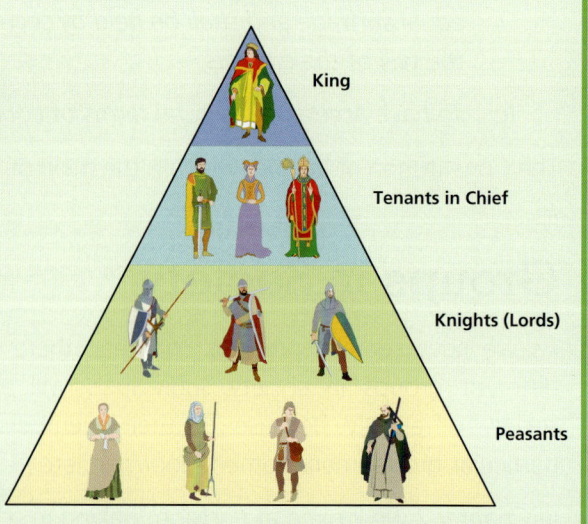

Fig. 3.11 Social stratification during the Middle Ages

KEY THINKERS

Social conflict theorists take a different view. They see society as a place of inequality that generates conflict and social change. Karl Marx is considered the 'father' of social conflict theory. For Marx, society is based on the existence of two main classes: the bourgeoisie and the proletariat. The system of capitalism requires this class-based social stratification. Marxists base social stratification on class alone. However, theorists such as Max Weber argue that society is more complex. For Weber, the hierarchy of groups in society is based on many aspects, including class, status (prestige) and political power (the ability to influence decisions and actions in society).

Tip:
Look back to Chapter 1 and revise what you learned about structural functionalism and social conflict theory. Answer the questions below before you read about social stratification in Ireland (page 80).

Fig. 3.12 The 1911 'Pyramid of Capitalist System' is an example of a socialist critique of capitalism and of social stratification

QUESTIONS

1. Do you agree with the structural functionalist view that stratification is necessary for society to function properly? Give reasons to support your answer.

2. How does Max Weber's view of social stratification differ from that of traditional Marxists?

3. Can you think of examples of occupations in Ireland that have relatively high economic status (i.e. a high income) but are assigned a lower social status (i.e. categorised as lower middle class or working class)? Make a list of them.

4. Can you think of examples of occupations in Ireland that have relatively low economic status (i.e. a low income) but are assigned a higher social status (i.e. categorised as middle class or upper class)? Make a list of them.

5. Are there any other factors, not already mentioned, that determine social stratification in Ireland?

Social Stratification in Ireland

WHAT THE RESEARCH SAYS!

CHERISHING ALL EQUALLY – ECONOMIC INEQUALITY IN IRELAND, NAT O'CONNOR AND CORMAC STAUNTON (TASC, 2015)

Class

In 2015, TASC (Think-tank for Action on Social Change) published the first detailed report on economic inequality in Ireland. Traditionally, researchers have focused on income as the main measure of economic inequality. However, *Cherishing All Equally* widened the definition of economic inequality to include a range of other areas, such as: whether or not people have equal access to public services, people's family composition, and the costs of goods and services. The research examined a variety of existing data and statistics from the CSO, OECD and other sources to provide an overview of economic inequality in Ireland.

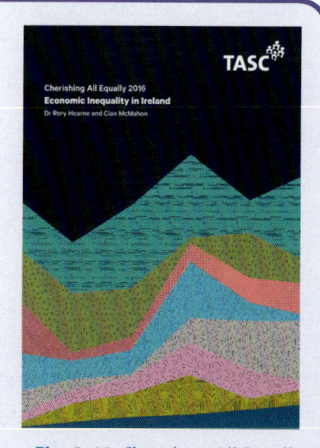

Fig. 3.13 Cherishing All Equally

Income/Wealth

- Wealth is much more unequally distributed than income. The top 10 per cent potentially hold more than half of Ireland's wealth, while the half of society on the lowest incomes has only 12 per cent of the wealth. Wealth includes all economic assets, such as home ownership, car ownership, valuables, savings and shares in companies.

- The 'living wage' is the term used to describe the full-time rate of pay necessary to sustain a basic but decent standard of living. In Ireland, the legal minimum wage (now €9.55 per hour) is far less than the living wage of €11.70 per hour (see www.livingwage.ie). At the same time, the cost of living in Ireland is 20 per cent more expensive than the EU average.

Public Services

In Ireland many public services are free of charge; however, too often people are asked to pay fees or to purchase services privately.

For example, childcare fees in Ireland are the second highest in the EU: Irish families on average wages often pay over a quarter of their income for childcare.

Nationally, 13 of the 20 best-performing boys' schools and 10 of the 20 best-performing girls' schools are fee-paying.

Many EU countries offer more public services free of charge, but they can only do so because social security payments and taxes are much higher in these countries. Social security payments (PRSI) in Ireland are the second lowest in the EU and are less than half of the EU average.

Non-Income

- 'Material deprivation' means that a person cannot afford some of the basic necessities, such as a warm coat, home heating and the capacity to replace worn furniture. More than one in four adults in Ireland – an estimated 968,000 adults – currently experience at least two forms of material deprivation.

- In 2012, one in ten individuals could not afford new (as opposed to second-hand) clothes. One in 20 could not afford two pairs of strong shoes. One in 27 could not afford a warm, waterproof coat.

- In 2009, one in five households in Ireland experienced 'energy poverty'. Of this group, one-quarter (one in 20 of the population) experienced 'extreme' levels of energy poverty.

- Ireland has one of the highest rates of overweight adults in Europe (three in five adults), which represents 2.2 million adults whose food and drink consumption patterns are unhealthy. Income inequality has been shown to be related to the incidence of obesity: unhealthy processed and sugar-sweetened foods are often cheaper than healthy foods.
- Food deprivation affects up to one in 13 people. Some 179,400 individuals (3.9 per cent) report the inability to afford a meal with meat or fish every second day.
- Lone parents (85 per cent of whom are women) are more likely to experience deprivation. It is more difficult for lone parents than couples to qualify for the Back to School Clothing and Footwear Allowance, even though their children have the same needs.
- Deprivation is more likely for certain groups: people who rent, households with lower educational attainment, and households with a greater than average number of children.

WHAT THE RESEARCH SAYS!

WOMEN AND MEN IN IRELAND (CSO, 2013)

Gender

According to the *Women and Men in Ireland* report from the CSO, Irish women are more likely to have a third-level qualification than men. However, women still face significant inequalities in Ireland.

- Women are significantly under-represented in decision-making structures in Ireland at both national and regional levels. In 2013 only 15.7 per cent of TDs in Dáil Éireann were women. Also, women accounted for less than one-fifth of members of local authorities and just over one-third of the membership of Vocational Education Committees. The average female representation in national parliaments in the EU was 27.5 per cent in 2013.
- The Gender Equality Index shows that Ireland was ninth-highest out of 27 EU member states in 2010, with a score of 55.2. This was slightly above the EU average score of 54, where 1 indicates total inequality and 100 indicates gender equality.
- In 2013 in Ireland, men were more likely than women to be in the labour force: seven out of ten men aged 15 and over were in employment, compared to five out of ten women. More than 98 per cent of those looking after home/family were women: almost 500,000 women looked after home/family, compared to only 8,700 men in this same role.
- Over one-third of women at work in Ireland in 2012 were working in the health and education sectors. Women accounted for four out of five employees in the health sector and three-quarters in the education sector. The sectors with the highest proportions of men in 2012 were construction, agriculture and transport. In primary education 85 per cent of teachers are female. In secondary education 68 per cent of teachers are female.
- Women are not well represented at senior management levels: despite making up three-quarters of the workforce in the education sector, women account for 44 per cent of primary school managers and 41 per cent of post-primary school managers. Despite making up one-fifth of health sector professionals, only 37 per cent of medical and dental consultants are women.
- Women's income in 2011 in Ireland was about three-quarters of men's income. After adjusting for the longer hours worked by men, women's hourly earnings were around 94 per cent of men's in 2011.

Note:
The **Gender Equality Index** measures differences between men and women in EU member states across a number of areas, including work, money, knowledge, health and power. It is produced by the European Institute for Gender Equality (EIGE). The index ranges from 1 (total inequality) to 100 (gender equality).

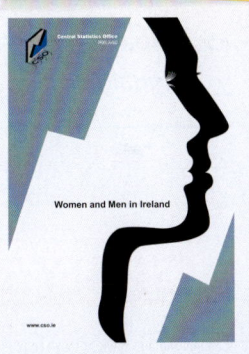

Fig. 3.14 *Women and Men in Ireland*

QUESTIONS

1. Define the term 'social class'. (Refer to page 12 to help you with your answer.)
2. Examine the findings of the TASC report *Cherishing All Equally* (on pages 80–81) and list the data that shows how inequality is a growing problem in Ireland today.
3. How does Ireland compare to the rest of the EU in relation to the cost of living and provision of services?
4. Find evidence in the TASC report that highlights the relationship between income levels and educational attainment levels.
5. What is meant by the term 'material deprivation'?
6. Identify from the TASC report any **three** groups that are most likely to experience deprivation in Ireland.
7. In relation to the CSO report *Women and Men in Ireland*, explain the term 'patriarchy'. (Refer to the Feminism section on page 9 of Chapter 1 to help you with your answer.)
8. Do the statistics in *Women and Men in Ireland* prove that Ireland is a patriarchy? Explain your answer.
9. In your opinion, why is there such a low percentage of women involved in national politics?
10. What barriers prevent women from rising to managerial positions in health, education and other sectors of the Irish economy?
11. In relation to both the TASC and CSO reports, do any of the statistics surprise you? Why/why not?
12. Is social stratification in Ireland determined more by class or gender? Make reference to the reports on pages 80–81 and your own experiences at school and in your community.
13. What are the strengths of the research methodology used for the TASC report *Cherishing All Equally*?

ACTIVITY 3.1

This activity explores how social class impacts on life chances and opportunities. Your teacher will assign you a character profile. You take on the role of the character while taking part in a race to the front of the class. You will take steps forward or backwards, depending on your response to questions asked by your teacher.

ACTIVITY 3.2

This activity explores classification and categorisation according to social class. Your teacher will give your group several images. Your group will divide the images into two categories: working class or upper/middle class.

SKILLS BOOK LINK 3.4

Go to pages 30–36 of your Skills Book to complete Skill Task 3.4 on social stratification in Dublin and Ireland.

See RESEARCH TIPS on page 33.

ACTIVITY 3.3

Your teacher will give your group several images of objects and occupations. Your group will categorise the images according to gender roles: male-related images in one group and female-related images in another.

ACTIVITY 3.4

Your teacher will call out several statements concerning gender. You will take part in a 'moving debate' where you express your opinion on each of the ten arguments put forward.

SKILLS BOOK LINK 3.5

Go to pages 37–40 of your Skills Book to complete Skill Task 3.5 on social class.

See RESEARCH TIPS on page 33.

SKILLS BOOK LINK 3.6

Go to pages 41–42 of your Skills Book to complete Skill Task 3.6 on female employment.

See RESEARCH TIPS on page 33.

SKILLS BOOK LINK 3.7

Go to pages 43–44 of your Skills Book to complete Skill Task 3.7 on gender inequality.

See RESEARCH TIPS on page 33.

RESEARCH ASSIGNMENT 3.2

Conduct a 'media watch' and gather recent examples of news stories that could be classified as issues of either gender or social class. Write a short report on the main findings of your media watch. Include the following in your report:
- A summary of two news stories related to gender. Interpret and explain how these stories can be linked to feminist theory (see page 9)
- A summary of two stories related to social class. Interpret and explain how these stories can be linked to theories on social class or social stratification (see pages 12–13)

KEY THINKERS

SOCIAL DIVISIONS AND POWER STRUGGLES

Karl Marx

'The executive of the modern state is but a committee for managing the common affairs of the whole bourgeoisie.' In Marx's analysis, government acts to ensure the dominance of one class over another. Government represents the bourgeoisie (upper) class.

Sylvia Walby

In Walby's theory, gender regimes are one of the important regimes of inequality in society, alongside class and ethnicity. Gender inequality can be found in the economy (for example, unequal pay), the polity (for example, fewer women than men in parliament), civil society (for example, sexualised images of women) and violence (for example, domestic violence).

Max Weber

Weber identified three sources of social organisation and power: class, status and party. Class relates to one's economic position in society. Social status or 'social honour' is broader than wealth. Status can be understood as the things that society values, which will affect our life chances (our education or occupation). Although wealth is often associated with status, the two elements are separate. A person with a lower class can have high social status, e.g. if they are not born wealthy but they attend a prestigious college. When classes or social status groups organise themselves to obtain power or to influence action in society, they become 'parties'. Examples of parties include trade unions, religious institutions, professional associations and political parties. A person can obtain power from membership in a party, even if they have a lower social class or status.

Kathleen Lynch

Lynch has looked at the position of different social groups in the Irish education system. In her research, she highlights the importance of looking at the different experiences of students on the basis of social class, gender, sexual orientation, ethnicity and religion. The education system is viewed as a reflection of wider Irish society: existing inequalities in society are present in the education system.

Complete your next Reflective Journal entry (page 10)

QUESTIONS

1. According to Marx, what is the role of the government? Who are the bourgeoisie?
2. Can you think of any actions taken by the Irish government in recent years that would support Marx's analysis?
3. Explain Weber's **three** sources of social organisation and power. In your opinion, which of the three is the most important for gaining power in Ireland?
4. Do you agree with Walby that society can be viewed as a patriarchy? Describe **two** aspects of Irish society that support her view, and **two** aspects that contradict her view.
5. Do you agree with the claim made by Kathleen Lynch that 'existing inequalities in society are present in the education system'? Give reasons to support your answer.

ACTIVITY 3.5

Is modern Irish society a patriarchy, where men dominate all areas of society: political, social, economic, moral and cultural (as Walby suggests)?

Your group will be assigned one area of Irish society (e.g. sport or religion). As a group, you will research the main institutions within that sector. Examine the gender composition of the membership and management structure of each institution, and conclude whether or not it represents a patriarchy. Present your findings to the class.

ACTIVITY 3.6

Your group will be assigned one of the key thinkers from page 84 by your teacher. You will be given extracts written by your assigned key thinker on the topics of social class or gender. You will read the extracts and write a concise summary of the key ideas of this thinker. You will then present your group's summary to another group using the jigsaw method.

SKILLS BOOK LINK 3.8

Go to page 45 of your Skills Book to complete Skill Task 3.8 on the Inequality Tree.

Representation Through Civil Society Bodies

Society is often considered as having three main sectors: public (e.g. government), private (e.g. businesses) and civil society. The civil society sector is made up of a variety of bodies (community groups, charities, unions, associations) that represent the interests of citizens. A civil society body will often represent a particular issue (e.g. poverty, environment, mental health) or a particular group (e.g. women, teachers, students, Traveller community, elderly, people with disabilities). In Ireland there are over 19,000 civil society bodies. They deliver important services to communities and citizens across a wide range of areas: education, health, housing, poverty relief, environment, sports and culture.

These bodies also play an important role in representing the interests and concerns of their constituent groups to political decision-makers. ICTU is the largest civil society body on the island of Ireland – with approximately 750,000 members, north and south.

Fig. 3.15 Some of the civil society bodies currently active in Ireland

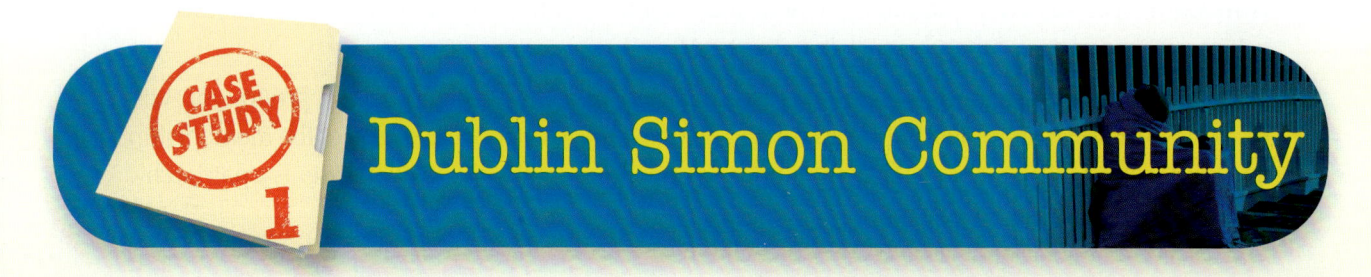

Case Study 1: Dublin Simon Community

Homelessness is a major issue of concern in Irish society. The official figures present a steady rise in the numbers of homeless people since the 2008 banking crisis and financial crash. According to the 2016 population census, in Dublin alone 4,262 people were counted in homeless shelters or as sleeping rough on the streets. The homeless community is an important and often unheard group in Irish society.

Fig. 3.16 Homelessness in Dublin

The Dublin Simon Community was founded by a group of Trinity and UCD students in 1969, who began by providing much-needed soup and sandwiches to people who were sleeping rough in Dublin city centre. The Simon Community now operates in Dublin, Kildare, Wicklow and Meath and provides additional services such as emergency accommodation, social activities, and health and support services to address some of the reasons that may have led to homelessness. The organisation also supports people who are at risk of becoming homeless. It helps these people to secure and sustain a home of their own, by providing advice and information on their right to housing. The Simon Community also strives to ensure that the concerns and needs of the homeless population are understood and included in government decision-making. The organisation produces research and reports on the homeless problem, proposes solutions, runs campaigns to raise public awareness, and aims to influence government decision-making.

RESEARCH ASSIGNMENT 3.3

Choose one of the social groups or any interest group in Irish society (e.g. homeless, immigrants, LGBTQ+, unemployed). Research and make a list of the main civil society bodies that represent the interests of your chosen group. Write a short report on the main findings of your research. Include the following in your report:

- Name of social group/interest group
- Name of civil society bodies that represent this group
- Aims of these civil society bodies
- Strategies and methods used to represent the group
- Effectiveness of this representation: whether or not it is successful, and why.

Representation Through Political Parties

In most Western democracies, political parties provide a link between citizens, or different interest groups, and the government. Although citizens can be represented by politicians who have no affiliation with a political party (i.e. independents), the majority of political systems in Western democracies are organised on the basis of political parties. The notion of political parties developed in the nineteenth century, with the concept of 'like-minded' politicians and the advent of representative democracy. The spectrum of political parties varies from country to country. Political parties are often a reflection of the particular social and political history and development of a society. For example, in Ireland the two main political parties – Fine Gael and Fianna Fáil – initially developed on the basis of a split and civil war between those who supported and those who opposed the Anglo-Irish Treaty. In modern times, the People Before Profit Alliance developed in response to growing inequality and the economic crash of 2008. Political parties can be viewed on the basis of their general position in relation to, for example, the left–right spectrum, a particular ideology (e.g. Christian, socialist, Nazi) or an issue or group (e.g. the environment, women's rights). In current global politics, however, some parties can be considered 'populist' political parties: they adopt positions that are general enough to appeal to the largest possible number of citizens, and are not tied to any specific ideology. Whatever their ideology, political parties aim to win power in government, thus providing citizens with political representation in government institutions.

Fig. 3.17 At election time, citizens vote for the political party that will best represent their interests

KEY THINKERS

PARTY SYSTEMS AND SOCIAL DIVISIONS

Lipset and Rokkan

In 1967, political scientists **Seymour Martin Lipset** and **Stein Rokkan** identified four main social divisions, or cleavages, which they believed determined the development of all political parties in Europe.

- **Centre versus Periphery:** Differences between elites living in urban areas (the dominant culture) and people in peripheral areas (subordinate cultures) give rise to distinct political parties. For example, regional groups in Spain have given rise to political parties including the Basque Nationalist Party and the Republican Left of Catalonia (ERC).

- **State versus Church:** Political parties representing religious voters or secular voters have emerged in some countries. Up to the

POLITICAL REPRESENTATION 87

KEY THINKERS

1970s the five major parties in the Netherlands consisted of three religious-based parties – the Catholic People's Party (KVP), the Protestant Anti-Revolutionary Party (ARP) and the Christian Historical Union (CHU) – and two secular parties – the social democratic Dutch Labour Party (PvdA) and the liberal People's Party for Freedom and Democracy (VVD).

- **Owner versus Worker:** This social cleavage is based on class and gave rise to parties of the left and right. Almost all European countries have parties representing both sides of the political spectrum.

- **Urban versus Rural:** This social cleavage is based on differences between urban and rural or industrial and agricultural interest groups and communities.

Lipset and Rokkan's party cleavage framework is one of the best-known and most applied models in analyses of party systems. However, it has been criticised for not being applicable to all countries (e.g. Finland, Ireland). With the rise of political parties based on new issues and ideologies (e.g. environmentalism, globalisation, feminism), some people question the validity of the Lipset and Rokkan theory.

QUESTIONS

1. What is the difference between a civil society body and a political party?
2. Explain the Centre versus Periphery social cleavage (division). Could this cleavage be applied to the ways in which different political parties have evolved in the UK in recent times? Explain why.
3. Which of the four social cleavages is most applicable to the divisions between the political parties in Ireland today? Give reasons to support your answer.

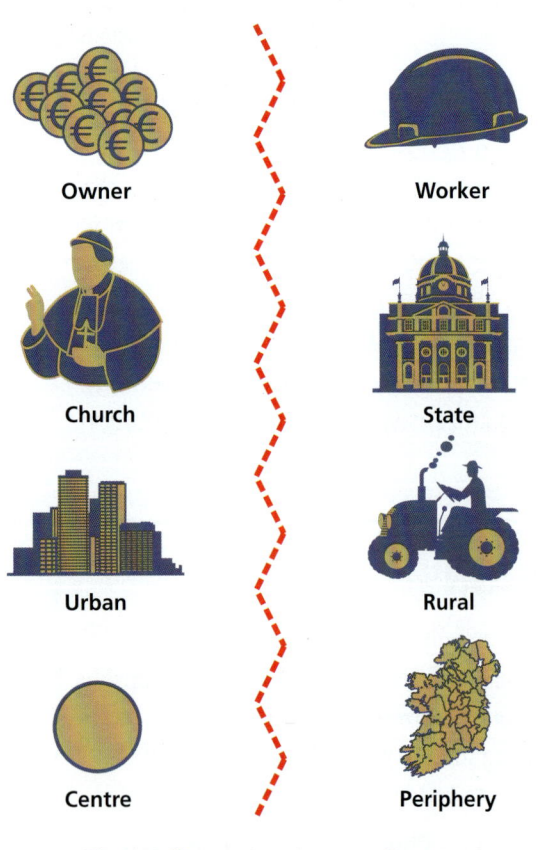

Fig. 3.18 Cleavages in society, according to Lipset and Rokkan

Fine Gael		Anti-Austerity Alliance/People Before Profit	
Fianna Fáil		Independents 4 Change	
Sinn Féin		Social Democrats	
Labour		Green Party	
Workers and Unemployed Action (No official emblem)		Independent Alliance* (No official emblem)	
*The Independent Alliance is not a political party. The Alliance consists of a number of independent (non-partisan) politicians (six TDs and 15 councillors) who are working in collaboration.			
*Other independents: There are 18 TDs, nine senators, three MEPs and almost 200 councillors who are independent.			

Table 3.1 Political parties who won seats in the Irish General Election, May 2016

POWER AND PEOPLE

ACTIVITY 3.7

Your group will be assigned one political party by your teacher. As a group, examine the party's website and conduct research on the party. Assess the extent to which this party represents all the groups in Irish society. Are there any groups that this party does not represent?

See **RESEARCH TIPS** on page 33.

Tip:
You could divide up the roles in your group so that each member assesses the party from one of the following perspectives: age, gender, social class, LGBTQ+, religion/ethnicity/race. For example, from a gender perspective, you could research the following questions: What percentage of the elected representatives are male/female? Does this party have aims or policies in relation to gender equality?

Voting Patterns

Voting patterns (how a society votes) give us an insight into the link between society and politics, i.e. the political choices a society makes. But what determines voter preference? Is it possible to identify support for certain political parties on the basis of class, gender or other social categories? As a woman, am I more likely to support a particular party over another? What if I am from the working class in my society? What influences my choice of political party then?

Since the 1960s, many political scientists have studied voting patterns as a means to examine the relationship between individuals, society and politics. There is a wide variety of different and competing theories on the main determinants of voter preferences.

Individual Determinants: Rational Choice

Rational choice theory states that voter preference is based on individual self-interest (i.e. Party A will best deliver my needs). Voters act like consumers and select the party with the manifesto and policies that best serve the individual interests of the voter. For example, a business owner may vote for the party that supports a low rate of corporate tax or other policies that support commercial activities. A person who is caring for an elderly or ill family member may prefer the party that supports an increase in social benefits such as the Carer's Allowance. This type of voting is also known as 'issue voting'. In this theory, voters will not select a party on the basis of loyalty or ideology, but on the basis of this party's positions on specific issues of importance to the voter. This theory helps to explain the phenomenon of **floating voters**.

Fig. 3.19 Floating voter

KEY TERM

A **floating voter** is someone who does not always vote for the same party in each election. Such voters do not demonstrate loyalty to a particular party: they may choose to change their party preference between elections.

Social Determinants: Class, Religion, Gender and Age

Social theories of voting behaviour point to membership of a particular social group as a major influence. In the 1960s many researchers focused on social class and religion as key determinants of voter behaviour. These researchers pointed to examples such as the UK, which had a party system dominated by two main political parties representing the upper and middle classes (Conservative Party) and the working classes (Labour Party). Similarly, religion was found to be an important influence in voter choice in countries including Belgium, France, Italy and the Netherlands.

POLITICAL REPRESENTATION

Modernisation theories on voting behaviour later emerged. In these theories, social class and religion lose significance as determinants of voting behaviour. This process is known as **dealignment**. Additional social factors – gender, age, education, ethnicity – are considered to play a role in influencing voter choices. With respect to gender, for example, research has found that more women than men align themselves to the parties of the left in many countries. Women are believed to support left-wing parties because of their policies on health, education and childcare. The same has been found with respect to age in some countries: younger voters tend to support left-wing parties.

> ### KEY TERM
> **Dealignment** describes the weakening of the relationship between a particular factor and a person's choice of political party. These factors can include class (class dealignment) and party loyalty (partisan dealignment).

Party Identification

Voters sometimes identify strongly with a particular political party. These voters demonstrate loyalty to 'their' party: voting for them in all/most elections. This is known as *partisan voting*. Voters may inherit their party preference from their family (i.e. our family supports Party A). Party identification and loyalty may then be reinforced by membership of a particular social group or identity. Until quite recently, voter preference in Ireland was primarily based on partisan voting and traditional family loyalties.

Political Ideologies

Voters may select a party on the basis of its ideological leaning: left, right, conservative, liberal, environmental, feminist, etc. However, in countries that do not offer a choice of parties with distinct ideologies, this may not be as relevant to the voter.

Voting Patterns in Ireland

What do we know about voting patterns in Ireland? Ireland has traditionally been considered as somewhat unusual in the European context. In the past in Ireland, factors such as class, religion and left–right ideologies played a less prominent role in determining voter behaviour. Until recently, voting in Ireland was heavily influenced by political history. Since the foundation of the Irish Free State in 1922, Irish politics has been dominated by just two political parties: Fianna Fáil and Fine Gael. These parties owe their origins to the political split over the Anglo-Irish Treaty, which led to the Irish Civil War in 1922. However, just as societies change, so too do political landscapes. The traditional Civil War politics of Ireland has been challenged by the growth of parties such as Labour and Sinn Féin, the increase in support for Independents, and the emergence of new parties and alliances (e.g. Anti-Austerity Alliance/People Before Profit). Researchers and analysts continue to investigate the behaviour of the Irish voter.

Fig. 3.20 Behaviour of the Irish voter

WHAT THE RESEARCH SAYS!

VOTING PATTERNS IN THE 2002 GENERAL ELECTION

The first-ever study of electoral behaviour in Ireland was conducted between 2002 and 2007. The Irish National Election Survey (INES) was conducted by the ESRI, Trinity College Dublin and University College Dublin. The survey was made up of interviews with 2,663 people of voting age after the 2002 and 2007 elections. The survey results demonstrated some interesting findings in relation to Irish voter behaviour.

Class
In terms of household income and educational attainment, the poorest and least educated respondents voted for Fianna Fáil, followed by Sinn Féin, Fine Gael and Labour. The party with the richest and most well-educated supporters was the Green Party.

Age
The average age of a supporter of Fine Gael was 48, followed by the Progressive Democrats (47.5) and Fianna Fáil (47). The parties with the youngest supporters were Sinn Féin (36) and the Green Party (35).

Gender
The most 'male' party was Sinn Féin (58 per cent of its supporters were men). The most 'female' party was the Green Party (55 per cent of its supporters were women). Gender differences were not significant within support for the other parties.

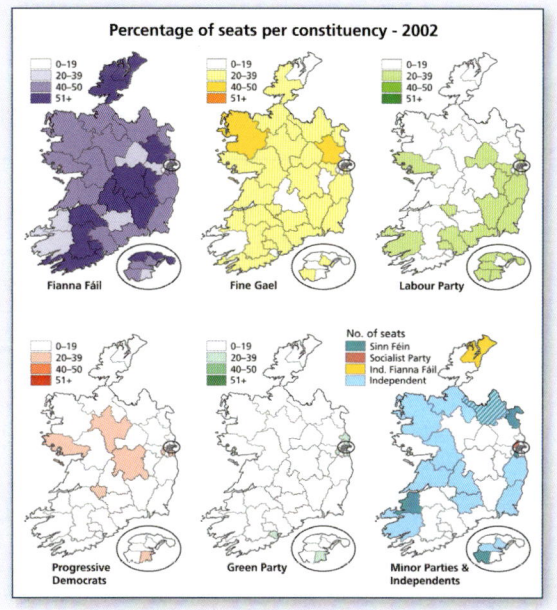

Fig. 3.21 Voting patterns in Ireland: percentage of seats per constituency

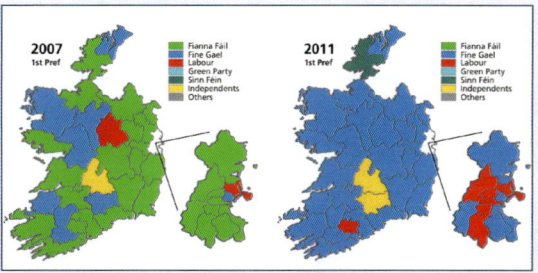

Rural/Urban
Combined support for Fianna Fáil and Fine Gael was 76 per cent in rural areas and just 44 per cent in Co. Dublin. Support for 'alternative' parties – Labour, Green Party, Sinn Féin and Others (i.e. Socialist Party, Workers' Party, Socialist Workers' Party) – was much stronger in Dublin than the rest of the country. These alternative parties received a combined 47 per cent of all votes cast in Dublin.

Fig. 3.22 A major shift in voting patterns took place between the 2007 and 2011 General Elections in Ireland

QUESTIONS

1. In your opinion, which of the factors (class, age, gender or rural/urban) had the biggest influence on voting patterns in the 2016 General Election? Explain your answer.
2. What other background factors influence voters in Ireland today?
3. Explain the following terms in relation to voting patterns: 'floating voter', 'rational choice theory', 'modernisation theory' and 'partisan voting'.
4. To what extent would your choice of political party or candidate be influenced by the preferences of your family members? What factors influence how you would vote?

POLITICAL REPRESENTATION

RESEARCH ASSIGNMENT 3.4

Your teacher will provide you with a list of useful sources and web links for this exercise.

Examine the 2011 and 2016 General Election results and analyse whether any clear voting trends emerge in relation to social class, gender, geographical location or any other significant category.

See **RESEARCH TIPS** on page 33.

RESEARCH ASSIGNMENT 3.5

Prepare a speech that you will give to your local TDs at a public meeting on this topic: 'Improving Political Representation and Ending Inequality in Ireland'. Ensure that your speech is persuasive and that it contains quotes from key thinkers as well as relevant, research-based evidence.

Fig. 3.23 Key Word cloud

SUMMARY

- Political representation refers to the ways in which the opinions and views of citizens are included in political decision-making processes.
- Fair political representation does not exist under certain forms of government, e.g. autocracies and oligarchies.
- Direct democracy is the purest form of democracy: in it, all sections of society are given a direct say in decision-making.
- The majority of countries in the world today are representative democracies, in which the people elect representatives to national parliaments to legislate and govern on their behalf.
- Modern society can be divided into different social groups with different interests that often compete with each other for power.
- Sociologists and political scientists agree that social class and gender are two important social categories that determine access to power.
- In free-market capitalist countries such as Ireland, inequality is evident between the various social classes.
- Many feminists propose that modern societies, such as Ireland, are patriarchies, where men dominate the powerful positions in the country's main cultural, economic and political institutions.
- Individuals/social groups use civil society bodies and political parties as two mechanisms through which they can have their views represented.

REVISION QUESTIONS

1. Describe the different types of government and explain the strengths and weaknesses of each type.
2. Define the following terms: 'social class', 'capitalism', 'patriarchy' and 'civil society'.
3. What is the role of civil society bodies in Ireland?
4. List **three** facts that illustrate how socio-economic opportunities and access to power in Ireland are determined by social class.
5. List **three** facts that show that gender inequality is a major problem in Ireland.
6. Explain the main ideas of Karl Marx and Max Weber on social class, power, and political representation.
7. Explain the main ideas of Sylvia Walby's feminist theories.
8. Summarise the main theories on the factors that influence voting patterns.
9. Write an account of the main factors that influence voting patterns in Ireland.
10. Write a letter to the Taoiseach, outlining any concerns that you have as a result of your learning in this chapter. Set out your points of concern and ensure that you back them up with evidence.

DATA-BASED QUESTIONS

Complete the qualitative and quantitative research data-based questions exercise on pages 46–48 of your Skills Book.

EXAM FOCUS — Section B of LC Exam

REVISION EXERCISES

Complete the revision exercises on pages 49–51 of your Skills Book.

EXAM FOCUS — Section A of LC Exam

DISCURSIVE ESSAY TOPICS

1. 'Representative democracy is the best, fairest and most efficient form of government.' Evaluate this statement with reference to at least two key thinkers.
2. 'Social class is the greatest barrier to achieving power and equality.' Discuss this statement with reference to the writings of Karl Marx and Max Weber, as well as relevant research evidence from Ireland.
3. 'Modern Irish society is a patriarchy.' Evaluate this statement with reference to at least **two** key thinkers. Use relevant research evidence to support your argument.

EXAM FOCUS — Section C of LC Exam

Reflective Practice

Ensure that you have completed all the Reflective Journal entries for this chapter (page 10 of your Reflective Journal and Learning Portfolio) before moving on to the next chapter.

Complete the Learning Portfolio activities on pages 11–13 of your Reflective Journal and Learning Portfolio. This will help you to self-assess the extent to which you have achieved the learning intentions for this chapter, and will help you to monitor your progress.

POLITICAL REPRESENTATION

CHAPTER 4
Selecting Our Representatives

'[Democracy] is the government of the people, by the people, for the people.'
Abraham Lincoln

KEY TERMS

- Government institution
- Constitution
- Referendum
- State
- Legislature
- Executive
- Judiciary
- Separation of powers
- Checks and balances
- Unconstitutional
- Party whip system
- Constituent
- Constituency
- PR-STV
- Parliamentary democracy
- Coalition
- Unionist
- Nationalist
- Devolution
- Power-sharing
- Member of the Legislative Assembly (MLA)
- Programme for government
- Veto

Introduction

In a democracy, citizens are represented through **government institutions**. These institutions have responsibility for making decisions and rules about how our society is organised and governed. But what are these institutions? Who are our representatives within them, and how are they selected? If political representation is central to democracy, then the way in which our representatives are selected is a critical issue.

On the island of Ireland, we have a variety of political structures that represent citizens at local, national and European levels: the Government of Ireland, the Northern Ireland Executive and the institutions of the European Union. Each of these institutions is made up of different parts, and representatives are chosen in a range of different ways.

In a democratic country such as Ireland, citizens select their representatives. However, as we will see, there are many different forms of selection process. Representatives can be directly or indirectly selected. The system that a country uses for selecting its representatives to government institutions is of fundamental importance. This system will determine exactly how representative the government is of citizens and social groups.

KEY TERM

A **government institution** is an established organisation or structure devoted to the effective running of government, e.g. a legislative parliament in a democracy.

94 POWER AND PEOPLE

By the end of this chapter you will be able to:
- Explain the term 'separation of powers' and outline the roles of the legislature, the executive and the judicial branches of government in a typical democratic republic.
- Describe the Oireachtas and explain the roles of Seanad Éireann, Dáil Éireann and the President in the national law-making process.
- Describe the role of the Taoiseach and the Cabinet of Ministers.
- Explain the PR-STV system of voting and assess its strengths and weaknesses.
- Explain how members of the Seanad and the Dáil are selected.
- Explain how the Taoiseach and the President of Ireland are selected.
- Summarise research evidence on the effectiveness of the Irish system of elections in representing the will of all the people.
- Define the terms 'devolution', 'devolved government' and 'power-sharing'.
- Describe the roles of the Northern Ireland Assembly and Executive in the law-making process in Northern Ireland.
- Explain how the Northern Ireland Assembly and Executive are selected.
- Explain the role of ministers in the Northern Ireland Executive.
- Provide one example of government in a non-democratic country and describe this system.
- Compare the different methods of selecting an executive and evaluate the effectiveness of these methods.
- Describe the roles of the European Parliament, the European Commission and the Council of the EU.
- Explain how the European Parliament, the European Commission and the Council of the EU are selected and composed.
- Draw upon different viewpoints, the ideas of key thinkers and relevant evidence to examine whether the Irish system of government is effective in representing the will of all the people.

By the end of this chapter you will have developed the following skills:
- Communication skills and the ability to present information and ideas verbally.
- Interpersonal skills and the ability to work effectively with small and large groups to reach agreed conclusions and achieve consensus.
- Research skills and information processing on a variety of issues related to the roles of government institutions and the methods of selecting them.
- Critical and creative thinking skills in relation to the strengths, weaknesses and limitations of key pieces of research and important viewpoints on different types of election and how governments are selected.

KEY THINKERS

SELECTION OF GOVERNMENT

Thomas Hobbes
The first and only task of political society is to name the sovereign. The sovereign then has absolute power and citizens must be completely obedient. Popular sovereignty is only temporary at the beginning of civilisation.

John Stuart Mill
'Rulers and ruling classes are under a necessity of considering the interests of those who have the suffrage [the right to vote]; but of those who are excluded, it is in their opinion whether they will do so or not.' The people who have the right to vote have the right to have their interests represented by the people they elect ('rulers').

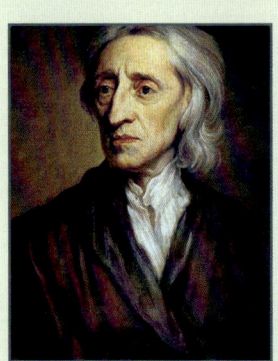

John Locke
'The liberty of man in society is to be under no other legislative power but that established by consent in the commonwealth.' People's freedom should be limited only by government that has been established by the agreement of the people.

Karl Marx
'The oppressed are allowed once every few years to decide which particular representatives of the oppressing class are to represent and repress them.'

Plato
The Ancient Greek philosopher Plato believed that the 'best' – and not the 'most' – should govern. The majority of people in society do not have the knowledge and expertise to be rulers. Democracy inevitably leads to a situation of 'rule of the mob', i.e. society would be ruled on the basis of simple and popular ideas and impulsive action. Government should be left to those in society who have the necessary qualifications and knowledge (of politics, military strategy, leadership, etc.).

QUESTIONS

1. Do you agree with Hobbes's claim that the only political task society has is to select a government and then remain 'completely obedient'? In the modern era, what other tasks and political responsibilities should society take on? Apart from voting in elections, what other actions can citizens take to ensure that the government hears their voice and represents them?

2. To what extent is Mill's view an accurate portrayal of government in Ireland? Are any groups in Irish society denied suffrage (the right to vote)? Does the government ignore the interests of any group?

3. Do you agree with Marx's pessimistic view of elections? Give examples to support your argument.

4. What do you think of Plato's view on who should be allowed to govern? Give **one** argument in favour and **one** argument against Plato's view.

5. Create your own philosophical quotation related to the selection of government and explain its meaning. The quotation should be no more than a single sentence.

96 POWER AND PEOPLE

ACTIVITY 4.1

Your teacher will call out several statements concerning the right to vote and how the government should be selected. You will take part in a 'moving debate' where you express your opinion on each of the arguments put forward.

SKILLS BOOK LINK 4.1

After the debate, go to pages 52–53 of your Skills Book to complete Skill Task 4.1 on the right to vote and how the government should be selected.

Political Representation Through Government Institutions

Fig. 4.1 Emblems of the Government of Ireland, the Northern Ireland Executive and the European Union

The Government of Ireland

The **Constitution** of Ireland (Bunreacht na hÉireann, 1937) outlines our system of government in the Republic of Ireland and the constitutional rights we have as Irish citizens. The Irish **state** is divided into three separate branches: **legislative**, **executive** and **judicial** (see Fig. 4.2). This structure is based on the idea of **separation of powers**, which means that no single part of government should have absolute power without adequate **checks and balances** by the other parts. In Ireland, the head of state is the President, and the head of government is the Taoiseach. This is different from the US system, for example, where the President is both head of state and head of government.

KEY TERMS

A **constitution** is a legal document that contains the fundamental laws and principles by which a state is to be governed. We can think of it as a 'rule book' for government. It outlines the roles of the main institutions of the state and lists the fundamental freedoms for all citizens in the state. A constitution can be amended (changed) to reflect new circumstances in society. In Ireland, the constitution can be amended if the majority of Irish citizens vote to do so in a **referendum**. Since 1937 there have been over 30 amendments to the Irish constitution, including the legalisation of divorce (1994), the transfer of certain powers to the EU, and the legal recognition of same-sex marriage (2015).

State is the term used to describe an organised political community living under one system of government, e.g. the Republic of Ireland is a state because it has its own government.

The **legislature** is the law-making body of government. In most democracies, the national parliament is the legislature.

The **executive** is the part of government responsible for enforcing and putting into practice the laws and decisions made.

The **judiciary** is the branch of government responsible for interpreting and upholding the law.

Separation of powers means that no single part of government should have absolute power without adequate **checks and balances** by the other parts.

SELECTING OUR REPRESENTATIVES

Separation of Powers in Ireland

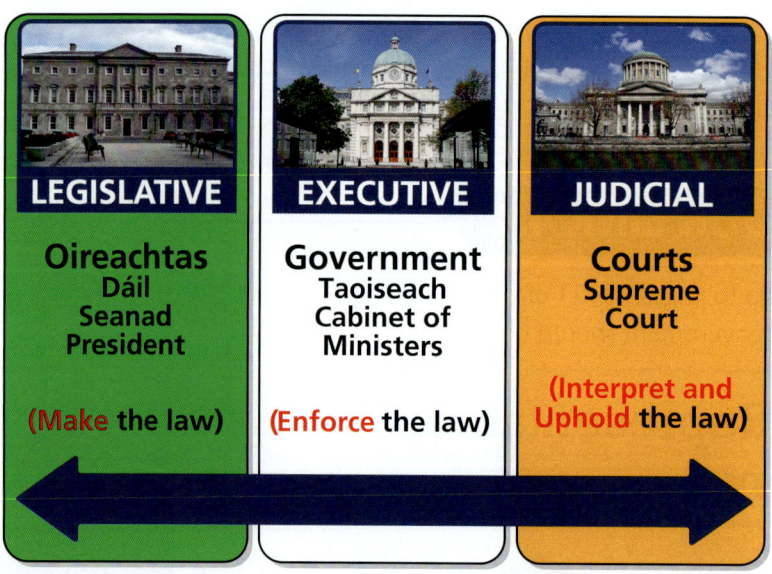

LEGISLATIVE
Oireachtas
Dáil
Seanad
President

(Make the law)

EXECUTIVE
Government
Taoiseach
Cabinet of Ministers

(Enforce the law)

JUDICIAL
Courts
Supreme Court

(Interpret and Uphold the law)

Fig. 4.2 The three branches of government in Ireland

KEY THINKERS: SEPARATION OF POWERS

The concept of 'separation of powers' first originated in ancient Greece and was used in the Roman Republic. It was further developed by French Enlightenment political philosopher **Baron de Montesquieu**. Montesquieu's ideas influenced the system of government in many modern Western democracies, including Ireland. In this system, power is divided between three branches: a legislature (parliament), an executive (government) and a judiciary (the courts). Each branch is granted certain powers which allow it to 'check' the power of the other branches. This is to ensure that no branch will ever become too powerful or gain complete control over the others. This system of 'checks and balances' is vital to the functioning of a healthy democracy, as it protects against the possible emergence of an oligarchy or dictatorship.

Baron de Montesquieu

Bunreacht na hÉireann

The separation of powers and the role of each branch of the Irish government is clearly outlined in the Constitution of Ireland, *Bunreacht na hÉireann*.

- *Legislative power* is the power to make laws, i.e. to introduce, remove or change legislation. Articles 15 to 27 of the Irish constitution give this power to the national parliament or the Oireachtas. The Oireachtas consists of Dáil Éireann, Seanad Éireann and the President.

- *Executive power* is the power to carry laws into effect, i.e. to execute or carry out the laws with the assistance of a police force, a military force and the civil service. Article 28 of the Irish constitution gives this power to the government (the Taoiseach, the Tánaiste and the Cabinet of Ministers).

- *Judicial power* is the power to interpret and apply the law to disputes and conflicts that arise between the state and individual citizens, as well as any disputes between citizens. Articles 34 to 37 of the Irish constitution give this power to the courts.

Fig. 4.3 Bunreacht na hÉireann

How Does the System of 'Checks and Balances' Work in Ireland?

- The Supreme Court (judicial branch) can declare a law passed by the Oireachtas (legislative branch) to be **unconstitutional**. This would mean that the law is not compatible with the important rules and democratic principles outlined in Ireland's constitution. If the Supreme Court declares a law unconstitutional, the law must be amended or removed completely. The Supreme Court also has the power to declare that a minister (from the executive branch) has exceeded or abused his or her powers or did not follow a legal procedure properly.

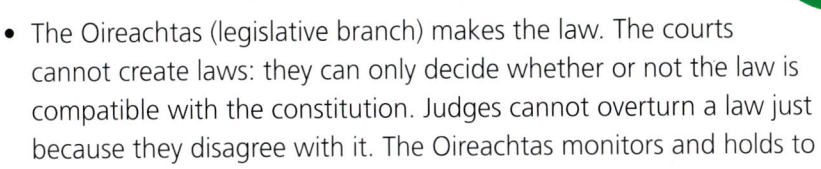

- The Oireachtas (legislative branch) makes the law. The courts cannot create laws: they can only decide whether or not the law is compatible with the constitution. Judges cannot overturn a law just because they disagree with it. The Oireachtas monitors and holds to account the government (executive branch) for its actions. The parliament (Dáil) does this through a series of powers, including posing questions which the Taoiseach and ministers must answer. The Oireachtas can also remove the Taoiseach and/or a minister by passing a 'motion of no confidence'.

Fig. 4.4 The three branches of government

This system sounds great in theory. However, in practice there can be some challenges. The parliamentary system of government which exists under the Irish constitution allows members of the government (executive) to also be members of the Oireachtas (legislative). For example, the Minister for Education in Ireland is also a member of parliament (Dáil).

As in the UK, members of parliament in Ireland must vote in the same way as their political party or risk being expelled. This is known as the **party whip system**. Therefore, if a party wins an overall majority in the Oireachtas (legislative) its members will form the government (executive). This makes it easier for the government to have laws passed without much scrutiny. The party whip system ensures that all members of the legislative branch who are members of the governing party will remain loyal to the government position. The threat of expulsion from the party acts as a strong disincentive to ever vote against party policy, and this ensures that the government retains its majority in the Oireachtas.

KEY TERMS

Unconstitutional: Any law passed by the legislature, or any action taken by the executive, which is in clear violation of the constitution is considered to be unconstitutional. Citizens are entitled to take a case to the Supreme Court if they believe that a specific law or government action goes against the rules outlined in the constitution. If the Supreme Court rules that a law is unconstitutional, it must be changed (amended) or scrapped by the government.

The party whip system: All political parties in Ireland have a 'party whip'. He or she enforces discipline within the party to ensure that all elected members vote according to the official party line. If a TD (Teachta Dála, meaning member of parliament) does not vote as instructed by the party whip, he or she is usually expelled from the party and is said to have 'lost the party whip'. This has happened to several TDs from various political parties in recent years. The whip system operates in many parliamentary democracies, but it is most strictly enforced in Ireland.

Supporters of the whip system claim that it leads to more stable and effective government, with laws being passed more efficiently. Critics of the system point out that it is an undemocratic practice to force TDs to vote against their own conscience or personal beliefs. Opponents of the whip system also claim that it is responsible for bad law-making because important laws often get voted quickly through parliament without much scrutiny. Critics state that this allows the government to ignore opposition parties, even if they make strong arguments for improving government legislation.

SELECTING OUR REPRESENTATIVES

Fig. 4.5 The separation of powers in Ireland

Executive Branch (Government)

Legislative Branch (Oireachtas)

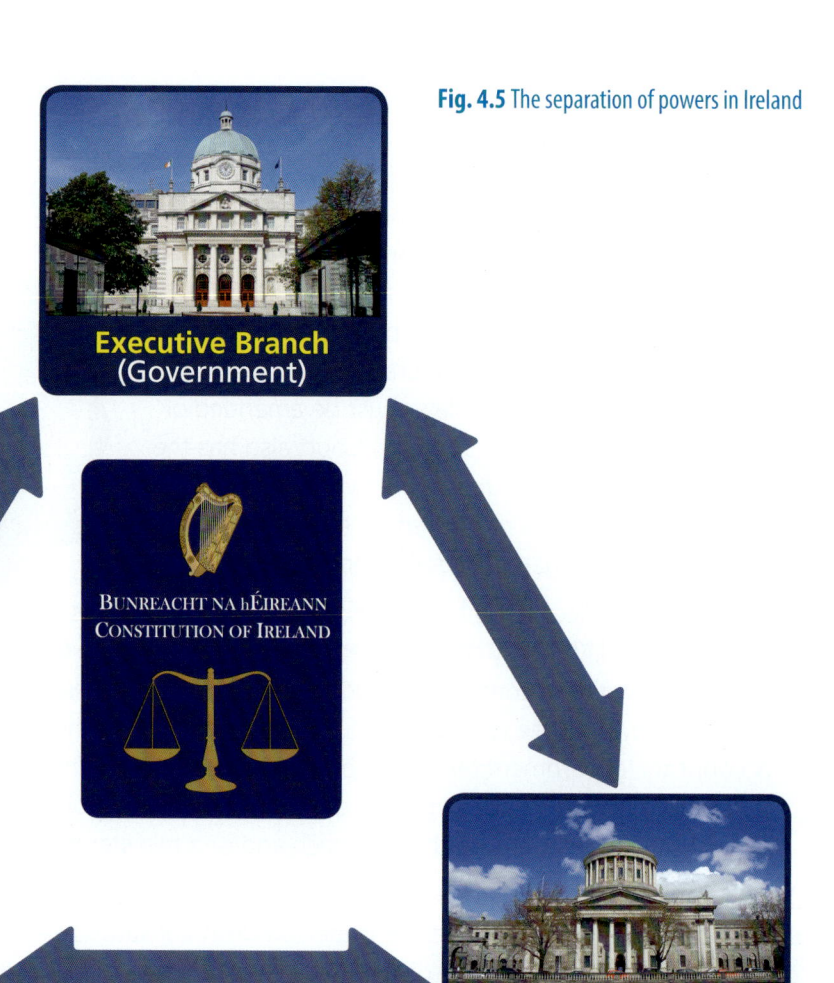

Judicial Branch (Supreme Court)

BUNREACHT NA hÉIREANN
CONSTITUTION OF IRELAND

QUESTIONS

1. What is a constitution?
2. What is the official name given to the Constitution of Ireland, and when was it created?
3. What is a referendum?
4. List **two** amendments made to the Constitution of Ireland following referendums.
5. Explain the democratic concept of 'separation of powers'. How does it safeguard democracy?
6. Describe the roles of the legislature, the executive and the judiciary as outlined in the Constitution of Ireland.
7. How does the system of 'checks and balances' operate in the Republic of Ireland?
8. What is a party whip?
9. Explain **one** benefit and **one** disadvantage of Ireland's party whip system.
10. Fig. 4.5 illustrates the separation of powers in Ireland. Can you explain the relationship between each branch of government displayed in this diagram? In your opinion, why is the constitution placed in the centre of the diagram?

ACTIVITY 4.2

Work with your partner to complete the following activity.

1. Think individually for a moment about how policies are created and enforced in your school. Is it possible to identify a separation of powers and the three branches of government in the management structure of your school? *(Think)*

2. With your partner, list all the stakeholders involved in the creation and implementation of policies at your school. Create a table with three columns – one for each branch (executive, legislature and judiciary). Discuss and decide to which branch each stakeholder belongs. List the stakeholders in the appropriate column. *(Pair)*

3. Share your list with the rest of the class. *(Share)*

SKILLS BOOK LINK 4.2

Go to pages 53–54 of your Skills Book to complete Skill Task 4.2 on checks and balances in Ireland.

See **RESEARCH TIPS** on page 33.

SKILLS BOOK LINK 4.3

Go to pages 55–57 of your Skills Book to complete Skill Task 4.3 on the party whip system.

See **RESEARCH TIPS** on page 33.

Complete your next Reflective Journal entry (pages 14–16)

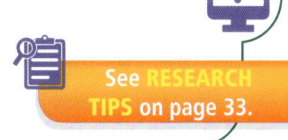

Fig. 4.6 The Four Courts, Dublin where the Supreme Court presides

The Oireachtas

What Is the Oireachtas?

Fig. 4.7 Dáil chamber

Fig. 4.8 Seanad

The legislative (law-making) branch of government in Ireland is called the Oireachtas (meaning 'deliberative assembly').

The Oireachtas is made up of three parts:

- Dáil Éireann (lower house of parliament)
- Seanad Éireann (upper house of parliament)
- The President, resident in Áras an Uachtaráin.

Fig. 4.9 Leinster House, where the Dáil and Seanad meet

What Does the Oireachtas Do?

The Oireachtas has the sole and exclusive power to make laws for Ireland, with two exceptions:

- Laws made at the European level on the basis of Ireland's membership of the EU
- Laws on local issues made by local government.

Dáil Éireann

Dáil Éireann is the main body of the Oireachtas. Dáil Éireann has the most power of the legislature in Ireland. The Dáil is our parliament, similar to the House of Representatives in the US and the House of Commons (Westminster) in the UK. The Dáil plays many important roles. Its primary function is to legislate: it proposes new laws (bills), debates new laws, makes amendments if necessary, and votes to pass these bills into law.

The Dáil also monitors the work of the executive (government) and ensures it is accountable to the people for its actions. The Dáil debates issues of importance to the country and approves public spending (budget). Since there are so many elected representatives in the Dáil, a committee system is used to ensure more efficient discussion and decision-making (see box on page 103).

The Seanad

The Seanad (senate) is the second house of the legislature in Ireland. It is similar to the Senate in the US and the House of Lords in the UK. The idea of having a second house is based on the principle of ensuring sufficient debate and deliberation on new laws. Ultimately, the aim is to improve the law-making process. The Seanad reviews bills from the Dáil and proposes amendments, if necessary.

The Seanad can also propose laws, with the exception of budget-related matters. However, the Dáil can reject the Seanad's proposals and amendments. The Seanad plays an advisory role and can only delay bills (usually for a maximum of 90 days), if it disagrees with them. If the Seanad rejects a bill passed by the Dáil, after 90 days the Dáil has the power to pass a resolution declaring that the bill is deemed to have been passed by both Houses. This provision means that the Seanad generally cannot stop the Dáil from making new laws. For a bill to become law in Ireland, it must be passed by both the Dáil and Seanad.

The Seanad has some of the same powers as the Dáil, e.g. the removal from office of the President, a judge of the Supreme Court or High Court or the Comptroller and Auditor General. The Seanad can declare and terminate a state of emergency. However, the Seanad has limited power in relation to the budget and government spending. Members of the Dáil can put official questions to ministers of government, but members of the Seanad cannot do this.

The fact that the Seanad has such limited powers has caused some politicians and journalists to question the necessity of having a Seanad at all. They have called for the Seanad to be abolished, claiming that it is ineffective and a waste of tax-payers' money. A 2013 referendum proposal to abolish the Seanad was marginally rejected by 51.7 per cent of voters. Since then, the Fine Gael government has pledged to reform the Seanad. The Seanad Reform Bill was introduced by a group of Independent senators in June 2016.

The Committee System

Since the 1990s the Oireachtas, to improve its efficiency, has used a committee system to look more closely at specific issues of special concern to the country at any particular time, (e.g. health, homelessness). Members of the Dáil and Seanad sign up to the committees of most interest to them. The Dáil and the Seanad can each have specific committees, known as *select committees*. The Dáil and the Seanad may also create committees together: these committees include members from both houses and are known as *joint committees*.

Fig. 4.10 An Oireachtas Committee meeting

See pages 162–164 for more information on the development and publication of bills.

When a proposal for a law (bill) is developed, it normally goes to one of these specialised committees. The committee examines and scrutinises the contents of the bill. Committees usually meet over several weeks or months, during which they listen to advice from experts in the sector, discuss research findings and debate proposals. Committees are usually dissolved after they have successfully produced a report of key findings and recommendations.

Committees also provide a space for members of parliament to interact with the public. Civil society bodies, voluntary organisations and community groups often ask for the opportunity to make a presentation on a particular issue to an Oireachtas committee. In this way, the views of the public are taken into consideration and given an important role in the decision-making process.

Fig. 4.11 Áras an Uachtaráin – the official residence of the President of Ireland

The President

The Constitution of Ireland gives the President some limited but important powers. All legislation passed by the Dáil and the Seanad must be signed by the President before becoming law.

- The President can send a bill to the Supreme Court to seek its legal opinion if he or she has concerns about whether or not a bill conflicts with the constitution.
- The President formally appoints the Taoiseach and other members of the government.
- The Dáil is established and dissolved by the President on the advice of the Taoiseach.
- The President is also Commander-in-Chief of the Irish Defence Forces.
- The President plays a representative role and is the chief ambassador for the country at relevant global events and occasions.

DID YOU KNOW?

The Oireachtas has its own TV channel, Oireachtas TV, which shows live debates from the Dáil and Seanad, as well as live coverage of all Committee sittings. Oireachtas TV is streamed online at **https://educateplus.ie/go/oireachtas-tv**. Oireachtas TV is also broadcast throughout Ireland on Saorview, Sky, Virgin Media and eir Vision.

RESEARCH ASSIGNMENT 4.1

Watch Oireachtas TV one evening and report back to your class on what you observed. Answer the following questions in a short report:

- Where was the broadcast from: Dáil, Seanad or Committee Room?
- What topic was discussed?
- Who were the main participants in the discussion?
- Why was the discussion taking place and what was its purpose?

QUESTIONS

1. What is the Oireachtas? Name the three bodies that make up the Oireachtas.
2. Explain **three** roles of Dáil Éireann.
3. Why was the committee system set up? Explain its purpose.
4. What is the difference between a select committee and a joint committee?
5. Explain **two** positive benefits of the committee system for law-making.
6. What is the primary function of Seanad Éireann?
7. List **three** roles of the President of Ireland.
8. What is the function of the judiciary? Why is it important that the judiciary is independent from the executive and legislative branches of government?

SKILLS BOOK LINK 4.4

Go to pages 57–58 of your Skills Book to complete Skill Task 4.4 on Seanad Éireann and the US Senate.

See RESEARCH TIPS on page 33.

SKILLS BOOK LINK 4.5

Go to pages 58–59 of your Skills Book to complete Skill Task 4.5 on the Seanad.

See RESEARCH TIPS on page 33.

Who Are the Representatives in the Oireachtas?

- The Dáil plays an important function in representing the will of the people. Members of Dáil Éireann are known as TDs ('Teachtaí Dála' means members of parliament). There are 158 TDs in the Dáil.
- The Seanad (Senate) is the second house of the legislature in Ireland. It consists of 60 members known as senators.
- The President is the head of state and represents Ireland. He or she is not the head of government. In the US, for example, the President is the head of state *and* the head of government. The role of President of Ireland is symbolic in this sense.

The Role of a TD

A TD could be said to have two different jobs and two different places of work. On the one hand, TDs are elected to legislate and discuss issues of national importance in Dáil Éireann. At the same time, they are expected to meet their **constituents** at home, represent their interests and deal with local issues in their **constituencies**. This dual function can prove to be a major challenge for TDs.

Fig. 4.12 TDs in Dáil Éireann

The work of a TD at Dáil Éireann involves meeting in plenary session in the Dáil chamber every Tuesday, Wednesday and Thursday, as well as the first Friday of each month. A plenary session of the Dáil is one which all TDs are expected to attend. A typical day's work includes researching and preparing speeches for debates on social, economic, financial and budgetary issues. TDs examine proposals for new legislation (bills) that are introduced in the Dáil. They propose and draft changes (amendments) to bills. TDs contribute to debates about new legislation and other important matters. TDs must vote on issues and bills in the Dáil chamber. They also attend Question Time, where they pose questions to the Taoiseach and government ministers of the day. TDs make written or oral representations to ministers or government departments on behalf of their constituents. TDs also participate in Oireachtas committee work.

As well as work at the Dáil and on committees, TDs work within their own constituencies. TDs hold regular advice clinics in different towns throughout their constituencies so that voters can meet them personally. TDs often provide assistance to constituents with a family/personal problem relating to a government department. TDs usually assign Mondays and Fridays as 'constituency days', although most also meet their constituents and attend local community meetings at weekends.

Who Do TDs Really Represent: Their Local Constituents or the Entire Irish Nation?

A common criticism of the Irish electoral system is that it leads to a narrow focus by TDs on local constituency concerns, which means that pressing issues of national importance may be neglected. Because of the competitive nature of the PR-STV system, TDs are often forced to prioritise local constituency concerns over national issues in order to protect their seats. Many TDs adopt the mantra: 'All politics is local.' These TDs will spend hours of their time meeting constituents, listening to their concerns, and making applications, representations and appeals on their behalf to public authorities or state bodies. Often, the focus of a TD can be dominated by local issues that have little or no connection with the TD's role in the Dáil. An Oireachtas survey carried out in 2010 found that Dáil deputies spend 53 per cent of their time on constituency matters and just 38 per cent on legislative work. The majority of TDs surveyed said that they were in parliament to represent the interests of voters in their particular constituencies, rather than citizens across the country. A majority of TDs also rated constituency activities as more important than legislative work. This is despite the fact that the Constitution of Ireland clearly states that the primary function of a TD should be to legislate (make laws) in the national interest.

Fig. 4.13 A large amount of a TD's time is consumed by constituency-level issues

See page 108 for more information on the PR-STV system.

IN THE MEDIA

Fig. 4.14 Politics in Ireland: local and national

KEY TERMS

A **constituent** is a person who is eligible to vote in a particular constituency. The term 'constituents' may also refer to a group of voters who share something in common (e.g. rural constituents, urban constituents, young constituents, female constituents).

A **constituency** is a geographical area of a country that elects a set number of political representatives to the national parliament in proportion to its population. For example, Dublin Central and Galway East each elect three TDs.

RESEARCH ASSIGNMENT 4.2

Conduct online research to find evidence to answer the following question: Is the role of a TD more like that of a delegate or a trustee?

Revise the views of James Madison and Edmund Burke (page 75) to help you answer this question. You may also draw upon the information in The Role of a TD on page 106.

This post on politics.ie outlines the pros and cons of the Delegate and Trustee models of political representation: **https://educateplus.ie/go/forum-post1**

This article in the Stanford Encyclopaedia of Philosophy provides more details on the models of political representation: **https://educateplus.ie/go/delegate-trustee**

This blog by Matthew Wall in the Irish Politics Forum provides interesting details from an Oireachtas survey: **https://educateplus.ie/go/tds**

This *Irish Examiner* article reveals the extent of 'constituency work' that TDs engage in: **https://educateplus.ie/go/td-requests**

How Are Representatives Selected for the Oireachtas?

Each of the three institutions that make up the Oireachtas has its own method of selecting its representatives.

Dáil Éireann

TDs are *directly elected* by citizens aged 18 or over during general elections. A general election must take place at least every five years, according to law. Ireland is divided into electoral areas known as constituencies (see Fig. 4.16). The 40 constituencies vary in size, and the number of TDs each constituency can elect to the Dáil differs. The number of TDs per constituency is loosely based on the population size: the constitution demands at least one TD for every 20,000–30,000 people. The electoral system used for Irish general elections is known as **Proportional Representation by Single Transferable Vote (PR-STV)**. As we will see, there are many arguments for and against PR-STV as an election system.

Fig. 4.15 Voter casting her ballot in a general election

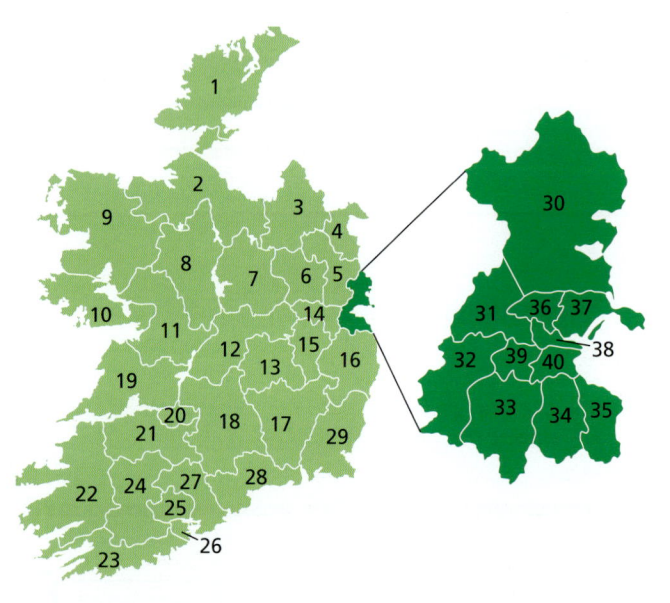

1. Donegal (5)
2. Sligo-Leitrim (4)
3. Cavan-Monaghan (4)
4. Louth (5)
5. Meath East (3)
6. Meath West (3)
7. Longford-Westmeath (4)
8. Roscommon-Galway (3)
9. Mayo (4)
10. Galway West (5)
11. Galway East (3)
12. Offaly (3)
13. Laois (3)
14. Kildare North (4)
15. Kildare South (3)
16. Wicklow (5)
17. Carlow-Kilkenny (5)
18. Tipperary (5)
19. Clare (4)
20. Limerick City (4)
21. Limerick (3)
22. Kerry (5)
23. Cork South West (3)
24. Cork North West (3)
25. Cork North Central (4)
26. Cork South Central (4)
27. Cork East (4)
28. Waterford (4)
29. Wexford (5)
30. Dublin Fingal (5)
31. Dublin West (4)
32. Dublin Mid-West (4)
33. Dublin South-West (5)
34. Dublin Rathdown (3)
35. Dún Laoghaire (4)
36. Dublin North-West (3)
37. Dublin Bay North (5)
38. Dublin Central (3)
39. Dublin South Central (4)
40. Dublin Bay South (4)

Fig. 4.16 Number of TDs per constituency

SKILLS BOOK LINK 4.6

Go to pages 59–60 of your Skills Book to complete Skill Task 4.6 on an electoral profile of your constituency.

See **RESEARCH TIPS** on page 33.

Proportional Representation by Single Transferable Vote (PR-STV)

- PR-STV is a voting system whereby voters rank candidates in order of preference. It is used by Ireland and Malta to directly elect individual members of national parliament, as well as to elect members of the European Parliament.

> **KEY TERM**
>
> **PR-STV** is a voting system whereby voters rank candidates in order of preference.

- In the PR-STV system, voters give a number 1 for their most preferred candidate to win, a number 2 for their second, and so on.

- First past the post (FPTP) is the system of voting whereby the candidate or party with the most votes is the winner. The losing candidates or parties do not win any seats or representation. FPTP is also known as *simple majority voting* and it is the system used in UK parliamentary elections.

- PR-STV was designed to ensure a more proportionally representative result. It is thought to give voters a wider choice. A person can vote for candidates from different parties, or without giving any consideration to political party affiliation.

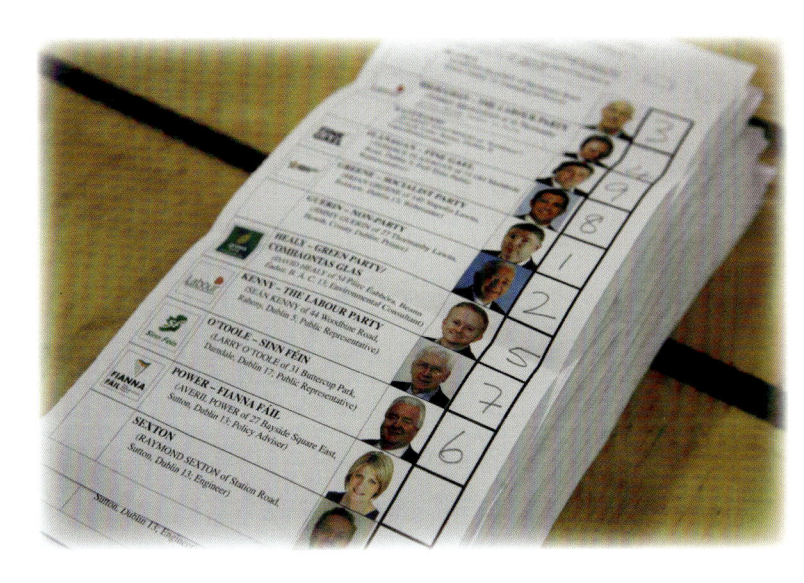

Fig. 4.17 A ballot paper with preferential ranking of candidates

Single transferable vote

- PR-STV is considered to provide smaller groups in society with a better chance of representation as it does not follow a simple 'majority rule'.
- The way in which PR-STV votes are counted will differ from country to country, but all PR-STV systems are based on a quota system. The quota is the minimum number of votes a candidate needs to get elected. Once a candidate receives enough number 1 votes to exceed the quota, all of his or her surplus number 1 votes will then be transferred to the candidate who received a number 2 vote on his or her ballots. And once any of these candidates reach the quota, the count of number 3 votes begins, and so on. Therefore, if you give a number 1 vote to a candidate who does not need it (because he or she has already received enough number 1 votes to meet the quota), your vote gets used again: it is given to your number 2 choice.
- In Ireland the PR-STV system is protected in our constitution, but the system has not been without its critics. In 1959 and 1968 referendums took place on a proposal to replace the PR-STV with a system similar to that in the UK. On both occasions, the people of Ireland rejected the proposal.

For	Against
Irish political culture is primarily 'local': citizens expect parliamentarians (TDs) to represent their individual and community concerns.	PR-STV system promotes a focus on constituency loyalty rather than national policy positions.
Local government in Ireland is comparatively less powerful than in other European countries: many local issues still require the support or action of a TD.	PR-STV generates electoral competition between candidates of the same party, which can lead to divisions within political parties.
The importance of local constituencies to the PR-STV system ensures that national politicians are never 'out of touch' with the realities of their local electorate.	Given the strong focus on local constituencies, TDs are less likely to make hard but necessary choices in the national interest.
Society is made up of diverse interests and groups: PR-STV achieves a broader and more representative parliament where minority groups are represented.	The system is associated with producing weak coalition governments and can create political instability.
PR-STV guarantees a high degree of party proportionality and ensures that smaller parties and independent candidates can win seats.	Although it happens rarely, the PR-STV system can lead to a candidate winning a seat with fewer first preference votes than a rival.

Table 4.1 The PR-STV system in Ireland: arguments for and against

SELECTING OUR REPRESENTATIVES

ACTIVITY 4.3

Hold a mock general election using:

(a) The Irish PR-STV system of voting

(b) The British FPTP system.

SKILLS BOOK LINK 4.7

Go to pages 60–62 of your Skills Book to complete Skill Task 4.7 on electoral systems.

ACTIVITY 4.4

Hold a classroom debate on the following motion:

'PR-STV should be abolished and replaced with a new electoral system.'

Seanad Éireann

Senators are not directly elected by the citizens of Ireland in the same way as TDs are elected. The selection process must take place no later than 90 days following the formal ending or dismissal (dissolution) of the Dáil. The selection of senators involves a mixed approach: *election and nomination*. The election process follows the PR-STV system used by the Dáil:

- Of the 60 senators in total, 43 are elected by the TDs of the new Dáil, members of the outgoing Seanad, and members of county councils and city councils.

- These 43 Seanad seats are divided among five thematic groups, known as panels. Each Seanad candidate must choose to run for election in one of the panels:

    - Administrative Panel (public administration and social services)
    - Agricultural Panel
    - Cultural and Educational Panel
    - Industrial and Commerical Panel
    - Labour Panel.

- There are also six Seanad seats decided by graduates of certain universities in Ireland. Three senators are elected by graduates of the National University of Ireland (NUI) and another three by graduates of the University of Dublin (Trinity College). Voters must be over 18 years of age and have a degree from either NUI or Trinity College.

- For the remaining 11 Seanad seats, senators are not elected: they are nominated directly by the Taoiseach.

The system of selecting senators in Ireland has been, and continues to be, the focus of much debate. The Seanad election process is just one element of a wider debate on whether or not the Seanad needs to be reformed.

For	Against
The selection process means that the Seanad represents a diversity of views, minority voices and specialist experience and expertise.	The Seanad is an elitist institution: the selection system is undemocratic, as it excludes the majority of citizens from voting.
Senators have different skills from TDs. The Seanad is the best system for selecting senators with technical skills and expertise on the different policy and law-making areas.	The system does not guarantee that selection is based on skill and expertise. Selection is, in fact, highly political.
If senators are directly elected (as TDs are), the Seanad will simply mirror the Dáil in its composition.	It is unfair that TDs who lose their seats in a democratic general election are often rewarded with a seat in the Seanad, if their party leader becomes Taoiseach.
Irish politics is already parochial enough, without allowing local constituencies to directly elect their senators.	Given that the Seanad voting system is not based on geographic constituencies, it is not geographically representative in the same way as the Dáil.

Table 4.2 The Seanad election system: Arguments for and against

IN THE MEDIA

Fig. 4.18 Discussions on Seanad reform

SELECTING OUR REPRESENTATIVES 111

> **SKILLS BOOK LINK 4.8**
>
> Go to pages 62–63 of your Skills Book to complete Skill Task 4.8 on proposals for reform of the Seanad electoral system.
>
> *See RESEARCH TIPS on page 33.*

The President

- As with TDs, the President is *directly* elected by citizens aged 18 years or over.
- For presidential elections, Ireland is not divided into constituencies: the nation as a whole is treated as a single constituency.
- To be a candidate for President of Ireland you must be an Irish citizen and aged 35 years or over. In 2015 a referendum to lower the eligible candidate age from 35 to 21 years was defeated by 73.1 per cent.
- Elections must take place by the date the current President's term in office expires but cannot take place more than 60 days before this.
- The term of the presidency is seven years.
- A president cannot serve for more than two terms.

Fig. 4.19 President Michael D. Higgins is Head of the Irish Defence Forces.

> **ACTIVITY 4.5**
>
> Hold a classroom debate on the following motion:
>
> 'Seanad Éireann should be abolished – it is not fit for purpose and is a waste of tax-payers' money.'

> **QUESTIONS**
>
> 1. How many TDs are in the Dáil and how many senators are in the Seanad?
> 2. Describe **three** roles of a TD.
> 3. How often must a general election take place in Ireland?
> 4. Explain the PR-STV system of voting.
> 5. Explain **two** arguments for and **two** arguments against the use of PR-STV for Irish general elections.
> 6. (a) Describe the process for electing Ireland's 60 senators.
>   (b) In your opinion, is this a good system? Explain your answer with reference to relevant research or evidence.
>   (c) List your own recommendations for how the Seanad could be reformed.
> 7. What age must you be to run for the office of President of Ireland? Do you think this is a good idea? Why/why not?
> 8. How long can the President of Ireland serve in office?
> 9. Should the office of President of Ireland be abolished, or should its powers be extended? Give reasons to support your answer.

Complete your next Reflective Journal entry (pages 14–16)

The Executive: Taoiseach and Government

What Is the Executive?

The executive branch of government is responsible for enforcing the law and implementing the programmes and policies of the elected government. In Ireland it consists of:

- The Taoiseach (prime minister)
- The Cabinet of Ministers.

What Does the Executive Do?

Together, the Taoiseach and ministers make up the government. They are responsible for making decisions and proposing policies and laws on a wide range of issues covering almost all areas of the lives of citizens (education, health, the economy, etc.). The government is responsible for ensuring that law and order is maintained, and that the needs, interests and safety of citizens are served.

Fig. 4.20 Former Taoiseach Enda Kenny with his new ministers during the first cabinet meeting of the new government in 2016

Who Are the Representatives of the Executive?

The Taoiseach (prime minister) is the head of government in Ireland. The Tánaiste is the deputy prime minister. Currently in office are 14 ministers and the Taoiseach, which is the maximum number allowed by our constitution. Together they make up what is referred to as the cabinet. Each minister has responsibility for a government department. The usual government departments are listed in Table 4.3. Department names can vary from cabinet to cabinet, even though the role of the department stays the same (e.g. the Department of Agriculture, Food and the Marine was formerly known as the Department of Agriculture, Fisheries and Food).

Department of An Taoiseach
Department of Agriculture, Food and the Marine
Department of Business, Enterprise and Innovation
Department of Culture, Heritage and the Gaeltacht
Department of Children and Youth Affairs
Department of Communications, Climate Action and Environment
Department of Defence
Department of Education and Skills
Department of Employment Affairs and Social Protection
Department of Finance
Department of Foreign Affairs and Trade
Department of Health
Department of Housing, Planning, Community and Local Government
Department of Justice and Equality
Department of Public Expenditure and Reform
Department of Rural and Community Development
Department of Transport, Tourism and Sport

Note: In the current Government, the Department of Defence is under the responsibility of the Taoiseach, while the Department of Foreign Affairs and Trade is under the responsibility of the Tánaiste.

Table 4.3 Departments of the Irish government, 2018

SELECTING OUR REPRESENTATIVES

Ministers of state, also called junior ministers, should not be confused with ministers. Ministers of state are not members of the Taoiseach's cabinet and therefore do not make executive decisions. They are appointed to provide assistance to a minister of a government department. Each minister also has a special adviser and a team of senior civil servants in his or her department.

How Are Representatives Selected for the Executive?

- As Ireland is a **parliamentary democracy**, the parliament (Dáil) is the starting point for government formation. Citizens directly elect TDs, and some of these TDs are then selected to form the executive. In this sense, the citizens indirectly elect the executive. This is different from systems where citizens directly or semi-directly elect the head of government.

> **KEY TERM**
>
> **Parliamentary democracy** is the form of government where those with the greatest representation in parliament form the government. Parliamentary democracies are normally organised by political parties.

- The Dáil (parliament) is responsible for selecting the Taoiseach (head of government) in Ireland. If the government fails to keep the support of the majority of TDs in the Dáil, this could result in either the dissolution (termination) of the Dáil and a general election being called, or the formation of a replacement government.

- After every general election a vote is held in the Dáil to nominate the Taoiseach. To become Taoiseach, a nominee needs the support of a simple majority of TDs (at least 80 votes). As a result, the elected leader of the largest political party will become Taoiseach if his or her party wins over 50 per cent (80 seats or more) in the general election.

- If no party wins a majority of the seats, a **coalition** government will be required. The leader of the largest party in the coalition will usually be nominated as Taoiseach.

> **KEY TERM**
>
> A **coalition** is when two or more parties or alliances of independents come together in an alliance to create a majority and form a government.

- After a successful vote in the Dáil, the President formalises the nomination of the Taoiseach and officially appoints him or her.

- The Taoiseach nominates the ministers, and the President formally appoints them.

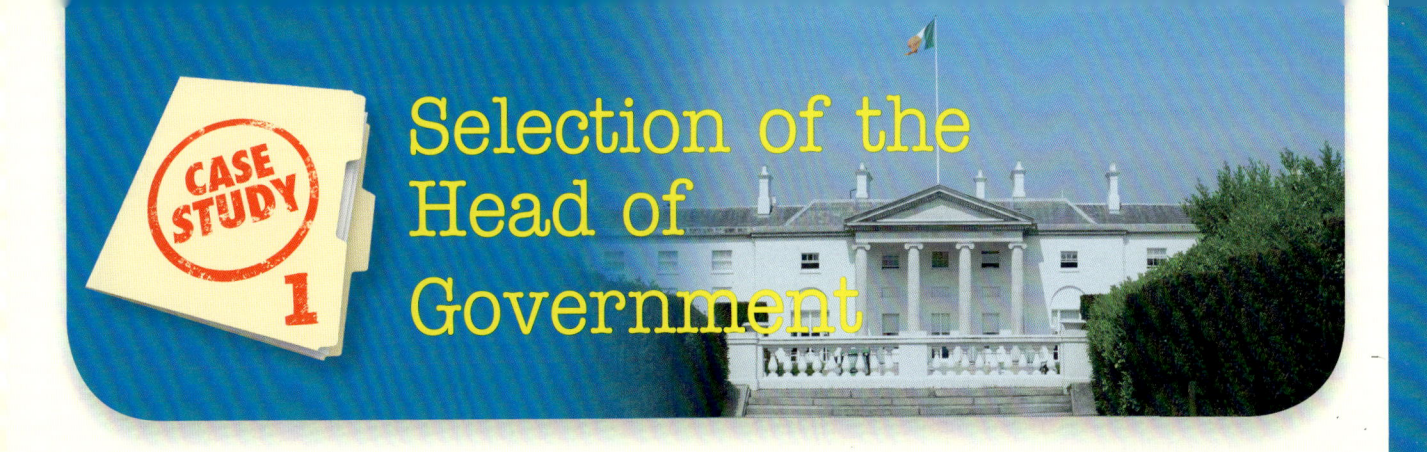

Case Study 1: Selection of the Head of Government

Direct Selection – President of Indonesia

In Indonesia, the president is both the head of state and the head of government. Since 2004, the president and vice-president are directly elected by the citizens. The president then appoints the other members of the executive (the cabinet). Unlike in Ireland, members of the cabinet do not have to be elected members of the legislature.

Fig. 4.21 President Joko Widodo of Indonesia

Semi-Direct Selection – President of the US

In the US, the citizens do not select their president by a direct vote. Instead, they select *electors* who will make the final selection on their behalf. The *electoral college system* in the US is, therefore, a form of semi-direct election.

The electoral college is made up of appointed electors from each of the 50 states, plus Washington DC. The number of electors a US state has is based on its population size. The electoral college makes the final selection of the president in the elections. The system was established by the founding fathers of the US as a way to avoid 'mob rule' (they believed the majority of US citizens were not educated enough to make a direct choice) and to ensure that the voices of minority groups would be included.

Fig. 4.22 US President Donald Trump

In the US constitution, members of the electoral college are not obliged to vote according to the results of the popular vote in their state, but they almost always do. In the US, the candidate who wins the popular vote in each state (even if this is by a small margin) is usually given all the available electoral votes from that state ('winner takes all'). In the 2016 US presidential elections, five Democratic and two Republican members of the electoral college voted against the popular vote in their state. When this happens, these members are popularly referred to as 'faithless electors'.

Five US presidents have been elected on the basis of winning the electoral college vote *without* winning the overall national popular vote. This was the case in 2016, when Hillary Clinton won the overall popular vote but did not become president.

Indirect Selection – Prime Minister of the UK

Although the UK is a parliamentary democracy, it also has a monarchy. This mixed system is known as a constitutional monarchy. Citizens directly elect members of parliament (MPs) in general elections. However, the monarch (king or queen) appoints the prime minister. The leader of the party with the majority in parliament is normally selected and appointed; however, no formal nomination by parliament is required in the UK.

Fig. 4.23 The Elizabeth Tower (which houses Big Ben) and Houses of Parliament in London

ACTIVITY 4.6

Your group will be assigned one country by your teacher. As a group, research the electoral system used for selecting the executive and write a short report on it. Include the following information:

- How the executive is selected
- How the legislature is selected
- The strengths and weaknesses of the system.

SKILLS BOOK LINK 4.9

Go to pages 63–64 of your Skills Book to complete Skill Task 4.9 on systems for selecting the executive in Ireland and in the US.

RESEARCH ASSIGNMENT 4.3

Write a speech to be delivered to an Oireachtas committee on electoral reform. In the speech, outline your suggestions on how to make the Irish system of elections more representative.

The Courts

The justice system is responsible for interpreting and upholding the law and our legal rights.

- In Ireland, the justice system includes four main courts: the District Court, the Circuit Court, the High Court and the Supreme Court.
- There are also a Special Criminal Court and a Court of Appeal.
- The Supreme Court is the *court of final appeal*. On the request of the president, the Supreme Court has the power to decide whether a bill passed by the Oireachtas is compatible with the constitution. If the Supreme Court deems a bill to be unconstitutional, the bill cannot be enacted and the Supreme Court's decision is final.
- All judges are appointed by the president on the advice of the government. The government receives recommendations from the Judicial Appointments Advisory Board, and the government normally follows these nominations. This process was established to ensure the courts' independence.
- Because Ireland is a member of the EU, the Court of Justice of the EU is also part of our justice system. This court interprets EU laws and ensures that they are applied equally across all EU states, including Ireland.

Complete your next Reflective Journal entry (pages 14–16)

QUESTIONS

1. Who makes up the executive in Ireland?
2. What does the executive do?
3. What is the cabinet?
4. Explain the process for selecting the Taoiseach and cabinet.
5. Is this process an example of direct or indirect election?
6. In your opinion, is the system for selecting the Taoiseach fair and representative? Give reasons for your answer.
7. Explain the difference between direct and semi-direct elections of executives, with reference to two countries you have studied.
8. In your opinion, what is the best way to select an executive? Give reasons to support your answer.
9. Name the four main courts that make up the Irish justice system.
10. What power does the Supreme Court have and why is this important for democracy?

Government in Northern Ireland

The system of government in Northern Ireland is unique: it is different from the democratic systems in place in most other countries in the world today. The current governmental structures in Northern Ireland are a direct result of the peace settlement that ended the violent conflict which had divided the two main communities in Northern Ireland: **unionist** and **nationalist**.

A peace agreement called the Good Friday Agreement (also known as the Belfast Agreement) was signed in 1998 and it established the system of government in Northern Ireland. In 1998, following referendums in Northern Ireland and in the Republic of Ireland to ratify (accept) the Good Friday Agreement, the UK parliament transferred a range of powers to Northern Ireland so that it could govern itself in relation to specific areas. This is known as **devolution**. However, the UK government still retains control over national policy on all matters that have not been devolved, e.g. foreign affairs, defence, currency and trade. Similar to the Republic of Ireland, the system of government in Northern Ireland consists of a legislature – the Northern Ireland Assembly – and an Executive – the Northern Ireland Executive. However, unlike in the Republic, the elected representatives from the main nationalist and unionist parties in Northern Ireland must take part in a coalition known as **power-sharing**.

Fig. 4.24 Stormont, Belfast

> ## KEY TERMS
> In Northern Ireland, a **unionist** is someone who supports the continuation of the union between Northern Ireland and Britain. A **nationalist** supports the reunification of Northern Ireland with the Republic of Ireland.
>
> **Devolution** is the transfer of power in certain areas (e.g. transport, education) from a central government to local or regional authorities. Devolved power can be withdrawn by the central government. For example, devolution to Northern Ireland was suspended in October 2002 and restored on 8 May 2007. This occurred when the DUP refused to share power with Sinn Féin as a result of two key issues – the decommissioning of IRA weaponry and the devolution of powers of justice and policing.
>
> **Power-sharing** is a term used to describe a system of governance in which all major segments of society are afforded a permanent share of power. This system is often contrasted with *government versus opposition* systems, in which ruling coalitions rotate among various social groups over time.
>
> The basic principles of power-sharing include:
> - Grand coalition governments in which nearly all political parties have appointments
> - Protection of minority rights for groups
> - Decentralisation of power
> - Decision-making by cross-party consensus.
>
> A **Member of the Legislative Assembly (MLA)** is an elected representative to the Northern Irish Assembly.

The Northern Ireland Assembly

What is the Northern Ireland Assembly?

The Assembly is the law-making body of Northern Ireland.

What does the Northern Ireland Assembly Do?

The Northern Ireland Assembly makes laws in relation to the policy areas devolved to it by the UK government. The areas over which the Northern Ireland Assembly has full legislative power include: health and social services, education, employment and skills, agriculture, social security, pensions and child support, housing, economic development, local government, environmental issues, planning, transport, culture and sport, the Northern Ireland civil service, equal opportunities, and justice and policing.

Fig. 4.25 Northern Ireland Assembly, Commons Chamber, Stormont, Belfast

Who are the Representatives of the Northern Ireland Assembly?

Elected representatives to the Northern Ireland Assembly are known as **Members of the Legislative Assembly (MLAs)**. There are 108 MLAs in total. Because of the political history of Northern Ireland, each MLA must designate himself or herself as 'unionist', 'nationalist' or 'other'. This identification is important, as it facilitates power-sharing between the unionist and nationalist communities. MLAs play a role similar to that of TDs. They represent the views and make laws on behalf of the citizens of Northern Ireland. MLAs hold the executive to account by scrutinising its proposals for new laws and its decisions.

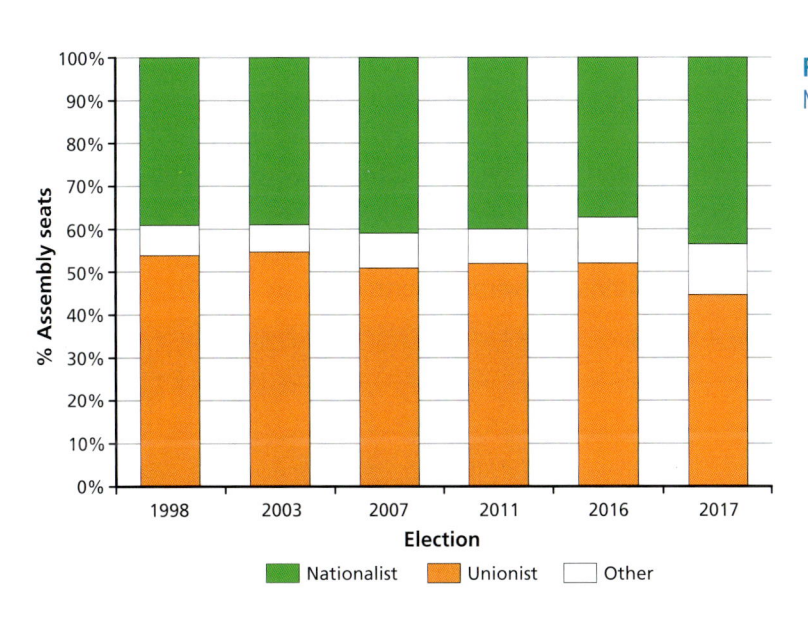

Fig. 4.26 Representatives of the Northern Ireland Assembly

How are Representatives Selected for the Northern Ireland Assembly?

Assembly elections take place every five years. Unlike constituency boundaries in the Republic, Northern Ireland is divided into 18 constituencies with relatively similar population sizes. The 18 constituencies elect six MLAs each. As with elections in the Republic of Ireland, PR-STV is used for Northern Ireland Assembly elections.

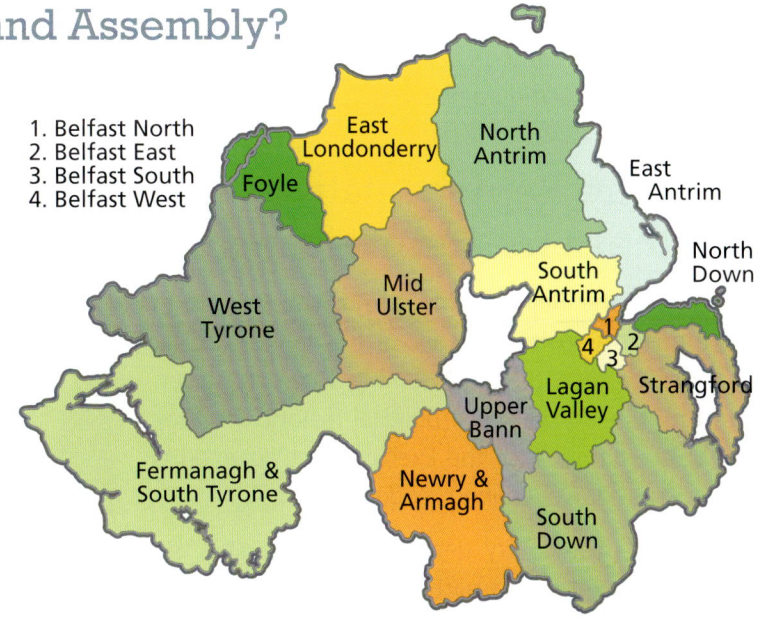

1. Belfast North
2. Belfast East
3. Belfast South
4. Belfast West

Fig. 4.27 The 18 constituencies in Northern Ireland

The Northern Ireland Executive

What is the Northern Ireland Executive?

The Northern Ireland Executive is the government of Northern Ireland.

What does the Northern Ireland Executive Do?

The executive develops and implements the **programme for government**. It develops a draft budget on the basis of the amount approved by the UK parliament. It also decides on the proposals of legislation to be sent to the Assembly for review and final approval.

> **KEY TERM**
>
> A **programme for government** is a government's overall plan of action. It outlines its goals and plans for what policies and actions it intends to make during its term.

SELECTING OUR REPRESENTATIVES

Who Are the Representatives of the Northern Ireland Executive?

The executive is led by the First Minister and Deputy First Minister, who are the joint heads of government and who have equal power. They must always act together. This is part of Northern Ireland's special power-sharing model. The executive also has two junior ministers and eight other ministers. The ministers are responsible for running several departments:

- Agriculture, Environment and Rural Affairs
- Communities
- Economy
- Education
- Finance
- Health
- Infrastructure
- Justice.

Fig. 4.28 Stormont Castle – meeting place of the Northern Ireland Executive

In addition to running their departments, ministers meet within the Executive Committee, similar to the Cabinet of Ministers in the Republic of Ireland. The number of ministerial posts any party can have is determined by the number of MLAs they have in the Assembly.

How Are Representatives Selected for the Northern Ireland Executive?

Similar to the Republic of Ireland, the formation of the Northern Ireland Executive is influenced by the composition of the Assembly. However, given Northern Ireland's special political history, the way in which members of the Executive are selected is based on a power-sharing model.

In most parliamentary democracies (including the Republic of Ireland), a party with a simple majority (50 per cent + 1) of seats can form the government alone and the other parties form an opposition. However, the power-sharing system in place in Northern Ireland ensures a mandatory (compulsory) coalition of all the elected parties. Therefore, unlike most functioning democracies, there is a lack of any real opposition in the Northern Ireland parliament: all the main parties are entitled to form part of the Executive.

Fig. 4.29 A Northern Ireland Executive meeting on 25 October 2016

The members of the Executive are selected using the *d'Hondt method*, which allocates positions among parties on the basis of the proportion of seats they have in the Assembly. The First Minister is taken from the largest party and the Deputy First Minister from the second largest party. Unlike in other countries, the First Minister and Deputy First Minister have equal power and must always act together.

DID YOU KNOW?

In January 2016 the Dáil agreed to the proportionate allocation of committee chairs using the d'Hondt method. This is intended to give opposition TDs a more powerful role in the Dáil and to reduce government control of the committees.

120 POWER AND PEOPLE

Power-Sharing in Northern Ireland

The Good Friday Agreement determined that the Executive Committee would be a power-sharing government, representing unionists and nationalists. It is based on the power-sharing, or consociational, model of democracy. The consociational model is often the preferred form of government in societies that are deeply divided, as it requires collaboration between the groups. Arend Lijphart, a Dutch political scientist, designed this model for societies emerging from, or with the potential for, conflict.

The main consociational features of the Northern Ireland power-sharing model are:

- *Cross-community power-sharing* at executive level through the joint office of First Minister and Deputy First Minister and a multi-party executive. The First and Deputy First Minister (one unionist and one nationalist) have equal powers. One cannot be in position without the other. The multi-party executive (cabinet or coalition) is made up of unionist and nationalist parties. The *d'Hondt method* determines the proportion of unionist and nationalist ministers appointed to the Executive, based on the number of seats a party wins in the election.

- *PR-STV* is used to elect members of the legislative assembly (MLAs). The d'Hondt method is used to allocate positions of power: ministers, chairs and deputy chairs of committees.

- *Cultural equality* for the two main traditions (e.g. development of the Irish language and Ulster Scots).

- *Special voting arrangements* give **veto** rights to the minority. Certain Assembly decisions require *cross-community support*: not just majority support, but the support of a certain percentage of nationalists and unionists. These decisions include:
  - Election of the Speaker and Deputy Speakers
  - Changes to the rules of the Assembly, known as Standing Orders
  - Budget allocations and other financial votes
  - Determination of the number of ministers and their responsibilities
  - Exclusion of ministers or members of political parties from holding office
  - Petitions of concern (30 MLAs can request that any decision be taken on a cross-community basis).

> **KEY TERM**
>
> **Veto** means a vote against. It is the power to reject a proposal or policy. In the United Nations Security Council – which is the UN body responsible for maintaining international peace and security – one single veto from any one of the five permanent members (China, France, Russia, the UK and the US) can mean that a decision or proposal is not approved. All five have exercised the right of veto at one time or another.

Northern Ireland's power-sharing executive is not without its critics. Opponents of the system claim that forcing parties into coalition and the absence of an opposition to hold the executive to account are undemocratic and contribute to a dysfunctional government. An interesting development was the decision by the UUP, SDLP and the Alliance parties to form an opposition and forgo their entitlement to representation on the executive in 2016. This has left the two main parties, the DUP and Sinn Féin, in complete control of the executive.

Fig. 4.30 Northern Ireland's First Minister Arlene Foster (right) with former Deputy First Minister, the late Martin McGuinness

RESEARCH ASSIGNMENT 4.4

Conduct further research on the power-sharing system of government in Northern Ireland. Imagine that the United Nations aims to implement a similar system as part of a peace settlement in a country emerging from a civil war. Write a report for the UN, including the following information:

- How power-sharing works
- Benefits of this system
- Disadvantages of this system
- Proposed changes to the system (if any)

ACTIVITY 4.7

Hold a classroom debate on the following motion:

'Power-sharing in Northern Ireland should be abolished – it is undemocratic and produces an ineffective system of government.'

QUESTIONS

1. Explain the following terms in relation to government in Northern Ireland:
   - Devolution
   - MLA
   - Power-sharing
   - d'Hondt method
2. How many constituencies are there in Northern Ireland?
3. What is the role of the Northern Ireland Assembly?
4. What system of voting is used for Assembly elections?
5. Apart from Assembly elections, name three other elections held in Northern Ireland.
6. Explain the composition of the Northern Ireland Executive.
7. Does the First Minister have more power than the Deputy First Minister?
8. Explain **two** benefits and **two** disadvantages of power-sharing for Northern Ireland.
9. In your opinion, how can the functioning of the democratic institutions in Northern Ireland be improved?

The systems for selecting government in Ireland and in Northern Ireland are democratic. In countries that do not follow such democratic principles, the structure of government and the selection processes can be very different.

Complete your next Reflective Journal entry (pages 14–16)

Case Study 2: Government in a Non-Democratic Country

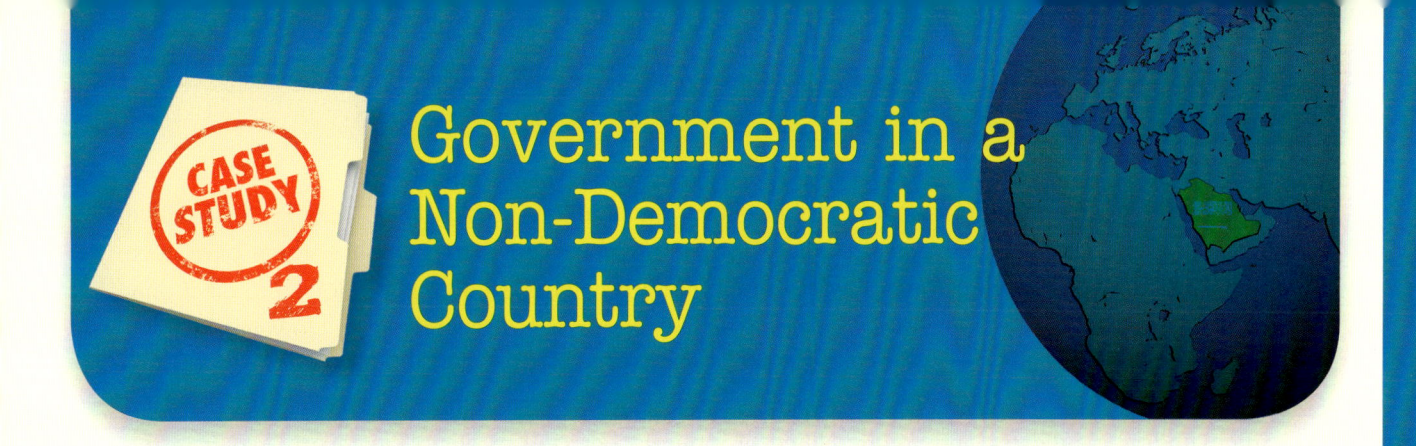

The Kingdom of Saudi Arabia

Fig. 4.31 King Salman of Saudi Arabia

Fig. 4.32 Location of Saudi Arabia

Saudi Arabia, formally known as the Kingdom of Saudi Arabia, is ruled by a hereditary monarchy. Citizens do not elect the government. Saudi Arabia was established in 1932 by King Abdulaziz (also known as Ibn Saud), who was a direct descendent of the last ruler of the family that had controlled most of the Arabian peninsula for more than 300 years. In 1953 he was succeeded by his eldest son. Since then the throne has passed through several sons in descending order of age.

The current King of Saudi Arabia is Salman bin Abdulaziz Al Saud (King Salman). The King appoints a Crown Prince to assist him in governing the country. There are no popular elections and no official political parties.

Executive Branch

The King is also the prime minister, chief of state, head of government, and commander in chief of the military of Saudi Arabia. The King's Cabinet (Council of Ministers) is appointed by the King every four years, and includes many family members. There are 22 government ministries that are part of the cabinet. In 2009, the first female cabinet member, Norah Al-Fayez, was appointed as Deputy Minister for Women's Education.

Legislative Branch

A Consultative Council (also known as Majlis as-Shura or Shura Council) advises the King on issues that are important to Saudi Arabia. It consists of 150 members, all of whom are appointed by the King every four years. Members are divided between 12 committees: human rights, education, culture, information, health and social affairs, services and public utilities, foreign affairs, security, administration, Islamic affairs, economy and industry, and finance.

In 2013, following the passing of a law by the King that women should make up 20 per cent of the membership of the Consultative Council, the King appointed 30 women.

CASE STUDY: Government in a Non-Democratic Country

At a local level, provincial and local assemblies cover the country's 13 provinces. In 2003, the Council announced plans to allow citizens to elect half of the members of these assemblies. There have been a total of three local elections since then. In 2005 and 2011, the electorate was allowed to elect only half the members of the assemblies (the other half were appointed by the King). However, women were not allowed to participate as candidates or voters in either election. The third, and most recent, election in 2015 saw two-thirds of the seats in Assemblies being elected and, for the first time, women participated as candidates and voters. However, only 47 per cent of eligible voters took part in the election. Commentators pointed to the limited powers of local assemblies, as well as scepticism about the elections, as causes for such low voter turnout.

Judicial Branch

The rule of law in Saudi Arabia is based on Islamic law (shariah). Justice is administered by a system of religious courts. The judges are appointed by the King on the recommendation of the Supreme Judicial Council. The King acts as the highest court of appeal and has the power to pardon any crime or offence.

QUESTIONS

1. Explain how the executive is selected in Saudi Arabia.
2. What is the role of the Consultative Council? How does it differ from Dáil Éireann?
3. Is Saudi Arabia a theocracy? Explain your answer. (Refer to page 73.)
4. Does the government of Saudi Arabia display any democratic characteristics?
5. What are the pros and cons of this system of government?

RESEARCH ASSIGNMENT 4.5

Choose a non-democratic country, other than Saudi Arabia, for your assignment. Research how the government is put in place in this country. Present your findings to the rest of the class.

European Union

As Irish citizens, the European Union (EU) is very much a part of our political representation. Ireland joined the EU, then known as the European Economic Community, in 1973. Ireland, like all 28* EU member states, is sovereign and independent: the governments of these states are the decision-makers. However, over the years, we have given some decision-making power to the institutions of the EU through a series of agreements known as *treaties*. As a result, the laws and policies made by our government must comply with EU legislation, i.e. the law that is common to all member states in the EU. The EU has many bodies within its structure. The three main institutions are the European Parliament, the Council of the EU and the European Commission.

Fig. 4.33 The three main institutions of the EU

*This includes the UK, which is in the process of leaving the EU.

European Parliament: The Voice of the People

What Is the European Parliament?

The European Parliament is part of the legislative arm of the EU. It officially sits in Strasbourg (France) but also works in Brussels (Belgium) and Luxembourg.

What Does the European Parliament Do?

Together with the Council (see below) it passes the laws which must be followed by all member states. The European Parliament plays three main roles, which are similar to those of the Oireachtas in Ireland.

- The Parliament passes laws in partnership with the Council through a process known as co-decision. Unlike the Oireachtas, it does not have the power to initiate legislation.

- The Parliament oversees the work of all EU institutions, i.e. the Commission. It does this by examining reports from the Commission and raising questions on its proposals and work. It also regularly questions the work of the Council. However, the Council alone has power of decision-making on some areas, such as common foreign and security policy. Citizens of the EU can raise petitions to the Parliament if they have concerns about the application of an EU law or wish the Parliament to adopt a certain position on a matter, e.g. if a state or company has infringed upon environmental or consumer rights.

Fig. 4.34 European Parliament

Fig. 4.35 European Parliament building, Brussels

- The Parliament has power to influence how EU money is spent. Once the EU budget proposal is prepared by the Commission, the Parliament and the Council then reject or approve it. The final budget must be approved and signed by the President of the Parliament.

Who are the Representatives of the European Parliament?

The Parliament is made up of 751 members who are called MEPs (Members of the European Parliament), and a President who represents the Parliament in interactions with other EU institutions and the outside world.

There are MEPs to represent the interests of citizens from all 28 EU member states. In terms of representation, the number of MEPs per country is based on population size. As EU membership has grown, the number of MEPs per country has changed: 751 is the maximum total number of MEPs allowed by law.

For 2014–2019, Ireland has 11 MEPs representing three constituencies: South (4), Midlands and North West (4), and Dublin (3). Prior to 2014, and the entry of Croatia to the EU, Ireland had 13 MEPs. Germany currently has the largest number of MEPs (96).

In the Parliament, MEPs are organised by political groups sharing similar political views. There are eight political groups in the European Parliament. In order of size, these are as follows.

- European People's Party (EPP, sometimes referred to as 'Christian Democrats')
- Progressive Alliance of Socialists and Democrats (S&D)
- European Conservatives and Reformists (ECR)
- Alliance of Liberals and Democrats for Europe (ALDE)
- European United Left–Nordic Green Left (GUE–NGL)
- The Greens–European Free Alliance (EGP–EFA)
- Europe of Freedom and Direct Democracy (EDDD)
- Europe of Nations and Freedom (ENL)
- Non-Inscrits (NI, known as 'non-attached').

RESEARCH ASSIGNMENT 4.6

Your group will be assigned one political group from the European Parliament by your teacher. As a group, visit the political group's website to research and compile a report. Include the following information:

- The ideology of the political group
- Key priorities and policies of the group
- Position of the party on the left–right political spectrum
- Number of MEPs in the group
- Names and political parties of any Irish MEPs in the group.

SKILLS BOOK LINK 4.10

Go to page 65 of your Skills Book to complete Skill Task 4.10 on political groupings in the European Parliament.

Is Representation in the European Parliament Unequal?

The European Parliament is sometimes criticised for being unrepresentative. Voters in smaller member states are believed to be overrepresented. This contributes to what critics call a 'structural democratic deficit' for the European Parliament. Critics also point to the lack of power of the European Parliament in comparison to other EU institutions.

The European Union gives disproportionate weight to smaller countries, stipulating that 'no representation of citizens should be degressively proportional, with a minimum threshold of six members [of the European Parliament] per [EU] Member State. No Member State shall be allocated more than ninety-six seats.' The latest apportionment decision was adopted on 28 June 2013 in the run-up to the accession of Croatia as the European Union's 28th member state.

The European Parliament's representation of European voters is compared with that of the national parliaments of large or medium-sized democratic countries. Fig. 4.36 presents a comparison between the representation of voters in the European Parliament and several national parliaments in democratic countries. A high percentage (%) suggests a high degree of voting power inequality among citizens eligible to vote.

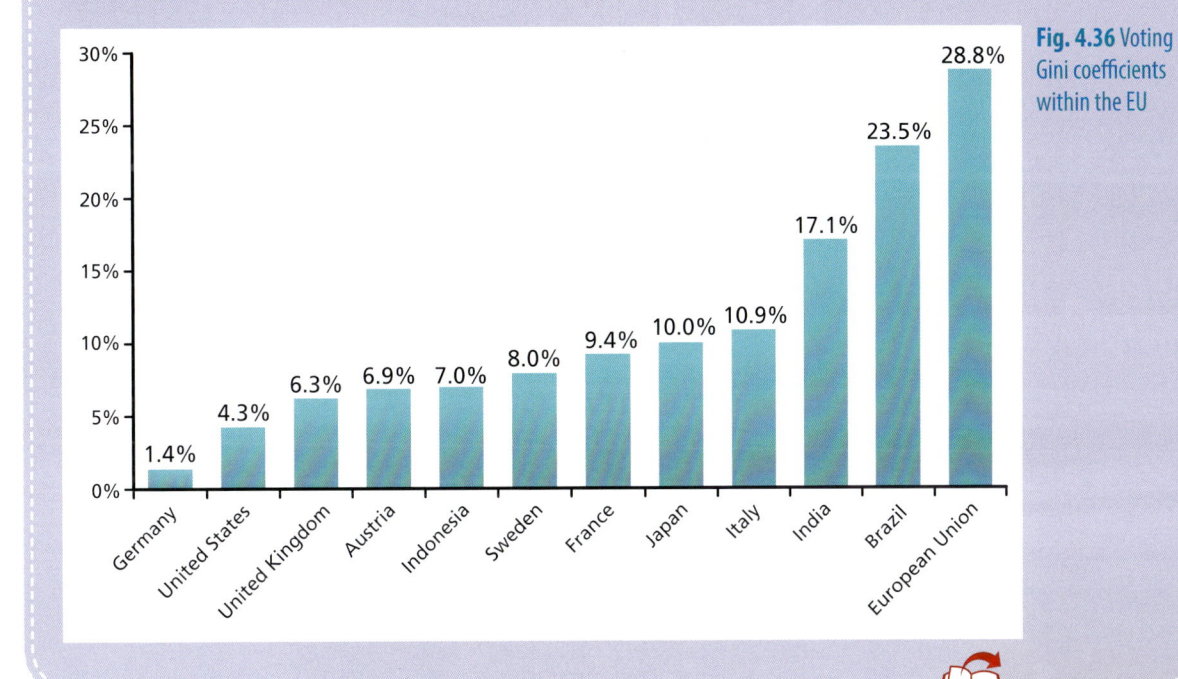

Fig. 4.36 Voting Gini coefficients within the EU

Country	%
Germany	1.4%
United States	4.3%
United Kingdom	6.3%
Austria	6.9%
Indonesia	7.0%
Sweden	8.0%
France	9.4%
Japan	10.0%
Italy	10.9%
India	17.1%
Brazil	23.5%
European Union	28.8%

The Gini coefficient is a tool used to measure inequality within a country or region. See p.386.

SKILLS BOOK LINK 4.11

Go to pages 65–67 of your Skills Book to complete Skill Task 4.11 on the European Parliament.

How Are Representatives Selected for the European Parliament?

MEPs are directly elected by the citizens of their respective EU country every five years. Relatively low voter turnout has been a feature of the elections (see Fig. 4.38). The exact voting system differs between the 28 member states, but all voting systems must be based on some form of proportional representation. In Ireland, we use the same PR-STV voting system to elect MEPs and TDs.

Fig. 4.37 MEPs are directly elected by the citizens of their respective EU country

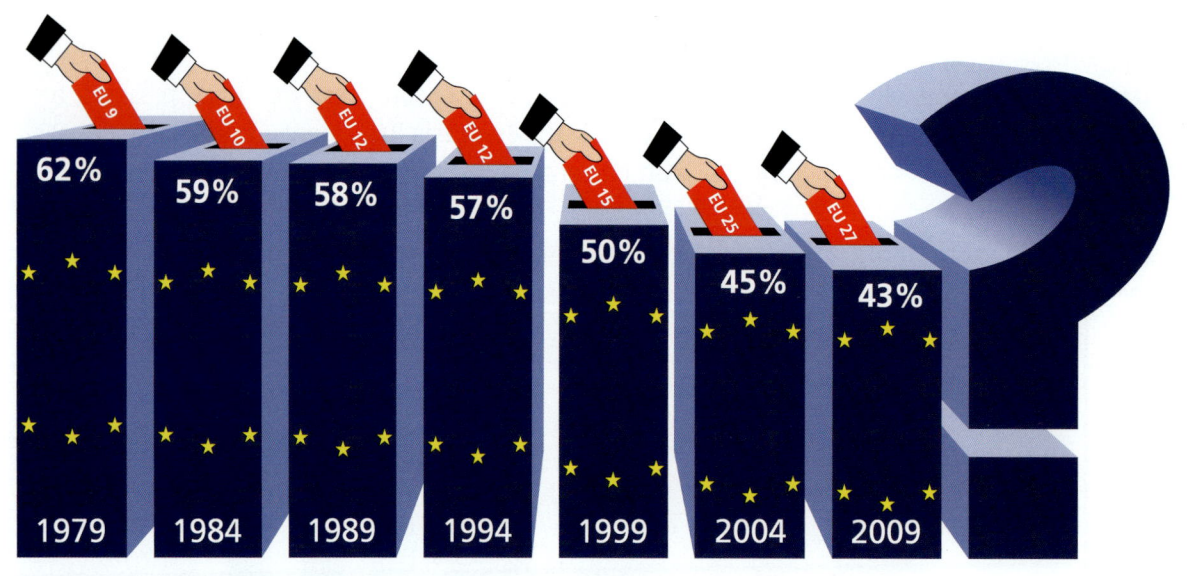

Fig. 4.38 Caring less: turnout at EU elections, as a percentage of registered voters

Fig. 4.39 MEPs voting in parliament

QUESTIONS

Examine Fig. 4.38 and answer the following questions.

1. What trend can be observed in this image?
2. Why, in your opinion, is voter turnout so low for European elections?
3. What impact is this likely to have on the composition and legitimacy of the European Parliament?

Council of the European Union: The Ministers of the Member States

What Is the Council of the European Union?

The Council forms part of the legislative branch of the EU, alongside the European Parliament. It is commonly referred to as 'the Council' but should not be confused with the European Council, which forms part of the executive of the EU.

128 POWER AND PEOPLE

Fig. 4.40 A meeting of the Council of the EU

Fig. 4.41 European Council building

> The EU has **two** institutions with 'Council' in their title. These two institutions play very different roles.
>
> - The *Council of the EU* shares responsibility with the European Parliament for law-making in the EU. It is made up of ministers from the national governments of the member states. There are different Council configurations depending on the issue (transport, environment, health, etc.).
>
> - The *European Council* consists of the heads of state or government of the member states, along with the President of the European Council and the President of the European Commission. It is responsible for guiding the political direction of the EU on big issues, (migration, new trade agreement, economic policy, etc.). It usually meets twice a year and these meetings are called *summits*.

What does the Council of the European Union Do?

Different councils exist depending on the issue. These are known as configurations. If, for example, the council is discussing agriculture and fisheries issues, the meeting will be attended by the relevant minister from each EU member state, and will be known as the Agriculture and Fisheries Council. The council has a number of important functions:

- The Council of the European Union discusses, reviews and passes European laws, in partnership with the European Parliament.
- The Council coordinates the national policies of member states.
- On the basis of guidance from the European Council, the Council develops the EU's common foreign and security policy.
- The Council is responsible for finalising international agreements between the EU and other countries (e.g. the United States) or international organisations (e.g. the United Nations).
- The Council shares power with the Parliament to approve or reject the EU's budget.

Who are the Representatives on the Council of the European Union?

The Council consists of the relevant ministers (depending on the issue) from the 28 member states.

SELECTING OUR REPRESENTATIVES

How are Representatives Selected for the Council of the European Union?

The acting minister for the relevant issue from each member state will represent his or her country in the Council.

European Commission: Executive Body of the EU

Fig. 4.42 The 28 members of the EU Commission

What is the European Commission?

The Commission is the executive arm of the EU.

What does the European Commission Do?

The European Commission is the body responsible for proposing the laws and policies to be reviewed and passed by the Parliament and Council. Similar to the government (Taoiseach and cabinet) in Ireland, the European Commission ensures that the decisions, programmes and policies of the EU are implemented by member states. The Commission, together with the President of the European Council, represents the EU to the outside world. Also, alongside the Court of Justice of the EU, it is responsible for ensuring member states comply with European law.

Although the Commission is quite powerful, it must ultimately answer to the Parliament. It participates in all the sessions of the Parliament, where it is questioned on its policies. The Parliament can dismiss the Commission by what is called a 'motion of censure'.

The Commission is often guided by the European Council. The European Council consists of the leaders (i.e. the Taoiseach) of the 28 member states, as well as the European Council President and the President of the Commission.

Who are the Representatives of the European Commission?

The members of the Commission are known as Commissioners. They come from all 28 member states. However, they represent the interests of the EU as a whole and do not represent the interests of their individual national governments.

The Commission consists of the Commission President and 27 Commissioners (also known as 'the College of Commissioners'). Seven of

Fig. 4.43 The Berlaymont building, Brussels: headquarters of the European Commission

POWER AND PEOPLE

the Commissioners are also appointed as Vice-Presidents by the Commission President, to support him or her.

Like our ministers in Ireland, each Commissioner is responsible for a particular area (trade, health and food safety, etc.). The departments are known as Directorate-Generals or DGs.

As with the special advisers to our ministers in Ireland, each Commissioner appoints a team of counsellors (cabinet) to help him or her to prepare for Commission decision-making processes.

How are Representatives Selected for the European Commission?

The President of the Commission is nominated by agreement of the governments of the member states (European Council) in consultation with the European Parliament. Each member state then nominates one of the 27 Commissioners. In Ireland, the Taoiseach makes this nomination. The European Parliament then votes by secret ballot to approve or reject the nominations of the President and all 27 Commissioners. The Commission President is responsible for assigning the specific policy areas (portfolios) between the other 27 Commissioners. The entire selection process takes place every five years.

The UK and the EU: Brexit

On 23 June 2016 a referendum on whether the UK should leave or remain part of the EU was held in England, Wales, Scotland and Northern Ireland. The referendum, commonly referred to as 'Brexit', resulted in an overall 'Leave' campaign win – by 52 per cent to 48 per cent. However, both Scotland and Northern Ireland voted to remain part of the EU, with 62 per cent and 55.8 per cent respectively. The UK has two years to leave the EU, following the formal confirmation of its plan to leave. This confirmation of the plan to leave is referred to as 'triggering Article 50' (an article in the Lisbon Treaty which outlines the process for a EU member state to withdraw from the EU). The UK triggered Article 50 on 29 March 2017.

Fig. 4.44 Brexit

Fig. 4.45 Prominent pro-Brexit supporters: (left) Boris Johnson, the Conservative Party, and (right) Nigel Farage, UKIP

RESEARCH ASSIGNMENT 4.7

Conduct further research on the powers of the European Commission, the process for the selection of the President, and the assignment of portfolios to Commissioners. Use this information to write a letter to your local MEP outlining the flaws in this system and your own proposals to reform it.

RESEARCH ASSIGNMENT 4.8

Examine the reasons why people in the UK voted to leave the EU. Write a newspaper article outlining the various reasons why the majority of people in the UK voted Leave. Include an appropriate caption, picture(s), relevant statistics and quotations from those who campaigned to leave.

ACTIVITY 4.8

Hold a classroom debate on the following motion:

'Ireland should withdraw from the EU because it is an undemocratic body run by an unrepresentative and unelected elite.'

QUESTIONS

1. What do the letters MEP stand for?
2. Describe **three** roles of the European Parliament.
3. What does the term 'co-decision' refer to?
4. How is the European Parliament elected?
5. Explain the difference between the Council of the EU and the European Council. Describe the roles of both of these institutions.
6. Explain the role and powers of the European Commission.
7. Describe how the European Commission is selected and composed.
8. How is the President of the Commission selected?
9. In your opinion, is the European Commission a democratic and representative institution? Explain your answer.
10. Select **two** key thinkers of your choice. In your opinion, how would each of these key thinkers view the EU institutions?

Electoral Systems and Issues of Representation

When we think about representation and government, there are two ways to approach the issue. First, we can look at whether or not the way in which we select our political leaders results in a representative government. Second, we can look at whether or not the voices of citizens and different social groups are included in the decision-making processes.

Complete your next Reflective Journal entry (pages 14–16)

As we have seen, the PR-STV system is used in general elections in the Republic of Ireland, in Northern Ireland Assembly elections, and to elect MEPs to the European Parliament. PR-STV is offered as an alternative to systems based on majority voting (e.g. first past the post in parliamentary elections in the UK, the system for electing the US president). PR-STV is said to avoid the 'tyranny of the majority' and ensure a broader representation of citizen and minority group interests. However, is this really the case? The system *can* lead to broader representation in parliament – but *does* it? In Ireland, for example, certain minority groups (e.g. members of the Traveller community) have never held a seat in the Dáil. What about women? Women represent approximately half the population. Does it follow that women have half the seats in the Dáil? The claim that PR-STV results in a representative parliament in Ireland has been the focus of much research in Ireland. The lack of representation in government of certain groups in society has led to the development of important initiatives and programmes.

WHAT THE RESEARCH SAYS!

ELECTING WOMEN TO THE DÁIL

In the 2007 Irish general election, only 22 of the 165 members elected to Dáil Éireann were women: exactly the same number as had been elected in 2002. Despite progressive social change in Ireland, including a significant increase in women's participation in the workforce, the percentage of women elected as TDs has remained low over the last two decades. In 2016, a total of 35 women were elected to the Dáil. Within the European Union, only Hungary, Romania, Cyprus and Malta have lower proportions of women in their national parliaments.

There has been much international research on gender and politics. One of the common findings is the very positive impact of proportional electoral systems (PR) on women's representation, with PR almost universally acknowledged to increase the number of women in elected office. It is surprising, then, that Ireland has been overtaken in the past decade by the United Kingdom and France (single-member district electoral systems) in the international rankings of women in parliament. The recent surge in the numbers of women in the national parliament in the UK (32%) and France (47%) has not been mirrored in Ireland (22%).

Fig. 4.46 Women remain under-represented in Irish politics, accounting for just 35 out of the 158 TDs (22 per cent) elected to the Dáil in the 2016 General Election

SELECTING OUR REPRESENTATIVES 133

Promoting More Women and Youth in Parliament

Gender Quotas for Political Party Candidates

In 2012 gender quota legislation was introduced in Ireland. The Electoral (Amendment) (Political Funding) Act 2012 means that political parties must ensure that at least 30 per cent of their candidates for election are female. Failure to comply with the quota rule results in a 50 per cent cut in the amount of state funding received by the party.

Promoting Young Candidates to Run for the Dáil

Future Voices Ireland is a youth charity in Ireland that works with young people from disadvantaged backgrounds. In 2015 it launched a programme entitled Youth:Elect, with the aim of increasing the level of youth representation in political life in Ireland. The programme supported 30 young people under the age of 30 from marginalised backgrounds to run as candidates in the 2016 general election.

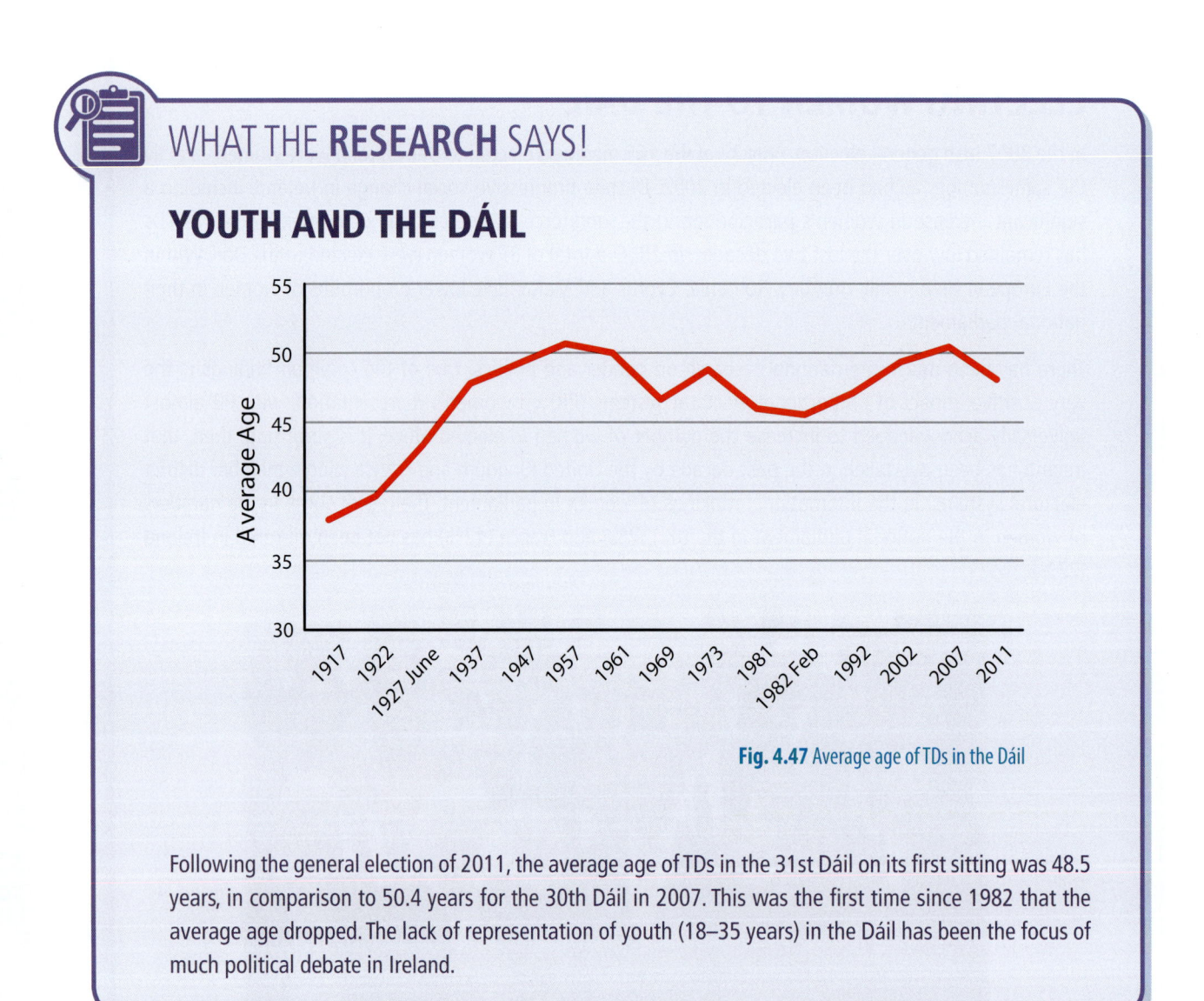

WHAT THE RESEARCH SAYS!

YOUTH AND THE DÁIL

Fig. 4.47 Average age of TDs in the Dáil

Following the general election of 2011, the average age of TDs in the 31st Dáil on its first sitting was 48.5 years, in comparison to 50.4 years for the 30th Dáil in 2007. This was the first time since 1982 that the average age dropped. The lack of representation of youth (18–35 years) in the Dáil has been the focus of much political debate in Ireland.

SKILLS BOOK LINK 4.12

Go to pages 68–69 of your Skills Book to complete Skill Task 4.12 on Ireland's level of female representation in parliament.

SKILLS BOOK LINK 4.13

Go to pages 69–70 of your Skills Book to complete Skill Task 4.13 on lack of female representation in parliament.

RESEARCH ASSIGNMENT 4.9

Write a summary report for a Dáil Committee entitled: 'Addressing Gender Inequality In Politics'. Include the following in your report:

- The most up-to-date statistics on female representation in local government and the Oireachtas
- Research-based evidence on the reasons for the under-representation of females in Irish politics
- Possible solutions and proposals to address the gender imbalance.

ACTIVITY 4.9

Hold a classroom debate on the following motion:

'Gender quotas in elections are undemocratic and should be abolished.'

SKILLS BOOK LINK 4.14

Go to pages 70–71 of your Skills Book to complete Skill Task 4.14 on representation of groups in the Dáil.

SKILLS BOOK LINK 4.15

Go to page 72 of your Skills Book to complete Skill Task 4.15 on why young people are under-represented in Irish politics.

ACTIVITY 4.10

Hold a classroom debate on the following motion:

'Dáil candidate quotas should be extended to include other under-represented groups in Irish society, such as young people and members of the Traveller community.'

SELECTING OUR REPRESENTATIVES

SUMMARY

Government in the Republic of Ireland

- Ireland is a parliamentary democracy bound by a constitution.
- Government in Ireland has three branches: the executive, the legislature and the judiciary. These three branches are also present in the UK and US systems of government.
- A system of 'checks and balances' ensures that no single branch can completely dominate and control all power.
- The Oireachtas is the legislative branch of government in Ireland. The Oireachtas is made up of three parts: Dáil Éireann, Seanad Éireann and the President.
- 158 TDs are elected to the Dáil from 40 constituencies using a voting system known as Proportional Representation by Single Transferable Vote (PR-STV).
- PR-STV benefits smaller parties and independents and leads to a more representative outcome in elections compared to majority systems of voting (e.g. first past the post in the UK).
- The Dáil is responsible for proposing and debating new policies, voting on bills (proposed new laws), considering amendments to bills (proposed changes), and holding the executive to account.
- An increasing amount of Dáil work is done through the committee system, where smaller groups of TDs tackle specific issues (e.g. public health) in select committees.
- The Seanad is made up of 60 senators:
  - 43 are elected from five different panels by an electorate comprising all sitting TDs, councillors and outgoing senators
  - Three are elected by graduates of the National University of Ireland (NUI)
  - Three are elected by the graduates of Trinity College Dublin
  - 11 are nominated directly by the Taoiseach.
- The Seanad is responsible for reviewing bills passed by the Dáil, and proposing amendments.
- All bills that become law must be passed by a majority vote in both the Dáil and Seanad. If the Seanad rejects a bill but the Dáil has approved it, the Dáil can use its power to pass a resolution declaring that the bill is deemed to have been passed by both Houses.
- The Seanad can introduce bills, with the exception of bills on budget-related matters.
- The President of Ireland is elected directly by all Irish citizens over the age of 18. Presidential candidates must be over the age of 35.
- The President of Ireland is head of state but not head of government.
- The President must sign all bills passed by the Dáil and Seanad into law, or else send the bills to the Supreme Court to test their constitutionality (i.e. that the proposed law is not illegal according to the constitution).
- The Taoiseach and the Cabinet of Ministers make up the executive branch of government.
- Unlike in the US, ministers in the Taoiseach's cabinet can be chosen only from members elected to the Oireachtas.
- The cabinet is responsible for creating a 'programme for government', implementing policies and enforcing the law.
- The judiciary is an independent branch of government that ensures that all laws passed are in keeping with the Constitution of Ireland.

Government in Northern Ireland

- The devolved power-sharing system of government in Northern Ireland was agreed under the Good Friday Agreement in 1998.
- 'Devolution' refers to the transfer of certain powers (on issues such as health, transport, education and policing) from the British government to the Northern Ireland Assembly and Executive.
- 'Power-sharing' refers to the consociational model of democracy developed by Arend Lijphart and used in Northern Ireland, where all the main parties enter into a mandatory coalition form of government.
- There are 108 Members of the Legislative Assembly (MLAs) elected to the Northern Ireland Assembly.
- The Assembly is the legislative branch of the Northern Ireland government and is similar to Dáil Éireann.

Government in the EU

- The European Union (EU) is an international governing body made up of 28 member states.
- The European Parliament is one part of the legislative arm of the EU.
- 751 Members of the European Parliament (MEPs) are directly elected to the European Parliament by the citizens of the EU.
- MEPs become members of one of the eight political groups within the European Parliament.
- The Council of the EU reviews and passes European laws in partnership with the European Parliament.
- The Council of the EU is made up of the relevant ministers from each member state (finance ministers for financial issues, agriculture ministers for agricultural issues, etc.).
- The European Council is made up of the heads of state of each EU member state and the president of the European Commission. It is responsible for guiding the general direction of EU policy.
- The European Commission is the executive arm of the EU and is responsible for proposing the laws and policies that are to be passed by the European Parliament and Council of the EU.
- The European Commission is made up of 28 Commissioners – one nominated by each member state.
- The president of the European Commission is selected with the agreement of each member state and the European Parliament.

Electoral Systems and Issues of Representation

- Certain groups are under-represented in politics, such as women and young people.
- Mechanisms such as gender quotas have been introduced in some countries, including Ireland, to ensure that more female candidates run for election.

Fig. 4.48 Mind map

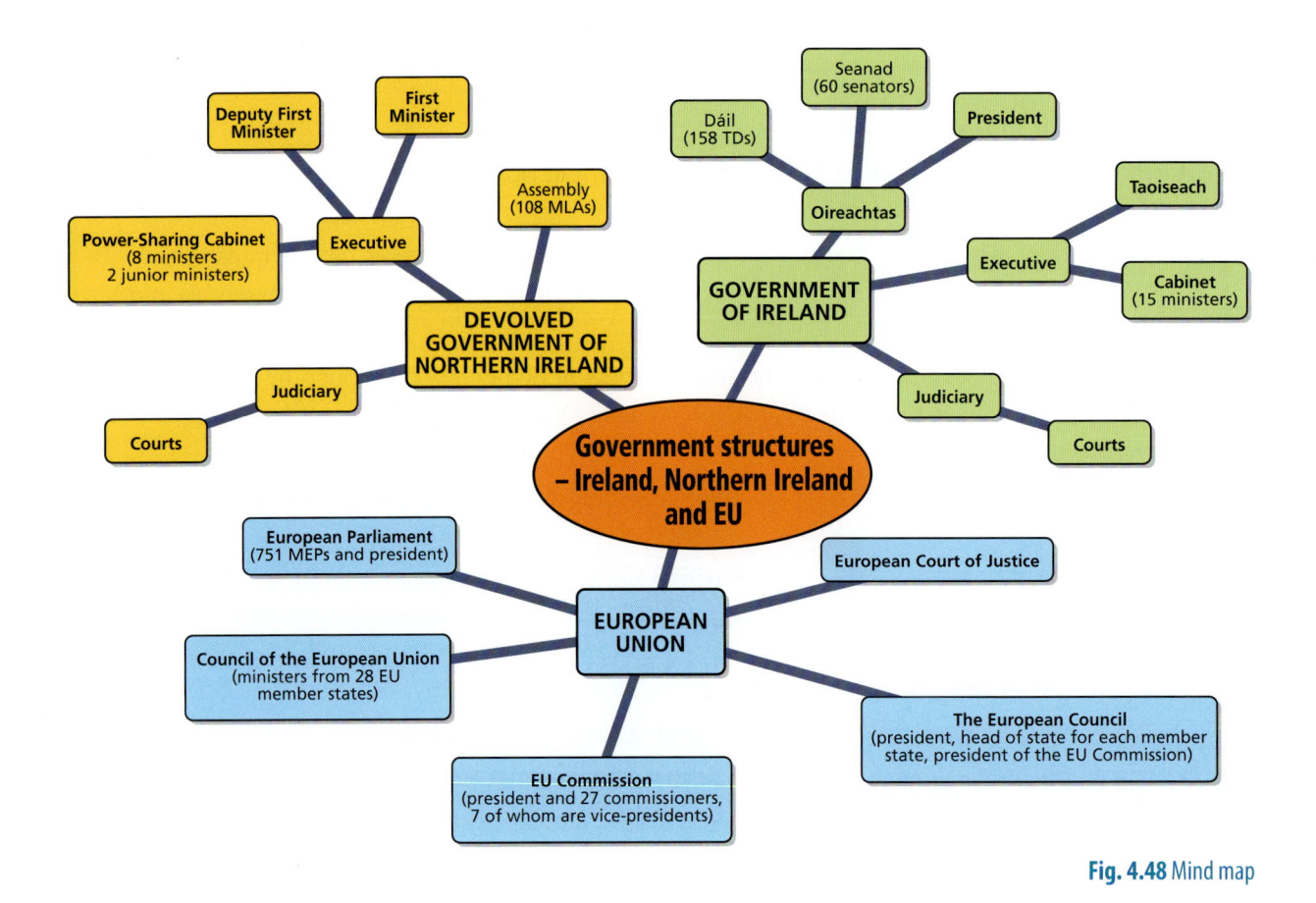

Fig. 4.49 Key Word cloud

138　POWER AND PEOPLE

REVISION QUESTIONS

1. Describe the main characteristics of a parliamentary democracy in a typical republic.
2. List the similarities and differences between the systems of government in the US and the Republic of Ireland.
3. Explain the importance of the following for protecting democracy in Ireland:
   (a) The Constitution
   (b) Referendums
   (c) The system of checks and balances
4. Explain the benefits and disadvantages of the party whip system in Irish politics.
5. What is the Oireachtas?
6. Name the main institutions/people that make up the following branches of government in Ireland:
   (a) The judiciary
   (b) The legislature
   (c) The executive.
7. What role does the President of Ireland play in government?
8. What is the primary function of a TD?
9. Describe the dual role that each TD must fulfil as part of his or her job.
10. Explain how the PR-STV system of voting works. What are the advantages and disadvantages of this system?
11. Do you agree that the Seanad is in need of reform? Give reasons for your answer.
12. Explain how the executive is selected in:
    (a) Ireland
    (b) The US
    (c) Indonesia
    (d) Saudi Arabia.
13. Explain how the executive in Northern Ireland is selected. Make specific reference to the power-sharing model and the d'Hondt method.
14. In your opinion, which is the best system for selecting an executive? Give reasons for your answer.
15. What is the role of MEPs and how are they selected?
16. Name three Irish MEPs.
17. What is the function of:
    (a) The Council of Europe
    (b) The European Council?
18. What is the function of the European Commission and how is it selected?
19. Name the current Irish European Commissioner.
20. Name the current President of the European Commission.
21. Name any **two** groups that are under-represented in Irish politics. In each case, give one reason why the group is under-represented.
22. What are gender quotas? Do you agree with them?

DATA-BASED QUESTIONS

Complete the qualitative and quantitative research data-based questions exercise on pages 73–74 of your Skills Book.

EXAM FOCUS — Section B of LC Exam

REVISION EXERCISES

Complete the revision exercises on pages 75–77 of your Skills Book.

EXAM FOCUS: Section A of LC Exam

DISCURSIVE ESSAY TOPICS

1. 'The Irish electoral system is in need of reform.' Discuss.
2. 'The PR-STV electoral system results in a more representative government.' Discuss, using examples from both the Republic of Ireland and Northern Ireland.
3. Examine the processes for electing a government in the Republic of Ireland and one other country of your choice. Make reference to the advantages and disadvantages of each system.
4. Compare and contrast the approaches to selecting the executive branches of the government of Ireland and the European Union.
5. Examine the causes of, and possible solutions to, the under-representation of women and/or youth in Irish politics.

EXAM FOCUS: Section C of LC Exam

Reflective Practice

Ensure that you have completed all the Reflective Journal entries for this chapter (pages 14–16 of your Reflective Journal and Learning Portfolio) before moving on to the next chapter.

Complete the Learning Portfolio activities on pages 16–18 of your Reflective Journal and Learning Portfolio. This will help you to self-assess the extent to which you have achieved the learning intentions for this chapter, and will help you to monitor your progress.

POWER AND PEOPLE

CHAPTER 5
Policy-making

'Democracy cannot function or survive without a sufficient medium by which citizens remain informed and engaged in public policy debates.' Nancy Snow

KEY TERMS
- Policy
- Law
- Public policy
- Electoral manifesto
- State agency
- Civil service
- Minority government
- Lobby
- Lobbyist
- Primary legislation
- Secondary legislation
- Bill
- Act
- Statutory instrument

Introduction

We select our government to make decisions on how our society should be governed to address our problems and meet our needs. Just as decisions made in school result in rules, government decisions result in **policies** and **laws**. We have policies and laws covering almost every aspect of our lives (e.g. health, education, transport, etc.). Some policies are developed to address particular problems or issues in society (e.g. road traffic deaths, obesity, literacy levels), while other policies are designed to address the unfair or unequal position of certain groups in society (e.g. women, low-income people, minority groups).

Fig. 5.1 Enda Kenny and Leo Varadkar launch Fine Gael's new health policy in advance of the 2016 General Election. We will learn how such policies become national policy, and who influences and shapes them

KEY TERMS

A **policy** is an agreed plan of action or set of ideas on how to deal with an issue or situation.

A **law** is a formal rule established by government to regulate the actions of members of society. Breaking a law can result in the imposition of a penalty or punishment.

'Legislation' is a term also used to describe a law or set of laws.

In Chapter 2, we learned how a variety of actors can participate in decision-making at school. Similarly, a variety of actors are involved in developing our national policies and laws. Some actors are *decision-makers*. Others are *influencers* who attempt to have their voices heard in the decision-making process. In this chapter, we will examine different decision-makers at national and European levels. We will pay particular attention to policy- and law-making processes at the national level, and the role of the different branches of government. Finally, we will look at examples of citizen participation in policy-making and the spaces that exist, or are created, to ensure that our policies and laws reflect the views of citizens.

By the end of this chapter you will be able to:
- Explain the difference between policies and laws.
- Identify the different decision-makers that are directly involved in the creation and implementation of national policy, e.g. government, civil service, statutory bodies.
- Identify the organisations and groups in society that play a role in influencing the development of national policy, e.g. political parties, media, research institutes, civil society bodies, lobbyists.
- Describe the process of decision-making at national level and the roles played by various decision-makers and influencers in the development of national policy.
- Explain how the institutions of the European Union impact on the development of national policy and laws in Ireland.
- Explain how supranational agreements, such as the United Nations Convention on the Rights of the Child, impact on the development of national policy and laws.
- Describe the key stages of a bill (proposed law) as it passes through the Oireachtas to become an Act (official law).
- Explain the difference between primary legislation and secondary legislation.
- List and describe the various ways in which individual citizens can influence and participate in the development of national policy.
- Describe the process of decision-making in relation to a specific policy that has a direct impact on young people in Ireland today.
- Examine and evaluate different evidence and viewpoints to assess whether the Irish system of government is effective in representing the will of the Irish people.

By the end of this chapter you will have developed the following skills:
- Communication skills and the ability to present information and ideas verbally.
- Interpersonal skills and the ability to work effectively with small and large groups to reach agreed conclusions and achieve consensus.
- Research skills and the ability to evaluate quantitative and qualitative evidence concerning the policy-making process.
- Action planning to formulate ideas, set goals and develop, implement and evaluate an action plan.
- Active citizenship: the ability to actively participate in a community-based project.

Policies: The 'Fruits of Government Decision-Making'

Governments make decisions on many different issues that affect society: the design of our education system, what and how we should recycle, how we deal with mental health issues, public safety, etc. Governments analyse the different needs or problems of a society, look at possible solutions, and make decisions. The results or 'fruits' of these decisions become our public policies. **Public policy** is the term used to describe how the government has decided to respond to the needs of its citizens: in other words, the government's plan of action. Public policy is not contained in a single document: rather it is a collection of rules, regulations and strategies with respect to a specific issue or area. Although the government is the primary decision-maker, public policy is also shaped by important national events or crises, such as overcrowding in hospitals, the deaths of homeless people and the housing crisis. The direction of public policy is also heavily influenced by public opinion and the media. Public policy is dynamic – it often changes in response to national events and the reactions of citizens to these events (see Fig. 5.3).

When we want to research the different policies in relation to an issue, we may need to use a variety of official and media sources (see page 144).

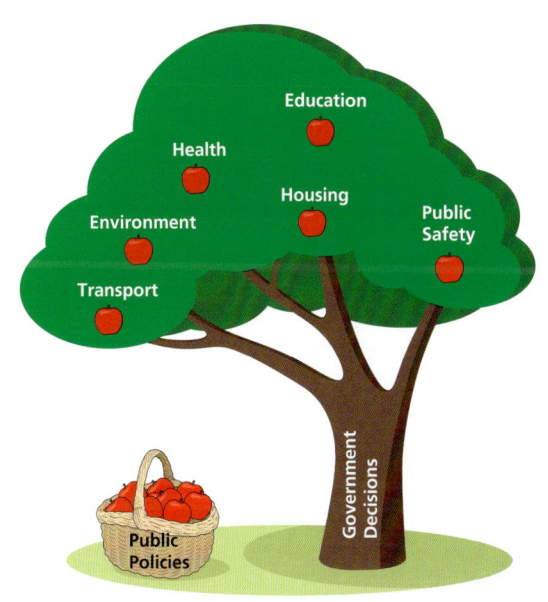

Fig. 5.2 The 'fruits of government decision-making'

> **KEY TERM**
>
> **Public policy** is a set of principles, guidelines and regulatory measures adopted by the executive branch of the government when it acts to address the needs of its citizens. Public policy is also known as 'national policy'.

Policies are not the same as laws. However, sometimes a law must be passed to allow a policy to be implemented. If a proposed policy involves a significant change from current practice and law, a new law will be needed.

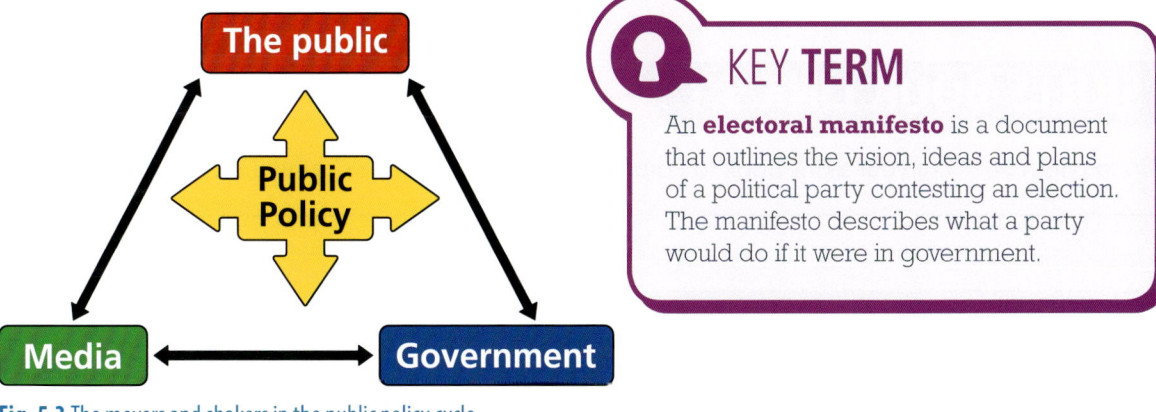

> **KEY TERM**
>
> An **electoral manifesto** is a document that outlines the vision, ideas and plans of a political party contesting an election. The manifesto describes what a party would do if it were in government.

Fig. 5.3 The movers and shakers in the public policy cycle

POLICY-MAKING   143

How to Research a Policy

We can use the following resources to research a policy:

- The programme for government: This is the government's 'work plan' for its period in office. The programme for government is usually based on the promises made in a political party's **electoral manifesto** before an election. Programmes for government change once a new government takes office. You can find the current programme for government at **www.merrionstreet.ie**

- The budget: This shows how much money the government has committed to different policies.

- National plans from government departments, public bodies or agencies: These often set out targets, objectives and performance indicators.

- Laws and regulations, including Acts of the Oireachtas, legislation and statutory instruments.

- Government department consultation papers and proposals. These include Green Papers and White Papers.

- Government circulars: These provide information, guidance, rules, and/or background information on policy and procedural matters. Examples include circulars issued by the Health Service Executive.

- Parliamentary statements made by government ministers, and answers to parliamentary questions.

- Media statements made by government ministers, or announcements in official press releases or speeches. These include the regular stream of announcements from the government Press Office at **www.merrionstreet.ie**

- Reports or analysis by public agencies.

- Reports or analysis from international bodies, such as the EU, UN or OECD.

- Reports or analysis by the media on a particular topic or issue. The media includes social media and alternative media.

- Academic books or papers with up-to-date reviews of topics and issues.

- Published research or analysis of a topic by activists or interest groups.

- Official statistics, including public spending data.

- Testimony by people who have first-hand experience of an issue. This information may be reported in the media or may be available from community organisations.

SKILLS BOOK LINK 5.1

Go to pages 78-79 of your Skills Book to complete Skill Task 5.1 on a County Development Plan.

SKILLS BOOK LINK 5.2

Go to pages 80–81 of your Skills Book to complete Skill Task 5.2 on crime prevention policies at local council level.

Public policy is like a jigsaw puzzle with many pieces. We need to gather all the pieces together to see the whole picture of public policy on an issue! For example, the official website of the Department of Health in Ireland lists a range of policies covering over 80 areas, such as dental health, food safety, medical cards and obesity. Within each area of government (e.g. education, health, environment), there will be an overall strategy that outlines the general objectives of the government. For example, the National Statement of Strategy for Health for 2015–2017 states that it is government policy to 'improve the health and wellbeing of people in Ireland by keeping people healthy, providing the healthcare people need, delivering high-quality services, and getting best value from health system resources'.

IN THE MEDIA

Fig. 5.4 The media regularly reports on government policies

Sometimes the term 'policy' can also refer to the positions, goals or aspirations of political parties that are outlined in their electoral manifestos. The overall strategy or vision of a political party will, in theory, inform the subsequent policies it proposes, develops or changes. Since there are several different ways to view any problem, different policy options will be proposed by the government, the parties in opposition and other groups. Sometimes it is possible to identify these differences on the basis of the overall political visions and ideologies of the government or political parties (e.g. left/right, liberal/conservative, feminist). Different views have been put forward on the objectives and limitations of government policy-making. Some people take the view that government policy should be limited to protecting the individual rights of life, liberty and property. Other people take the view that government policy should focus on protecting the vulnerable in society.

POLICY-MAKING 145

Examples of Education Policies and Laws in Ireland

Policies

Policies in Ireland include:
- Literacy and Numeracy for Learning and Life, 2011–2020
- 20-Year Strategy for the Irish Language, 2010–2030 … Delivering Equality of Opportunity In Schools – An Action Plan for Educational Inclusion
- Digital Strategy for Schools, 2015–2020
- Anti-Bullying Procedures for Primary and Post-Primary Schools

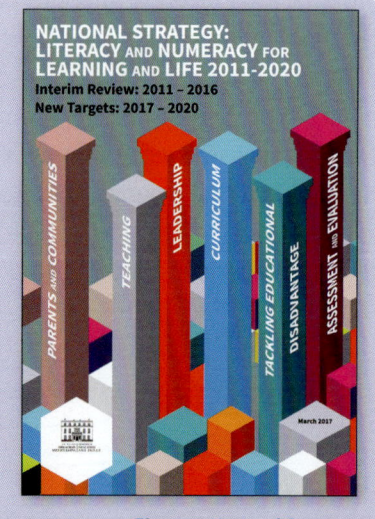

Fig. 5.5 *National Strategy: Literacy and Numeracy for Learning and Life 2011–2020 Interim Review: 2011 – 2016, New Targets: 2017 – 2020*

Laws

Laws in Ireland include:
- Education Act, 1998
- Teaching Council Act, 2001
- Education for Persons with Special Educational Needs 2004 (the EPSEN Act)
- Student Support Act 2011

Fig. 5.6 Ireland's Education Act, 1998

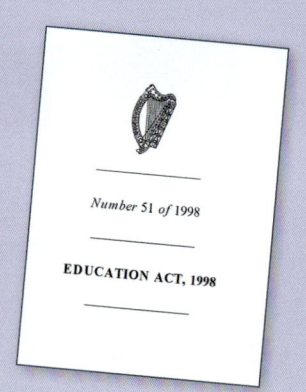

SKILLS BOOK LINK 5.3

Go to page 82 of your Skills Book to complete Skill Task 5.3 on the educational legislation.

See RESEARCH TIPS on page 33.

SKILLS BOOK LINK 5.4

Go to pages 82–83 of your Skills Book to complete Skill Task 5.4 on researching national policies in Ireland.

See RESEARCH TIPS on page 33.

RESEARCH ASSIGNMENT 5.1

Go to the official website of the Department of Health to find the department's list of policies. Go to **https://educateplus.ie/go/health-policy**. Choose **one** policy from the list that directly affects young people. Write a summary of the policy.

See RESEARCH TIPS on page 33.

Addressing Inequality Through Policy

Fig. 5.7 Several policies in Ireland aim to address inequality in access to third-level education

Inequality in Access to Third-Level Education

In Ireland, there are several strategies and policies that aim to make access to third-level education more equal. For example, the Undergraduate Maintenance Grant System and the Student Assistance Fund Scheme support low-income students who attend third-level educational institutions. Many universities (e.g. DCU, TCD, UCD) have government-funded 'access programmes'. The Mature Students Admissions Pathway (MSAP) programme provides a range of supports to youth and adults from socio-economic, ethnic minority or Traveller community groups who would normally be under-represented at university.

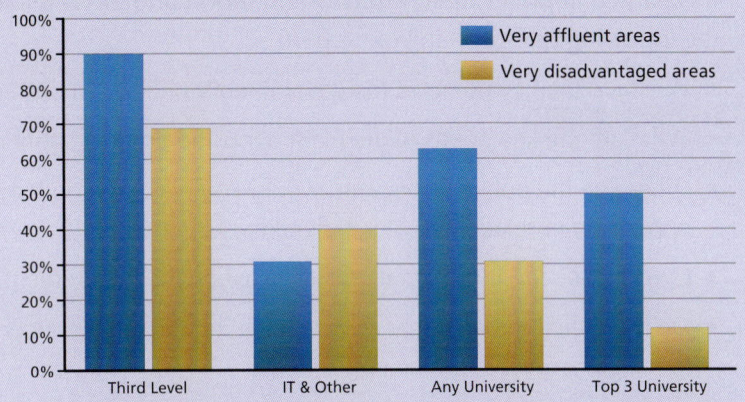

Fig. 5.8 Percentage of students from affluent and disadvantaged areas attending third level, by institution type (2014)

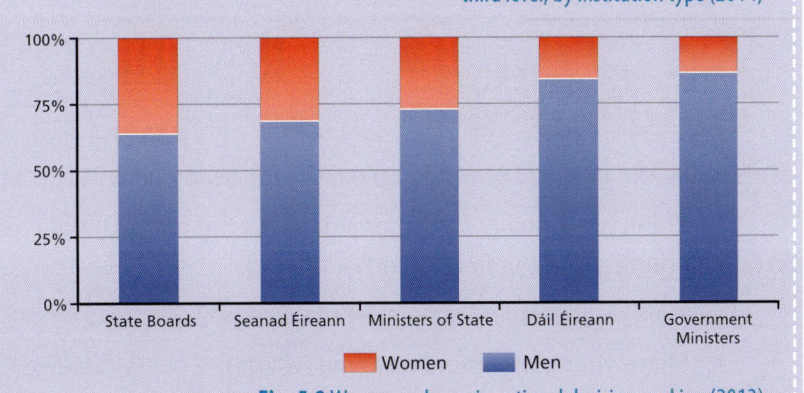

Gender Equality

The Central Statistics Office (CSO) regularly produces data on the position of women and men in Ireland. Women face many challenges in many areas, such as in the workforce and in political representation. Several policies have been developed to address these issues. The provision of the free preschool year is intended to provide a financial support for mothers who wish to return to the workforce. Public funding to political parties is now tied to gender quotas. It is hoped that this will increase the representation of women in politics.

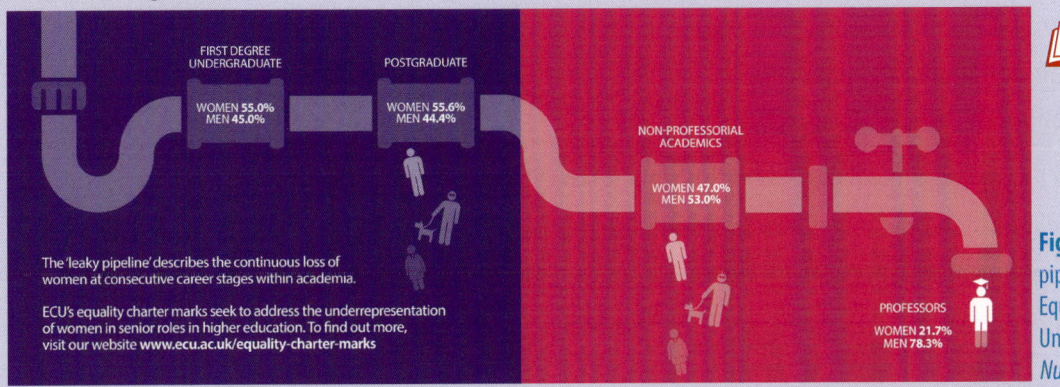

Fig. 5.9 Women and men in national decision-making (2013)

See page 133 for more information on gender quotas for political parties in Ireland.

Fig. 5.10 The 'leaky pipeline' taken from Equality Challenge Unit's 2014 *Know Your Numbers* report

FIRST DEGREE UNDERGRADUATE — WOMEN 55.0% MEN 45.0%
POSTGRADUATE — WOMEN 55.6% MEN 44.4%
NON-PROFESSORIAL ACADEMICS — WOMEN 47.0% MEN 53.0%
PROFESSORS — WOMEN 21.7% MEN 78.3%

The 'leaky pipeline' describes the continuous loss of women at consecutive career stages within academia.

ECU's equality charter marks seek to address the underrepresentation of women in senior roles in higher education. To find out more, visit our website www.ecu.ac.uk/equality-charter-marks

POLICY-MAKING

QUESTIONS

1. Examine Fig. 5.8, Fig. 5.9 and Fig. 5.10. What does the data tell us about **(a)** socio-economic inequality and **(b)** gender inequality in Ireland today?
2. How is government policy currently addressing these inequalities?
3. Can you think of any other policies that could be implemented to reduce inequality in Ireland today?

ACTIVITY 5.1

Your group will be assigned one policy area by your teacher (e.g. health, education). As a group, research the positions of the government and of the main opposition parties on this particular policy area. Write a short report and present it to another group. Address the following questions in your report:

- What are the key points of the government's policies in this area?
- What are the key points of the main opposition parties' policies in this area?
- Where on the political spectrum would you place the policies of the government *and* of the opposition in relation to your assigned policy area?
- Can you see ideological differences between the government and the opposition on this policy area?
- Do the policies adequately represent the interests and concerns of young people? Answer in relation to the government and the opposition.
- Do the policies ignore the concerns of any social groups in Ireland? Answer in relation to the government and the opposition.

ACTIVITY 5.2

Work with your partner to complete the following activity.

1. Think individually for a moment about the national policies that are of most significance to young people in Ireland today. *(Think)*
2. With your partner, agree a list of these policies. *(Pair)*
3. Share your conclusions with the rest of the class. *(Share)*

RESEARCH ASSIGNMENT 5.2

Choose **one** important national policy/law that has a direct impact on the lives of young people. Research the positions of the main political parties on this policy/law. Write a summary report that covers the following points:

- Name and description of the policy/law
- How this policy/law affects young people
- Positions of the main political parties on this policy/law
- Recommendations on how this policy/law could be improved
- Summary of the interest groups that should have an input in developing this policy/law, and why.

See **RESEARCH TIPS** on page 33.

POWER AND PEOPLE

KEY THINKERS

SOCIAL DIVISIONS AND POWER STRUGGLES

Revise the Key Thinkers boxes on pages 50 and 84 to help you with these questions.

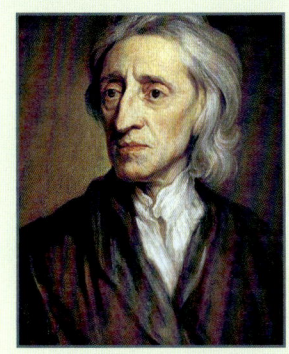

John Locke

Karl Marx

Max Weber

Sylvia Walby

Kathleen Lynch

QUESTIONS

1. According to Locke, humans will give up certain freedoms in return for protection from others. Can you think of any examples of policies that reflect Locke's position? Does the government have a duty to implement policies that protect the rights of all citizens, even if that means restricting individual freedom and autonomy? Why/why not?

2. According to Marx, the history of all societies can be viewed as a class struggle between two groups – the powerful bourgeoisie and the exploited proletariat. What policies can be adopted to ensure that the modern-day proletariat (worker) is protected from exploitation by the bourgeoisie (business owner)?

3. Does current national policy in Ireland adequately represent the concerns of those from lower socio-economic groups?

4. According to Weber, the position of a person in society is not determined by class alone but by status and power as well. In your opinion, does social status determine one's ability to influence policy-making in Ireland today? The Irish government is more likely to listen to which group(s) in Irish society? In your opinion, why is this?

5. What current national policies are increasing gender inequality and which ones are decreasing inequality? Does this support or contradict Walby's theory of transformations of the form of gender regimes?

6. Kathleen Lynch has examined inequalities in society. How can we ensure that the voices of the most vulnerable groups in Irish society are heard in the policy-making process?

7. Is the decision-making process at your school a good example of how policy-making should take place at national level? Why/why not?

POLICY-MAKING

KEY THINKERS

ROBERT NOZICK AND THE 'MINIMAL STATE'

Robert Nozick was an American political philosopher. He is best known for his book *Anarchy, State, and Utopia* (1974). In it, he argues for a minimal state: a state/government that limits its interventions to protect the individual rights of life, liberty and property. Nozick is often contrasted with his contemporary, **John Rawls**, who argued that ensuring equality is the primary purpose of government, and this requires more state intervention. Nozick and Rawls were writing during a time of growing disillusionment among Americans towards the US political system. Events such as the Vietnam War and high-level political scandals such as Watergate prompted new thinking on government and political models. Nozick was against the idea of wealth redistribution that was supported by egalitarian liberals such as Rawls. Nozick's logic was based on the idea that we are entitled (have a right) to the money we earn from our labour (work) and, as such, having to pay a compulsory (involuntary) tax would amount to forced labour, a type of slavery. Given such a view, it is unsurprising that Nozick was not a supporter of the 'welfare state' in which the government plays an active role (through regulation, laws and policies) in ensuring the protection of the economic and social wellbeing of its citizens. In fact,

Robert Nozick

Nozick viewed the welfare state as immoral. For Nozick, the social and economic benefit schemes (e.g. minimum wage, unemployment benefits) that we have in many of today's social democracies, including Ireland, amount to a type of 'theft' of legitimately earned wealth. Nozick argued instead for a minimal state, where government acts only to protect the individual from physical harm (e.g. protection of the police and military) and from unlawful fraud or theft of one's property (e.g. protection in the courts of law).

QUESTIONS

1. Do you agree with Nozick's argument for limited government intervention and a minimal state? Explain your reasons.
2. Is Ireland a minimal state? Why/why not?
3. Name **one** strength and **one** weakness of Nozick's argument for a minimal state.
4. What group(s) in society are likely to support Nozick's call for a minimal state?
5. Where on the political spectrum do the ideas of Nozick and Rawls lie?

Decision-Makers and Influencers: Who Makes Our Policies and Laws?

A variety of actors play a role in making public policy and laws in Ireland. Some actors are decision-makers. Other actors are influencers. Decision-makers will differ, depending on whether it is a policy or a law being made. They also differ depending on the issue (e.g. environment, health, education) and depending on the level (e.g. local, national, European). We will now learn about the decision-makers and influencers in Ireland.

Complete your next Reflective Journal entry (pages 19–20)

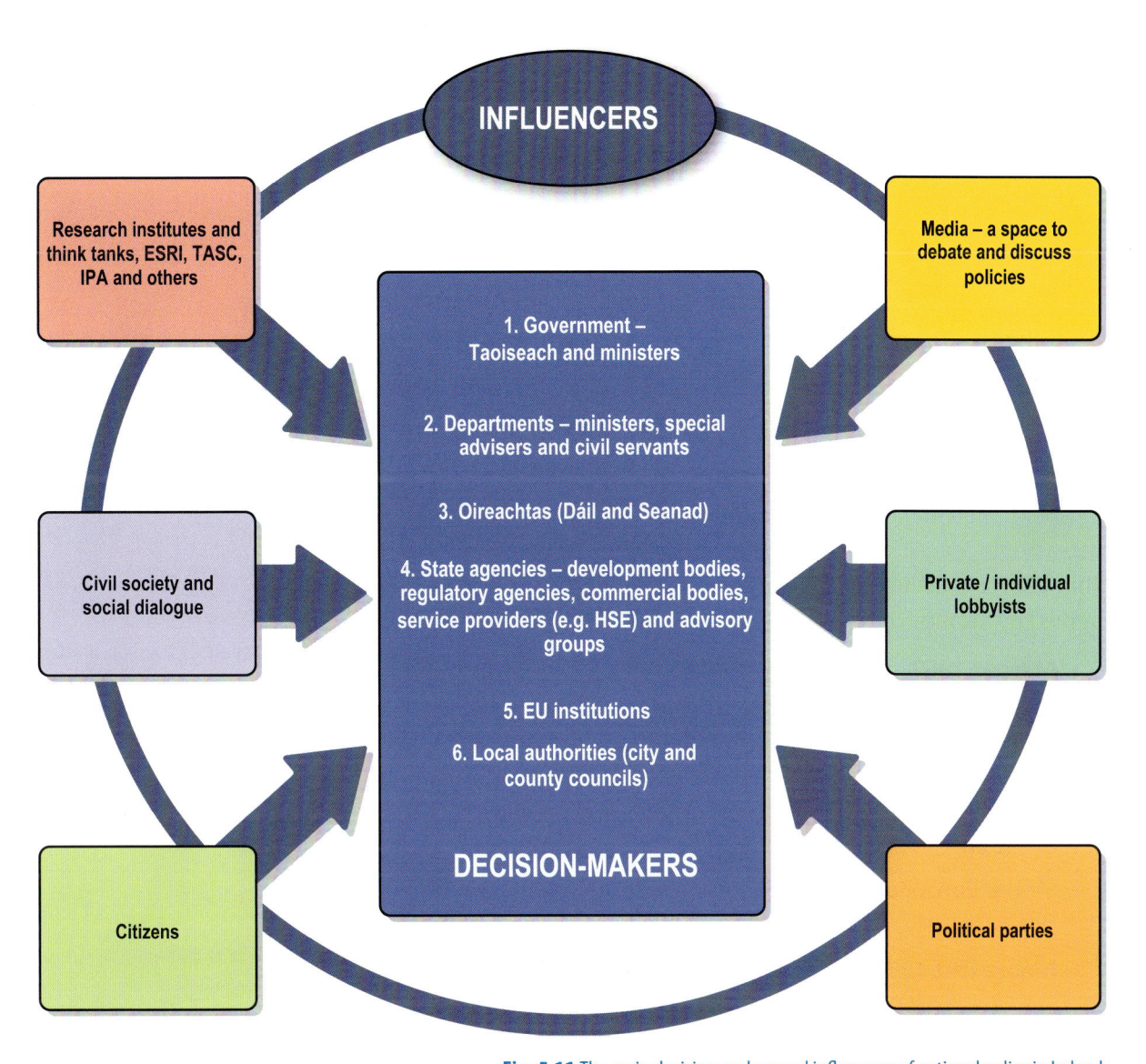

Fig. 5.11 The main decision-makers and influencers of national policy in Ireland

Decision-Makers

Government (Executive)

As we learned in Chapter 4, the government (Taoiseach and ministers) is the main decision-maker in the Irish system of national policy-making. The policies proposed by the government are based on a document called the programme for government. This is a type of action plan agreed by members of a new government and is based on the electoral manifestos of their respective political parties.

Each party holds a certain vision of how society should be, and makes proposals for different policy areas (e.g. health, education, economy, taxation). These proposals are presented in the party's manifestos, strategies and position documents. Political parties that form the government aim to have most of their policy positions turned into national policies. When a government is made up of more than one political party (coalition government), the parties negotiate on these different positions and agree on a final policy.

Fig. 5.12 The Programme for Government 2016–2021

European Union

As a member of the EU, Ireland must comply with certain decisions made by EU institutions on issues such as trade, environment, agriculture, employment, etc. A significant proportion of our policies and laws originate from Ireland's EU membership. The fundamental laws of the EU are set out in treaties that must be ratified (accepted) by the parliaments of all member states. The following EU treaties have been ratified by Ireland.

Fig. 5.13 The European Commission, Brussels

- **Merger 1967:** merged three bodies of European cooperation – European Coal and Steel Community (ECSC), European Atomic Energy Community (Euratom) and European Economic Community (EEC) – into a single institutional structure; regarded as the beginning of the EU

See page 125 for more information on the institutions of the EU.

- **Single European Act 1986:** created the single market

- **Maastricht 1992:** strengthened political and economic union among member states

- **Amsterdam 1997:** changed the powers of EU institutions and paved the way for EU enlargement

Fig. 5.14 Many of the EU laws that affect Ireland begin in the European Commission

- **Nice 2001:** made further changes to the powers and structures of EU institutions to facilitate enlargement

- **Lisbon 2007:** came into effect on 1 December 2009 and changed how decisions are made at EU level.

Treaties are the primary source of EU law. There are also secondary sources of EU law. The EU institutions have the power to make legislation that affects policy-making in Ireland. This power is shared between the European Commission, the Council of the EU and the European Parliament.

Because of Ireland's membership of the EU, some decision-making takes place at the European level, in areas such as the environment, health, education, trade and the economy. Decision-making at EU level involves various institutions:

- European Parliament
- European Council (heads of government)
- Council of the EU (ministers of member states)
- European Commission.

The European Council defines the general political direction and priorities of the EU but it does not 'make law'. Generally, it is the European Commission that proposes new laws, and it is the European Parliament and the Council of the EU that adopt these laws. The member states and the European Commission then implement the laws.

KEY TERM

State agency is the term used to describe a public or governmental organisation that plays a role in policy-making and the delivery of services on behalf of the government. Ireland has several different types of state agencies, such as commissions, advisory bodies, statutory and non-statutory corporations, and tribunals. At the end of 2015, there were approximately 600 state agencies in Ireland, covering all policy areas (social welfare, health, environment, etc.). The agencies are structured and managed in different ways, but each agency will report to one of the 15 government ministers and departments.

State agencies provide services to the public. They design and implement day-to-day strategies, policies and rules. They research, monitor and enforce the national policies under their responsibility. Examples of state agencies include:

- Competition and Consumer Protection Commission
- Food Safety Authority of Ireland
- Health Service Executive
- Irish Human Rights and Equality Commission
- National Disability Authority
- National Economic and Social Council
- Tusla: the Child and Family Agency

See page 260 for more information on the Irish Human Rights and Equality Commission.

Cabinet, Departments and State Agencies

Most decisions on policies will be made by the relevant minister (e.g. Minister for Transport, Minister for Health) in consultation with the Taoiseach and the cabinet. The day-to-day design and implementation of strategies and policies will be done by the relevant Department (e.g. Department of Children and Youth Affairs) and the associated **state agencies** (e.g. Tusla – the Child and Family Agency). In the Irish system of government, the minister is responsible for his or her department. This means that the minister takes full responsibility for the actions of the Department, including any wrongdoings, such as corruption, even if he or she was not directly involved. This is known as the doctrine of ministerial responsibility. The cabinet as a whole is bound by *collective responsibility*: all members of the cabinet must support and take joint responsibility for government decisions. Collective responsibility means that if a government loses the support of the majority of Dáil members through a motion of no confidence and the government is dissolved, all the ministers will be removed from their positions.

Fig. 5.15 Department of the Taoiseach, Government Buildings, Dublin

Civil Service

The policy proposals that are presented by ministers and discussed at weekly cabinet meetings are often created and developed by the **civil service** – senior staff and special advisers who work in the Department of Education,

KEY TERM

The **civil service** is the large body of government employees entrusted with the administration of the government and mandated to implement the national policies as decided by government. In Ireland, the civil service is divided into Departments that work under Government ministers (e.g. the Department of Finance).

POLICY-MAKING 153

for example. Ministers can change from election to election, but senior civil servants usually remain in permanent positions for life. Because of this, ministers rely heavily on the advice, experience and technical expertise of the leading civil servants in a department. As a result, some critics claim that senior civil servants play a more influential role in the creation of national policy than even the ministers themselves.

Oireachtas and County Councils

Sometimes a policy that is proposed is significantly different from existing practice and requires a change to an existing law (an amendment) or a new law. When this happens, the Oireachtas – the main law-making body in Ireland – becomes part of the decision-making. For local issues (e.g. the management of beaches and public parks) it is the city councils and county councils (local authorities) who make the decisions.

Fig. 5.16 Department of Finance

Fig. 5.17 Senior civil servants play an influential role in formulating national policies

RESEARCH ASSIGNMENT 5.3

Research and list all the decision-makers involved in creating the national policy/law that you examined in Research Assignment 5.2. Find out the names of the minister, Department, state agencies, etc. that created the policy or law.

See **RESEARCH TIPS** on page 33.

QUESTIONS

1. What is a policy? Give **one** example of a national policy in Ireland.
2. What is a law? Give **one** example of a law in Ireland.
3. Explain the following terms:
   - (a) Public policy
   - (b) Legislation
   - (c) State agency
   - (d) Civil service.
4. What is a manifesto? Explain the difference between a manifesto and a programme for government.
5. Write an account of the main decision-makers involved in the development of national policies and laws. Make reference to the roles of the government, EU, cabinet, state agencies and the civil service.
6. How might the power of the civil service undermine democracy?

Influencers

In a democracy, decision-making processes are inclusive and involve the participation of many different actors. This is based on the principle of ensuring that the voice of the people is present in government (see page 132). In Ireland, different actors and groups provide important inputs into the making of policies. Although they are not formal decision-makers for policies, they attempt to influence the decisions made by government. Actors can influence through formal or informal processes. Each actor will have its own interests, concerns and expertise, which are used to influence and contribute to government policy-making. There are many different influencers present in any democracy. Broadly speaking, however, we can identify five main categories of influencer: political parties; the media; research institutes, think tanks and universities; civil society bodies; and lobbyists.

Political Parties

A political party could be either a decision-maker or an influencer, depending on whether it has won or lost an election. When a party is in opposition, it does not have government power – this can restrict the influence it has in policy-making. When a government has a majority in parliament, the parliament usually passes all proposed legislation without challenge. However, if the government is a **minority government**, this increases the potential influence of all political parties with seats in parliament. In return for supporting a minority government, opposition political parties will aim to have their positions reflected in the final policies that are voted through the Oireachtas.

> **KEY TERMS**
>
> A **minority government** is formed if the governing party or parties do not have an overall majority of seats in parliament. It usually requires the support of the main opposition party. Government legislation can only be passed with the support of other members of the parliament to make up the required majority.

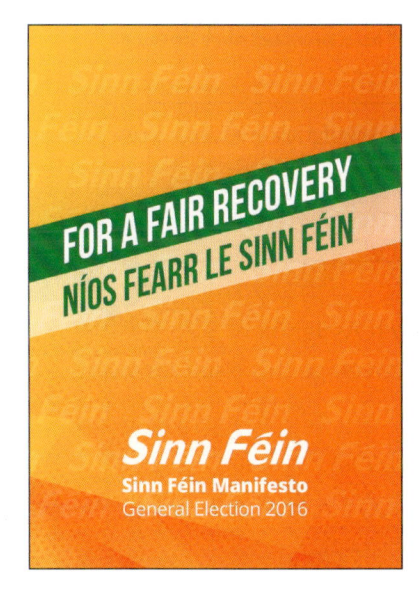

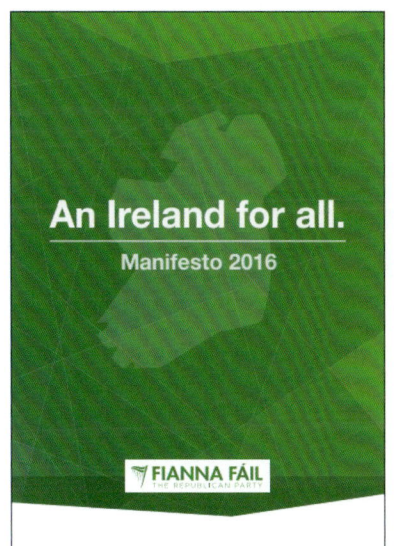

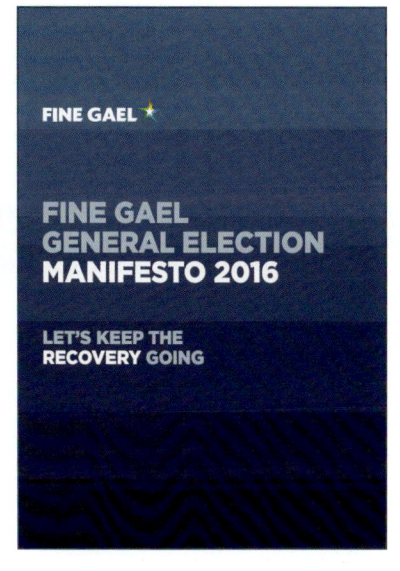

Fig. 5.18 Examples of manifestos of political parties in Ireland

The Media

The media – print, radio, TV and online – can play a powerful role in focusing the attention of policy-makers on certain issues and opinions. The media acts as a direct influencer, and also provides a platform for others to influence policy-making. Both the general public and the decision-makers will pay attention to the media. In Ireland, the media has played a pivotal role in highlighting major political issues, shaping public opinion, and applying pressure for government action on issues such as the Catholic Church abuse scandals, political corruption and discrimination against members of the Traveller and LGBTQ+ communities. Different actors attempt to use the media as a tool to get their message across. A media campaign is a common tool in politics. Governments and parties will use the media to launch a policy or test it against public opinion. Interest groups and civil society bodies will also use the media to raise their concerns. With the growing influence of social media (Twitter, Facebook, etc.), we have entered an age of 'citizen media' whereby anyone with access to digital media can voice their concerns, ideas and opinions. In Chapter 6, we will examine in more detail the role of the media in politics and society.

Fig. 5.19 The media plays a powerful role in influencing policy-making

RESEARCH ASSIGNMENT 5.4

Keeping with the national policy/law that your group chose in Research Assignment 5.2, research newspaper articles and media sites to discover what media coverage this issue received. Discuss the following questions in your group:

- Did the policy receive the media coverage it deserved?
- What stance did the media take on the policy?
- Was there a general consensus among the media on this issue?
- Was the media in favour or against the government policy?
- In your opinion, how powerful was the media in influencing the outcome of this policy?

Research Institutes, Think Tanks and Universities

Good policy relies on strong evidence and facts about the problem or issue. Institutions that produce reliable and objective research on social, economic and political issues play a critical role in policy-making in most countries. In Ireland, a variety of research institutes (e.g. ESRI: Economic and Social Research Institute), think tanks (e.g. TASC: Think-tank for Action on Social Change) and universities regularly produce research and reports on important issues. This research is used by policy-makers when they design new policies and laws. Sometimes the government commissions a particular piece of research so that it can design subsequent policy. However, research institutes and universities also conduct research independently in an effort to provide data that can be used to influence policy-making. The ESRI, for example, produces reports on a range of policy areas, including: education, social inclusion and equality, health and quality of life, energy and the environment, and the economy.

Fig. 5.20 Economic and Social Research Institute

IN THE MEDIA

Fig. 5.21 Research institutes, think tanks and universities influence policy-making

RESEARCH ASSIGNMENT 5.5

Keeping with the national policy/law that your group chose in Research Assignment 5.2, conduct online research to find out if any institutes carried out research into this national policy itself or any issues that are related to it. If so, write down the name of the research institute and briefly summarise the recommendations that it made.

POLICY-MAKING 157

Civil Society Bodies

See page 85 for more information on political representation through civil society bodies.

In Chapter 3, we saw how citizens can be represented through a range of bodies that work with different social issues or groups. Collectively, these bodies are known as civil society. They work closely with groups facing a particular social challenge, such as poverty, homelessness or discrimination based on race, ethnicity or sexual orientation. In Ireland, examples of civil bodies working with children and youth include Barnardos, Youth Work Ireland, and the Children's Rights Alliance. Community organisations, charities, unions and other civil society bodies can provide a rich source of expertise and knowledge to our decision-makers on a variety of policy issues. These bodies help to ensure that the voices of different groups are included in policy-making.

RESEARCH ASSIGNMENT 5.6

Building on your work in Research Assignment 5.5, use the internet to locate and identify any civil society bodies that represent the interests of those affected by the policy/law which your group chose. Select one of these organisations and provide a brief description of any recent campaigns they have had on the policy/issue.

In Ireland, for many years, formal participation of civil society and other sectors in policy-making was facilitated through the 'social partnership model'. Civil society bodies in Ireland attempt to influence decision-makers in a variety of ways.

Social Partnership in Ireland

The social partnership process in Ireland began in the 1980s as a way to facilitate discussion among different sectors of society on a variety of social and economic policy issues. When it started, membership was initially limited to the government and three pillars: business, trade unions and farmers. In 1996, civil society bodies working with people living in poverty protested that they should be involved in the process. The government added a fourth pillar to social partnership: the community and voluntary sector. Organisations representing the unemployed and those experiencing poverty and inequality argued that their members did not benefit from the agreements, and so they began to **lobby** to be included in the 1996 negotiations. In 2009 the government added a fifth pillar to include organisations working on the environment. Between 1987 and 2006, the social partnership process resulted in seven agreements. The agreements covered a range of policy issues: agreements on welfare, education, health, national wages and other employment issues. However, following the economic crash in 2008, the social partnership process collapsed and no formal arrangement has replaced it. The various sectors continue to influence policy-making through a variety of formal means, such as meetings, consultations and campaigns.

POWER AND PEOPLE

Lobbyists

Different private interest groups or **lobbyists** can also influence policy-making. These lobbyists attempt to ensure that the laws or policies of government are favourable to (or do not impact negatively on) their interests. In countries such as the US, lobbying is a big industry: over 13,000 registered lobbyists represent a variety of interests in the US, such as pharmaceutical companies, the food industry and religious institutions. Lobbyists use a variety of methods to attempt to influence political decision-makers: from arranging one-to-one meetings with politicians, to actively fundraising for and supporting the election campaigns of politicians in return for favourable access. In 2016, lobby groups in the US spent over $3.1 billion trying to buy influence. Among the biggest spenders each year are the American Chamber of Commerce, the oil and mining industry, the pharmaceutical lobby, the technology lobby and the defence industry. Former US President Barack Obama claimed that the biggest disappointment of his eight years in office was his failure to persuade Congress to pass stricter gun control legislation. The National Rifle Association (NRA) is one of the most powerful lobby groups in the US: the NRA's successful lobbying of Congress members had a stronger influence than that of the President. In Ireland, a series of tribunals and public investigations revealed that lobbying is also a big part of Irish politics. In March 2015, Ireland introduced a new law in an attempt to regulate lobbying and increase transparency. The Regulation of Lobbying Act 2015 ensures that the public has information on who is conducting lobbying, the issues being discussed, what the lobbyists are asking for, and with which government official, politician or public servant they are dealing. The new law covers all private individuals, charities and social groups, unions, businesses and companies conducting lobbying activities. The Irish Farmers' Association and IBEC (Ireland's business and employer association) are among the biggest lobbyists in Ireland. Lobbyists must now register their activities and the information is made available online at **www.lobbying.ie** The register gives us some insight into who is attempting to influence our policy-making.

KEY TERMS

To **lobby** is to take actions aimed at influencing the outcome of decisions. In politics, lobbying involves paid activity in which special interest groups hire well-connected professional advocates or lawyers called **lobbyists** to represent their interests to decision-makers. A lobbyist may be hired to persuade politicians to introduce new legislation that would be beneficial to the interest group. Lobbyists may also be hired to influence politicians to reject a bill (proposed law) that the interest group does not want.

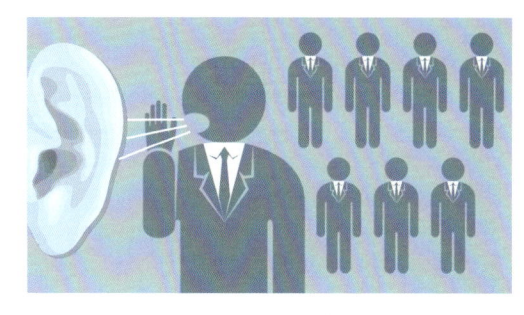

Fig. 5.22 Lobbying

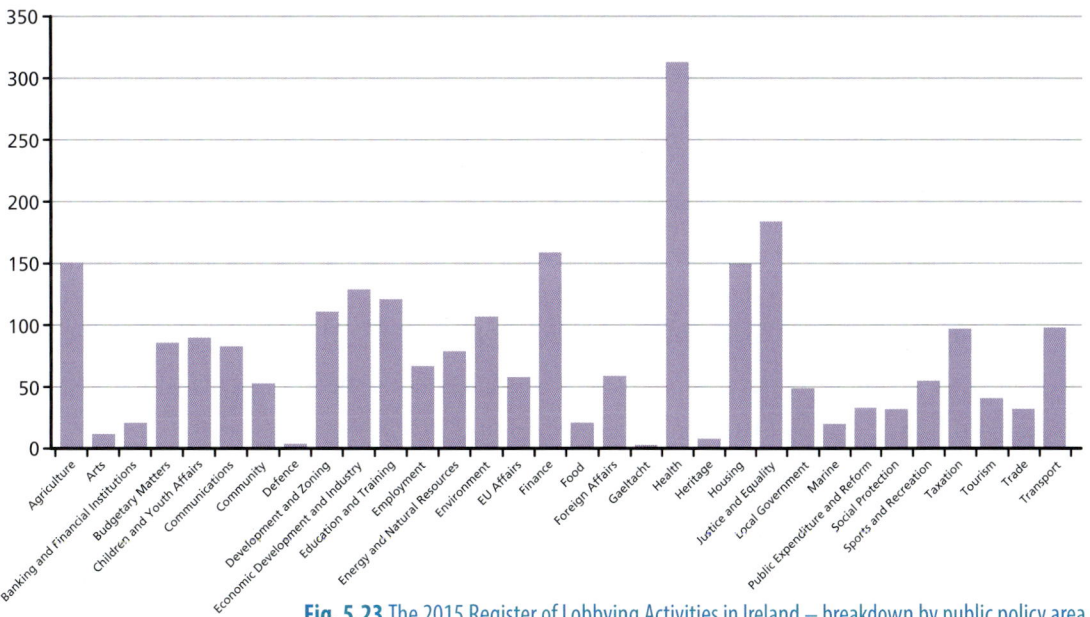

Fig. 5.23 The 2015 Register of Lobbying Activities in Ireland – breakdown by public policy area

POLICY-MAKING

Fig. 5.24 Lobbying in politics

QUESTIONS

1. Examine Fig. 5.23 and answer the following questions.
   (a) What area had the highest recorded instances of lobbying? In your opinion, why is there such a high level of lobbying in this area compared to other areas?
   (b) Name the **three** areas in which instances of lobbying were lowest. In your opinion, why was there such a lack of lobbying recorded in these areas?
   (c) Do lobbyists have much power to influence Irish politicians? What methods can they use?
   (d) Why is it important that lobbyists are required to register their lobbying activities in this way?
2. Examine Fig. 5.24 and answer the following questions.
   (a) What is the message of this cartoon? Give evidence from the cartoon to support your answer.
   (b) How is lobbying a danger to democracy?
3. What is a minority government?
4. What is the difference between a minority government and a coalition government?
5. Explain how the media can influence government policy.
6. Can you think of any occasion when the media influenced a government decision?
7. Why is it important that the government consults research institutes before making laws?
8. Name **one** important research institute in Ireland.
9. What is a civil society body? Name **one** civil society body that represents young people.
10. Explain how social partnership operated in Ireland in the past.
11. Name the **five** pillars of the former social partnership model.
12. Give **one** advantage and **one** disadvantage of social partnership.

Complete your next Reflective Journal entry (pages 19–20)

The Policy-Making Process

Policy is continually made and changed by ministers, civil servants, political parties and public bodies. Different interest groups, lobbyists, civil society, research institutes and media also influence the process. In Ireland, the three strands of the government – Taoiseach, Tánaiste and ministers – have collective responsibility for making national policy. Collective responsibility means that they share responsibility for the decisions and policies made. The process of actually making national policy is not always the same, however.

Generally, a policy proposal will be developed by the relevant department, such as the Department of Education and Skills. The policy proposal is a discussion document that is sometimes called a Green Paper. The document outlines the issue that the policy aims to tackle (e.g. literacy in primary schools). It outlines the range of possible solutions for the issue (e.g. alphabetic versus phonetic approaches). It examines their respective advantages and disadvantages. Sometimes a public consultation will be held and individuals and groups (e.g. teachers, educational experts) can send written responses to share their views on the options.

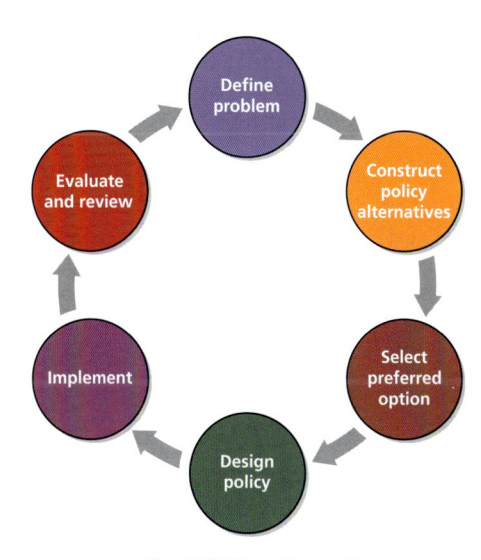

Fig. 5.25 The policy-making process

Good policy needs to be based on strong evidence and research. In Ireland, as elsewhere in Europe, the government makes use of research, data and statistics produced by the Central Statistics Office (CSO) and a range of research institutes when designing policy.

The next step in the policy-making cycle is when the government develops its final policy. The final policy can be referred to as a White Paper (e.g. White Paper on Improving Literacy Levels in Primary Schools), a strategy or a policy. If the policy does not require any change in the law, it is ready to be implemented immediately.

The Watchful Eye of the Oireachtas

Although the government is the main decision-maker when it comes to national policy, the houses of the Oireachtas (Dáil and Seanad) play an important role in monitoring government policies. Each opposition party appoints what is called 'front bench spokespersons' in the Dáil and Seanad. They each follow a specific minister's work (e.g. Minister for Defence). In the Dáil, TDs can ask these ministers questions or raise concerns about current or planned policies. Also, ministers can be asked to attend a meeting of the relevant Joint Committee (e.g. Joint Committee on Jobs, Enterprise and Innovation). The Oireachtas website has archived footage of Dáil, Seanad and Committee debates at **https://educateplus.ie/go/playback**

Fig. 5.26 The watchful eye of the Oireachtas

The Law-Making Process

Policies are not the same as laws, but sometimes a law will need to be passed to allow a policy to be implemented. Society is constantly evolving: new issues, problems and needs emerge all the time. Governments respond to these changes with new policies. If a proposed policy involves a significant change from current practice, it usually requires a change to an existing law or the creation of a new law. For example, in 2016 a new law was needed to allow the government to introduce a penalty against the use of worn tyres on vehicles. Policy decisions that require new laws result in one of two types of legislation: **primary legislation** or **secondary legislation**.

> **KEY TERMS**
>
> **Primary legislation** consists of the main laws of a country. They are approved by parliament. Examples in Ireland include the Education Act, 1998 and the Mental Health Act, 2001.
>
> **Secondary legislation** consists of laws that detail how primary laws are to be implemented. They are developed by the executive without approval of the legislature.

Primary Legislation

In a democratic society, rules are based on laws. The main laws of our country are collectively known as primary legislation. In Ireland, the constitution (Bunreacht na hÉireann) is our 'mother' law. It states what rights we have and how our system of government works. Ireland must also follow important European and international laws which protect human rights. The introduction of any new laws cannot conflict with the constitution or human rights laws. Laws cover almost all aspects of our lives, such as education, health, employment and justice. In a democracy, the legislature has the exclusive responsibility for making our laws. In Ireland, the legislature is made up of the two houses of the Oireachtas (Dáil and Seanad) and the President. Because of Ireland's membership of the EU, some of our primary legislation is made at European level.

> See page 97 for more information on the legislature and the separation of powers.

Development and Publication of a Bill

In Ireland, a law starts its life as a **bill**. Once a bill is developed, it goes through both houses of the Oireachtas in six stages before it becomes an **Act** of law.

The majority of bills come from government. The relevant minister (e.g. Minister for Transport) is the final decision-maker with respect to draft laws. However, his or her senior civil servants, advisers and the heads of state agencies all play important roles in developing the content of bills. During the development of a bill, a consultation is usually held with other government departments and interested stakeholders that may be affected by the proposed law. For example, the Department of Education and Skills may invite education groups to share their views during the development of a School Admissions Bill. Sometimes the process involves public consultation, and sometimes not. If a consultation is part of the process, it normally starts with a Green Paper. The public is then invited to express its views in relation to the discussion document. Consultations can take many forms, but are usually through written submissions. Once the consultation process has been finalised, the minister then develops what is called a *Heads of Bill* or *General Scheme*. This is an outline of the main objectives of the proposed new law, which is presented to the government for approval. Since 2011, the Heads of Bill is usually also sent to the relevant Joint Oireachtas Committee for its review. For example, bills related to education will be dealt with by the

> **KEY TERMS**
>
> A **bill** is a proposal for a law. An **Act** is a bill that has been passed into law.

Joint Committee on Education and Social Protection. The public can also submit its views on the proposal to the Committee at this stage. The Committee makes a report with its opinions and recommendations. The minister can accept or reject these. In the final step in this first stage, the minister presents the Heads of Bill at one of the weekly cabinet meetings for government approval. Once approved, bill is drafted and it starts the six stages in the Oireachtas.

Fig. 5.27 A bill undergoes much scrutiny before it becomes an Act of law

Private Members' Bills

Since the 1970s, there has been a tradition of individual members or opposition parties introducing legislation through what are called *private members' bills*. Important changes in social policy have been the outcome of private members' bills, mainly in the Seanad (e.g. animal welfare, homelessness, freedom of information and family planning). Although most policy comes from government, members in opposition in both houses of the Oireachtas (Dáil and Seanad) can initiate a proposal for legislation through a private member's bill. However, there have only been a few successful cases of private members' bills being passed into law. Examples include: a 2014 law to prevent people smoking inside a car in the presence of children, and a 1980 law which established the Office of the Ombudsman to deal with complaints about public services. For the most part, however, the houses of the Oireachtas debate and pass legislation that comes from the government, rather than from private members' bills (the opposition).

How a Bill Becomes an Act

How a Bill becomes an Act

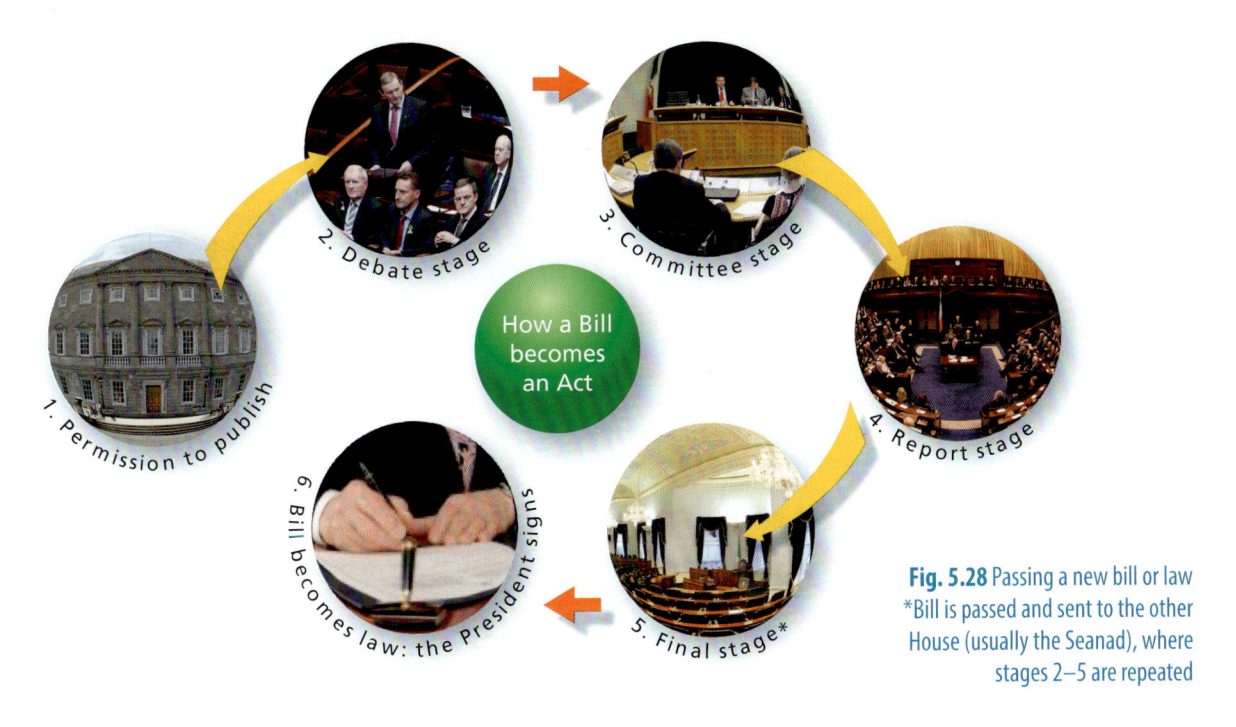

1. Permission to publish
2. Debate stage
3. Committee stage
4. Report stage
5. Final stage*
6. Bill becomes law: the President signs

Fig. 5.28 Passing a new bill or law
*Bill is passed and sent to the other House (usually the Seanad), where stages 2–5 are repeated

1. Permission to Publish

Permission to publish means that a bill can be formally presented to the Oireachtas. Governments can start bills in either of the houses of the Oireachtas (Dáil or Seanad). For example, the School Admissions Bill (2015) started in the Dáil, while the Gender Recognition Bill (2014) started in the Seanad. However, most bills start in the Dáil. In fact, constitutional amendment bills and any bills related to finance must be started in the Dáil. Once the bill completes all stages and is passed by one house, it then completes the same process in the other house. Government bills do not require permission to publish. They are automatically presented to the Oireachtas. However, private members' bills must obtain formal permission to publish. The bill is then sent for printing.

Limited Powers of the Seanad

The constitution gives primary law-making power to the Dáil, since it is the directly elected house. While the Seanad provides an additional opportunity to analyse and debate legislation, it cannot delay indefinitely the passing of new laws. Constitutional amendment bills and any bills related to finance can be initiated only in the Dáil. The Seanad can make recommendations (but not amendments) to bills related to finance. These recommendations must be made within 21 days.

2. Debate Stage

The second stage of the process is where initial discussion of the bill begins. There is a general debate on the bill: TDs and senators have an opportunity to speak and share their views on it. The discussion is normally on the overall objectives of the bill and what it covers, but not the finer detail of the bill. Once the debate is finished, a vote is taken. If passed, the bill then goes to the third stage. If the government has a majority in parliament, a private members' bill is unlikely to pass. Most private members' bills do not make it past this stage.

Fig. 5.29 During the debate stage, TDs and senators express and share their views on a bill

RESEARCH ASSIGNMENT 5.7

Go to **https://educateplus.ie/go/bills** to find out what bills have been debated in the Dáil most recently.

3. Committee Stage

The third stage is where the committee system of the Oireachtas comes into play. The relevant committee will look at the bill in detail and will develop a report which includes recommendations for any changes to the bill.

POWER AND PEOPLE

Committees exist for different issues. For example, a bill in relation to children will go to the Committee on Children and Youth Affairs, while a bill on transport will go to the Committee on Transport, Tourism and Sport.

Stage 3, the Committee Stage, is the most important stage of the process. The committee considers every detail of the bill (line by line) and there is a lot of debate and discussion. It is during this stage that the public can have its say, by contacting members of the committee (TDs and senators). Normally, the committee formally invites interested groups, such as civil society bodies, to provide expert inputs. The bill may go through many changes during this process, as each member strives to have his or her ideas included. In the end, there is a vote on the final position the committee takes in respect to the bill, including any changes it would like to see made. If the vote passes, the committee reports back to the Dáil or Seanad.

Fig. 5.30 An Oireachtas Committee meeting

See page 103 for more information on the committee system of the Oireachtas.

SKILLS BOOK LINK 5.5

Go to pages 83–84 of your Skills Book to complete Skill Task 5.5 on the committee system.

4. Report Stage

The committee presents to the Dáil/Seanad its recommendations on the bill, along with any proposed changes. There is general discussion again and new amendments can be proposed by any TD or senator.

Fig. 5.31 During the report stage, new amendments can be proposed by any member of the Dáil or Seanad

RESEARCH ASSIGNMENT 5.8

Go to **https://educateplus.ie/go/committees** and scroll to the bottom of the page. You will see a list of the most recent reports published by Oireachtas committees. Choose one committee report and list any **three** important recommendations made in it.

POLICY-MAKING

5. Final Stage

The final stage involves a debate on the final content of the bill. This is followed by a vote on whether to pass the bill. Because of the party whip system (see below), it is extremely rare for a government-supported bill to be defeated in a vote. Once the bill is passed in one house, it goes to the other house for approval. Most bills go through the Dáil first and then the Seanad. In such cases, the Seanad usually has 90 days to consider the bill. The Seanad can pass the bill without amendment, reject the bill, or propose amendments. If the Seanad rejects the bill or proposes amendments that the Dáil does not accept, the Dáil has the power to consider the bill as being passed. Therefore, the Seanad has the power to delay legislation, but not to stop it.

Fig. 5.32 During the final stage, a vote is taken on whether to pass the bill

Party Whip System

One of the first uses of a whip system in a parliamentary democracy was in 1884, when Charles Stewart Parnell, nationalist leader of the Irish Home Rule Party, imposed a party pledge on all elected members of his party at Westminster. His Home Rule MPs had to swear a pledge to 'sit, act and vote' as instructed, or else resign. This tradition continues in Irish politics today: TDs are expected to vote according to the party position. Although the party whip system is not a formal procedure of the Dáil, it is used by all the main political parties to ensure loyalty and discipline. If a TD votes against the party position, the TD may be expelled from his or her party. This happened to four Fine Gael TDs in 2013, after they voted against legislation allowing abortion in limited circumstances.

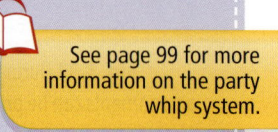

See page 99 for more information on the party whip system.

RESEARCH ASSIGNMENT 5.9

Look again at the research paper by Dr Brian Hunt from Skill Task 5.5 at pages 83–84 of your Skills Book. Read pages 23–4 of the research paper and answer the following question:

'How does the whip system impact on the scrutiny of legislation?'

6. Bill Becomes Law: The President Signs

Once the bill has passed, the Taoiseach sends the bill to the President for signature. The President has the power to send a bill to the Supreme Court for its legal opinion, if the President believes that the Bill could conflict with our constitution. (It is rare for the President to do this, however.) Once signed by the President, the bill becomes an Act and it is now the law. The case study (below) on the Gender Recognition Act 2015 provides a useful example of the entire process.

Fig. 5.33 A bill becomes law when the President signs it

QUESTIONS

1. Explain the process involved in the development of national policy. Make specific reference to the following:
   - (a) Green Paper
   - (b) Public consultation
   - (c) Research institutes
   - (d) White Paper.

2. Explain the following terms:
   - (a) Primary legislation
   - (b) Secondary legislation
   - (c) Statutory instrument.

3. What is the difference between a bill and an Act?
4. List and describe the main stages that a bill goes through to become an Act.
5. What are the benefits of the committee system?
6. Is the party whip system undemocratic? How does it impact on the role of a TD? In your answer, refer to the views of James Madison and Edmund Burke on page 75.

CASE STUDY 1: Gender Recognition: From a Bill to an Act

In 2015, Ireland introduced a law that provided legal means and protection for citizens to select their preferred gender. The Gender Recognition Act 2015 provides an interesting example of the steps and time involved in developing a piece of primary legislation in Ireland.

A Matter of Human Rights

In 2007 the European Commissioner for Human Rights, Thomas Hammarberg, urged member states to ensure that transgender citizens could select their preferred gender. Ireland was among the last countries in the EU to permit legal recognition of transgender people. In the same year in Ireland, a transgender Irish citizen, Dr Lydia Foy, took a case to the

Fig. 5.34 In 2015, Ireland introduced the Gender Recognition Act

POLICY-MAKING **167**

Case Study: Gender Recognition: From a Bill to an Act

High Court because the state would not provide her with a new birth certificate for her preferred gender. The High Court ruled against the state and confirmed that the state had failed to comply with its obligations under the European Convention on Human Rights (ECHR). Because of this High Court ruling, Ireland now needed to make a new law.

First Steps Towards Preparing a Government Bill

In May 2010 the Minister for Social Protection set up the Gender Recognition Advisory Group (GRAG) to look at the issue. GRAG held consultations, conducted research and published a report in 2011. The report outlined a proposal, including criteria for permitting legal gender recognition.

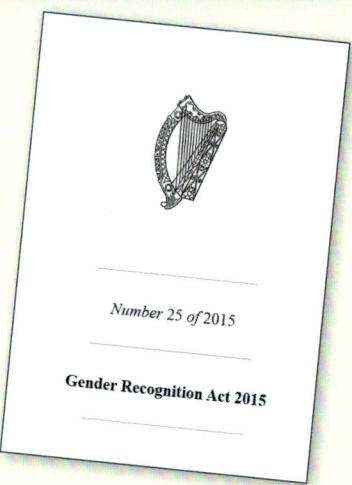

Fig. 5.35 Gender Recognition Act 2015

Civil Society Lobbying

Civil society groups, such as Transgender Equality Network Ireland (TENI), criticised the report. Of particular concern to the groups was the requirement that a medical diagnosis be one of the criteria, and that the law would only cover unmarried transgender individuals.

Private Members' Bills

In 2013, because of delays in the development of the government bill, two private members' bills were introduced. In the Dáil, on 23 May 2013, Deputy Aengus Ó Snodaigh launched his Gender Recognition Bill 2013. It was modelled on Argentinian legislation and would allow individuals to 'self-declare' their preferred gender. In the Seanad, on 27 June 2013, Senator Katherine Zappone launched the Legal Recognition of Gender Bill 2013. TENI had worked with Senator Zappone on the drafting of her bill. This bill would make the rights available to all transgender and intersex people, irrespective of their marital or civil partnership status. The introduction of the two bills put pressure on the government to take action.

Draft Heads of Bill

In July 2013, the Minister for Social Protection finally published the draft Heads of Bill. This was sent for review to the Joint Oireachtas Committee on Education and Social Protection. In September 2013, the committee requested written submissions from groups and individuals, and also held two days of public hearings in October. The committee then published its report in January 2014. The report highlighted some weaknesses in the draft Heads of Bill, and was debated in the Dáil by TDs and the minister.

Gender Recognition Bill 2014

In June 2014, the Minister for Social Protection received cabinet approval for a revised Heads of Bill, and this was published. The revised version addressed many of the concerns raised by civil society groups and TDs, including a process for 16- and 17-year-olds to seek legal recognition, and the removal of the phrase 'medical diagnosis'. The general scheme of the bill was then referred to the Office of the Parliamentary Counsel for drafting. The Gender Recognition Bill 2014 was published in December 2014.

CASE STUDY: Gender Recognition: From a Bill to an Act

Seanad Debate

The Gender Recognition Bill was introduced in the Seanad on 21 January 2015 for the second stage debate, which continued to a second debate on 28 January. The bill entered committee stage on 3 February and was debated over two days. The bill entered the final/report stage on 17 February and was passed. In this process, a review clause was included in the legislation and the words 'medical evaluation' were removed.

Dáil Debate

On 5 March the Gender Recognition Bill was then debated in the Dáil. This was a historic moment: 26 TDs from all parties spoke on the bill. All TDs broadly welcomed the introduction of the legislation but called on the government to improve the bill. TDs from constituencies across Ireland spoke on the bill, including Independents (9) and members of Fine Gael (8), Labour (4), Sinn Féin (4) and Fianna Fáil (1). TDs criticised several elements of the bill, such as the requirement that a medical practitioner affirm an applicant's identity, the need for applicants to be single, and the exclusion of young transgender and intersex people.

Review of the Bill

The Minister agreed to review the bill. On 3 June, it was announced that transgender people over the age of 18 would be able to self-declare their gender identity and there would be no requirement of certification from a medical practitioner. The bill was revised in the select sub-committee meeting on 17 June and all medical criteria for individuals over 18 was removed.

Gender Recognition Act 2015

By 15 July 2015 the Gender Recognition Bill had been approved by both houses of the Oireachtas and was sent to the President for signature.

RESEARCH ASSIGNMENT 5.10

Choose one law that affects young people in Ireland today. (You may choose the law your group worked on in Research Assignment 5.2.) Using the archives at **www.oireachtas.ie**, write a report on the process involved in developing this law. Write a report that covers the following points:

- Name and description of the law
- Date when the law was first introduced to the Oireachtas as a bill, and by whom
- Influencers involved: describe the input of any civil society bodies, media or lobbyists who may have influenced the development of the law
- Stages of development in the Oireachtas: list the dates when the bill went through each stage, describe the nature of the Dáil debates, identify the committee recommendations and any amendments proposed
- Outcome: evaluate the extent to which the law addressed the concerns of all the main groups in society, and whether or not the law is successful today.

See RESEARCH TIPS on page 144.

Complete your next Reflective Journal entry (pages 19–20)

EU Legislation

Process

The most common process for making EU legislation is called the *ordinary legislative procedure* — also known as the *co-decision procedure*. The European Parliament and the Council of the EU have equal power, and the laws passed using this procedure are joint acts of the Council and the Parliament. It applies to the majority of EU legislation, covering a wide range of areas, such as consumer rights, environmental protection and transport. Under the ordinary legislative procedure, the Commission makes a proposal which must be approved by both the Parliament and the Council.

Fig. 5.36 The most common process for making EU legislation is called the ordinary legislative procedure

Policy Areas

The EU treaties (agreements) list the policy areas in which the EU can take decisions. In some policy areas, the EU has exclusive responsibility, which means that decisions are taken at EU level by the member states meeting in the Council and the European Parliament. These policy areas cover trade, customs, competition rules, monetary policy for the euro area, and the conservation of fish. In other policy areas, the decision-making competences are shared between the EU and the member states. This means that if legislation is passed at EU level, then these laws have priority. However, if no legislation is adopted at EU level, then individual member states may make their own laws at national level. Shared responsibility applies in many policy areas, such as the internal market, agriculture, the environment, consumer protection and transport.

Fig. 5.37 Shared responsibility applies in many policy areas within the EU

Types of EU Laws and Policies

There are several types of legislation, which are applied in different ways.

- A **regulation** is a law that member states are obliged to implement directly. It does not need to be passed into national law by the Oireachtas, although changes to existing national laws might be required to avoid conflict with the regulations. An example of a regulation is the 2011 Regulation on the provision of food information to consumers. With this regulation, we now have a common approach to food labelling across the EU.

- A **directive** is a law that requires the member states to achieve a particular objective (e.g. ending discrimination based on race or ethnic origin) but without stating *how* this is to be done. Directives normally require the development of legislation by the Oireachtas.

- A **decision** is a rule that is normally made jointly by the European Parliament and the Council of the EU. Sometimes the power to make decisions is delegated to the Commission. Decisions can be made in relation to a member state or an individual (e.g. in 2004 a decision was made against Microsoft for being anti-competitive). In other cases, decisions are not legislative/law (e.g. when decisions are made by the European Council, the Council of the EU or the Commission).

- **Recommendations and opinions** are sometimes issued from the EU. Member states are not obliged to follow these, but recommendations and opinions can often be influential in subsequent policy-making. In 2016 the European Commission issued an opinion that Ireland had given the tech company Apple special treatment in relation to taxes.

ACTIVITY 5.3

Go to the EUR-Lex (Access to European Union law) website at **https://educateplus.ie/go/eu-law** and use the search engine to find summaries of the following EU legislation:

- Good-quality water in Europe (EU Water Directive) – (Directive 2000/60/EC): **https://educateplus.ie/go/water-directive**
- Promotion of the use of energy from renewable sources (Directive 2009/28/EC): **https://educateplus.ie/go/renewable**
- Education and skills agenda for young people (Communication 2010/477): **https://educateplus.ie/go/education-skills**
- Tackling the pay gap between men and women (Communication 2007/424): **https://educateplus.ie/go/pay-gap**
- The corrective arm: the excessive deficit procedure (Council Regulation (EC) No 1467/97): **https://educateplus.ie/go/corrective-arm**

Read the summaries and answer the following questions:

1. What aspects of these EU laws do you agree with? Why?
2. What aspects of these EU laws do you disagree with? Why?
3. What impact do these laws have on Irish sovereignty?
4. Should limits be imposed on the extent to which the EU can influence national policy and legislation in Ireland? In what areas should the Irish government retain complete sovereignty?

Tip: Focus on the 'Key Points' in each of the online summaries

Secondary Legislation

Sometimes we need additional rules regarding exactly how different national policies and laws will be implemented. For example, exactly what rules must we have in place to protect our land, seas and air according to the primary laws we have in relation to the environment? Such decisions result in what is known as secondary legislation or **statutory instruments**.

KEY TERM

A **statutory instrument** is a tool used by government to make secondary legislation. Examples include regulations for speed limits on our roads and regulations for food hygiene practices. There are five types of statutory instruments: orders, regulations, rules, by-laws and schemes.

Government ministers approve secondary legislation that is created by government departments and public agencies/bodies. Government Departments and public agencies/bodies have the power to make secondary legislation to allow for the implementation of existing national policies and laws. They cannot, however, make new laws: this is the role of the Oireachtas. For example, the Minister for the Environment cannot make a regulation on waste collection permits (secondary legislation) without there being a Waste Management Act (primary legislation). Statutory instruments are commonly used by ministers to ensure that Ireland complies with new EU laws. City councils and county councils also produce secondary legislation, known as by-laws, to deal with local issues (e.g. local parks, beaches).

Examples of Secondary Legislation in Ireland

We need rules to implement our main laws across a range of issues. These rules come in many forms: orders, regulations, rules, by-laws and schemes. Secondary legislation cannot exist without a primary law. In Ireland, our primary laws come from national and European levels. Below are some examples of secondary legislation in Ireland:

- **Student Grant Scheme 2016:** The scheme outlines financial support arrangements available for students at third level. The primary law is the Student Support Act 2011.

- **Irish Water Customer Registration Order 2015:** The order requires citizens to register their households with Irish Water. The primary law is the Water Services Act 2014.

- **Social Welfare and Pensions Order 2014:** The order established the Pension Authority and the Pensions Council to regulate pensions and provide advice to the Minister of Social Protection on pension matters. The primary law is the Social Welfare and Pensions Act 2016.

- **Road Traffic (National Car Test) Regulations 2014:** The regulation allows car owners to put their car through the NCT car test any time before the normal NCT due date for their car. Before this regulation, cars could not take the test earlier than 90 days prior to the due date. The primary laws are the Road Traffic Act 2006 and a series of laws from the EU between 1996 and 2009.

Process

The main laws in our country identify who has the power to make secondary legislation in any given area. For example, the Health Insurance Act, 1994 gives the Minister for Health powers to make rules on the health insurance system in Ireland. In addition, the European Communities Act, 1972 (the law which formally made Ireland a part of the EU) states that ministers have the power to issue any legislation that is needed to ensure that Ireland complies with EU law. Apart from ministers, certain institutions in Ireland have the power to make secondary legislation, e.g. the Commission for Telecommunications Regulation (ComReg), the Law Society, and the Medical Council.

The processes of making secondary legislation can differ greatly. Sometimes the process involves public consultation and sometimes not. Once a statutory instrument has been finalised, the minister passes it to the Dáil. Unless it is revoked, it is considered as 'passed' within 21 days. In this sense, the Oireachtas plays a somewhat passive role in secondary legislation. However, both the Dáil and Seanad can cancel secondary legislation by a simple majority.

Complete your next Reflective Journal entry (pages 19–20)

> **QUESTIONS**
>
> 1. What is the difference between primary legislation and secondary legislation?
> 2. Why is secondary legislation needed?
> 3. Why does secondary legislation not go through the same lengthy process as primary legislation?
> 4. Is there a danger that ministers could abuse their power to use statutory instruments to pass controversial legislation without debate?

Citizen Participation in Decision-Making

'Active citizenship requires the will and the opportunity to participate at every level and in every way – to be the arrow; not the target.' President Michael D. Higgins

The role of the citizen does not end with voting. In a representative democracy, we elect members of government to make the laws and policies that safeguard our interests and protect our rights. However, many modern democracies recognise the need to facilitate continued citizen participation in policy-making. Citizen participation in decision-making can be viewed as both a right (the right to be involved in decision-making on issues that affect us) and as a means to ensure the policies developed by government best respond to the needs of society and the realities faced by citizens (the citizen is an invaluable source of information). There are many ways in which citizens can influence policy-making, including direct contact with their local TD, senator or MEP. To be effective in influencing policy-making and decision-making, citizens must use their skills and give careful consideration to the most appropriate strategy. Sometimes, formal public consultations are held, which provide an opportunity for people to have their say on a policy issue. Deliberative democracy is currently very popular among democratic theorists.

> See page 21 for more information on deliberative democracy.

Deliberative democracy is based on the belief that ongoing public debate should form a central part of policy-making. Sometimes, however, it is not possible or effective for citizens to have their views on policy-making heard through the official and formal routes. This may be because the issue is not yet viewed as a priority by policy-makers. It may be because the issue is a controversial one and decision-makers are not quite ready to listen. In such cases, citizens can make use of a range of methods to create their own space to influence policy, e.g. public protests, petitioning and social media campaigns.

SKILLS BOOK LINK 5.6

Go to pages 84–85 of your Skills Book to complete Skill Task 5.6 on active citizenship.

KEY THINKERS

POLITICAL REPRESENTATION

Revise the Key Thinkers box on page 76 to help you with these questions.

Thomas Hobbes | **John Locke** | **Montesquieu** | **Jean-Jacques Rousseau** | **Karl Marx**

QUESTIONS

1. Which of the key thinkers would be against the idea of direct citizen participation in national policy-making? Explain.
2. Which of the key thinkers would be in favour of some form of deliberative democracy? Explain.
3. Compare and contrast the views of Locke, Montesquieu and Rousseau. Which view is most relevant to the way in which laws are passed in Ireland today?
4. Rousseau argues for the direct participation of all citizens in the development of national laws. How practicable is this? How could this be achieved in Ireland today?
5. Which view do you most agree with? Why?

Citizen Voice in Irish Policy-Making

In addition to formal public consultations on national policies, there are several government initiatives to promote citizen voice in policy-making at national and local levels.

National

Citizens' Assembly and the Constitutional Convention

Deliberative democracy is based on the idea that ongoing citizen discussion and debate on issues affecting society and policy-making will improve democracy. Many countries have experimented with different forms of deliberative democracy (e.g. the G1000 group in Belgium, the National Assembly of Iceland, the Power Inquiry in Britain, and AmericaSpeaks in the US).

Ireland's first experience of a citizens' assembly took place in 2011, at a time when the government was looking at changes we might need to make to our constitution. A group called We The Citizens organised a meeting of 100 randomly selected citizens over the age of 18 for a weekend of deliberations. The Citizens' Assembly took place in June 2011. Participants discussed and debated upcoming political and constitutional reforms on issues such as the economy, the role of the Seanad, and women's representation in politics. The format of the assembly influenced the design of a subsequent Constitutional Convention organised by the Irish government in 2012 to discuss proposed changes (amendments) to the Constitution of Ireland. The convention had 100 members: a chairperson; 29 members of the Oireachtas; four representatives of Northern Ireland political parties; and 66 randomly selected citizens of Ireland. At the convention, a total of 10 issues were discussed, eight of which were pre-determined by the government. The government was not obliged to act on the recommendations of the convention, but it was obliged to provide a formal response. Two of the convention's proposals were put to a referendum in May 2015: the proposal to legalise same-sex marriage and the proposal to reduce the age of eligibility for the presidency from 35 to 21.

Fig. 5.38 We The Citizens

Dáil na nÓg

Dáil na nÓg is the national parliament for young people aged 12–18 years. The Department of Children and Youth Affairs funds and hosts it every two years as part of the National Youth Strategy and in response to its obligations under the United Nations Convention on the Rights of the Child (UNCRC). The event is attended by delegates from across the country who are selected by their local youth councils (Comhairle na nÓg). Comhairle na nÓg is an organisation of child and youth councils in the 31 local authority areas of Ireland. Dáil na nÓg provides young people with an opportunity to have their voices heard on matters of importance to them. Past Dáil na nÓg events have been attended by ministers, such as the Minister for Education. The main recommendation from the 2015 event was that young people should have more say in what happens in the classroom and in school decision-making.

Dáil na nÓg has had some impact in terms of influencing policy. For example, in 2010 the Minister for Health took on board a recommendation to start the cervical cancer vaccine programme for 12-year-old girls.

Fig. 5.39 Dáil na nÓg

Local

Fingal County Council's Online Consultation Portal

Since 2015, Fingal County Council in Dublin has been facilitating ongoing public consultations on proposed local policies through its website **(https://educateplus.ie/go/consult-fingal)**. The consultation portal is based on a project developed by TCD, UCC and Kilkenny County Council called SOWIT (Social Web for Inclusive and Transparent democracy). The council has used the portal to enable citizens to have a voice in relation to local policies on issues such as economic planning, housing development projects and traffic measures. Citizens and civil society organisations that register on the website can have direct input into local policies through discussion in online forums. They can also participate in formal consultations, presenting their views in relation to a planned project or policy. During the council meetings, time is allocated to discuss the forum discussions and responses to consultations. The feedback from the council is then posted to the website.

Fig. 5.40 Fingal County Council's Online Consultation Portal

Public Participation Networks (PPNs)

To encourage and support greater citizen and community participation in decision-making at the local level in Ireland, the Local Government Reform Act 2014 established Public Participation Networks (PPNs). The PPNs provide a space for organisations (such as environmental, social inclusion, community and voluntary groups) to discuss issues of importance to the community with the local authorities. PPNs have now been established in every local authority area in Ireland. PPNs are relatively new but are beginning to influence the decision-making of local authorities.

QUESTIONS

1. Do you think that the Citizens' Assembly is a positive development for Irish democracy? Will it lead to better policy-making? What are the benefits of having a Citizens' Assembly?

2. What are the weaknesses of the Citizens' Assembly? How representative is it? Could the Assembly be prone to lobbying or the influence of others? In your opinion, is there a concern that certain groups could be excluded?

3. Conduct online research to see what issue is currently being discussed by the Citizens' Assembly. How much should the Assembly be allowed to influence decision-making on this issue? Why?

4. Why is Dáil na nÓg an important government initiative? How could its influence be strengthened?

5. Should online consultation forums, similar to Fingal County Council's Online Consultation Portal, be adopted at national level? How could they be used in the development of national policy-making and law-making?

6. Does a Public Participation Network exist in your area? Do you know of any local authority decisions it has successfully influenced?

7. Examine the Ladder of Participation (Fig. 2.10 on page 53) and the Pyramid of Student Voice (Fig. 2.13 on page 55). At what stage and level is each of the following:
   (a) Citizens' Assembly
   (b) Dáil na nÓg
   (c) PPN?

CASE STUDY 2: Creating Our Own Space to Influence Policy

Sometimes the space does not yet exist to raise our particular issue of concern. Sometimes a space does exist, but a particular group may be excluded from participating in it. In such cases, citizens and civil society bodies can take several different actions to have their voices heard.

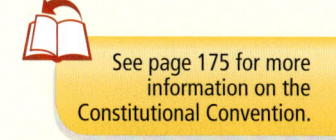

Bringing Young Voices into the Constitutional Convention

See page 175 for more information on the Constitutional Convention.

The Constitutional Convention organised by the government in 2012 did not involve young people. Participants had to be over 18 years of age. Two civil society bodies working with young people, Youth Work Ireland and the Voices of Youth Group, decided to create a space for young people to have their say. The Children's and Young People's Constitutional Convention was held on 20 April 2013, with 50 young people from around Ireland. The chairperson of the government's Constitutional Convention attended the event to listen to the views of young people. The young

Fig. 5.41 Bringing young voices into the Constitutional Convention

CASE STUDY: Creating Our Own Space to Influence Policy

people discussed and voted on the same eight proposed constitutional amendments that were the focus of the government convention, including lowering the voting age to 16, legalising same-sex marriage, and increasing the participation of women in politics. In addition, young people requested that several other issues be discussed at the government convention (e.g. making free education a reality, and reviewing abortion laws). Representatives from the Children's and Young People's Constitutional Convention were subsequently invited to the Constitutional Convention to present the views of young people.

CASE STUDY 3: Protest, People Power and Water Charges

A series of large public protests in Ireland in 2014 and 2015 on the introduction of water charges led to eventual changes in government policy on the matter. Following the economic crash, the Irish government signed a bailout agreement in 2010 with the EU, International Monetary Fund (IMF) and the European Central Bank (ECB) – the so-called Troika. Part of the agreement included the requirement that the Irish government would introduce water charges. The Water Services (No.2) Bill 2013 was rushed through all stages in the Dáil in a record time of four hours on 19 December 2013. Public discontent grew as

Fig. 5.42 The Right2Water campaign was established in September 2014

the media reported the high cost of government spending to set up the water charge system and the body responsible for managing the system: Irish Water. Small protests on the installation of water meters began to take place in communities across Ireland. As public discontent and opposition to water charges grew, the Right2Water campaign was established in September 2014. The campaign was made up of citizens, activists, community groups, political parties and trade unionists calling for the government to recognise access to water as a human right and to abolish water charges. Right2Water started its campaign with a petition and collected over 35,000 signatures. This was followed by a national protest in Dublin in October 2014. Over 80,000 people participated. At the same time, many households refused to register with Irish Water, which was a requirement of the new law. On 1 November one of the largest public protests in Irish history took place: over 100 demonstrations took place and over 150,000 people participated. As a result, on 19 November the government announced that charges would be reduced. However, protests continued into 2015. Water charges became a key election issue in the 2016 General Election. The new government voted to suspend water charges for 9 months until March 2017. An expert commission was established to review the water charges issue and to make recommendations for how to fund water services in the future. The Right2Water campaign has been criticised by the government for some of its tactics, such as the harassment of some Irish Water personnel attempting to install water meters, and the treatment received by then Tánaiste Joan Burton, who was forced to lock herself in her car at a water protest. However, the water protests were mainly peaceful with significant nationwide support.

Fig. 5.43 Right2Water demonstrators

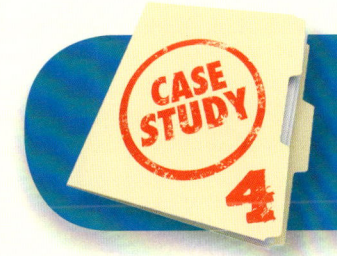

CASE STUDY 4: Uplift – Pledge a Bed for Refugees

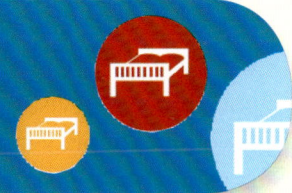

Online and social media (e.g. Facebook, Twitter) can be powerful tools for raising issues and pushing for political change. A famous and recent example is the success of the Yes campaign for the 2015 Marriage Equality referendum in Ireland. Another interesting case is the 2015 Pledge A Bed online campaign run by Uplift in the wake of increasing numbers of refugees from war-torn countries seeking refuge in Ireland. Uplift is an Irish campaigning organisation that enables thousands of people to take action on a variety of social justice issues. In 2015, in an attempt to push the Irish government to adopt a policy to increase refugee numbers entering Ireland, Uplift allowed Irish citizens to register on its website an offer of accommodation for refugees. In just a few days, over 14,000 offers of beds were made. A further 38,000 people signed an online petition calling on Taoiseach Enda Kenny 'to commit to allowing thousands not hundreds of refugees seek refuge in Ireland'. Hundreds of people paid for a full page ad in a national newspaper as a powerful way to deliver the campaign's message to the government. As a result of the public outcry and the coordinated action taken by Uplift, the government quickly agreed to increase the number of refugees allowed in Ireland from 600 to 4,000.

Fig. 5.44 Uplift's Pledge A Bed campaign

Uplift also supports citizens to run their own petitions and campaigns through its website: **www.myuplift.ie**. Uplift members in Co. Clare successfully campaigned to get Clare County Council to pass a motion against a trade deal called TTIP being negotiated within the EU. If approved, TTIP could mean that many of the protections of health, environment and other rights in EU member states could be set aside in trade agreements with the US. Other campaigns that are popular on **www.myuplift.ie** are the Love Not Hate campaign (which calls for the introduction of legislation in Ireland on the issue of hate crimes), campaigns for animal rights and campaigns on environmental issues.

QUESTIONS

1. Describe the different strategies used by the participants in each of the case studies (above) to ensure that their voices were heard.
2. Which strategy, do you think, is the most effective? Why?
3. What are the advantages and disadvantages of using public protest to influence government decisions?
4. Explain how social media can be used to influence government decisions.

ACTIVITY 5.4

With your group, choose one issue that you believe needs to be immediately addressed by the government. Devise a citizenship project that your group could carry out to positively influence government policy in this area. Include the following in your project:

- Description of the issue: refer to available statistics and evidence to highlight the extent of the problem.
- Solution(s) to the issue: explain the rationale for your proposed solution
- Ideas for action: explain the strategy and tactics to be adopted and list the specific objectives
- Plan of action: include a step-by-step guide of all the actions to be taken, and a realistic timeframe for them
- Evaluation: include guidelines for assessing the success of your citizenship project.

Refer to the following two boxes to help you create this citizenship project.

ACTIVE CITIZENSHIP: Ideas for Action

Citizenship Project – Ideas for Action!

Citizens can take many actions to raise a concern with decision-makers or to influence a change in policy. The issue can be national or local (e.g. in our school or community). Below are some examples of actions that can be taken by citizens. Can you use any of these actions in your citizenship project for Activity 5.4?

- Conduct a survey or do research to find out more about an issue or problem.
- Organise a 'public hearing' or meeting on an issue and invite the relevant decision-maker(s) to attend.
- Write letters/articles for newspapers/magazines and write social media posts to raise awareness.
- Start a petition.
- Start a social media campaign.
- Write letters to elected representatives.
- Attend community meetings to gain information, discuss issues and lend support to other campaigners.
- Attend or watch Oireachtas debates and committee hearings.
- If there is a public consultation on your issue, make a submission to it.
- Contact your local PPN to have your issue discussed at city/county council meetings.
- Demonstrate through marches, boycotts, sit-ins or other forms of protest.
- Design your own solution to the problem and implement it. Be the change you want to see!

Ingredients for Successful Policy Influencing

- **Good communication skills:** It is vital to have the ability to clearly and respectfully communicate your concern or proposal.
- **Evidence-based argument:** The person you are trying to influence will want to know that you have done your research. Back up your argument with facts and figures!

- **Motivation:** Try to find out what might motivate the decision-maker to take the desired action. Will they be rewarded with positive public attention as a result? Is there an upcoming election for which your vote might be sought? Is it in the interests of the decision-maker to listen to your views?
- **Planning:** Successful campaigns are based on strong planning. Have a clear and realistic goal and evaluate the best strategies to achieve it.

SKILLS BOOK LINK 5.7

Go to page 86 of your Skills Book to complete Skill Task 5.7 on the roles of stakeholders in decision-making at national level.

ACTIVITY 5.5

Your teacher will call out eleven statements concerning policy-making and decision-making at national level. You will take part in a moving debate where you express your opinion on each of the arguments put forward.

SKILLS BOOK LINK 5.8

Go to pages 87–88 of your Skills Book to complete Skill Task 5.8 on policy-making and decision-making at national level.

ACTIVITY 5.6

Hold a classroom debate on the following motion:

'It is time for a radical overhaul of the decision-making processes at national level: the voices of ordinary citizens are not being listened to by the executive.'

Civil society Secondary legislation Primary legislation Bill Deliberative democracy Minority government Act Civil society Bill Act Bill Statutory instrument Lobbyist State agency Citizen participation Act Bill Citizen action Act Primary legislation

Fig. 5.45 Key Word cloud

POLICY-MAKING 181

SUMMARY

- Public policy is a set of principles, guidelines and regulatory measures adopted by the executive branch of government when it acts to address the needs of its citizens.
- Public policy may or may not result in new legislation.
- Various actors are involved in the policy-making process at national level. These actors can be categorised into decision-makers and influencers.
- Decision-makers are directly involved in the creation and implementation of national policy. Decision-makers include the government, the civil service and statutory bodies.
- Influencers attempt to shape and influence the nature of national policies. Influencers include political parties, the media, research institutes, civil society bodies and lobbyists.
- When a *majority government* is formed in Ireland, the Taoiseach and his or her Cabinet of Ministers will have greater autonomy to implement their policies and create the laws they desire, without much scrutiny from the Oireachtas (once these policies are constitutional).
- When a *minority government* is formed (as occurred after the 2016 General Election), the government will need the support of the opposition to pass laws. Therefore, government policies will tend to focus on issues of national consensus.
- For a bill to become a law, it goes through six stages in the Oireachtas:
  1. **Permission to publish:** After cabinet approval of the *Heads of Bill*, the bill is drafted in detail, published and formally presented to the Oireachtas.
  2. **Debate stage:** The bill is debated in either the Dáil or Seanad, depending on which house it is introduced to first.
  3. **Committee stage:** A special *select committee* or *joint committee* will be tasked with examining the bill in detail and developing a report with recommendations. It is during this stage that relevant members of the public, interest groups and civil society bodies will be invited to make representations.
  4. **Report stage:** The committee presents to the Dáil/Seanad its position and its proposed changes to the bill. A general discussion is held and proposed amendments are voted on.
  5. **Final voting stage:** A debate is held on the final content of the bill. This is followed by a vote to accept or reject it. Once the bill is passed in one house, it is sent to the other house for approval.
  6. **President signs:** The President signs the bill into law if he or she deems it to be constitutional.
- The institutions of the EU pass laws that affect Ireland through a process known as *co-decision*, whereby the European Parliament and the Council of the EU share equal power to vote on and pass/reject any laws proposed by the Commission.
- EU treaties are implemented through various types of EU laws, some of which are binding on member states and some of which are not. EU legislation includes regulations, directives, decisions and recommendations.
- Secondary legislation is passed by the executive using *statutory instruments*. Secondary legislation implements the aims of the primary legislation.

REVISION QUESTIONS

1. Explain the term 'public policy'.
2. List **five** different sources of information that can be used to research public policy.
3. What is the difference between a policy and a law?
4. Compare and contrast the views of any **two** key thinkers on the development of public policy.
5. Identify all the main institutions, groups and bodies involved in the policy-making process in Ireland. Briefly explain their respective roles in the process.
6. In relation to policy-making, what is the difference between a Green Paper and a White Paper?
7. What is a minority government? What impact does it have on the nature of law-making in the Oireachtas?
8. What is the difference between primary legislation and secondary legislation?
9. What is a statutory instrument?
10. What is the difference between a bill and an Act?
11. Describe the various stages that a bill must go through to become an Act.
12. Describe the process of policy development and law-making in the EU.
13. Explain the following terms in relation to the EU:
    - (a) Regulation
    - (b) Directive
    - (c) Decision
    - (d) Recommendation.
14. What is deliberative democracy? Give examples of deliberative democracy in Ireland.
15. List the various ways in which you can become actively involved in influencing national policy-making in Ireland today.

DATA-BASED QUESTIONS

Complete the qualitative and quantitative research data-based questions exercise on pages 89–91 of your Skills Book.

EXAM FOCUS — Section B of LC Exam

REVISION EXERCISES

Complete the revision exercises on pages 92–94 of your Skills Book.

EXAM FOCUS — Section A of LC Exam

DISCURSIVE ESSAY TOPICS

1. The Irish policy-making system involves many actors. Examine the role(s) of each actor and critically assess which actor(s) have the most power and influence. Support your answer with relevant facts and evidence.

2. Examine the process and effectiveness of national policy-making in Ireland with reference to at least **one** policy you have studied.

3. How effective is the Irish system of policy-making in representing the will of all the Irish people? Support your answer with reference to different viewpoints and evidence.

4. 'In Ireland, the government develops policies and laws to protect the most vulnerable groups in society (e.g. the elderly and the poor).' Do you agree with this statement? Support your answer with relevant examples and evidence.

EXAM FOCUS — Section C of LC Exam

Reflective Practice

Ensure that you have completed all the Reflective Journal entries for this chapter (pages 19–20 of your Reflective Journal and Learning Portfolio) before moving on to the next chapter.

Complete the Learning Portfolio activities on pages 20–22 of your Reflective Journal and Learning Portfolio. This will help you to self-assess the extent to which you have achieved the learning intentions for this chapter, and will help you to monitor your progress.

CHAPTER 6

The Role of the Media

'Were it left to me to decide whether we should have a government without newspapers or newspapers without a government, I should not hesitate for a moment to prefer the latter.'
Thomas Jefferson

KEY TERMS

- Media
- Social media
- Mass media
- Traditional media
- Digital media
- Content analysis
- Media consumption
- Watchdog
- Agenda-setting theory
- Framing
- Propaganda
- Stereotyping
- Freedom of the press
- Social responsibility
- Defamation
- Libel
- Gatekeepers
- Public service broadcaster
- Public relations (PR) companies
- Spin doctor
- Media consolidation
- Media pluralism

Introduction

The **media** plays an important role in society. It shapes our ideas and opinions, and can even influence government action and promote social change. Media is all around us: the shows we watch on television, the music we listen to on the radio, the newspapers we read, the websites we visit, and the **social media** we use. Society's use of media continues to evolve over time. We have several different media types, each with its own particular characteristics. The 'digital age' has given rise to new **mass media** forms which have transformed how content is developed, received and used. This era has challenged traditional definitions of audience: citizens have become

KEY TERMS

Media is the collective term used to describe all the main forms of communication (information, news, education, entertainment, etc.) in a society. **Social media** is technology such as websites and other applications which facilitate social networking and the creation and sharing of content among users. **Mass media** refers to the agencies that transmit this communication to large (mass) audiences.

both the consumers and the producers of media content. At the same time, **traditional media** still dominates. Traditional media outlets have adapted themselves to the digital age. This chapter will address many important questions on the role of the media in politics and society. Who controls information in the media? What role is played by advertising? How does the media present information to us? What impact can this have on society? In a democracy, we have certain expectations regarding how the media should act. Two important principles for media democracy are *freedom of the press*, and *social responsibility*. The role of the media in power and decision-making is a widely researched and debated topic.

> **KEY TERM**
>
> **Traditional media** (also known as 'old media') refers to any form of mass communication available before the advent of digital media. Traditional media includes books, newspapers, magazines, radio and television.

See page 208 for more information on freedom of the press and social responsibility.

By the end of this chapter you will be able to:

- List and define the various types of media, such as traditional media, digital media and social media.
- Describe the key characteristics of the main types of media in use today.
- Identify where media information originates.
- Identify who controls the information presented in various types of media.
- Explain modern-day media consumption patterns.
- Explain the function of the media and assess its role in society, with reference to Marxist, functionalist and feminist perspectives.
- Examine and evaluate the power of the media to influence public opinion and national politics, with reference to agenda-setting theory, framing techniques and stereotyping.
- Describe the democratic rights and responsibilities of the media, with reference to concepts such as freedom of the press, social responsibility and accountability.
- Examine the ownership and control of the media and explain how this impacts on media coverage and content.
- Assess the power of advertising and consumer-targeting strategies to shape ideas, reinforce social norms and promote certain ideologies over others.
- Describe the challenges of regulating the media.

By the end of this chapter you will have developed the following skills:

- Communication skills and the ability to present information and ideas verbally.
- Interpersonal skills and the ability to work effectively with small and large groups to reach agreed conclusions and achieve consensus.
- Research skills and information processing on issues linked to the role of the media in society.
- Critical and creative thinking skills in relation to the strengths, weaknesses and limitations of key pieces of research and ideological viewpoints on the role of the media.

ACTIVITY 6.1

Work with your partner to complete the following activity.

1. Think individually for a moment about the types of media that you consume in an average week. List all the types and rank them from 'used most often' to 'used least often'. *(Think)*

2. With your partner, compare your lists. Discuss the following questions. *(Pair)*
   - Which media type do you use most frequently? Why?
   - Which media type do you use least frequently? Why?
   - Is there any media type that you never use? If so, why?
   - Which media types are most accessible to you? Which are least accessible to you?
   - Which media types provide information that is most reliable? Which provide information that is least reliable?

3. Share your conclusions with the rest of the class. *(Share)*

ACTIVITY 6.2

Your teacher will read out several statements regarding the media. You will take part in a 'moving debate' where you express your opinion on each of the statements.

SKILLS BOOK LINK 6.1

Go to pages 95–96 of your Skills Book to complete Skill Task 6.1 on the media.

What is the Media?

Every day we hear the term 'media' used in conversations about politics and society. Who or what is 'the media'? The media is the collective term used to describe agencies involved in transmitting communication (concerning news, education, information, entertainment, advertising, etc.) to a large audience. There are three main types of media:

- **Print media:** newspapers, magazines, comics, books and print-based advertising (e.g. posters, billboards)
- **Broadcast media:** television, radio, cinema, DVDs and music
- **Digital media:** internet-based media, including interactive social networking sites such as Facebook and Twitter.

Print and broadcast media are sometimes referred to as 'traditional' media forms. Internet-based or digital forms are sometimes referred to as 'new media'. Each type of media has its own general characteristics.

> **KEY TERM**
>
> **Digital media** (also known as 'new media') refers to content that is used and stored via computer technology. The use of such technology (e.g. computer networks) makes digital media easier to share and distribute widely.

Media type	Key characteristics
Print	• Traditional media form • Newspapers, magazines, comics, books and print-based advertising • Multi-purpose: news, education, entertainment and advertising • Broadsheet newspaper: higher text content than image content. It usually provides detailed and in-depth analysis of major issues (e.g. *The Irish Times*). • Tabloid newspaper: smaller newspaper with higher image content than text content. It usually focuses on entertainment news and attention-grabbing headlines (e.g. *The Star*). • Advertising: high image content, with a focus on the product for sale • Costs for advertising: newspaper advertising costs less than other forms (e.g. billboards) • Low audience involvement in origination and display of content • Control and management of content is high
Broadcast	• Traditional media form • Television, radio, cinema, DVDs and music • Multi-purpose • Television is a powerful medium for appealing to mass audiences, reaching people regardless of age, sex, income or educational level • Television offers sight and sound, and makes dramatic and lifelike representations of people, lifestyles and products • Radio stations/programmes are normally differentiated on target audiences (listener age, taste and gender) • Audience involvement in content can be low (television) or medium (radio) • Control and management of content can be high (television) or medium (radio) • Costs for advertising can be high (television) or medium (radio)
Digital media	• New media form • Internet-based, including interactive online news (e.g. www.thejournal.ie, *The Guardian* newspaper online), news commentary and discussion forums • Social media: social networking sites (e.g. Facebook, Twitter) • Multi-purpose

RESEARCH ASSIGNMENT 6.1

Your group will be assigned one type of contemporary media (e.g. newspaper, television station, radio station, social media site). As a group, research the characteristics of the media type and create a table to display the following information:

- Geographic reach
- Target audience
- Sources of revenue
- Accessibility
- Strengths and weaknesses as a source of information

See **RESEARCH TIPS** on page 33.

SKILLS BOOK LINK 6.2

Go to pages 96–97 of your Skills Book to complete Skill Task 6.2 on the characteristics of **one** media type.

188 POWER AND PEOPLE

Researching the Mass Media: Content Analysis

The main method used by researchers to analyse media content is called **content analysis**. This can mean analysing text or visuals (images, photographs, etc.) in media reports. It involves counting the frequency of particular words, themes or images. For example, if a person is conducting research on how the media reports on crime within the Traveller community, they might search the content for terms such as 'crime' 'robbery' or 'Traveller'. Researchers analyse the content of media reports to identify themes and patterns. Researchers aim to point out the ways in which stories are presented, the use of certain words or phrases, etc.

> **KEY TERM**
>
> **Content analysis** is the main method used by researchers for analysing media reports (text or visuals). Content analysis often involves counting the frequency of words, themes or images.

Media Consumption Patterns

Fig. 6.1 Media consumption patterns

The invention of the printing press in the fifteenth century enabled some of the first forms of mass communication, through mass publication of books, newspapers and other print media. Historically, the newspaper was the main source of news and information in society. However, **media consumption** patterns have since evolved. New mass media forms emerged, such as radio in the 1920s, television in

> **KEY TERM**
>
> **Media consumption** describes the media that an individual or group uses in daily life. Research on media consumption patterns will focus on the different types of media we use as well as the purposes for which we use them.

THE ROLE OF THE MEDIA   189

the 1940s and the internet in the 1990s. Media consumption patterns identify the *types* of media used by society and the *purposes* for which they are being used. Print, audio-visual and digital media can be used by individuals in different ways. For example, we can use radio, television and digital media for information, entertainment, news, education, or a combination of these.

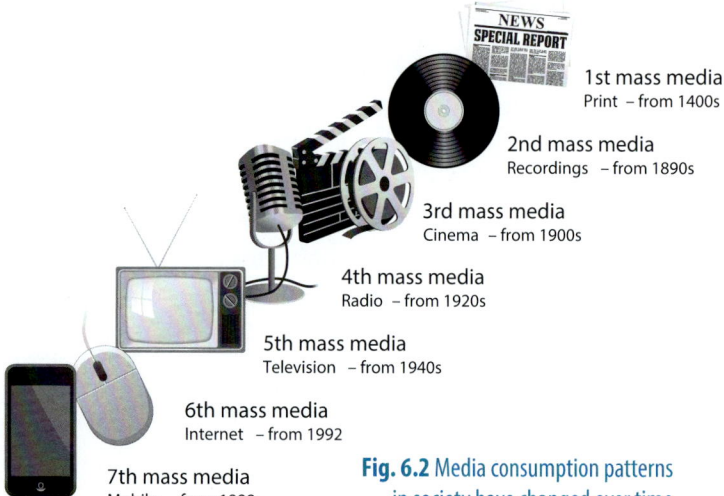

The media consumption patterns of a society can change over time. Nowadays, people may have a lower consumption of news from traditional forms, such as newspapers. People may be exposed to more advertising through social media sites, such as Twitter. All media types are multi-purpose; however, the way in which a media type presents and transmits information is influenced by its specific characteristics. If we analyse how the same news item (e.g. an election) is covered by television, radio, newspapers and social media networks, we start to see the differences between these media types. The type of media we use also impacts on the way we 'experience' information – whether that is in a passive or an interactive way.

1st mass media Print – from 1400s
2nd mass media Recordings – from 1890s
3rd mass media Cinema – from 1900s
4th mass media Radio – from 1920s
5th mass media Television – from 1940s
6th mass media Internet – from 1992
7th mass media Mobile – from 1998

Fig. 6.2 Media consumption patterns in society have changed over time

WHAT THE RESEARCH SAYS!

GLOBAL MEDIA CONSUMPTION PATTERNS

The Reuters Institute for the Study of Journalism is an international research centre in comparative journalism study at the University of Oxford. Each year, the institute produces an annual Digital News Report. The report is based on the largest comparative international survey that analyses changing news habits across 36 countries, including Ireland. Fig. 6.3 presents the global findings with respect to media sources of news between 2012 and 2016.

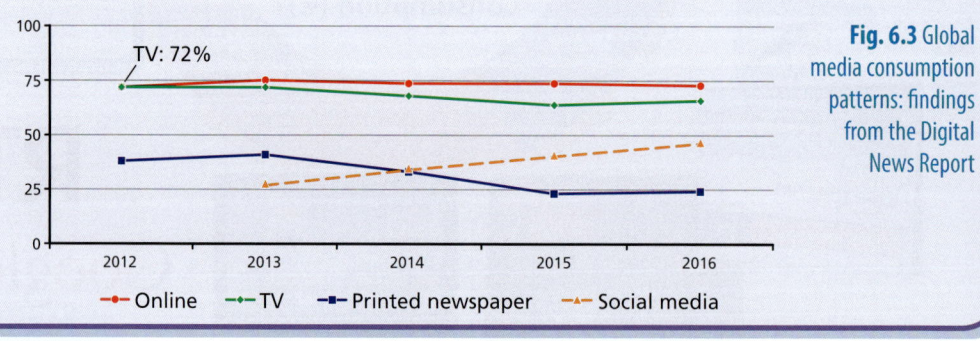

Fig. 6.3 Global media consumption patterns: findings from the Digital News Report

— Online   — TV   — Printed newspaper   — Social media

QUESTIONS

Examine Fig. 6.3 and answer the following questions.

1. Which media type was the most popular source of news in 2016?
2. Which media type suffered the biggest decline as a source of news?
3. Which media type witnessed the largest increase as a source of news?
4. What conclusions can be drawn in relation to traditional media versus new media?
5. What are the weaknesses and limitations of the above research?

Tips for Question 5:
- Visit **https://educateplus.ie/go/digital-news-report** to find a list of the countries surveyed in the Digital News Report from the Reuters Institute for the Study of Journalism – are they representative?
- Do the average figures disguise variations between and within countries?
- Are all the surveyed countries equally developed? Do they all have the same level of internet access/broadband coverage?

POWER AND PEOPLE

RESEARCH ASSIGNMENT 6.2

Go to **www.digitalnewsreport.org** to see the most recent Digital News Report from the Reuters Institute.

1. Summarise the main findings of the report.
2. Critically evaluate the methodology used by analysing the reliability of the data gathered and its limitations.
3. Write a summary on the main findings of the country-based report for Ireland.
4. Using the data in the report, draw a suitable graph to compare any **three** important statistics relating to news usage in:
   (a) Ireland
   (b) Two other named countries
   (c) The average of all countries combined.

Media Consumption: Social Media and the News

WHAT THE RESEARCH SAYS!

SOCIAL MEDIA AND NEWS CONSUMPTION IN THE US

The Pew Research Center is an independent think tank based in Washington DC that conducts public opinion polling, demographic research, content analysis and other data-driven social science research. The Journalism Project at the Pew Center conducted a series of surveys between 2013 and 2014 about how news is functioning within social media spaces (such as Twitter, Facebook and Reddit). Some of the main findings are listed here.

- Half of Facebook and Twitter users get news on those sites, as do 62 per cent of Reddit users.
- Only 34 per cent of Facebook news consumers 'like' a news organisation or individual journalist, which suggests that the news that Facebook users consume is coming from friends.

Fig. 6.4 Social media has a major impact on news consumption

THE ROLE OF THE MEDIA 191

- Facebook news consumers list 'entertainment news' as their most viewed news topic. This is followed by:
  - People and events in my community
  - Sports
  - National government and politics
  - Crime
  - Health and medicine
  - Local government and politics.
- Not only are social network users sharing (50 per cent) and discussing (46 per cent) news stories, but a certain proportion of users contribute to reporting by taking photos (14 per cent) or videos (12 per cent). This has given rise to what is called 'citizen journalism'.
- Regarding news and information about government and politics, Facebook users are more likely to post and respond to content. Twitter users are more likely to follow news organisations.
- Opinions expressed on Twitter do not always reflect broad public opinion. With respect to gun control, an analysis of Twitter conversations showed 64 per cent in favour of stricter gun control. This contrasts with the Pew Center's results from a public opinion poll during the same period, where 49 per cent of people surveyed were in favour of stricter gun control.
- Facebook is an important channel for bringing users to news sites, but people who come to a news site from Facebook spend on average less time per visit (1 minute 41 seconds) than those who visit it directly (4 minutes 36 seconds).

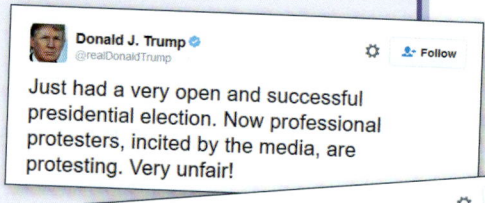

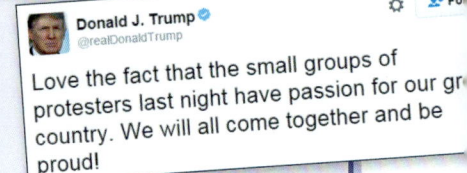

Fig. 6.5 Donald Trump's tweets regarding public protests on the result of the 2016 US election: immediately after he was elected US President (top) and a day later (bottom)

WHAT THE RESEARCH SAYS!

EUROBAROMETER – SOCIAL NETWORKS AND NEWS CONSUMPTION ACROSS THE EU

The Public Opinion Analysis sector of the European Commission has been monitoring the evolution of public opinion in the member states since 1973. Eurobarometer surveys track public opinion across a broad range of issue areas, including EU citizenship, EU enlargement, health, culture, information technology, environment, the euro, defence, etc. The Media Use in the European Union Eurobarometer report is published annually. It tracks media consumption patterns and levels of trust across the EU in relation to five different media types (television, radio, written press, the internet and online social networks). The reports present EU averages as well as the individual results from each country. The EU findings in relation to social networks from the 2015 report included the following.

- Television remains the main source of national political news (81 per cent). This is followed by:
  - Print (41 per cent)
  - Radio (41 per cent)
  - Internet (38 per cent)
  - Social networks (13 per cent).
- The majority of EU citizens agree that 'online social networks can get people interested in political affairs' (52 per cent agree; 22 per cent disagree).
- The majority also believe that online social networks are 'a good way to have your say on political issues' (51 per cent agree; 23 per cent disagree).
- The majority of EU citizens also say that 'information on political affairs from online social networks cannot be trusted' (47 per cent agree; 23 per cent disagree).
- EU citizens with the highest use of online social networks have a greater tendency to see these networks as 'politically relevant' (72 per cent agree; 52 per cent disagree) but also criticise their 'lack of reliability' (59 per cent agree; 47 per cent disagree).

WHAT THE RESEARCH SAYS!

PARTICIPATION IN THE NEWS – IRELAND

The Institute for Future Media and Journalism (FuJo) at Dublin City University (DCU) and the Broadcasting Authority of Ireland (BAI) produce an annual report based on the findings of the Digital News Report by the Reuters Institute. Part of this annual report examines how Irish people participate in news. The 2016 report found that 72 per cent of people share or participate in news coverage during an average week. Fig. 6.6 presents the different ways in which people participate in the news.

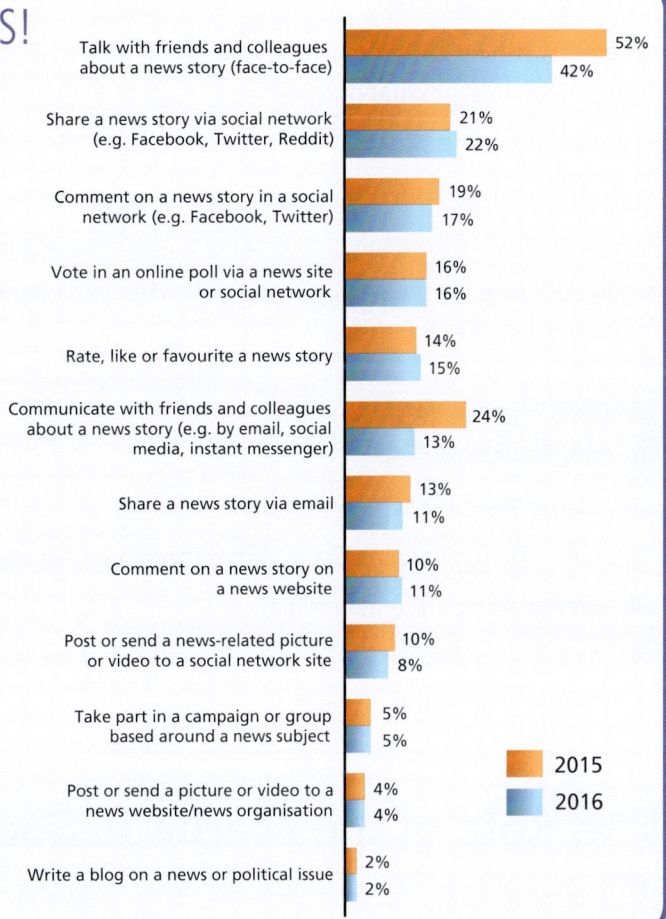

Activity	2015	2016
Talk with friends and colleagues about a news story (face-to-face)	52%	42%
Share a news story via social network (e.g. Facebook, Twitter, Reddit)	21%	22%
Comment on a news story in a social network (e.g. Facebook, Twitter)	19%	17%
Vote in an online poll via a news site or social network	16%	16%
Rate, like or favourite a news story	14%	15%
Communicate with friends and colleagues about a news story (e.g. by email, social media, instant messenger)	24%	13%
Share a news story via email	13%	11%
Comment on a news story on a news website	10%	11%
Post or send a news-related picture or video to a social network site	10%	8%
Take part in a campaign or group based around a news subject	5%	5%
Post or send a picture or video to a news website/news organisation	4%	4%
Write a blog on a news or political issue	2%	2%

Fig. 6.6 Irish media consumption patterns: findings from the Digital News Report

QUESTIONS

1. Look at the research piece on Social Media and News Consumption in the US. According to the Pew's Center's journalism surveys, how many Facebook and Twitter users report getting news from these respective sites?
2. What percentage of social media users share and discuss news stories via social media?
3. Many Facebook users access news sites through Facebook (e.g. by clicking on links/stories that have been shared with them). What is the average time that they spend on these news sites?
4. The Pew Center notes that 'citizen journalism' is on the rise. In your opinion, what are the benefits and dangers of this trend?
5. The Pew Center notes that opinions expressed on Twitter do not always reflect broad public opinion. Why might an analysis of social media posts not be an accurate indicator of broader public opinion?
6. What are the advantages and disadvantages of using Twitter as a source of news?
7. Look at the research piece on Social Networks and News Consumption Across the EU. According to the Eurobarometer report, what do most respondents believe to be the positive and negative aspects of social media news?
8. Look at the research piece on Participation in the News – Ireland. Apart from talking about a news story with friends face to face, what were the next **two** most popular ways in which Irish people actively participated in news in 2016?
9. Examine Fig. 6.6. List all the different ways in which you have ever participated in news.
10. In your opinion, what type of media is the most reliable when it comes to sourcing accurate information on politics or current affairs? Give a reason for your answer.

Complete your next Reflective Journal entry (pages 23–24)

ACTIVITY 6.3

Conduct a survey to find out what different types of media are used by students in your school and for what purposes.

- Work with your group to create a suitable list of questions/statements for the survey.
- Decide on how many students to survey (e.g. one class, one year group or the whole school).
- Agree on the best sampling method (e.g. random sampling or stratified sampling).
- After carrying out the survey, analyse the data and create a suitable presentation, with graphs and charts, to display the results.

QUESTIONS

1. Name the **three** types of media.
2. Describe the characteristics of the **three** types of media.
3. Define the term 'mass media'.
4. What is content analysis? Content analysis of the media is used for what purpose?
5. Write a paragraph on media consumption trends in Ireland.

The Role of the Media in Society

The media is an important institution in society and it plays several roles. It informs, educates and connects society. It gives us a wider view of the world, beyond our individual and family environments. Through the media, we can see different places around the world, learn about different cultures, and listen to the stories of different people without ever leaving home. The media distributes information about local, national and global politics. The media has a vital role to play in supporting a functioning democracy. In democratic societies, the media acts as a **watchdog** to ensure that governments and other sectors are acting ethically.

An independent media guarantees freedom of speech and gives a voice to ordinary people, including those from disadvantaged communities and minority groups. The media can ensure that governments consider public opinion during their decision-making processes. In the key thinkers box (page 195), we can see how the role of the media can be viewed from different sociological perspectives.

> **KEY TERM**
>
> A **watchdog** is a person or organisation that monitors the actions or behaviour of a person, organisation or situation to ensure they are not illegal or unethical.

Role of the Media

- Provides news and information
- Educates the public
- Supports democracy: informs the public about government policies; explains how these policies can be useful to citizens; acts as a channel for ordinary people to voice their concerns and opinions
- Acts as a watchdog: monitors the activities of different sectors of society
- Entertains people
- Connects people: locally, nationally and globally
- Promotes trade, commerce and industry through advertisements
- Promotes social and political change.

KEY THINKERS

THE ROLE OF THE MEDIA IN SOCIETY

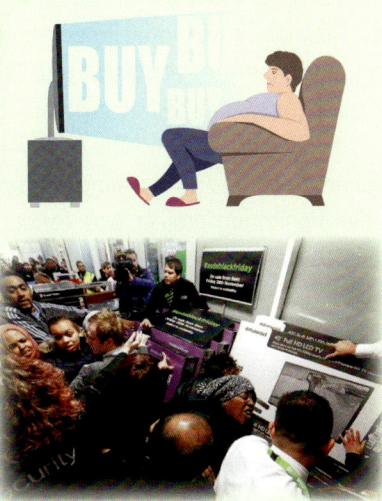

Fig. 6.7 The media can be analysed from a Marxist perspective

Marxist Perspective

Media is part of what Marx termed the 'superstructure'. It is used to present a picture of society that supports the existing social order and makes inequality and injustice seem natural. The media does not give space to alternative ideas or perspectives that would challenge the dominant ideology. The media promotes two main messages: life is about working hard for a wage; and people should consume capitalist products. Some Marxist theorists point to the under-representation of working-class stories or voices in the media. Theorists have analysed the depictions of the working class: positive (i.e. good hard-working people) and negative (i.e. lazy communities with drug and crime problems). Theorists also point to the dominant presence of advertising in the media and its role in creating consumers for the capitalist system. Theorists from the Frankfurt School branch of Marxism have noted the excessive use of entertainment that is not thought-provoking as a means to silence and control society.

Functionalist Perspective

According to functionalists, the media plays many roles in society. It entertains, educates and informs. Functionalists point out that, like education, the media plays a role in the socialisation process. The media enforces social norms and values and provides a 'collective' experience for individuals to create necessary bonds in society (e.g. many citizens in a nation coming together to watch an international sporting event). As part of the socialisation process, the media teaches us about what types of actions and behaviours receive reward or punishment. Media coverage of crime and justice issues teach us about what is 'right' or 'wrong'. The media, and particularly digital media, acts to build and reinforce mini-communities in society. For example, digital media is used to develop communities around a certain group (e.g. LGBTQ+), social issue (e.g. the environment) or cultural product (e.g. a musician).

Fig. 6.8 From the functionalist perspective, the media teaches us about what types of actions receive reward or punishment

THE ROLE OF THE MEDIA 195

Feminist Perspective

As a 'conflict theory', feminist theory views the media as a tool that reinforces patriarchy in society (male dominance). Feminist theorists focus on media messages about men and women. Theorists have noted how women are under-represented in media content, and how they are portrayed. Theorists such as Gaye Tuchman have described the ways in which women are ignored or condemned by the media as a 'symbolic annihilation'. The relatively poor media coverage of women's GAA games in Ireland is an example of symbolic annihilation. An Irish national media monitoring project was conducted in February 2013 by Dr Jane Suiter and funded by the Broadcasting Authority of Ireland (BAI). The research monitored women's participation rates in news programmes on commercial and public radio. It found that women's participation rate was 32.9 per cent, compared with 67.1 per cent for men.

Feminists also point to the role the media plays in the gender socialisation process in terms of teaching us our 'appropriate' gender roles (e.g. domestic and childcare roles of women). The media produces and reinforces gender-based **stereotypes**. Women are more often portrayed as 'victims' and men as 'aggressors'; women as 'emotional' and men as 'rational'; women as 'weak' and men as 'strong', etc. Finally, feminists also argue that women are sexually objectified in the media, especially in advertising. The media caters to a male audience in this sense.

Fig. 6.9 From the feminist perspective, the media reinforces patriarchy

QUESTIONS

1. Can you think of any recent news reports, advertisements, films or programmes that could be used as evidence to support the Marxist perspective? Explain your answer.
2. Can you think of any recent news reports, advertisements, films or programmes that could be used as evidence to support the functionalist perspective? Explain your answer.
3. Can you think of any recent news reports, advertisements, films or programmes that could be used as evidence to support the feminist perspective? Explain your answer.
4. In your opinion, which perspective is most relevant to the role of the media in Irish society today? Give reasons to support your answer.

RESEARCH ASSIGNMENT 6.3

Your group will be assigned one of the three perspectives (Marxist, functionalist or feminist) on the role of the media. Each group member will monitor one media type for a week and gather as much evidence as possible to support the perspective that your group is assigned. The evidence can include pictures, recordings, newspaper clips and written summaries.

At the end of the week, your group presents its research findings to the rest of the class.

See **RESEARCH TIPS** on page 33.

SKILLS BOOK LINK 6.3

Go to page 97 of your Skills Book to complete Skill Task 6.3 on monitoring the media.

See **RESEARCH TIPS** on page 33.

The Power and Influence of the Media

The media presents us with stories and coverage of different issues in society. However, the media can only ever show us a *part* of reality. Even when we are viewing live footage of a protest, for example, we are limited by what the camera captures. It is not possible to cover every aspect of the event or every person involved. *What* the media covers (and does not cover) and *how* stories are covered raises important questions about media power. We often think about news production as responding to real-life situations or events. Our perception is that media responds to events as they happen (e.g. war, natural disasters, political crises). However, is this always the case? When looking at media content, we need to be aware of the *what* and the *how* of media coverage. There are many important communication theories and concepts that we can use to understand the power and influence of the media.

> *[The press] may not be successful at telling people what to think, but it is stunningly successful in telling its readers what to think about.'* Bernard Cohen

Agenda-setting theory was first explained by American communication theorists Maxwell McCombs and Donald Shaw in 1972. In their study of media messages and voter perspectives during presidential elections between 1968 and 1976, they found a strong correlation between what voters considered major issues during the campaign and media coverage. The theory is based on the idea that the more coverage an issue gets in the media, the more it is considered a priority issue by society. We assess the importance of an issue on the basis of whether or not, or how often, it is covered by the media. This can mean that the public never discusses certain issues because these issues are not in the media.

Fig. 6.10 The power of the media in agenda-setting

> **KEY TERM**
>
> **Agenda-setting theory** states that the media has power and influence in establishing the public agenda. The more coverage an issue or topic receives in the media, the more it is considered a public priority.

Examples of agenda-setting in the US include the extensive media coverage of the O.J. Simpson murder case and the Clinton–Lewinsky scandal. In Ireland, some critics, such as journalist John Waters, claim that a general anti-Catholic Church and pro-liberal agenda is being pursued by certain sections of the media. Anti-abortion campaigners also claim that the mainstream Irish media promotes a liberal pro-abortion bias. On 11 March 2015, a large-scale anti-abortion rally was held outside the gates of Leinster House to protest what the campaigners called a 'pro-abortion bias within the media'. The anti-abortion campaigners maintained that over a two-week period, national newspapers had printed 33 articles that were 'pro-abortion', and only one article that was 'anti-abortion'.

See page 60 for more information on 'setting the agenda' and Steven Lukes' types of power.

A 2004 study on the 'political preferences and value orientations of Irish journalists' by Professor of Sociology at Maynooth University Mary P. Corcoran revealed that most Irish journalists positioned themselves as 'left of centre' with liberal tendencies.

Agenda-setting can also be influenced by other factors. Whether an issue or story gets covered by the media can be based on what are known as 'news values'. In the 1960s, media researchers Johan Galtung and Mari Holmboe Ruge analysed international news stories to see if they could identify common characteristics which could explain what is considered 'newsworthy'. Galtung and Ruge identified 12 factors they termed 'news values'. For example, the international media considered stories 'newsworthy' if they were *negative* (i.e. concerning crime, war or corruption), *close to home*, focused on a *personality* (i.e. an individual character) or about a powerful or *elite* nation or person.

News Values	
Frequency	Short-term news stories (e.g. a murder) are preferred to long-term trends (e.g. poverty).
Threshold	The size of an event dictates its importance: the bigger the event (e.g. the more victims in a natural disaster) the more newsworthy it becomes.
Unambiguity	The more clearly an issue or story can be understood by the public, the more likely it is to make the news.
Meaningfulness	Issues or events that speak to our sense of culture or identity, or take place close to home, hold more meaning for us.
Consonance/ Correspondence	The unfolding of an issue or story corresponds to the public's prediction of what it wants or expects to happen.
Unexpectedness	Bizarre or interesting headlines get the audience's attention (e.g. 'Cat goes snowboarding' or 'Woman donates entire €20 million lottery win').
Continuity	Events that will live beyond a day or a week (e.g. the World Cup or a war) are deemed newsworthy.
Composition	Stories that may not otherwise be newsworthy are selected to achieve balance. For example, if the media covers a story of institutional racism within the police, they are likely to balance this with a story on an anti-racism initiative.
Elite nations	Stories from powerful nations are often covered by media across the world (e.g. coverage of the US presidential elections).
Elite people	The actions of elite people are deemed to be more newsworthy than the actions of ordinary people.
Reference to individuals	Stories that personify issues (e.g. the issue of poverty or a national disaster) by presenting them as 'acts of free will' or human action are deemed newsworthy.
Negativity	Bad news (e.g. death, tragedy, political or economic crises) is valued more than good news.

Table 6.1 News values, according to Galtung and Ruge

QUESTIONS

1. Would you agree that the media values and promotes negativity/bad news over good news? Give recent examples to support your answer.
2. Does the Irish media display a negative bias when representing Irish youth in news stories?
3. What topics/issues in the news currently have currency in Ireland? In your opinion, why do these topics still have currency?
4. What types of newspapers in Ireland focus primarily on these media values: personality, simplicity, exclusivity and size?
5. In your opinion, do the news values of Galtung and Ruge support or hinder the media in playing its role in a democracy? Does the mainstream Irish media focus too much on certain news values and neglect others?

Whatever the reason behind agenda-setting, the media's agenda can influence public opinion and government policy or action. The media holds a lot of power in this respect. The agenda-setting theory of McCombs and Shaw was developed prior to the emergence of digital media – when print, television and radio were the dominant media types. With the emergence of social media and the rise of citizen journalism, many theorists argue that the practice of media agenda-setting is more democratic now than it has been in the past.

The CNN Effect

The CNN effect is a theory in media studies and political science, based on the idea that mainstream news media has an effect on foreign policy. The theory developed in the early 1990s in response to the extensive coverage by global media actors, such as CNN, of several different political and humanitarian crises. With close to 24-hour media coverage, startling images of famine and conflict overtook news programmes, radio programmes and newspaper articles. A theory began to emerge that the heavy coverage of such events by organisations such as CNN led to the US government's decision to intervene in certain events: the Kurdish crisis (1991), Somalia (1992–3) and Bosnia (1995).

Fig. 6.11 The CNN effect is a much-debated theory in media studies

The theory is not without its critics, and some argue that the news media was simply following the lead of US government officials who wanted to draw attention to these crises. Modern critics also point to the dominance of the 'war on terror' ideology of the US government in media coverage of the wars in Iraq, Afghanistan, Libya and Syria after the September 11 attacks in the US. These theorists propose that the presence of the phrase 'war on terror' in media stories during this time is evidence that the media is influenced by government, rather than the other way around.

With the emergence of new communication technology, the widespread use of digital cameras and smartphones, and the rise of citizen journalism, the CNN effect theory has been somewhat challenged. Some people argue that developments such as WikiLeaks and events such as the 'Arab Spring' point to the erosion of power of the mainstream media. Citizen journalism now has an influence on government decision-making.

RESEARCH ASSIGNMENT 6.4

This evening, watch the news on RTÉ and on TV3. Also examine **one** national tabloid newspaper and **one** national broadsheet newspaper. For each of the four media, make a list of the top **five** stories that were covered, in order of the importance given to them. Then answer the following questions.

1. Did all four media organisations have the same main headline story? If not, give possible reasons for the differences in the prioritisation of the news stories.
2. For each of the four media, do you agree with the ordering of the top five stories?

See **RESEARCH TIPS** on page 33.

Tips:
- Did the main story deserve to be front page news or reported on first?
- Were other stories more deserving of front page news?
- Were there any important stories (national or international) that were completely omitted? In your opinion, why might that be?

Citizen Journalism: The End of Agenda-Setting Theory?

Social media, blogs and the rise of citizen journalism are said to have changed the traditional agenda-setting processes of the media. Citizen journalism provides an alternative source of news. In a 2001 article entitled 'The End of Mass Communication?', communication theorists Steven H. Chaffee and Miriam J. Metzger argued that people (rather than mass media outlets) will start setting the agenda. The 'new media' is seen as the end of mass communication because it places control in the hands of the user. Everyone now has equal opportunity to participate in

THE ROLE OF THE MEDIA

creating news, which involves a distribution of agenda-setting power from the few to the many. Not only can people interact in different ways with the media (e.g. comment sections, blogs, forums), people can produce their own 'news' content and spread it through personal blogs or social media (e.g. Twitter, Facebook, YouTube).

New media has created an alternative flow of information that is increasingly taken into account by traditional media. There are many cases of stories or comments in forums that have become so popular ('going viral') that they were eventually reported on by traditional media. Citizen journalism has been responsible for breaking stories such as US soldier abuse of detainees in the Abu Ghraib jails in Iraq. During the Iranian uprising of 2009, there was a government ban on reporting by media outlets; however, citizens used Twitter and other social media sites to spread information, images and footage. These acts of citizen journalism forced the public and political leaders to pay attention and eventually to take action.

Some critics, however, have warned against the simple view of citizen journalism as 'democratisation' of the media. Some studies on news creation and engagement habits of social media users have pointed to the dominance of entertainment and celebrity news over political or social issues. With smartphones, most citizens *can* be citizen journalists – but this does not necessarily mean that citizens *want* to engage in journalism or politics in this way. Critics have also noted that, since we choose to follow/unfollow news organisations or items, we can actually censor out the news stories that we prefer not to see. Studies have also shown that, despite the diverse choices we have for alternative sources of news, we tend to limit ourselves to a handful of news media organisations to which we 'tune in'.

All of this means that our views can still be heavily influenced by traditional media. A 2015 study by the Pew Research Center found that, while most people say they use 2–5 online news sources, approximately 21 per cent of people routinely rely on just one online news source. The question of *who* is setting the agenda – traditional media or citizen journalists – remains a topic of much debate and research.

Fig. 6.12 Representations of citizen journalism

ACTIVITY 6.4

Hold a classroom debate on the following motion:
'It is the media – not the ordinary citizens – that sets the political agenda in Ireland.'

Framing

Agenda-setting is about *what* issues get media coverage. **Framing** is about *how* issues are presented – in other words, the specific text or images used to 'frame' our ideas or opinions on an issue. In this sense, media messaging is not always objective or neutral. The same issue (e.g. drugs, homelessness) can be presented in different ways. For example, a news article on drugs could look at the topic as

> **KEY TERM**
>
> In media studies, **framing** refers to the particular angle or perspective from which a story or issue is presented.

a crime issue, a health issue or a symptom of underlying social causes. In imposing a particular angle or slant on an issue, the media influences how the audience develops its own understanding of the topic. Framing in the news media will influence how a story is investigated and reported (e.g. who the journalist chooses to speak with, the questions he or she asks and how the information is eventually reported). Framing is evident in the text chosen for a report. Word choice will have a powerful impact on how we read a story. A reporter may describe the same person as 'low-income' or 'dole recipient', as 'drug user' or 'addict', as 'sex worker' or 'prostitute', as 'youth' or 'delinquents', as 'terrorist' or 'rebel fighter', etc.

Framing can be intentional or unintentional: it is usually underpinned by unconscious or conscious ideologies and interests. In this sense, the media transmits a certain ideology (e.g. 'war on terror' or 'immigration and insecurity').

Fig. 6.13 Media messaging is not always neutral

Framing can also be used to ensure support of government policies. In the Irish context, the mainstream media is sometimes criticised for acting as an uncritical platform for the government. Two recent examples are cited by critics. Following the financial crash in the mid-2000s, much of the media coverage involved communicating the official government position and rationale for its extensive austerity programme. Austerity was framed as 'necessary', 'responsible', and 'the right thing to do'. Another recent issue in the Irish context was media coverage of the protests against water charges. Much of the media coverage is said to have downplayed the significance of the protests and presented it as part of a 'leftist' agenda, rather than a popular movement. The deliberate use of mass communication to promote or demote certain values, views or perceptions is known as **propaganda**.

KEY TERM

Propaganda is information that is biased and is used to promote a political cause or point of view. The use of propaganda by the Nazis during World War II is a famous example.

Fig. 6.14 Media coverage of austerity and water protests in Ireland

Framing is evident with use of images as well as text. As we know, a picture paints a thousand words. Visual communication is a powerful tool used by newspapers, television, film and digital media. It can greatly influence how we view an issue.

The images that accompany a media report on any particular issue will often contain just as much messaging as the text. Particular attention has been given to the use of images in advertising. The chosen images are designed to make us want to purchase a product or buy into a lifestyle or concept (e.g. travel) that is being presented.

Fig. 6.15 Visual communication in advertising

THE ROLE OF THE MEDIA   201

CASE STUDY 1: Media Framing

Image A and Image B (below) were featured separately in online articles from two of the UK's main newspapers about BP's oil spill in the Gulf of Mexico in 2010.

Fig. 6.16 Representations of BP's oil spill in the Gulf of Mexico in 2010

CASE STUDY 2: Media Framing

Images C–F below were published in newspapers reporting on the Iraq War in 2003. Images C and D appeared on countless front pages of newspapers around the world beneath headlines such as 'End of Dictatorship – Beginning of Democracy!' and 'Mission Accomplished – Bush Declares Victory in Iraq!'

Images such as E and F were subsequently published in newspapers that reported the ongoing violence in Iraq in the days, months and years that followed.

Fig. 6.17 Representations of the Iraq War in 2003 and its aftermath

QUESTIONS

1. Look at Case Study 1.
   (a) Explain how images A and B might frame one's perspective on the BP oil spill.
   (b) Which picture is most likely to gain sympathy for BP? Why?
   (c) Which picture is most likely to encourage public criticism of BP? Why?

2. Look at Case Study 2.
   (a) Explain how images C and D might have influenced the public's perception of the progress of the Iraq War in 2003.
   (b) Do images E and F appear to contradict the way in which images C and D have been framed? Explain.
   (c) Have you ever been influenced by the way in which news headlines and associated images are framed?

SKILLS BOOK LINK 6.4

Go to page 98 of your Skills Book to complete Skill Task 6.4 on a newspaper article.

Representations and Stereotyping

Closely linked to framing is the idea that the media represents certain groups in society in a particular way. When we make generalisations about individuals or groups who appear to share a particular characteristic (age, gender, ethnicity, etc.) this is known as **stereotyping**. The following statements are examples of stereotyping: 'Women are more emotional than men', 'The poor are lazy', 'All Italians are great cooks', 'Young people are selfish'. Stereotypes can be positive or negative. The media is full of stereotypes. Some stereotypes are explicit, such as the sexual objectification of women. Some stereotypes are implicit, such as the deliberate linking of certain groups (e.g. Travellers) with certain issues (e.g. crime). Much research has looked at how the media represents and stereotypes different groups.

KEY TERM

Stereotyping involves believing that individuals or groups who appear to share a particular characteristic (such as age, gender, disability or ethnicity) are all the same.

ACTIVITY 6.5

Work with your partner to complete the following activity.

1. Think individually for a moment about stereotypes that are promoted or reinforced by the media. *(Think)*
2. With your partner, agree a list of these stereotypes. *(Pair)*
3. Share your conclusions with the rest of the class. *(Share)*

THE ROLE OF THE MEDIA

IN THE MEDIA

Fig. 6.18 Stereotyping in the media

Media Stereotyping

WHAT THE RESEARCH SAYS!

GENDER INEQUALITY IN THE NEWS 1995–2015

The Global Media Monitoring Project (GMMP) is an organisation that aims to change how women are represented in the news media. Since 2005, it has produced reports that examine how women are represented in media organisations, media decision-making, and media content. The 2015 report involved an analysis of news media in 114 countries spanning two decades (1995–2015). The report found that gender stereotypes remained firmly embedded in news media content during that period. Only 4 per cent of stories were found to explicitly challenge gender stereotypes; this was a mere one per cent rise since 2005. The report also analysed the different topics in media reports with respect to where women were most likely and least likely to be the focus. The results present interesting data on gender stereotyping by the media.

Top 10 topics in which women are most likely to be central, 2015

1. Women's participation in economic processes
2. Birth control, fertility, sterilisation, termination
3. Family relations, intergenerational conflict, parents
4. Beauty contests, models, fashion, cosmetic surgery
5. Gender violence based on culture, family and interpersonal relations, feminicide, harassment, rape, sexual assault, trafficking, female genital mutilation
6. Changing gender relations (outside the home)
7. Women politicians, women electoral candidates
8. Women's movement, activism, demonstrations, etc.
9. Human rights, women's rights, rights of sexual minorities, rights of religious minorities, etc.
10. Celebrity news

Women's centrality: the bottom 10 stories

1. Other development issues, sustainability, etc.
2. Climate change, global warming
3. Gender violence perpetuated by the state
4. Other stories on economy
5. Economic crisis, state bailouts of companies, company takeovers and mergers, etc.
6. Economic policies, strategies, modules, indicators, stock markets, etc.
7. Peace, negotiations, treaties
8. Transport, traffic, roads, etc.
9. Consumer issues, consumer protection, fraud, etc.
10. Other labour issues (strikes, trade unions, etc.)

Fig. 6.19 Gender inequality in the news

WHAT THE RESEARCH SAYS!

MEDIA STEREOTYPING OF YOUNG PEOPLE IN IRELAND

In 2006 the Equality Authority and the National Youth Council of Ireland published a report on inequality and stereotyping faced by young people in Ireland. The qualitative study involved interviewing young people in Ireland to discuss their experiences of stereotyping, within the family, community and media. Most of the young people surveyed pointed to the media as one of the main sources of youth stereotyping. The stereotyping was viewed as negative. As one survey participant, Christopher, stated: *'It's all trouble, vandalism, joyriding, drinking, drugs, smoking. They never have any of the good stuff we do in it'.*

When the survey participants were asked if this stereotyping of young people in Ireland was accurate, a range of different responses were recorded. Some participants felt that the representation of youth was completely false, as it treated the behaviours of a minority as 'typical' behaviour of all youths. Other participants believed that, although the stereotype might be somewhat true, it was unfair to exclusively associate issues such as drugs and alcohol abuse with the youth alone, since these are issues for wider Irish society. Young Travellers were believed to face additional challenges with media stereotyping, since they would continue to face media stereotyping as adults. This was described by one youth: *'It'd be the same no matter what it is, young, old or middle-aged. Whatever happens with a Traveller it's on the front page headline news.'*

WHAT THE RESEARCH SAYS!

MIGRANT COMMUNITIES

The Media For Diversity And Migrant Integration (MEDIVA) Project at the European University Institute was established to promote positive media practices in relation to the coverage of immigration issues and communities within the EU. The project conducted research involving a review of studies published across Europe between 2000 and 2010 on the representation of migrants in the media, as well as interviews with media professionals in Ireland, Britain, the Netherlands, Italy, Greece and Poland. The 2011 report contained the following findings.

- Media coverage of migrants is frequently based on a contrast between a positive 'us' and a negative 'them'.
- Migrants are frequently represented as a 'group' rather than individuals.
- Migrants are usually attributed characteristics of threat, or associated with problems, such as crime and conflicts.
- Migrants are more negatively represented than non-migrants, when covering the same type of news.
- The stereotyping of Muslim migrants is a specific finding. Muslim men are associated with religious fundamentalism. Muslim women are portrayed as victims of a backward and subordinating culture. Islam is predominantly presented as a threat to security and the culture and values of 'the West'.

QUESTIONS

1. Look at the research piece on Gender Inequality in the News. Explain how these statistics could be used to support the feminist perspective on the role of the media.

2. Look at the research piece on Media Stereotyping of Young People in Ireland. Do you believe that the Irish media presents a negative stereotype of young people? Provide recent examples to support your answer.

3. Look at the research piece on Migrant Communities. In what ways are migrants stereotyped?

4. Revise the research pieces on Gender Inequality in the News and on Migrant Communities. Compare and contrast the research methodologies adopted. Which methodology is stronger? What implications does this have for the outcome of the research?

Tip: Revise page 205 to help you with this question.

SKILLS BOOK LINK 6.5

Go to page 99 of your Skills Book to complete Skill Task 6.5 on how the media represents groups in Irish society.

See **RESEARCH TIPS** on page 33.

RESEARCH ASSIGNMENT 6.5

Your group will be assigned an issue that is currently in the media. As a group, research and analyse how this issue is covered across various types of media. Each member of your group chooses one type of media to analyse (e.g. TV, radio, print) and writes a short report that covers the following questions:

- What type of media did you research/analyse?
- What potential influence does this type of media have on the public? (Consider the target audience, geographic reach, effectiveness of communication style and capacity to engage the audience.)
- What level of participation/engagement with the public was reached by this type of media?
- Choose two contrasting reports from the type of media you analysed. Describe two contrasting views that were expressed on the same issue.
- How in-depth was the reporting in this type of media?
- Focus on two contrasting reports in this type of media. In each case, what was the evidence of research undertaken to support the argument put forth on the issue?
- Did you observe bias, framing or stereotyping in this type of media? Give examples.
- Were alternative views represented in this type of media? Give examples.

With your group, share your findings and discuss. Prepare a group presentation for the rest of the class entitled 'Comparative Analysis of How Different Media Types Cover the Same Issue'.

See **RESEARCH TIPS** on page 33.

SKILLS BOOK LINK 6.6

Go to page 100 of your Skills Book to complete Skill Task 6.6 on left-wing and right-wing ideologies in the media.

See **RESEARCH TIPS** on page 33.

RESEARCH ASSIGNMENT 6.6

Choose any national newspaper and examine its content over a one-week period. Assess the extent to which it could be termed a left-wing or right-wing newspaper. Consider the following in your examination of the newspaper:

- Agenda-setting and priority given to specific topics or issues
- Use of framing, representation and stereotyping
- The 'editorial section' and the views of the newspaper's journalists.

See **RESEARCH TIPS** on page 33.

Complete your next Reflective Journal entry (pages 23–24)

THE ROLE OF THE MEDIA 207

QUESTIONS

1. Describe **two** ways in which the media contributes to the functioning of democracy.
2. Explain the Marxist perspective on the role of the media in society.
3. In what ways does the media contribute to what functionalists term 'the socialisation process'?
4. Do you agree with feminist views on the role of the media in society? Explain your answer.
5. Explain agenda-setting theory and the CNN effect.
6. Do you think the Irish media has much influence on the political agenda in Ireland? Give reasons to support your answer.
7. What is citizen journalism? What are the positive and negative effects of the rise of citizen journalism?
8. What is framing? How can it be used by the media to influence public opinion?
9. What is stereotyping? Can you think of any people or groups who suffer from media stereotyping on a regular basis?

The Rights and Responsibilities of the Media in a Democracy

Different societies have different expectations regarding how the media should perform its role. In non-democratic countries, the mainstream media is usually state-owned or operates under tight government control. In many cases, the government will dictate the information that media outlets can produce. This is known as propaganda. The use of media to communicate propaganda has been, and continues to be, one of the most powerful tools used by dictatorships and other non-democratic political systems around the world. However, propaganda has also been used in democratic countries – particularly during times of political or economic crisis (e.g. war, famine, natural disasters, economic collapse). Propaganda was used heavily in Nazi Germany, in coverage of the Cold War by Russian and US media outlets, in anti-American cartoons published in North Korea, etc. Despite this, in democratic societies, the media is expected to act in a way that reflects our democratic values. These expectations are underpinned by two important principles: **freedom of the press**, and **social responsibility**.

Media in a Democracy

In a democracy, we expect the media to:

- Provide a factual and objective view on events and issues
- Inform the public about important social issues so that citizens can make better political, social and economic choices
- Provide a channel for government to explain its policies and decisions
- Support greater public participation in decision-making by provoking public debates and providing a channel between citizen and government
- Investigate and report on abuses of power in society
- Promote positive social and political change
- Raise public awareness and mobilise support for humanitarian causes or social injustices
- Promote political pluralism by providing a platform for different and alternative views, ideas and perspectives on issues

KEY TERMS

Freedom of the press is the right of media professionals to report the news and circulate opinions without censorship by the government.

While the media has a right to operate freely in a democratic society, it must show **social responsibility**: it must act in a responsible manner. The media is responsible for ensuring that it functions to serve 'the public good'.

Freedom of the press is considered one of the most important aspects of a functioning democracy. The ability of the media to operate freely ensures that the public is informed on government policy and action. Freedom of the press allows the media to perform its watchdog role without interference from government. The concept of freedom of the press is based on fundamental human rights of *freedom of expression* and the *right to information*, which are protected by several international and national human rights laws. 'Press freedom theory' developed from sixteenth-century libertarian political ideas. In this theory, the media is not restricted in what issues it covers, or how it covers them. Since everyone has a right to information, there is no control or censorship whatsoever. The theory sees people as rational actors capable of judging whether information is good or bad, factual or not. Therefore, the media should not restrict any information, even if the information is negative or provocative. In practice, however, press freedom does not operate like this in modern democracies: with rights come responsibilities.

Fig. 6.20 Free speech

See page 8 for more information on libertarian ideas.

ACTIVITY 6.6

Work with your partner to complete the following activity.

1. Think individually for a moment about what limits, if any, should be placed on the right to freedom of the press. Does the press need to exercise caution when writing/reporting on certain controversial issues? *(Think)*

2. Discuss with your partner. *(Pair)*

3. Share your conclusions with the rest of the class. *(Share)*

Universal Declaration of Human Rights (1948)

Article 19:
'Everyone has the right to freedom of opinion and expression; this right includes freedom to hold opinions without interference and to seek, receive and impart information and ideas through any media and regardless of frontiers.'

International Covenant on Civil and Political Rights (1966)

Article 19:
'Everyone shall have the right to hold opinions without interference … Everyone shall have the right to freedom of expression; this right shall include freedom to seek, receive and impart information and ideas of all kinds, regardless of frontiers, either orally, in writing or in print, in the form of art or through any other media of his choice.'

The European Convention on Human Rights (1950)

Article 10:
'Everyone has the right to freedom of expression. This right shall include freedom to hold opinions and to receive and impart information and ideas without interference by public authority and regardless of frontiers.'

Bunreacht na hÉireann (1937)

Article 40.6(1):
'The state guarantees liberty for the exercise of the following rights, subject to public order and morality:
- The right of the citizens to express freely their convictions and opinions
- The education of public opinion.'

THE ROLE OF THE MEDIA

Social Responsibility and Accountability

The concept of social responsibility developed in the US during World War II. The concept places certain limits on press freedom. The basic idea is that, while the media has a right to operate freely in a democratic society, it must act in a responsible manner. The media is responsible for ensuring that it functions to serve 'the public good'.

In the concept of social responsibility, the media has many obligations to society. The media must ensure that its reporting is accurate, objective and balanced, allowing citizens to develop well-informed opinions or decisions. This means, for example, that journalists need to maintain a clear distinction between facts and opinion, and reporting and analysis, and properly check sources for news items. It also means that the media should present political issues in an unbiased manner, explaining the issues without oversimplifying or sensationalising. The media must be 'pluralistic': it must provide a variety of perspectives that represent the diversity of society. Finally, the media must balance its responsibility to provide information to the public with its other responsibilities of ensuring security and stability in society. This means, for example, that the media should not report on state secrets, use information that could be harmful to national security, or report any details that could put people in danger.

Ultimately, the media is accountable to society. Social responsibility is achieved through compliance with professional codes of ethics, self-regulation and state regulation. Because of the power it holds, the failure of the media to act responsibly can have serious consequences for individuals and society. Indeed, the growth of social media and citizen journalism has also had an impact on media social responsibility, since media content now comes from a much wider range of sources. The principles of freedom of the press, and social responsibility, are the principles on which the media operates in democratic societies. However, these principles often come into conflict.

Commission on Freedom of the Press

The Hutchins Commission (whose official name was the Commission on Freedom of the Press) was established in the US during World War II in a response to growing public and government criticism over media ownership. Between 1943 and 1947 the commission examined what role the media should play in a democratic society. It concluded that the media had a duty to contribute to the development and stability of modern societies and, as such, had certain responsibilities. Above all, the media should consider the needs of society and the greater good when deciding what stories or issues to cover. This gave birth to the concept of social responsibility and accountability of the media. It also inspired the idea that codes of ethics and professional standards should be developed and implemented by the mass media.

Social Responsibility of the Media in the Constitution of Ireland

Article 40.6 of the Constitution of Ireland protects freedom of expression. However, it places certain limits on this freedom in the interest of the 'common good':

'The state shall endeavour to ensure that organs of public opinion, such as the radio, the press, the cinema, while preserving their rightful liberty of expression, including criticism of government policy, shall not be used to undermine public order or morality or the authority of the state. The publication or utterance of blasphemous, seditious, or indecent matter is an offence which shall be punishable in accordance with law.'

The Defamation Act 2009

Section 36 of the Defamation Act 2009 deals specifically with the crime of blasphemy:

1. A person who publishes or utters blasphemous matter shall be guilty of an offence and shall be liable upon conviction on indictment to a fine not exceeding €25,000.

2. For the purposes of this section, a person publishes or utters blasphemous matter if:

    (a) he or she publishes or utters matter that is grossly abusive or insulting in relation to matters held sacred by any religion, thereby causing outrage among a substantial number of the adherents of that religion, and

    (b) he or she intends, by the publication or utterance of the matter concerned, to cause such outrage.'

Several groups have campaigned for the removal of section 36 from the Defamation Act and the Constitutional Convention recommended that the government call a referendum to remove article 40.6 from the Irish Constitution. The main argument put forward for the removal of Irish blasphemy law is that it discriminates unfairly against atheists and others who do not practise religion.

> **KEY TERM**
>
> **Defamation** is the act of damaging someone's reputation through a false accusation or communication that is usually of a public nature.

ACTIVITY 6.7

Hold a classroom debate on the following motion:

'Ireland's blasphemy laws should be abolished – the rights to freedom of the press and freedom of speech must be guaranteed.'

CASE STUDY 3: RTÉ and Fr Kevin Reynolds

In May 2011 RTÉ aired 'Mission to Prey'. This edition of the *Prime Time* programme claimed that an Irish missionary priest, Fr Kevin Reynolds, had been involved in the rape and impregnation of a Kenyan teenager. Because of the programme and the negative public backlash, Fr Reynolds was removed from his parish post and forced to leave his home. The allegations were found to be false and the government conducted an investigation into RTÉ through the Broadcasting Authority of Ireland. Among other things, the investigation discovered that prior to the broadcasting of the show by RTÉ, Fr Reynolds had offered to have a DNA test to prove his innocence. However, RTÉ refused the offer.

As a result of the scandal, *Prime Time* was temporarily suspended, RTÉ was fined by the Broadcasting Authority and Fr Reynolds received compensation in a **libel** case he brought against RTÉ. Director General of RTÉ Noel Curran admitted that the 'Mission to Prey' programme constituted 'one of the gravest editorial mistakes ever made'.

> **KEY TERM**
>
> **Libel** is a published false accusation or a 'written' defamation (e.g. in a newspaper).

THE ROLE OF THE MEDIA

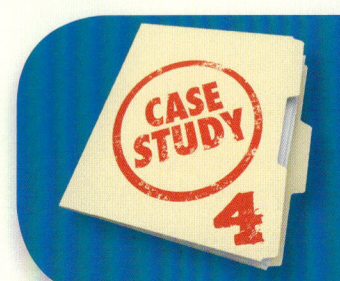

Media Reports and Xenophobic Attacks in South Africa

CASE STUDY 4

In 2015, South Africa was hit by a wave of violence against foreign nationals. Most of those affected were from Malawi, Zimbabwe, Somalia and the Democratic Republic of Congo. Between May and March, violent attacks against immigrant communities took place in the province of Kwazulu-Natal and in the capital city, Johannesburg. The businesses of immigrants were looted and their homes were ransacked. Thousands of people were forced to flee to seek refuge in makeshift camps. The violence left seven people dead and 5,000 displaced. A government-commissioned inquiry took place, headed by Judge Navi Pillay, former UN High Commissioner for Human Rights. In April 2016, the commission published its report, which found that media organisations had played a role in the outbreak of violence. The report stated that a series of sensational headlines and the dissemination of false information on social media were to blame: 'The failure of media houses to contextualise the violent occurrences sent shock waves across the country and around the world … The spreading of misinformation on social media platforms contributed to widespread panic at the height of the attacks in April 2015.'

SKILLS BOOK LINK 6.7

Go to pages 100–102 of your Skills Book to complete Skill Task 6.7 on newspaper headlines.

RESEARCH ASSIGNMENT 6.7

Go to **https://educateplus.ie/go/journalism-guidelines** for RTÉ's Journalism Guidelines (revised September 2014). Read Section 10: Serving the Public Interest and answer the following question.

List and explain any passages contained in Section 10 that relate to:

(a) The general role of the media in a democracy

(b) Freedom of the press and freedom of speech

(c) The social responsibility of the media.

RESEARCH ASSIGNMENT 6.8

Research examples of occasions (other than those discussed in this chapter) when the media acted in a socially irresponsible manner. Write a report on the main findings of your research.

Tip:
You could look at occasions when the media:
- Wrongfully defamed politicians/celebrities by printing false or misleading information
- Stoked up societal, religious or racial tensions
- Promoted xenophobia
- Interfered in the legal process by publishing sensitive evidence during or before a criminal trial (search for 'media in contempt of court').

Complete your next Reflective Journal entry (pages 23–24)

POWER AND PEOPLE

> **ACTIVITY 6.8**
>
> Imagine that the Irish government has decided to introduce new legislation to regulate the media in Ireland. Devise proposals for a new bill to be introduced to the Dáil. Your proposals will include safeguards to protect the freedom of the press, and regulations concerning the social responsibility and accountability of the media.

Ownership and Control of the Media

The media can play a powerful role in shaping our ideas, opinions and world view, as well as influencing government policy and action. As we have seen, this can be achieved through several means: agenda-setting, framing or reinforcing stereotypes. Given that the media has such power, a key issue to be considered is *who* owns or controls the media. Who are the media **gatekeepers**? What are the different models of media ownership and control in Ireland and globally? How do these influence press freedom and social responsibility of the media? What about the rise of 'new media'? These are vital questions to ask in any analysis of the power of the media and its impact on politics and society.

> **KEY TERM**
>
> Gatekeeping refers to the process of filtering information before it is disseminated by the mass media. For example, in traditional news media, we think of editors and journalists as the **gatekeepers**.

Media Ownership and Control in Ireland

In Ireland, as in many of today's modern democratic societies, we have public and private models of media ownership.

Public

Raidió Teilifís Éireann (RTÉ) is Ireland's national **public service broadcaster (PSB)**. It consists of four television stations, nine radio stations and a range of digital media (RTÉ news app, YouTube channel, etc.). RTÉ is a semi-state company: it is partly owned by the Irish state. RTÉ has two sources of revenue: television licence fees and commercial advertising. It is regulated by the Broadcasting Authority of Ireland (BAI), which is a state body. TG4 is the Irish-language PSB in Ireland.

> **KEY TERM**
>
> A **public service broadcaster** is a media outlet that transmits communication in the service of the public. Examples include the BBC in the UK, and RTÉ in Ireland.

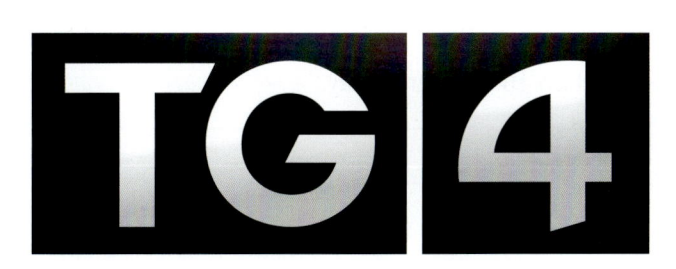

Fig. 6.21 Logos of RTÉ and TG4: public service broadcasters in Ireland

THE ROLE OF THE MEDIA

Broadcasting Authority of Ireland

'We are committed to being an effective regulator, trusted by the public, broadcasters and legislators to serve the viewing and listening needs of the people of Ireland, now and in the future.'

The Broadcasting Authority of Ireland (BAI) is Ireland's national regulator of broadcasting, both public and private. The BAI is responsible for several regulatory tasks. It:

- Awards licences to broadcast to television and radio stations
- Develops broadcasting rules and codes
- Monitors the annual performance of RTÉ and TG4 in meeting their public service objectives and use of public funds
- Monitors and enforces compliance of all broadcasters – public and private – with the broadcasting codes and rules
- Receives and decides on complaints from viewers and listeners on content.

The BAI can reject or uphold a complaint. One example was when the BAI upheld a complaint against *The Ray D'Arcy Show* on RTÉ Radio 1 for unfair bias towards the pro-choice perspective during a programme on fatal foetal abnormality and abortion.

Fig. 6.22 BAI logo

SKILLS BOOK LINK 6.8

Go to pages 102–103 of your Skills Book to complete Skill Task 6.8 on the BAI.

RESEARCH ASSIGNMENT 6.9

Go to **https://educateplus.ie/go/journalism-guidelines** for RTÉ's journalism guidelines. Write a summary report on the following sections:

- Section 8: Impartiality
- Section 9: Editorial Integrity and Independence
- Appendix 1: RTÉ and Political Coverage/Studio Election Debates
- Section 16: Accountability.

Private

The Irish media landscape also includes many private (commercially owned) print, radio, television and digital media outlets. There are over 30 commercially owned radio stations and one commercially owned television station (TV3) in Ireland. With respect to commercially owned newspapers (print and online), Ireland has eight daily and seven weekly national publications, over 50 local newspapers, a variety of magazines and three online-only news publications (such as **www.thejournal.ie**). The press in Ireland is regulated by the Press Council of Ireland (Office of the Press Ombudsman). Similar to the BAI, the council monitors the press to ensure that it acts ethically. It promotes journalistic standards such as accuracy, privacy and fairness, which are set out in its code of practice. It also handles complaints made against the press.

Fig. 6.23 TV3 logo

Who Controls Media Content?

Whether publicly or privately owned, the question of *who* really controls media content remains a topic of debate. There are several perspectives on the issue.

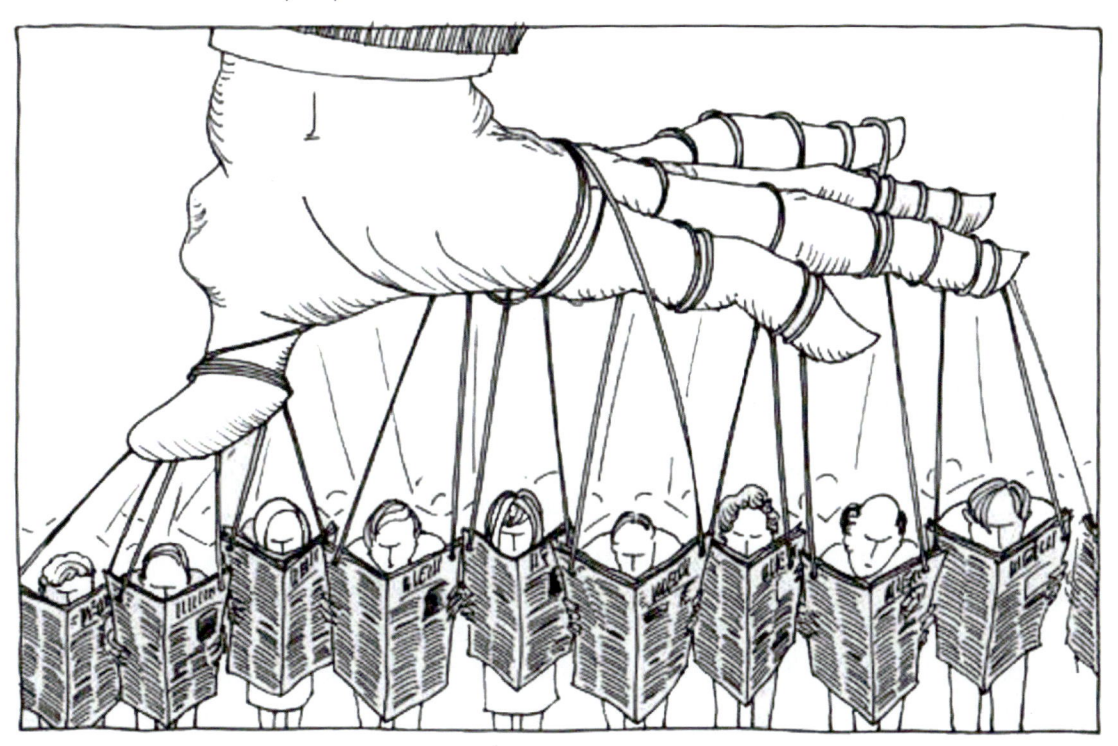

Fig. 6.24 Who controls media content?

- Some people argue that it is a simple case of free market economics, i.e. the public dictates what gets printed. According to this perspective, if journalists ignore what the public demand and fail to satisfy their appetite for news, then the resulting news will not sell, the media organisation will lose money and the journalists will be replaced. Therefore, media content is developed to meet public demand.

- Other people claim that it is the owners who exercise most influence in determining what content gets coverage in their media organisations. Like every individual, media owners have their own ideological outlook and political leanings. They may impose their personal ideals on their staff through agenda-setting and the hiring and firing of editors and journalists.

THE ROLE OF THE MEDIA

```
                          EXTERNAL INFLUENCERS

       Advertisers      Public opinion      Government      Public relations
```

                                    Publisher
                                       |
                                    Editor — Additional page editor
                                       | |
                                    Managing   Editorial writers
                                     editor

City editor	State/reg editor	Business editor	Sports editor	Lifestyles editor	Design editor
Assistant city editor	Assistant state/reg editor	Assistant business editor	Assistant sports editor	Assistant lifestyles editor	Layout editors
Reporters	Reporters	Reporters	Reporters	Reporters	
		Chief copy-editor	Photo editor	Graphics editor	
		Copy-editors	Photographers	Graphics reporters/artists	

Fig. 6.25 Who influences media content?

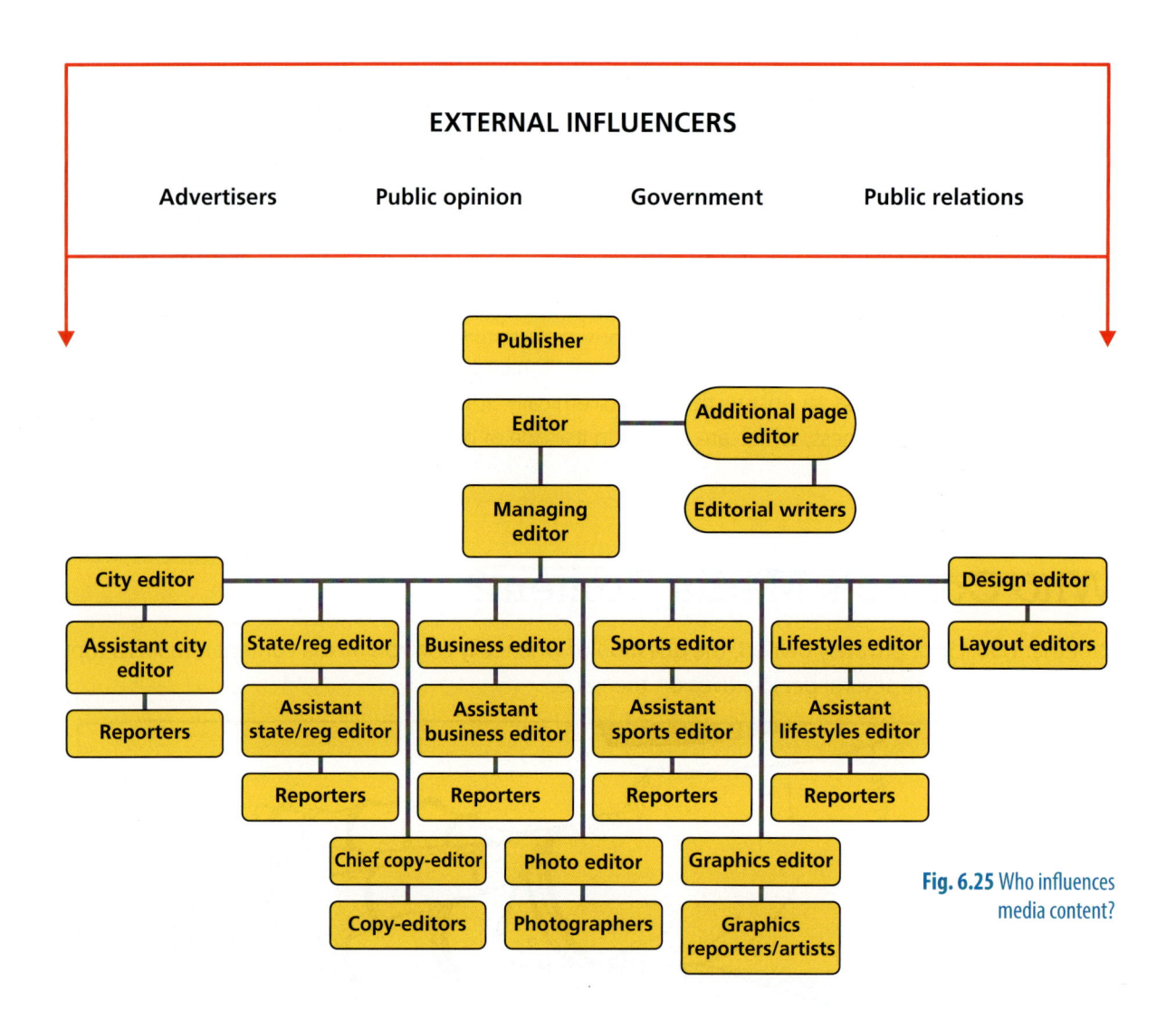

- Several commentators have pointed to the power of advertisers in exercising undue influence over media content. The vast bulk of media organisations are heavily dependent on revenue from advertising for their survival. Because of this economic dependence, media organisations can be reluctant to print anything that might upset their main advertisers.

- **Public relations (PR) companies** and **spin doctors** have become increasingly influential in dictating media coverage of issues. These communications professionals develop and disseminate 'pre-packaged' news for journalists. With increasing pressure on journalists to report more stories in a shorter space of time, PR materials can influence the agenda and framing of media content.

- For public media, such as RTÉ, media content is regulated by norms and values serving the public interest. Formal rules are established by institutions such as the Broadcasting Authority of Ireland.

KEY TERMS

Public relations (PR) companies are hired to develop, produce and manage messages to the public, usually through the media. The messages are usually intended to change the public's attitudes or behaviours. For example, health is one of the biggest PR sectors, as pharmaceutical companies and governments attempt to influence the public's health behaviour (e.g. promotion of healthy lifestyle choices or specific branded drugs).

Spin doctor is a term used to describe a PR person who tries to manage negative publicity by publicising a 'positive spin' or interpretation of an event or issue linked to a company, party, government or celebrity.

WHAT THE RESEARCH SAYS!
MEDIA COVERAGE OF GENERAL ELECTION 2011

The 2011 General Election in Ireland marked a significant change in the regulation of broadcast media coverage of elections. In 2009, new legislation had for the first time given power to the BAI to regulate public broadcasters (e.g. RTÉ) and private broadcasters (e.g. TV3). The law also contained rules to specifically deal with news and current affairs coverage, including the coverage of elections. All broadcasters were required to:

Fig. 6.26 Media coverage of the 2011 General Election

- Report and present news in an objective and impartial manner and without any expression of the broadcaster's own views
- Transmit free party political broadcasts (PPBs) provided that in the allocation, no party receives preferential treatment over its rivals
- Comply with the long-standing ban on paid broadcast political advertising.

The BAI Code on Election Coverage did not contain any practical guidelines on how broadcasters were to ensure that their election coverage was fair, objective and impartial. In effect, each broadcaster was free to decide how to apply the rules.

Research conducted by Prof. Kevin Rafter at DCU examined how Ireland's public service broadcaster, RTÉ, implemented the code in its coverage of the 2011 General Election. The research involved the examination of internal RTÉ documents, including the minutes of meetings held by RTÉ's Election Steering Committee (SC) and data on RTÉ's electoral coverage. The SC was set up to provide internal advice to RTÉ programme makers on election matters and to monitor how RTÉ's programmes were covering elections, in order to ensure objective, impartial and fair coverage. Three main areas of RTÉ's election coverage were assessed: election news coverage, political advertising and leader debates. The findings provide insight into the challenges of balanced election coverage, the importance of media regulation during election times, and the experience of one broadcaster attempting to implement the BAI regulations.

General Code of Conduct

In the run-up to the 2011 General Election, RTÉ provided staff with advice on how to ensure balanced, objective and fair media coverage.

- Staff were advised to avoid giving personal, partisan or biased opinions on election-related matters on RTÉ programmes, in other media (e.g. newspaper columns) or on personal social media accounts.
- Current affairs programme presenters and journalists were advised to play 'a more moderating-a-debate role rather than confrontational interviewer role'.
- Programme-makers were advised to ensure the use of commentators (e.g. audience members) representing an even spread of different views/opinions.
- Makers of satirical programmes (e.g. *The Savage Eye*) were advised to ensure that 'any ridicule was spread across the political spectrum'.

Election News Coverage

RTÉ's long-established practice in allocating air time to competing parties and candidates was to use the first preference vote secured by parties in the previous general election. Parties that had won more first preference votes would be given more air time. However, prior to the 2011 election, RTÉ reviewed this approach and invited academics to develop new proposals for fair and impartial allocation of air time during the upcoming election. BAI did not appear to have been part of these discussions. RTÉ added several additional criteria, including the results of the 2009 European and local elections, and opinion poll results between 2007 and 2011. A guideline was then developed which provided the percentage of air time to be allotted to each political party in RTÉ's election coverage for 2011. A researcher was hired to closely monitor the on-air contributions of, and coverage given to, each political party. Halfway through the election campaign, the SC reviewed RTÉ's election coverage. The data showed that coverage to both Fianna Fáil and Fine Gael was close to the guideline. However, Labour received above its air-time ratio and independent candidates below theirs. Table 6.2 below presents the actual media coverage in comparison to the RTÉ guideline for each party.

Fig. 6.27 RTÉ's Leaders' Debate from the 2011 General Election

Political Party	RTÉ coverage: Guideline 2011 (per cent)	RTÉ coverage: Actual 2011 (per cent)	Final coverage: Differential 2011 (per cent)
Fianna Fáil	31.2	26.6	– 4.6
Fine Gael	27.0	27.14	+ 0.14
Independents	15.7	7.21	– 8.49
Labour	12.6	20.0	+ 7.40
Sinn Féin	6.7	9.10	+ 2.40
Green Party	4.7	6.61	+ 1.91
Socialist Party	1.0	2.31	+ 1.31
Workers' Party	0.4	0.07	– 0.33
People Before Profit	0.5	0.90	+ 0.40
Christian Solidarity	0.4	0.06	– 0.34

Table 6.2 RTÉ's coverage of General Election 2011

Leader Debates

Televised leader debates are one of the main media events for political parties during election campaigns. Traditionally, in Ireland only the two largest parties, Fianna Fáil and Fine Gael, participated in televised leader debates. RTÉ was the only broadcaster that held a leaders' debate during elections, and it was a single broadcast only. In 2011, there were four debates in total (two on RTÉ, and one each on TV3 and TG4). The most important change in 2011 was an increase in the number of participating party leaders. The leader of the Labour Party, traditionally the third largest party, participated in all four debates and one of the debates involved five candidates representing all parties with a minimum representation in the outgoing Dáil. RTÉ advised the five political parties that the programme would 'aim to give a reasonable equivalence in time to each leader and to vary the order in which contributions are made so that no party leader is placed at a significant disadvantage'. However, one party subsequently received advice that the programme would allocate air time on the basis of the established ratios.

Party Political Broadcasts

Party political broadcasts (PPBs) are the only opportunity for political parties to deliver an unmediated televised message to potential voters. According to the BAI, PPBs can be provided only to political parties listed on the Register of Political Parties. RTÉ, however, decided that parties must also have at least seven nominated election candidates. This rule resulted in the exclusion of several smaller parties, such as the Workers' Party, the Communist Party of Ireland and the Socialist Party. The BAI also requires broadcasters to ensure that no party receives an unfair advantage when allocating time to PPBs. RTÉ allocated the total PPB time for each party on the basis of first preference votes received during the 2007 elections: Fianna Fáil (48 minutes), Fine Gael (31 minutes), Labour (12 minutes), Sinn Féin (8 minutes), Greens (9 minutes), and Others (9 minutes). With respect to the different times of day for PPBs, the slots with higher viewership numbers (i.e. after 6 p.m.) were given to the larger parties. This was despite the BAI election code that requires broadcasters to ensure that PPBs are transmitted 'at times that are aimed at achieving a similar audience for all such broadcasts'.

QUESTIONS

1. What rules did the 2009 legislation establish in relation to news media coverage in Ireland?
2. Name **three** elements of RTÉ's General Code of Conduct for coverage of the 2011 General Election.
3. What method did RTÉ use to establish the media coverage each political party should receive during the election campaign? Do you think it was fair? Why was it necessary?
4. Analyse the data presented in Table 6.2. What does it tell us about the media coverage for each political party?
5. How would you describe RTÉ's coverage of the 2011 General Election? In your opinion, how could it have been improved?

THE ROLE OF THE MEDIA

Case Study 5: Irish Media and the Banking Crisis

'Print and broadcast media in Ireland played an immeasurable but almost certainly significant role in the inflation of the property bubble and the legitimation of risky behaviour by the financial services sector in the lead-up to the crisis of 2007–8, and did so partly by ignoring or marginalising scepticism about these phenomena.'

Opening statement of Harry Browne to the Banking Inquiry, February 2015

The Committee of Inquiry into the Banking Crisis (the Banking Inquiry) was a joint committee of the Houses of the Oireachtas established in November 2014. The Banking Inquiry was set up to look into the factors that contributed to Ireland's banking crisis. In March 2015, the Oireachtas Banking Inquiry received expert submissions from media academics in relation to media coverage of the Irish economy before and after the financial crash. Harry Browne of Dublin Institute of Technology and Dr Julien Mercille of University College Dublin were among those who provided analyses. The inquiry heard how media professionalism had been compromised in an effort to avoid antagonising major advertisers. Both Browne and Mercille pointed to the limited coverage – and in some cases 'denial' – given to the 'property bubble' by the media in the lead-up to the crash. Newspapers such as *The Irish Times* and *Irish Independent* were receiving significant revenue from advertisers related to the property market. Property revenue accounted for 17 per cent of the total revenue of *The Irish Times* and 14 per cent of the total revenue of Independent News and Media. Such revenue ranged from €10 million in 2002 to €22 million in 2006. This was believed to have influenced coverage that downplayed the growing dangers and risks for the economy, as well as encouraged the continued development of the property market.

Geraldine Kennedy, former editor of *The Irish Times*, gave evidence that she was aware that many telephone calls were made by the property sector to the editorial team of *The Irish Times*. She stated that she was aware of the view held in the property sector that '*The Irish Times* would never get an advertisement again after the publication of an article by Professor Morgan Kelly which predicted a drop in property prices'. However, editors denied that their advertising relationships had influenced editorial independence.

QUESTIONS

1. According to Harry Browne and Dr Julien Mercille, why did the media give limited coverage to (and even deny allegations about) a property bubble in the run-up to the economic crash?
2. What facts and statistics support their view that there was a strong relationship between the media and the property market?
3. Apart from the construction sector, can you think of any other sectors or bodies that may have an influence over the media through advertising contracts or other means?

WHAT THE RESEARCH SAYS!
PUBLIC RELATIONS AND MEDIA CONTENT IN THE UK

Fig. 6.28 Public relations materials influence media content.

In 2008 Prof. Bob Franklin, Prof. Justin Lewis and Dr Andrew Williams published the first piece of research to look systematically at the role of PR in news production and the ability of journalists to maintain journalistic independence in the UK. The study involved a 'content analysis' of news coverage over a two-week period in 2006. The study covered the UK's main national 'quality' newspapers (2207 items in *The Guardian*, *The Times*, *The Independent*, *The Daily Telegraph* and the mid-market *Daily Mail*) and radio and television news reports (402 items broadcast by BBC Radio 4, BBC News, ITV News and Sky News). The researchers compared media content with materials produced by public relations companies and government bodies, and reports provided by the UK Press Association ('news agency copy') to identify the level of influence these had on the final coverage in published and broadcast news contents. The study's findings highlighted a significant link between public relations materials and media content.

Influence of Press Agency Copy (Text of a Story Supplied By a Press Agency)

- Newspaper articles: 30 per cent of the stories analysed replicated agency service copy almost verbatim (word for word), with a further 19 per cent being largely dependent on these materials. In other words, nearly half of all press stories appeared to come wholly or mainly from agency services. However, only 1 per cent of these directly attributed the source of information to the Press Association (PA) or relevant agency services.
- Broadcast news (television and radio): The influence of agencies and other media was less apparent in broadcast news. Nonetheless, 27 per cent contained information that appeared to be mainly or wholly derived from agency copy or other media.

Influence of Public Relations Materials

- Overall, at least 41 per cent of press articles and 52 per cent of broadcast news items were found to contain PR materials that play an agenda-setting role or where PR material makes up the bulk of the story.
- If we are to include those stories in which the involvement of PR was found to be 'likely' but could not be verified, then a majority of stories are informed by PR: 54 per cent of print stories and 58 per cent of broadcast new stories.

- Examples: A story in *The Times* headlined 'George Cross for Iraq War Hero' repeated almost verbatim a press release issued by the UK Ministry of Defence. Similarly, an article about a new hay fever vaccine in the *Daily Mail* reproduced a private press release from the drug company (Cytos) without adding any original material.
- For newspaper articles in which the news story is based on specific factual claims, only 5 per cent had obtained corroboration from other sources (such as academics or scientists).

Main Sources of PR Content

- The area with the most PR-generated material is health, where 37 per cent of stories are based mainly or wholly on PR material coming from healthcare and pharmaceutical companies.
- The most successful 'spin doctors' came from business rather than from non-governmental organisations (NGOs), charities or pressure groups. The business sector produced 38 per cent of PR material that was used in the media, as opposed to only 11 per cent coming from the NGO sector.
- When it comes to governmental PR, there is a significant difference between print and broadcast news: on TV and radio, 39 per cent of PR material used came from government sources; whereas in newspapers, 21 per cent of PR material used came from government sources. This may reflect the style of BBC journalism: research suggests that this style of journalism tends to favour 'official' sources, often government sources.
- Citizen-generated PR is by far the smallest category of public relations material encountered. In only 2 per cent of cases when PR was used in the composition of a story, the content originated from members of the public.
- The study concluded that the relationship between PR and media is a linear process in which PR material is reproduced by agency journalists whose copy is, in turn, reproduced in the news media.

The study concluded that the reliance of journalists on these news sources is extensive and raises significant questions.

QUESTIONS

1. Look at the research piece on Public Relations and Media Content in the UK. According to the research, what percentage of newspaper articles contained content that was either completely or mostly copied from press agencies? Why might this be a cause for concern for the public?
2. What percentage of broadcast news items were found to contain PR materials which play an agenda-setting role or where PR material makes up the bulk of the story?
3. What percentage of news articles containing facts were found to have corroborated their sources? Why might this be a major cause of concern?
4. Name the **two** main sources of PR content. How might this impact on the responsibility of the media to be independent and impartial?
5. Examine the methodology used for this research. What are the strengths and weaknesses of the methodology used?

MEDIA OWNERSHIP AND CONTROL: DOES IT MATTER?

YES

Marxist Perspective

There is a direct relationship between ownership and control. The mass media, like education, is a form of deliberate social control in society. This means that the media acts to ensure that the working class accepts the capitalist system. The ruling class are the owners of the media and they use it to maintain domination over the working class as well as to make every citizen into a consumer who will buy their products and use their services. This is achieved through media messaging as well as advertising. The media will not cover stories that might lead to a rejection of the capitalist system (e.g. the underlying causes of poverty). Media ownership is based on hierarchical relationships between the owner, the editor, the journalists and the public. The dominant ideas and values of capitalism are filtered down through this system.

Neo-Marxist Perspective

Capitalism still exists in modern society but it is more 'discrete'. Control is more complex and indirect. For example, instead of the owners being in control, it is the editor or even the journalist. However, these people hold the beliefs and interests of the ruling class. The media appears to present all views and challenge the ruling class. However, it presents alternative or challenging views as somewhat weaker or in a less favourable light, thus creating bias for the audience towards accepting the dominant class ideology of society. In the mid-1970s, the Glasgow University Media Group (GUMG) conducted one of the first surveys of British media content. It found that, while media content did support capitalist views, content was based more on the predominantly white middle-class social background of media personnel (editors, broadcasters, journalists) and economic considerations (e.g. extremist views tend not to sell) than a deliberate strategy as professed by classic Marxism. Neo-Marxists are also concerned with the rise of global media organisations and their effect on eroding regional cultures in favour of Western norms and values.

NO

Pluralist Perspective

Media ownership and control is shaped by consumer demand. It is about economics and not politics. Media content is based on what the public want. Our media preferences (whether we want entertainment media, current affairs or education) are *products* in this sense. Owners, editors and journalists are businesspeople. If they ignore the preferences of their customers, people will simply stop using or buying their media products (newspapers, television programmes, websites, etc.). The audience holds the real power in this sense. Pluralists also believe that given the apolitical nature of the mass media, it plays an important role in democracy and acts in a socially responsible manner. Private media organisations adopt professional ethics and codes of conduct to ensure this, and public (state-owned) media are regulated by the government. Public media will balance any possible bias in the private media, and the government can act to regulate media ownership to ensure that no single person can own too many media outlets or too many different types of media.

Postmodernist Perspective

We live in a society with infinite sources of media and it has become an integral part of our lives. We have reached saturation point. We now confuse reality with what is presented to us, and what we present, in the media. Media messages can be interpreted in different ways by different people. Media messages can even be interpreted differently by the same person from one day to the next. Media ownership does not mean control. It does not matter who owns the media. In a sense, all of us control the media.

QUESTIONS

1. Do you agree with the Marxist perspective that the media acts to ensure that the working class accepts the capitalist system? In your answer, give examples that support *and* contradict this view.
2. Compare and contrast the Marxist and neo-Marxist perspectives. Explain **one** similarity and **one** difference between the two views.
3. Would you agree with the pluralist analysis of the media? Is media content simply based on what the public want? Use examples and evidence to support your answer.
4. In your opinion, has media consumption reached 'saturation point', as claimed by the postmodernists?
5. Postmodernists claim that media messages can be interpreted in different ways by different people. Do you agree? Give examples in your answer.

Modern Trends and Debates on Media Ownership and Control

Two recent global – and opposing – trends have sparked debate on how the ownership and control of the media will influence freedom of the press and social responsibility. On the one hand, there is a growing concentration in media ownership, with a smaller number of individuals or single companies owning multiple media outlets. At the same time, however, we have witnessed the explosion of social media platforms and the rise of citizen journalism. If we have fewer 'owners' of the media, how does this affect freedom of the press? As a result of these trends, is the media more likely or less likely to act in a socially responsible way? To whom are the media accountable in such circumstances? These are the key issues in an exploration of how the media functions in a democratic society.

Growing Concentration of Media Ownership

Concentration of media ownership, also known as **media consolidation** or convergence, means that a smaller number of corporations control an increasing number of media outlets. In 1983, 50 corporations controlled the majority of news media in the US. By 2014, just five giant media corporations owned 90 per cent of US mass media. This trend is taking place across the world, including Ireland.

> **KEY TERM**
>
> **Media consolidation** (also known as media 'concentration' or 'convergence') is a term used to describe the phenomenon of media ownership being increasingly concentrated in the hands of fewer individuals or organisations.

Concentration of media ownership can be vertical or horizontal. Vertical media concentration happens when a media company owns many companies in the same line of production or distribution. For example, 21st Century Fox owns film studios in Hollywood, cinemas and television channels. Horizontal or cross-ownership is when a media company expands its ownership into different types of media (e.g. newspaper, television and radio). Horizontal concentration is the most common type of media concentration.

Media concentration presents challenges to press freedom and social responsibility in many ways. First, if we have only a few media companies in control, this can negatively affect the diversity of information available in the mass media. Many people have argued that media concentration will result in the mass media representing only the interests of a small number of elites. **Media pluralism** is threatened. Although it may appear that we have a diversity of media options (many different newspapers, radio stations and online outlets), many of these companies are owned and controlled by the same parent company. Concentrated ownership can act to filter the information we receive in the mass media.

Second, media concentration can lead to mass media being commercially driven, rather than serving the public interest. The argument is that the media is loyal and accountable to its 'sponsors' (i.e. advertisers and government) rather than the public. Even when stories are in the public interest, they may be suppressed if they are in opposition to the interests of the sponsors. Several examples in Ireland and beyond demonstrate the influence that media ownership can have on press freedom and social responsibility.

> ### KEY TERM
> **Media pluralism** refers to the existence of multiple media outlets owned by different groups, characterised by a plurality of voices and range of diverse opinions.

WHAT THE RESEARCH SAYS!

CONCENTRATION OF MEDIA OWNERSHIP IN IRELAND

Since 2014 the European University Institute has produced the annual Media Pluralism Monitor report, which examines media ownership in 19 EU countries, including Ireland. The report rates the following indicators into low-, medium- and high-risk categories: media concentration, political independence and social inclusiveness. In Ireland, the research is conducted in collaboration with DCU. The 2015 report found that none of the 19 surveyed countries was free from risks to media pluralism. Ireland received a 'high risk' rating for concentration of media ownership. The high risk was attributed because of the lack of strong legislation regulating media ownership in Ireland. No maximum ownership thresholds have been established in Ireland, as has been done in countries such as Germany. The 2014 Competition and Consumer Protection Act refers to the 'undesirability of allowing any one undertaking to hold significant interests [20 per cent share] within a sector or across different sectors of media business in the state'. Businessman Denis O'Brien owns 29.9 per cent of shares in Independent News & Media (INM), Ireland's largest print media group. He is also the director and main shareholder of Communicorp, which controls 20 per cent of the radio market in Ireland. INM owns the two biggest-selling newspapers in Ireland (*Irish Independent* and *Sunday Independent*) as well as the *Sunday World* and *The Herald*. It also owns 50 per cent of the *Irish Daily Star* and owns 14 local newspapers across the country. In the radio sector, Communicorp owns Ireland's two main commercial talk radio stations (Newstalk and Today FM) and a number of other stations (e.g. Dublin's 98FM, SPIN 1038). Ireland received a medium-risk rating for political independence and for social inclusiveness of the media.

RESEARCH ASSIGNMENT 6.10

Conduct a comparative analysis of media concentration and ownership in Ireland and the UK. Write a summary report on the topic.

> The Centre for Media Pluralism and Media Freedom (CMPF) publishes reports by country each year. These reports can be accessed at:
> https://educateplus.ie/go/mpm

The Propaganda Model

In 1988 Edward S. Herman and Noam Chomsky developed the *propaganda model* to explain how a profit-driven system can influence news content. The model states that corporate-owned news media will produce content that serves the interests of economic and political power in society. In the model, media content passes through five filters:

1. **Ownership:** Media concentration and profit orientation means that mass media has an interest in maintaining an economic and political climate that is favourable to them and ensures their continued profitability.

2. **Advertising:** As the main source of revenue for commercial mass media, the interests of advertisers act as a content filter. The media is unlikely to produce content that opposes its main advertisers.

3. **'Expert' sources:** The people who gather the news often rely on content that is easily and readily available. Elites facilitate this process through press conferences, press releases and other public relations products. The government, politicians and business leaders are also considered 'official' or 'authoritative' sources for stories.

4. **Flak:** This refers to disciplinary actions or negative commentary that can be used against journalists who do not 'toe the line'. Lawsuits, libel cases and complaints are examples of 'flak'.

5. **Creation of an 'external enemy or threat':** To discourage alternative or opposing perspectives, the mass media can set the limits of the debate on issues. This is achieved by establishing a common threat or enemy that will appeal to mass public opinion (e.g. communism or terrorism). Any alternative opinions are likely to be viewed as being 'in support of the enemy' and are heavily criticised as a result.

Fig. 6.29 Propaganda

CASE STUDY 6: The Impact of Media Concentration on Press Freedom

Rupert Murdoch is an Australian-born American media tycoon who built up and controls the most powerful media empire in the world. Murdoch owns two giant corporations called News Corp and 21st Century Fox, which control dozens of film, television and media companies across the globe. Fox News, *The New York Times* and *The Wall Street Journal* are just a few of the influential media outlets owned by Murdoch in America. In Britain, *The Sun*, *The Times*, *The Sunday Times* and Sky Television are among the media organisations that he owns. Murdoch has drawn wide criticism for what some consider a monopolisation of control over international media.

> **CASE STUDY**
> **The Impact of Media Concentration on Press Freedom**

In the 1990s Murdoch faced criticism in Britain over *The Sun* newspaper's ultra-aggressive campaign against the Labour Party and its leader, Neil Kinnock, in the run-up to the 1992 General Election. Labour was widely tipped to win the election but John Major became Prime Minister after the Conservatives achieved an unexpected victory. *The Sun* famously claimed credit for the Conservative victory.

Fig. 6.30 *The Sun* newspaper targets Labour leader Neil Kinnock and claims credit for the Conservatives' victory in the 1992 General Election

Research by the Media Standards Trust in the UK found that in the run-up to the 2015 General Election in the UK, *The Sun* targeted the Labour Party even more aggressively than it had in the 1992 election. The research found that 95 per cent of the paper's editorials were anti-Labour, with most of them directly attacking the Labour leader, Ed Miliband. Again, Labour lost the election. During the election campaign Murdoch is said to have berated his journalists in *The Sun* for not doing enough to stop Labour winning the election and warned of the consequences of a Miliband win for the future of News Corp. Prior to this, Miliband had signalled his intention to take action against the amount of power wielded by Murdoch in a review of rules regulating media ownership in the UK.

The Rise of Social Media and Citizen Journalism

Social media platforms and other types of 'new media' offer an alternative to traditional mass media. They are not replacing traditional media and journalism; instead, they operate alongside and with them. Content origination (where stories come from) has become democratised. Through our posts, shares, comments and engagements in online discussion forums, we have all become contributors to media content.

THE ROLE OF THE MEDIA   227

Citizen journalism offers both challenges and opportunities to media in modern democracies. It supports media pluralism by enabling ordinary people to have their voices and opinions heard in both new and traditional media. Radio programmes such as Joe Duffy's popular *Liveline* programme offer citizens the opportunity to set the political agenda via live phone-ins.

By removing traditional gatekeepers and filters, social media increases the potential for a richer and more diverse range of perspectives to be presented in the media. It has also facilitated the speedy gathering and dissemination of local- or individual-level analysis of breaking news. Many of our current big news stories first break on Twitter and other platforms. Social media has positively supported press freedom in political contexts where traditional journalism has been prevented from doing so (e.g. in political and civil crises).

However, the social media explosion has also presented society with important challenges. Critics of citizen journalism are particularly concerned with how it influences the principle of social responsibility for the media. Traditional media outlets in modern democracies are regulated to ensure a balance between press freedom and social responsibility. This is not the case with new media, which is almost entirely unregulated. Citizen journalists are not required to operate with the same ethical or professional standards as traditional journalists. Traditional journalists are also increasingly using social media to gather content for reporting. Facing pressure to publish as quickly as possible in the digital age has led to the practice of 'publish first and correct later'. Journalistic ethics and standards that are practised in traditional media forms (print or broadcasting media) are sometimes compromised as journalism is driven by 'views and clicks'. This can result in several negative consequences, including inaccurate reporting of facts, personal bias, inducing panic or incitement to hatred. The modern debate on the role of social media and citizen journalism in modern democracy centres on this balance between press freedom and social responsibility.

Citizen Journalism and Media Democracy

Case Study 7: Supporting Press Freedom

On 3 May 2011, the United Nations marked World Press Freedom Day, giving special attention to the role of social media and citizen journalism in 'contributing to freedom of expression, democratic governance and sustainable development'. The spread of popular uprisings in the Middle East and North Africa (the 'Arab Spring') was one of the first high-profile cases of the supportive role social media can provide to democracy and news media reporting. Initial reporting on the Arab Spring did not come in the form of traditional newspaper or television reporting, but through amateur videos, images and posts on social networking sites such as Facebook and Twitter. Given the lack of traditional journalists on the ground, as well as the government restrictions, many of the global news media outlets relied on this content for their initial coverage of the unfolding events. A Channel 4 documentary entitled *Syria's Torture Machine* used approximately 30,000 clips that had been uploaded on various social network sites. Since then, citizen journalism has continued to rise, providing coverage and alternative sources for many stories that later become major news headlines (tsunami disaster in Japan, police shootings in the US, etc.).

Case Study 8: Promoting Social Change: Marriage Equality

On 22 May 2015, Ireland said Yes to Marriage Equality in a referendum on same-sex marriage. While it is not possible to attribute the success of the Yes campaign to any single one of its campaign tools, social media is believed to have played a significant role. The Yes campaign implemented a widespread social media strategy across a variety of platforms, including Facebook, Twitter, WhatsApp and YouTube. The marriage equality issue was one that was close to the hearts and minds of young people, and social media is their domain. *The Irish Times* reported impressive social media statistics in the run-up to the referendum: 1.6 million Facebook posts in the week prior to the poll, and over 2 million Yes Equality hashtags every 48 hours. Social media users also developed their own campaigns, such as #hometovote, which encouraged many from the Irish diaspora to return to vote Yes. The social media strategy also prompted young voters to register for the first time. Approximately 65,000 first-time voters turned out for the referendum. The role of social media in the Yes campaign is now the focus of much research in Ireland and beyond.

Socially Irresponsible Reporting: The Boston Bomber

CASE STUDY 9

A powerful example of the dangers of social media can be seen in the tragic case of American student Sunil Tripathi, who was falsely accused on the Reddit social network of having committed the Boston Marathon bombings on 15 April 2013. Sunil had gone missing one month prior to the bombing, after dropping out of college. As part of a search appeal, his family had set up a Facebook page ('Help Us Find Sunil Tripathi'), which contained his photo. In the days following the Boston Marathon bombings, the FBI released the photographs of two suspects. A user on the Reddit social network then re-posted the FBI photos alongside the photo of Sunil Tripathi and a social media frenzy ensued. The post went viral and spread to Facebook, Twitter and other social media platforms. Mainstream media journalists began to take up the story, including retweets that Sunil was an official suspect in police investigations. Sunil's family began to receive threats and hate messages through the Facebook page that had been set up to find their son. Within 12 hours, hundreds of thousands of social media users believed that Sunil was responsible for the bombings. It was only the next day, when the NBC television network confirmed Sunil was not in fact a suspect that the fiasco ended. On 23 April, Sunil was found dead in Boston's Providence River. The details of Sunil's death remain unknown.

QUESTIONS

1. What are the advantages and disadvantages of social media as a source of information?
2. Does social media affect the distribution of power between different groups in society? Give examples from Ireland in your answer.
3. Do you participate in, or are you influenced by, social media campaigns and citizen journalism? If so, explain how and why.
4. What regulations could be imposed to counter the irresponsible use of social media?

ACTIVITY 6.9

Hold a classroom debate on the following motion:

'Citizen journalism is a danger to society – news reporting should be left to the professionals in the media.'

✓ SUMMARY

- There are three main types of media:
  - Print (e.g. newspapers)
  - Broadcast (e.g. television and radio)
  - Digital (internet-based).
- 'Traditional media' generally refers to print and audio-visual media. 'New media' refers to digital media.
- Each type of media has different characteristics that can be defined by the origination of content, purpose, style, level of audience involvement and level of content control.
- The media has a powerful and important role to play in democratic society. It:
  - Provides information and news to the public
  - Investigates abuses of power and holds those with power accountable for their decisions
  - Provides a platform for citizens to challenge government policy
  - Raises awareness of global injustices
  - Can promote social and political change.
- The media has the power to influence our thoughts and opinions through agenda-setting, framing and stereotyping.
- Freedom of the press is essential in a democracy.
- Freedom of the press must be balanced with the social responsibility of the media to act in the public interest in a balanced manner.
- The ownership and control of the media is an issue of vital importance, as it can impact on what content gets coverage and what content is ignored.
- Owners, advertisers and the public all have some influence on media content.
- There are two main types of media ownership in Ireland: public (RTÉ) and private (TV3, for example).
- The role of the media in society can be viewed through different ideological lenses.
- Marxists argue that the media functions as part of the 'superstructure' which upholds the dominant ideology of the elite: capitalism.
- Functionalists argue that the media is an integral part of the 'socialisation process': it imparts shared values and norms, which bonds a society.
- Feminists argue that the media reinforces traditional gender roles and promotes patriarchy.
- The current trend towards media consolidation has led to fears that there may be a lack of diversity of views in the media.
- Citizen journalism, through social media, is on the rise. This trend has led to the democratisation of access to, and the creation of, news and information.

Fig. 6.31 Key Word cloud

THE ROLE OF THE MEDIA

REVISION QUESTIONS

1. What does the term 'mass media' mean?
2. Name and give examples of the **three** main types of media.
3. Compare and contrast the key characteristics of print media and social media.
4. Explain the following terms in relation to the media:
   - Media consumption
   - Agenda-setting
   - Stereotyping
   - Watchdog
   - Framing
   - Media consolidation.
5. How has the rise of social networking and citizen journalism impacted on the media in relation to content origination, agenda-setting and public involvement in the news?
6. In your opinion, what role should the media play in a democratic society?
7. Compare and contrast Marxist and feminist perspectives on the role of the media in society.
8. Explain how the media can be viewed from a functionalist perspective.
9. Why is freedom of the press one of the most important aspects of a functioning democracy?
10. Name **three** international agreements that protect the right to freedom of the press.
11. Explain the concept of social responsibility of the media. Why is it important?
12. Describe **two** examples of occasions when the media acted in a socially irresponsible manner.
13. Explain the difference between public and private ownership of the media and give an example of each type in Ireland.
14. What are the benefits of having a public service broadcaster?
15. Explain the purpose of the Broadcasting Authority of Ireland. How does it promote standards in the media and hold RTÉ accountable?
16. Describe the role played by PR companies and spin doctors in agenda-setting and influencing media output.
17. How does a neo-Marxist interpretation differ from a traditional Marxist interpretation of media ownership and control?
18. Explain the pluralist view on media ownership and control.
19. How do postmodernists view the media?
20. What dangers does the process of media consolidation pose to society?
21. Explain the propaganda model developed by Herman and Chomsky.
22. What are the positive and negative aspects of the current trend towards citizen journalism via social media?
23. Draw up a list of regulations that should be imposed on the media.

DATA-BASED QUESTIONS

Complete the qualitative and quantitative research data-based questions exercise on pages 104–106 of your Skills Book.

EXAM FOCUS — Section B of LC Exam

REVISION EXERCISES

Complete the revision exercises on pages 107–109 of your Skills Book.

EXAM FOCUS — Section A of LC Exam

232 POWER AND PEOPLE

DISCURSIVE ESSAY TOPICS

1. Explain the concepts of freedom of the press, and social responsibility of the press. Use examples in your explanation. In your answer, refer to the ways in which these concepts are influenced by two or more of the following:
   - Ownership and control of the media
   - The role of advertising in the media
   - Origination of media content
   - Consumer-targeting strategies adopted by the media.

2. Critically examine the role of the press in a democracy.

3. 'The rise of citizen journalism poses as many problems as opportunities.' Discuss.

EXAM FOCUS — Section C of LC Exam

Reflective Practice

Ensure that you have completed all the Reflective Journal entries for this chapter (pages 23–24 of your Reflective Journal and Learning Portfolio) before moving on to the next chapter.

Complete the Learning Portfolio activities on pages 25–27 of your Reflective Journal and Learning Portfolio. This will help you to self-assess the extent to which you have achieved the learning intentions for this chapter, and will help you to monitor your progress.

ACTIVE CITIZENSHIP: Ideas for Action

Can you use any of these actions in a citizenship project?

- Devise a 'citizenship project' that your group will carry out to identify one way in which you can promote the role of media in democracy. Include the following in your project:
  - Description of the issue: refer to available statistics and evidence
  - Solution(s) to the issue: explain the rationale for your proposed solution
  - Ideas for action: explain the strategy and tactics to be adopted, list the specific objectives, and include a realistic timeframe to achieve them
  - Plan of action: include a step-by-step guide of all the actions to be taken
  - Evaluation: include guidelines for assessing the success of your citizenship project.
- Design and conduct a media campaign to raise awareness of an important issue of your choice. The issue can be local or national.
- Conduct a 'media watch' on local or national newspapers to examine how young people are represented. Write to the relevant newspapers with your findings and recommendations.
- Conduct an awareness campaign in your school on the dangers of the irresponsible use of social media.

THE ROLE OF THE MEDIA

CHAPTER 7
Human Rights and Responsibilities in Ireland

'To deny any person their human rights is to challenge their very humanity.' Nelson Mandela

HUMAN RIGHTS – WE'RE ALL ENTITLED TO THEM

HOPE | RULE OF LAW | DIGNITY | EQUALITY | PROSPERITY | PEACE | FREEDOM | JUSTICE

KEY TERMS

- Human rights
- Needs
- Wants
- Universal Declaration of Human Rights (UDHR)
- Universal
- Civil and political rights
- Economic, social and cultural rights
- Inalienable
- Indivisible
- Absolute rights
- Limited rights
- Qualified rights
- Rights holder
- Duty bearer
- Immediate obligation
- Progressive realisation
- UN Convention on the Rights of the Child (UNCRC)
- Equality of condition
- Direct discrimination
- Indirect discrimination
- Periodic reports

Introduction

Human rights are a cornerstone of modern democratic societies, such as Ireland. In a democracy, government policy-making (see Chapter 5) and social order are based on ensuring that the rights of individuals and groups are respected and protected. But what exactly are human rights? Who has them? Who is responsible for providing them? Does everyone enjoy them equally? What mechanisms do we have in place to ensure that they are respected? Through a focus on the right to education, we will examine these questions and explore important concepts and principles of human rights. We will look at the exact detail of our right to education, issues related to equality and non-discrimination, and research and engage with the question of whether or not education is enjoyed equally by everyone in Ireland.

By the end of this chapter you will be able to:

- Define human rights.
- Explain the difference between needs, wants and rights.
- Identify the rights to education as described in Bunreacht na hÉireann, the Universal Declaration of Human Rights and the UN Convention on the Rights of the Child.
- Identify rights holders and duty bearers in different contexts.
- Explain the difference between immediate obligation and progressive realisation.
- Explain key human rights terms and concepts, such as 'universal', 'inalienable', 'indivisible', 'absolute rights', 'limited rights', 'qualified rights', 'negative rights' and 'positive rights'.
- Distinguish between civil and political rights, and economic, social and cultural rights.
- Describe the nine grounds under which discrimination is illegal according to Irish law.
- Explain the difference between direct and indirect discrimination.
- Describe the patterns of diversity that exist on the island of Ireland in relation to ethnicity, language, religion, sexual orientation and disability.
- Present and debate various arguments about rights, with reference to evidence and different ideological perspectives.
- Describe the roles and functions of human rights bodies in Ireland, north and south.
- Use research evidence to evaluate whether the right to education is enjoyed equally by everyone in Ireland.

By the end of this chapter you will have developed the following skills:

- Active listening skills by listening carefully, summarising accurately, and responding critically to alternative viewpoints aired during class discussions and debate.
- Communication skills by putting forward and presenting your own evidence-based arguments on different human rights issues in Ireland.
- Dialogue skills by engaging in a moving debate and allowing your opinions to be challenged and even changed in the light of better arguments.
- Research skills by sourcing and compiling suitable evidence for various research assignments on human rights in Ireland.
- Teamwork skills by working effectively with others on different group tasks and participating constructively in a role play.
- Active citizenship skills by participating in an active citizenship project with the rest of your class.

KEY TERM

Human rights are the basic universal rights and fundamental freedoms that all humans are considered to be entitled to by virtue of the fact of being human. Human rights are often expressed and guaranteed by law. International human rights law lays down obligations for governments to act in certain ways – or to refrain from certain acts – in order to promote and protect the human rights and fundamental freedoms of individuals or groups.

What are Human Rights?

Fig. 7.1 Citizens demonstrating for human rights

We have expectations of how we can and cannot be treated in society, and of what freedoms we can enjoy. We use the term 'rights' in everyday conversation: 'It's my right!', 'Everyone has a right to their opinion', etc. But what exactly do we mean by human rights? At their basic level, human rights are the things we are entitled to because we are human. Human rights are the things we are allowed to have (e.g. health), to do (e.g. practise our religion) or to be (e.g. free and safe). Human rights can be positive or negative. For example, we have the right *to* education (positive right) and we have the right to be free *from* violence (negative right). Unlike a privilege, a right cannot be taken away: it is guaranteed. Many of our human rights relate to our basic **needs** (life, shelter, health, education, etc.) but not necessarily our **wants** (e.g. a sun holiday, the latest smartphone).

There are 30 basic human rights that every person has. These rights are contained in an important international document known as the **Universal Declaration of Human Rights**, which can be considered a type of international human rights constitution. At the national level, the Constitution of Ireland sets out our basic rights in Ireland. Today we may take the existence of human rights for granted, but they are a relatively recent development in human history.

KEY TERMS

Needs are the personal, physiological and socio-economic requirements necessary for humans to survive and function properly. For example, our basic needs for survival include access to food, clean water and shelter.

Wants are the goods and services that we desire, which are not necessary for survival and development. For example, we may want the latest designer jeans but we do not need them in order to survive and develop.

KEY TERM

The **Universal Declaration of Human Rights (UDHR)** is an international document that states basic rights and fundamental freedoms to which all human beings are entitled. It was adopted by the General Assembly of the United Nations on 10 December 1948. Motivated by the experiences of the preceding world wars, many countries came together to agree on a comprehensive list of human rights that were to be guaranteed to all people, everywhere.

ACTIVITY 7.1

Your teacher will give your group cards that display a variety of different needs and wants. Sort the cards into two categories: needs and wants.

SKILLS BOOK LINK 7.1

Go to page 110 of your Skills Book to complete Skill Task 7.1 on the human rights charter.

IN THE MEDIA

Having a home is a basic human right that thousands in our State are denied
Niamh Randall — PUBLISHED 23/03/2016 | 02:30

Student fees plan is 'an attack on the right to education'
Critics say proposed rise in third-level fees would hit people from poorer backgrounds
Sat, May 28, 2016, 19:50 — Mark Hilliard

Right to life of the mother takes precedence
Tue, Sep 4, 2012, 01:00 — Jacky Jones

SECOND OPINION: Will the church really seek an absolute ban on abortion?

ARE CITIZENS going to be subjected to another round of specious arguments and "mental reservations" by the Catholic hierarchy? The European Court of Human Rights gave its judgment on abortion in the case of A, B and C v. Ireland in December 2010. Article 8 of the Convention for the Protection of Human Rights and Fundamental Freedoms ("the Convention") protects personal autonomy, physical and psychological integrity, and the right to respect for private and family life.

Former TD's right to fair trial breached, court hears
Wednesday, December 07, 2011 — By Vivion Kilfeather

FORMER Fine Gael TD Liam Cosgrave has begun an appeal aimed at halting his criminal trial in connect with alleged corrupt payments concerning land rezonings in Co Dublin.

Mr Cosgrave and businessman James Kennedy are separately seeking orders from the Supreme Court stopping their trials over alleged corrupt payments in relation to rezoning of lands in Carrickmines, own by Jackson Way Properties in 1992 and the successful rezoning of part of these lands in 1997.

In the High Court last July, Mr Justice John Hedigan rejected both men's separate judicial review applicat and their appeals against that decision came before the Supreme Court yesterday.

However, the court said it would hear only Mr Cosgrave's appeal at this stage and would adjourn Mr Kennedy's appeal to January.

Mr Cosgrave, of Merrion Park, Blackrock, Co Dublin, has denied charges of receiving sums between June and June 29, 1992; on December 23, 1997, at Buswell's Hotel, Dublin; and on October 30, 1997, at the

Fig. 7.2 Human rights in the media

HUMAN RIGHTS AND RESPONSIBILITIES IN IRELAND

Universal Declaration of Human Rights (1948)

1. Everyone is born free and has dignity because they are human.
2. Everyone has equal rights regardless of differences between people, such as gender, colour, religion, language, wealth or political opinion.
3. Everyone has the right to life and the right to live in freedom and safety.
4. No one shall be held in slavery.
5. Everyone has the right not to be hurt, tortured or treated cruelly.
6. Everyone has the right to be treated as a person under the law, everywhere.
7. The law is the same for everyone and should protect everyone equally.
8. Everyone has the right to ask for legal help when their basic rights are not respected.
9. No one should be arrested, imprisoned or expelled from their country without good reason.
10. Everyone has the right to a fair trial, if accused of a crime.
11. Everyone has the right to be presumed innocent until proven guilty, if accused of a crime.
12. Everyone has the right to privacy.
13. Everyone has the right to travel within and outside their own country.
14. Everyone has the right to seek asylum in another country, if they are being persecuted in their own country.
15. Everyone has the right to a nationality.
16. Everyone has the right to marry and have a family.
17. Everyone has the right to own property on their own or with others. No one should have their property taken from them without good cause.
18. Everyone has the right to their own free thoughts, conscience and religion, including the right to practise their religion privately or in public.
19. Everyone has the right to say what they think and to share information with others.
20. Everyone has the right to meet with others publicly and privately and to freely form and join peaceful associations.
21. Everyone has the right to vote in regular democratic elections and to take part in the government of their country.
22. Every country must do its best to ensure that everyone has enough to live a life of dignity.
23. Everyone has the right to work for a fair wage in a safe environment, and also has the right to join a trade union.
24. Everyone has the right to rest and leisure time.
25. Everyone has the right to a home, enough food and healthcare.
26. Everyone has the right to education and to free primary education.

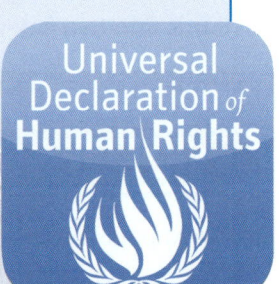

> Watch the following video clips before examining the text below:
> **Clip 1** – Eleanor Roosevelt and the origins and development of the UDHR: https://educateplus.ie/go/roosevelt
> **Clip 2** – Explanation of the 30 articles of the UDHR: https://educateplus.ie/go/declaration

27. Everyone has the right to take part in the cultural life of their community and the right to benefit from scientific and artistic learning.
28. National and international laws and institutions must make possible the rights and freedoms set out in this declaration.
29. Everyone has the responsibility to respect and uphold the rights of others in their community and the wider world.
30. No one has the right to take away any of the rights in this declaration.
(Simplified version of UDHR, Amnesty International Ireland)

QUESTION

Why do you think simplified versions of the UDHR are produced and circulated?

ACTIVITY 7.2

You will be assigned a selection of images by your teacher. Each image depicts one human right. Match the image to the human right it depicts.

SKILLS BOOK LINK 7.2

Go to pages 111–112 of your Skills Book to complete Skill Task 7.2 on character profiles.

RESEARCH ASSIGNMENT 7.1

Investigate a case from Ireland or around the world where human rights have been denied. Compile a report on the case. Include the following in your report:

- Geographic location: Name the country, region and locality.
- Human rights: List the specific UDHR articles being violated.
- Situation: Explain how the individual or group involved is being denied their human rights.
- Conflicting perspectives: Compare and contrast the views of the media, the government, the UN (examine any relevant UN reports) and human rights organisations on the issue.
- Advocacy campaigns: Assess the effectiveness of any campaigns on the issue.
- Solutions: Describe how the issue could/should be resolved.

See RESEARCH TIPS on page 33.

Human Rights Timeline

Human rights were not always universal. In the past, rights were enjoyed by a privileged few (e.g. kings, queens, noblemen). The first known declaration of human rights was produced by Cyrus the Great after conquering Babylon in 539 BCE. This declaration – the Cyrus Cylinder – was written on a clay tablet. It freed the slaves, gave people the right to choose their own religion, and established racial equality. Human rights quickly spread to India, Greece and Rome. The most significant moments in our modern human rights timeline include the following.

Watch 'The Story of Human Rights' at https://educateplus.ie/go/human-rights

1215: **The Magna Carta**
King John of England signed the 'Great Charter' which gave people individual rights and made the king subject to the law.

1776: **The United States Declaration of Independence**
The declaration of independence from Britain included protections for the right to life, liberty and the pursuit of happiness.

1789: **The Declaration of the Rights of Man and of the Citizen**
The French Revolution resulted in this declaration, which stated that all citizens are equal under the law.

1864–1907: **Geneva and Hague Conventions**
A series of international treaties protecting the rights of soldiers and establishing rules and customs of war.

Fig. 7.3 Declarations of human rights

1914–1919: **World War I and the League of Nations**
Following World War I, the Treaty of Versailles established rights of national sovereignty and self-determination and led to the creation of the League of Nations.

1939–1945: **World War II and the United Nations Charter**
With scores of millions dead and inconceivable atrocities committed, including the Nazi concentration camps, 51 of the world's leaders signed the United Nations Charter. A main aim was to promote 'respect for human rights and for fundamental freedoms for all without distinction as to race, sex, language or religion'.

POWER AND PEOPLE

1937: **Bunreacht na hÉireann**
Following Irish independence, the Constitution of Ireland was established, which sets out the fundamental rights of Irish citizens.

1945–1949: **Nuremberg and Tokyo trials**
War criminals were prosecuted for crimes against humanity committed during World War II.

1946: **Commission on Human Rights**
The United Nations established the Commission on Human Rights and made Eleanor Roosevelt the chairperson.

Fig. 7.4 Eleanor Roosevelt – diplomat, human rights activist and former First Lady of the United States – presents the UDHR

1948: **Universal Declaration of Human Rights**
The first globally accepted document of **universal** human rights was developed and was adopted by the United Nations on 10 December 1948.

1966: **International Human Rights Covenants**
Two international covenants were established: **Civil and political rights**, and **Economic, social and cultural rights**.

KEY TERMS

Human rights apply to everyone, everywhere. They are **universal**.

Civil and political rights is the term used to classify the group of rights which generally restrict the power of government in interfering with the rights of the individual, his or her autonomy and participation in civil and/or political life.

Civil and political rights are sometimes referred to as 'first generation rights'.

Economic, social and cultural rights is the term used to classify the group of rights which relate to the economic, social or cultural aspects of human life. They are sometimes referred to as 'second generation rights'.

Types of Human Rights

In Chapter 5, we learned how legislation in Ireland sets out in more detail the rights that are stated in the Constitution of Ireland. Similarly, we have a series of laws that flow from the Universal Declaration of Human Rights. In the 1960s, many states began to sign additional agreements known as *covenants* that expanded on the basic rights contained in the Universal Declaration of Human Rights. The International Covenant on Civil and Political Rights, and the International Covenant on Economic, Social and Cultural Rights were established in 1966 and gave rise to a distinction between two broad groups of rights.

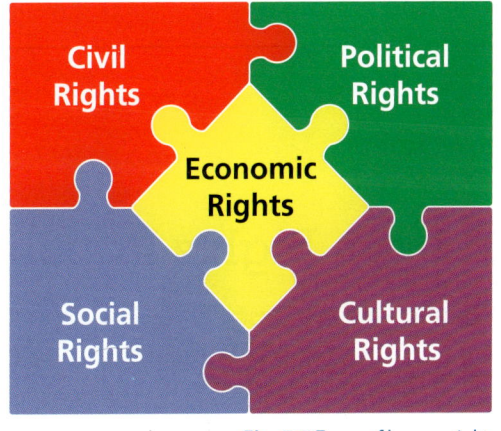

Fig. 7.5 Types of human rights

HUMAN RIGHTS AND RESPONSIBILITIES IN IRELAND   241

Type	Definition	Examples
(i) Civil and Political		
Civil	Rights that guarantee personal liberties, fair treatment and social equality for all individuals	• Life, liberty and security of the person • Protection from physical violence, torture and inhuman treatment, arbitrary arrest, detention, exile, slavery and servitude • Respect for privacy, right of ownership, freedom of movement • Freedom of thought, conscience and religion • Public hearing, presumption of innocence, and legal assistance
Political	Rights that enable individuals to participate freely in the political process	• Freedom of expression • Freedom of association and assembly • Take part in government, vote, and stand for election by democratic secret ballot
(ii) Economic, Social and Cultural		
Economic	Rights that create the conditions necessary for prosperity and wellbeing	• Property • Right to work, a fair wage and reasonable working hours • Trade union rights
Social	Rights that are necessary for an adequate standard of living	• Health • Shelter • Food • Social care • Education
Cultural	Right to participate freely in the cultural life of the community	• Share in scientific advancement • Protect scientific, literary or artistic materials

Table 7.1 Types of human rights

ACTIVITY 7.3

Re-examine the 30 articles of the UDHR and categorise each article into either **(i)** Civil and political rights or **(ii)** Economic, social and cultural rights.

SKILLS BOOK LINK 7.3

Go to page 113 of your Skills Book to complete Skill Task 7.3 on human rights denied in Ireland.

See **RESEARCH TIPS** on page 33.

Human Rights Principles

Human rights are based on several important principles. These principles apply to all types of human rights. Understanding these principles will help us to see how our human rights are meant to be put into practice.

Universal

Human rights are universal. This means that they apply to everyone everywhere. Each of us is a citizen of the world and each of us has these rights.

Fig. 7.6 Human rights are universal

Equality and Non-discrimination

We are all equal as human beings and we should all have equal access and opportunity to exercise our rights. Human rights should be guaranteed to everyone, regardless of race, ethnicity, gender, age, language, sexual orientation, disability, religion, political or other opinion, national or social origin, property, birth or other status.

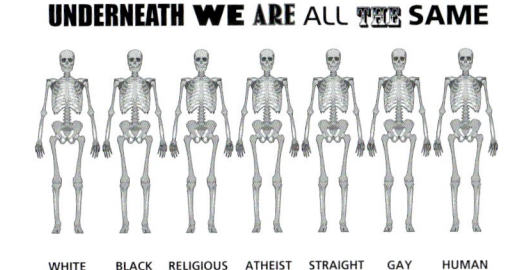

Fig. 7.7 Equality and non-discrimination

Dignity and Respect

Each of us has value and worth as a human being. Human rights are based on this principle of dignity. Dignity is about how we treat each other. When we treat someone in a way that respects their value and worth, we treat them with dignity. We must respect the dignity of each person, regardless of who they are or where they are from.

Inalienable

When we say that human rights are **inalienable**, this means that these rights cannot be taken away without a good reason and a proper process. Rights must be respected. We always have rights. If they are taken away from us, this is a violation.

Fig. 7.8 Human rights are based on the principle of dignity

> **KEY TERM**
>
> When a right is said to be **inalienable**, this means that it cannot be taken away without good reason and due process.

> Any law which violates the inalienable rights of man is essentially unjust and tyrannical; it is not a law at all.
>
> **Maximilien Robespierre**

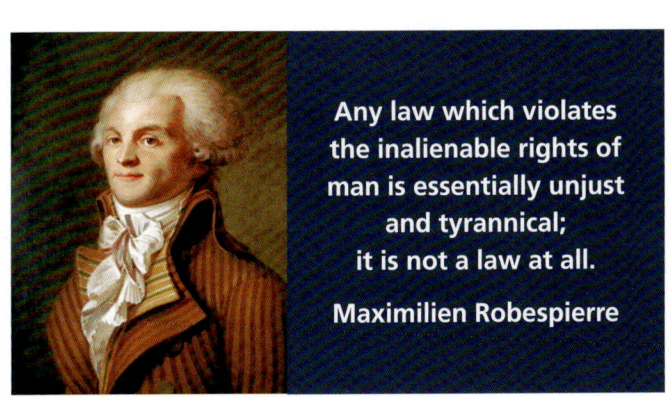

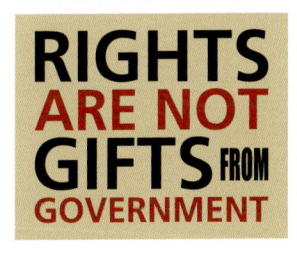

Fig. 7.9 Human rights are inalienable

HUMAN RIGHTS AND RESPONSIBILITIES IN IRELAND

Human rights can only be taken away in special circumstances and only after a fair and just process. For example, our right to freedom (liberty) can be restricted if we are found guilty by a court of law of committing a crime. There are three different categories of rights – absolute, limited and qualified – and the principle of inalienability is applied somewhat differently between these categories.

Indivisible

We cannot separate our human rights: they are **indivisible**. All our rights are interdependent: our enjoyment of one right is dependent on other rights. For example, if we do not have enough food or shelter or good health, we will be unable to fully exercise our right to education or our right to work.

As we will see, several key thinkers have made important contributions to the development of human rights.

> **KEY TERM**
>
> Human rights are **indivisible**: they are connected. We cannot enjoy one right fully without the others being fulfilled also.

Are Our Rights Inalienable at all Times?

Human rights are inalienable: they cannot be taken away. Some rights can never be taken away – these are **absolute rights**. Other rights can be withheld under special circumstances – these are *non-absolute rights*, such as **limited rights** or **qualified rights**.

Absolute Rights

Certain rights (e.g. the right to protection from torture) can never, under any circumstances, be taken away. These fundamental rights are said to be absolute.

Fig. 7.10 The right to protection from torture can never be taken away

Limited Rights

Some rights (e.g. the right to liberty or freedom of movement) can be restricted under special circumstances. For example, if we commit a crime and are found guilty by a court of law, our right to liberty will be temporarily restricted. Freedom of movement can also be restricted during times of public health or security crises.

Qualified Rights

These are rights that the government can decide to withhold or alter in special circumstances, and only when absolutely necessary in a democratic society. The interference must: fulfil a pressing social need, pursue a legitimate aim, and be proportionate. This usually happens when the government needs to restrict certain rights to protect the 'common good' or in the interest of public security. Some rights are complicated because the exercise of them might negatively affect the needs of wider society or democracy. For example, in Chapter 6 we saw how 'freedom of expression' in the media is

> **KEY TERMS**
>
> **Absolute rights** are rights that can never, under any circumstances, be taken away (e.g. freedom from torture).
>
> **Limited rights** are rights that can be restricted under special circumstances (e.g. if we commit a crime, our right to freedom will be temporarily suspended).
>
> **Qualified rights** are rights that the government can decide to withhold or alter in special circumstances, and only when absolutely necessary in a democratic society (e.g. freedom of movement during a public health pandemic).

Fig. 7.11 Some rights are limited: they can be restricted under special circumstances

regulated to ensure that the media acts responsibly. For many governments today, the threat of terrorism causes complications. Governments must protect the right of the media to freedom of expression, but they must also protect sensitive information that could be considered a security threat.

Another example of a qualified right is the right to practise one's religion. In France, for example, there are bans on many religious symbols in public spaces. Critics of such bans argue that this negatively impacts on the rights of people to practise their religion, e.g. Muslim women cannot wear full face veils in public spaces in France.

Interference (*derogation*) in qualified rights must be based on a *legitimate* objective, such as protecting the rights of wider society (i.e. security) or upholding a democratic principle. As you can imagine, the interpretation of qualified rights and any interference with qualified rights will bring much debate.

Most rights are considered to be *non-absolute* because they can often be in conflict with other important rights, and may or may not be upheld depending on the situation. Sometimes there can be a clash of rights between individuals. For example, you have the right to freedom of speech but you have a responsibility not to incite hatred or promote racism. In such circumstances, a compromise is needed. One right may be upheld over another, in the interests of the common good or the rights of the majority. With rights come responsibilities. By exercising human rights in a socially responsible manner, individuals can minimise the potential for conflict.

KEY THINKERS

HUMAN RIGHTS

John Locke and Jean-Jacques Rousseau made significant contributions to the development of human rights.

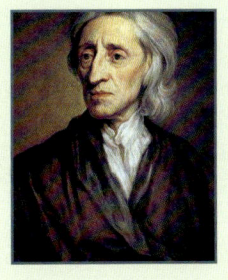

John Locke
Everyone is born free and equal. Each person has a number of natural rights, including the right to preserve one's life and to acquire and protect goods necessary for one's survival (i.e. property). There is no natural justification for the submission of one's rights to another.

Jean-Jacques Rousseau
'Man is born free.' Human beings are free in their natural state, as they are 'naturally good'. Preserving oneself does not necessarily conflict with the preservation of others. Rights are natural: everybody has rights.

QUESTIONS

1. Do you agree with Locke that there is 'no natural justification for the submission of one's rights to another'? Under what circumstances might it be necessary to limit or deny an individual his or her human rights? Give examples.

2. Rousseau claims that 'preserving oneself does not necessarily conflict with the preservation of others'. However, sometimes our freedom to exercise a right *can* lead to conflict with other people's rights. Can you think of examples where one set of human rights is in conflict with another set of human rights?

ACTIVITY 7.4

List all the rights that you have at your school. Categorise these rights into **(i)** absolute and **(ii)** non-absolute.

SKILLS BOOK LINK 7.4

Go to pages 113–114 of your Skills Book to complete Skill Task 7.4 on the UDHR.

ACTIVITY 7.5

Your teacher will assign two students to perform a role play based on a 'rights in conflict' scenario. Listen carefully to the arguments put forward by each actor. Decide who is in the right and how the conflict should be resolved.

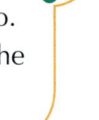

SKILLS BOOK LINK 7.5

Go to pages 114–116 of your Skills Book to complete Skill Task 7.5 on rights in conflict.

Rights Holders and Duty Bearers

When we talk about human rights, we are implying that someone *possesses* rights. **Rights holder** is the term that we use for the person who has rights. And since human rights are universal, each of us is a rights holder. In the context of the right to education, children and young people are the main rights holders.

If we 'have' a right, then there must be a person who is responsible for providing it. The UDHR places primary responsibility to 'respect, protect and fulfil' our human rights with the state (see Fig. 7.12). It is the government that has primary responsibility. However, depending on the context, private individuals, groups or organisations can also be responsible. We call those responsible **duty bearers**. With respect to children's rights, for example, the duty bearers could be parents, teachers and the Minister for Education.

> **KEY TERMS**
>
> **Rights holder** is the term we use to identify a person who has rights. Rights holders can be individuals or groups, depending on the right in question. For example, women are the rights holders when we are talking about women's rights.
>
> **Duty bearer** is the actor who has a particular obligation or responsibility to respect, promote and fulfil human rights and to refrain from human rights violations.

Duty bearers have obligations to ensure that we can fully exercise our rights. The obligations of duty bearers involve different strands, e.g. the obligation to *respect*, the obligation to *protect* and the obligation to *fulfil*.

An example with respect to the right to education could be:

- **Respect:** The state must respect the freedom of parents to choose schools for their children.
- **Protect:** The state must ensure that no one, including parents, can prevent children from going to school.
- **Fulfil:** The state must take positive measures to ensure that education is culturally appropriate for minorities and indigenous peoples, and that education is of good quality for all people.

Human Rights Obligations

The government has to

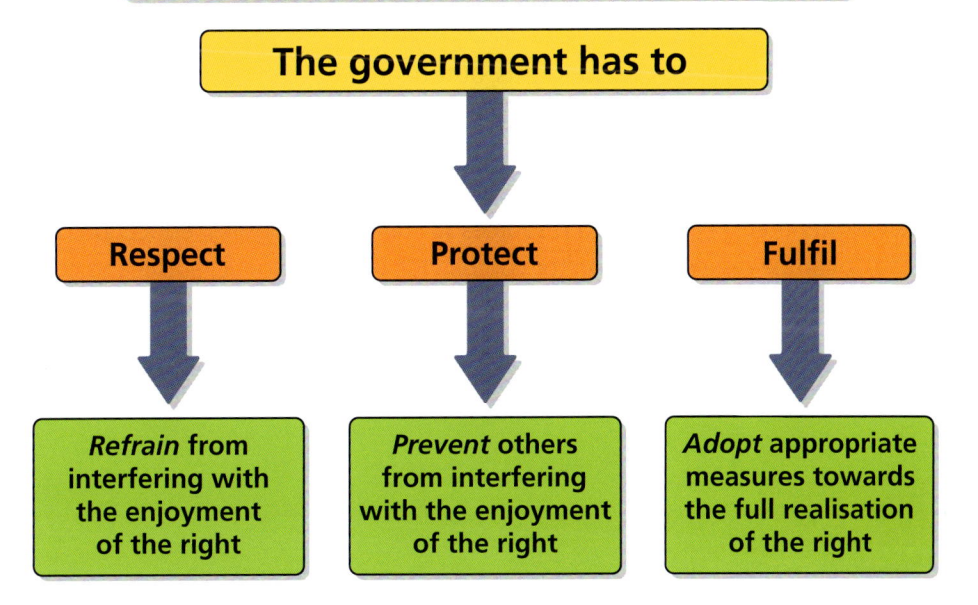

- **Respect** → *Refrain* from interfering with the enjoyment of the right
- **Protect** → *Prevent* others from interfering with the enjoyment of the right
- **Fulfil** → *Adopt* appropriate measures towards the full realisation of the right

Fig. 7.12 The government as duty bearer

QUESTIONS

1. Identify the rights holders and the duty bearers in each of the following cases:
   (a) In a prison
   (b) In your school
   (c) In a workplace.
2. Research and write a short account on any recent examples when the Irish government upheld its responsibilities as a duty bearer to: (a) respect, (b) protect and (c) fulfil the right(s) of an individual or group.

The Nature of Duty Bearer Obligations

Duty bearers, such as our governments, are obliged to ensure the conditions necessary for us, the rights holders, to fully exercise and enjoy our human rights. However, the exact nature of the obligation can differ depending on the type of rights we are talking about. Duty bearer obligations can be **immediate obligations** or **progressive realisations**.

Immediate Obligation

Civil and political rights carry an immediate obligation for their respect. This means that governments and other duty bearers are obliged to respect and protect certain rights with immediate effect, e.g. the right to life, freedom from violence and freedom of expression. This obligation is contained in the

KEY TERMS

Immediate obligation means that governments and other duty bearers are obliged to respect and protect certain rights with immediate effect, e.g. the right to life, freedom from violence and freedom of expression (civil and political rights).

Progressive realisation means that governments and other duty bearers have an obligation to work progressively towards the realisation of certain rights (usually economic, social or cultural). Duty bearers must ensure that they are respecting and fulfilling these rights to the best of their abilities and 'to the maximum extent of their available resources'.

International Covenant of Civil and Political Rights (ICCPR). Certain economic, social and cultural rights also have immediate obligations, e.g. free and compulsory primary education for all.

Progressive Realisation

With respect to economic, social and cultural rights, duty bearers have an obligation to work progressively towards the realisation of these rights. Duty bearers must ensure that they are respecting and fulfilling these rights to the best of their abilities and 'to the maximum extent of their available resources'. It does not mean that a lack of resources allows inaction, but it is based on the understanding that there are certain rights that take time and resources to fulfil (e.g. housing, education, healthcare). As you can imagine, it can be difficult to monitor compliance with economic, social and cultural rights. It involves assessing a government's current performance and deciding whether or not it is doing its best to implement these rights. During times of political or economic crises, it can be especially difficult to assess whether or not a government is fulfilling its obligation of progressive realisation.

ACTIVITY 7.6

Re-examine the UDHR and identify which articles should be designated for **(i)** immediate obligation and **(ii)** progressive realisation.

ACTIVITY 7.7

Create a puzzle (such as a wordsearch or crossword) that includes the following key terms:

universal, inalienable, indivisible, absolute rights, qualified rights, rights holders, duty bearers, immediate obligation, progressive realisation.

Swap your group's puzzle with another group's puzzle. Complete the puzzle.

Visit the Discovery Education Puzzlemaker site at https://educateplus.ie/go/puzzle-maker

SKILLS BOOK LINK 7.6

Go to page 117 of your Skills Book to complete Skill Task 7.6 on limitations placed by the Irish government on human rights.

See **RESEARCH TIPS** on page 33.

Complete your next Reflective Journal entry (pages 28–29)

248   POWER AND PEOPLE

Human Right in Focus: The Right to Education in Ireland

We have many different human rights. One right which is of particular concern in relation to children and young people is the right to education. An examination of the right to education allows us to explore human rights – instruments, principles and obligations – in more detail. When we want to understand the exact content of a right, and what it entails, we need to look to the law. The right to education in Ireland is protected by national and international law. At the national level, the Constitution of Ireland protects this right. At the international level, the UDHR and the **UN Convention on the Rights of the Child (UNCRC)** are key documents. The relationship between the UDHR and UNCRC is quite like that between the Irish Constitution and the Education Act. The UDHR states that we have the right to education, and the UNCRC provides more detail on the exact nature of the right. A key difference between the UDHR and the UNCRC is that the UNCRC is a legally binding agreement, whereas the UDHR is not.

> **KEY TERM**
>
> The **UN Convention on the Rights of the Child (UNCRC)** is a legally binding international agreement that establishes the civil, political, economic, social and cultural rights of every child, regardless of their race, religion or abilities.

Article 42 of Bunreacht na hÉireann (the Constitution of Ireland) describes the right to education for people living in Ireland.

1. The state acknowledges that the primary and natural educator of the child is the family and guarantees to respect the inalienable right and duty of parents to provide, according to their means, for the religious and moral, intellectual, physical and social education of their children.

2. Parents shall be free to provide this education in their homes or in private schools or in schools recognised or established by the state.

3. The state shall not oblige parents in violation of their conscience and lawful preference to send their children to schools established by the state, or to any particular type of school designated by the state.

4. The state shall, however, as guardian of the common good, require in view of actual conditions that the children receive a certain minimum education, moral, intellectual and social.

5. The state shall provide for free primary education and shall endeavour to supplement and give reasonable aid to private and corporate educational initiative, and, when the public good requires it, provide other educational facilities or institutions with due regard, however, for the rights of parents, especially in the matter of religious and moral formation.

Fig. 7.13 The right to education in Ireland is enshrined in Bunreacht na hÉireann

SKILLS BOOK LINK 7.7

Go to page 118 of your Skills Book to complete Skill Task 7.7 on the right to education as outlined in the Constitution of Ireland.

RESEARCH ASSIGNMENT 7.2

Study article 42 of Bunreacht na hÉireann and write a detailed report on it for submission to a special United Nations Committee on the Right to Education. Include the following in your report:

- Write a summary of the key points in article 42.
- Identify the rights holders, duty bearers and those with responsibility.
- List the aspects of article 42 that require immediate obligation or progressive realisation.
- Describe the overall strengths and weaknesses from a UN human rights perspective.
- Provide recommendations on how article 42 can be improved or amended.

See RESEARCH TIPS on page 33.

ACTIVITY 7.8

Hold a classroom debate on the following motion:

'Home schooling in Ireland should be outlawed – the state is better equipped than the family to provide for the right to education.'

In preparation for the debate, conduct research on the pros and cons of home schooling. In particular, you could examine research evidence from countries where home schooling is more prevalent (e.g. Australia, Canada, the US, the UK). You may also examine the reasons why home schooling is illegal in other countries (e.g. Sweden, Germany).

The Right to Education: International Instruments

Article 26 of the Universal Declaration of Human Rights

1. Everyone has the right to education. Education shall be free, at least in the elementary and fundamental stages. Elementary education shall be compulsory. Technical and professional education shall be made generally available and higher education shall be equally accessible to all on the basis of merit.

2. Education shall be directed to the full development of the human personality and to the strengthening of respect for human rights and fundamental freedoms. It shall promote understanding, tolerance and friendship among all nations, racial or religious groups, and shall further the activities of the United Nations for the maintenance of peace.

3. Parents have a prior right to choose the kind of education that shall be given to their children.

Articles 28 and 29 of the UN Convention on the Rights of the Child

Article 28: Education

1. States parties recognise the right of the child to education, and with a view to achieving this right progressively and on the basis of equal opportunity, they shall, in particular:

    (a) Make primary education compulsory and available free to all;

    (b) Encourage the development of different forms of secondary education, including general and vocational education, make them available and accessible to every child, and take appropriate measures such as the introduction of free education and offering financial assistance in case of need;

- (i) Make higher education accessible to all on the basis of capacity by every appropriate means;
- (ii) Make educational and vocational information and guidance available and accessible to all children;
- (iii) Take measures to encourage regular attendance at schools and the reduction of drop-out rates.

2. States parties shall take all appropriate measures to ensure that school discipline is administered in a manner consistent with the child's human dignity and in conformity with the present Convention.

3. States parties shall promote and encourage international cooperation in matters relating to education, in particular with a view to contributing to the elimination of ignorance and illiteracy throughout the world and facilitating access to scientific and technical knowledge and modern teaching methods. In this regard, particular account shall be taken of the needs of developing countries.

Article 29: Aim of Education

1. States parties agree that the education of the child shall be directed to:
   - (a) The development of the child's personality, talents and mental and physical abilities to their fullest potential;
   - (b) The development of respect for human rights and fundamental freedoms, and for the principles enshrined in the Charter of the United Nations;
   - (c) The development of respect for the child's parents, his or her own cultural identity, language and values, for the national values of the country in which the child is living, the country from which he or she may originate, and for civilizations different from his or her own;
   - (d) The preparation of the child for responsible life in a free society, in the spirit of understanding, peace, tolerance, equality of sexes, and friendship among all peoples, ethnic, national and religious groups and persons of indigenous origin;
   - (e) The development of respect for the natural environment.

No part of the present article or article 28 shall be construed so as to interfere with the liberty of individuals and bodies to establish and direct educational institutions, subject always to the observance of the principle set forth in paragraph 1 of the present article and to the requirements that the education given in such institutions shall conform to such minimum standards as may be laid down by the state.

SKILLS BOOK LINK 7.8

Go to page 119 of your Skills Book to complete Skill Task 7.8 on a comparison of the UDHR and UNCRC.

RESEARCH ASSIGNMENT 7.3

Write a speech to be delivered to an Oireachtas committee on reform of the education system. In your speech:

- Include a summary of the right to education as outlined in the UDHR and articles 28 and 29 of the UNCRC.
- Provide an explanation of the state's responsibility as the primary duty bearer to respect, protect and fulfil these rights.
- Highlight areas where the state is fulfilling its responsibilities in relation to the right to education
- Highlight areas where the state is failing to fulfil its responsibilities in relation to the right to education.
- Describe your own proposals to be included in a new Education Act to reform the Irish education system.
- Include aims and objectives that require **(i)** immediate obligation and **(ii)** progressive realisation.
- Outline any amendments that may need to be made to the Constitution of Ireland (article 42).

See **RESEARCH TIPS** on page 33.

State Obligations Under the Right to Education: The 4 As

In an effort to provide more detail to states on their exact obligations with respect to the right to education, the United Nations issued further guidance in 1999. The document is known as *General Comment No. 13*. It identifies four elements of state responsibility: the 4 As.

1. Availability

Functioning educational institutions and programmes must be available in sufficient quantity (e.g. appropriate class sizes). This includes appropriate physical infrastructure, such as buildings, sanitation facilities, safe drinking water, libraries, computer facilities and other relevant technologies.

2. Accessibility

Educational institutions and programmes must be accessible to everyone, without discrimination. Accessibility has three dimensions:

- Non-discrimination: Education must be accessible to all, especially the most vulnerable groups, without discrimination on any of the prohibited grounds (e.g. admission policies should not discriminate).
- Physical accessibility: Education must be within safe physical reach, either by convenient geographic location (e.g. a neighbourhood school) or via modern technology (e.g. access to a 'distance learning' programme).
- Economic accessibility: Education must be affordable for everyone. Primary education is made immediately available and free to all. And states are required to progressively (eventually) introduce free secondary and higher education.

3. Acceptability

The form and substance of education, including curricula and teaching methods, must be acceptable to students. Education must be relevant, culturally appropriate and of good quality.

4. Adaptability
Education must be flexible so that it can adapt to the needs of changing societies and communities, and respond to the needs of students within their diverse social and cultural settings (e.g. minority children, migrant children, children from the Traveller community, children with disabilities).

QUESTIONS

1. To what extent are the 4 As provided for at your school?
2. To what extent has the Irish government fulfilled its obligation to uphold the 4 As nationally? With which of the As are they succeeding? With which of the As are they failing?

WHAT THE RESEARCH SAYS!
AUSTERITY AND THE RIGHT TO EDUCATION IN IRELAND

Progressive realisation means that states have an obligation to fulfil rights 'to the maximum extent of their available resources'. But what happens during times of economic crisis? In 2014 the European Parliament commissioned a study to research the impact of the economic crisis and the austerity measures introduced by the Irish government on a number of fundamental human rights. The report was published in 2015. It found that austerity measures and successive budget cuts between 2009 and 2014 had seriously affected a number of fundamental rights, including education.

Fig. 7.14 Teachers demonstrating for the right to education in Ireland

Reduction in Teacher Numbers
The pupil–teacher ratio increased in primary schools from 27 to 28 per class and in secondary schools from 18 to 19 per class from September 2009. This resulted in 200 fewer primary teachers and 200 fewer post-primary teachers. Other important posts, such as educational psychologists, language support teachers, and the visiting teacher service for Travellers were also affected.

Abolition of School Grants
Grants were removed in many areas of education, such as music, language support and Transition Year. Children from poorer backgrounds and children from the Traveller community were particularly affected by the removal of specialised support grants.

Increase in School Transport Costs
The 2014 budget increased the post-primary school transport charges by €100 per annum and introduced a €100 charge for primary school transport. In 2011, the rural transport coordination service for 331 rural DEIS primary schools was removed.

Reduction of Clothing and Footwear Allowance
The 2013 budget reduced the Back to School Clothing and Footwear Allowance from €250 to €200 for children aged 12–17 and from €150 to €100 for children aged 4–11.

The report concluded that the budget cuts had impacted negatively on the right to education in several important ways, resulting in early school leaving and an increase in the pupil–teacher ratio. Children with disabilities, immigrant children and Traveller children were found to be particularly affected.

Note: In Budget 2018, the figures for Back to School Clothing and Footwear Allowance were €125 for primary school and €250 for post-primary school.

QUESTIONS

1. Explain progressive realisation.
2. In what ways did the austerity measures during the recent economic recession impact on the standard of education in Ireland?
3. According to the European Parliament report, how did the budget cuts affect the right to education in Ireland? What groups in society suffered from this the most?
4. When it comes to progressive realisation, should the right to education be prioritised over other economic, social and cultural rights? Since rights are indivisible, what other rights should be prioritised by the government? Explain your answer.
5. Look back at the 4 As on page 252. Can you identify evidence from the European Parliament report to show that the Irish government had failed on any of these?

RESEARCH ASSIGNMENT 7.4

The Children's Rights Alliance produces an annual 'Report Card' which assesses the Irish government's performance in meeting its obligations under the UNCRC. Research the most up-to-date report card (for the current year) and write a summary of the evidence concerning the government's performance in relation to the right to education.

See **RESEARCH TIPS** on page 33.

Visit **www.childrensrights.ie** and click on 'report card'.

The Right to Education: Equality and Non-discrimination

Human rights are universal and are based on the principle of equality and non-discrimination. However, some groups in society do not fully enjoy their rights in an equal way. As we have seen, society is made up of diverse groups on the basis of different social categories, such as gender, age and ethnicity (see pages 77–78). Simply by being a member of a particular group (e.g. being female, an immigrant or a member of the Traveller community) a person may face discrimination in relation to their rights. Therefore, we need laws to safeguard equality and non-discrimination. In Ireland, we legally recognise nine categories or grounds of discrimination. Discrimination on the basis of any of these nine grounds is illegal. The concept of non-discrimination is upheld and protected by important laws known as the Equal Status Acts.

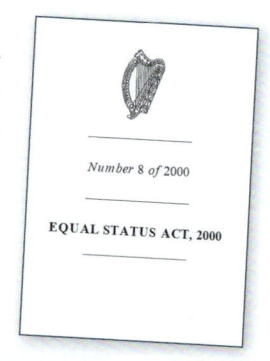

Fig. 7.15 Equal Status Act, 2000

Equality: The Different Dimensions

When we think about equality, what do we mean? Equality has many different dimensions that we need to analyse.

Access

Equality of access refers to whether or not people have equal access to a right. For example, does each person have a primary school relatively close to where they live? Does each school have enough teachers?

Participation

Equality of participation is about whether or not people can exercise a right in the same way and unhindered. For example, does each person have the same opportunity to participate in school, i.e. during the lessons, in mock exams, in sport and cultural activities and in Transition Year?

Outcome

Human rights are ultimately about having positive impacts on our lives in some way. The right to healthcare will contribute to our wellbeing. The right to housing will help us to find shelter that keeps us safe and warm. Equality of outcome looks at whether or not everyone is enjoying the positive impacts of a human right in an equal way. If people are not experiencing these positive impacts, we must find out why this is so. For example, does each person get the benefits of a good education, e.g. skills, knowledge, capabilities, good grades and the prospect of a good job?

Equality of Condition

Kathleen Lynch and John Baker at the UCD Centre for Equality Studies developed the term **equality of condition** to explain why having equal access to a right does not always lead to having equal outcome (benefits). Lynch and Baker define equality of condition as 'people's real options'. People's real options – or lack of options – are rooted in wider society. Existing inequalities in society will have an impact on whether or not a group has *real* access to a right, and whether or not this group can enjoy the associated positive outcomes. For example, I may have access to the same school and classes as everyone, but this does not necessarily mean that I have the same benefits or results. This is because I may not have the same conditions as others in my class, e.g. respect from my teachers or fellow students, money for grinds, time to study or a supportive family environment. All of these conditions affect how I can access my right to education.

> **KEY TERM**
>
> **Equality of condition** is an egalitarian principle that seeks to achieve equality in material (e.g. income) and non-material (e.g. familial or social support networks) conditions of individuals or groups in society.

Affective Equality

The nurturing that produces love, care and solidarity constitutes a unique system of affective relations. Affective relations are not social derivatives, subordinate to economic, political or cultural relations in matters of social justice. Rather, they are productive, materialist human relations that constitute people mentally, emotionally, physically and socially. Affective relations are sites of political importance, therefore, for the realisation of social justice. Lynch argues that it is impossible to have gender justice without relational justice in loving and caring. Moreover, if love is to thrive as a valued social practice, public policies need to be directed by norms of love, care and solidarity rather than norms of capital accumulation. To promote equality in the affective domains of loving and caring, she argues for a four-dimensional rather than a three-dimensional model of social justice (one that recognises the importance of relational justice (affective equality) as well as the redistribution of wealth, recognition of differences and parity of representation in the exercise of power.

QUESTIONS

1. Do all the people in your community enjoy the right to equality of access and participation in education? Why/why not?
2. Explain why equality of access does not guarantee equality of outcome.
3. What measures could the government take to progress towards equality of outcome for all participants in education?
4. Can equality of outcome ever be fully realised?
5. In your opinion, is it the government's responsibility to ensure equality of outcome, or does the government's responsibility extend only to ensuring equality of access?

RESEARCH ASSIGNMENT 7.5

Create a profile of Ireland's diversity. Using the most up-to-date census statistics, create a profile on the patterns of diversity on the island of Ireland. Include statistics on and evidence of diversity. Use the following headings in your profile:

- Ethnic diversity and membership of the Traveller community
- Religious diversity
- Language diversity
- Diversity of ability and disability.

Create a graph to illustrate the key points of your profile.

See **RESEARCH TIPS** on page 33.

- Visit **https://educateplus.ie/go/census-reports** for the Ir 2016 Census Report
- Visit **https://educateplus.ie/go/ni-census** for informatio about the Northern Ireland census

Equal Status Acts 2000 to 2015

The Equal Status Acts 2000 to 2015 provide us with important legal protection against discrimination outside the workplace in Ireland. For workplace-related discrimination in Ireland, we have separate laws known as the Employment Equality Acts 1998–2015.

The Equal Status Acts provide us with the legal definition of discrimination in Ireland. Discrimination happens when a person is treated less favourably than another person in the same situation on the basis of one or more of the following grounds:

- Gender
- Marital status
- Family status
- Sexual orientation
- Religion
- Age
- Disability
- Race
- Membership of the Traveller community.

See page 64 for more information on discrimination.

Missing Grounds?

As of 1 January 2016, the Equality Act 2015 introduced 'housing assistance' as a new discriminatory ground. It is now illegal for landlords to refuse to accept tenants because of rental allowance.

Irish equality legislation continues to evolve. However, it does not contain several grounds that are mentioned in international instruments such as the UDHR and UNCRC. These include language, political or other opinion, social origin, property, birth or other status.

Discrimination: Direct and Indirect

Direct discrimination happens when a person receives unfair treatment because of their membership of one of the official grounds. An example of direct discrimination in the case of education would be if a school excluded a child from enrolling because of their race. **Indirect discrimination** happens when the outcome is unfavourable even if the action does not seem to be discriminatory at first. An example of indirect discrimination would be if a school advised a student who is a wheelchair user that they could not attend the school tour to a local museum because the building is not wheelchair accessible. If it was found that there was an alternative option, reasonably close by, which is wheelchair accessible but the school did not investigate that option, this would amount to indirect discrimination.

KEY TERMS

Direct discrimination happens when a person, or a group of people, is treated less favourably than another person or group based on certain characteristics or origin. In Ireland we officially recognise nine grounds for discrimination.

Indirect discrimination happens when a practice, policy or rule which applies to everyone in the same way has a worse effect on some people or groups than others, placing them at an unfair disadvantage. In Ireland, the same nine grounds are officially recognised, whether for direct or indirect discrimination.

POWER AND PEOPLE

Equality does not mean that everyone needs to be treated in exactly the same way. It means that everyone should be able to enjoy their rights equally. This means that certain groups may need special measures to allow this to happen. Duty bearers (e.g. schools) must make special arrangements to ensure that people with disabilities can enjoy their rights in an equal manner. This is known as 'reasonable accommodation'. Examples of reasonable accommodation in the context of education include learning and language supports in schools.

Discrimination in School

The Equal Status Acts identify four specific areas in which a school must not discriminate:

- The admission of a student, including the terms or conditions of the admission of a student
- The access of a student to a course, facility or benefit provided by the school
- Any other term or condition of participation in the school, e.g. sporting events
- The expulsion of a student or any other sanction.

QUESTIONS

1. Look at the nine grounds of discrimination that are legally recognised in Ireland. Compare this list with the UN list of groups who should not be discriminated against (see page 256). Should any of these groups be added to the Equal Status Acts? In your opinion, why has the Irish government not added them?
2. Are there any other groups that should be legally protected against discrimination in Ireland?
3. What is the difference between direct and indirect discrimination?
4. Give examples of direct and indirect discrimination that you have experienced or are aware of today.
5. Can you think of any examples from history of direct discrimination that was used to bring benefit to some groups over other groups?
6. Can you think of examples when discrimination was used as a basis by those in power to promote a certain ideology or to influence social norms?

SKILLS BOOK LINK 7.9

Go to pages 120–124 of your Skills Book to complete Skill Task 7.9 on discrimination.

ACTIVITY 7.9

Your group will be assigned one of the nine grounds under which discrimination is outlawed in Ireland. Research the human rights advocacy groups or civil society bodies that work in Ireland to protect human rights in this area. Write a short report and present it to your class. Include the following in your report:

- Name the ground your group investigated.
- Name the civil society bodies that focus on this area.
- Describe the current campaigns being conducted by these groups: the types of discrimination they address and the recommendations they advocate.

Discrimination in Education: Ireland and Northern Ireland

CASE STUDY 1: Grounds for Discrimination: Religion

School Admissions Policy: Ireland

In 2015 the School Admissions Bill was introduced by the government in an effort to address concerns over discriminatory practices in school admission policies. Many civil society groups and UN treaty bodies had long called for legislative measures to address school admission practices that excluded certain groups of children, such as children with special needs, children of immigrants and Traveller communities. Once passed, the bill will require school management to:

- Admit every student that applies to schools not over-subscribed (i.e. that have places available)
- Ban waiting lists and fees
- Publish school admission policies
- Include an explicit reference to the nine grounds of discrimination in their admission policy.

The bill will provide important protections against discriminatory admissions practices. One area of continued debate, however, is the protected right of religious schools (a right granted by the Equal Status Act, 2000) to give preference to children of a particular faith in their admission policies. If the school can prove that the refusal of admission of a student is required to maintain the ethos of the school, this is permitted. This exemption has been criticised by the UN Committee on the Rights of the Child, the UN Committee on Economic, Social and Cultural Rights, the Irish Human Rights and Equality Commission, and the Ombudsman for Children.

CASE STUDY 2: Grounds for Discrimination: Disability

Northern Ireland

In 2007 the Equality Commission in Northern Ireland received a complaint against a secondary school for discriminatory treatment against a 17-year-old girl with spinal muscular atrophy. The girl was a wheelchair user with some hearing difficulties. Three months before her GCSE results, her parents looked at Sixth Form options for her at several schools but were told to wait until after the GSCE results. The young woman did very well in her GSCE exams and decided to take three A levels, including Biology and Chemistry. Her parents found a school with suitable wheelchair and disability access which offered these subjects. It turned out, however, that a lot of paperwork was required by the Education and Library Board before

POWER AND PEOPLE

Case Study: Discrimination in Education: Ireland and Northern Ireland

the girl could start. Because of her disability, a formal request to attend the school had to be written. Then an occupational therapist's report on the school had to be completed. Nobody in the Education Board could advise on how long this process would take – and by this stage, the school term was due to start the following week. Neither the girl nor her parents had been given any prior advice about these procedures. Because it was likely the young woman would be disadvantaged by missing time at the start of term, she decided she would go back to her old school. Unfortunately, this meant that she could not study Chemistry: her former school did not offer this subject. Her parents felt that their daughter was treated in a discriminatory manner because of her disability: if she had been non-disabled, she would have been at the school she had chosen. Her parents asked the Education Board to provide home tuition in Chemistry, but the Board refused. The case went to tribunal under SENDO (Special Educational Needs Disability Order) law and was settled in 2008. The Education Board agreed to provide Chemistry teaching. They apologised for what had happened. They restated their commitment to equality under the disability laws and agreed to ensure that their procedures reflected this. They agreed to meet with the Equality Commission to check this and to provide disability awareness training to all staff.

SKILLS BOOK LINK 7.10

Go to page 124 of your Skills Book to complete Skill Task 7.10 on discriminatory practices in the Irish education system.

See RESEARCH TIPS on page 33.

How are Human Rights Monitored and Protected?

We have several bodies and mechanisms in place to ensure that our human rights are respected and protected. At the national level, special state bodies play an important role. At the international level, states are required to regularly report on their human rights obligations.

State Bodies for Human Rights on the Island of Ireland

States must establish independent bodies that can monitor whether or not human rights are being respected and fulfilled. These bodies are known as national human rights institutions (NHRIs) and they exist in every member state of the United Nations. On the island of Ireland, the Irish Human Rights and Equality Commission (IHREC) and the Northern Ireland Human Rights Commission (NIHRC) are our NHRIs. They perform important functions which ensure that we know our rights, that our laws and policies respect these rights, and that we have access to remedy when violations occur. Children and youth rights are handled by two specific bodies: the Ombudsman for Children Office and the Northern Irish Commissioner for Children and Young People.

Coimisiún na hÉireann um Chearta an Duine agus Comhionannas
Irish Human Rights and Equality Commission

Fig. 7.16 Logo of the Irish Human Rights and Equality Commission

Complete your next Reflective Journal entry (pages 28–29)

National Human Rights Institutions on the Island of Ireland

Irish Human Rights and Equality Commission

In 2014 the Irish Human Rights and Equality Commission (IHREC) was established following the amalgamation of the Equality Authority and the Irish Human Rights Commission. The IHREC is the national human rights organisation in Ireland. It is also Ireland's equality board for a range of EU anti-discrimination measures. It promotes and protects human rights and equality in several ways. It:

- Provides the public with information and training on human rights and equality
- Conducts and commissions research on human rights and equality issues in Ireland
- Monitors and reviews our laws and government actions to ensure that these are in compliance with human rights
- Provides legal assistance and takes cases on behalf of people attempting to vindicate their rights
- Receives complaints from the public and conducts inquiries into cases of human rights violations or discrimination.

Northern Ireland Human Rights Commission

The Northern Ireland Human Rights Commission was established as part of the Northern Ireland peace process. The commission has several functions. It:

- Provides advice to government departments on what they need to do to ensure that they are complying with their human rights obligations
- Provides legal support on behalf of people in cases of human rights violations
- Conducts investigations into possible human rights violations
- Educates the public on their rights and trains staff of public bodies so that they can perform their duties in a way that respects human rights.

Fig. 7.17 Logo of the Northern Ireland Human Rights Commission

RESEARCH ASSIGNMENT 7.6

Investigate the work done by the IHREC and the NIHRC over the past year. Include the following in a written report:

- Describe the roles of the two bodies.
- Explain how both bodies operate (describe their activities).

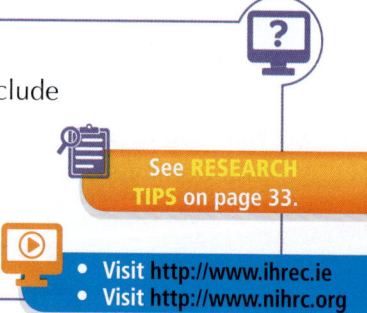

See **RESEARCH TIPS** on page 33.

- Visit http://www.ihrec.ie
- Visit http://www.nihrc.org

ACTIVITY 7.10

Design a poster to illustrate the right to education as outlined in the Constitution of Ireland.

Rights of the Child and Youth

The Irish Ombudsman for Children's Office (OCO) was established in 2014 with the responsibility to promote and protect the rights of children and young people under 18 living in Ireland. The OCO performs a number of tasks. It:

- Investigates complaints made by children and young people against public entities
- Advises government on how to ensure that laws and policies respect the rights of children
- Conducts research to better understand human rights issues for children and young people
- Educates the public about the rights of children and young people.

The Northern Irish Commissioner for Children and Young People is the body in Northern Ireland that performs tasks similar to the OCO in the Republic of Ireland.

Fig. 7.18 Logo of Irish Ombudsman for Children's Office (OCO)

Reporting to the United Nations

When a state *ratifies* an international human rights treaty, it formally finalises an agreement that makes the treaty legally binding. The state then has an obligation to present **periodic reports** to the United Nations detailing how the rights in that treaty are being implemented. Each treaty has a special committee which receives and examines the report. Committees include: the Committee on the Rights of the Child; the Committee on Economic, Social and Cultural Rights; the Committee on the Elimination of Discrimination Against Women, etc. The general human rights situation of each state is reviewed every 4–5 years by a mechanism known as the Universal Periodic Review (UPR). States are required to present reports to the special committees and the UPR. In addition to the state report, the UN will also receive reports from other sources, including the National Human Rights Institutions (NHRIs), and civil society groups. For example, the Children's Rights Alliance presents a report when Ireland is being reviewed by the Committee on the Rights of the Child. The committee takes all the reports and holds a session with the state to discuss the situation. It then develops a document or report known as 'Concluding Observations', which outlines its concerns and recommendations with respect to the human rights situation being reviewed. This human rights reporting mechanism can be a useful opportunity for governments and civil society bodies to highlight any human rights issues and to propose ways to address them.

> **KEY TERM**
>
> **Periodic reports** is a term used to describe the regular reports that states must present to the United Nations detailing how they are implementing their obligations under a treaty (e.g. UNCRC).

RESEARCH ASSIGNMENT 7.7

Write a report assessing Ireland's performance in fulfilling its obligations under the UN Convention on the Rights of the Child. Include the following in your report:

- Aspects of the UNCRC that Ireland is fulfilling well
- Aspects of the UNCRC that Ireland is not fulfilling adequately
- Concerns voiced by civil society bodies
- Position of the Irish government
- Up-to-date recommendations by the UN Committee on the Rights of the Child
- Recommendations which the state has an immediate obligation to implement, and those that can be progressively realised
- Overall challenges in fully implementing the recommendations.

The link below provides access to all relevant UN commissioned reports concerning Ireland's performance in upholding its human rights obligations (including the concluding observations by the Committee on the Rights of the Child):
https://educateplus.ie/go/ireland-human-rights

KEY THINKERS

DEBATES ON HUMAN RIGHTS

Several key thinkers have made important contributions to our understanding of human rights and equality. Their differences of opinion on certain issues have resulted in major debates.

See page 150 for more information on Robert Nozick and the 'minimal state'.

Debate 1: Individual Liberty versus Equality

American political philosophers **John Rawls** and **Robert Nozick** took different points of view on the balance between respecting individual rights and ensuring equality for all. Writing in the 1920s, Rawls, a liberal philosopher, argued that the main goal of government is to ensure equality in society. This means that government intervention should be based on re-balancing inequalities in relation to rights. Individual rights should be balanced with equality. For example, the rich should only be able to get richer if the poorer in society would not be left behind. In the 1970s, Robert Nozick challenged Rawl's ideas. Nozick argued against government intervention, which he felt would affect the individual rights and liberty of people in society. For example, he believed that forcibly taxing the wealthy was a violation of their economic rights and individual liberty. Nozick advocated for what he called the 'minimal state', where the government would act only to maintain law and order.

Debate 2: Individual Rights versus Common Good

A common debate in human rights is the balance between individual rights and the common good of society. The **classic liberal** view, such as that of **John Locke**, is that individual rights must be protected and respected above all else. This view initially developed as a reaction against authoritarian governments which acted to limit or violate human rights.

By contrast, the **communitarian** perspective is based on the belief that one cannot separate the individual from society. **Jean-Jacques Rousseau** believed that ensuring the common good is the most important goal of a society. In this perspective, we need to have a balance between rights and responsibilities in society, and between our individual freedoms and the wider needs of our society. One famous example is the debate that ensued over military conscription in the US in the 1960s during the Vietnam War. While the US government and US army argued that conscription was necessary to safeguard security and democratic freedom globally (i.e. the common good), many citizens protested that it amounted to a violation of their individual rights, such as freedom from forced servitude. In modern society, we continue to face challenges in balancing the rights of the individual and the rights of the majority (collective rights).

Debate 3: Equality of What? Access, Opportunity and Outcome

When it comes to equality, every person has human rights. However, there are different views on where to draw the line with respect to the responsibilities of duty bearers. For some, duty bearers should focus only on ensuring that everyone has equal access and opportunity in relation to exercising their rights. In this sense, governments and other duty bearers cannot be held responsible for the final outcome (i.e. whether or not a person subsequently enjoys the benefits associated with their rights). For example, if a government ensures that every child has access to a school, is this sufficient?

Conservative American economist and Nobel laureate **Milton Friedman** famously wrote that 'a society that puts equality before freedom will get neither'. Friedman believed that the freedom of individuals to use their capacities and to avail of opportunities should be the main goal of society. In Friedman's view, designing policies to target equality of outcome is a type of socialism. Similar to Nozick, Friedman did not support government intervention that would go beyond this, as he believed that this would amount to an attack on an individual's economic freedom.

Critics of this view, however, point to the fact that effectively addressing inequality requires us to look beyond equality of access and opportunity. People need certain things to be able to truly enjoy their rights. In the 1980s, Indian economist, **Amartya Sen**, first asked the question: 'Equality of what?'

See page 299 for more information on Amartya Sen.

HUMAN RIGHTS AND RESPONSIBILITIES IN IRELAND

KEY THINKERS

Sen was concerned about how we measure development in poor countries and the limitations with focusing on economic growth alone. He was primarily concerned about whether or not vulnerable groups (e.g. women, poor people) could really avail of apparent opportunities (education, health, jobs, etc.). Sen argued that we must look at 'capabilities' when assessing equality. Capabilities are not just 'opportunities' but are the *real* possibilities a person has based on their life situation. For example, what is the real possibility of a child living in poverty to have equal opportunity of education, if that child has no clothing, food or shelter?

Martha Nussbaum, an American philosopher and Law Professor at the University of Chicago, further developed Sen's approach when she asked: 'What are people able to do and be?' Nussbaum identified ten central capabilities she believed need to be protected to ensure people have equality in society:
- Life: not dying prematurely
- Bodily health: including good health, nutrition and shelter
- Bodily integrity: including freedom of movement, freedom from violence, reproductive rights
- Freedom to imagine, think and reason
- Freedom to have and express our emotions
- Freedom to engage in critical reflection
- Freedom to have personal and social affiliations
- Ability to co-exist with nature and other species (i.e. animals)
- Ability to enjoy play, recreation and leisure
- Control over one's environment, both political (i.e. participation) and material (i.e. owning property).

If people do not have these ten things, they will not enjoy their rights equally in society. The idea of capabilities has been integrated into international policy, such as the Human Development Index of the United Nations, as well as national poverty policies in countries such as Germany.

Debate 4: Human Rights and Power

The relationship between human rights and power is the source of another important debate. For liberal thinkers, human rights is an important tool that can be used against the abuse of power or to counteract power imbalances in society (e.g. between rich and poor, or men and women). The ills that human rights seek to end, such as torture and unfair imprisonment, all result from harmful or dominating misuses of power. Those who support this view believe that human rights are independent of political ideologies because they can be applied by any ideology (universal) as long as the application does not involve an abuse of the rights.

By contrast, radical political theorists such as **Marx**, and sociologists such as **Foucault**, have argued that human rights are not immune to being used as tools of political power. They can be used as instruments of power to regulate or dominate society or certain groups or uphold certain ideologies. Human rights can be used by those who hold power to maintain their position of power. The selective application of human rights to support certain interests or ideologies can act to weaken their overall power and enforceability. A modern example of this is the violation of the right to freedom of movement in the name of national security and the fight against terrorism.

See page 61 for more information on Michel Foucault.

QUESTIONS

1. Which political philosopher do you agree with more: John Rawls or Robert Nozick? Give reasons to support your answer.
2. Can you think of any positive rights that help some individuals at the expense of others?
3. What would be the advantages and disadvantages of living in Nozick's 'minimal state'?
4. Explain the relationship between Nozick's ideas and right-wing political philosophy.
5. Would you agree that sometimes the rights of the individual have to be set aside to protect the rights of the majority? Give examples of occasions when individual rights have to be sacrificed for 'the common good'.
6. Explain why those who advocate for measures to achieve equality of outcome are often labelled as socialists or left-wing.
7. In your opinion, is it the duty of the government to ensure equality of participation and equality of outcome?
8. Explain the views of Amartya Sen and Martha Nussbaum.
9. List the 'capabilities' needed to avail of equal rights and opportunities in Ireland today.
10. Explain how the selective application of human rights can be used by those in power to maintain power.
11. Do certain human rights benefit some groups more than others? Can you think of examples in Ireland of how the selective application of human rights has given some groups an unfair advantage over others? Explain your answer.
12. In what ways have human rights influenced the behaviours, actions and attitudes of modern Irish society? What types of alternative behaviours, actions and attitudes have been silenced by the promotion of human rights in Ireland?

ACTIVITY 7.11

Your teacher will read out several statements concerning human rights. You will take part in a 'moving debate' where you express your opinion on each of the statements.

After the debate, complete Skill Task 7.11.

SKILLS BOOK LINK 7.11

Go to pages 125–126 of your Skills Book to complete Skill Task 7.11 on human rights.

ACTIVITY 7.12

Your group will be assigned one argument about human rights. Work together to evaluate this argument. Include the following in a presentation to your class:

- A clear explanation of the exact meaning of the argument
- Evidence that supports this argument
- Evidence that contradicts or undermines this argument
- Where this argument is situated on the left–right political spectrum
- Key thinkers who would support this argument.

RESEARCH ASSIGNMENT 7.8

Is Ireland ensuring the right to education for all? Summarise research evidence to assess the extent to which the right to education is enjoyed equally by everyone in Ireland.

See **RESEARCH TIPS** on page 33.

- Research papers from 'Our Voice, Our Rights':
  https://educateplus.ie/go/right-education
- OECD indicators:
  https://educateplus.ie/go/education
- Education at a Glance OECD Report:
  https://educateplus.ie/go/oecd-report

✓ SUMMARY

- Human rights are the rights that all individuals are entitled to because they are human.
- Human rights can be divided into two categories: civil and political rights; and economic, social and cultural rights.
- Negative rights are rights that protect us from the potential negative actions of others (e.g. the right not to be tortured or enslaved).
- Positive rights are rights that oblige positive actions that help us to develop (e.g. the right to education).
- The UN Convention on the Rights of the Child (UNCRC) builds on the Universal Declaration of Human Rights (UDHR) by elaborating on all the rights to which everyone under the age of 18 is entitled.
- Many of the human rights listed in the UDHR and the UNCRC are enshrined in the Constitution of Ireland, Bunreacht na hÉireann.
- Duty bearers are those deemed responsible for respecting, protecting and fulfilling their human rights obligations (e.g. the Irish government).
- Rights holders are those who are entitled to human rights.
- Immediate obligation means that the government has to implement a human right with immediate effect.
- Progressive realisation means that the government is given time to fully implement a human right in line with the maximum extent of their available resources.
- Absolute rights are rights that can never be taken away (e.g. the right not to be subject to torture).
- Limited or qualified rights can be restricted or taken away from time to time in the interest of public safety or the common good.
- There are nine grounds under which discrimination is illegal in Ireland.
- Direct discrimination is when an individual is treated unfairly because of their membership of a particular group.
- Indirect discrimination occurs when a law or action has disproportionately negative impact on one group compared to all others.

- Ireland is obliged to submit periodic reports to the UN to show how it is implementing human rights.
- All UN member states must establish independent bodies known as National Human Rights Institutions (NHRIs) to monitor whether or not human rights are being respected and fulfilled.
- The Irish Human Rights and Equality Commission (IHREC) and the Northern Ireland Human Rights Commission (NIHRC) are the two NHRIs on the island of Ireland.
- Research suggests that not everybody in Ireland enjoys an equal right to education in terms of equality of access, opportunity and outcome.

Fig. 7.19 Key Word cloud

REVISION QUESTIONS

1. What are human rights?
2. Explain the difference between a need, a want and a right.
3. List the rights to education as outlined in Bunreacht na hÉireann.
4. List **three** important civil and political rights contained in the UDHR.
5. List **three** important economic, social and cultural rights contained in the UDHR.
6. Compare and contrast the right to education as outlined in the UDHR and the UNCRC.
7. Identify the similarities and differences between Bunreacht na hÉireann and the UNCRC in relation to the right to education.
8. Define the terms 'rights holder' and 'duty bearer'.
9. What is the difference between immediate obligation and progressive realisation in relation to the implementation of human rights?
10. Explain the following concepts:
    - Universal
    - Indivisible
    - Limited rights
    - Negative rights
    - Inalienable
    - Absolute rights
    - Qualified rights
    - Positive rights.
11. What is the difference between civil and political rights, and economic, social and cultural rights?
12. List the nine grounds under which discrimination is illegal according to Irish law.
13. Explain the difference between direct and indirect discrimination.

HUMAN RIGHTS AND RESPONSIBILITIES IN IRELAND

DATA-BASED QUESTIONS

Complete the qualitative and quantitative research data-based questions exercise on pages 127–129 of your Skills Book.

EXAM FOCUS: Section B of LC Exam

REVISION EXERCISES

Complete the exercises on pages 130–131 of your Skills Book.

EXAM FOCUS: Section A of LC Exam

DISCURSIVE ESSAY TOPICS

1. Critically examine the extent to which the right to education is enjoyed equally by all in Ireland.
2. 'Sometimes the rights of the individual need to be set aside to protect the rights of the majority.' Discuss.

EXAM FOCUS: Section C of LC Exam

Reflective Practice

Ensure that you have completed all the Reflective Journal entries for this chapter (pages 28–29 of your Reflective Journal and Learning Portfolio) before moving on to the next chapter.

Complete the Learning Portfolio activities on pages 29–31 of your Reflective Journal and Learning Portfolio. This will help you to self-assess the extent to which you have achieved the learning intentions for this chapter, and will help you to monitor your progress.

ACTIVE CITIZENSHIP: Ideas for Action

Here are some ideas for actions that you could take to engage in active citizenship. These ideas could be used to form the basis of a Citizenship Project.

- Conduct a survey in your school to find out differences in student experiences of the right to education. In your survey, assess equality of opportunity, participation and outcome in relation to the right to education. Use the **4 As** model to design your questionnaire (see page 252). Write a report on the main findings of the survey and include recommendations. Present the report to your school's board of management.

- Identify one of the nine grounds of discrimination and conduct research to find out the extent to which this group suffers from direct or indirect discrimination in your local area. As part of your research, you could ask members of the local community to complete a questionnaire or face-to-face interview. Write a report on the main findings of your research. Organise an action campaign (e.g. lobbying your local TD) or an awareness-raising campaign (e.g. using social media).

CHAPTER 8
Human Rights and Responsibilities in Europe and Beyond

'The rights of every man are diminished when the rights of one man are threatened.'
John F. Kennedy

KEY TERMS

- European Convention on Human Rights (ECHR)
- Developing country
- Ratification
- Implementation
- National human rights institutions (NHRIs)
- Child mortality
- Sanitation
- Honour killing
- Female genital mutilation (FGM)
- Genocide
- Corporal punishment
- Refugee
- Asylum seeker
- Direct provision
- Council of Europe
- Protocol
- European Court of Human Rights
- Western concept
- Cultural imperialism
- Sustainable Development Goals (SDGs)

Introduction

Human rights are global. The international human rights framework is made up of many different laws (conventions), bodies and mechanisms. In Chapter 7, we began our exploration of human rights with a focus on the right to education in Ireland. We examined the right to education across several important United Nations treaties, including the UDHR and the UNCRC. We looked at important human rights principles and concepts, and we learned how state bodies and reporting mechanisms work to ensure that human rights are implemented. Chapter 8 will build on this by looking at how human rights are implemented beyond Ireland. We will explore a broader set of rights from the UNCRC and we will look at different case studies, which focus on the extent to which these rights are being implemented around the world.

We will examine the **European Convention on Human Rights** and the specific mechanisms it provides to ensure that our rights are respected, protected and fulfilled. We will then investigate how economic, social and cultural human rights influence international cooperation in the fight against poverty and exclusion in **developing countries**. Finally, we will further engage with many of the controversial arguments and contemporary debates concerning human rights.

KEY TERMS

The **European Convention on Human Rights** was developed by the Council of Europe. It protects the rights of all citizens living within the 47 member states that signed and ratified it.

A **developing country** is a country with a low standard of living, underdeveloped industrial base, and moderate/low rating on the human development index (HDI). The HDI is a comparative measure of poverty, literacy, education, life expectancy and other indicators of development. Developing countries are also commonly referred to as 'low-income' or 'middle-income' countries.

By the end of this chapter you will be able to:

- Explain the main rights contained in the UN Convention on the Rights of the Child (UNCRC).
- Summarise research evidence on the extent to which the following rights from the UNCRC are being implemented around the world:
  - Article 6 of the UNCRC – *the right to survival and development*
  - Article 14 of the UNCRC – *the right to freedom of thought, conscience and to have or manifest a religion or beliefs*
  - Article 19 of the UNCRC – *the right to protection from physical or mental violence, injury, neglect or abuse*
  - Article 31 of the UNCRC – *the right to rest, leisure, play and recreation*
- Explain the main rights contained in the European Convention on Human Rights (ECHR).
- Describe the mechanisms that people can use to have their rights in the ECHR protected and implemented.
- Critically evaluate qualitative and quantitative research on the implementation of human rights.
- Evaluate various arguments about human rights by engaging in debate, examining different viewpoints and assessing relevant research-based evidence.
- Discuss and evaluate the argument that human rights are a western idea and the imposition of them across the globe is a form of 'cultural imperialism'.
- Discuss and evaluate the argument that it is justifiable for a government to put political rights aside temporarily to enable its country to develop and to provide for its citizens.
- Describe recent efforts of international cooperation in implementing economic, social and cultural rights.
- Identify the main elements of the UN Declaration on the Right to Development.
- Explain the main aspects of the Sustainable Development Goals (SDGs).

By the end of this chapter you will have developed the following skills:

- Active listening skills by listening carefully, summarising accurately, and responding critically to alternative viewpoints aired during class discussions and debate.
- Communication skills by putting forward and presenting your own evidence-based arguments and by delivering group presentations to the class.
- Dialogue skills by engaging in debates and allowing your opinions to be challenged and even changed in the light of better arguments.
- Research skills by sourcing, compiling and evaluating suitable evidence for research assignments on the topic of human rights.
- Teamwork skills by working effectively with others on different group tasks and role plays.
- Action-planning skills by reviewing your progress, reflecting on your learning, setting goals and developing an action plan to achieve these goals.

The Rights of the Child around the World

Human rights are universal. We all have the rights outlined in the UDHR, and, as we have learned, the specific rights of children and young people are contained in the UNCRC. In Chapter 7, we looked at what the UNCRC says about our right to education (Articles 28 and 29). However, the right to education is just one of many child rights. The UNCRC contains over 40 rights in many different areas:

- Economic, e.g. protection from child labour
- Social, e.g. right to health
- Cultural, e.g. right to play and recreation
- Civil, e.g. right to a nationality
- Political, e.g. freedom of expression and association.

See page 238 for more information about the UDHR.

ACTIVITY 8.1

Your group will be assigned a selection of images by your teacher. Each image depicts one right contained in the UNCRC. Match the image to the human right it depicts.

ACTIVITY 8.2

Your group will be assigned one section of the UNCRC by your teacher. Examine and discuss the Articles contained in this section. As a group, write a report that each member of your group will present to other groups in your class. Include the following in your report:

- Define and explain the right contained in the Article
- Explain the categories to which this right belongs: economic, social, political, cultural or civil; negative or positive; absolute, limited or qualified.
- List the strengths and weaknesses of the right.
- Examine the extent to which this right is being implemented (a) in Ireland and (b) around the world.

SKILLS BOOK LINK 8.1

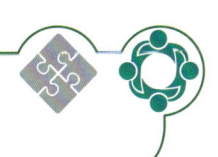

Go to page 132 of your Skills Book to complete Skill Task 8.1 on the UNCRC.

UN Convention on the Rights of the Child in child-friendly language

'Rights' are things that every child should have or be able to do.
All children have the same rights, which are
listed in the UN Convention on the Rights of the Child.

Almost every country has agreed to these rights.
All the rights are connected to each other, and all are equally important.
Sometimes, we have to think about the rights in terms of what is the best
for children in a situation and what is critical to life and protection from harm.
As you grow, you have more responsibility to make choices and exercise your rights.

Article 1
Everyone under eighteen has these rights.

Article 2
All children have these rights – no matter who they are, where they live, what their parents do, what language they speak, what their religion is, what their culture is, and whether or not they are a boy or girl, have a disability, or are rich or poor. No child should be treated unfairly on any basis.

Article 3
All adults should do what is best for you. When adults make decisions, they should think about how their decisions will affect children.

Article 4
The government has a responsibility to make sure your rights are protected. They must help your family to protect your rights and create an environment where you can grow and reach your potential.

Article 5
Your family has the responsibility to help you learn to exercise your rights and to ensure that your rights are protected.

Article 6
You have the right to be alive.

Article 7
You have the right to a name, and this should be officially recognised by the government. You have the right to a nationality (to belong to a country).

Article 8
You have the right to an identity – an official record of who you are. No one should take this away from you.

Article 9
You have the right to live with your parent(s), unless it is bad for you. You have the right to live with a family who cares for you.

Article 10
If you live in a different country than your parents, you have the right to be together in the same place.

Article 11
You have the right to be protected from kidnapping.

Article 12
You have the right to give your opinion, and for adults to listen and take it seriously.

Article 13
You have the right to find out things and share what you think with others, by talking, drawing, writing or in any other way, unless it harms or offends other people.

Article 14
You have the right to choose your own religion and beliefs. Your parents should help you decide what is right and wrong, and what is best for you.

Article 15
You have the right to choose your own friends and join or set up groups, as long as they aren't harmful to others.

Article 16
You have the right to privacy.

Article 17
You have the right to get information that is important to your wellbeing from radio, newspapers, books, computers and other sources. Adults should make sure that the information you are getting is not harmful, and they should help you find and understand the information you need.

Article 18
You have the right to be raised by your parent(s) if possible.

Article 19
You have the right to be protected from being hurt or mistreated, in body or mind.

Article 20
You have the right to special care and help if you cannot live with your parents.

Article 21
You have the right to care and protection if you are adopted or in foster care.

Article 22
You have the right to special protection and help if you are a refugee (if you have been forced to leave your home and live in another country), as well as all the rights in this convention.

Article 23
You have the right to special education and care if you have a disability, as well as all the rights in this convention, so that you can live a full life.

Article 24
You have the right to the best health care possible, to safe water to drink, nutritious food, a clean and safe environment, and information to help you stay well.

Article 25
If you live in care or in other situations away from home, you have the right to have these living arrangements looked at regularly to see if they are the most appropriate.

Article 26
You have the right to help from the government if you are poor or in need.

Article 27
You have the right to food, clothing, a safe place to live and to have your basic needs met. You should not be disadvantaged so that you can't do many of the things other kids can do.

Article 28
You have the right to a good-quality education. You should be encouraged to go to school to the highest level you can.

Article 29
Your education should help you use and develop your talents and abilities. It should also help you learn to live peacefully, protect the environment and respect other people.

Article 30
You have the right to practise your own culture, language and religion – or any you choose. Minority and indigenous groups need special protection of this right.

Article 31
You have the right to play and rest.

Article 32
You have the right to protection from work that harms you, and that is bad for your health and education. If you work, you have the right to be safe and paid fairly.

Article 33
You have the right to protection from harmful drugs and from the drug trade.

Article 34
You have the right to be free from sexual abuse.

Article 35
No one is allowed to kidnap or sell you.

Article 36
You have the right to protection from any kind of exploitation (being taken advantage of).

Article 37
No one is allowed to punish you in a cruel or harmful way.

Article 38
You have the right to protection and freedom from war. Children under fifteen cannot be forced to go into the army or take part in war

Article 39
You have the right to help if you've been hurt, neglected or badly treated.

Article 40
You have the right to legal help and fair treatment in the justice system that respects your rights.

Article 41
If the laws of your country provide better protection of your right than the articles in this convention, then those laws should apply.

Article 42
You have the right to know your rights! Adults should know about these rights and help you learn about them, too.

Article 43–54
These articles explain how governments and international organisations, like UNICEF will work to ensure children are protected with their rights.

Fig. 8.1 Summary of the UN Convention on the Rights of the Child (UNCRC)

ACTIVITY 8.3

Your teacher will assign different students to act out some of the rights contained in the UNCRC. You will observe and identify the right being acted out.

Global Implementation of the UNCRC

Once a state has **ratified** a human rights convention, the state is obliged to **implement** it. But how do we know if duty bearers are fulfilling their obligations? If we want to assess how well a human rights convention is being implemented around the world, we need to look at a variety of sources. The UN human rights framework provides us with several formal mechanisms that provide information on how states are implementing their obligations. In Chapter 7, we briefly looked at the reporting system in the UN. **National human rights institutions (NHRIs)**, UN agencies, civil society bodies and human rights organisations also produce regular theme-based (e.g. health) and country-based (e.g. Ireland) reports, which are useful sources of information. So how are we doing globally with respect to the implementation of the UNCRC? Are some countries performing better than others? Are we doing well on some rights, but not on others? Are all children benefiting equally from the UNCRC? As one might expect, the implementation and the enjoyment of the rights contained in the UNCRC varies greatly from place to place. This becomes clear when we examine these four rights from the UNCRC:

> **KEY TERMS**
>
> After a state signs a human rights convention or agreement, it must then formally accept or approve it. When this happens, the convention is said to have been **ratified** by the state.
>
> When a state **implements** a human rights convention, the state puts in place the national laws, regulations and practices required to adhere to the convention.
>
> States must establish independent bodies to monitor whether or not human rights are being respected and fulfilled. These bodies are known as **national human rights institutions (NHRIs)**.

- The right to survival and development (Article 6): see Case Study 1 on page 276.
- The right to freedom of thought, conscience, and to have and manifest their religion or beliefs (Article 14): see Case Study 2 on page 282.
- The right to protection from physical or mental violence, injury, neglect or abuse (Article 19): see Case Study 3 on page 285.
- The right to rest, leisure, play and recreation (Article 31): see Case Study 4 on page 289.

See page 260 for more information on NHRIs on the island of Ireland.

See page 261 for more information on the reporting system in the UN.

Fig. 8.2 *Article 6*: Survival and Development

Children and young people have the right:

1. to grow up in conditions that support their physical and mental wellbeing and development.
2. to have their own ideas, thoughts, opinions and beliefs. They also have the right to follow whatever religion they want, with parental guidance.
3. to be protected from being hurt or treated badly, whether that is physically, sexually or mentally.
4. to relax through sport, music, drama or other activities.

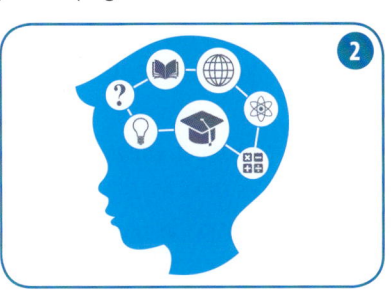

Fig. 8.3 *Article 14*: Freedom of Thought, Conscience and Religion

Fig. 8.4 *Article 19*: Protection from Neglect and Abuse

Fig. 8.5 *Article 31*: Leisure, Recreation and Culture

WHAT THE RESEARCH SAYS!

RESEARCHING THE IMPLEMENTATION OF HUMAN RIGHTS CONVENTIONS

Periodic Reporting to UN Treaty Bodies

Nine UN human rights conventions have monitoring bodies to oversee the implementation of the treaties. These monitoring bodies are composed of Independent Experts who review the reports submitted by states. They also examine individual complaints or communications related to the human rights relevant to the specific treaty. Following their review of all these documents and reports, the monitoring body produces important documents which are useful sources for assessing a country's performance in relation to the right(s), e.g. 'Concluding Observations' and 'General Comments'. Links to all the documents for each country are available on the website of the Office of the High Commissioner for Human Rights (OHCHR): https://educateplus.ie/go/hrc

Fig. 8.6 A UN Independent Expert

Reports of Special Rapporteurs and Working Groups

The United Nations Human Rights Council supports human rights monitoring through special working groups and independent experts. It appoints individual experts to monitor human rights conditions in relation to priority areas, such as education, violence against women, child protection and the right to food. These experts are known as Special Rapporteurs. They receive reports and information from civil society bodies and visit countries to report on the human rights situation there. You can find the reports of the working groups and the Special Rapporteurs on the OHCHR website: https://educateplus.ie/go/annual-reports

Fig. 8.7 Dr Geoffrey Shannon, Special Rapporteur on Child Protection

Universal Periodic Review (UPR)

Every 4–5 years the overall human rights situation of each UN member state must be reviewed in a process known as the Universal Periodic Review (UPR). Ireland was reviewed in February 2016 and will next be reviewed in 2021. The UPR is a 'peer review'. This means that other member states examine the report presented by the state under review, as well as any reports received from civil society bodies. There is a live session in Geneva, normally lasting three hours per country, during which different member states raise their concerns on any human rights issues and make recommendations for how the state under review can improve. In 2016, Ireland received 262 recommendations from other UN member states. The process results in a final 'Outcome Report', which lists all the concerns and recommendations made with respect to the country's human rights situation. The country that is being reviewed must then submit a report in response to the final recommendations, stating which recommendations it accepts. This document and the level of progress the state has made in relation to the accepted recommendations will then be considered during its next review. The documents and reports are available on the UPR website: https://educateplus.ie/go/upr

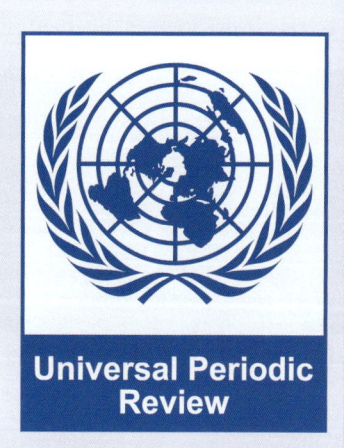

Fig. 8.8 Universal Periodic Review (UPR)

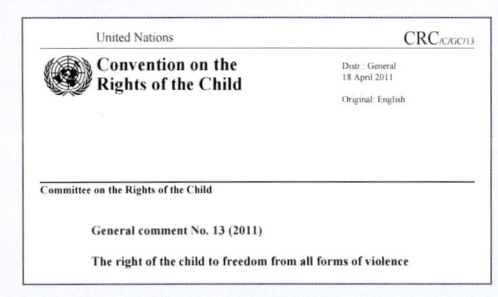

UN General Comments

A General Comment is a document which is produced by one of the UN Treaty Bodies (e.g. the Committee on the Rights of the Child). A General Comment will provide further detail with respect to a convention. It can provide a detailed interpretation of a specific Article and detailed guidance to states on what they need to do to implement them. Examples of General Comments under the UNCRC include:

- Comment 1: The aims of education (2001)
- Comment 3: HIV/AIDS and the rights of the child (2003)
- Comment 9: The rights of children with disabilities (2006)
- Comment 10: Children's rights in juvenile justice (2007)
- Comment 12: The right to be heard (2009)
- Comment 13: The right of the child to freedom from all forms of violence (2011)
- Comment 17: The right of the child to rest, leisure, play, recreational activities, cultural life and the arts (2013).

General Comments are useful sources for interpreting the full detail and implications of a right. They are available on the OHCHR website: **https://educateplus.ie/go/general-comments**

Fig. 8.9 UN General Comment

The Right to Survival and Development: Article 6

All children have the right to conditions that support their survival and development. Implementing this right involves several aspects, such as reducing child death (**child mortality**) and providing healthcare, nutrition, **sanitation** and drinking water. It also means that harmful practices are stopped, such as early marriage, **honour killings**, **female genital mutilation** and the use of child soldiers. The basic measurement used globally to evaluate the implementation of Article 6 is the rate of child mortality. Since the 1990s, significant progress has been made in reducing the number of deaths of children under the age of 5: in fact, this figure has been halved. In 2015 the global average was 42.5 deaths for every 1,000 children born, compared to 90.6 in 1990. More children around the world are surviving. However, progress is unequal and child survival and development remains an unfulfilled right in some parts of the world.

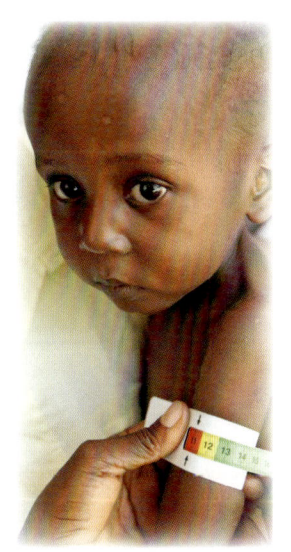

Fig. 8.10 Garsiline Koko, 3, who suffers from malnutrition, has his arms measured at the Pipeline health centre in Monrovia

KEY TERMS

Child mortality is also known as under-5 mortality or child death. It is the basic measurement used globally to evaluate implementation of Article 6 of the UNCRC.

Sanitation refers to the promotion of hygiene and the prevention of disease (e.g. clean drinking water and safe disposal of sewage).

An **honour killing** is the killing of a relative – usually a girl or woman – who is thought to have 'dishonoured' or 'shamed' the family in some way.

Female genital mutilation (FGM) is the practice of injuring or removing female genital organs for non-medical reasons.

HUMAN RIGHTS AND RESPONSIBILITIES IN EUROPE AND BEYOND

ACTIVITY 8.4

Your group will examine the meaning of Article 6 as outlined in pages 83–94 of UNICEF's *Implementation Handbook for the Convention on the Rights of the Child*, 3rd edition.

Create a presentation on Article 6 and deliver it to your class. Include the following in your presentation:

- Define Article 6 and explain what type of right it is: economic, social, political, cultural or civil; negative or positive; absolute, limited or qualified
- Summarise the main aspects of Article 6 and how they are to be implemented
- Create a poster or other visual to represent the main aspects of Article 6.

Tip: Distribute the relevant pages in the handbook equally among the members of your group. In this way, each group member can focus on one or two aspects of Article 6 before collaborating with the rest of the group to compile all the information into a single presentation.

SKILLS BOOK LINK 8.2

Go to page 133 of your Skills Book to complete Skill Task 8.2 on the meaning of Article 6 of the UNCRC.

CASE STUDY 1: Implementation of Article 6 UNCRC

Angola

Angola is an oil-rich country located in southwest Africa. Despite its wealth of natural resources, Angola earned the title of 'deadliest country in the world for children' in 2015 because it had the highest child mortality rate in the world: 157 children per 1,000 born die before they reach the age of 5. By comparison, the child mortality rate in 2015 in Ireland was 4 per 1,000. The European average was between 3 and 4 per 1,000. There is significant global inequality with respect to the right to child survival and development. According to a 2016 UNICEF report entitled *State of the World's Children*, 'a child born in a low-income country is, on average, 11 times as likely to die before the age of 5 as a child in a high-income country'.

Fig. 8.11 Angola and surrounding countries

Case Study: Implementation of Article 6 UNCRC

With respect to nutrition – another critical component of child survival and development – 29 per cent of Angolan children suffer from stunted growth. The majority of Angolans do not have access to adequate healthcare. Only 14 per cent of children (aged 0–14 years) who are HIV positive are receiving necessary treatment. Government expenditure on healthcare in Angola in 2014 was only 3.3 per cent of the overall budget. Waterborne diseases such as cholera are major killers in Angola, and only 21 per cent of households have access to piped drinking water.

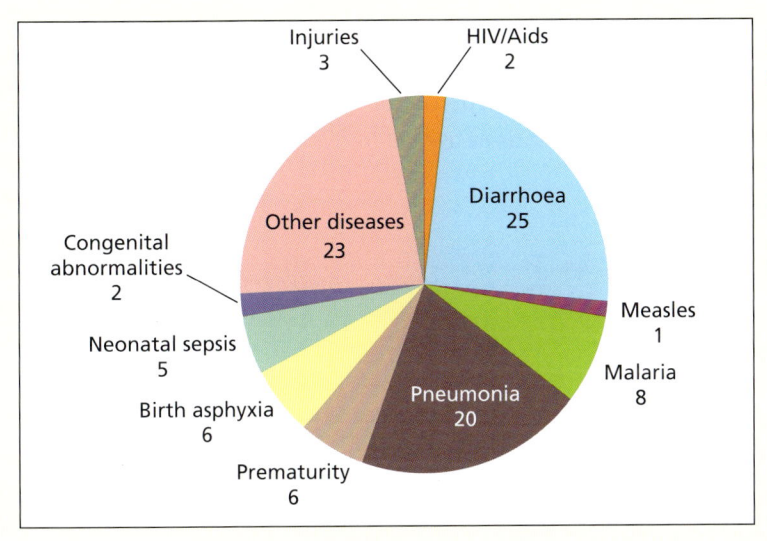

Fig. 8.12 Distribution of causes of death among children aged <5 years (%) in Angola

Source: African Health Observatory - World Health Organization Regional Office for Africa

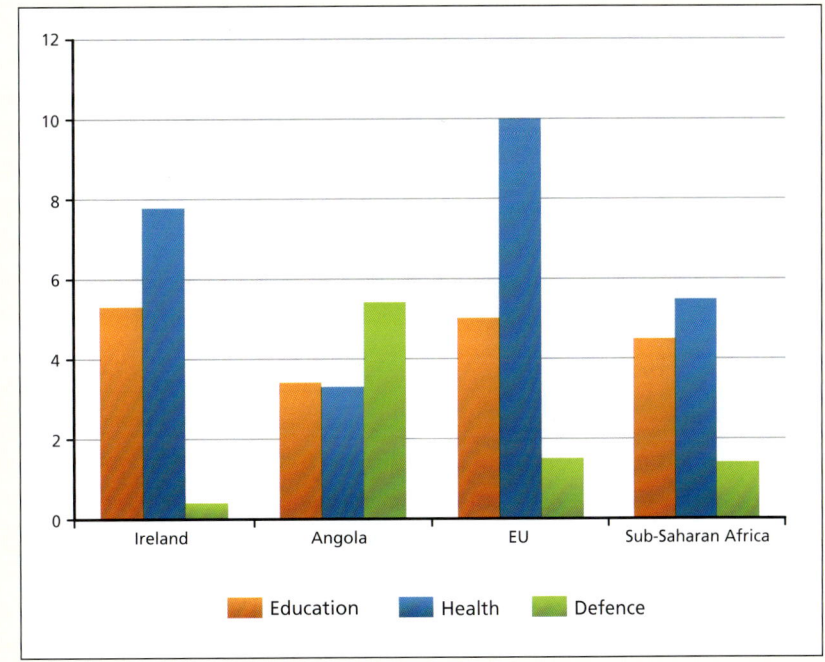

Fig. 8.13 Education, health and defence expenditures as a total % of GDP (2014)

United Nations Monitoring System

Angola failed to present its scheduled report to the Committee on the Rights of the Child in 2015. During its review of Angola in 2010, the committee raised several concerns about Angola's implementation of its obligations under Article 6:

- Government spending on health, education and child protection remains low.
- Child mortality rates are high.
- Certain groups of children, such as minority ethnic groups or children living with disabilities or HIV, face discrimination that affects their ability to enjoy their rights.

HUMAN RIGHTS AND RESPONSIBILITIES IN EUROPE AND BEYOND

The committee has no power to impose sanctions on states that fail to implement the recommendations made in the concluding observations. Equally, the committee has no power to force states to submit periodic reports.

Reasons for Failure to Implement Human Rights Obligations

Angola suffered from nearly three decades of a violent civil war between 1975 and 2002. The war destroyed basic infrastructure, such as roads, schools and hospitals. This has presented the government with significant challenges. However, many civil society bodies and human rights organisations have also pointed to massive corruption and undemocratic practices by the government as factors contributing to Angola's failure to fulfil its human rights obligations. In global indices, Angola is consistently ranked one of the most corrupt and least free countries. In 2015 it ranked 163 out of 168 countries on Transparency International's Corruption Perception Index and was categorised as 'not free' by Freedom House.

Fig. 8.14 An Angolan family look through a large hole in their home caused by an artillery shell during the civil war

QUESTIONS

1. The government of Angola is failing to fulfil its obligation to implement Article 6 of the UNCRC. Choose relevant facts from the case study to support this view.
2. What factors have contributed to Angola's poor record on implementing Article 6?
3. List **two** weaknesses of the UN committee system which limit the UN's ability to implement the UNCRC around the world.
4. According to Fig. 8.12, apart from 'other diseases', what are the top **three** named causes of child mortality in Angola?
5. Examine Fig. 8.13. Compare and contrast Angola's expenditure with that of Ireland and of the EU. What impact is this likely to have on the implementation of Article 6?
6. What are the limitations of the research? Do you believe that there are statistics and information *not* included in the case study that would provide us with a better picture of the extent to which Article 6 is, or is not, being implemented in Angola?
7. As a homework assignment, research and list additional statistics and evidence that could be added to this case study to show the extent to which Article 6 is being implemented in Angola.

IN THE MEDIA

'DEADLIEST COUNTRY FOR KIDS'

by Nicholas Kristof, *The New York Times*, **19 March 2015 (abridged)**

LUBANGO, Angola – This is a country laden with oil, diamonds, Porsche-driving millionaires and toddlers starving to death. New UNICEF figures show this well-off but corrupt African nation is ranked No. 1 in the world in the rate at which children die before the age of five.

'Child mortality' is a sterile phrase, but what it means here is wizened, malnourished children with twig limbs, discoloured hair and peeling skin. Here in Lubango in southern Angola, I stepped into a clinic and found a mother carrying a small child who seemed near death. He was unconscious, his eyes rolling, his skin cold and his breathing laboured, so I led the mom to the overburdened nurses.

Just then, 20 feet away, a different mother began screaming. Her malnourished son, José, had just died.

One child in six in this country will die by the age of five. That's only the tip of the suffering. Because of widespread malnutrition, more than one-quarter of Angolan children are physically stunted. Women have a 1-in-35 lifetime risk of dying in childbirth.

In a Lubango hospital, I met a 7-year-old boy, Longuti, fighting for his life with cerebral malaria. He weighed 35 pounds. His mother, Hilaria Elias, who had already lost two of her four children, didn't know that mosquitoes cause malaria. When Longuti first became sick, she took him to a clinic, but it lacked any medicine and didn't do a malaria test. Now Longuti is so sick that doctors say that even if he survives, he has suffered neurological damage and may have trouble walking and speaking again.

Yet kids like Longuti who are seen by a doctor are the lucky ones. Only about 40 per cent to 50 per cent of Angola's population has access to the healthcare system, says Dr Samson Agbo, a UNICEF paediatrics expert.

Fig. 8.15 Angola has the highest child mortality rates in the world

Some of the poorest countries, such as Mauritania and Burkina Faso, fortify flour with micronutrients – one of the cheapest ways possible to save lives – yet Angolan President dos Santos hasn't tried that. He invests roughly three times as much on defence and security as on health.

'Children die because there is no medicine,' lamented Alfred Nambua, a village chief in a thatch-roof village on a rutted dirt road near the northern city of Malanje. The village has no school, no latrine, no bed nets. The only drinking water is a contaminated creek an hour's hike away.

There are many ways for a leader to kill his people, and although dos Santos isn't committing **genocide** he is presiding over the systematic looting of his state and neglect of his people. As a result, 150,000 Angolan children die annually. Let's hold dos Santos accountable and recognise that extreme corruption and negligence can be something close to a mass atrocity.

KEY TERM

Genocide is the deliberate killing of a large group of people (e.g. a nation or ethnic group).

QUESTIONS

1. The article on page 279 refers to research data. List **two** pieces of quantitative data and **two** pieces of qualitative data contained in the article.

2. What might be some of the strengths and weaknesses of using news articles such as this when researching an issue or topic? In your answer make reference to any facts, opinions, possible exaggeration or potential bias contained in the article.

RESEARCH ASSIGNMENT 8.1

Investigate the extent to which Article 6 of the UNCRC is being implemented in Ireland today. Develop your own case study on the topic (similar to the case study on Angola). Include the following in your case study:

- Brief background information on Ireland's global status/ranking in terms of:

  (a) Economic development: refer to GDP and HDI score

  (b) Political stability: refer to World Bank political stability index

  (c) Commitment to human rights: refer to global human rights rankings.

- Summary of the aspects of Article 6 that are being implemented well
- Summary of the aspects of Article 6 that are not being fully implemented
- UN recommendations for better implementation of Article 6
- Reasons for the success or failure of the government in implementing each aspect of Article 6.

Three valuable sources of information for this assignment are:
- Ireland's consolidated 3rd and 4th Periodic Reports to the UN Committee on the Rights of the Child (2013): **https://educateplus.ie/go/report-2013** (focus on Chapter 3, Part C, Numbers 284–99, pp. 58–61).
- Report by the UN Committee on the Rights of the Child – Concluding Observations on the combined 3rd and 4th Periodic Reports of Ireland (2016): **https://educateplus.ie/go/concluding-observations** (focus on Section III, Parts C and G on Article 6)
- The Children's Rights Alliance Report Card (2017): **https://educateplus.ie/go/report-card** (focus on Chapter 1 – standard of living and Chapter 6 – health)

See **RESEARCH TIPS** on page 33.

RESEARCH ASSIGNMENT 8.2

Examine the following Human Rights Watch report on the impact of early marriages in Nepal on the rights of young girls: **https://educateplus.ie/go/child-marriage**

Write a summary report that includes the following points:

- Statistics on the rate of early marriages in Nepal
- Causes of early marriage
- Effects of early marriage
- Recommendations on how the situation can be improved.

See **RESEARCH TIPS** on page 33.

Complete your next Reflective Journal entry (pages 32–33)

POWER AND PEOPLE

The Right to Freedom of Thought, Conscience and Religion: Article 14

Children and young people have the right to have and express their ideas, thoughts, opinions and beliefs, while respecting the rights and freedoms of others. With parental guidance, children should be able to practise any religion they choose. However, children should not be harmed – physically or mentally – as a result of a belief. The UNCRC recognises that childhood ends at 18 years of age. As children mature and form their own views, they may begin to question certain religious practices or cultural traditions. Children should not be forced to hold certain beliefs, nor should they be prevented from holding their own beliefs.

Fig. 8.16 Young Muslim women protest outside London's French embassy at proposed ban on wearing of the hijab in French state schools

The *Implementation Handbook for the Convention on the Rights of the Child* is available at **https://educateplus.ie/go/child-rights**

The report by the Special Rapporteur on the Freedom of Religion and Belief is available at **https://educateplus.ie/go/freedom-religion**

ACTIVITY 8.5

Your group will examine the meaning of Article 14 as outlined in pages 185–94 of UNICEF's *Implementation Handbook for the Convention on the Rights of the Child*, 3rd edition.

Your group will also examine a report by the Special Rapporteur on the Freedom of Religion and Belief, which provides a detailed interpretation of Article 14.

Create a presentation on Article 14 and deliver it to your class. Use page 134 of your Skills Book and include the following in your presentation:

- Define Article 14 and explain what type of right it is: economic, social, political, cultural or civil; negative or positive; absolute, limited or qualified
- Summarise the main aspects of Article 14 and how they are to be implemented.
- Create a poster or other visual to represent the main aspects of Article 14.

Tip: Distribute the relevant pages in the handbook equally among the members of your group. In this way, each group member can focus on one or two aspects of Article 14 before collaborating with the rest of the group to compile all the information into a single presentation.

SKILLS BOOK LINK 8.3

Go to page 134 of your Skills Book to complete Skill Task 8.3 on the meaning of Article 14 of the UNCRC.

CASE STUDY 2: Implementation of Article 14 UNCRC

Ireland

The education system in Ireland has a long history of religious patronage. The vast majority (90 per cent) of primary schools in Ireland, for example, are owned by the Catholic Church. Reports from the Irish Human Rights and Equality Commission and children's rights organisations, such as the Children's Rights Alliance, raised concerns that the lack of non-denominational schools in Ireland may affect children's rights under Article 14 of the UNCRC. In particular, it was highlighted that few alternatives are made available for children who do not want to take part in religious instruction or religious events at school (e.g. Mass). Concerns have also been raised by several UN treaty bodies, including the Committee on the Rights of the Child and the Committee on Economic, Social and Cultural Rights.

In 2015, Ireland's implementation of the UNCRC was reviewed and resulted in a committee recommendation that Ireland 'ensure accessible options for children to opt out of religious classes and access appropriate alternatives to such classes, in accordance with the needs of children of minority faith or non-faith background'.

Ireland offers an example of how failure to accommodate children who do not hold or practise a particular religious belief can impinge upon their freedom of thought and beliefs. However, Article 14 also protects the right of the child to freely practise their religious beliefs. This right is not respected in some parts of the world, such as China, where the government has placed restrictions on certain religious groups.

Fig. 8.17 There is a long history of religious patronage in Irish schools

IN THE MEDIA

'SHE FEELS EXCLUDED AND DIFFERENT'

by Kitty Holland, *The Irish Times*, 11 December 2015

Valentine Doyle (6) sits at the back of her class for 30 minutes every day and 'draws', while her classmates are taught religion.

'She feels left out, different, excluded,' says her father, Devin. 'She says she wants to "do the God thing" now because the other kids are doing it. They were doing the sign of the cross and some of them told her she should do it too. So she wants to.'

Devin, from Dublin, and his French wife, Nanou, returned to Ireland earlier this year. They had met in Ireland and lived for a time in Australia and France. They have a younger daughter, Juliette (2).

'Vallie went to school in France. There you just go to the local school. It's completely secular. If parents want their children to do religious education, they go to Sunday school or private schools. We knew there would be an issue here, so we put Vallie's name down for a lot of Educate Together schools, but she didn't get in. They were all full.'

Living in Dublin 7, they secured a place for her in the Christ the King National School in Cabra. 'It has to be said they have been great,' says Devin. 'They have acceded to our request that she opt out of religion and they have done their best to make her feel included.'

However, opting out of religious instruction means sitting at the back of the class for 30 minutes each day. 'She draws. She sits on her own and she doesn't like it. She feels excluded and different. We'd really like religion taken out of the main school day,' says Devin. 'If parents want religious instruction, that's fine, but let it be at the end of the school day. This is not about there not being enough school places. Vallie's school is not oversubscribed and still she has to sit at the back of her class for half an hour every day, feeling different.'

QUESTIONS

1. What step was taken by Christ the King National School to facilitate Vallie's right to freedom of thought and conscience?
2. What alternative measures could the school take in the future to support the rights of non-faith pupils under Article 14 of the UNCRC?
3. What specific right of the child is affected by the lack of non-denominational schools in Ireland?
4. What recommendation did the UN Committee on the Rights of the Child make in 2015?
5. Give arguments in favour of and against the religious patronage of schools in Ireland.
6. Should religious education and instruction be removed from the curriculum? Give reasons to support your answer.

ACTIVITY 8.6

Hold a classroom debate on the following motion:

'Religious education and instruction should be removed from the curriculum in Ireland, as it is contrary to Article 14 of the UNCRC.'

ACTIVITY 8.7

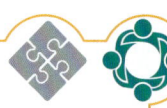

Your group will be assigned a country by your teacher. Research the extent to which Article 14 of the UNCRC is being implemented in this country. As a group, write a report. Present your report to another group in your class. Include the following in your report:

- Brief background information on the country's global status/ranking in terms of:
    - (a) Economic development: refer to GDP and HDI score
    - (b) Political stability: refer to World Bank political stability index
    - (c) Commitment to human rights: refer to global human rights rankings.
- Summary of the aspects of Article 14 that are being implemented well
- Summary of the aspects of Article 14 that are not being fully implemented
- Recommendations for better implementation of Article 14
- Reasons for the success or failure of the government in implementing each aspect of Article 14.

RESEARCH ASSIGNMENT 8.3

Compare and contrast how Article 14 of the UNCRC has been implemented in any two countries of your choice.

See **RESEARCH TIPS** on page 33.

The Right to Protection from Abuse and Neglect: Article 19

Children and youth have the right to protection from all forms of violence – physical, mental and sexual. Governments must have laws in place that prohibit violence, and proactively ensure the protection of children. Violence against children can take place in the home or within public institutions. The UNCRC prohibits violence in all forms and in all settings of a child's life. There are many different types of violence. **Corporal punishment** remains one of the most common forms of violence experienced by children around the world.

> **KEY TERM**
>
> **Corporal punishment** is physical punishment (e.g. slapping or hitting).

Complete your next Reflective Journal entry (pages 32–33)

ACTIVITY 8.8

Your group will examine the meaning of **Article 19** as outlined in pages 249–274 of UNICEF's *Implementation Handbook for the Convention on the Rights of the Child*, 3rd edition.

Your group will also examine a 2006 UN study on violence against children, which outlines all forms of violence.

Create a presentation on Article 19 and deliver it to your class. Include the following in your presentation:

- Define Article 19 and explain what type of right it is: economic, social, cultural or civil; negative or positive; absolute, limited or qualified?
- Summarise the main aspects of Article 19 and how they are to be implemented
- Create a poster or other visual to represent the main aspects of Article 19.

Tip: Distribute the relevant pages in the handbook equally among the members of your group. In this way, each group member can focus on one or two aspects of Article 19 before collaborating with the rest of the group to compile all the information into a single presentation.

The *Implementation Handbook for the Convention on the Rights of the Child* is available at **https://educateplus.ie/go/handbook**

The 2006 UN study on violence against children is available at **http://www.unviolencestudy.org/**

SKILLS BOOK LINK 8.4

Go to page 135 of your Skills Book to complete Skill Task 8.4 on Article 19 of the UNCRC.

CASE STUDY 3: Implementation of Article 19 UNCRC

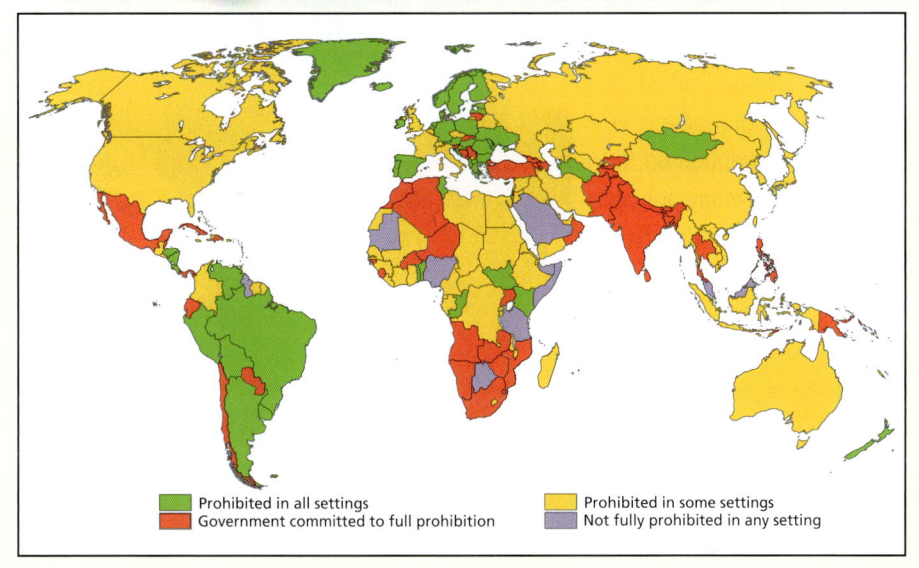

Fig. 8.18 The use of corporal punishment globally

Legend:
- Prohibited in all settings
- Government committed to full prohibition
- Prohibited in some settings
- Not fully prohibited in any setting

Global

According to the Global Initiative to End All Corporal Punishment of Children, as of October 2015, 46 states had formally prohibited all forms of corporal punishment of children in all settings, including the home, and at least 57 more states had expressed a commitment to making corporal punishment illegal. In Norway, for example, corporal punishment is prohibited through a series of laws covering the home,

> **CASE STUDY**
>
> **Implementation of Article 19 UNCRC**

alternative care settings (i.e. foster homes), day care and schools. A 2010 revision to Norway's Parent and Child Act made illegal the use of any form of violence in the 'upbringing of the child'.

However, in 2015 there remained 92 states where governments had not yet made any commitment to ending the most common type of violence experienced by children – corporal punishment.

Many countries have only partially banned corporal punishment in certain settings (e.g. at school) but have failed to protect children from violence in the home. Children in countries such as Lebanon, the Dominican Republic, Italy and Angola have no legal protection in their countries in such instances. In a significant number of countries (36 countries), whipping, flogging, caning and other forms of physical violence are recognised as lawful forms of punishment for crimes committed by juveniles.

QUESTIONS

1. As of October 2015, corporal punishment was illegal in how many countries in the world?
2. How many countries have made no commitment to ending corporal punishment?
3. List the types of corporal punishment that are legal in 36 countries.
4. What alternative measures are used in your school to discipline students for breaches of school rules?

IN THE MEDIA

'BEATINGS FOR ASKING FOR HELP: CORPORAL PUNISHMENT IN INDIA'S SCHOOLS'

by Virginia Morrow, *The Guardian*, 22 May 2015 (abridged)

Despite widespread concern about the effects of corporal punishment on children, it persists in schools across the world. Its eradication in many countries is proving difficult, and India is no exception. India ratified the UN Convention on the Rights of the Child in 1992, and has many policies that ban corporal punishment in schools. But these seem out of kilter with everyday realities. The government of India commissioned research that included more than 3,000 children aged from 5 to 18, asking about physical abuse by teachers. In all age groups, 65% reported being beaten at school. Younger children (aged 7–8) were significantly more likely to have witnessed and experienced corporal punishment than the 14- to 15-year-old cohort, with over two-thirds of the younger children having been physically punished at school in the past week, compared with one-third of the older young people. Poorer children were more likely than less poor children to be punished.

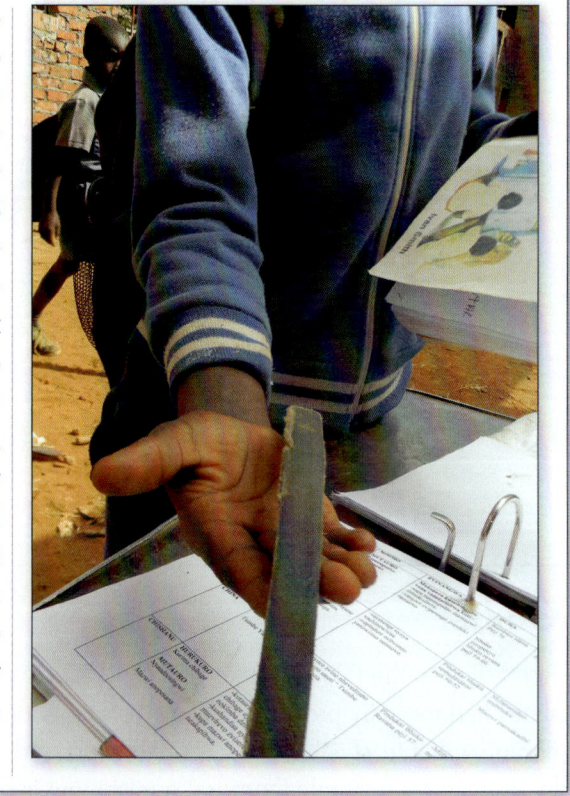

286 POWER AND PEOPLE

Girls and boys spoke of a range of reasons for punishment, including being absent from school due to work, illness or attending family celebrations, missing classes, not doing their homework, not reading well, making mistakes, receiving poor marks in exams, not wearing a uniform, not having the right equipment, or not paying the teacher for extra lessons. One girl, aged 10, said:

'If we don't study, they beat us. If we ask other children for help, they beat [us]. I went to drink water without asking sir, so he beat me that time. They said all children should come back to class by the time they count 10 after the interval. But I went home [to use the toilet]. After coming back to school, he beat me.'

In global policy debates, much emphasis has been placed on the role of education as the solution not only to reducing cycles of poverty in developing countries, but also to addressing gender violence.

However, the evidence presented here suggests that we must question this, at least in the Indian context. All children, regardless of gender, experience high levels of physical violence in schools. But it is teenage boys who experience the most.

But blaming specific groups (teachers, and/or parents) will not enable progress to be made, and risks alienating teachers already under pressure because of overcrowded classrooms, poor infrastructure, and poverty situations.

Approaches need to develop not only from the top down, but from communities, families and teachers to find ways of working together to change practices.

QUESTIONS

1. What percentage of 5- to 18-year-olds reported being beaten at school in India?
2. Name **two** groups that were more likely to be the victims of corporal punishment. In your opinion, why have these groups suffered more than other groups?
3. For what reasons are children punished?
4. What alternative forms of punishment could be used in Indian schools?

ACTIVITY 8.9

Your group will be assigned a country by your teacher. Research the extent to which Article 19 of the UNCRC is being implemented in this country. As a group, write a report. Present your report to another group in your class. Include the following in your report:

- Brief background information on the country's global status/ranking in terms of:
    (a) Economic development: refer to GDP and HDI score
    (b) Political stability: refer to World Bank political stability index
    (c) Commitment to human rights: refer to global human rights rankings.
- Summary of the aspects of Article 19 that are being implemented well
- Summary of the aspects of Article 19 that are not being fully implemented
- Recommendations for better implementation of Article 19
- Reasons for the success or failure of the government in implementing each aspect of Article 19.

Complete your next Reflective Journal entry (pages 32–33)

RESEARCH ASSIGNMENT 8.4

Compare and contrast how Article 19 of the UNCRC has been implemented in any two countries of your choice.

See **RESEARCH TIPS** on page 33.

ACTIVITY 8.10

Hold a classroom debate on the following motion:

'Corporal punishment is sometimes necessary and can be justified under certain conditions.'

The Right to Rest, Leisure and Play: Article 31

Children's right to play is not a 'luxury': it is recognised as an essential part of child development. Children have the right to play and to participate in recreational and cultural activities. The implementation of this right includes many aspects, such as ensuring access to recreational facilities (e.g. parks, youth clubs, sports facilities) and achieving a balance between work or study and rest or play. We often take rest and play for granted, but in some parts of the world this right is not enjoyed. Poverty and conflict are two common reasons why rest and play are not enjoyed by all children.

Fig. 8.19 Children have the right to rest, leisure and play

ACTIVITY 8.11

Your group will examine the meaning of Article 31 as outlined in pages 469–477 of UNICEF's *Implementation Handbook for the Convention on the Rights of the Child*, 3rd edition.

Create a presentation on Article 31 and deliver it to your class. Include the following in your presentation:

- Define Article 31 and explain what type of right it is: economic, social, cultural or civil; negative or positive; absolute, limited or qualified.
- Summarise the main aspects of Article 31 and how they are to be implemented
- Create a poster or other visual to represent the main aspects of Article 31.

Tip: Distribute the relevant pages in the handbook equally among the members of your group. In this way, each group member can focus on one or two aspects of Article 31 before collaborating with the rest of the group to compile all the information into a single presentation.

The Implementation Handbook for the Convention on the Rights of the Child is available at **https://educateplus.ie/go/handbook**

SKILLS BOOK LINK 8.5

Go to page 136 of your Skills Book to complete Skill Task 8.5 on Article 31 of the UNCRC.

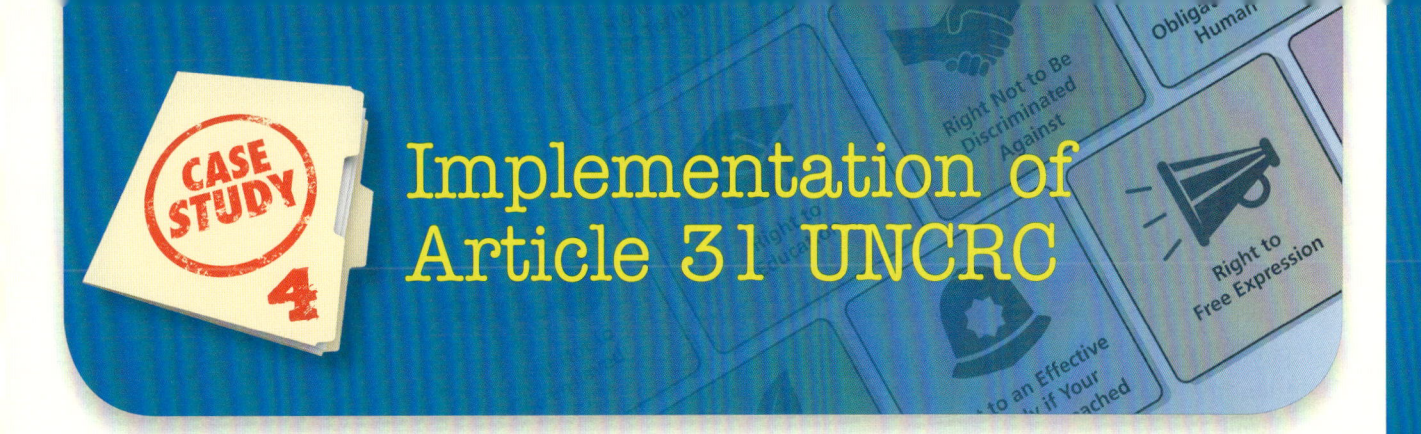

Case Study 4: Implementation of Article 31 UNCRC

Global

The right to rest and play is not enjoyed equally in all parts of the world. In some countries, urban sprawl and development remove the green spaces and parks that are essential for children and youth to enjoy their rights. Financial crises can lead to budget cuts, which reduces government spending on facilities such as youth clubs or public swimming pools. In some parts of the world, persistent poverty and conflict mean that children and young people never get to play.

Child Labour

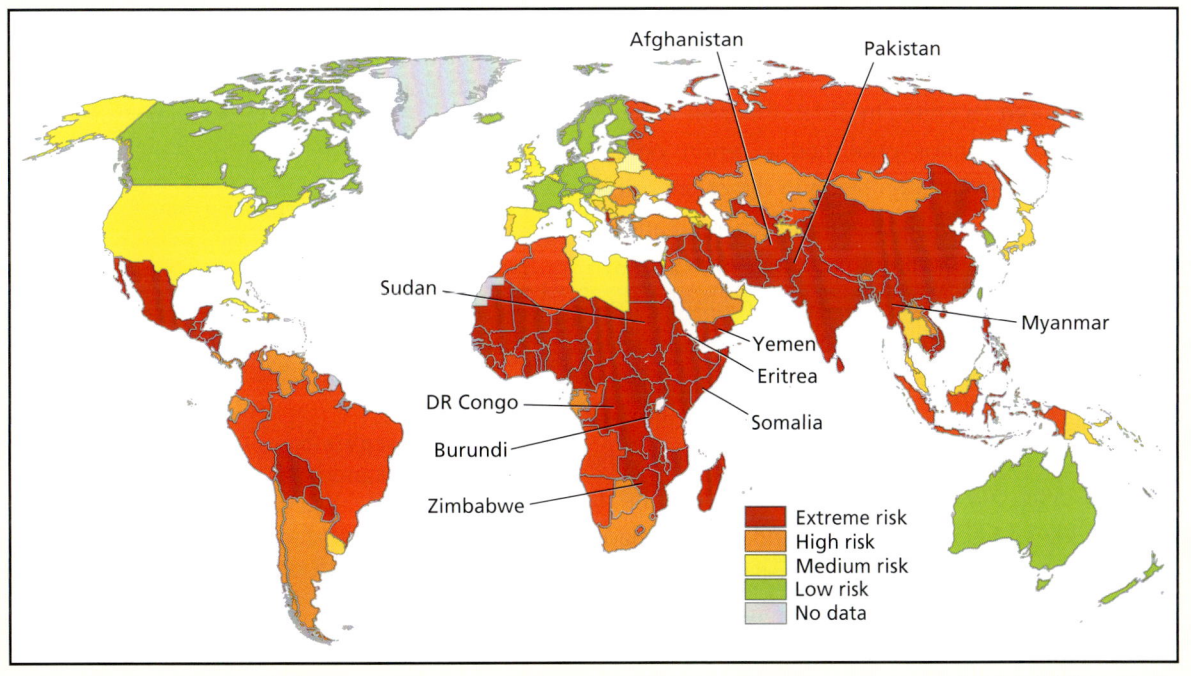

Fig. 8.20 Child labour index

According to the International Labour Organization, in 2013 there were 168 million children engaged in child labour around the world. More than half of these children are involved in hazardous work in dangerous and unhealthy conditions. This includes construction, mining and agriculture industries, where children are in regular contact with chemical substances. Sub-Saharan Africa still has the highest rate of child labour: 21 per cent of the child population is engaged in labour. Other high rates include Asia and the Pacific region (9.3 per cent), Latin America and the Caribbean region (8.8 per cent) and the Middle East and North Africa (8.4 per cent).

Asylum Seekers: Children in Direct Provision

The UN Refugee Agency (UNHCR) estimated that by the end of 2015 there were over 60 million forcibly displaced people in the world. Because of conflict, political and economic crises, and natural disasters, people are forced to flee their homes and countries. Conflicts in Syria, Afghanistan, Somalia and South

CASE STUDY: Implementation of Article 31 UNCRC

Sudan contributed to most of the **refugee** population in 2015. Over half of the refugee population (51 per cent) are under the age of the 18. Before a person is granted official refugee status – the right to stay in their host country – they are considered an **asylum seeker**. In Ireland, asylum seekers waiting for their application to be processed by the government are placed in a system and accommodation known as **direct provision**.

Civil society bodies such as NASC (the Irish Immigrant Support Centre) and the Irish Refugee Council have criticised the system and conditions of direct provision. They have reported that most asylum seekers spend three years in direct provision, and many more wait over seven years. The conditions of the accommodation have been criticised for being restrictive: people have to cook at certain times, adults and children share bedrooms, and residents share bathroom facilities. In 2012, the Irish Refugee Council and Barnados published a report on the situation faced by children living in direct provision. One of the concerns raised was the lack of recreational facilities. Children in direct provision did not have access to safe play areas and were prohibited from inviting friends living outside of direct provision to visit. This impacts negatively on their psychological wellbeing and their ability to integrate socially and make friends. These concerns were also raised by the UN Committee on the Rights of the Child during its 2015 review of Ireland. It recommended that Ireland 'ensure asylum and refugee centres have facilities including recreation areas that are appropriate for young children and families'.

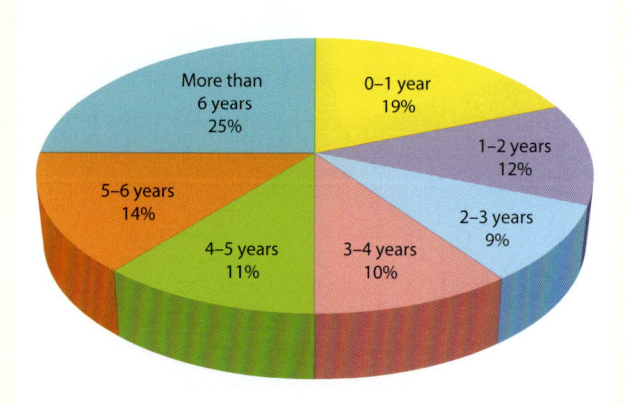

Fig. 8.21 Length of time spent in direct provision (2013)

- More than 6 years: 25%
- 0–1 year: 19%
- 1–2 years: 12%
- 2–3 years: 9%
- 3–4 years: 10%
- 4–5 years: 11%
- 5–6 years: 14%

KEY TERMS

A **refugee** is a person who has had their right to receive protection and remain in another state officially recognised. Refugees can face persecution in their home countries for several reasons: race, ethnicity, religion, nationality, membership of a particular social group (e.g. LGBTQ+) or certain political views. Under international law, states are obliged to provide protection to refugees.

An **asylum seeker** is a person who has fled his or her home country in search of sanctuary or protection. An asylum seeker is a person waiting to be recognised as a refugee.

Direct provision is the system in Ireland that accommodates asylum seekers as they wait for their request for refugee status to be processed. In direct provision, asylum seekers are provided with state-run accommodation and a small allowance. They cannot seek employment, choose where to live, or leave the direct provision system while their application is in process.

QUESTIONS

1. What factors prevent children around the world from enjoying their right to rest, leisure and play?
2. How many children were engaged in child labour in 2013?
3. Name the **two** regions of the world that have the highest rates of child labour.
4. Look at Fig. 8.21. In 2013, what percentage of asylum seekers in Ireland had been in direct provision for at least three years?
5. How many refugees were in the world in 2015?
6. What percentage of the refugee population are children?
7. What is the difference between an asylum seeker and a refugee?
8. Name **two** civil society bodies in Ireland that advocate for refugee rights.
9. Explain how the quality of direct provision impacts on children's rights.

IN THE MEDIA

'LIVES IN LIMBO'
by Carl O'Brien, *The Irish Times*, August 2014 (series of articles, abridged)

It was supposed to provide shelter for just six months. Today, many asylum seekers in the state's direct provision system spend years in conditions which most agree are damaging to the health, welfare and life-chances of those forced to endure them. Asylum seekers are not allowed to work. They are not entitled to social welfare. And they are excluded from social housing and free third-level education. In all, more than 4,300 people, including 1,600 children, live in 34 accommodation centres spread across the state. The centres, which include former hostels, hotels and a mobile home park, are run by private contractors who receive about €50 million in State funding annually.

The state-run Reception and Integration Agency says it ensures the basic needs of all residents are met. But the United Nations and international human rights groups have heavily criticised the system. Former Supreme Court judge Catherine McGuinness has predicted that a future government will end up publicly apologising for damage done by the direct provision system. The voices of asylum seekers are rarely heard. Many are fearful that speaking out will damage their request for refugee status. But their personal stories provide a rare insight into the impact of the system on these lives in limbo.

More than 1,600 children are growing up in the direct provision system with limited access to play or recreation. The state's Special Rapporteur on Child Protection, Dr Geoffrey Shannon, has raised concerns that many children are living in state-sanctioned poverty and in environments that could prove highly damaging. 'We are in a situation where we treat children in direct provision as being second-class citizens,' he says.

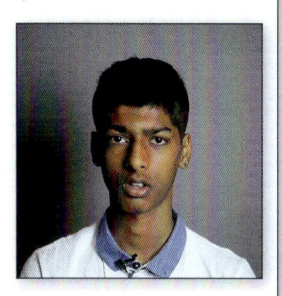

Waleed, 14, shares a hotel room with his parents and younger brothers. 'I feel I can't tell my friends where I live,' he says. 'Even if they come over, they're not allowed come to my room. I've nowhere to play.' In the room, his mother and father sleep on a mattress on the floor. He, along with his two younger brothers, sleep on beds surrounding them. 'I just did my Junior Certificate. It was really hard for me because I wasn't able to study properly – because my brothers are fighting and disturbing me all the time.'

Natasha, 12, is used to coming up with excuses. Whenever her friends at school plan a sleepover or a trip away, she knows she won't be able to go. So she makes up a story about why she can't. 'Sometimes I tell my friends that I'm going somewhere, or I can't go because my mom is sick,' she says. She lives in a mobile home in a direct provision centre in Athlone, along with her mother and brother. Visitors to the site must pass through a security barrier and sign in at a reception desk. 'I'm ashamed that if they see where I live I'll get bullied,' she says.

QUESTIONS

1. Dr Geoffrey Shannon, the State Special Rapporteur on Child Protection, claims that 'we treat children in direct provision as being second-class citizens'. Give evidence from the article to support this claim.
2. Other than the right to play and leisure, what other rights of Waleed and Natasha might be affected by the direct provision system? Do you think this is fair?

HUMAN RIGHTS AND RESPONSIBILITIES IN EUROPE AND BEYOND

ACTIVITY 8.12

Your group will be assigned a country by your teacher. Research the extent to which Article 31 of the UNCRC is being implemented in this country. As a group, write a report. Present your report to another group in your class. Include the following in your report:

- Brief background information on the country's global status/ranking in terms of:
  (a) Economic development: refer to GDP and HDI score
  (b) Political stability: refer to World Bank political stability index
  (c) Commitment to human rights: refer to global human rights rankings.
- Summary of the aspects of Article 31 that are being implemented well
- Summary of the aspects of Article 31 that are not being fully implemented
- Reasons for the success or failure of the government in implementing each aspect of Article 31
- Recommendations for better implementation of Article 31.

RESEARCH ASSIGNMENT 8.5

Compare and contrast how Article 31 of the UNCRC has been implemented in any two countries of your choice.

See **RESEARCH TIPS** on page 33.

Human Rights in Europe

As we have seen, many of our human rights come from the UDHR and the UN Conventions. In Europe, we also have another important document that protects our rights and freedoms. The European Convention on Human Rights was developed by the **Council of Europe** and came into existence on 4 November 1950.

Complete your next Reflective Journal entry (pages 32–33)

KEY TERM

The **Council of Europe** is an international organisation based in Strasbourg. It promotes human rights, democracy and the rule of law in Europe. It has 47 member states, 28 of which are members of the European Union. The council monitors the human rights obligations of member states, provides legal advice to member states to assist them in making necessary changes to national laws, and conducts campaigns to promote human rights. As with the UN, the Council of Europe was established following the end of World War II. The founding states of the council, including Ireland, developed the European Convention of Human Rights in 1950. Since then, the Council of Europe is responsible for developing one of the most advanced human rights protection mechanisms in the world.

Note: The Council of Europe is not to be confused with the Council of the European Union.

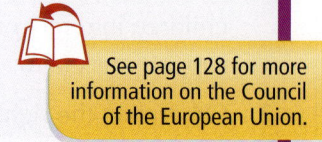

See page 128 for more information on the Council of the European Union.

Fig. 8.22 The Council of Europe

European Convention on Human Rights

The European Convention on Human Rights was initially intended to focus on several *civil and political* rights contained in the UDHR. It drew rights mainly from the first half of the UDHR, such as the right to life, freedom and security, freedom of expression, the right to a fair trial and respect for privacy.

Since 1950, additional rights – including social and economic rights, such as the right to education – have been added to the convention through what are known as **protocols**. One of the main mechanisms we have in place to enforce the rights contained in the convention is the **European Court of Human Rights**. The court has made some important rulings that have resulted in the protection of rights in Ireland and elsewhere.

KEY TERMS

A **protocol** is a piece of text that is added to and changes the original convention by introducing a new right or amending an existing one. To date there have been 15 protocols added to the European Convention on Human Rights.

The **European Court of Human Rights** is the main mechanism for enforcing the rights contained in the European Convention on Human Rights.

Convention for the Protection of Human Rights and Fundamental Freedoms

The European Convention on Human Rights, as it is commonly referred to, contains 59 articles. Articles 1–18 detail the rights we have under the convention. The remaining articles establish the mechanisms and important procedures to ensure implementation and enforcement of the convention, the most important of which is the establishment of the European Court of Human Rights.

Some of the main rights contained in the convention include:
- Article 1 Respecting rights
- Article 2 Right to life
- Article 3 Prohibition of torture, ill-treatment
- Article 4 Prohibition of slavery and forced labour
- Article 5 Right to liberty and security
- Article 6 Right to a fair trial
- Article 7 No punishment without law

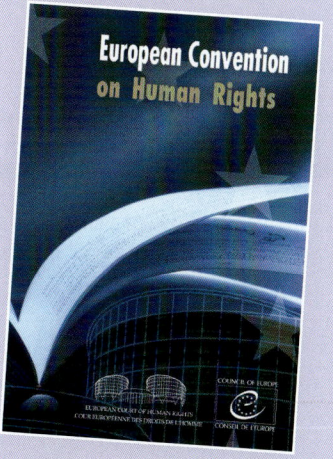

Fig. 8.23 European Convention on Human Rights

HUMAN RIGHTS AND RESPONSIBILITIES IN EUROPE AND BEYOND

- Article 8 Right to respect for private and family life
- Article 9 Freedom of thought, conscience and religion
- Article 10 Freedom of expression
- Article 11 Freedom of assembly and association
- Article 12 Right to marriage
- Article 13 Right to an effective remedy
- Article 14 Prohibition of discrimination

Protocols

The European Convention on Human Rights is an evolving document. Down through the years, protocols have added new rights and changes to the procedures to ensure that states implement the convention. For example, in 1952 the first protocol to the convention added the right to education, free elections, and protection of private property.

ACTIVITY 8.13

Your group will be assigned two rights from the European Convention on Human Rights by your teacher. Research the rights and discuss what they mean in practice. As a group, write a summary report on each right. Present your report to another group in your class. Include the following in your report:

- Name of the right and article in the ECHR
- Explanation of what this right means in practice
- Details of any decisions made by the European Court of Human Rights concerning this right.

Council of Europe, student-friendly resource
The European Convention on Human Rights – Rights and Freedoms in Practice (2013)
https://educateplus.ie/go/european-convention

Irish Council for Civil Liberties, user-friendly handbook on ECHR
Know your rights – European Convention on Human Rights:
https://educateplus.ie/go/know-your-rights

SKILLS BOOK LINK 8.6

Go to page 137 of your Skills Book to complete Skill Task 8.6 on one article of the European Convention on Human Rights.

European Court of Human Rights

The European Convention on Human Rights established several important mechanisms to ensure respect for the rights contained within it. The European Court of Human Rights is a vital mechanism. The court, which sits in Strasbourg, ensures that everyone living in the countries that have signed the convention is guaranteed these rights. If a right is not respected or is violated, a case can be brought to the court. This can be by an individual or a state. The first inter-state case taken to court was the unsuccessful case taken by Ireland in 1978 against the UK with respect to torture and ill-treatment of men who were interned in Northern Ireland by members of the British Army and Royal Ulster Constabulary (RUC). To date, the vast majority of cases have been brought by individuals rather than states.

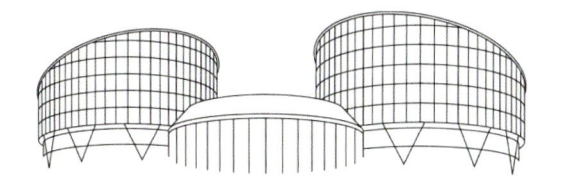

Before a case can be brought to the European Court of Human Rights, all attempts to resolve the issue at the national level must have been made. This is known as *exhausting all domestic remedies*. For example, in Ireland, a person must first have tried to take their case through our national court system and usually as far as the Supreme Court (the highest court in our country).

The decisions of the European court are *binding*: its judgement must be followed. If the court finds that a violation has occurred, the offending state must rectify the situation for the victim and take necessary actions to ensure that a similar violation does not happen in the future. Sometimes a change to a law or policy is needed. The court's rulings often include a small compensation award for the victim.

Human Rights Debates in the Wider World

Fig. 8.24 European Court of Human Rights

Committee of Ministers

The implementation of court rulings is monitored by a body known as the Committee of Ministers. This Committee consists of the Ministers of Foreign Affairs of all the member states and their diplomatic representation to the Council of Europe.

The European Court of Human Rights plays a vital role in safeguarding human rights and freedoms in Europe. Its judgements have made significant impacts in Ireland and elsewhere. It has resulted in the decriminalisation of homosexual acts in Ireland, the prohibition of corporal punishment in schools in the UK, and improvements in the temporary living conditions of foreigners who have not been granted stay in Greece while they await deportation.

Fig. 8.25 Committee of Ministers

QUESTIONS

1. Where does the European Court of Human Rights sit?
2. Why was the court set up?
3. Who can take a case to the court?
4. Explain the following phrases in relation to the European Court of Human Rights:
   - Exhausting all domestic remedies
   - Decisions are binding
   - The Committee of Ministers.
5. Explain how the court has had an impact on laws in: **(a)** Ireland **(b)** another European country.

SKILLS BOOK LINK 8.7

Go to pages 137–138 of your Skills Book to complete Skill Task 8.7 on taking a case to the European Court of Human Rights.

SKILLS BOOK LINK 8.8

Go to pages 139–140 of your Skills Book to complete Skill Task 8.8 on the European Court of Human Rights case studies.

RESEARCH ASSIGNMENT 8.6

Write a speech on the European Convention on Human Rights.

Target audience: The speech is to be delivered to a group of refugees who have recently been granted Irish citizenship after fleeing persecution in their home country.

What to include: Summarise all the main rights guaranteed under the European Convention on Human Rights and describe the mechanisms through which these people can take cases to the European Court of Human Rights to have their rights protected.

The European Court of Human Rights: Impacts in Ireland

CASE STUDY 5

The European Court of Human Rights has made several important rulings in cases brought by Irish citizens.

Norris v. Ireland (1988)

In 1983 David Norris (now a senator) took a case to the European Court against the Irish state for laws that criminalised homosexual acts. Norris argued that the laws were a violation of Article 8 of the European Convention, which protects the right to respect private and family life. In 1988 the European Court ruled in favour of Norris's case. The ruling eventually led to the removal in 1993 of the laws which had criminalised homosexual acts.

A, B & C v. Ireland (2010)

Three women – known as A, B and C – presented a case to the European Court in 2005 against Ireland's abortion laws. Each of the three women had travelled abroad for abortion services. The women argued that the criminalisation of abortion in Ireland had put their health and wellbeing at risk. In December 2010 the court ruled that Ireland's failure to implement the existing constitutional right to a lawful abortion in Ireland when a woman's life is at risk violated Article 8 of the European Convention on Human Rights. As a result of this ruling, a new law protecting the life of women during pregnancy was introduced in Ireland in 2014.

O'Keeffe v. Ireland (2014)

In the late 1990s, Louise O'Keeffe, a victim of child abuse by her primary school principal in the early 1970s, took a case to the High Court against the Irish state. However, the High Court found that the state was not liable, a ruling which was also upheld by the Supreme Court upon appeal. Ms O'Keeffe took the case to the European Court of Human Rights, which ruled in 2014 that the Irish state was in fact liable for having failed to protect her from sexual abuse in school.

RESEARCH ASSIGNMENT 8.7

Research decisions made by the European Court of Human Rights concerning other cases brought by individuals or groups against European states. Write a summary on the details and the outcome of **three** cases brought to the court.

Complete your next Reflective Journal entry (pages 32–33)

HUMAN RIGHTS AND RESPONSIBILITIES IN EUROPE AND BEYOND

Human Rights in the Wider World

The world is made up of countries and regions with a diverse range of political systems, levels of social and economic development, and cultures. How do human rights operate in such a global context? Several ongoing debates demonstrate some of the challenges associated with applying human rights in the wider world.

KEY THINKERS

DEBATES ABOUT HUMAN RIGHTS IN THE WIDER WORLD

Debate 1: Are Human Rights a Western concept?

Human rights are universal. The UDHR declares that everyone has human rights 'with no distinction given to their race, colour, sex, language, religion, political or other opinion, national or social origin, property, birth or other status'. However, our world is full of diverse societies and cultures with different ideas and beliefs about life and moral standards. These two facts have led to a debate on exactly how 'universal' human rights are.

Human Rights are Western

Critics of the universality of human rights argue that human rights are ultimately a **western concept**. Critics believe that human rights are based on western cultural traditions and beliefs that value 'individualism' and protect rights associated with the capitalist model (e.g. the right to private property). Human rights are considered to have developed in the western world, from the ideas of European philosophers such as Locke and Rousseau, to their integration in the Constitutions that followed the French Revolution and the American Revolution.

Human rights do not fit easily within non-western cultural belief systems. There are varying interpretations of human rights between western and non-western societies. In the theory of *cultural relativism*, culture is the main factor that determines what becomes a moral right or rule. What is morally right in one culture may not be in another.

Confucianism, Hinduism, Islam and African religions each have their own approaches to concepts of dignity and equality. For example, in the Confucian tradition or so-called 'Asian values', duties and responsibilities, and social stability, are afforded more importance than rights. In African traditions, communal or group rights are more important than individual rights.

Women's rights are a particularly difficult area, since the position of women in certain cultures does not follow the equality principle of human rights. Human rights are sometimes viewed as part of a wider 'neo-colonial' agenda. In this perspective, western countries use human rights as a type of 'Trojan horse' – forcing their values and ideology on other cultures, and using human rights as an excuse to interfere in the affairs of countries around the world.

Human Rights are Universal

Supporters of the universalism of human rights, such as American human rights theorist Jack Donnelly, argue that human rights are essentially about dignity: the value and worth of humanity. They are essential minimum standards for a life of dignity. This transcends culture and unites us all. Modern human rights came from the UDHR, which was developed by the nations of the world, including non-western societies. In fact, two-thirds of the countries that voted to support the UDHR were non-western. The Canadian former politician and global human rights academic Michael Ignatieff argues that those who believe human rights are a form of western **cultural imperialism** are almost always the leaders of non-democratic and dictatorial countries guilty of grave human rights abuses.

KEY TERMS

Critics of the universality of human rights argue that human rights are a **western concept**, meaning that they take into consideration western rules and norms only.

Cultural imperialism is the cultivation of unequal relationships between civilisations, with the aim of keeping the more powerful civilisation in the dominant position.

298 POWER AND PEOPLE

KEY THINKERS

Debate 2: Do Human Rights Help or Hinder Development?

The world is made up of countries with different levels of economic development: there are developed countries and developing countries. Can a developing country afford to respect all human rights when it is involved in the task of building its economy and state structures?

Political Rights can be Suspended During the Development Phase

Political and civil rights sometimes need to be set aside to facilitate economic growth and allow a country to escape poverty. Following the process of decolonisation, beginning in the 1950s and 1960s, some leaders of developing nations argued that human rights are for developed nations. The focus of these post-colonial states was to address their lack of economic development. You need to eat before you can vote! Only when economic development has been achieved, can a country realise human rights.

The rapid economic development of countries in East Asia since the 1970s is often used as evidence in support of this position. Politically repressive countries such as Indonesia, Taiwan, China, Singapore and South Korea advanced their economic development at the expense of guaranteeing citizens political rights and freedoms. For many developing countries, the 'Asian approach' to economic development has been offered as an alternative to the western approach. Values such as obedience to authority and a strong work ethic replace democratic values and individual liberties. Certain political rights, such as the right to be a member of a trade union, for example, can have a negative impact on a country's economic growth.

Human Rights are Development!

On the other side of the debate are writers such as Amartya Sen. He argues that a country cannot truly develop without respecting all human rights. Human rights are indivisible and cannot be separated. For example, without freedom of expression, citizens cannot discuss their economic needs and support the development of the economy. Sen also argues that the rapid growth of East Asian countries also relied on policies associated with democracy, such as access to international markets, openness to competition, reforms that gave citizens access to land, and many others. Sen also points to the economic failure of other politically repressive countries, such as Ethiopia, Uganda and Myanmar, as evidence that the suspension of political and civil rights does not lead to economic growth and development. Scandinavian countries, such as Norway and Sweden, that are highly developed and have a strong human rights tradition are presented as evidence that, rather than being incompatible, human rights and development are interconnected. Finally, even if human rights are not vital to economic development, they are an *end* in themselves.

QUESTIONS

1. Would you agree that human rights are primarily a western idea? Give **one** argument that supports this belief and **one** argument that contradicts it.
2. What specific rights in the UDHR or UNCRC promote capitalism or western values?
3. Which human rights are incompatible with other cultures and religious beliefs in the world?
4. Which human rights hinder economic development?
5. Would you agree that certain human rights can and should be set aside to enable poorer countries in the world to focus on economic development?
6. What evidence does Amartya Sen use to support his opinion that a country cannot fully develop without respecting all human rights?

HUMAN RIGHTS AND RESPONSIBILITIES IN EUROPE AND BEYOND

SKILLS BOOK LINK 8.9

Go to pages 140–141 of your Skills Book to complete Skill Task 8.9 on human rights as a 'western idea'.

See RESEARCH TIPS on page 33.

ACTIVITY 8.14

Hold a classroom debate on the following motion:

'Human rights are a western idea and imposing this idea on non-western countries is a form of cultural imperialism.'

SKILLS BOOK LINK 8.10

Go to page 142 of your Skills Book to complete Skill Task 8.10 on human rights and economic growth.

ACTIVITY 8.15

Hold a classroom debate on the following motion:

'Human rights hinder economic development and therefore must be set aside in the poorest countries to enable them to develop fully.'

Global Poverty and Development

Global poverty and inequality have long been a feature of human history. From the sixteenth century, European powers carried out colonial actions throughout Africa, South America, Asia and other parts of the world. The slave trade and natural resource grab in Africa, for example, was used to fuel the industrialisation and economic growth of colonial powers, including France and the UK. This resulted in a state of uneven development and a world of developed and developing countries. Our world today remains unequal.

Complete your next Reflective Journal entry (pages 32–33)

WHAT THE RESEARCH SAYS!

UNEQUAL GLOBAL DEVELOPMENT, 2015

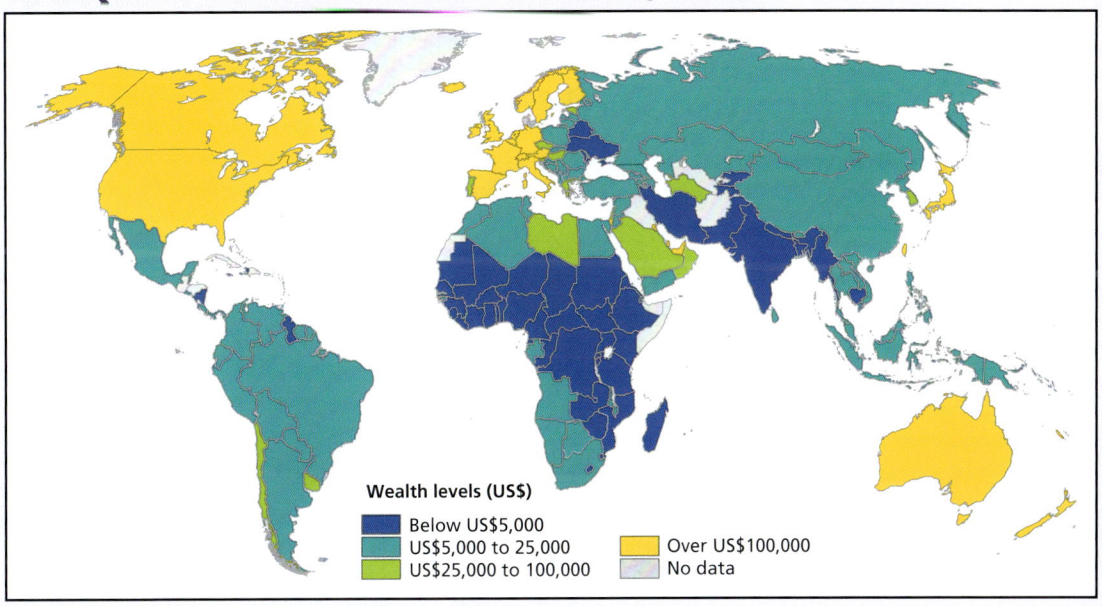

Wealth levels (US$)
- Below US$5,000
- US$5,000 to 25,000
- US$25,000 to 100,000
- Over US$100,000
- No data

Fig. 8.26 Unequal global development (Note: The term wealth is defined as the value of financial assets plus real estate (housing) owned by the households, less their debts throughout the Credit Suisse Wealth Report. The study focuses on the wealth held by the adult population across more than 200 countries, from billionaires at the top of the wealth pyramid to the middle and bottom sections of the pyramid. The analysis comprised the wealth holdings of 4.8 billion adults. It did not include the relatively small amount of wealth owned by children on their accounts.)

Source: *Credit Suisse Global Wealth Databook 2015*

Income Poverty

- 71 per cent of the world holds only 3 per cent of global wealth.
- The world's wealthiest individuals make up only 8.1 per cent of the global population but own 84.6 per cent of its wealth.
- Africa is now home to more than 160,000 people with personal fortunes worth in excess of $1m (£642,000 or €811,000). However, the number of poor people in Africa – living on less than $1.25 a day – increased from 411.3 million in 2010 to 415.8 million in 2011.
- The number of people in extreme poverty by continent: 551 million in Asia; 436 million in Africa; 15 million in South America; 5.9 million in North America; 0.3 million in Europe; and 50,000 in Oceania.

Hunger

- One in nine people in the world were suffering from chronic undernourishment in the period 2014–16. Almost all the hungry people, 780 million, live in developing countries, representing 12.9 per cent of the population of developing counties.

Health

- Global life expectancy at birth in 2015 was 60.0 years in the African region and 76.8 years in the European region.

Education

- One-third of all out-of-school children of primary school age live in West and Central Africa.
- Out-of-school rates were lowest in:
  - South Asia, and Latin America and the Caribbean – 6 per cent
  - Central and Eastern Europe and the Commonwealth of Independent States (CEE/CIS), and East Asia and the Pacific – 5 per cent
- Western Europe, North America and Australasia – 4 per cent.

ACTIVITY 8.16

Research additional data on poverty and unequal development in the world today. Design a poster or other visual to display the information.

A Matter of Human Rights: The Right to Development

What do poverty and development have to do with human rights? When we view development as a human right, we can see that it is based on legal entitlements and obligations rather than goodwill or charity. Just as we have a right to education or health, we also have a right to development. However, development has not always been considered a human right.

Development – Three Main Approaches

Our understanding of development has evolved over the years. The three main approaches are: the charity approach, the needs-based approach and the rights-based approach.

Charity Approach

The earliest efforts to support development in poor nations were based on a 'charity' model. This model was based on making donations of aid or support to help the 'needy'. Donors identify the needs of the poor. Development efforts under this model include money donations, food, clothing, shelter and medical care. It meets the immediate needs of those living in poverty but does not address the underlying causes of poverty. The charity approach is often used to address emergencies such as famines, wars and natural disasters.

Fig. 8.27 The charity approach to development often occurs after natural disasters

Needs-Based Approach

From the middle of the twentieth century, the international community began to shift its focus to addressing the 'basic needs' as identified by the poor themselves. This was a significant improvement on the charity model, as it recognised that poor people themselves are best placed to identify their development needs. However, the needs-based approach still failed to address the underlying causes of poverty. Development was still seen as a matter of choice rather than a right or obligation.

Rights-Based Approach

Since the late 1980s, development is now recognised as a human right. The rights-based approach to development differs greatly from the charity approach and the needs-based approach. Development is based on a full range of formal and recognised human rights (economic, social, cultural, political and civil). They are legal entitlements and are non-negotiable. They apply to everyone everywhere. States no longer have a 'choice': they are obligated to fulfil their duties. This approach addresses the structural causes of poverty, including discrimination and inequality.

QUESTIONS

1. Explain the advantages and disadvantages of the charity approach as a solution to unequal global development.
2. 'Give a man a fish and you feed him for a day. Teach a man how to fish and you feed him for a lifetime.' Explain how this old proverb can be used to explain the needs-based approach.
3. Why is the rights-based approach the best solution to unequal global development?

Evolution of the Right to Development

The right to development began to be discussed in the UN as early as the 1950s and 1960s. During the process of decolonisation, newly independent developing countries began to join the UN. Of major concern for these nations was the idea of development. Through this, the concept of the 'right to development' began to grow. These countries believed that their former colonisers had a moral duty to redress the development imbalance that had been caused in large part by colonialism. However, it was not until 1986 that the UN formally recognised the right to development. In fact, the right was first recognised not by the United Nations but by a regional human rights instrument – the African Charter on Human and Peoples' Rights – in 1981.

Development is a human right and belongs to everyone

UN Declaration on the Right to Development

The UN adopted the Declaration on the Right to Development in 1986. Prior to this, *development* had been understood in very narrow, economic terms. Many governments around the world had violated the basic rights of their people in the name of economic growth. People had been evicted and denied basic rights such as food, water, sanitation, education, housing and health. The Declaration on the Right to Development widened the definition of development as an 'economic, social, cultural and political process', confirmed it as a human right, and placed *people* at the centre of development. Rather than focus on economic growth, the development process would now be aimed at the wellbeing of the entire population. Each person has the right to reach his or her full potential. The right to development became firmly connected to the realisation of economic, social and cultural rights, as well as political and civil freedoms. Development is about rights, and rights are about development.

Key Elements of the UN Declaration on the Right to Development

The Right to Development is about:

- **Putting people at the centre of development**

  What this means: Development is about people. They should be the main focus of development policies. People are the subject, participant and beneficiary of development.

- **Ensuring free, active and meaningful participation**

  What this means: People are not only the targets of development but are active participants in their own development and that of their society. Women are a commonly excluded group. The participation of women should be ensured.

- **Securing non-discrimination**

  What this means: Every person, regardless of race, colour, gender or any other category, has the right to development.

- **Fairly distributing the benefits of development**

  What this means: Growing inequalities need be addressed. Everyone should enjoy a fair distribution of the benefits of development.

- **Respecting self-determination, and sovereignty over natural resources**

  What this means: Countries and peoples have the right to freely choose the ways and means to achieve their development. They should have full ownership and control of their natural wealth and resources.

- **All in a process that advances other civil, political, economic, social and cultural rights**

  What this means: The right to development consists of all types of rights. They should be given 'equal attention'. Human rights are inalienable and indivisible (see pages 243—244). Rights cannot be separated, and one right cannot be denied in the pursuit of another.

ACTIVITY 8.17

Your group will be assigned a section of the UN Declaration on the Right to Development. Summarise the main points in the section. Ensure that you clearly explain the meaning of articles, rights and any key terms.

Create a presentation and deliver it to your class.

The full text of the UN Declaration of the Right to Development is available at https://educateplus.ie/go/right-development

RESEARCH ASSIGNMENT 8.8

Imagine that you are a UN Special Rapporteur on the Right to Development and you are on a visit to a country. You have been asked by the country's government to answer the following questions concerning the UN Declaration of the Right to Development:

1. What is the right to development? What are its key elements?
2. Who are the rights holders and duty bearers of the right to development?
3. Is the Declaration of the Right to Development legally binding on the government?
4. How can the right to development be implemented in this country?

> The answers to the above questions can be found in Fact Sheet No. 37, 'Frequently asked questions on the right to development' UN Office of the High Commissioner (2016): https://educateplus.ie/go/faq

International Cooperation

'States have the duty to cooperate with each other in ensuring development and eliminating obstacles to development.'
Article 3, Declaration on the Right to Development

The Declaration on the Right to Development imposes duties on individual states and on the collective international community. At a national level, individual states are required to make policies and programmes that ensure that their populations are benefiting from development (e.g. national poverty reduction programmes). The declaration also recognised the global dimension to development. The global transfer of information, communication, people and goods means that we are all connected. We are interdependent. Many of the challenges and barriers to development are global in nature and require a global response (e.g. climate change, unfair trade, tax injustice).

Fig. 8.28 Development depends on international cooperation

In recognition of this fact, the declaration also requires states and international organisations (e.g. UN agencies) to cooperate. International cooperation to implement the right to development has been based on many different international frameworks down through the years. The current global framework for international cooperation on development is Agenda 2030 and the **Sustainable Development Goals** (also known as the *Global Goals*). International cooperation can involve many different actions.

KEY TERM

There are 17 **Sustainable Development Goals (SDGs)**. They cover a range of human rights – economic, social, cultural and political.

> See Chapters 10 and 11 (pages 371–457) for more information on climate change, unfair trade and tax injustice.

HUMAN RIGHTS AND RESPONSIBILITIES IN EUROPE AND BEYOND

CASE STUDY 6: International Cooperation: Implementing the Right to Development

Agenda 2030 and the Sustainable Development Goals

In 2000 the Millennium Development Goals (MDGs) were developed. This was the first ever common framework agreed by UN member states to address global development. Before the MDGs, international cooperation was not coordinated in such a global manner. The MDGs consisted of eight goals the international community was committed to achieving by 2015. The MDGs covered many important economic, social and cultural rights, such as halving levels of extreme poverty, preventing the spread of HIV/AIDS and providing universal primary education.

From 2000 to 2015, the MDGs gave direction to international development cooperation. Development aid programmes, such as Ireland's (Irish Aid), were guided by these eight goals. Developing countries in Africa, Asia, Latin America and elsewhere designed their national poverty reduction programmes on this basis too. By 2015, the MDGs had been partially achieved and significant progress had been made in relation to a number of targets. The number of people living on less than $1.25 a day had been reduced (Goal 1) from 1.9 billion in 1990 to 836 million. Primary school enrolment (Goal 2) had increased from 83 per cent in 2000 to 91 per cent. The child mortality rate had reduced (Goal 4) by more than half. The target of halving the proportion of people without access to improved sources of water (Goal 7) has been achieved. However, many of the targets had not been achieved and many criticised the MDGs for leaving out important human rights areas, such as climate change, environmental rights and women's rights. The international community began to discuss what should replace the MDGs after 2015.

In September 2015, world leaders met at the United Nations Sustainable Development Summit and adopted the 2030 Agenda for Sustainable Development. They committed to achieving 17 Sustainable Development Goals (SDGs). The SDGs, also known as the **Global Goals**, replaced the Millennium Development Goals and cover a wider range of economic, social, cultural and political rights.

The international community, states and international organisations have committed to achieving these goals together. This means providing resources, training and expertise, and ensuring that laws and policies promote the achievement of these goals.

Fig. 8.29 The 17 Sustainable Development Goals (SDGs)

ACTIVITY 8.18

Your group will be assigned one of the Sustainable Development Goals (SDGs) to investigate in more detail. Prepare a short report on the SDG and present it to your class. Include the following in your report:

- Describe and explain the meaning of the goal
- Explain the exact targets and deadline for achieving the goal
- Identify which human rights are linked to the goal
- Discuss whether the goal is achievable or if it could be more ambitious.

Sustainable Development Goals are explained in this *Guardian* article from 19 January 2015: https://educateplus.ie/go/goals-interactive

CASE STUDY 7: Irish Aid

Ireland played a leading global role in negotiating the SDGs. Appointed by the President of the UN General Assembly, as Co-Chair of this process, Ireland worked with colleagues in all relevant government departments and civil society bodies to ensure that Ireland's priorities of ending hunger and poverty, promoting gender equality and women's empowerment, and promoting good governance and the rule of law were represented in the new goals.

The SDGs provide a compass for national governments, such as the Irish government, to set programmes and strategies that will contribute to the achievement of the goals by 2030. Irish Aid is the Irish government's programme for overseas development, managed within the Department of Foreign Affairs and Trade. Irish Aid's programmes and projects contribute to the achievement of the SDGs.

- In Ethiopia, hundreds of thousands of people affected by drought received support to adapt their agricultural practices to climate change. This contributed to **SDG 13: Climate Action**.

- In Liberia, Irish Aid supported immunisation projects to expand protection against disease and disability in children. This contributed to **SDG 3: Good Health and Well-being.**

- In South Africa, civil society bodies are being supported to address gender-based violence. This contributed to **SDG 5: Gender Equality** and **SDG 16: Peace, Justice and Strong Institutions.**

- In Zambia, Irish Aid supported projects to improve nutrition for children. This contributed to **SDG 2: Zero Hunger**.

- In Uganda, Irish Aid provided financial support to vulnerable children and adolescents to attend secondary school. This contributed to **SDG 4: Quality Education**.

Irish Aid
An Roinn Gnóthaí Eachtracha agus Trádála
Department of Foreign Affairs and Trade

Fig. 8.30 Ireland's Permanent Representative to the United Nations, David Donoghue (right) with former United Nations Secretary General, Ban Ki-moon (left)

Fig. 8.31 Hills in Northern Tigray, Ethiopia, are terraced with a series of small dams to improve natural irrigation and raise the water table

Fig. 8.32 Shefena Kahsay, surrounded by the rocky terrain of her home in Northern Tigray, Ethiopia

A central component to Irish Aid's programmes is the promotion of **good governance**. Irish Aid believes that good governance is a vital ingredient in efforts to reduce poverty and hunger, and to support development that is inclusive and sustainable. Irish Aid programmes promote increased participation of citizens in government decision-making, and the protection and promotion of human rights.

Global Goal 17: Partnerships for the Goals

The final Global Goal of Agenda 2030 identifies exactly how states and the international community need to support the delivery of the goals. It provides an example of the different aspects of international cooperation.

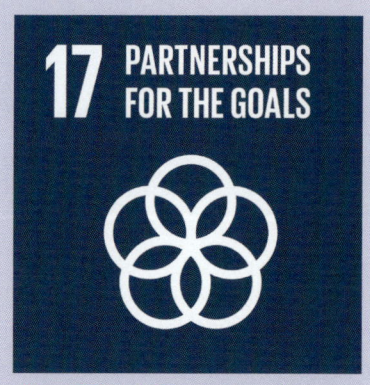

Fig. 8.33 Goal 17 articulates what states need to do to deliver on the SDGs

Finance

States must ensure that adequate funds are available to support global development. This includes:

- Ensuring that developed countries, such as Ireland, meet their commitment to provide overseas development assistance to developing countries: 0.7 per cent of GNP.
- Ensuring tax justice: supporting developed countries to strengthen their tax systems, and addressing tax avoidance globally.
- Supporting developing countries to deal with their debt situation by providing conditions that are fairer and more sustainable.

See page 451 for more information on tax justice.

Technology

Supporting global development is about more than funding. Development requires skills, knowledge and technology. States must ensure the fair distribution of information, communication and scientific knowledge, and technologies that are environmentally sustainable.

Knowledge and Skills

The international community should provide training and support to developing countries in developing and implementing their national programmes and plans to achieve the global goals. For example, the training of doctors and nurses could be used to help a country achieve good health (Goal 3) or training on nutrition might be shared to help achieve an end to hunger (Goal 2).

Trade

The international community should address unfair trade rules that have resulted in the low market access and smaller share of trade for developing and least developed countries.

See page 400 for more information on unfair trade rules.

RESEARCH ASSIGNMENT 8.9

Explain the responsibilities and duties of each state to implement economic, social and cultural rights within the framework of international cooperation.

Tips:
- Refer to the Global Goal 17 box above.
- Read 'Frequently asked questions on the right to development' (Fact sheet 37) from the UN Office of the High Commissioner (2016), with particular focus on the answers to Questions 7, 8, 10 and 14: https://educateplus.ie/go/faq

SUMMARY

- States that signed and ratified the UNCRC have a legal obligation to fully implement all the rights contained in the convention.
- The implementation and the enjoyment of the rights contained in the UNCRC varies greatly from place to place.
- Globally, the rate of child mortality has been greatly reduced. However, many children still do not have the right to survival and development, especially in developing countries such as Angola.
- The right to freedom of thought, conscience and religion is protected by laws or enshrined in the constitutions of most western democracies. At the same time, certain practices and laws can undermine that right.
- In theocracies (e.g. Iran) and atheist states (e.g. China) many people are denied the right to freedom of thought, conscience and religion.
- The right to protection from all forms of abuse and violence – physical, mental and sexual – is one of the most important rights contained in the UNCRC.
- Corporal punishment is still permitted in most states in the world. In certain countries, large numbers of children suffer from severe abuse as child labourers (e.g. sub-Saharan Africa and South East Asia), child soldiers (e.g. Somalia, Syria, Sudan) and sex workers (e.g. India).
- Poverty and war are the two most common barriers that prevent children from enjoying the right to rest, leisure, play and recreation. Child labourers, child soldiers and refugees are three groups that are denied this right throughout the world.
- The European Convention on Human Rights was developed by the Council of Europe. It protects the rights of all citizens living within the 47 member states that signed and ratified it.
- If your human rights are denied in Ireland, you can take a case to the European Court of Human Rights – once you have exhausted all avenues of the Irish judicial system.
- Some critics of human rights argue that human rights are a western concept and that imposing them on the non-western world is a form of cultural imperialism.
- Supporters of human rights argue that human rights were carefully developed by western and non-western countries to be universal and cross-cultural.
- Some political analysts and economists claim that human rights hinder economic development and should be set aside in developing countries to enable these states to develop faster.
- Critics of this view argue that economic development is inseparable from social and political development, and that all three strands are compatible with sustainable development.
- Under the Sustainable Development Goals (2015–30), states have an obligation to enter into a framework of international cooperation to implement economic, social and cultural rights throughout the world.

REVISION QUESTIONS

1. What is the UN Convention on the Rights of the Child?
2. What is the main difference between the UNCRC and the Universal Declaration of Human Rights?
3. Explain clearly and give examples of the following key rights in the UNCRC:
   (a) The right to survival and development (Article 6)
   (b) The right to freedom of thought, conscience and religion (Article 14)
   (c) The right to protection from all forms of violence, neglect or abuse (Article 19)
   (d) The right to rest, leisure, play and recreation (Article 31).
4. Describe **three** reputable official sources that can be used to conduct research on the implementation of human rights in different countries.
5. What is the Council of Europe?
6. Describe **five** important rights contained in the European Convention of Human Rights (ECHR).
7. In relation to the ECHR, what is a protocol?
8. What is the function of the European Court of Human Rights?
9. Describe the steps involved in taking a case to the European Court of Human Rights.
10. Give **two** examples of decisions made by the European Court of Human Rights in cases taken by Irish citizens.
11. Who is responsible for implementing and enforcing the decisions taken by the European Court of Human Rights?
12. 'Human rights are a western concept and a form of cultural imperialism.' Give **two** arguments or pieces of evidence that support this view, and **two** arguments or pieces of evidence that contradict this view.
13. 'Human rights hinder economic development.' Give **two** arguments or pieces of evidence that support this view, and **two** arguments or pieces of evidence that contradict this view.
14. List **three** statistics that illustrate global inequality in the world today.
15. Describe the **three** approaches to development (the development models).
16. Why is a rights-based approach to development more effective than the charity approach?
17. How does the UN Declaration on the Right to Development define 'development'?
18. Describe the main elements of the UN Declaration on the Right to Development.
19. What are the Sustainable Development Goals?
20. Explain how the Irish government can cooperate with the international community in implementing economic, social and cultural rights throughout the world.

Fig. 8.34 Key Word cloud

DATA-BASED QUESTIONS

Complete the qualitative and quantitative research data-based questions exercise on pages 143–145 of your Skills Book.

EXAM FOCUS: Section B of LC Exam

REVISION EXERCISES

Complete the revision exercises on pages 146–147 of your Skills Book.

EXAM FOCUS: Section A of LC Exam

DISCURSIVE ESSAY TOPICS

1. Critically examine the extent to which one or more of the rights listed in the UN Convention on the Rights of the Child is implemented around the world.
2. 'Human rights can bring positive change to the world but the concept is not without its critics.' Discuss.

EXAM FOCUS: Section C of LC Exam

Reflective Practice

Ensure that you have completed all the Reflective Journal entries for this chapter (pages 32–33 of your Reflective Journal and Learning Portfolio) before moving on to the next chapter.

Complete the Learning Portfolio activities on pages 34–36 of your Reflective Journal and Learning Portfolio. This will help you to self-assess the extent to which you have achieved the learning intentions for this chapter, and will help you to monitor your progress.

HUMAN RIGHTS AND RESPONSIBILITIES IN EUROPE AND BEYOND

CHAPTER 9
Identity in a Global Age

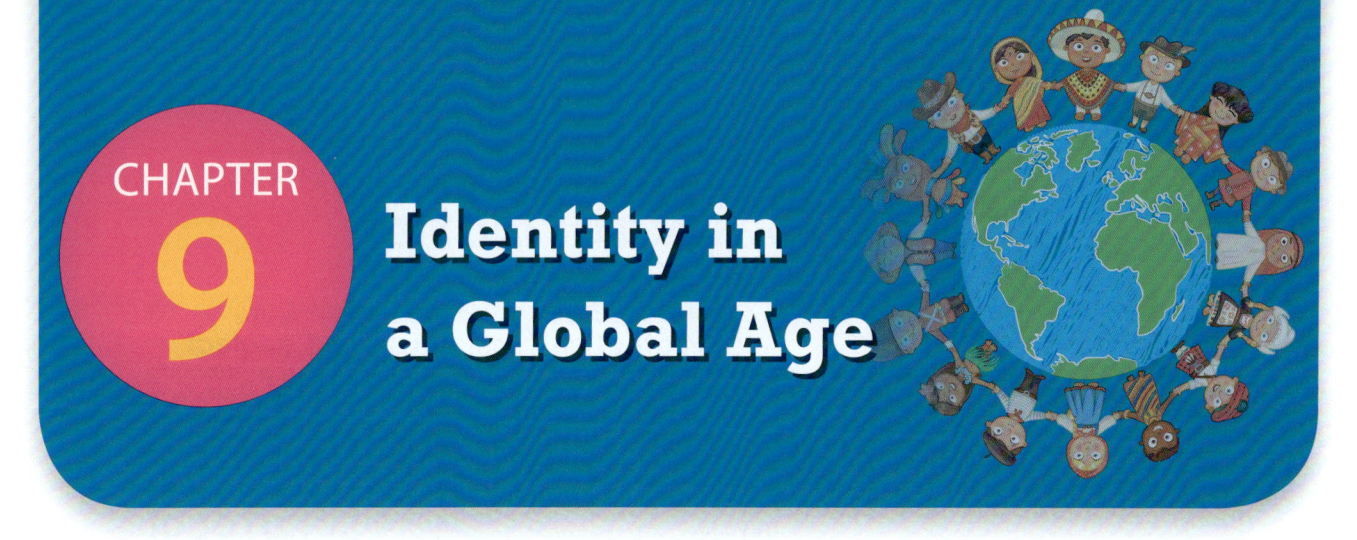

'Our ability to reach unity in diversity will be the beauty and the test of our civilisation.'
Mahatma Gandhi

KEY TERMS

- Globalisation
- Monoculturalism
- Multiculturalism
- Cultural diversity
- Identity
- Western culture
- Non-western culture
- Culture
- Popular culture
- Dominant culture
- Subculture
- Mass culture
- Segregation
- Sectarianism
- Cultural integration
- Cultural diffusion
- Cultural convergence
- Cultural divergence
- Cultural hybridisation
- Cultural appropriation
- Cultural integration policy
- Cultural assimilation
- Sovereignty
- Political globalisation
- Supranational organisations

Introduction

One of the key features of our modern societies is our interconnectedness. **Globalisation** has resulted in closer connections and links between societies and populations around the world. With the mass movement of people, goods and services, and information, our pathways – real and virtual – are constantly crossing. But what impact does globalisation have on our society? Cultural identity is one area that has changed significantly in our interconnected world. **Monoculturalism** has given way to **multiculturalism**: our societies have more **cultural diversity** than ever before. We can sample cuisine from any part of the world in our local restaurants and hear a diverse range of languages being spoken on the streets of our cities. We can interact with people from all corners of the globe, who bring with them their unique cultures and rituals. In this chapter, we will examine identity and culture in Ireland and Europe. We will look at patterns of diversity and engage with debates in relation to where identity comes from and how it is maintained and adapted. We will explore both sides of the 'identity paradox'. On the one hand, globalisation is said to have threatened the survival of local and traditional culture. At the same time, we have also witnessed the rise of identity politics, as cultures revitalise and reassert themselves in the face of perceived threats to their existence.

KEY TERMS

Globalisation is the process by which the world has become increasingly interconnected. These interconnections are based on trade, migration and communication technology.

Monoculturalism is the promotion and preservation of a dominant homogeneous (same) culture among all members of a society. Monoculturalism is based on the exclusion or assimilation of all other minority cultures within the country. In the world today, there are very few examples of truly monocultural countries.

Multiculturalism is the acceptance and promotion of multiple cultural traditions within a single jurisdiction (area).

Cultural diversity is the existence of a variety of cultural or ethnic groups within a society. New York is an example of a culturally diverse society where inhabitants from Africa, Asia and other parts of the world practise and celebrate their unique cultures.

By the end of this chapter you will be able to:

- Define key terms, such as 'globalisation', 'cultural diversity', 'multiculturalism' and 'monoculturalism'.
- Explain identity and culture, and describe how they are socially constructed.
- Describe how Irish identity has been represented in the Irish school curriculum.
- Summarise research evidence on the relationship between education and identity in Northern Ireland.
- Engage with different viewpoints and evaluate evidence to assess the role played by education in shaping a sense of national identity in Ireland, north and south.
- Provide examples and research-based evidence to illustrate how cultures develop and change in the process of cultural mixing and adaptation.
- Draw on relevant examples and examine qualitative and quantitative research to evaluate the role of the following phenomena in the process of cultural mixing and adaptation:
  - ICT and media
  - Migration and travel.
- Describe the patterns of cultural, linguistic and religious diversity that exist within the EU.
- Describe patterns of ethnic diversity within states and across the EU.
- Evaluate evidence and engage with different viewpoints to assess the following arguments about national and ethnic identity:
  - National and ethnic groups share a common culture, values and beliefs.
  - National and ethnic groups are 'imagined communities' that are socially constructed.
- Evaluate evidence and engage with different viewpoints to assess the argument that national and ethnic groups are 'imagined communities' which are socially constructed.
- Explain the positive and negative effects of developing a sense of ethnic identity.
- Explain and evaluate various arguments concerning the interaction between western and non-western cultures.
- Describe the role of supranational bodies in the decision-making process relating to one policy that affects young people.
- Evaluate the argument that power is moving from national governments to supranational bodies.
- Critically evaluate one piece of quantitative and one piece of qualitative research on cultural change and identity, making reference to the quality of the evidence and conclusions drawn in the research pieces.
- Describe the contribution of key thinkers to debates concerning culture and identity.

By the end of this chapter you will have developed the following skills:
- Interpersonal and teamwork skills by working effectively with small and large groups to complete tasks, solve problems and achieve consensus.
- Research skills and information processing on content related to culture and identity.
- Critical and creative thinking skills in relation to the strengths, weaknesses and limitations of key pieces of research and ideological viewpoints on culture and identity in the modern world.
- Communication and active listening skills by engaging constructively in dialogue and debate.

Identity and Culture

Identity is how individuals or groups define themselves or are defined by others. Identity is the label we give to ourselves, or are given by others – and it is the label we give to other individuals and groups. This label can involve many strands, such as language, ethnicity, gender, nationality, religion, class and lifestyle. In Chapter 3, we looked at some of these categories with respect to political representation. In Chapter 6, we looked at how different groups can be stereotyped in the mass media. We have seen how each person has multiple identities – one element can be stronger than other elements, depending on the circumstances. For example, as an Irish Muslim woman, my Irish identity may become stronger during the Olympic Games, my Muslim identity may be particularly important to me during Ramadan, and on International Women's Day, I may identify most strongly with being a woman.

Identity is important because it affects how we view ourselves and others. It can shape how we perceive and interact with others in society (social relations). We view ourselves and others in certain ways, depending on the labels (identities) we assign. If we think of age, for example, we view young people and the elderly in very different ways. And the meaning we assign to certain groups can differ across cultures, e.g. **western cultures** and **non-western cultures**. The elderly in many African cultures are given a very high status as sources of wisdom and authority. In many western cultures, youth is considered a thing of beauty and power. When we give an identity label to an individual or group, we show that we hold certain expectations or assumptions about their characteristics and behaviour.

KEY TERMS

Identity is the term we use to describe how an individual or group will view and define themselves. Identity can involve many strands, such as language, ethnicity, gender, nationality, religion, class and lifestyle.

Western culture is a term used to describe the shared cultures and traditions of North America and Western Europe. Elements of western culture include capitalism, consumerism, human rights and individualism.

Non-western culture refers to cultures which do not originate in the west and do not imitate typical 'western' cultural values or practices. Non-western cultures are traditionally found in Asia, Africa, India, Latin America and the Middle East.

ACTIVITY 9.1

Work with your partner to complete the following activity.

1. Think individually for a moment about your identity. List the different aspects of your identity, such as language, ethnicity, gender, nationality, religion, class and lifestyle. *(Think)*
2. With your partner, compare your lists. Discuss how each aspect of your identity makes you feel, act and behave. *(Pair)*
3. Share your conclusions with the rest of the class. *(Share)*

SKILLS BOOK LINK 9.1

Go to page 148 of your Skills Book to complete Skill Task 9.1 on identity.

Culture refers to a shared way of life of a society or group. Culture consists of many elements, such as language, values and norms, beliefs, customs and traditions, dress, cuisine, arts, literature and sports. Culture can be based on language, ethnicity, nationality, religion or social factors (i.e. consumer or **popular culture**). Culture can be visible and invisible. In society, we normally have a **dominant culture**, which is the main way of life accepted by the majority. We also have **subcultures**. These are the smaller cultures of groups in society that differ from the dominant culture. For example, in Ireland we have a rich diversity of subcultures, including the Traveller community, other ethnic minority groups, the LGBTQ+ community, and many more. Culture can be passed from one generation to the next through institutions such as the family, education and the media. Culture is not biologically programmed. Culture is not permanent or static: it can be created and changed.

KEY TERMS

Culture refers to the accepted and familiar beliefs, customs and behaviours of a society or group.

Popular culture consists of cultural activities, products and services that are considered to appeal primarily to non-elite groups in society (traditionally considered the working and middle classes). Examples include soap operas and popular music genres (e.g. pop music, hip hop).

Dominant culture is the main way of life accepted by the majority in a society.

Subcultures are the cultures of groups that differ from the dominant culture in a society. Examples of subcultures in modern societies include ethnic minority groups and LGBTQ+ communities.

Mass culture refers to a set of common ideas and values that are produced and distributed via the mass media, news sources, music and art.

What is the Difference Between Race and Ethnicity?

Race is an outdated concept that was used to classify and categorise people according to their physical characteristics and variations in genetics. It was based on what people inherited biologically – our physical characteristics, such as skin colour, hair type, height and physique. In the modern scientific community, there is broad consensus that we are all essentially the same genetically. In this sense, there is only one race: the human race.

Ethnicity is a more useful concept when studying differences within the human race. Ethnicity refers to the culturally defined differences between groups in society. Differences in language, religious beliefs, historical experiences, customs, culture and traditions can be used to categorise people into distinctive ethnic groups.

Fig. 9.1 There is only one race: the human race

Markers of Culture

Religion

Religion provides a system of beliefs, values, symbols and rituals. In some cases, religion influences our choices with respect to clothing, food and other aspects of daily life. Religion crosses national borders. The main world religions are Buddhism, Christianity, Hinduism, Islam, and Judaism.

Fig. 9.2 Religion is a marker of culture

Language

Traditionally, groups and societies have shared a common language. Language plays an important role in creating cultural bonds and in establishing boundaries with 'other' linguistic groups. We use language to communicate with each other and to transmit our heritage – our beliefs, customs and traditions – between generations. Examples of dominant linguistic cultures that cross 'national' borders include Arabic, English, French, Mandarin, Russian and Spanish.

Fig. 9.3 Language is a marker of culture

Ethnicity

'Ethnicity' is the term we use to describe groups that share a common identity based on a similar ancestral lineage or social, cultural and national experiences. Examples include the Tatars in Russia, the Roma people within Europe, Native Americans, Hispanic populations and Basque and Catalan people in Spain.

Fig. 9.4 Ethnicity is a marker of culture

Ethnicity in Modern Ireland

Several minority ethnic groups exist in modern Ireland, such as the Polish community, the Traveller community, etc. However, according to the 2016 census a large majority of the population in Ireland (82.2 per cent) claim a 'White Irish' ethnicity. The roots of this dominant ethnic group can be traced to the indigenous Gaelic clans who controlled the country before the English conquest of Ireland. Following the arrival of the Normans in 1169 CE, an Anglo-Saxon ethnicity developed and spread throughout the east and south of the country. In the decades that followed, the Anglo-Irish intermarried with the Gaelic Irish and began to adopt Gaelic customs, traditions and language. Eventually the two groups became indistinguishable, as the Anglo-Saxons were assimilated into Gaelic society. During the late sixteenth and early seventeenth centuries, the British adopted a policy of plantation (an organised migration of English and Scottish Protestants to Ireland) in an attempt to support colonial rule and eradicate Gaelic culture. The most successful of these plantations was the Plantation of Ulster, which saw the arrival of thousands of Scottish Presbyterians to many parts of the north. The three groups – Gaelic Irish, Anglo-Saxon and Planter – have shaped one another over the centuries to create the 'White Irish' ethnic identity claimed by the majority of people living in the Republic of Ireland.

Fig. 9.5 Irish schools benefit from increased ethnic diversity

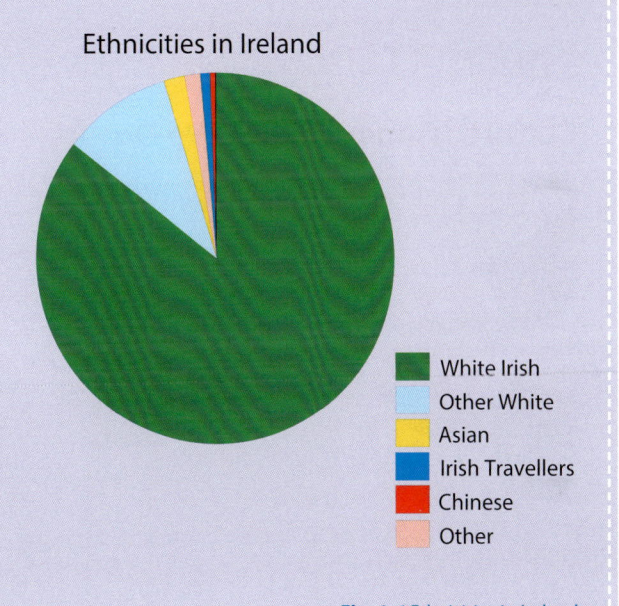

Fig. 9.6 Ethnicities in Ireland

QUESTIONS

1. Explain how globalisation has contributed to cultural diversity.
2. Explain the difference between multiculturalism and monoculturalism.
3. Define and give an example of:
   (a) Monoculture
   (b) Mass culture
   (c) Subculture.
4. What is the difference between race and ethnicity?
5. Name and describe **three** markers of culture.
6. According to the census, what ethnicity do the vast majority of people living in the Republic of Ireland claim to be?
7. Name **two** minority ethnic groups in Ireland today.
8. Name and describe the **three** main ethnic groups that existed in Ireland in the seventeenth century.

IDENTITY IN A GLOBAL AGE

SKILLS BOOK LINK 9.2

Go to page 149 of your Skills Book to complete Skill Task 9.2 on culture in Ireland.

SKILLS BOOK LINK 9.3

Go to page 150 of your Skills Book to complete Skill Task 9.3 on a culture outside of Ireland.

See **RESEARCH TIPS** on page 33.

Cultural Differences in Everyday Things

Culture is About What We Do

Fig. 9.7 Business card etiquette in Asia: Business cards should be presented facing upwards with both hands. It is considered rude if the recipient does not inspect a business card before putting it away

- In the Middle East and East Asia it is considered an insult to point your feet at a person (particularly the soles) or to display your feet in any way, e.g. by resting with your feet up.
- In Asia it is considered an insult to crumple a business card that someone has given to you. The business card is viewed as an extension of that person and it is therefore extremely rude to handle it in a careless way.
- In China, when you are eating with company, you should not clear your plate. Your host is obliged to keep refilling it. Leaving some food on your plate is a sign that your host is generous.

- In the US and the UK, a strong handshake is considered friendly. In countries such as the Philippines, it can be viewed as a sign of aggression.
- In Greece, displaying your palm and extended fingers towards a person is an insulting gesture known as the *mountza*.
- In most Arab countries, the left hand is considered unclean. It is extremely rude to offer it for a handshake or to use it to feed yourself.

Fig. 9.8 In the Philippines, a strong handshake may be viewed as a sign of aggression

318 POWER AND PEOPLE

Culture is About What We Say

- Together, approximately 95 per cent of the world's people speak fewer than 100 of the 6,000 different languages that exist.
- Linguists predict that as many as 90 per cent of all world languages will be extinct or nearing extinction within the next 100 years. Each language represents a distinct style of thought and expression. Therefore, when a language becomes extinct, this amounts to more than a loss of particular words and phrases.

QUESTIONS

1. Can you think of any other examples of everyday cultural practices that are unique to certain cultures?
2. Can you think of cultural practices that are uniquely Irish?

ACTIVITY 9.2

Discuss the characteristics of a 'typical Irish person' with your group. Your teacher will give your group a large blank sheet. Use the sheet to draw a portrait of a typical Irish person, with his or her cultural traits and characteristics clearly labelled. Present your portrait to the class.

Tip: You could draw the outline of a face and list the 'typical Irish person' traits within it.

SKILLS BOOK LINK 9.4

Go to pages 150–151 of your Skills Book to complete Skill Task 9.4 on stereotypical Irish traits.

SKILLS BOOK LINK 9.5

Go to page 151 of your Skills Book to complete Skill Task 9.5 on identity, dominant culture and diversity.

IDENTITY IN A GLOBAL AGE

KEY THINKERS

CULTURAL ICEBERG

In 1976 **Edward T. Hall** developed the concept of the 'cultural iceberg'. According to Hall, culture is composed of visible and invisible elements. The visible component makes up about 10 per cent of culture. It includes elements of culture that can be easily observed, such as music, clothing, food and games. The remaining 90 per cent of culture, however, consists of things that are not immediately visible, such as values, beliefs and attitudes.

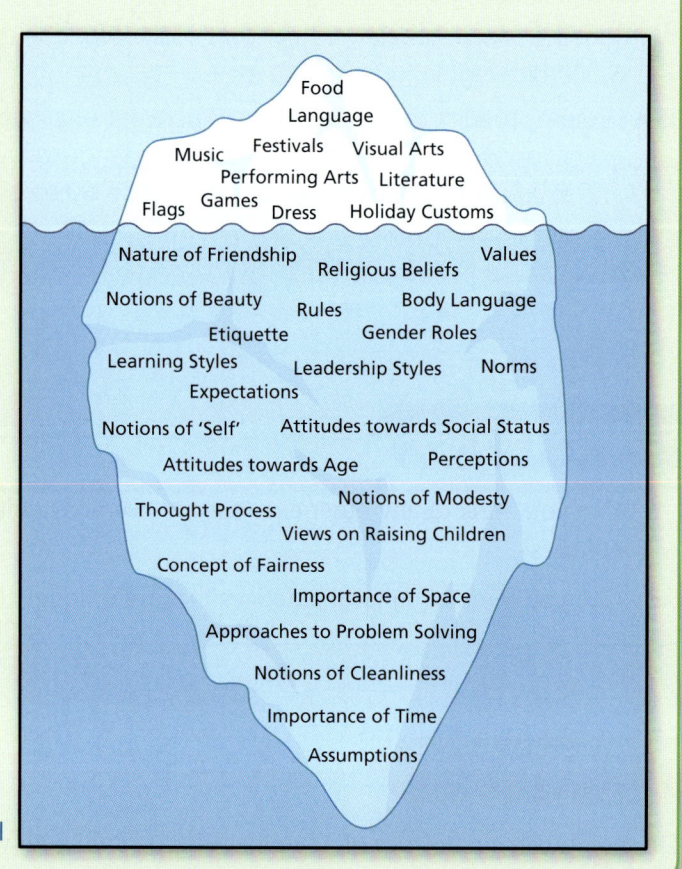

Fig. 9.9 The 'cultural iceberg' as described by Edward T. Hall

QUESTIONS

1. Explain the term 'visible culture'.
2. Explain the term 'invisible culture'.
3. Divide a page in your copybook into two columns: one entitled 'visible culture' and the other entitled 'invisible culture'. List aspects of Irish culture under each column.
4. Can people's perception of Irish culture be influenced by stereotyping? What aspects of Irish culture are often stereotyped by the media or other groups?

ACTIVITY 9.3

Draw a cultural iceberg to represent the visible and invisible aspects of Irish culture.

National Identities on the Island of Ireland

National identity remains a strong form of identity in our modern world. We assign national identities to help us to identify and distinguish between groups of people from different geographic territories. Nations are not the same as states: several different nations can exist within the same state. Nationalism is a shared identity. As with culture, national identity is not a biological fact. We are not born with a sense of being Irish, Nigerian, Chinese or Pakistani. These identities are socially constructed.

What is the Difference Between a Nation and a State?

The terms 'nation' and 'state' are often used interchangeably. However, they mean different things.

A **nation** is a group or community of people who share a sense of common identity. This identity can be based on different elements, such as language, religion or customs. Examples of national groups include French, Kurds, Basques, etc.

A **state** is a political unit. It is an independent and sovereign territory. We normally use the term 'country' to refer to a state. The UN currently recognises over 200 states.

Most states contain multiple nations or national groups. For example, Northern Ireland contains three dominant national groups: Irish, British and Northern Irish. The term 'nation-state' refers to a situation where the boundaries of a state and those of a nation are perfectly aligned. This rarely exists, however. Japan and Iceland are examples of nation-states.

KEY THINKERS

NATIONAL IDENTITY

Benedict Anderson

Benedict Anderson was an Irish political scientist, born in China to an Anglo-Irish father and English mother. In 1983 he developed the concept of **'imagined communities'** to describe his theory of nationalism and national identity. Anderson believed that people born within a certain geographic territory have a sense of belonging to an imagined community – the nation. This sense of belonging is based on a shared history or language among the people. Nations are different from states. A state can have multiple nations within it. For example, Belgium, Switzerland and Canada have multiple nations within their states, based on language. There is nothing biological about nationality. Anderson states that the printing press and the first forms of mass communication (e.g. newspapers) were responsible for cultivating a sense of shared national identity. Communities living in the same geographical territory may never meet, but because they read information about each other that is presented as 'common' or 'shared', a national identity is formed. Nations are invented.

Ernest Gellner

Ernest Gellner is one of the most influential modern theorists on nations and nationalism. His most famous book, *Nations and Nationalism*, was written in 1983. Gellner argued that nationalism is a recent phenomenon. It is a product of modernisation and industrialisation. He defined a nation as being a cultural group of people who see themselves as alike. They share a common language, belief system and sense of shared history. Nationalism, for Gellner, is the belief that all members of a nation should be part of the same political unit. Industrialisation made the growth of nationalism possible because it brought with it standardised education and a national administration. Like Durkheim, Gellner argued that education was the most important of these modern developments. Villages that had lived in relative isolation began to develop cultural similarities. As people began to concentrate in urban centres and became cut off from their roots, they began to develop a collective identity. For Gellner, states with a single nation (nation-states) are more stable politically than states with multiple nations.

IDENTITY IN A GLOBAL AGE

QUESTIONS

1. Would you agree with Anderson's claim that nations are 'imagined communities'? Give reasons to support your answer.

2. Is the concept of an Irish nation a modern invention? When did a common Irish identity first emerge? Did an ancient bond exist among the inhabitants of the island before Christianity came to Ireland? What aspects of Irish identity and culture are ancient? What aspects of Irish identity and culture are modern-day inventions?

3. What is a nation, according to Gellner? What characteristics do nations share?

4. How did industrialisation lead to the growth and spread of nationalism?

5. Do you agree with Gellner that nation-states are stronger than states containing multiple nations? Give reasons and examples to support your answer.

To help you answer Question 2:
- See page 324 for more information on the role of commemorations in shaping Irish national identity.
- See page 326 for more information on the role of education in shaping Irish national identity.

Who and What Shapes National Identity?

If national identity is something that is imagined and socially constructed, then who or what is responsible for creating it? Where do we get our sense of Irishness? In Chapter 2 and in Chapter 6, we learned about the role of social institutions (e.g. family, media, education) in reinforcing norms and values in society and in getting us to act in certain ways. These institutions also play a role in developing our sense of national identity. Governments play a fundamental role in shaping our sense of national identity. Throughout the world, governments promote specific national symbols, sporting events, festivals, heritage and traditions to reinforce a distinctive national identity among a nation's citizens. National days of commemoration and the education system are two important mechanisms through which a government can promote and shape the national identity of its people.

KEY THINKERS

THE ROLE OF EDUCATION IN FORMING IDENTITY

Functionalist Perspective

Émile Durkheim

According to functionalists such as Durkheim, social institutions (e.g. family, religion, media, education) play a role in the socialisation process. These institutions prepare individuals to contribute to the functioning of society. Education is part of the secondary socialisation process. With respect to identity formation, the education system gives pupils a shared sense of identity. Through subjects such as History, English and Civic Education, students develop a common sense of history and learn about the dominant values and traits associated with this identity. In school, we learn about our national symbols, anthem and traditions. National identity serves an important function in society in creating bonds between individuals. These bonds are necessary for the functioning of society.

POWER AND PEOPLE

> **QUESTIONS**
>
> 1. Would you agree that the Irish education system has influenced your sense of identity? If so, in what ways has this occurred?
> 2. What other social institutions have shaped your identity?
> 3. In your opinion, what was the single biggest influence in shaping your identity?
> 4. What do you think the following perspectives would say about the role of education in forming identity?
>   (a) Marxist perspective
>   (b) Feminist perspective.

The Role of the Government in Shaping Traditional Irish Identity

Fig. 9.10 Key aspects of traditional Irish identity

What do we mean by Irish identity? What does it mean to be Irish? Since the foundation of the Irish state, traditional depictions of Irish national identity have been based on common elements. Irish identity was characterised by images of rural Ireland, the Irish language, dancing, folklore (storytelling), Gaelic games, Catholicism and a 'white' ethnic population. Successive Irish governments promoted this distinct national identity through various means, including national days of commemoration and the education system.

IDENTITY IN A GLOBAL AGE

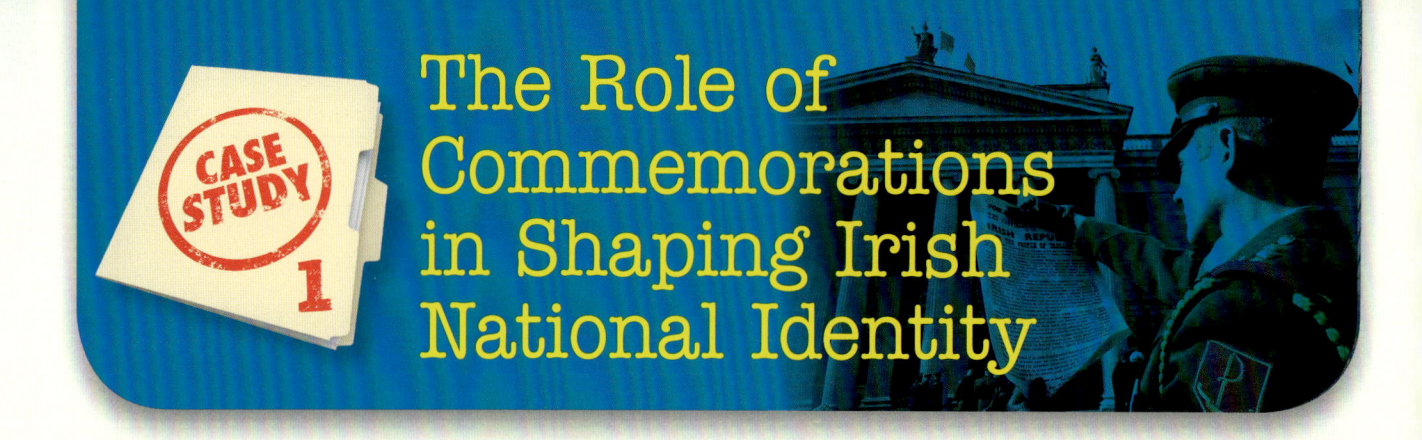

The Role of Commemorations in Shaping Irish National Identity

CASE STUDY 1

The Politics of Commemoration

Hosting annual state commemorations is arguably the most effective method used by governments to influence (and even to alter) the national identity of a country. National identity is socially constructed and is based on all members of the nation professing a shared collective memory or interpretation of their past (a common history). Because of this, what the government chooses to commemorate – and how they choose to commemorate it – are vital political issues. The historical events that a government chooses to commemorate become engrained in the collective memory of its people and can define national identity. The specific events that Irish governments have chosen to commemorate in the past have influenced many aspects of traditional Irish national identity.

Fig. 9.11 Commemoration of the 1916 Rising, O'Connell Street, Dublin

Commemorating the 1916 Easter Rising

Since gaining independence, the Irish state has prioritised the commemoration of the 1916 Rising over other equally important rebellions in Irish history, such as the United Irishmen rebellion of 1798. Consequently, the role played by Irish Protestants in Ireland's long struggle for independence has been neglected and downplayed. For example, in 1798 the United Irishmen were led by a Church of Ireland Protestant named Theobald Wolfe Tone, and Presbyterians led the rebellion in Ulster. However, during the early decades of independence, Irish governments focused on commemorating the 1916 Rising. Particular emphasis was placed on its pious Catholic leaders and their selfless sacrifice. For example, the message of Patrick Pearse's devout Catholicism and enthusiasm for the Irish language was promoted over James Connolly's atheism and socialist values. This was part of the government's agenda to develop a distinctively Catholic and Gaelic national identity for the new state. In 1966, the Golden Jubilee of the Easter Rising was marked by a fortnight of official state ceremonies and commemorative events. Some historians claimed that the government was guilty of legitimising the physical force used by republican rebels and promoting the ideals of 'blood sacrifice' and honourable uprising through the commemoration. In contrast, the

Fig. 9.12 The Proclamation is read aloud during the 2015 Easter Rising commemorations

ÉIRE IRELAND 19 20 16

CASE STUDY: The Role of Commemorations in Shaping Irish National Identity

government used the recent centenary celebrations in 2016 as an opportunity to promote the message of shared histories and identities on the island of Ireland. For example, all Irish people who died in 1916, including those who fought for the British Army in World War I, were remembered in a much more inclusive commemoration than any ever held before. This illustrates how national identity in Ireland is evolving to include all traditions on the island.

Taoiseach Éamon de Valera's St Patrick's Day broadcast, 1943

In 1943 Taoiseach Éamon de Valera used the national St Patrick's Day commemoration as an opportunity to promote his vision of an ideal Ireland and a distinctive national identity. He outlined this vision in his famous 'The Ireland that we dreamed of' speech, which was broadcast to the nation.

The Ireland That We Dreamed Of

The ideal Ireland that we would have, the Ireland that we dreamed of, would be the home of a people who valued material wealth only as a basis for right living, of a people who, satisfied with frugal comfort, devoted their leisure to the things of the spirit – a land whose countryside would be bright with cosy homesteads, whose fields and villages would be joyous with the sounds of industry, with the romping of sturdy children, the contest of athletic youths and the laughter of happy maidens, whose firesides would be forums for the wisdom of serene old age. The home, in short, of a people living the life that God desires that men should live. With the tidings that make such an Ireland possible, St Patrick came to our ancestors fifteen hundred years ago promising happiness here no less than happiness hereafter. It was the pursuit of such an Ireland that later made our country worthy to be called the island of saints and scholars. It was the idea of such an Ireland – happy, vigorous, spiritual – that fired the imagination of our poets; that made successive generations of patriotic men give their lives to win religious and political liberty; and that will urge men in our own and future generations to die, if need be, so that these liberties may be preserved.

Fig. 9.13 Éamon de Valera's St Patrick's Day broadcast in 1943 described 'the Ireland that we dreamed of'

QUESTIONS

1. Explain how early commemorations of the 1916 Rising helped to shape Irish national identity during the formative years of the Irish state.
2. How have recent commemorations of the 1916 Rising become more inclusive?
3. What are the key characteristics of Éamon de Valera's vision of Irish identity, as presented in his St Patrick's Day speech in 1943?
4. To what extent is this vision a reality today? Does it exist in any parts of the country? In what ways does the Ireland of today differ from de Valera's vision?
5. What groups in Ireland today might feel excluded from de Valera's vision of Ireland? Explain.

Complete your next Reflective Journal entry (pages 37–38)

CASE STUDY 2: The Role of Education in Shaping Irish National Identity

The Politics of Education

Schools serve many important functions in society, beyond providing us with academic knowledge and skills. One important function of education is the transmission of cultural norms and values to new generations. Schools provide us with a shared sense of national identity through representations of history, culture, beliefs and values. In Ireland, as elsewhere, the education curriculum has been used by the government to cultivate a sense of national identity.

Fig. 9.14 Education transmits cultural norms and values to new generations

The Role of Education in Influencing Irish Identity in the Pre-Independence Period

During the late nineteenth and early twentieth centuries, the control and patronage of Irish schools was divided along religious lines, despite the efforts of the British government to encourage multidenominational schooling. Both the Catholic and Protestant Churches received state aid for setting up and providing schools. Different Catholic orders ran schools throughout the country: the Jesuits, Franciscans, Dominicans and Christian Brothers (for boys), and the Mercy, Loreto and Presentation Sisters (for girls). Apart from instilling Catholic beliefs and values, these orders also promoted the Irish language and other aspects of traditional Irish identity during the Irish cultural revival, which preceded the Irish War of Independence. One Catholic order in particular, the Christian Brothers, played a leading role in incorporating aspects of the cultural revival into their curricula in schools. For instance, from 1878, Irish was taught in the Christian Brothers schools. By the turn of the century, the Christian Brothers were considered the 'Irish-Ireland' teaching institution. They promoted an Irish cultural nationalism built on Catholic and Gaelic values. Their overtly nationalist approach to teaching Irish history and geography also fostered their reputation as the 'Irish-Ireland' teaching institution. Past pupils of Christian Brothers schools are notable for the leading roles they played in the Gaelic League, nationalist organisations and the events of the Irish Revolution. For example, seven of the fourteen leaders executed after the 1916 Rising had formerly attended Christian Brothers schools. A relatively high percentage of IRA volunteers who took part in the War of Independence had also been former students of the Christian Brothers.

Patrick Pearse – Educational Philosopher and Founder of St Enda's

Patrick Pearse, a leader of the 1916 Rising, was a former student of the Christian Brothers and he was keenly aware of the powerful role that schooling could play in promoting a nationalist identity. Pearse was highly critical of the English-imposed system of education that existed in Ireland during his time. Referring to it as 'the murder machine', he criticised both the values and methods of the system. He criticised the education system for promoting English history and Victorian values at the expense of

POWER AND PEOPLE

CASE STUDY: The Role of Education in Shaping Irish National Identity

Irish history and native Gaelic values. He was particularly critical of the system of rote learning used by teachers, which he claimed stymied the freedom of thought and natural creativity of young students.

Pearse developed a progressive educational philosophy which was shaped by his studies of modern educational theorists such as Maria Montessori and his visits to bilingual schools in Belgium. He called for a complete overhaul of the Irish education system, asking for a child-centred and exploratory approach to replace indoctrination and the rote learning method. He also argued that the Irish education system should foster patriotism and a distinctive Irish nationalist identity instead of an anglicised one. Writing in *An Claidheamh Soluis* (the Gaelic League's Irish-language newspaper) from 1903 to 1909, Pearse repeatedly emphasised the need for education reform to secure 'the intellectual and political independence of Ireland'. He claimed that any teacher 'who cannot arouse a patriotic spirit in the breasts of Irish boys and girls is not worth his salt'. He believed that the entire education system – from nursery to university – should 'in spirit and complexion, be Irish and national'. For Pearse, language was 'the largest and most important of all the elements that go up to make a nation'.

Fig. 9.15 Patrick Pearse

In 1908 Pearse established his own bilingual school, St Enda's in Ranelagh, for the purpose of promoting his vision. Pearse and his fellow teachers at St Enda's instilled a love of the Irish language, Gaelic culture and traditions among their pupils. Irish history and folklore were brought to life through drama, as students were allowed to explore and re-enact famous stories and Celtic legends. The sense of patriotism, heroism and self-sacrifice was fostered through the study of Irish heroic figures such as Fionn MacCumhaill and Cúchulainn, as well as modern revolutionary patriots such as Robert Emmet. Given this patriotic emphasis, it is hardly surprising that many former pupils of St Enda's took part in the fighting during the 1916 Rising and the subsequent War of Independence. Three teachers at the school, Thomas MacDonagh, Con Colbert and Pearse himself, were executed for their leading roles in the Easter rebellion.

Fig. 9.16 Hurling team, St Enda's

IDENTITY IN A GLOBAL AGE

CASE STUDY: The Role of Education in Shaping Irish National Identity

The Role of Education in Influencing Irish Identity in the Post-Independence Period

Following independence in 1921, Ireland had the opportunity to develop its own education system for the first time. From the beginning, Ireland's education programme has been tied to cultivating a national identity based on a common history, language and religion. Ireland's first Chief Executive Officer for Education, Pádraig Ó Brolcháin, expressed this view: 'It is the intention of the new government to work with all its might for the strengthening of the national fibre by giving the language, history, music and tradition of Ireland their natural place in the life of Irish schools'. During the 1920s, Cumann na nGaedheal (the first government of the Irish Free State) introduced a series of education reforms to implement this vision.

History

- The history of Ireland was taught, instead of the history of England.
- A more traditional and nationalistic interpretation of Irish history was promoted in the syllabus. The history books used in class presented a general picture of Irish history as eight centuries of brave, patriotic struggle by a poor and oppressed people against a foreign invader.
- In the English-language syllabus, European authors replaced Anglo-Saxon authors.

Irish Language

- Irish was made obligatory for at least one hour per day in primary schools. From 1928, students had to pass Irish to be awarded the newly established Inter Certificate. In the 1930s, this was extended to include the Leaving Certificate.
- Teachers were instructed to teach all subjects through the medium of Irish, wherever possible.

Catholic Faith

- The state continued to protect the patronage and management role of the Catholic Church.
- The Rules for National Schools were published in 1965. Rule 68 stated: 'Of all the parts of a school curriculum, Religious Instruction is by far the most important.' Religion was made a compulsory subject in all schools.

Fig. 9.17 Irish society has become more diverse

The Role of Education in Influencing Irish identity in the Post-Celtic Tiger Period

Since the mid-1990s, Ireland has experienced significant immigration. This has helped to create a rich, multicultural society. Irish society has become more diverse in its nationalities, ethnicities, languages, cultures and religious affiliations. But has this been reflected in the curriculum or school system?

QUESTIONS

1. Explain how **(a)** the Christian Brothers and **(b)** Patrick Pearse used the Irish education system to promote a distinctive Irish identity prior to independence.

2. In what ways did the Cumann na nGaedheal government use the education system to shape Irish identity post-independence?

3. In your opinion, do governments have a right to use their education systems to promote a sense of national identity? What are the benefits and disadvantages of this approach to education?

4. Does the current post-primary curriculum reflect modern Irish identity? To what extent does it promote a narrow vision of Irish identity or a multicultural one?

ACTIVITY 9.4

Hold a classroom debate on the following motion.

'Irish should not be a compulsory subject at secondary school.'

RESEARCH ASSIGNMENT 9.1

Examine the current Junior Cycle curriculum and write a report entitled 'How Irish Identity is Represented in the Curriculum'. Include the following in your report:

- List all subjects that have topics or content relating to identity.

- In your view, are there aspects of certain subjects that promote a traditional, narrow or exclusive type of Irish identity? Explain your view.

- In your view, are there aspects of certain subjects that promote cultural diversity and inclusion? Explain your view.

- In your view, are there any minority groups in Ireland who are excluded from the general 'Irish' identity that is represented in the curriculum?

- Give recommendations on how the overall curriculum might be improved to represent Irish identity today.

See **RESEARCH TIPS** on page 33.

Tip: Details of the Junior Cycle curriculum can be found at on the Curriculum Online website: https://educateplus.ie/go/junior-cycle

National Identity in Modern Ireland

Ireland has changed significantly since the time of de Valera's 'The Ireland that we dreamed of' speech. We have experienced significant inward and outward migration, and a rich multicultural society has emerged. Ireland has always had a rich history of emigration, which has resulted in an enormous Irish diaspora: estimates vary widely, between 3 million and 70 million people. Since the mid-1990s, Ireland has also benefited from a significant increase in inward migration. This has made Ireland more culturally diverse than ever before. Irish society now includes many different nationalities, languages, cultures, ethnicities and religious affiliations.

Ireland – Cultural Diversity

Population Census 2016
Ethnic and Cultural Background

Ethnic and cultural background	%
White Irish	82.2
Any other White background	9.5
Non-Chinese Asian	1.7
Other, including mixed backgrounds	1.5
Irish Traveller	0.7
Chinese	0.4

Table 9.1 Population census 2016: Some of the groups included in the census under the profile 'Ethnic and cultural background'.
Source: Central Statistics Office (CSO)

Fig. 9.18 Cultural diversity in Ireland

Ethnic and cultural background: The largest group in 2016 was 'White Irish' with 3,854,226 (82.2%) usual residents. This was followed by 'Any other White background' (9.5%), non-Chinese Asian (1.7%) and 'Other, including mixed background' (1.5%). Irish Travellers (30,987) made up 0.7 per cent of the usually resident population while Chinese (19,447) made up just 0.4 per cent.

Religion

2016 – Religion	Pop. No.	%
Total	4,761.8	100.0
Catholic	3,729.1	78.3
No religion	468.4	9.8
Church of Ireland	126.4	2.7
Muslim (Islamic)	63.4	1.3
Orthodox	62.2	1.3
Christian	37.4	0.8
Presbyterian	24.2	0.5
Hindu	14.3	0.3
Apostolic or Pentecostal	13.4	0.3
Other	97.7	2.1
Not stated	125.3	2.6

Fig. 9.19 Cultural diversity on the high streets of Ireland

Table 9.2 Population census 2016: Religion.
Source: Central Statistics Office (CSO)

Language

Census 2016 revealed that 612,018 residents spoke a language other than Irish or English at home, an increase of 19.1% since 2011. Of these 243,911 were Irish nationals. French (41,241 persons), Polish (22,077), German (17,596) and Spanish (16,803) were the most common languages spoken in Irish homes, reflecting the most common foreign languages taught in Irish schools. The top languages spoken by non-Irish nationals were Polish (113,225), Lithuanian (30,502) Romanian (26,645) and Portuguese (16,737). Amongst Asian nationals, Chinese was the most common language spoken at home, followed by Urdu (Pakistani), Arabic and Malayalam (Indian). Amongst African nationals Arabic was the most common language spoken, followed by French. Yoruba and Igbo (Nigerian), together with Afrikaans, also featured strongly.

RESEARCH ASSIGNMENT 9.2

1. What percentage of the population was Catholic in 2016?
2. What was the second largest group by religious category in 2016?
3. In your opinion is 'White Irish' a suitable ethnic category? What additional ethnic categories could the CSO consider adopting in the next census?
4. Examine the same statistical categories above in the 2011 Census and write an account on changes in diversity in Ireland under the following headings:

    (a) Changes in Ethnic Diversity (2011–2016)

    (b) Changes in Religious Diversity (2011–2016)

    (c) Changes in Linguistic Diversity (2011–2016)

Census 2011 Profile 7 Religion, Ethnicity and Irish Travellers – Ethnic and cultural background in Ireland: **https://educateplus.ie/go/census-profile7**

ACTIVITY 9.5

Design and conduct a survey on the different identities, cultures, religions and languages of students in your school. Write a summary report on the main findings of your survey. Include the following in your report:

- Conduct a comparative analysis with the most recent census figures. Show whether the percentage of each cultural group in your school is above or below the national average.
- Create a graph or table to illustrate the cultural diversity of your school.

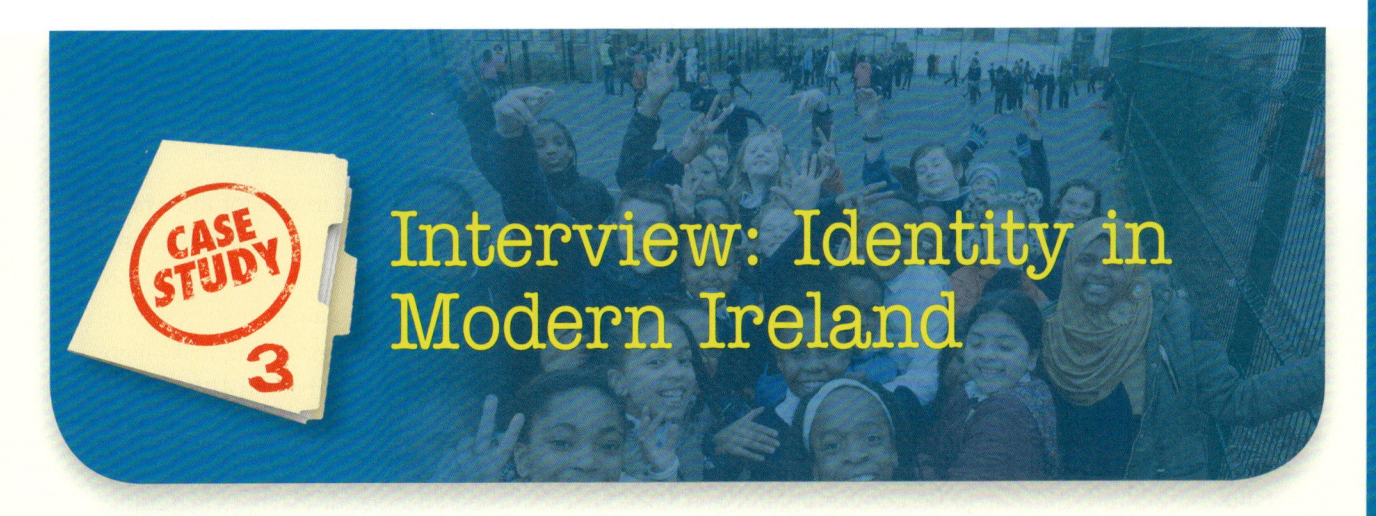

CASE STUDY 3: Interview: Identity in Modern Ireland

1. Tell us a little about yourself – your early life and your life today. When, how and why did you move to Ireland?

Elham: My name is Elham Osman. I'm 24 years of age. I was born in Tripoli in Libya. My parents are originally Egyptian, and my paternal granddad is originally Turkish. I lived in Libya until the age of 2 and then moved to Cairo in Egypt, where we lived until I was 8. Then I moved to Dublin. My father moved to Dublin in 1999 on a work permit and myself and my siblings came two years later with our mother. I completed my primary, secondary and university education in Dublin. I speak Arabic and English fluently, along with intermediate French and beginner-level Turkish. I currently work for CPL on-site Facebook in the Arabic market as a content moderator.

IDENTITY IN A GLOBAL AGE

Case Study: Interview: Identity in Modern Ireland

Filip: My name is Filip Czuk. I'm 16 years old and I'm Polish. I was born in Zabrze, a city in Poland. We moved here, to Ireland, in 2007, when I was 7 years old. We emigrated to Ireland because my dad found a job here that paid better than in Poland. We now live in Carrigart, a small town in north Co. Donegal, and I go to school to Loreto Community School in Milford.

2. When did you become an Irish citizen?

Elham: I became an Irish citizen in December 2012.

Filip: I am not an Irish citizen. I am a Polish citizen.

3. How would you describe your identity/identities?

Elham: I consider myself Egyptian, obviously, because of my roots and my family – and the Egyptian Arabic dialect we speak at home. We are still connected with our family back in Cairo and, therefore, we go to visit whenever possible. I also consider myself Irish because I actually am – on paper. I was naturalised and given Irish citizenship. And also, Ireland is where I grew up and where I made friends and where I learned to speak English (in a Dublin accent). I also consider understanding Irish humour as part of the Irish identity, which is something I love about the Irish culture. I cannot say I am of one fixed identity. Rather, I am a mix of both and am proud of that.

Filip: I consider myself to be 100 per cent Polish. That's where I was born and where my family are from and all our ancestors. Even though I've lived most of my life in Ireland I don't consider myself to be Irish. Maybe if I had Irish citizenship I would consider myself partially Irish. I would describe my culture to be modern with some Slavic and European traditions. I am a Christian and regularly go to church. And I respect all the major religions and see many similarities between them. I would describe myself as an open-minded free spirit, hungry to explore new ideas and contemplate theories and searching for enlightenment as I wait to see what life throws at me.

4. What does 'Irishness' mean to you?

Elham: Irishness means: getting on the bus and seeing familiar smiling faces that talk to you for the whole journey, asking about how you are getting on and talking about how bad the weather is. It also means going to Dublin city centre, seeing all the Gaelic souvenir stores and so many tourists looking around. It is also the sense of humour and community: family is a very important factor for the Irish nation. Irish is seeing Christmas lights on Grafton Street and seeing people do last-minute shopping. Understanding Irish lingo and explaining it to 'non-Irish' people is part of being Irish, in my opinion. Being proud of the 1916 Easter Rising and the fact it is celebrated every year is a very important factor.

Filip: I think to be Irish is to be born in Ireland and have ancestral roots in Ireland. Having citizenship makes a person legally Irish, but I think you are from where you were born and/or have roots. I think that, traditionally, Irish people enjoy going to the pub to socialise and playing football (Gaelic) to keep fit and entertain themselves.

5. What traits have you adopted that you would consider to be 'Irish'?

Elham: Saying 'sorry' when I bump into people has become a norm and is done automatically. Eating spuds and gravy (one of my favourite dishes) and eating a full Irish breakfast (excluding sausages and rashers, for religious reasons). Turning any situation into a joke to lighten up the mood. Saying 'God bless' when saying

Case Study

Interview: Identity in Modern Ireland

goodbye to someone. Complaining about how bad the weather is, after 16 long years of living here. And having a cup of tea in the evening is a must.

Filip: From living in Ireland I have surely adopted a few traits that would be considered Irish. I enjoy meeting up with friends to watch a really important Gaelic match. I've learned the basics of the Irish language in school. And I've picked up a few little things, like saying 'Good luck' as a farewell, and drinking tea with milk.

6. What traits/customs from your non-Irish culture are you proud of? Which do you continue to practise?

Elham: Family comes number one in our culture, regardless of the situation, so this is something I must say I am proud of having. Helping people in need whenever I can – to me, that is an obligation. If I can do something to help someone, I will do it. Religion-wise, Ramadan and Eid are a big thing in the Middle East in general. And in Egypt, how people prepare for Ramadan, with all the street lights – the so-called 'Ramadan lanterns' – is a culture that has developed over the years. Eid is also a massive celebration, where families get together and the elders give the young ones 'Eidya' – which is money, basically. I am also proud of retaining my religion and striving to be a good person before anything else.

Filip: I am continuing to speak the Polish language with my family, as well as practising Polish traditions and eating Polish food. I am also very interested in Polish history and I often find myself reading about it in my spare time. I am proud of my Slavic heritage.

7. Do you think Ireland is now a multicultural society? Have you found Ireland to be welcoming and tolerant? What challenges remain, in your view?

Elham: Ireland has now become very multicultural, in comparison to what it was like just 15 years ago. That is noticeable, even with the amount of takeaways that vary from Chinese to Italian to Turkish to Vietnamese. That in itself is multiculturalism, since food is such a part of culture. Companies now seek speakers of foreign languages, which gives more people of different backgrounds a chance to work and reside in Ireland. Irish people are very welcoming and amazing hosts to other people who are non-Irish. Obviously, there is the odd person who does not like the idea of other people coming to their country and, according to them, 'taking their jobs'. I myself have experienced a racial attack by a group of girls whose ages varied from 15 to about 17, all because of the headscarf I wear. It was both physical and verbal, and very vulgar language was used. In my opinion, more knowledge about other cultures is needed so that people can be more tolerant and open to the idea of multiculturalism.

Filip: I think that Ireland is definitely a multicultural society and is very welcoming and tolerant. People here are really nice and welcoming to strangers and I think most are tolerant of different cultures. From living in Ireland, I have never encountered racism (other than a bit of friendly teasing among friends) and am very comfortable in this society and I think anyone would be. I think the only problem for people that move to live in Ireland, especially if English isn't their first language, is the language barrier. There are many different accents in Ireland which can be difficult for an outsider to understand, even if they speak good English. I had the advantage of moving here at a young age which made me used to the Donegal accent, but even looking at my parents I can tell that even they sometimes have difficulty understanding some people – even though they have lived here a long time. So that would be the only big challenge I could think of for an outsider to participate in Irish society.

QUESTIONS

1. Do you agree with Filip that to be Irish 'is to be born in Ireland and have ancestral roots in Ireland'?
2. Elham is Egyptian–Irish. What elements of both cultures does she consider as being part of her identity?
3. What are the characteristics and cultural traits of Irish identity, according to both Elham and Filip? Do you agree with them?
4. What do you think of both Elham and Filip's opinions on whether or not Ireland is a welcoming place for immigrant communities?

ACTIVITY 9.6

Your teacher will give your group cards showing statements about Irish identity. Sort the cards into three categories:

- Statements that describe a vision of Irish identity from the past
- Statements that describe the reality of Irish identity today
- Statements that describe a vision of Ireland that you would like to see in the future.

RESEARCH ASSIGNMENT 9.3

Write a research report entitled 'How Irish Culture and Identity Has Changed'.

Include the following in your report:

- Describe the main characteristics of Irish culture in the past.
- Explain how some of these characteristics have been changed or diminished today.
- Describe the main characteristics of modern Irish culture and identity.
- Explain the main influences on Irish culture and identity today.

See **RESEARCH TIPS** on page 33.

Northern Ireland – Identity and Education

Northern Ireland presents an interesting example of the role that education can play in shaping identity. Traditionally, society in Northern Ireland has been divided into two dominant traditions based on religious and ethnonational identities: Protestant/unionist and Catholic/nationalist. Since its foundation, Northern Ireland has had two separate education systems to cater for these communities. While there has been an end to conflict and a peace process in

Fig. 9.20 Nationalists living in Northern Ireland maintain a distinctive Irish identity

place since 1998, school attendance for most children in Northern Ireland continues to be **segregated** along religious lines. Much research has been conducted into Northern Ireland's education system and its impact on the formation and maintenance of national identities.

> **KEY TERM**
>
> **Segregation** is the separation or isolation of a group or groups (e.g. race, class or ethnic group). It can be forced or voluntary.

Fig. 9.21 Unionists in Northern Ireland promote a distinctive British identity

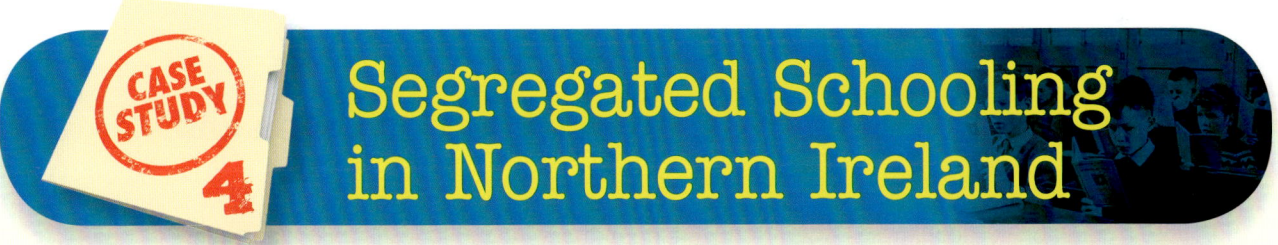

CASE STUDY 4: Segregated Schooling in Northern Ireland

Education in Northern Ireland is segregated at primary level and at secondary level. According to 2014 data, 87 per cent of Catholic students attend a Catholic school and 79 per cent of Protestants attend state schools, which are traditionally identified as Protestant. Since the founding of Northern Ireland in 1921, segregated schooling has been in place. At the time, the first Minister of Education, Lord Londonderry, proposed the establishment of integrated primary schooling. However, this was rejected by both the Protestant and Catholic Churches: both wanted segregated education.

Fig. 9.22 The extent of sectarianism and segregation in parts of Northern Ireland was highlighted in 2001 when the British Army had to be called in to protect Catholic school children from being attacked by loyalist protesters on their way to school in Ardoyne, North Belfast

IDENTITY IN A GLOBAL AGE

Case Study: Segregated Schooling in Northern Ireland

The Role of Segregated Schools in Reinforcing Community Identity and Cultural Divisions

Segregation in education in Northern Ireland enabled both communities to develop the curriculum and to offer an education that promoted their own cultural identity and values. Traditionally, Catholic schools tended to promote Irish nationalism, and state schools tended to promote British culture. The distinct cultural identities in Northern Ireland were maintained in part by the cultural values, symbols, language and sports taught at different schools.

History
- Up until 1989, the teaching of Irish history was not encouraged in state schools. British history made up half the official History curriculum and Irish history was included only as a small sub-set within that. Consequently, in the majority of state schools, little or no Irish history was taught.
- In contrast, Catholic schools traditionally placed more emphasis on Irish history, covering events such as the United Irishmen rebellion and other aspects of the Anglo–Irish conflict.

Irish Language
- Since the founding of Northern Ireland in 1921, Irish has been taught in all Catholic schools in Northern Ireland. Among the compulsory core curriculum subjects at second level is a requirement to study at least one modern language. Irish is recognised as a modern language for this purpose.
- After French, Irish is the most commonly taught language in Northern Ireland. It is taught exclusively in Catholic and integrated schools.

Sport
- Although some sports (such as soccer) are played at both Catholic and state schools, certain sports that are associated with Britishness or with Irishness are exclusive to each denomination.
- Gaelic games (football and hurling) are played in all Catholic schools, and are usually not available in state schools.
- Rugby and cricket are played mainly in state schools.

A Common Curriculum: Towards Social Reconciliation and Shared Identities

In 1989, a common curriculum was first introduced in Northern Ireland to foster a common sense of history and mutual respect for both traditions. The common curriculum included the compulsory teaching of Irish history in all schools. The new History curriculum in Northern Ireland is now highly regarded by other societies in conflict (or recently emerged from it). Two features are praised in particular:

- The prescribed curriculum ensures that all children, regardless of community background, are taught a broadly common programme, which includes Irish history in a British and European framework.
- The enquiry-based approach to teaching enables pupils to engage with different perspectives. Nowadays, blatant partisanship (bias) is hard to find in textbooks or in classrooms in Northern Ireland.

However, even though the History curriculum was designed to promote cultural tolerance and social reconciliation, much of the research indicates that, in practice, many teachers are cautious of this goal – or even dismissive of it. Most History teachers tend to avoid controversial topics that link the past with the present situation in Northern Ireland: they are afraid of enticing emotional or **sectarian** outbursts in their classrooms. A particular concern of teachers interviewed by Margaret Conway in 1991 (while the Troubles were ongoing) was that teaching more contemporary Irish history might 'bring the troubles of the streets into the classroom'.

The research also indicates that teachers are careful not to challenge the aspects of their students' identities or the interpretations of modern Irish history that have been learned at home or within the community.

> **KEY TERM**
> **Sectarian** means strongly supporting a particular religious group and being unwilling to accept other religious beliefs or groups.

WHAT THE RESEARCH SAYS!

EDUCATION AND IDENTITY IN NORTHERN IRELAND

Integration, Segregation and Mixing

In 2014 the Integrated Education Fund (IEF) explored the attitudes of young people from Northern Ireland aged 16–24 years on the topics of integration, segregation and mixing. The research involved over 2,000 people aged 16–24, through opinion polls, focus groups, political hustings or round-table discussions. Respondents were asked how *divided* Northern Ireland was in terms of religion, skin colour and/or language, ethnicity, cultural traditions and festivals, sports, schools attended, rich/poor and social class. These were some of the main findings.

- A large majority (81 per cent) of secondary school respondents saw religion as the main source of division in Northern Ireland.
- 36 per cent of respondents stated that people's choice of school is a divisive factor.
- 75 per cent felt that there should be more integration in relation to religion.
- 56 per cent felt that there should be more integration in relation to sport.
- More than 83 per cent agreed that an education system where children of all faiths and none go to the same school would be an important step in combating sectarianism.
- 73.6 per cent stated that they would prefer for their own children to go to school with other children of all traditions and backgrounds.

Type of Education

- In 2007, researchers Bernadette Hayes, Ian McAllister and Lizanne Dowds examined whether the *type of school* a person in Northern Ireland attended had made any impact on their identity as an adult. The study looked at three types of schools:
  - Integrated: schools with a minimum threshold of 30 per cent representation of the 'minority' grouping
  - Mixed: mixed schools that do not meet the formal 30 per cent threshold
  - Segregated schools.
- The study analysed data from the Northern Ireland Life and Times and Electoral Surveys. Table 9.3 summarises the main results.

Identities and type of education by religion in Northern Ireland

	Protestant				Catholic			
	Integrated	Mixed	Segregated	All	Integrated	Mixed	Segregated	All
National identity								
British	63.4	71.5	72.2	72.0	11.1	12.1	9.3	9.5
Irish	3.7	2.8	2.5	2.6	59.3	56.3	64.8	64.0
Ulster	3.7	5.6	8.2	7.8	1.2	0.5	0.6	0.6
Northern Irish	24.4	17.9	15.3	15.7	27.2	29.5	24.0	24.5
Other	4.9	2.1	1.8	1.8	1.2	1.6	1.4	1.4
Total	100.0	100.0	100.0	100.0	100.0	100.0	100.0	100.0
(N)	(82)	(780)	(5,903)	(6,765)	(81)	(380)	(4,186)	(4,647)
Political identity								
Unionist	54.3	71.2	73.2	72.2	0.0	1.6	1.0	1.0
Nationalist	2.5	0.7	0.8	0.8	58.5	57.9	66.4	65.6
Neither	43.2	28.1	26.0	26.5	41.5	40.4	32.6	33.4
Total	100.0	100.0	100.0	100.0	100.0	100.0	100.0	100.0
(N)	(81)	(768)	(5,843)	(6,692)	(82)	(375)	(4,166)	(4,623)

Table 9.3 Identities and type of education by religion in Northern Ireland

ACTIVITY 9.7

Analyse Table 9.3 and list **three** important conclusions that can be drawn from the data.

ACTIVITY 9.8

Your teacher will assign your group a piece of research on the teaching of History in Northern Ireland. Examine the research and write a summary report. Present this report to another group. Include the following in your report:

- Provide the topic of the research and the name of the author(s).
- Rationale of the research: What question(s) did the author(s) hope to answer?
- Methodology: Explain the research method used and how the data was derived. Evaluate whether this has a positive or negative impact on the overall quality of the findings.
- Describe the main findings of the research.

SKILLS BOOK LINK 9.6

Go to pages 152–153 of your Skills Book to complete Skill Task 9.6 on the role of education in shaping Irish identity – north and south.

See RESEARCH TIPS on page 33.

Diversity and Cultural Change

Culture and identity are neither fixed nor unchanging. They are created. Because they consist of learned beliefs and patterns of behaviour, they can be *unlearned*. Culture and identity are influenced by changes in our society. Cultural change happens when something new (e.g. air travel, smartphones) opens society to new ideas and new ways of living. It is likely that our sense of culture and identity differs from that of our parents, and differs significantly from that of our grandparents. In the past, societies and cultures remained relatively isolated from one another: they shared little communication. In the absence of interaction between societies, culture and identity passed relatively unchanged from one generation to the next. However, globalisation has forged new connections – real and virtual – between societies and people. This has influenced our culture and identity. Technological changes (e.g. the spread of social media, the influence of mass culture, the increase in migration and travel) have contributed to adapting and shaping modern cultures and identities. Globalisation has allowed for greater exchange between cultures. Two aspects of globalisation – migration/travel and media/communication – have contributed greatly to cultural change and diversity.

Complete your next Reflective Journal entry (pages 37–38)

POWER AND PEOPLE

Globalisation

Globalisation is the process by which the world is becoming increasingly interconnected. Anthony Giddens, a prominent globalisation theorist, defines it as 'the intensification of worldwide social relations which link distant localities in such a way that local happenings are shaped by events occurring many miles away, and vice versa'. Globalisation has resulted in the world becoming a smaller place – a type of 'global village'. This apparent shrinking of the world has come about with the increasingly rapid flow of goods, services, information, communication and people around the world. Globalisation has been taking place for centuries – since the foundation of capitalism and colonialism. However, the pace of globalisation greatly increased during the mid-twentieth century. Globalisation involves economic, political, social and **cultural integration**. Because of globalisation, trade and financial transactions now cross traditional national borders. Globalisation has given rise to global multilateral institutions (e.g. UN, EU, IMF, World Bank) and the emergence of multicultural societies in many of our countries.

Fig. 9.23 The world becomes increasingly interconnected through globalisation

KEY TERM

Cultural integration is when one group adopts the beliefs, practices and rituals of another group without sacrificing the characteristics of its own culture.

Globalisation has four main dimensions:

- **Political:** We have increased and intensified political cooperation, coordination and shared decision-making. We have many international and multilateral organisations (e.g. UN, EU, IMF, World Bank).
- **Social:** Aspects of people's daily lives (e.g. education, work opportunities, health) are greatly impacted by globalisation. These impacts can be positive (e.g. increased education and work opportunities) and negative (e.g. the spread of unhealthy products, such as tobacco).
- **Economic:** Our national economies are tied to the global economy. We have increased global trade, common markets and currencies (e.g. the euro).
- **Environmental:** Globalisation has negatively impacted on our natural resources and environment.

Globalisation Data

- In 2015, 244 million people – 3.3 per cent of the world's population – lived outside their country of origin.
- In 2013, over three-quarters of a million people who were born in Ireland (771,572 people) were reported to be living abroad – in 72 other countries.
- In the April 2016 census, 535,475 non-Irish people – of 200 nationalities – were resident in Ireland.
- As of 2014, world trade in goods has been valued at more than $18.5 trillion. World trade in services has been valued at approximately $5 trillion.
- As of 2016, there were more than 36,000 McDonald's outlets in 100 different countries. There were over 24,000 Starbucks outlets in 70 different countries.
- Taylor Swift's album *1989* topped iTunes sales charts in over 95 countries.
- Close to half of the Irish government's international aid fund (49 per cent) is channelled through multilateral organisations (e.g. UN, EU).

Globalisation: What Happens to Culture?

There are different views on the impact of globalisation on culture.

Cultural Diffusion

Cultural diffusion happens when the ideas or cultural elements of one society are borrowed and incorporated into the culture of another society. For example, there is a 'Chinatown' in almost every major city of the world.

Fig. 9.24 Globalisation has impacts on culture

Cultural Convergence

Cultural convergence is the theory that globalisation leads to 'sameness'. Cultures around the world are becoming more similar. We have developed global cultures based on mass media consumption, e.g. Hollywood, pop artists and consumer products (e.g. McDonald's, iPhone). Cultural convergence is also known as 'cultural globalisation' or 'McDonaldisation'. Traditionally, social scientists and anthropologists have used the 'melting pot' metaphor to describe a process whereby different cultures and peoples come together and blend into one society and culture. The United States was cited as an example. However, there are many critics of the 'melting pot' theory. Many theorists believe that no such society exists.

Cultural Divergence

Cultural divergence is the opposite of convergence. This is the idea that local or traditional cultures reassert themselves in the face of threats from a global culture.

Cultural Hybridisation

Jazz has been described as the product of a union of African and western cultures. In this way, it is an example of **cultural hybridisation**.

> **KEY TERMS**
>
> **Cultural diffusion** happens when the ideas or cultural elements of one society are borrowed and incorporated into the culture of another society.
>
> **Cultural convergence** is the theory that globalisation has led to cultures around the world becoming more and more similar.
>
> **Cultural divergence** is the opposite of convergence. Local or traditional cultures reassert themselves and become stronger in the face of threats from a global culture.
>
> **Cultural hybridisation** happens when two cultures are combined to produce a new cultural product (e.g. Spanglish or jazz music).

ACTIVITY 9.9

Research and list examples in Ireland and in other countries of each of the following:

- Cultural diffusion
- Cultural convergence
- Cultural divergence
- Cultural hybridisation.

RESEARCH ASSIGNMENT 9.4

Create appropriate case studies to illustrate any **two** of the following processes:

- Cultural diffusion
- Cultural convergence
- Cultural divergence
- Cultural hybridisation.

See **RESEARCH TIPS** on page 33.

Information and Communication Technology

Fig. 9.25 ICT is continually shaping not only how we think but also our identity and culture

The global nature of information and communication technologies (e.g. satellite TV, internet) has created a steady flow and exchange of ideas, concepts and images that connect audiences worldwide. Media and social media play a major role in shaping culture today. What we watch on television, read in magazines, and see and share online will influence our opinions, beliefs, interests, lifestyle choices, diet, dress and behaviour. Western culture has spread globally. Societies in Africa, Asia and Latin America embrace western music, dress and other cultural elements. Equally, western societies have been influenced by non-western cultures (e.g. religions such as Buddhism and Islam, and world music and cuisine). Social media has enabled audiences to develop, share and spread new ideas. This contributes to the continual adaptation and creation of new forms of culture.

MTV: Global Pop Culture

The global expansion of Music Television (MTV) is arguably one of the best examples from the late twentieth century of the cultural influences of ICT (Information Communication Technology). In 1981 MTV launched in the United States. Targeted at young people, MTV combined music and style, and quickly became the main source of American popular culture. When MTV launched, it aimed to be about more than music and fashion. It presented attitudes, beliefs, behaviours and even a new *language* that challenged the dominant culture in the US at that time. Artists and celebrities who appeared on the channel were presented as cultural role models. MTV was also the epitome of consumerism – a dominant element of American culture. The fashion, music and lifestyle presented on MTV were commodities sold to young viewers. Advertisers flocked to the channel. By June 1983, MTV had sold advertising time to 140 companies representing more than 240 consumer products. During the 1990s, MTV began its European expansion, launching first in Germany. Critics at that time warned against the potential 'Americanisation' of European societies and the dangers of creating a global youth culture. MTV's global expansion continued across Asia, Africa and Latin America. By 2015, MTV programming was received by 411.7 million households in over 160 countries. Young people around the world now share many similarities in fashion and style. Clothing companies such as Nike now sell on all six continents.

Fig. 9.26 MTV launched in the US in 1981

Fig. 9.27 MTV – cultural globalisation

However, the cultural impact of MTV has not just been to promote cultural convergence. MTV's approach to balancing international and local content across its channels (i.e. MTV India, MTV Latin, MTV Africa Base) has been responsible for cultural diffusion *and* cultural hybridisation. MTV has shared the music of non-western acts, such as Shakira, and has promoted and transmitted a fusion of western and non-western cultures, introducing music styles including Afro-beat, Asia-pop, Bollywood-electro and Latin-house.

Emoji Language: Social Media Changes How We Communicate

Language is one of the primary markers of any culture. In 2015, the *Oxford English Dictionary* (OED) word of the year was not a word but a pictograph: the 'face with tears of joy' emoji – 😂. According to OED, an emoji is 'a small digital image or icon used to express an idea or emotion in electronic communication'. Traditionally associated with youth and teenagers, the emoji is now mainstream: celebrities and politicians regularly integrate the emoji in their social media communications on Facebook, Snapchat, Twitter, etc. The emoji was developed in the early 1980s, but its usage has grown rapidly in line with the spread of social media. In particular, the launch of Apple's iOS6 in 2012 made the emoji an integral part of how we communicate with each other online. An estimated 6 billion emojis are sent globally every day. The average American sends 96 emojis every day. Researchers at Instagram have traced the evolution of our communication from internet slang (e.g. 'that made me laugh'), to abbreviations ('LOL'), to the emoji 😃. As we experience less face-to-face communication, the emoji provides context to our communications. It replaces traditional non-verbal communication, such as facial expressions. The same can be said of the 'hashtag' phenomenon. Use of emojis and the hashtag is transnational – it is a sign of our global culture. In 2015, Swiftkey (the creators of the popular emoji keyboard) conducted the first ever global analysis of emoji usage by analysing more than 1 billion emoji communications across sixteen languages. Researchers are now examining the impact of the emoji revolution in cross-cultural communication and understanding.

Fig. 9.28 Social media has changed how we communicate

ACTIVITY 9.10

Work with your partner to complete the following activity.

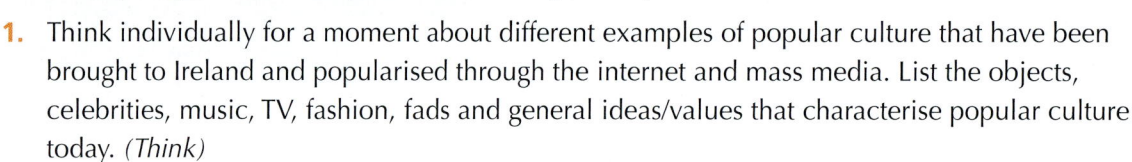

1. Think individually for a moment about different examples of popular culture that have been brought to Ireland and popularised through the internet and mass media. List the objects, celebrities, music, TV, fashion, fads and general ideas/values that characterise popular culture today. *(Think)*

2. With your partner, compare your lists. Discuss the extent to which these examples of popular culture influence your daily lifestyle and identity. *(Pair)*

3. Share your conclusions with the rest of the class. *(Share)*

SKILLS BOOK LINK 9.7

Go to page 154 of your Skills Book to complete Skill Task 9.7 on a media watch.

See **RESEARCH TIPS** on page 33.

ACTIVITY 9.11

Your group will be assigned one of the following processes by your teacher:

- Cultural diffusion
- Cultural convergence
- Cultural divergence
- Cultural hybridisation.

Examine how the media and ICT have contributed to this process. Create a presentation to illustrate this process to your class.

KEY THINKERS

CULTURE
In sociology, culture is sometimes divided into two categories: high culture and popular culture.

HIGH CULTURE
This includes cultural elements such as classical music, opera, ballet, live theatre and other activities usually associated with intellectual audiences. Members of the upper and upper-middle classes are often considered to have the necessary time, money and knowledge to appreciate and pursue high culture. French sociologist Pierre Bourdieu coined the term 'cultural capital' to describe the value placed on high culture. According to Bourdieu, the upper and upper-middle classes learn about high culture through higher education. People in lower classes are excluded from obtaining high culture. In this sense, culture can be used as a device to maintain a superior position in society.

POPULAR CULTURE
This consists of cultural activities, products and services that are considered to appeal primarily to members of the middle and working classes. Examples include Hollywood celebrity news, soap operas, reality TV, and music genres such as pop music, hip hop and R&B.

FUNCTIONALIST PERSPECTIVE
According to functionalists, popular culture serves an important function in society. It is the 'glue' that holds society together. It creates common bonds between individuals. Popular culture helps people to temporarily forget their problems.

MARXIST PERSPECTIVE
According to Marxists, corporations are the source of most popular culture. They create popular culture in the same way that they create any other product or service. In this sense, popular culture has been turned into a commodity that we purchase (e.g. fashion, music). Popular culture is designed to focus on consumerism and light entertainment to ensure that the working classes remain uncritical and unaware of their position in an unfair and unjust capitalist system.

FEMINIST PERSPECTIVE
Feminists are primarily concerned with how men, women and gender relations are portrayed in popular culture. Popular culture can create unfair and unrealistic ideals for men and for women. Popular culture often tells us how to act, based on the dominant gender stereotypes: men as strong and stoic, and women as weak and emotional. Even when a woman is portrayed as strong (e.g. superhero), she tends to be highly sexualised (e.g. Catwoman).

Fig. 9.29 Representations of high culture and popular culture

QUESTIONS

1. Do you think the distinction between high and popular culture is useful? Why/why not?
2. Can you think of examples of high culture and popular culture in Ireland today?
3. With which pespective on popular culture do you most agree – functionalist or Marxist? Give reasons for your answer.
4. According to the feminist perspective, popular culture is used to reinforce gender stereotypes. Do you agree? Give reasons for your answer.

IDENTITY IN A GLOBAL AGE

Migration and Travel

Migration is not a new or recent phenomenon. Migration and travel have long been a key feature of human history. Colonialism resulted in the migration of more than 60 million Europeans, as well as the movement of millions of Asians, Africans and Amerindians (native peoples of the Americas) to Europe. Much of this initial migration to Europe was involuntary, through the slave trade. Throughout history, migration flows have been influenced by the prevailing social and political order of the time. The process of decolonisation during the 1950s and 1960s, for example, resulted in the mass movement of populations from former European colonies to Europe. The demographic make-up of European countries began to change dramatically because of this process: people from India, Pakistan and the West Indies migrated to England, and people from Vietnam, Cambodia, Algeria, Tunisia and Morocco migrated to France.

Fig. 9.30 Migration and travel have impacts on culture

Migration has always been a part of global history. However, in recent decades, the world has witnessed a significant increase in migration and travel. Poverty, conflict and climate change are the most common modern 'push' factors, as people seek economic opportunities and political and environmental safety and security. At the same time, there are 'pull' factors that fuel migration: a desire to experience a new culture or way of life, or a better standard of living. Increased migration and travel have been supported by cheaper air travel and increased access to information about other cultures (i.e. we can learn about different cultures online). Travel and migration have produced multicultural societies, and have wide-ranging cultural impacts.

CASE STUDY 5: Hispanic Immigration and American Culture

In 2014, 46 per cent of the immigrant population of the US (19.4 million people) reported having Hispanic or Latino origins. Most Hispanics in the US are native born: only 35 per cent (19.4 million) of those who identified themselves as Hispanic were immigrants. Mexicans are the largest immigrant group in the US. The majority of Mexicans (83 per cent) settle in the states of Texas and California. Hispanic immigrant populations contribute greatly to the US economy. They also have a strong influence on many different elements of culture.

Language

According to a 2015 report by the Instituto Cervantes, more people in the US speak Spanish than ever before. The US has 41 million native Spanish speakers and 11 million more who are bilingual. This has made the US the second largest Spanish-speaking country after Mexico. Spanish-speaking immigration to the US has resulted in the development of a linguistic-hybrid known commonly as *Spanglish*. Spanglish can be considered a variety of Spanish with heavy use of English, or a variety of English with heavy use of Spanish. The language initially developed out of necessity to facilitate communication. It is now spoken in many areas of the US.

Fig. 9.31 Spanglish

> **CASE STUDY**
>
> **Hispanic Immigration and American Culture**

Food

In 2013 salsa overtook ketchup as America's number one condiment. Mexican and other traditional Hispanic food (e.g. enchiladas, tacos, tamales) has been adopted into the mainstream food culture of the US. The Tex-Mex style of cooking includes nachos, burritos, fajitas and tortillas. It is described as an American way of cooking Mexican food. It is an example of a cultural hybridisation that resulted from Mexican immigration to the US.

Fig. 9.32 Tex-Mex food

Music and Arts

Latino music has greatly influenced the pop music scene in the US and globally. Artists such as Carlos Santana, Enrique Iglesias, Cypress Hill, Ricky Martin, Kat DeLuna, Kid Frost, Marc Anthony, Tito El Bambino, Jennifer Lopez and Selena Gomez have exported Latino pop music. Few contemporary pop music genres can claim to be without some Latino influence. Rap music, house, electro and many other genres regularly fuse with Latino-inspired melodies and beats.

Fig. 9.33 Latino music

> **CASE STUDY 6**
>
> # The Rise of Buddhism, Yoga and Meditation: East Meets West

Buddhism

Buddhism is a world religion with roots in Asia. It was established in Northern India in the fifth century and Buddhists now represent approximately 7 per cent of the world's population. According to the Pew Center, the number of Buddhists around the world will increase between 2010 and 2030, from 488 million to 511 million people approximately. While most Buddhists will remain in Asia, Buddhism is rising in Europe and the US, with projections of 0.5 per cent and 1.2 per cent of total populations respectively. In Ireland, the number of Buddhists increased by almost 34 per cent between the 2006 and 2011 censuses; over one-third (37.9 per cent) of these people were Irish by nationality. The rise of Buddhism in the west is often linked to travel and migration between the west and Asia. European scholars of Buddhism travelled east during the nineteenth century to study in Buddhist monasteries. On their

Fig. 9.34 Buddhists represent approximately 7 per cent of the world's population

IDENTITY IN A GLOBAL AGE

CASE STUDY: The Rise of Buddhism, Yoga and Meditation: East Meets West

return, they established Buddhist centres in many of the main cities of Europe and America. Established in 1924, the Buddhist Society of London is the oldest and largest of these centres. In the 1950s and 1960s, many people from Tibet, Vietnam, Thailand and other Asian countries migrated to the west because of conflict and economic difficulties in their countries of origin. This contributed to the growth of Buddhism in the west. Many Buddhists in the west converted to Buddhism in adult life, having previously been part of organised religions. Buddhism can be viewed as a spiritual philosophy or way of life as opposed to an organised religion.

Yoga and Meditation

Closely linked to the growth of Buddhism in the US and Europe are the practices of yoga and meditation. Yoga originated as part of Hinduism. It was a spiritual practice involving meditation and body poses. Buddhism and yoga originated in the Indian subcontinent over 2,000 years ago. In recent decades, yoga has become a popular practice in the US and Europe. According to the US Center for Disease Control and Prevention, 10 per cent of adults and 3 per cent of children in the US participated regularly in yoga in 2012. In Europe, a growing number of yoga studios have been established in many urban areas. Yoga holidays and retreats have become a popular holiday choice for many westerners. Yoga as practised in western societies involves some adaptation of the ancient eastern tradition. 'Western yoga' is a commonly cited example of **cultural appropriation** – taking a traditional culture and adapting it to suit the needs and behaviours of the recipient culture. Cultural appropriation can result in the dilution (or even destruction) of the original roots and meaning of the cultural practice. Traditional variants of yoga are steeped in spiritual philosophies, such as Hinduism, Buddhism and Jainism. For many practitioners in the west, yoga is simply a physical exercise and relaxation method. Western yoga is the product of the appropriation of a spiritual practice by a predominantly secular western culture. In many western societies, yoga has become part of a wider subculture that includes dietary habits (e.g. organic or vegetarian diets), cultural events (e.g. yoga holidays and arts festivals) and dress (yoga-inspired clothing).

Fig. 9.35 Yoga is popular in the US and Europe

Fig. 9.36 Yoga holidays and retreats have become popular for westerners

> **KEY TERM**
>
> **Cultural appropriation** is the process of taking a traditional culture and adapting it to suit the needs and behaviours of the recipient culture.

SKILLS BOOK LINK 9.8

Go to page 155 of your Skills Book to complete Skill Task 9.8 on the cultural impact of immigrant communities on Ireland.

ACTIVITY 9.12

Your group will be assigned one of the following processes by your teacher:

- Cultural diffusion
- Cultural convergence
- Cultural divergence
- Cultural hybridisation.

Examine the impact of migration and travel on this process. Create a presentation to illustrate this process to your class.

SKILLS BOOK LINK 9.9

Go to pages 156–157 of your Skills Book to complete Skill Task 9.9 on cultural mixing and adaptation.

See **RESEARCH TIPS** on page 33.

Diversity in the European Union: United in Diversity

One of the founding principles of the European Union is respect for diversity. European history has been marked by political upheavals and violent conflicts fuelled by intra-state and inter-state ethnic and national divisions. World War II devastated Europe and produced unprecedented human and economic losses. The European project developed with this backdrop and aimed to create economic and political conditions that would promote cohesion (unity) while respecting the different religious, cultural, linguistic, ethnic and national identities within the European region. Diversity remains a pillar of the EU today. Growing diversity within the EU has been based on EU enlargement and on inward migration. These phenomena have contributed to an overall increase in diversity, as well as unique and changing patterns of diversity.

European Economic Community, 1958

The European Economic Community, the predecessor to the EU, was established with the signing of the Treaty of Rome (1957). The EEC had a total population of over 169 million people and consisted of six member states: Belgium, France, Italy, Luxembourg, the Netherlands and West Germany. From its inception, the European Community has been culturally diverse. The European Community comprised four languages: Dutch (spoken in the Netherlands and Belgium), French (spoken in France, Belgium, Italy and Luxembourg), German (spoken in West Germany, Belgium and Italy) and Italian (spoken in Italy). Some of these member states contained multiple linguistic and ethnic or national groups within their state borders, such as the Flemish and Walloons in Belgium. The original EEC lacked religious diversity: it had a predominantly Christian population.

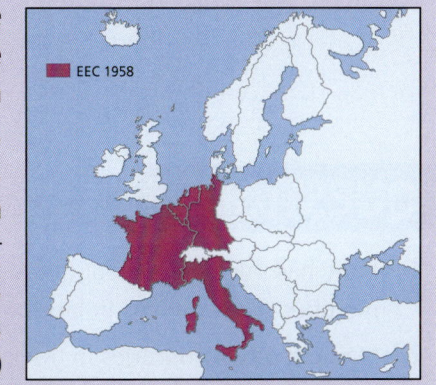

Fig. 9.37 The EEC in 1958

IDENTITY IN A GLOBAL AGE 347

Increasing Diversity within the European Union

Many factors contributed to the increase in diversity in the EU.

EU Enlargement

The EU has grown from the original six members to 28* member states today. The EU currently comprises: Austria, Belgium, Bulgaria, Croatia, Republic of Cyprus, Czech Republic, Denmark, Estonia, Finland, France, Germany, Greece, Hungary, Ireland, Italy, Latvia, Lithuania, Luxembourg, Malta, the Netherlands, Poland, Portugal, Romania, Slovakia, Slovenia, Spain, Sweden and the UK. Each member state brings a unique national and cultural identity, and religious and linguistic diversities.

(*This includes the UK, which is in the process of leaving the EU.)

Migration Flows in the EU

EU migration patterns are characterised by flows between EU member states (free movement area) and inward migration from non-EU countries. In 2014, EU data estimated:

- A total of 3.8 million immigrants migrated to and within the EU.
- 1.6 million citizens from non-EU member states migrated to EU member states.
- 1.3 million people with citizenship of one EU member state migrated to another EU member state.
- 870,000 people experienced return migration to the EU member state for which they have citizenship (e.g. returning nationals or nationals born abroad).
- There are 12,400 stateless people in the EU.
- The countries with the largest number of immigrants in descending order were Germany, the UK, France, Spain and Italy.
- Relative to the size of the resident population, Luxembourg recorded the highest rates of immigration in 2014 (40 immigrants per 1,000 persons), followed by Malta (21 immigrants per 1,000 persons) and Ireland (15 immigrants per 1,000 persons).
- As of 2013, the top five countries of origin of newly arrived non-EU nationals were: India, China, Morocco, Pakistan and Ukraine.
- In 2013, 871,293 non-EU nationals acquired citizenship in an EU country. The top five countries of origin were: Morocco, India, Turkey, Colombia and Albania.

Fig. 9.38 The map above shows the flag of the second largest nationality, by country of birth, living in each European country

QUESTIONS

1. How has the enlargement of the EU led to increased cultural diversity across the EU and within member states such as Ireland?
2. Name the **two** countries in the EU with the largest number of immigrants. In your opinion, why do so many people migrate to these two countries?
3. In 2014, where did Ireland rank in comparison to other EU member states in terms of the number of immigrants as a percentage of the total population?
4. Name the top **five** countries from which newly arrived non-EU citizens migrate. In your opinion, why do these people migrate from their home countries to Europe?

Migration Trends

- **1815–1930:** Approximately 50 million Europeans emigrated to countries such as the US, Canada, Australia, Brazil and Argentina.

- **1945–1970:** The end of World War II and the decolonisation process reversed the outward migration trend. Citizens of former colonies migrated to countries such as France and Britain. At the same time, post-war reconstruction attracted labour migration to countries such as Belgium, West Germany and the Netherlands. By 1960, the number of international migrants living in Europe had reached 14.4 million or 3.5 per cent of the total population.

- **1990s:** The fall of the Soviet Union led to high east–west migration (particularly to West Germany). The war in former Yugoslavia created large numbers of refugees. Economic growth in southern European countries such as Italy, Spain and Portugal led to increases in their migrant populations.

- **2000s:** Eastern enlargements of the EU in 2004 and 2007 further increased east–west migration. In 2009, recession led to increased intra-migration: citizens from the worst-affected member states travelled to the less affected states.

- **2015:** More than 1 million migrants and refugees crossed into Europe seeking asylum from violent conflicts in countries such as Syria, Afghanistan and Iraq.

QUESTIONS

1. Explain **two** reasons for the high rates of inward migration to Europe between 1945 and 1970.
2. Describe **three** different patterns of migration that have taken place in Europe since the 1990s.

Patterns of Diversity within the European Union

Ethnicity

Europe is an ethnically diverse continent. According to scholars Pan and Pfeil (2003), we can count a total of 87 'peoples of Europe'. A total of 60 million EU citizens – 12 per cent of the EU population – come from ethnic and religious minority groups. Almost all European countries are now multi-ethnic. The majority of EU member states have minority populations that account for approximately 20 per cent of their total population. Bosnia and Herzegovina, which applied for EU membership in 2016, is the only country where no absolute majority exists: Bosniaks, the largest ethnic group, comprise 44 per cent of the country's total population. Ethnic groups in Europe can be divided into four main categories.

National

These are ethnic or national groups who live within the territory of another state, such as the Greeks and Turks in Cyprus, the Albanians in Kosovo, the Hungarians in Romania and Slovakia, the nationalists in Northern Ireland. The 'creation' of ethnic minorities in Europe has come about because of the re-drawing of political borders within Europe after events such as the World Wars, the collapse of the Soviet Union, the dissolution of Czechoslovakia and the Balkan wars.

Transnational

This refers to ethnic groups whose 'homeland' stretches across several state borders but does not form a nation in any of them. Examples include the Basques and Catalans in France and Spain, and the Frisians in Germany and the Netherlands.

IDENTITY IN A GLOBAL AGE

Immigrant

This refers to ethnic and national groups who have entered the EU, such as North African people in France and Turkish people in Germany. It is estimated that at least 175 nationalities are present within the EU.

Indigenous

This refers to ethnic groups who reside in their ancestral homeland within a state, but do not form a nation, such as Bretons in France or Cornish in Britain.

Language

The EU now has over 500 million citizens, three alphabets and 24 official languages.

According to 2012 data (Eurobarometer) the most widely spoken mother tongue is German (16 per cent), followed by Italian and English (13 per cent each), French (12 per cent), and Spanish and Polish (8 per cent each). There is a lack of up-to-date data, but it is likely that languages such as Arabic have also grown, particularly in countries such as France and the Netherlands. In 2012, over half of Europeans (54 per cent) could hold a conversation in at least one additional language, a quarter of Europeans could hold a conversation in at least two additional languages, and one in ten Europeans were conversant in at least three additional languages. Within the EU, some 60 other languages are spoken in specific regions or by specific groups (e.g. Catalan, Basque, Irish and Yiddish). Non-EU immigrants have added to Europe's linguistic diversity. In Ireland, a total of 187 languages were recorded as spoken in the 2011 census.

Official Languages of the EU		
Bulgarian	French	Maltese
Croatian	German	Polish
Czech	Greek	Portuguese
Danish	Hungarian	Romanian
Dutch	Irish	Slovak
English	Italian	Slovenian
Estonian	Latvian	Spanish
Finnish	Lithuanian	Swedish

Table 9.4 The 24 official languages of the EU

Fig. 9.39 Map showing the distribution of languages in countries and regions of Europe

Religion

The EU remains predominantly Christian (72 per cent). Catholics accounted for the largest Christian group (48 per cent), followed by Protestants (12 per cent), and Eastern Orthodox (8 per cent).

The Muslim population accounted for 2 per cent of the total EU population, according to the 2012 Eurobarometer survey. A significant portion of survey respondents identified as agnostic (16 per cent) or atheist (7 per cent). Table 9.5 shows projections for 2050.

	2010 Estimated Population	% In 2010	2050 Projected Population	% In 2050	Population Growth 2010-2050	% Increase 2010-2050	Compound Annual Growth Rate (%)
Christian	553,280,000	74.5	454,090,000	65.2	−99,190,000	−17.9	−0.5
Unaffiliated	139,890,000	18.8	162,320,000	23.3	22,420,000	16.0	0.4
Muslims	43,470,000	5.9	70,870,000	10.2	27,400,000	63.0	1.2
Jews	1,420,000	0.2	1,200,000	0.2	−220,000	−15.2	−0.4
Hindus	1,380,000	0.2	2,660,000	0.4	1,280,000	92.9	1.7
Buddhists	1,350,000	0.2	2,490,000	0.4	1,140,000	85.0	1.5
Other religions	890,000	0.1	1,100,000	0.2	210,000	23.3	0.5
Folk religions	870,000	0.1	1,590,000	0.2	720,000	83.1	1.5
Regional Total	742,550,000	100.0	696,330,000	100.0	−46,220,000	−6.2	−0.2

Table 9.5 Size, projected growth of major religious groups in Europe, 2010–2050

QUESTIONS

1. What percentage of the EU population is composed of ethnic and religious minority groups?
2. Explain the difference between a national and a transnational ethnic group. Give examples of both groups in Europe.
3. What is an indigenous ethnic group?
4. Give an example of an indigenous ethnic group in **(a)** Ireland and **(b)** one other member state in the EU.
5. Name the top **three** languages spoken in the EU.
6. What percentage of EU citizens can speak more than one language?
7. How many languages are spoken in Ireland?
8. What is the largest religious group in Europe?
9. What percentage of the EU is:
    (a) Catholic
    (b) Protestant
    (c) Muslim?
10. What is predicted to be the second largest religion in Europe by 2050?
11. Which **two** religions are expected to experience the biggest percentage increase in membership?
12. In your view, are the identities within the EU best explained by Benedict Anderson's theory on 'imagined communities'?

See page 321 for more information on Benedict Anderson's theory on 'imagined communities'.

RESEARCH ASSIGNMENT 9.5

Examine the most up-to-date statistics on diversity in the EU at **https://educateplus.ie/go/eu-stats**
Create **three** suitable graphs to illustrate the following information:

(a) Ethnic diversity (b) Language diversity (c) Religious diversity.

See **RESEARCH TIPS** on page 33.

ACTIVITY 9.13

Select **one** country in the EU and create a diversity profile for that country. Include the following data:

- Number of immigrants/non-nationals as a percentage of the total population
- Main ethnic groups and minority groups within the country
- Main languages spoken and religious affiliations
- Patterns and trends: include statistics that show how the country has become more diverse within a particular period.

CASE STUDY 7: Ethnic Diversity in Focus

The Catalans

The Catalans are a national group residing in a region that takes in parts of France and Spain, along the northwest Mediterranean and eastern Pyrenees, known as Catalonia (*Catalunya*). Modernday Catalonia is located in north-east Spain and its major cities include Barcelona, Valencia and Palma de Mallorca.

Language and Culture

Catalan is a Romance language derived from Latin. It is closer to Provençal than to Castilian Spanish. Variants of Catalan are spoken throughout the region, from the Balearic Islands to parts of Aragon, Andorra, France and Sardinia. In addition to its own distinct language, Catalonia also hosts many unique cultural traditions and customs. The *correfocs* is a Catalan festival in which people dress up as devils and march through the streets with fireworks. During the spring festival, on 23 April, Catalans celebrate the *Dia Sant Jordi* (St George's Day): men give red roses to women, and women give men books in return. During festivals, Catalans make large 'human towers' known as *castells*. The practice has been included in the UNESCO World Heritage List.

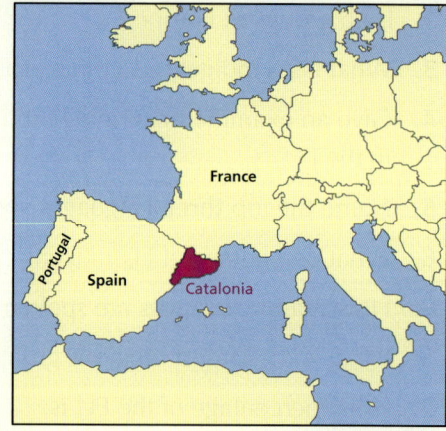

Fig. 9.40 Catalonia

Fig. 9.41 Catalonia

Case Study: Ethnic Diversity in Focus

Politics: Autonomy and Independence

Catalans have a strong sense of nationalism. Since losing independence in 1714, the Catalans have continued to fight for self-determination. In 1979, the region was finally granted some autonomy. Catalonia has a local parliament with several powers, including full control over education and the recognition of Catalan as the official language, alongside Spanish (Castilian). Each year, on 11 September, Catalans commemorate the 1714 siege of Barcelona by the Bourbon monarchy, which led to the loss of Catalan self-rule.

Fig. 9.42 Catalan flag

A nationalist movement arose in the nineteenth century as Catalonia became increasingly industrialised and prosperous. Today it remains one of Spain's wealthier regions. Catalonia is a major contributor to the Spanish economy: the region accounts for 19 per cent of Spain's GDP.

Since 2005, Catalonia has developed a movement for political independence. Between 2009 and 2011, several symbolic non-binding referendums on self-determination were held in over 540 towns across the region. Over 1.5 million people attended a demonstration under the banner 'Catalonia: Next State in Europe'. On 23 January 2013 the Catalan Sovereignty Declaration was adopted by the Catalan parliament. In 2014 the Spanish government rejected requests to permit a referendum on self-determination and the Supreme Court ruled to suspend the power of the Catalan parliament to hold a referendum. Despite the ruling, a vote was held in Catalonia in November 2014: 2.3 million votes were cast and the result was 80.76 per cent in favour of independence. The vote was criticised as 'political propaganda' by the Spanish government. In October 2017, another vote on independence was held by the government of Catalonia. Spanish police disrupted the planned vote, resulting in violent clashes with pro-Independence supporters which injured hundreds of people. The vote once again supported separation from Spain and the government of Catalonia declared independence. As a result, the government of Spain imposed direct rule, removed the Regional President, Carles Puigdemont, and his pro-Independence government from office, and called snap elections to be held in December. The question of Catalan independence remains a topical political issue and a modern-day example of a nation within a state.

Fig. 9.43 Catalonia has developed a movement for political independence

North African Migrant Community in France

France does not collect or present population data on ethnicity or race. According to Eurostat, as of January 2015, 5.7 million non-EU migrants were living in France, which accounts for 8.6 per cent of the total population. A large percentage of the immigrant community in France are believed to be from the former French colonies, particularly North Africa. In the 1960s, as part of the decolonisation process, the French government facilitated labour migration from former French colonies, such as Algeria, Morocco and Tunisia. These migrant workers supported the growing French economy by providing much-needed labour in the unskilled sectors. The pay conditions were poor and many of these

Fig. 9.44 France has a large North African migrant community

IDENTITY IN A GLOBAL AGE **353**

Case Study: Ethnic Diversity in Focus

Fig. 9.45 A 2004 French law banned the wearing of conspicuous religious symbols in public schools

migrants lived in poor housing conditions. As a result, cultural ghettoes of high-rise apartments were formed on the outskirts of many of France's major cities. Family members began to join the newly arrived migrants, and these communities grew, building mosques and developing local commercial districts. Despite the slow-down of the economy in the 1970s and the rising unemployment, the North African migrant communities remained in the country. France had become their adopted home and many of their children, born in France, had developed strong social ties.

Government Immigration Policies: Left-Right-Left …

During the 1960s and 1970s, France's policy toward immigrants was geared towards assimilating them into French society. Migrants were expected to adhere to traditional French values and culture. However, this policy failed and communities continued to practise their cultural beliefs and traditions, including the Muslim faith. From the mid-1980s, France pursued **cultural integration policies**.

The French government invested resources in organisations that promoted respect for distinctive cultures and traditions, while respecting the civil culture and laws of France. However, beginning in the 2000s, right-wing political leaders began to take advantage of, and influence, the growing hostility of public opinion towards immigrants in order to revive the **cultural assimilation** policies of the 1960s and 1970s. These politicians claimed that increasing crime rates were an 'immigration problem' and called for new laws to promote the assimilation of immigrants into French culture. This led, for example, to a 2004 law that banned the wearing of any conspicuous religious symbols in

KEY TERMS

There are two distinct approaches taken by governments who want to integrate immigrants and minority groups peacefully into their countries.

Cultural integration policies promote a two-way process, where the majority and the minority cultures are encouraged to interact and influence each other. Both cultures will change and adapt, so that the minority culture can be accepted alongside the majority culture. This is a process that requires acceptance of the laws and ways of the host country by the people of the minority culture, without these people giving up their own cultural values and identity. In this process, both cultures are modified.

Cultural assimilation is a process of absorbing minority cultures into the ways and views of the majority community. Unlike cultural integration, assimilation is a one-way process: the majority culture is imposed on the minority culture. The minority communities are expected to learn the customs and traditions of the majority community. This often involves giving up their own identity or modifying their culture to become acceptable to the majority community.

CASE STUDY: Ethnic Diversity in Focus

public schools. The ban included the hijab (headscarf worn by Muslim girls as a religious practice). Between 2007 and 2012, France returned to an integrationist policy, as French President Sarkozy appointed ministers from minority backgrounds and supported initiatives to promote the integration of minority communities into the private sector.

Tension and Unrest

Some French people developed a fear that French culture was under threat because of France's multicultural society. Xenophobic politicians gained ground in many local elections. Immigrant communities faced increasing discrimination in access to jobs and services. Unemployment and poverty led to tensions within immigrant communities. Violent riots broke out in some French cities in 2005 and again in 2012. The riots sent shockwaves throughout France, as images of burning cars and assaults on local businesses in French cities such as Marseille and Lyon appeared in the media.

Recent Developments

Terror attacks have been on the rise in France in recent years (e.g. the Charlie Hebdo killings and the Bataclan massacre). With this, Islamophobia is reportedly on the rise. Right-wing political views, such as those of the Front National, have gained some ground. Some commentators propose that French society has become more polarised, with extremist views developing in mainstream French society and in Muslim communities.

QUESTIONS

1. Explain some of the reasons why Catalans might claim that they are entitled to full independence from Spain.
2. What has been the impact of immigration and ethnic diversity on France?
3. How can ethnic tensions in France be best resolved by the government? In your answer, refer to the advantages and disadvantages of assimilation policies and integrationist policies.

Ethnic Identity: A Source of Community or Conflict?

Nationalism and ethnicity remain important sources of identity for many people in the world today. These aspects of identity continue to play a major role in our understanding of politics and society. However, are nationalism and ethnicity sources of community or of conflict? An examination of the past and the present demonstrates their potential for both. On the one hand, we have witnessed the destructive role that ethnicity and nationalism can play in societies. Tens of millions of men, women and children have lost their lives in conflicts such as the Armenian and Rwandan genocides, the Khmer Rouge campaign of terror in Cambodia, the Holocaust, the war in Bosnia, and genocide in Darfur.

At the same time, however, ethnic or national identity can provide a source of social and community cohesion. A shared sense of belonging to a particular group can produce positive benefits for the wellbeing of the group's members, as well as the community as a whole. It can provide us with a sense of security and belonging. In some cultures, ethnic identity can develop positive values and norms for society.

Ethnicity and nationalism can be sources of community or sources of conflict, depending on how they are interpreted and used.

Case Study 8: Ethnicity and Genocide

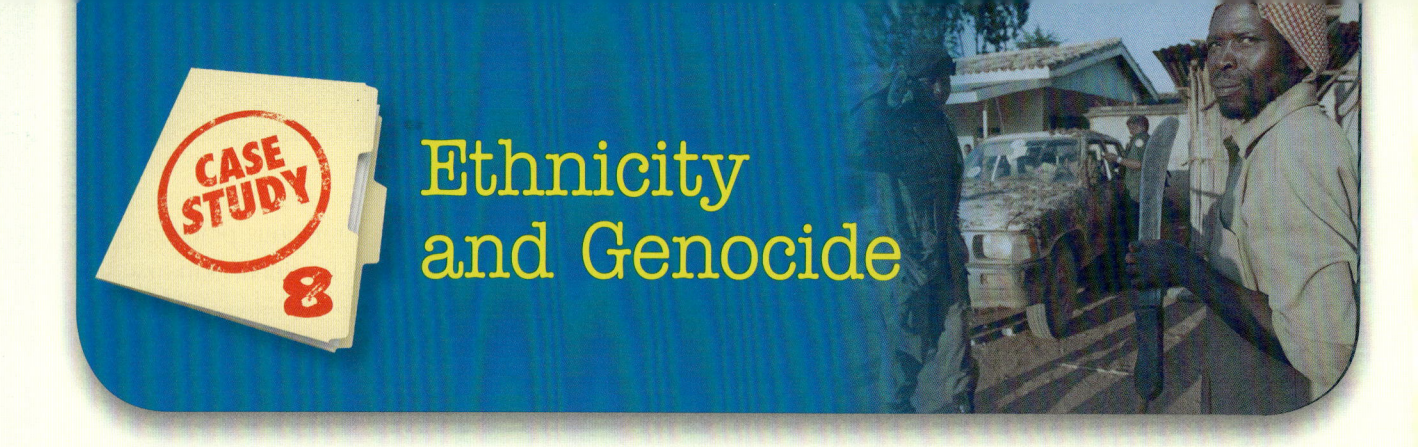

Rwanda

Rwanda is in Central Africa. The Rwandan genocide is one of the darkest events in modern human history. In a period of 100 days, 800,000 Tutsis and moderate Hutus were slaughtered across the country.

History

Rwanda was a colony of Belgium. Approximately 85 per cent of Rwandans are Hutus but the Tutsi minority had long been in power. The colonial power, Belgium, believed that the Tutsi group were superior to the Hutu group, and so had put the Tutsis in charge. Three years before Rwanda was due to obtain its independence, the majority ethnic group, the Hutus, overthrew the Tutsi King. Thousands of Tutsis were killed and over 150,000 were forced to flee to neighbouring countries, such as Uganda, Democratic Republic of Congo and Burundi. While in exile, the Tutsis formed the Rwandan Patriotic Front (RPF) and a civil war began in 1990. In April 1994, the Rwandan President Juvénal Habyarimana, a Tutsi, was assassinated. This sparked political tensions, and the Hutus organised a campaign of ethnic cleansing against the Tutsi population.

Fig. 9.46 In the Rwandan genocide, 800,000 people were killed over a period of 100 days

The Genocide

Shortly after the president's death, Hutu rebels surrounded the capital of Kigali. Tutsis – and anyone suspected of having any ties to a Tutsi – were killed. Radio was used as a weapon of the genocide. Radio stations broadcast details of Tutsi 'targets', including their names, addresses and license plate numbers. Hate speeches were used to encourage ordinary Hutus to take to the streets and 'exterminate' Tutsis. Tutsis were dehumanised in these broadcasts and were described in derogatory terms (e.g. as 'cockroaches'). In addition to the brutal mass killings, systematic rape was used as a weapon of war. It is estimated that between 250,000 and 500,000 women were raped. The UN and Belgium sent forces to Rwanda but the UN mission was, famously, not given any power to stop the killing. The Belgians and most UN peacekeepers pulled out soon after 10 Belgian soldiers were killed in fighting.

Fig. 9.47 Soldiers in the Rwandan conflict

CASE STUDY: Ethnicity and Genocide

Ending the Violence

The Tutsi RFP, backed by the Ugandan government, gained control of Kigali in July and an estimated 2 million Hutus fled the country. The genocide in Rwanda ended. However, it has directly led to two decades of violence and unrest in the neighbouring Democratic Republic of Congo: an estimated five million people have been killed in this conflict. Rwanda's government has twice invaded Democratic Republic of Congo, which it accuses of permitting the Hutu militias to operate on its territory. Rwanda has also armed local Congolese Tutsi forces.

Seeking Justice

The effect of the genocide on the people of Rwanda is incalculable. People were tortured, terrorised and slaughtered. An estimated 100,000 children were orphaned, abducted or abandoned; 26 per cent of the population suffer from post-traumatic stress disorder. In 1995 the UN established the International Criminal Tribunal for Rwanda (ICTR) to bring to justice those responsible for the genocide. The ICTR was the first ever international tribunal to deliver verdicts in relation to genocide. It was also the first international tribunal to define rape in international criminal law and to recognise rape

Fig. 9.48 UN International Criminal Tribunal for Rwanda (ICTR)

as a means of perpetrating genocide. Over the course of 10 years, the ICTR tried 93 cases involving high-ranking military and government officials, politicians, businessmen, as well as religious, militia and media leaders. In addition, traditional courts in Rwanda, known as *Gacaca*, were used to deal with over 1.2 million cases. The Rwandan genocide is one of the worst atrocities of our time and leaves us with important lessons on what can happen when views on ethnicity are manipulated.

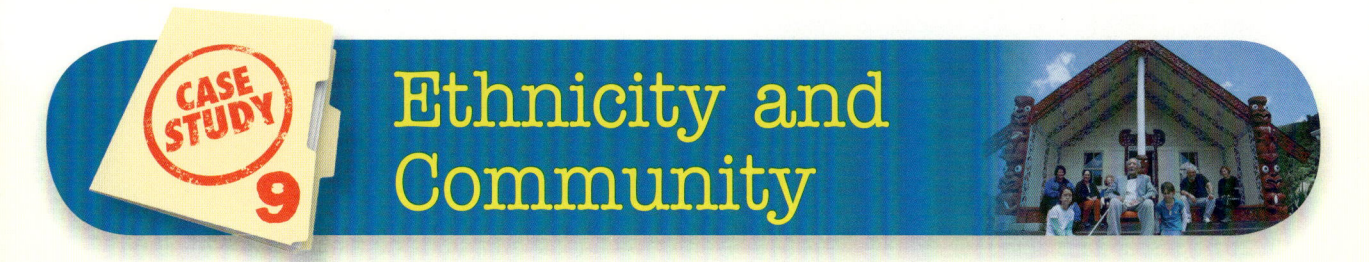

CASE STUDY 9: Ethnicity and Community

The Maori

The Maori of New Zealand are probably best known for giving us the *haka* – a tribal war dance which has become a common pre-match ritual of New Zealand's All Blacks rugby team. Maori culture is rich, and an examination of it demonstrates the positive effects of having a strong sense of ethnic identity.

Maori are the indigenous people (*tangata whenua*) of New Zealand. They arrived in New Zealand more than 1,000 years ago from their mythical Polynesian

Fig. 9.49 New Zealand's All Blacks perform the haka

IDENTITY IN A GLOBAL AGE

Ethnicity and Community

homeland of Hawaiki. The Maori now comprise 15 per cent of New Zealand's population. Their language – Te Reo – is an official national language, alongside English and sign language.

Cultural Values

Maori culture is based on a strong connection with and respect for the natural environment, and close familial and communal bonds. In traditional Maori culture, individuals are seen as a part of the group: what affects one member affects the whole group. Maori culture adopts a broad concept of family. Extended family members, cousins, aunts and uncles are also referred to as 'brother' and 'sister'. Several cultural concepts produce positive impacts for society in New Zealand as a whole.

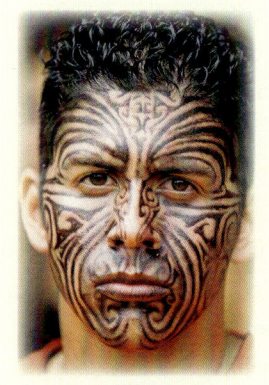

Fig. 9.50 Tā moko is the permanent body and face marking seen in Maori culture

Manaakitanga

Manaakitanga is a Maori word that loosely translates as 'hospitality'. It is a concept of kindness and inclusion. It sums up the act of welcoming and looking after others. Maori culture is based on mutual respect and extending love to all peoples.

Fig. 9.51 A Maori home

Kaitiakitanga

Kaitiakitanga loosely translates as 'guardianship' or 'protection'. The Maori have a strong sense of respect and responsibility for the natural environment. They believe that humans are part of nature: we are part of the forests, seas and waterways of our planet. People have a sacred connection to the natural environment, and the use of natural resources must be conducted under strict limitations (*rāhui*). For example, over-fishing that would result in a depletion of fish stocks is strongly prohibited in Maori culture.

Benefits of a Strong Sense of Maori Identity

In 2014, researchers at the Victoria University in Wellington published a study on the influence of ethnic identity on Maori adolescents. The research involved surveying 431 self-identified Maori (aged 10–15 years) once a year, for three years. The study found that, among Maori adolescents, a strong ethnic identity and higher levels of family connectedness are linked to greater psychological and social wellbeing. Maori teenagers experience the same adolescent pressures as teenagers in 'western societies' but their higher levels of connectedness and belonging lessen the effects of these pressures. Participation in cultural activities and traditions were found to lead to a stronger ethnic identity which, in turn, resulted in wellbeing over longer periods.

Fig. 9.52 Family connectedness is linked to greater wellbeing

QUESTIONS

1. Explain how ethnic divisions led to conflict in Rwanda.
2. What is genocide?
3. What were the effects of the genocide in Rwanda?
4. Who are the Maori?
5. Briefly explain some of the positive aspects of Maori culture and identity.

ACTIVITY 9.14

Work with your partner to complete the following activity.

1. Think individually for a moment about the following questions. *(Think)*
   - Describe your own ethnicity, culture and identity.
   - List the positive and negative characteristics of your identity.
   - List the benefits that you gain from your own sense of identity in relation to:
     (a) How you feel about yourself
     (b) How others perceive you and treat you as a result of your identity
     (c) How you treat others as a result of your identity.
2. With your partner, compare your conclusions. *(Pair)*
3. Share your conclusions with the rest of the class. *(Share)*

SKILLS BOOK LINK 9.10

Go to page 158 of your Skills Book to complete Skill Task 9.10 on inter-ethnic conflict.

See **RESEARCH TIPS** on page 33.

Identity and Culture in a Global Age: Key Debates

As we have seen, globalisation has connected different cultures of the world. Globalisation has produced different effects, from cultural convergence to divergence, and from diffusion to hybridisation. We are now more aware of other cultures than we have been during any other time in modern human history. Many of our societies are multicultural. Cultural diversity is increasing. Globalisation has increased and intensified the interaction between western and non-western cultures. All of this has led to several important debates.

Complete your next Reflective Journal entry (pages 37–38)

KEY THINKERS

WESTERN AND NON-WESTERN CULTURES

Edward Said: Orientalism – 'Us' and 'Them'

In his 1978 book, *Orientalism*, Edward Said argued that the 'west' develops particular cultural representations of the so-called 'east'. 'Orientalism' refers to how the west views 'the east'. 'Occidentalism' refers to the stereotypes of 'the west' which are held by non-western cultures. Said, a Palestinian scholar, was particularly interested in how the west depicts societies and peoples from Asia, North Africa and the Middle East. He examined the historical, cultural and political views of the east that are held by the west – and how these views developed from British and French colonial rule. His theory of Orientalism described how Arab culture is imagined, exaggerated and misrepresented by the west. Arab culture is presented as exotic, backward, uncivilised and at times dangerous. Images of flying carpets, maharishis wearing turbans, and knife-brandishing bandits crossing dangerous deserts are created and presented to western societies. Key elements of Orientalism include the following.

- The 'Orient' is presented as one homogenous cultural entity. No distinction is made between countries or their different cultures.

- We develop a sense of distinction between west and 'the Orient' based on 'us' and 'them'. Our understanding of Arab culture is egocentric: it comes from how we perceive them to be different from us.

- The west has assigned characteristics to 'us' and 'them'. The west is viewed as civilised, rational and superior. Arab societies are understood and presented as irrational, inferior and uncivilised.

Said's theories can be applied to much of our cultural interactions and the 'good west versus bad Islam' discourse of recent decades.

Kwame Anthony Appiah: Cosmopolitanism – Citizen of the World

Cosmopolitanism is the theory that all human beings belong to the international society. The word 'cosmopolitan' comes from the Greek word *kosmopolites*, which means 'citizen of the world'. The theory challenges traditional identities and attachments that are based on political, ethnic, national, religious or other cultural factors. Kwame Anthony Appiah, an American-Ghanaian cultural theorist, has used his writings to support the theory. Appiah defines cosmopolitanism as 'universality plus difference'. In our modern world, with increased travel, exchange of information and multicultural societies, we must respect one another's cultures. Appiah argues that we should inform and educate ourselves about the different cultures in our society and the wider world. A cosmopolitan might be someone who is multilingual and interested in the arts and cultures of different societies. We can celebrate our differences. To function and prosper, the world does not need everyone to be the same. At a minimum, we should tolerate and respect cultural differences. However, Appiah believes there is a limit to how much weight we give to cultural difference. We should respect cultures only in so far as they are not harmful to people. As cosmopolitans, we should prioritise our universal concern and responsibility for every human's life and wellbeing: 'the boundary of your state is not the boundary of your moral concern'. Appiah's main argument is that there are basic universals we need to respect (e.g. human rights) but outside of that, we should respect that different cultures have different ways of doing things. In cosmopolitan theory, we will see a reduction in the significance of cultural differences and people will be more influenced by multiculturalism and universal ideals.

KEY THINKERS

Samuel Huntington: Clash of Civilisations

'Clash of civilisations' is a theory that, in the post-Cold war world, people's cultural and religious identities will provide the main source of conflict. It was developed by American political scientist Samuel P. Huntington in the early 1990s. With the collapse of the Soviet Union, political theorists began to hypothesise what would replace the 'east–west' cultural division. Francis Fukuyama, a former student of Huntington, had argued that western democracy had triumphed and we had reached the 'end of history'. In response, Huntington presented his theory of the clash of civilisations. According to the theory, the world can be divided into 'major civilisations':

- Western civilisation: This includes the US and Canada, western and central Europe, Australia and Oceania. Huntington also suggested that some parts of Latin America (e.g. Mexico, Cuba) and the former member states of the Soviet Union could eventually be included, depending on their future direction.
- Latin America: Central and South America.
- Orthodox world: Parts of the former Soviet Union, the former Yugoslavia (except Croatia and Slovenia), Bulgaria, Cyprus, Greece and Romania.
- Eastern world: Buddhist, Chinese, Hindu and Japanese civilisations.
- Muslim world: Greater Middle East.
- Sub-Saharan Africa.

Huntington offered several reasons for the likelihood of conflict between civilisations. First, the differences between these civilisations are significant, and they will not disappear any time soon. Second, globalisation is making the world a smaller place and forcing civilisations to interact with one another. Third, religion is the most dominant source of identity: it unites people within each civilisation. Fourth, the west is gaining power and western culture is spreading. At the same time, local and traditional non-western cultures are reviving themselves. This creates a tension between western civilisation and the other civilisations. Finally, civilisations are developing their own regional models of economic cooperation (e.g. EU, ASEAN, COMESA). This will act to further strengthen their shared identity as a civilisation. Huntington argues that the future of world conflict will be based on western civilisation against 'the rest'.

Thomas Hylland Eriksen: 'Overheating' and the Rise of Identity Politics

Norwegian anthropologist Thomas Hylland Eriksen argues that globalisation has led to the politicisation of culture: culture has become more political. As traditional cultures feel threatened by the speedy import and spread of new technology and ideas, they resist. Hylland Eriksen referred to this as 'overheating'. Globalisation is happening at too fast a rate for local and traditional cultures. The result of globalisation's 'overheating' is the rise of identity politics. Religious fundamentalism and neo-nationalism are increasing. These movements have the aim of restoring or protecting tradition, religious fervour or ethnic or national identities. Eriksen points to several examples of identity politics. In Europe, the rise of ethnic nationalism in Croatia and Serbia, Scottish nationalism, and right-wing nationalism in France, Germany and the UK are examples. In Asia and the Middle East, the growth of the Taliban in Afghanistan and the Hindu nationalist party in India are offered as examples of this phenomenon.

IDENTITY IN A GLOBAL AGE

QUESTIONS

1. Would you agree with the central argument in Edward Said's *Orientalism* that we in the west tend to present ourselves as more civilised and superior in comparison to non-western civilisations in the world, which we often represent as different, backward and inferior? Give examples of how the media and/or western governments have contributed to this view:
   (a) In the past
   (b) Today.

2. Explain what Kwame Anthony Appiah means by 'cosmopolitanism'.

3. Do you think cosmopolitanism is an appropriate solution to ethnic divisions and conflict? Why/why not?

4. Is the process of globalisation breaking down national cultures and identities and contributing to a cosmopolitan culture and cosmopolitan identity? Provide examples in your answer.

5. Do you agree with Samuel Huntington's theory on the clash of civilisations? Is conflict between different cultures inevitable or can cultures live harmoniously side by side? Give reasons and examples to support your answer.

6. Explain what Thomas Hylland Eriksen means by 'overheating' and the 'rise of identity politics'.

7. Is western culture at risk from the increasingly rapid rate of population growth in non-western culture?

RESEARCH ASSIGNMENT 9.6

Critically evaluate the strengths and weaknesses of the following arguments about culture and identity in the wider world. Use appropriate research evidence and examples to back up your points.

1. The West has historically constructed itself ('us') in opposition to the non-western world ('them') and in doing so has imagined itself to be rational, civilised and mature, and has imagined the non-western world as irrational, depraved and child-like.

2. Processes of globalisation such as travel, commerce and ICT are breaking down national cultures and identities and creating a cosmopolitan identity.

3. There are many major civilisations in the modern world. Culturally, they are fundamentally different from and are in competition with one another.

4. If the west does not protect its culture of human rights and rational thought from other world civilisations, then western culture will be wiped out.

See RESEARCH TIPS on page 33.

ACTIVITY 9.15

Hold a classroom debate on the following motion.

'The clash of civilisation theory best explains the current state of the world.'

Complete your next Reflective Journal entry (pages 37–38)

Globalisation of Politics and Decision-making

Globalisation has multiple dimensions: cultural, social, political and environmental. Traditionally, politics and decision-making have been undertaken exclusively at the national level. States were largely independent and their political systems operated on the principle of **sovereignty**. Up until the mid-nineteenth century, national governments were solely responsible for maintaining the security and economic welfare of their citizens, protecting human rights, and caring for the environment on their territories. However, as the world became more interconnected, states began to face common challenges (e.g. environmental change, tax injustice, global conflict). States came together to develop common aspirations (e.g. economic cooperation and the promotion of universal human rights). With this, politics began to move from the national to the global level. **Political globalisation** has resulted in the establishment of **supranational organisations**. In Chapter 5, we learned about the EU. There are many other important international organisations in which an increasing number of national political and economic decisions are taken.

> ## KEY TERMS
>
> **Sovereignty** refers to the right and independent authority of a state to control its own government and decision-making.
>
> **Political globalisation** is the process whereby more and more government action takes place on a global level. Decision-making that was traditionally taken at a national level (e.g. welfare of citizens and management of the national economy) is now taken by supranational bodies at regional levels (e.g. EU) or international levels (e.g. UN, World Bank, IMF).
>
> **Supranational organisations** are bodies that states can join, where decision-making is shared on issues of common interest.

Global Economic Decision-making: Bretton Woods System

The International Monetary Fund (IMF), the World Bank and the World Trade Organization (WTO) are three important international organisations that make decisions affecting national economies and societies, particularly those of poorer nations or those with weaker economies. These organisations play an important role in decision-making. They provide loans (e.g. to Ireland and Greece following recent economic crashes). They give financial support to health, education and private sector projects in developing nations. They establish and adjudicate international trade agreements.

International Organisations
WTO, IMF and the World Bank

Bretton Woods Institutions

In 1944 the United Nations Monetary and Financial Conference was held in Bretton Woods, New Hampshire in the US. Following the Great Depression of the 1930s and World War II, the international financial system had been devastated. The global financial landscape was chaotic and many countries operated with rigid trade barriers. The Bretton Woods conference brought 44 nations together to develop a new international financial framework known as the Bretton Woods system. The conference gave rise to three institutions:

Fig. 9.53 The UN Monetary and Financial Conference in Bretton Woods, 1944

IDENTITY IN A GLOBAL AGE

- International Monetary Fund (IMF)
- International Bank for Reconstruction and Development, which later became the World Bank
- General Agreement on Tariffs and Trade (GATT), which eventually became the World Trade Organization (WTO)

The IMF and the World Bank

The IMF and the World Bank have little influence over wealthier countries, but they can affect developing countries and countries during times of economic crisis when those countries seek additional financial support. Financial support from the IMF and World Bank is tied to the acceptance of certain conditions.

Fig. 9.54 Representatives of the IMF

IMF

The IMF has 188 member countries, including Ireland. It monitors and produces an annual report on the health of the economies of its members. It provides technical advice to countries on the development of policies to manage their economies, including their tax systems. The IMF provides loans to countries during times of economic difficulty. However, these loans are dependent on the acceptance of conditions. In this sense, the IMF can play an important role in national decision-making with respect to how a country manages its national economy.

The World Bank

The World Bank's stated aim is to provide 'financial and technical assistance to developing countries around the world [to] reduce poverty and support development'. World Bank loans and grants finance many areas in developing countries, including education, health, infrastructure, financial and private sector development, agriculture, and environmental and natural resource management. The IMF and World Bank often work together with a particular developing country. As with IMF loans, World Bank loans are tied to the acceptance of certain conditions. Both the IMF and the World Bank have been criticised for the many conditions they impose on poor countries (e.g. trade liberalisation and the privatisation of basic services such as water and electricity). National priorities are often set aside to gain access to much-needed financial support. For example, in 2005 Burkina Faso – which has high rates of poverty – was forced to spend public money to train government staff on a new accounting software package in order to access World Bank finance.

World Trade Organization (WTO)

The WTO emerged out of the General Agreement on Tariffs and Trade (GATT) and was established in 1995. The WTO is responsible for establishing trade rules and agreements between countries. It is the forum for decision-making on trade. It establishes how much tax a government can place on imported goods (tariffs). It assesses the volume of imported goods (quotas). It gauges the supports that governments can provide to national industries and businesses to increase market competitiveness (subsidies).

The WTO also monitors compliance with trade agreements and provides a dispute resolution mechanism when conflicts arise between countries. In 2004 Brazil, Australia and Thailand lodged a complaint at the WTO against the EU for its sugar subsidies, which they claimed were in excess of the WTO trade agreement. In 2005 the WTO found that the EU was in breach of this agreement and the EU had to reform its sugar policy. The WTO's dispute resolution mechanism is a source of contention. Supporters argue that the WTO prevents trade wars and provides a fair adjudication mechanism. Critics argue that it has an unfair bias towards wealthier countries and it erodes national sovereignty.

QUESTIONS

1. Why did the UN host a Monetary and Financial Conference at Bretton Woods in 1944?
2. What was the outcome of the conference?
3. What is the IMF? What functions does it perform?
4. What is the aim of the World Bank? What types of loans does the bank provide?
5. Explain how the IMF and World Bank can influence national decision-making in developing countries. Is this fair?
6. What is GATT?
7. Describe the functions of the World Trade Organization.
8. Explain **one** benefit and **one** criticism of the WTO.

CASE STUDY 10: The IMF and Ireland

In December 2010 Ireland agreed a financial loan programme, commonly referred to as the 'Bailout Programme', with the EU and the IMF. Ireland's economy was in crisis from 2008, as a result of the housing market collapse, soaring unemployment and a banking crisis. Ireland's real GDP declined by 10 per cent between 2008 and 2009. By 2010 Ireland had a record deficit of 32 per cent of GDP. The Irish government was forced to seek assistance from the EU and the IMF. In late November 2010, the government agreed a multi-year funding deal with the EU and the IMF, which was overseen by the European Central Bank (ECB). These three institutions became known as 'the Troika' in this context.

Fig. 9.55 Former Minister for Finance in Ireland, Michael Noonan, and IMF Director, Christine Lagard, meet during Ireland's economic recession

The Bailout Agreement

The Bailout Programme initially provided funding commitments of €67.5 billion. In return for this funding, the Irish government agreed to make changes to the banking sector, reform economic policies and cut public spending. Ireland implemented an austerity programme on the basis of these conditions. Between 2008 and 2014, Ireland cut €18.5bn in public spending. This affected all sectors, including housing and health. According to *The Examiner* newspaper, government spending on health between 2008 and 2015 was cut by 27 per cent 'resulting in an 81 per cent increase in the number of patients waiting on trolleys and chairs in emergency departments'. By July 2015, over 1,000 children and 500 families were living in emergency accommodation in Dublin because of massive cuts to funding for local authority housing.

Impact on Children and Youth

Many families and children were pushed into poverty. The child poverty rate rose: from 18 per cent in 2008 to 29.1 per cent in 2013. The Children's Rights Alliance (CRA) produces an annual report analysing the National Budget from a children's rights perspective. In its 2012 report, the CRA found that children

CASE STUDY: The IMF and Ireland

and poorer families were the groups hardest hit by austerity measures: 'The decision to cut Child Benefit for families with three or more children, combined with the cut to the Back to School Clothing and Footwear Allowance and the increase in the cost of school transport, will have a real impact on families with children, already struggling to make ends meet.' In 2015, one year after Ireland had formally exited the IMF programme, the EU commissioned a study on the impact of austerity measures in countries including Ireland and Greece. The report found that the quality of primary and secondary education in Ireland had been affected by fewer teachers, a reduction in critical support services (i.e. special needs) and the abolition of school grants. The report linked an increase in the rate of early school leaving to the austerity measures.

Ireland's Corporate Tax Rate

One contentious issue during the EU-IMF bailout negotiations was Ireland's low rate of tax for corporations. Ireland's 12.5 per cent corporate tax rate is below the EU average (26.3 per cent) and the global average (16.3 per cent). During negotiations, the EU and IMF proposed an increase in Ireland's rate. However, the Irish government refused this proposal and the corporate tax rate remained unchanged in the final bailout agreement.

RESEARCH ASSIGNMENT 9.7

Drawing on evidence from your own research and from Case Study 10, critically evaluate the view that power is moving from national governments to supranational bodies.

See **RESEARCH TIPS** on page 33.

Globalisation and the United Nations Development Programme (UNDP)

The United Nations is one of the earliest examples of globalisation. It was established in 1945, after World War II and the atrocities of the Holocaust, when the nations of the world sought to promote political cooperation and ensure justice, freedom and human rights for all. The main objectives of the UN are to:

- Secure international peace
- Eliminate poverty
- Protect human rights.

The UN is not a 'world government'. Its purpose is to bring all nations of the world together to work for peace and sustainable development, based on the principles of justice, human dignity and the wellbeing of all people. The UN is made up of 193 countries known as 'member states'. The member states finance the UN's work and govern its activities.

The UN is made up of many bodies, each with a different function and remit. Two of the best-known bodies are the General Assembly and the Security Council.

Fig. 9.56 Logo of the UNDP

General Assembly

The UN's 193 member states meet in the General Assembly, which is the closest thing we have to a world parliament. Each country – large or small, rich or poor – has a single vote. While the assembly's decisions are not binding on member states, they carry the weight of world governmental opinion.

Security Council

The Security Council is responsible for maintaining peace, and tries to settle conflicts that threaten international security. All UN member states must respect and abide by the council's decisions. It can set up peacekeeping operations in countries experiencing conflict. These operations protect civilians and help warring parties to resolve their differences peacefully. The Security Council has 15 members, five of which are permanent: China, France, Russia, the UK and the USA. The permanent members can veto any major proposal in the Security Council.

The work of the United Nations reaches every corner of the world. Much of this work is carried out by UN funds, programmes and specialised agencies. These are part of the UN system but operate as independent bodies. One such body is the United Nations Development Programme (UNDP).

United Nations Development Programme (UNDP)

The UNDP is the United Nations programme to support global development and the fight against poverty and inequality. Its headquarters are in New York and it operates in almost 170 countries and territories. The UNDP works with countries to develop solutions to their development challenges and connect them to the necessary skills, technology and expertise. It is funded entirely by voluntary contributions from member nations, including Ireland. The UNDP has achieved many positive results. In 2015:

- **18.6 million people** (50 per cent women) benefited from improved economic activities (e.g. farming) in **115 countries**.
- **1.35 million new jobs** (42 per cent for women) were created in **94 countries**.
- Technology support was provided to **53 countries** to stop the use of gases that destroy the ozone layer.
- **2.1 million people** in **33 countries** were provided with access to legal aid services.
- **1.7 million people** (51 per cent women) living with HIV received antiretroviral treatment in **33 countries**.

QUESTIONS

1. Why was the United Nations set up in 1945?
2. List the **three** aims of the UN.
3. Describe the roles of the two main bodies in the UN.
4. Name the **five** permanent members that have a veto on the Security Council. What is the disadvantage of this veto system?
5. What is the UNDP? What is the primary aim of the programme?
6. List **three** achievements of the UNDP.
7. 'The United Nations is but one example of the positive effects of globalisation.' Do you agree with this statement? Give reasons for your answer.

SUMMARY

- Globalisation is the process whereby national and regional economies, societies, cultures and decision-making processes have become interconnected and integrated through the global network of trade, communication, immigration and transportation.
- Identity is how individuals or groups define themselves or are defined by others. Identity can be based on many categories, including language, ethnicity, nationality and gender.
- Culture refers to the accepted and familiar beliefs, customs and behaviours of a society or group.
- National or ethnic groups are those with a common culture based on shared values, beliefs, customs, language and history.
- Some political scientists such as Benedict Anderson argue that nations are invented over time and are 'imagined communities' which are socially constructed.
- Irish national identity has been heavily influenced by the Irish school curriculum, which promoted a traditional national identity based on a shared nationalistic history, rural culture and the Irish language.
- Ireland and the European Union have become increasingly diverse and multicultural.
- Mass media, ICT, migration and travel have contributed to the process of cultural mixing and adaptation.
- Globalisation has impacted on cultures across the world, resulting in different patterns of cultural diffusion, convergence, divergence and hybridisation.
- The EU comprises diverse cultures and ethnicities.
- EU enlargement, internal migration and external migration have resulted in greater ethnic, cultural, linguistic and religious diversity within EU member states.
- The development of a strong sense of national and ethnic identity can have positive and negative effects.
- The benefits of a secure and confident sense of one's ethnic identity include a strong communal or national spirit and the imparting of positive value systems.
- When ethnic identities are in competition for power within a region or are under threat, it can lead to inter-ethnic violence and even genocide.
- Historically, the west has constructed itself as rational, civilised and superior in comparison to the non-western world, which has been represented as irrational, backward and inferior.
- Some critics argue that certain cultures are fundamentally opposed and incompatible and that this will lead to a 'clash of cultures' and conflict in the future.
- Others argue that globalisation is resulting in the spread of cosmopolitanism, which has the potential to ease tensions between different cultures.
- National sovereignty has been somewhat weakened by globalisation, because of the rise of large supranational bodies such as the IMF, World Bank and World Trade Organization.

Fig. 9.57 Key Word cloud

REVISION QUESTIONS

1. What is globalisation?
2. Describe the key characteristics of culture.
3. What is the difference between multiculturalism and monoculturalism?
4. Define the following terms: 'popular culture', 'subculture' and 'dominant culture'.
5. Explain how Irish identity has been represented in the Irish school curriculum.
6. How does the segregated education system in Northern Ireland impact on cultural identity?
7. Describe how ICT and mass media have contributed to greater cultural mixing and adaptation.
8. Describe how migration and travel have contributed to greater cultural mixing and adaptation.
9. Explain how globalisation has impacted on cultures around the world in relation to:
    (a) Cultural diffusion
    (b) Cultural convergence
    (c) Cultural divergence
    (d) Cultural hybridisation.
10. Explain the difference between cultural assimilation and cultural integration. In your opinion, which of these two policies should be adopted in Ireland? Why?
11. Describe the patterns of cultural diversity that exist within the EU in relation to:
    (a) Ethnic diversity   (b) Linguistic diversity   (c) Religious diversity.
12. With reference to **one** example that you have studied, explain the benefits associated with achieving a secure and confident sense of one's ethnic identity.
13. With reference to **one** example that you have studied, explain how ethnicity can lead to conflict in a multi-ethnic society.
14. Describe and explain the **four** key arguments concerning interaction between western and non-western cultures.
15. To what extent is national identity and culture 'socially constructed' and imagined?
16. Name **three** supranational bodies that have the power to interfere with the sovereignty of the nation-state.
17. In relation to Irish politics, what was 'the Troika'? How did the Troika influence decision-making processes in Ireland during the last economic recession? What impact did this have on young people in Ireland?

IDENTITY IN A GLOBAL AGE

DATA-BASED QUESTIONS

Complete the qualitative and quantitative research data-based questions exercise on pages 159–163 of your Skills Book.

EXAM FOCUS — Section B of LC Exam

REVISION EXERCISES

Complete the exercises on pages 164–166 of your Skills Book.

EXAM FOCUS — Section A of LC Exam

DISCURSIVE ESSAY TOPICS

1. 'Cultures are the product of a process of mixing and adaptation and are continually evolving.' Discuss.

2. To what extent is the process of globalisation resulting in the destruction and/or replacement of minority cultures with mass culture?

3. 'Ethnic diversity and multiculturalism can have both positive and negative impacts on society'. Discuss this statement with reference to the EU and/or a member state within it.

4. To what extent does the development of a strong sense of ethnic identity create benefits and risks for society?

5. 'Conflict between western and non-western cultures is unavoidable. These cultures are fundamentally different, incompatible and in competition with one another.' Discuss.

EXAM FOCUS — Section C of LC Exam

Reflective Practice

Ensure that you have completed all the Reflective Journal entries for this chapter (pages 37–38 of your Reflective Journal and Learning Portfolio) before moving on to the next chapter.

Complete the Learning Portfolio activities on pages 39–41 of your Reflective Journal and Learning Portfolio. This will help you to self-assess the extent to which you have achieved the learning intentions for this chapter, and will help you to monitor your progress.

CHAPTER 10
Global Development

'Like slavery and apartheid, poverty is not natural. It is man-made and it can be overcome and eradicated by the actions of human beings.'
Nelson Mandela

KEY TERMS

- Development
- Gross domestic product (GDP)
- Human Development Index (HDI)
- Unsustainable development
- Lifestyle
- Climate change
- Global warming
- Carbon footprint
- Deforestation
- Overpopulation
- Consumer
- Gini coefficient
- Modernisation theory
- Dependency theory
- Colonialism
- Neocolonialism
- Tariff
- Tied aid
- Processor
- Retailer

Introduction

Globalisation has brought the world closer together through increased communication, technology, trade and travel. However, economic growth and people's quality of life still varies between countries. Globalisation contributes to the growth and **development** of countries in different ways. In this chapter, we will take a closer look at the concept of global development and consider some of the big questions in this field: What type of development pathway has the world followed? What are some of the resulting key global development issues we face? Why do we have global inequality? Why are some countries persistently poorer than others? What are the main causes of global poverty and inequality? What are the different ways we measure development? Throughout this chapter, we will engage with theories and research that attempt to explain development and the causes of underdevelopment, poverty and inequality.

KEY TERM

The term **development** describes how resources, wealth and quality of life are distributed between and within countries around the world.

By the end of this chapter you will be able to:
- Define global development.
- Assess the strengths and weaknesses of the different methods used to measure global development (including GDP and HDI).
- Describe some of the main global development challenges.
- Explain why the current capitalist model of economic development and modern-day consumption patterns are unsustainable.
- Explain why development is unequal across the world and why some regions are more developed than others.
- Describe the impact of unequal global development and inequality on the people of the world.
- Explain and critique the modernisation theory of development.
- Describe the impact of industrialisation on women and the local environment in developing countries.
- Explain and critique the dependency theory of development.
- Examine and assess the main causes of underdevelopment in the developing world, including unfair trade, tied aid, debt and corruption.

By the end of this chapter you will have developed the following skills:
- Communication skills by engaging in dialogue and debate and by formulating and presenting your own evidence-based arguments on global development.
- Teamwork and interpersonal skills by working effectively with others to complete group assignments.
- Information processing skills by analysing and evaluating both quantitative and qualitative data related to global development.
- Research skills by sourcing and compiling data relevant to global development.
- Action-planning skills by reviewing your progress, reflecting upon your learning, setting goals and developing an action plan to achieve these goals.

ACTIVITY 10.1

Your teacher will give your group cards showing statements about development. Rank the statements in order of importance. Discuss each statement carefully before agreeing where it should be placed in the ranking.

What is Development?

Development is essentially about how resources, wealth and quality of life are distributed between and within countries around the world. The term 'development' can be defined in different ways. How we *define* development will influence how we *measure* it. The two most common ways of measuring development are economic development and human development.

- Economic development is a measure of a country's wealth and how it is generated. Countries in which most of the population work in primary activities (e.g. agriculture, mining) are considered less economically developed than countries in which most of the population work in secondary activities (e.g. manufacturing) and tertiary activities (e.g. services). The level of a country's economic development is usually measured as **Gross Domestic Product (GDP)**.

- Human development measures the standard of living of the population (e.g. access to wealth, jobs, education, nutrition) *and* quality of life or wellbeing (e.g. health, leisure, safety). The **Human Development Index (HDI)** was devised by the UN to emphasise the importance of people's living standards and quality of life when measuring a country's level of development.

KEY TERMS

Gross domestic product (GDP) is a measurement of a country's overall economic activity. It is calculated by adding up the value of all the goods and services produced within a country, including all investments and exports, minus imports. The total figure is then divided by the country's population and expressed in a monetary value per capita. For example, Ireland's GDP per capita in 2016 was US$61,200 compared to Mali's GDP per capita of just US$720.

The **Human Development Index (HDI)** was developed by the UN as a method for assessing the social and economic development levels of countries. Four principal areas of examination are used to rank countries:

- Mean years of schooling
- Expected years of schooling
- Life expectancy at birth
- Gross national income per capita.

Countries are awarded an overall score ranging from 0.1 (very low development) to 1.0 (very high development). The HDI makes it possible to follow changes in development levels over time and to compare the development levels of different countries.

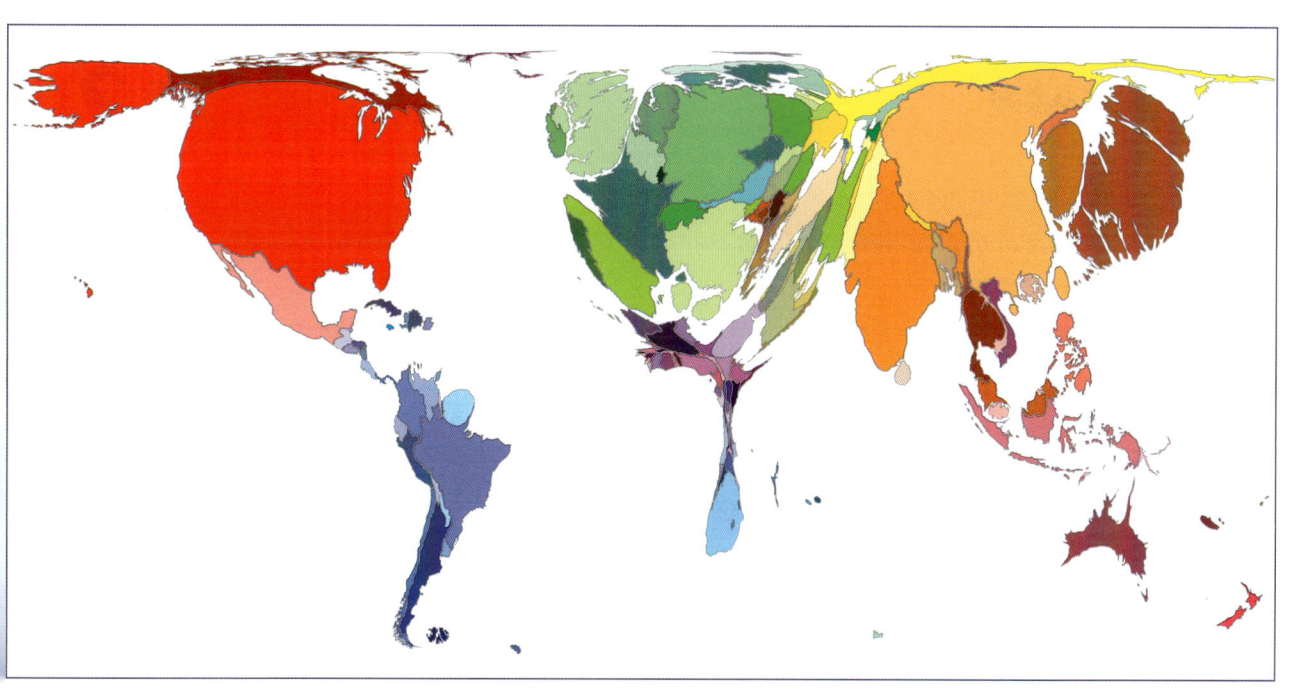

Fig. 10.1 Wealth map: a map of the world resized according to each country's total estimated GDP

Beyond Economic Growth

Examples of Human Development Indicators

- **Life expectancy** is the average age a person can expect to live in a given country.
- **Infant mortality rate** is the number of babies, per 1,000 live births, who die under the age of 1.
- **Poverty** indices count the percentage of people living below the poverty level, or on very low incomes.
- **Access to basic services** is the availability of services necessary for a healthy life, such as clean water and sanitation.
- **Access to healthcare** measures, for example, how many patients there are for every doctor.
- **Risk of disease rates** calculate the percentage of people with diseases such as AIDS, malaria and tuberculosis.
- **Access to education** measures how many people attend primary school, secondary school and higher education.
- **Literacy rate** is the percentage of adults who can read and write.
- **Access to technology** includes, for example, the percentage of people with access to phones, mobile phones, television and internet/broadband.
- **Gender equality** compares statistics such as literacy rates and employment rates between men and women.
- **Government spending priorities** compares health and education expenditure with military expenditure and paying off debts.

QUESTIONS

1. In your opinion, which is a more accurate measure of a country's development: GDP or HDI? Give reasons for your answer.
2. Can you think of any other indicators that could be added to the list above to assess a country's level of development?

Development takes place at different rates and is distributed unevenly within each country. As a result, overall/average national economic growth figures can be misleading because they disguise inequalities between different sections within a country's population. Therefore, it is important to look beyond the statistics and figures concerning a country's economy. Many countries with high GDPs also have very high rates of poverty.

Human development indicators can present us with a better overall picture because they also assess the non-economic elements of a country's development. The HDI, for example, involves a combination of three key indicators:

- Life expectancy
- Education levels
- Purchasing power parity.

The HDI is produced every year and it gives countries a measurement between 0.1 and 1.0. In 2015, Norway was ranked number 1 on the index, with a HDI of 0.944. Niger in western Africa had the lowest HDI at 0.348. The HDI groups countries into four categories based on their ranking:

- Very high development
- High development
- Medium development
- Low development.

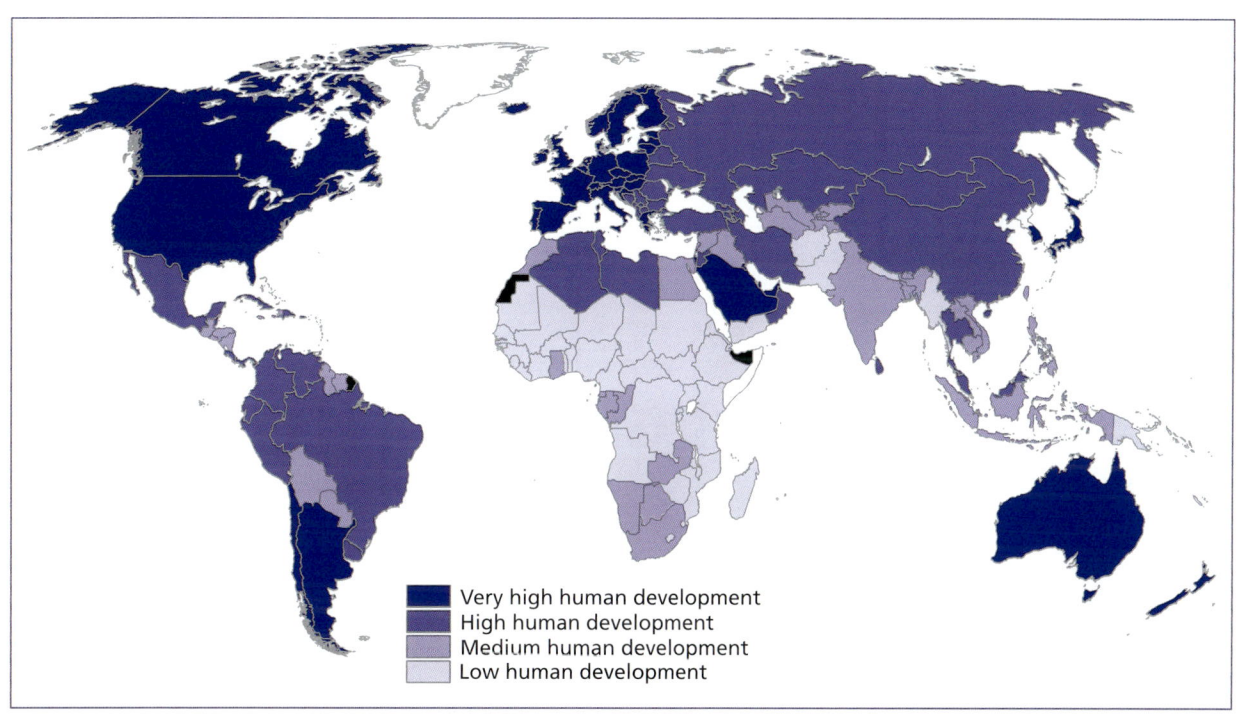

Fig. 10.2 HDI levels around the world

SKILLS BOOK LINK 10.1

Go to pages 167–168 of your Skills Book to complete Skill Task 10.1 on HDI rankings.

See **RESEARCH TIPS** on page 33.

- The 2015 HDI rankings can be viewed at: https://educateplus.ie/go/2015-report
- The most up-to-date annual rankings will be contained in the latest UN Human Development report, available at: https://educateplus.ie/go/2016-report

Unsustainable Development

KEY TERMS

Unsustainable means that it is impossible for something to be maintained at its current rate or level.

Unsustainable development occurs when human activities and urbanisation (the growth of cities) are based on the exploitation and over-consumption of important natural resources, without regard for the needs of future generations. Unsustainable development leads to environmental degradation because of the rapid depletion of natural resources. This generates waste and pollution. Unsustainable development has caused the rapid deforestation of the world's rainforests, the destruction of natural habitats, the extinction of species and the pollution of air and water supplies. All of this has put future generations at risk.

Fig. 10.3 Unsustainable development leads to environmental degradation

The traditional focus on economic development has meant that modern global development has followed a path of industrialisation, urbanisation and increased consumption. This model has produced many negative impacts. Our development is **unsustainable** because we are progressing at the expense of future generations. We have been meeting our needs and wants, without regard for the ability of future generations to meet their needs and wants.

WHAT THE RESEARCH SAYS!

GROWING CONSUMPTION

Following the Agricultural and Industrial Revolutions in the late eighteenth and early nineteenth centuries, the population of the world began to increase dramatically. In 1800 the total population of the world was just under 1 billion. By 1950 it had reached 2.5 billion. Today there are over 7.5 billion people living in the world and this is estimated to exceed 9.5 billion by 2050. This dramatic rise in the world's population has been labelled a 'population explosion'. Combined with unsustainable economic models of development based on over-consumption, the population explosion is one of the biggest challenges facing the world today. It has put a huge strain on vital global resources. According to the UN, we will need the equivalent of three planets to sustain current lifestyles.

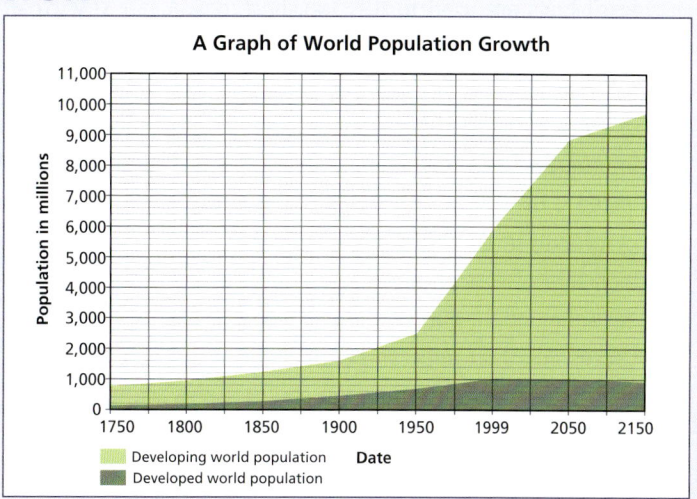

Fig. 10.4 World population growth

> **KEY TERM**
>
> **Lifestyle** is about how and where we live, spend our time and interact with others, where we travel and holiday, where we shop and what we consume.

Food

Over 90 per cent of annual global population growth is taking place in the developing world (see Fig. 10.4). This is a major cause for concern because localised food shortages are becoming more common with the higher frequency of droughts in many of these regions (e.g. the Sahel region of Africa and parts of Asia). Compounding this problem is the high rate of poverty in the developing world. Poor people in developing countries spend 60–80 per cent of their income on food and many struggle to afford a balanced diet. Approximately 165 million children across the world suffer from malnourishment. According to the Food and Agriculture Organization (FAO) of the UN, approximately one-third of the food produced in the world for human consumption every year – roughly 1.3 billion tonnes – is lost or wasted. It is estimated that Americans alone waste about 141 trillion calories worth of food every day.

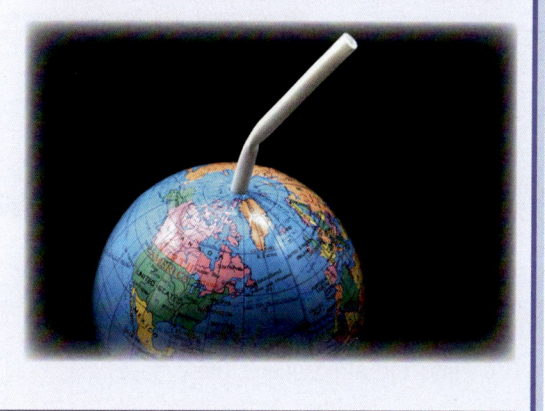

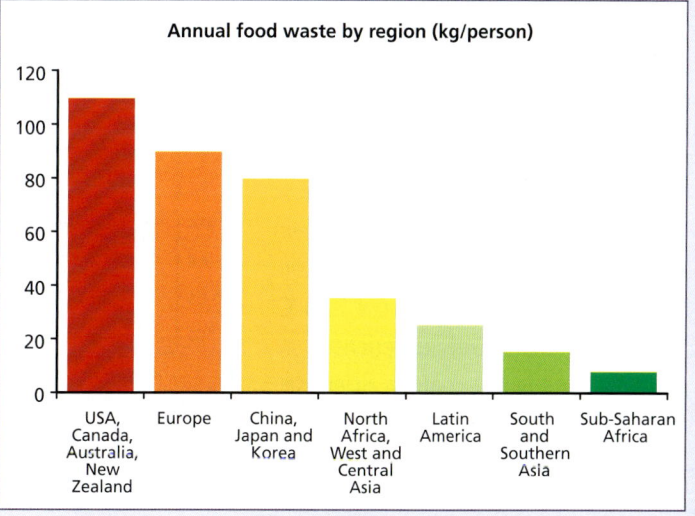

Fig. 10.5 Annual food waste by region (kg/person)

GLOBAL DEVELOPMENT 377

Energy

The world is heavily dependent on fossil fuels (e.g. coal, oil, gas) as sources of energy to promote economic development. These fossil fuels are used to fuel transport, power industry, create electricity and provide heating for our homes. However, fossil fuels are finite, non-renewable resources and the current rate of consumption is unsustainable. According to the US Energy Information Administration, world energy consumption will increase by 56 per cent by 2040. This will be driven primarily by growth in countries in Asia, such as China and India. The high rate of fossil fuel consumption is severely damaging the environment. The burning of fossil fuels pollutes the atmosphere, causes acid rain and can contaminate water supplies. It also contributes to **climate change** and **global warming**.

> **KEY TERMS**
>
> **Climate change** is a significant change in climate in a region, caused by natural and human factors.
>
> **Global warming** is the increase in the Earth's average surface temperature because of rising levels of greenhouse gases in the atmosphere, caused by human activities.

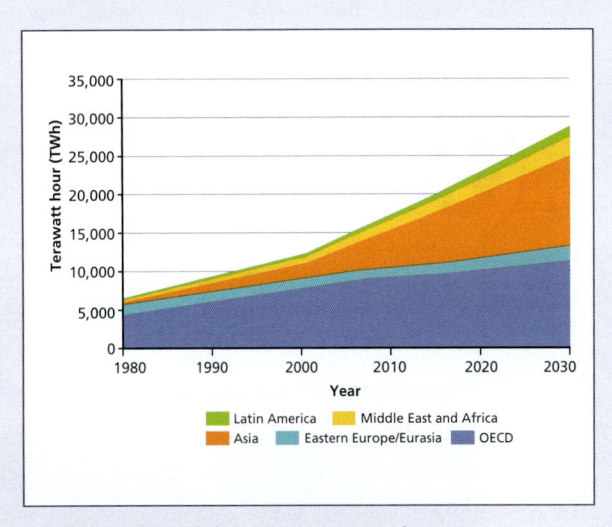

Fig. 10.7 World electricity consumption by region

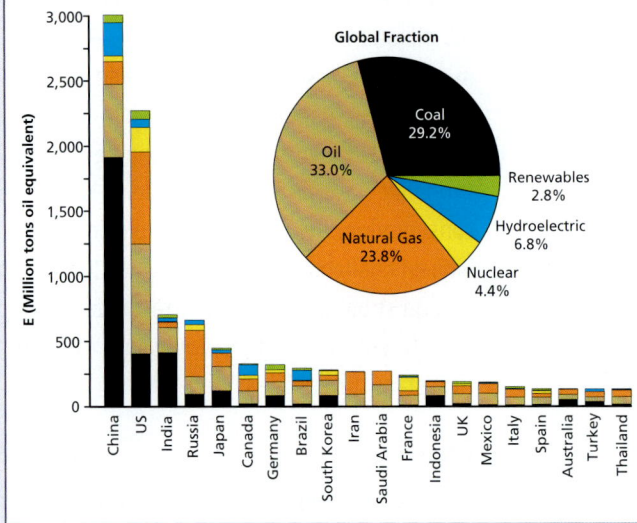

Fig. 10.6 Energy consumption by fuel, 2015 (BP data)

Climate Change and Global Warming

When fossil fuels are burned, they emit high quantities of greenhouse gases (e.g. carbon dioxide, CO_2) into the atmosphere. These gases linger in the atmosphere for decades and trap more heat from the sun, causing global warming. According to the UN's World Meteorological Organisation, the amount of CO_2 in the atmosphere in 2014 was 43 per cent more than pre-industrial levels. The average global temperature is now 1.38°C higher than levels experienced in the nineteenth century. Scientists at NASA claim that the world is warming at an unprecedentedly rapid rate (over 10 times faster than the historical average) and that 2016 was the hottest year on record.

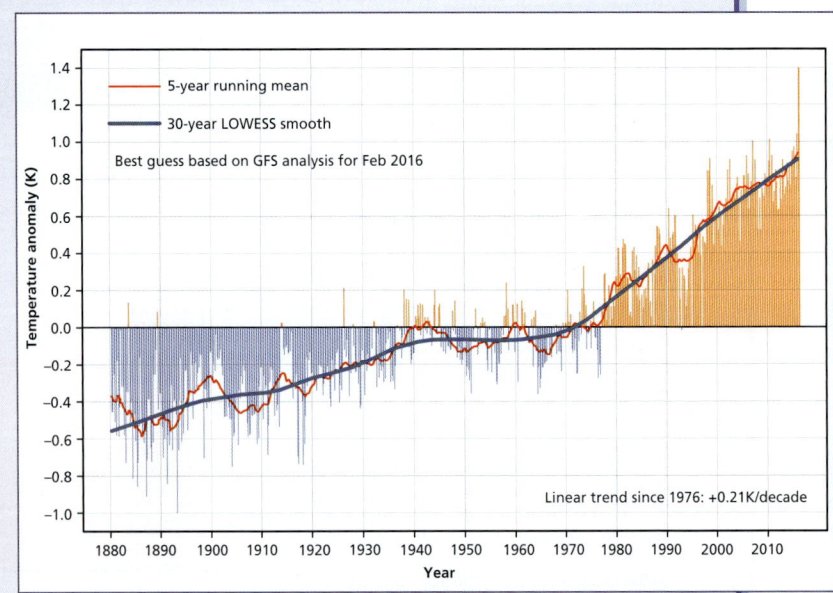

Fig. 10.8 Land seasonal temperature anomaly (March 1880–February 2016); baseline 1901–2000

The effects of climate change can be catastrophic.
- Floods and droughts are increasing and intensifying around the world (UN, 2014).
- Approximately 600,000 deaths occurred worldwide because of weather-related natural disasters in the 1990s (World Health Organization, 2005).
- Ice caps are melting and sea levels are rising, endangering more than half of the world's population who live on low-lying land within 60 km of the sea (UN, 2014).

Carbon Footprint

In response to this alarming rate of climate change, world leaders called a Climate Change Conference in Paris in December 2015. At the Paris Climate Change Conference, 195 countries adopted the first ever universal, legally binding global climate deal. In June 2017, US President Donald Trump announced that the US would pull out of the Paris Agreement. The Paris Agreement sets out a global action plan to put the world on track to avoid dangerous climate change by limiting global warming to well below 2°C. Under the agreement, each country has committed to cut its greenhouse gas emissions and to reduce its **carbon footprint**. The carbon footprint is the total amount of greenhouse gases that is produced to directly or indirectly support human activities. The carbon footprint is usually expressed in equivalent tonnes of carbon dioxide (CO_2).

KEY TERM

Carbon footprint is the total amount of greenhouse gases produced to support human activities. Carbon footprint is usually expressed in equivalent tonnes of carbon dioxide (CO_2).

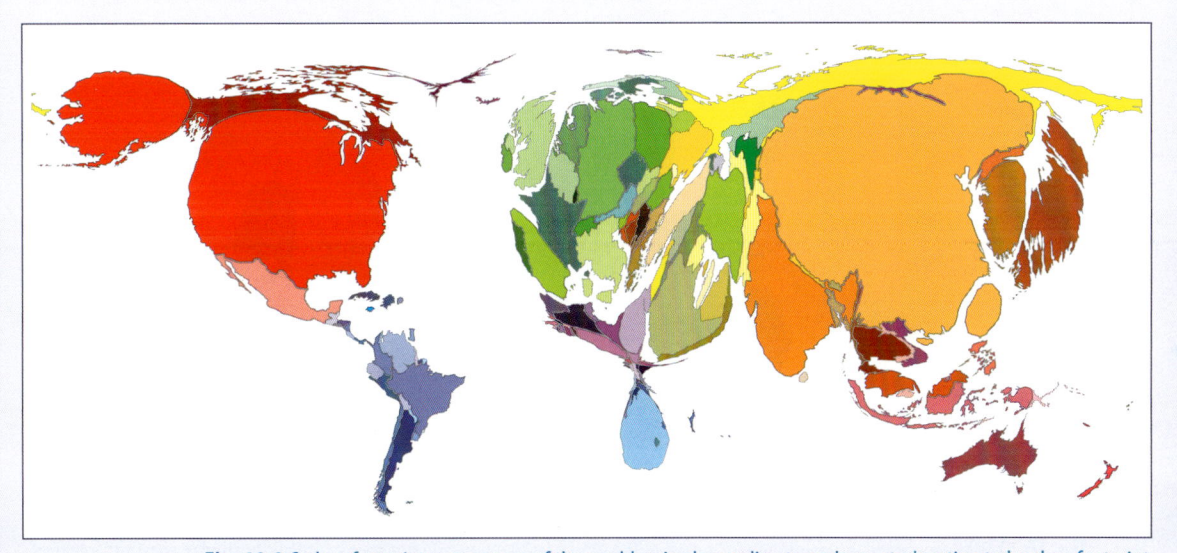

Fig. 10.9 Carbon footprint map: a map of the world resized according to each country's estimated carbon footprint

Water

If humans continue to use and pollute water as we have been doing, we will have only 60 per cent of the water we need in 2030 (UN, 2015).

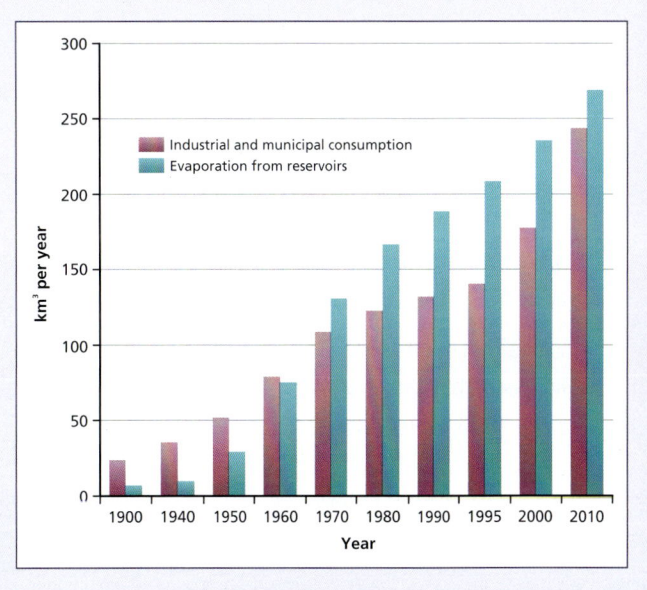

Fig. 10.10 Water consumption: industrial and domestic consumption compared with evaporation from reservoirs

GLOBAL DEVELOPMENT

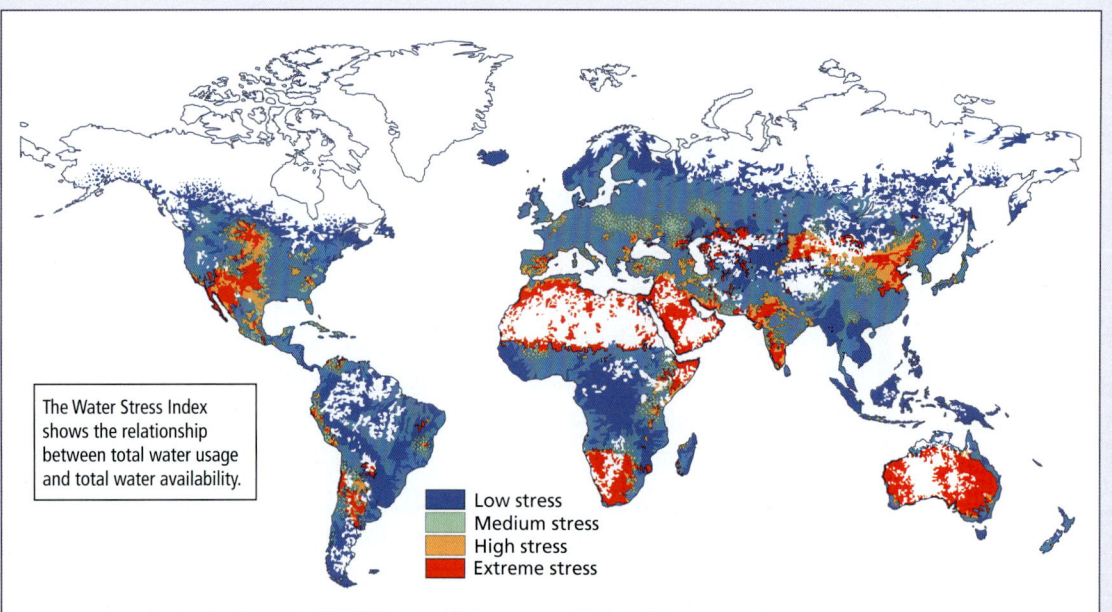

The Water Stress Index shows the relationship between total water usage and total water availability.

Low stress
Medium stress
High stress
Extreme stress

Fig. 10.11 Sub-national map of the Water Stress Index, 2011

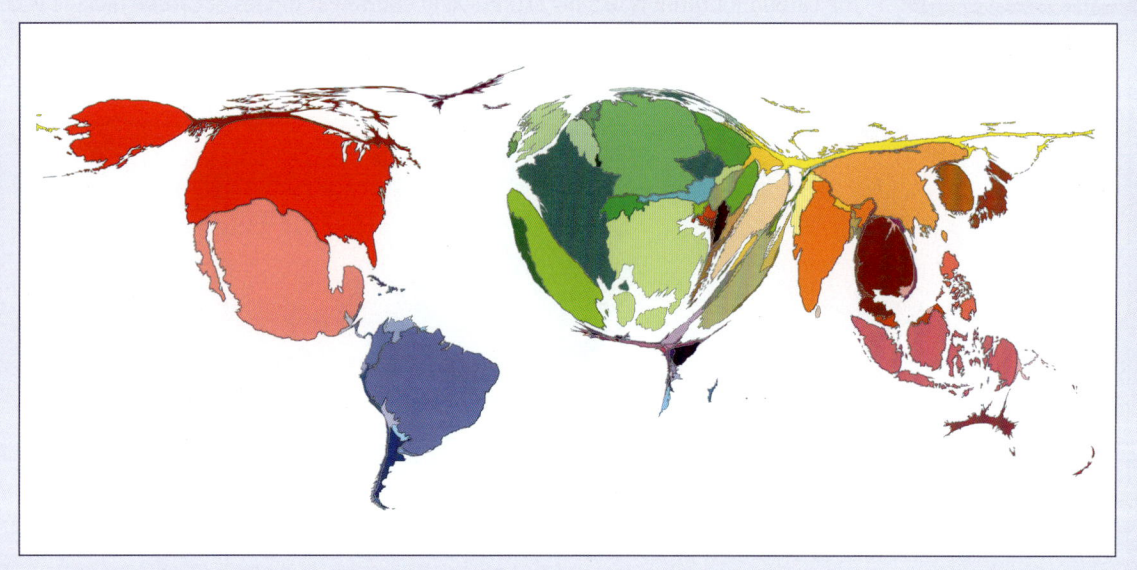

Fig. 10.12 Bottled water consumption map: a map of the world resized according to each country's bottled water consumption

Air

- There is more CO_2 in the atmosphere today than there has been at any point in the past 800,000 years. In 2015 there was 43 per cent more CO_2 than pre-industrial levels (UN, 2015).

- Global emissions of CO_2 have increased by almost 50 per cent since 1990. Emissions grew more quickly between 2000 and 2010 than in each of the three previous decades (UN, 2016).

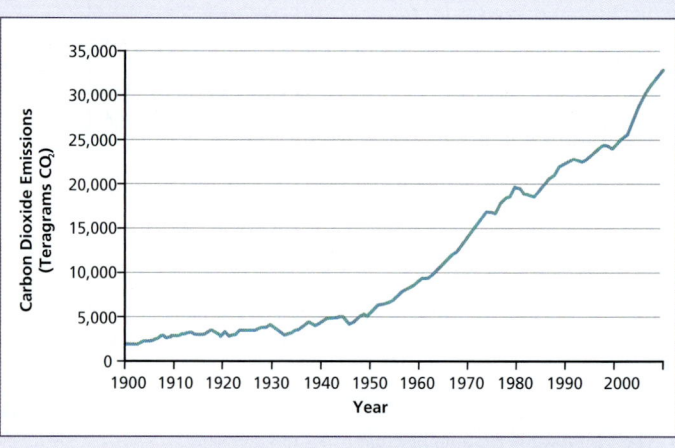

Fig. 10.13 Carbon dioxide emissions

380 POWER AND PEOPLE

Land

- Global natural resources are being depleted at a rate of 45 per cent per year (World Bank, 2014).
- Human activities such as urban development, industrialisation, commercial farming, logging and mining are responsible for much of this destruction.
- Valuable resources and minerals are in huge demand today and are used in the production of many of the luxury goods consumed by people, primarily in the developed world. Mobile phones are made from as many as 42 different minerals, including aluminium, copper and limestone. During manufacturing, a TV set requires 35 different minerals; a computer requires more than 30.

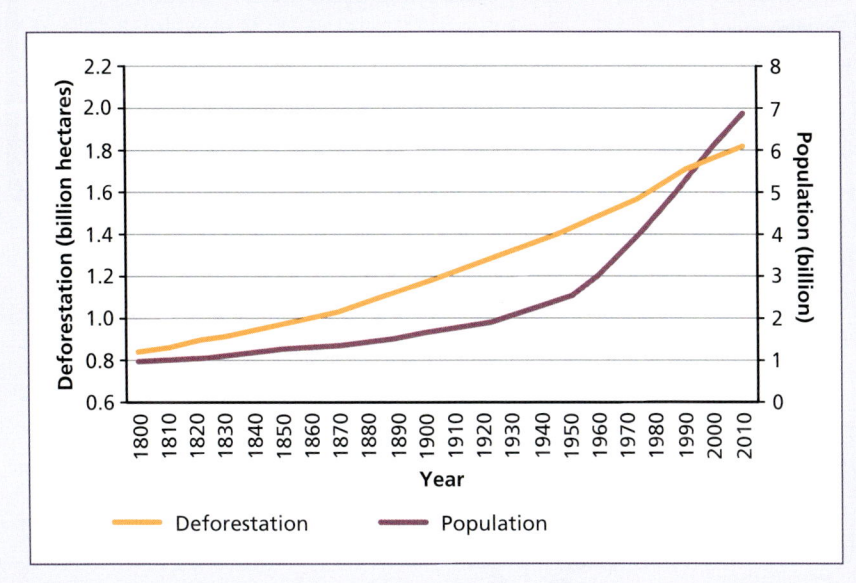

Fig. 10.14 World population and cumulative deforestation, 1800 to 2010

- **Deforestation** is taking place at an alarming rate. Trees are an important source of fresh water, as they contribute to the global water cycle via transpiration. The Amazon rainforest alone contains 20 per cent of the world's fresh water. Trees also play a vital role in consuming CO_2 and emitting clean oxygen. The Amazon rainforest has earned the nickname 'the lungs of the earth' because it produces over 20 per cent of the world's oxygen. Rainforests have been described as 'nature's medicine cabinet' because approximately 25 per cent of medicines, including over 120 prescription drugs, contain ingredients that are sourced directly from rainforest plants (World Wildlife Fund/World Wide Fund for Nature (WWF), 2016).

> **KEY TERM**
>
> **Deforestation** is the cutting down of trees and the permanent clearance of forests for alternative land uses, such as agriculture, industry or urban developments.

- Some 129 million hectares of forest – an area more than 15 times the size of the island of Ireland – has been lost since 1990 (FAO, 2015).
- Approximately 1.5 acres (an area the size of a football pitch) of rainforest is lost every second. If this rate of deforestation continues, there will be no rainforest left in just 40 years (WWF, 2016).

Overpopulation or Overconsumption?

- Some demographic experts claim that the current population of the world is unsustainable. They claim that the world is 'overpopulated'.

- Some commentators blame the high birth rates in the developing world for **overpopulation**. Others blame the high-consumption lifestyles of people in the developed world. David Satterthwaite, a senior fellow at the International Institute for Environment and Development in London, has stated: 'It is not the number of people on the planet that is the issue – but the number of **consumers** and the scale and nature of their consumption.' He supports the view famously put forward by Gandhi: 'The world has enough for everyone's need, but not enough for everyone's greed.'

KEY TERMS

Overpopulation occurs when the number of people in the world exceeds the world's carrying capacity; in other words, when there are not enough resources in the world (e.g. water, fertile land, food, energy) to sustain the world's population.

A **consumer** is a person who purchases goods and services for personal use.

Fig. 10.15 Overpopulation or high-consumption lifestyles?

QUESTIONS

1. Explain the following terms: 'lifestyle', 'population explosion', 'fossil fuels', 'climate change', 'carbon footprint', 'deforestation' and 'overpopulation'.

2. According to the research piece, where is most of the population growth taking place and why is this a cause for concern?

3. List **three** statistics that indicate that the current rate of consumption is unsustainable.

4. List the **three** most popular sources of energy used in 2015.

5. List the **five** countries that consumed the most energy in 2015.

6. Explain how the use of fossil fuels contributes to global warming.

7. Can you think of any clean/alternative sources of energy?

8. What is the current rate of rainforest deforestation?

9. Give **three** reasons why we should conserve what is left of the world's rainforests.

10. Explain how population growth affects the environment.

11. How reliable is the information contained in the above research piece? In your answer consider the following questions: Who produced the information contained in the research piece? List all the sources mentioned. For what purpose might these bodies have produced these statistics? Could they be biased?

ACTIVITY 10.2

In groups, create a carbon footprint poster. On your poster, draw the outline of a large foot and write two lists within it:

(a) All the things humans take from the earth (e.g. natural resources and minerals)

(b) All the human actions that are damaging the environment (e.g. waste, emissions).

Present and explain your poster to the other groups in your class.

SKILLS BOOK LINK 10.2

Go to page 168 of your Skills Book to complete Skill Task 10.2 on calculating your carbon footprint.

Unequal Development

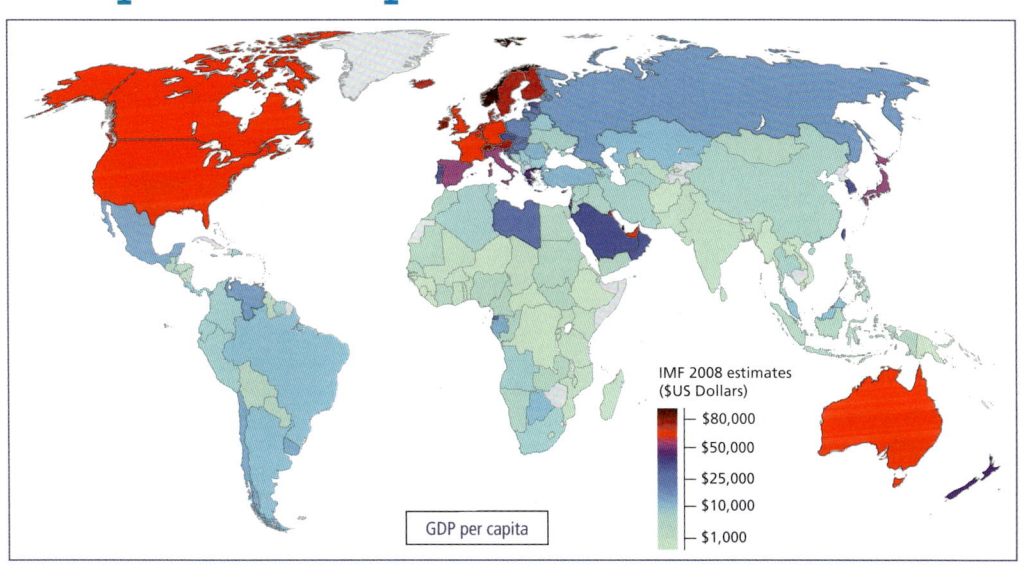

Fig. 10.16 Unequal development

Our model of development has also created and reinforced imbalances between and within our societies. Patterns of economic growth during the twentieth and twenty-first centuries (i.e. from agriculture, to manufacturing, to service and information exchange) have created and deepened global inequalities. Some countries have benefited more than others. Because of the model of development the world is following, the inequality gap between developing and developed countries is widening. In economic terms, the GDP of the richest country in 2015, Qatar, was 228 times that of the poorest, the Central African Republic. However, inequalities are not just economic. People living in developing countries face daily challenges in health and education, even in regions where economic growth has increased. The effects of climate change (e.g. droughts, floods) are experienced much more harshly in poorer nations and poorer communities.

ACTIVITY 10.3

Imagine the following scenario: the population of the world has been shrunk to the size of your class. Your class now represents the total world population.

Your teacher will call out a series of questions relating to the percentage/proportion of the world's population that have access to wealth, health, education and other standards of living. As a class, guess the correct answer to each question by arranging yourselves into representative proportions/groups.

WHAT THE RESEARCH SAYS!

INEQUALITY

Economic

- Since 2000, the poorest half of the world's population has received just 1 per cent of the increase in global wealth, while half of that increase has gone to the top 1 per cent (Oxfam, 2016).
- Since 1960, the wealth gap has grown between the US and the following regions by these percentages: Latin America (206 per cent), sub-Saharan Africa (207 per cent) and South Asia (196 per cent) (World Bank, 2016).
- 1 per cent of the world's population have more money than the remaining 99 per cent combined (Oxfam, 2016).
- The world's eight richest billionaires control the same wealth between them as the poorest half of the globe's population. Of the 62 richest people in the world, only 9 are women (Oxfam, 2017).

The top 1% controls over 50% of the world's wealth

Fig. 10.17 The wealth gap

Social

- In developing countries, children in the poorest 20 per cent of the population are up to three times more likely to die before their fifth birthday than children in the richest segment (UNICEF, 2013).
- 50 per cent of pregnant women in developing countries do not have access to proper maternity care. This results in approximately 300,000 deaths from childbirth each year (UNICEF, 2016).
- 88 per cent of all children and 60 per cent of all women living with HIV are in sub-Saharan Africa (UNAIDS, 2015).
- 795 million people – or one in nine people in the world – do not have enough to eat. Ninety-eight per cent of these people live in developing countries and 60 per cent are women (FAO, 2015).

Fig. 10.18 Inequality in the developing world: over 1 billion people live in slums similar to what is shown on the left of this photo

- Every year, consumers in rich countries waste almost as much food (222 million tonnes) as the entire net food production of sub-Saharan Africa (230 million tonnes) (FAO, 2016).
- 663 million people lack access to clean water and almost half of those live in sub-Saharan Africa (WHO, 2015).
- About 1.6 billion people live in substandard housing and 100 million are homeless, according to United Nations statistics (UN-Habitat, 2017).
- Today, a billion people – 32 per cent of the global urban population – live in urban slums (UN-Habitat, 2017).

Environmental

- While the poorest people live in areas most affected by climate change, the poorest half of the global population are contributing only 10 per cent of global carbon emissions. Meanwhile, the richest 1 per cent contribute up to 175 times that of the poorest 10 per cent (Oxfam, 2015).
- Approximately 95 per cent of deaths related to natural disasters in the 1990s happened in developing countries (WHO, 2015).
- Africa and South America had the highest net annual loss of forests in 2010–2015: 2.8 million and 2 million hectares respectively (FAO, 2015).

- The global average annual rate of natural resource depletion is 45 per cent. However, the rate is significantly higher in sub-Saharan Africa (88 per cent) and Latin America (57 per cent) (World Bank, 2014).

Technological

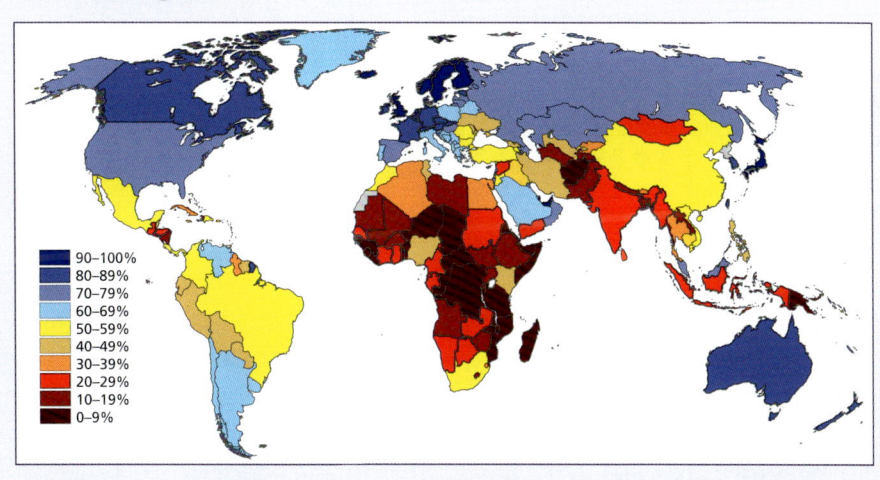

Fig. 10.19 Internet users in 2015 as a percentage of each country's population

- The Networked Readiness Index (NRI) measures the level of ICT penetration across 143 countries. NRI research shows that the global digital revolution has created new inequalities, with rich countries benefiting mainly. In 2015, 30 of the 31 sub-Saharan African countries were in the bottom half of the rankings. Mauritius was the only exception (World Economic Forum, 2015).

- Many parts of the developing world still have no access or limited access to the internet. In 2015 only 13 per cent of people living in the world's 48 least developed countries regularly used the internet. This compared to 80 per cent of people living in the EU (World Bank, 2015).

QUESTIONS

1. What number of the richest people in the world have the same wealth between them as the poorest half of the world's population?

2. Global economic inequality has increased in recent decades. Give **two** pieces of evidence from the research piece that support this view.

3. Which **two** groups are more likely to suffer from social inequality in the developing world?

4. What has been the environmental impact of development on the developing world?

5. In what ways can access to technology help to solve the developing world's socio-economic problems?

6. What are the strengths and weaknesses of the research piece?

RESEARCH ASSIGNMENT 10.1

Compare and contrast Ireland with one named country in the Global South (developing world), in relation to the following indicators of development:

- Life expectancy
- Infant mortality rate
- Adult literacy levels
- Expected years of schooling
- Gross domestic product.

The relevant information can be found in the UN Human Development Reports, accessible at: https://educateplus.ie/go/human-data

Measuring Inequality

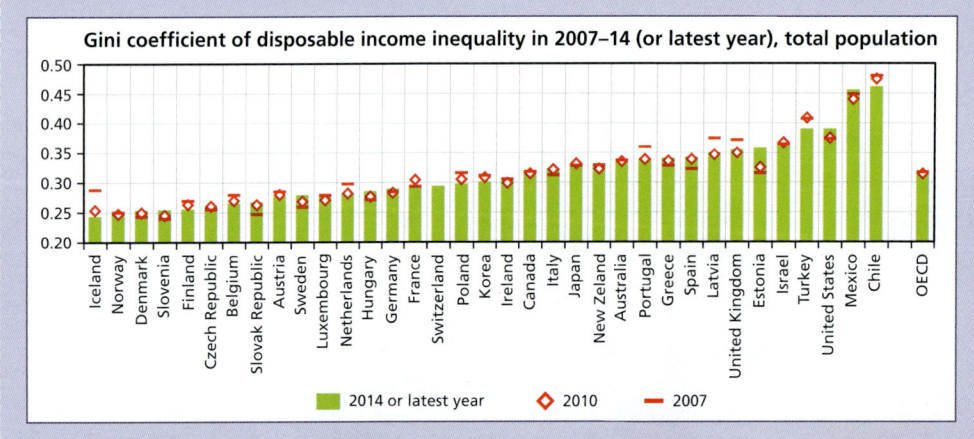

Fig. 10.20 The Gini coefficient

Gini coefficient of disposable income inequality in 2007–14 (or latest year), total population

Legend: 2014 or latest year | ◇ 2010 | — 2007

The **Gini coefficient** is a tool used to measure inequality within a country or region. It is commonly used to measure inequality of income, wealth or consumption. A value of 0 represents absolute equality and a value of 100 absolute inequality. In recent years, the Gini coefficient has also been used by researchers to measure inequalities in the areas of health and education.

In November 2016, the OECD published data on how the global economic recovery had impacted inequality across different countries. Fig. 10.20 represents the Gini coefficients per country in 2007, 2010 and 2014.

QUESTIONS

Examine Fig. 10.20 and answer the following questions.

1. Name the **three** countries with the highest levels of income inequality in 2010.
2. Name the **three** countries with the lowest levels of income inequality in 2007.
3. Which country has experienced the greatest decline in income inequality since 2007?
4. In which country has income inequality increased the most since 2007?
5. How does Ireland fare in income inequality when compared to the OECD average?

Theories of Development

There is a wide variety of theories and explanations of the causes of global poverty and what leads to development.

Modernisation Theory

Since the end of World War II, the world has struggled to address poverty in the so-called developing countries. Newly independent countries, the UN and industrialised countries promoted a model based on **modernisation theory**. Developing countries were encouraged to follow the path of developed countries and meet a 'western' standard of development. Investment in the form of aid was given to these countries to develop infrastructure and industry, expand education and transfer technology in order to grow their economies.

KEY TERMS

Gini coefficient is a tool used to measure inequality (e.g. of income, wealth or consumption) within a country or region.

Modernisation theory claims that developing countries must adopt a western, capitalist culture and will need more money and western technology in order to fully develop.

Complete your next Reflective Journal entry (page 42)

KEY THINKERS

MODERNISATION THEORY

Modernisation theory is based on the view that to develop means to become 'modern'. According to this theory, countries are underdeveloped because their traditional value systems and institutions hinder the development or modernisation process. These countries will become modern by adopting western cultural values and social institutions.

Walt Whitman Rostow

In 1960, American economist Walt Whitman Rostow suggested that development is an evolutionary process. He argued that countries progress up a development ladder of five stages.

1. Undeveloped societies are 'traditional societies' characterised by institutions such as families, tribes and clans. Roles are assigned (i.e. people are born into them) rather than achieved on merit. The economy is based on agriculture.
2. In the 'preconditions for take-off' stage, money and technology from the west are introduced to these societies in the form of capital investment by western companies and official development aid (ODA) by western governments.
3. The 'take-off stage' is the most important. In this stage, the traditional attitudes and values that have hindered development (e.g. witchcraft, communal values) are replaced by western ideals that support capitalism. These western concepts include: the idea that roles in society are based on merit and achievement (skills and ability) rather than tradition, and the erosion of 'communal' ties (clan, tribe) as people become defined by the capitalist model as workers.
4. The 'drive to maturity stage' is marked by the export of manufactured goods to the west. The country now joins the international trading system.
5. Development is achieved in the final stage – 'the age of high mass consumption'. In this stage, traditional societies mirror western industrial societies: most citizens live in urban rather than rural areas, and enjoy a higher standard of living. Life expectancy has increased and citizens have access to free education and adequate healthcare.

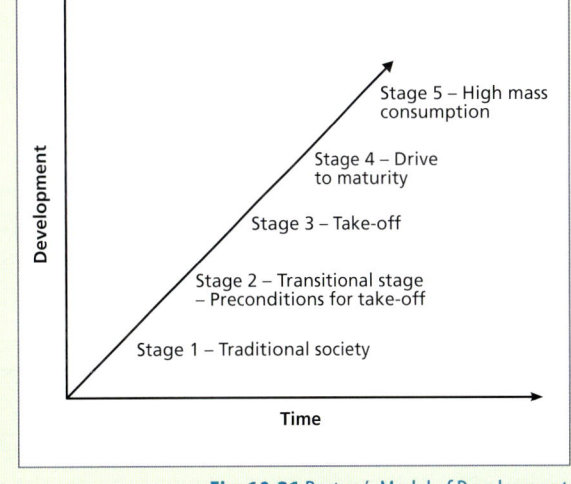

Fig. 10.21 Rostow's Model of Development

QUESTIONS

1. According to Rostow, what are the main characteristics of 'traditional societies'?
2. Rostow claims that these characteristics hinder development. In your opinion, why might this be so?
3. Can you think of any other specific aspects of non-western cultures that act as barriers to economic development?
4. In the 'take-off stage', what kinds of western values contribute to the development of prosperous economies?
5. In your opinion, do all countries have to adopt western ideals to develop fully? Can you think of any developed or rapidly developing countries that have retained their traditional societal values?
6. Do you agree with modernisation theory? Give reasons to support your answer.
7. Is modernisation theory based on a right-wing or left-wing perspective? Give reasons for your answer.

GLOBAL DEVELOPMENT   387

CASE STUDY 1: Modernisation Theory and Rwanda: A Success Story?

Modernisation theory has heavily influenced global development and aid interventions, as well as the national policies of developing countries across Africa, Asia and Latin America. Have these interventions been a success in ending poverty and underdevelopment? Many international development experts describe Rwanda as a modern success story. Two decades after a genocide claimed the lives of over 800,000 people, Rwanda's economy has grown significantly and is performing well in key social sectors.

See page 356 for more information on the Rwandan genocide.

Government Policies

President Paul Kagame, who has been in power since 2000, has followed a development pathway based on modernisation. Government policies are aimed at transforming Rwanda's low-income, agriculture-based economy. The goals include increasing agricultural productivity, tourism, technological growth and heavy investments in infrastructure. In 2015, financial services and manufacturing received the largest share of foreign direct investment (FDI): 25 per cent and 23 per cent respectively. ICT was the fourth largest FDI sector at 9 per cent.

Agriculture is the main economic activity for the people of Rwanda. It provides employment to approximately 86 per cent of the total population; 80% of these workers are women. One of Rwanda's main agricultural policies is the Crop Intensification Programme (CIP). It began in 2007 and has focused on modernising the agricultural practices of small-scale farmers. Through the programme, farmers can access fertilisers and technical training on modern farming techniques. The CIP has increased agricultural production and exports of tea and coffee. However, Rwanda's coffee exports are still primarily made up of unprocessed green (unroasted) coffee, which provides limited income potential. In 2015, the average selling price of a container of green beans was US$8,000, while the average selling price of a container of roasted, ground and packaged coffee was 12 times that figure.

Fig. 10.22 Modern infrastructure under construction in Rwanda

Fig. 10.23 Paul Kagame, President of Rwanda, on a tour of a redeveloped business district in Rwanda's capital, Kigali

Development Progress

Two decades after the Rwandan genocide, the country has achieved significant progress in economic growth as well as key social sectors of health and education:

- Rwanda's GDP per capita more than tripled from US$202 in 1994 to US$690 in 2015.
- Between 2001 and 2015, Rwanda experienced an average annual economic growth rate of 8 per cent.
- The child mortality rate was reduced from 151 per 1,000 live births in 1990 to 55 per 1,000 in 2012.

CASE STUDY: Modernisation Theory and Rwanda: A Success Story?

- Rwanda has the highest primary school enrolment rates in Africa: 97 per cent in 2012. Furthermore, girls and boys are benefiting equally: 98 per cent and 95 per cent respectively are enrolled in primary school.
- The school completion rate increased from 53 per cent in 2008 to 73 per cent in 2012.
- Rwanda has the highest percentage of female parliamentarians. The global average is 22 per cent; in Rwanda, it is almost 64 per cent.

Economic Growth Without Rights

Despite impressive economic growth and development, Rwanda's progress has not been without its critics. Amnesty International (among others) have raised concerns over President Kagame's politically repressive form of rule, arguing that 'journalists, human rights defenders and members of the opposition face a repressive environment'. When President Kagame won the election in 2010, three of the major opposition parties were prohibited from participating and some of the leaders were jailed. Rwanda's economy is still heavily dependent on foreign aid. It is estimated that 30–40 per cent of the national budget is still supported through foreign aid.

Fig. 10.24 Does modernisation produce benefits for all?

Economic growth has not benefited every citizen. Although poverty has been reduced, an estimated 63 per cent of Rwandans continue to live on less than US$1.25 a day and 82 per cent on less than US$2. Rwanda had a Gini coefficient of 50.8 when it was last measured in 2011. The top 10 per cent of the population gained 43 per cent of the country's income.

QUESTIONS

1. What specific strategies did the Rwandan government put in place which would appear to follow the 'modernisation' theory of development?
2. Give **three** pieces of evidence that illustrate the success of government policy under President Kagame.
3. What are the main criticisms regarding Rwanda's model of development?

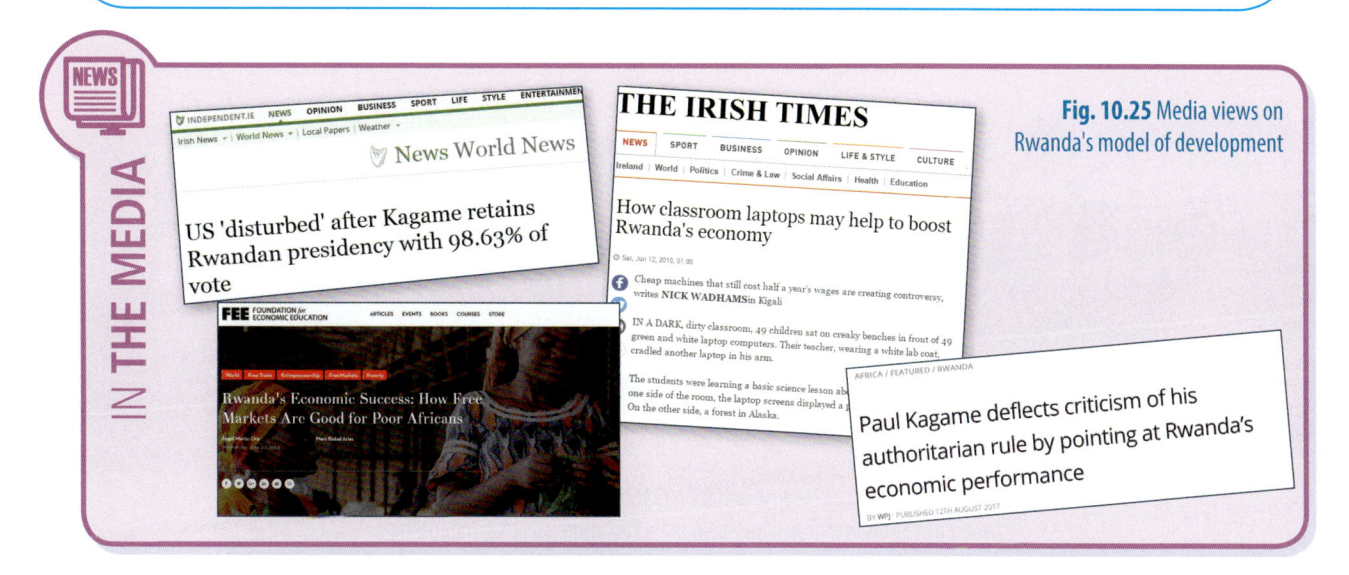

Fig. 10.25 Media views on Rwanda's model of development

GLOBAL DEVELOPMENT 389

ACTIVITY 10.4

Examine how the economic development of Ireland since the 1950s can be used to support modernisation theory. Your teacher will give your group an article to read concerning the economic development of Ireland since independence. Examine the article and take note of any evidence that supports modernisation theory. Write a summary of the evidence and present it to another group in your class.

RESEARCH ASSIGNMENT 10.2

Write a report on how modernisation theory can be used to explain the economic development of one named country of your choice. Include the following in your report:

- Name of the country
- List of sources consulted
- Brief explanation of modernisation theory
- Summary of the main findings and conclusions drawn.

See **RESEARCH TIPS** on page 33.

Women and Development

Modernisation theory states that industrialisation leads to economic growth, which in turn results in benefits for the entire population. However, in the 1970s it became evident that not only had economic growth failed to resolve poverty and inequality in many regions, it had also led to particular impacts for women. Industrialisation in developing countries brought significant changes to society. It shifted employment from an agricultural to a manufacturing base, and from rural to urban centres. It created a division of labour based on gender. In particular, women became a cheap source of labour for multinational corporations. It remains the case today that women are more likely than men to be employed in the informal, lower-paying sectors. Women provide the main supply of labour on assembly lines and in factories, particularly in Asia. Before industrialisation, many societies in developing countries were rural and based on agriculture. Women played a central role in cultivating the land, providing food for their families, and protecting the natural environment. Industrialisation affected these societies in two ways. First, many men and women were forced to migrate to urban centres to seek employment opportunities in the industrial sector. Second, with the commercialisation of agriculture, women farmers lost access to land and resources and were forced to cultivate smaller plots of less profitable crops. In many societies, women remain the primary caregivers in the home. This means that women's share of work is double that of men.

Fig. 10.26 Because of industrialisation in the developing world, more women are now working in low-paid manufacturing jobs than in farming

Women and Economic Development

Globally, women are paid less than men. Women in most countries earn on average only 60–75 per cent of men's wages. Women are more likely to be wage workers (rather than business owners) and unpaid family workers.

- Women are more likely than men to work in informal employment and without a proper contract. In South Asia, over 80 per cent of women in non-agricultural jobs are in informal employment; this figure is 74 per cent in sub-Saharan Africa, and 54 per cent in Latin America and the Caribbean.

- More women than men work in vulnerable, low-paid or undervalued jobs. As of 2013, 49.1 per cent of the world's working women were in vulnerable employment, often unprotected by labour legislation. This figure is 46.9 per cent for men.

- Women make up an average of 43 per cent of the agricultural labour force in developing countries. In these regions, women produce 60–80 per cent of the food but less than 20 per cent of landowners are women.

- Women farmers have limited access to important agricultural inputs, such as seeds and credit loans.

- Commercialisation of agriculture in developing countries has worsened the situation of women because men have gained control of the cash crops and the money generated from them.

Fig. 10.27 Women working at a Nike assembly line in Ho Chi Minh City in 2005

Global average, annual earnings

2006 — $6,000 / $11,000

2015 — $11,000 / $21,000

Fig. 10.28 Gender pay gap

QUESTIONS

1. Which region of the world has the highest percentage of women employed in the informal sector?
2. What is the informal sector?
3. In your opinion, why do women face difficulties in accessing loans in some countries?
4. List **three** statistics that support the view that women suffer from economic inequality.

GLOBAL DEVELOPMENT 391

WHAT THE RESEARCH SAYS!

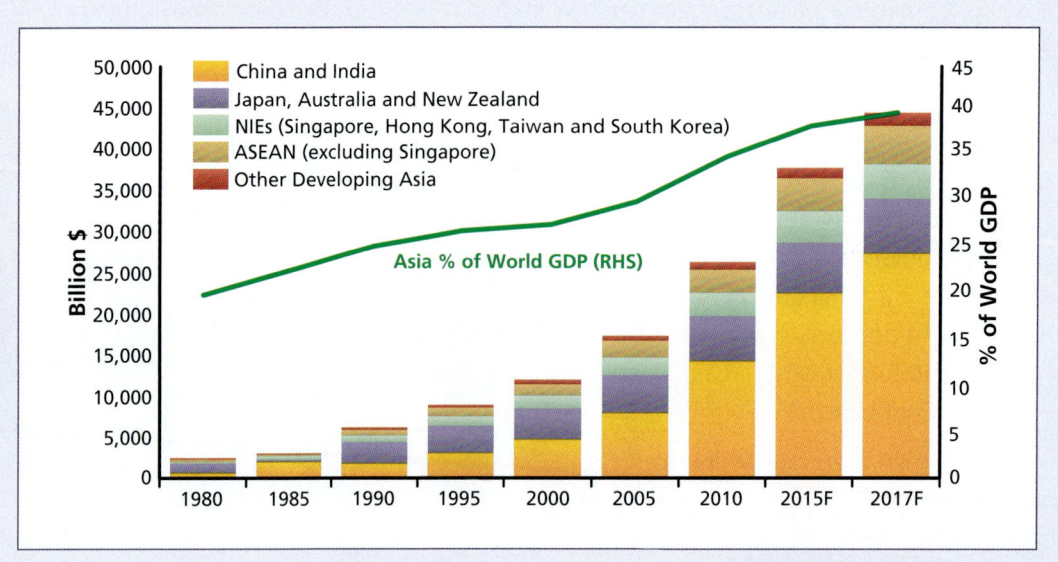

Fig. 10.29 Asian economic growth

OXFAM RESEARCH: ASIA'S ECONOMIC SUCCESS AT THE EXPENSE OF WOMEN

The Asia region is often cited as an economic success. Since the 1990s, economic growth has advanced many countries from low- to middle-income status. However, as elsewhere in the world, economic growth has not benefited everyone equally. Inequality in income and in social services (e.g. health and education) is a feature of many Asian countries. Women have been particularly affected by Asia's economic growth model, which has been heavily based on industrialisation. Asia has become a popular destination for multinational corporations in the food, clothing and electronics industries. Women and children provide the main source of labour in many of Asia's factories.

Oxfam Report

In 2016 Oxfam published a report about the impact of Asia's economic model on women. The report highlighted several negative consequences for women:

- To compete in the global market, many Asian countries have driven down wages and working conditions, particularly in sectors that employ women.
- Women's wages in the Asia region amount to just 70–90 per cent of men's wages.
- Many women are forced to work long hours in unsafe conditions and are denied benefits such as sick pay. Women are often fired if they become pregnant.
- Women in Asia work a 'double day'. On average, women in Asia do two and a half times more unpaid care work than men (e.g. cooking, cleaning, washing clothes, and caring for children and elderly family members).

Clothing Industry in Myanmar

The clothing industry in Myanmar is growing, as more and more international brands, including GAP, H&M, Primark and Adidas, use factories there. There are almost 300 clothing factories in Myanmar. Altogether the workforce in these factories is nearly 300,000 people, most of whom (90 per cent) are young women.

According to a survey of workers conducted by Oxfam in 2015, working conditions are poor. Workers are forced to work up to 11 hours a day, six days a week in dangerous conditions. They receive very low wages. More than one in three workers reported that they had been injured at work. The exits of factory buildings are often locked, and many workers are afraid of fires. In some factories, there are restrictions on the use of toilets. Workers face verbal abuse from managers who pressure them to work faster. Almost one in four workers reported doing forced overtime. Several workers reported doing unpaid overtime. Despite being legally entitled to paid sick leave, three out of four workers (76 per cent) reported having their pay cut if they are sick and miss a day of work.

Fig. 10.30 Female workers in Myanmar's clothing industry

WHAT THE RESEARCH SAYS!

ACTIONAID RESEARCH: SUGARCANE PLANTATION PROJECT, TANZANIA

Rural communities in the Bagamoyo district on the northern coast of Tanzania are opposing a sugarcane plantation project planned by EcoEnergy, a Swedish-owned company. The project involves the lease of 20,000 hectares of land for the next 99 years. The land is currently home to smallholder farming communities. EcoEnergy's plan to develop the sugarcane plantation is part of the New Alliance for Food Security and Nutrition, the G8's African agriculture initiative. The New Alliance is a set of agreements that give large corporations a key role in agricultural development in Africa. Under the agreement, African governments give incentives to agribusiness, adopt a 'high-tech' industrial model for agriculture, and increase corporate access to seeds, land, water, labour and markets. In Tanzania, the New Alliance is funded by the European Union and the British, French, German, Japanese, Russian and

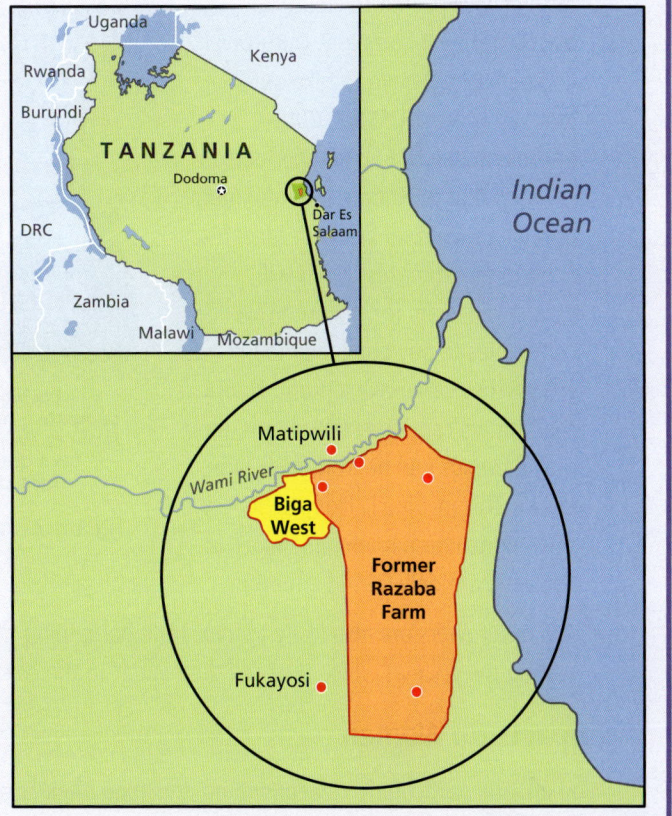

Fig. 10.31 Tanzania

GLOBAL DEVELOPMENT   393

US governments. EcoEnergy wants to establish an 'outgrower programme' in which 1,500 smallholder farmers will use village land to form 25–35 'block farms'. An average of 50 farmers per block farm will plant sugarcane and supply sugar to the company at an agreed price. In 2014, ActionAid conducted research on the impact of the project on the local affected communities through interviews and focus group discussions with 153 people, including local farmers, local government and EcoEnergy. The research highlighted important findings.

- While EcoEnergy has conducted consultations with the communities, people have not been offered the choice of whether or not to be resettled. They have been offered only the choice of whether to receive compensation in cash or land for being resettled. EcoEnergy denies these claims.

Fig. 10.32 Ally Ame and his wife, Pili Hassan Musa, in their field of cassava in Tanzania

- Each group of 50 smallholder farmers is expected to create its own outgrower company. Outgrower companies will have to take out loans of at least US$800,000 – approximately US$16,000 per person – a sum that is 30 times the minimum annual agricultural salary in Tanzania. EcoEnergy estimates that it will take seven years for the outgrower companies to pay back their loan before they can make a profit. Until the farmers can repay their loans, their only earnings will be from their farm labour. This income is likely to be low, since agricultural minimum wages in Tanzania are only US$44 a month.

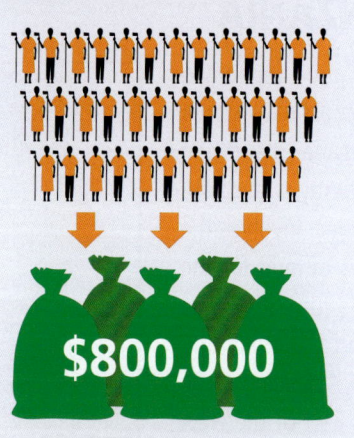

Each outgrower company - approximately 50 farmers - will be required to take out a loan of at least US$800,000.

Each farmer would be required to take out the equivalent of US$16,000.

Fig. 10.33 EcoEnergy's outgrower programme will place a significant debt burden on Tanzanian farmers

- The outgrowers are also likely to have little bargaining power in obtaining loans from the banks or in setting the price at which they sell their sugar to the company.

Impacts on Women

Women are particularly dependent on the land they use; however, women generally have less secure ownership and access to land. They are less involved in decision-making at different levels. The EcoEnergy project involves particular risks for women:

- In Bagamoyo district, women are the main suppliers of food for their families. When women face difficulties with access to land and the ability to farm, this results in food insecurity for the entire community. Women who grow food in this area generally focus on long-term (or perennial) crops (e.g. fruits, cashew nuts). However, since it has been announced that families may be relocated and their land given away for the EcoEnergy project, women in the area are reluctant to invest in crops in case they are forced to relocate.
- Previous research highlights that the outgrower model can increase inequality between men and women. A 2008 study from the Food and Agriculture Organization of the United Nations (FAO) found that, under a similar outgrower project by EcoEnergy in Swaziland, 'women's income-generating potential has been considerably reduced compared with that of men'. This happened because most of the men had claimed back land that was previously allocated to their wives. A further study carried out by the World Bank reviewed 24 agricultural investment projects in developing countries. It found that 'virtually all outgrowers were men' because 'only 1.5 per cent of outgrowers were women'.

ActionAid Recommendations

The ActionAid report made recommendations for governments and the EcoEnergy company.

The government of Tanzania should:

- Conduct a new process of consultations that respect the standard of free, prior and informed consent, with particular attention to women's participation and rights.
- Promote land management systems and models that respect the legitimate land rights of users, in particular women.

Governments supporting the New Alliance agreement should:

- Stop support for the New Alliance and replace it with initiatives that genuinely support small-scale food producers and advance sustainable agriculture.

QUESTIONS

1. Which **two** groups make up the main source of workers in Asian factories?
2. How has industrialisation in Asia had a negative impact on women?
3. Describe the typical working conditions of women working in Myanmar's clothing industry.
4. Explain the rationale and objectives behind EcoEnergy's sugarcane plantation project.
5. In your opinion, do the cases highlighted in the two research studies support modernisation theory?
6. According to the research conducted by ActionAid, how will the plantation impact on the local community?
7. In what ways has the project put women at risk?

Dependency Theory

In the 1960s and 1970s, modernisation theory received criticism from development theorists. Modernisation theory was viewed as a western-centric model that pushed a 'one size fits all' approach to development. The model is based on how European countries and the US have developed: it ignores the importance of different cultural interpretations of development. The biggest criticism came from Marxism. **Dependency theory** was offered as an alternative. Supporters of dependency theory argue that modernisation theory fails to acknowledge the active role of developed countries (the west) in causing global poverty and underdevelopment in poorer nations.

KEY TERMS

Dependency theory is a critique of modernisation theory. It claims that the west is responsible for the underdevelopment of developing countries by imposing colonialism, neocolonialism and an unfair global trading system.

Colonialism is the practice of acquiring full or partial political control over another country by occupying it with settlers and exploiting it economically. Several European countries adopted this policy and created colonies in Africa and other developing regions of the world from the sixteenth century onwards. Colonialism is sometimes referred to as *imperialism*.

KEY THINKERS

DEPENDENCY THEORY

Dependency theory is a critique of modernisation theory from a Marxist perspective. While modernisation theory blamed the traditional values and lack of modern knowledge and technology of developing countries for their underdevelopment, dependency theory places responsibility with the west. Supporters of dependency theory point to centuries of western exploitation of people and resources in Latin America, Asia and Africa. The west keeps developing countries in a state of poverty because this serves the economic and political interests of the west.

Andre Gunder Frank

One of the leading dependency theorists, Andre Gunder Frank, argues that the world can be viewed as a system that is divided between 'core nations' (developed countries, such as the US and UK) and 'peripheral nations' (developing nations). The core nations seek to maintain peripheral nations in a state of dependency because the core nations require cheap labour and raw materials. Frank based his theory on a historical examination of the relationship between core and peripheral nations from the period of slavery and colonialism up to the modern era of international trade and aid systems.

SLAVERY AND COLONIALISM

Andre Gunder Frank argues that the west gained a development advantage during **colonialism**, as it used the slave trade and exploitation of natural resources in developing countries to fuel the industrialisation of its societies. Colonial policies created poverty in developing nations. For example, land that was traditionally used to meet the food needs of the local population was confiscated for the production of cash crops to be exported to the colonial powers.

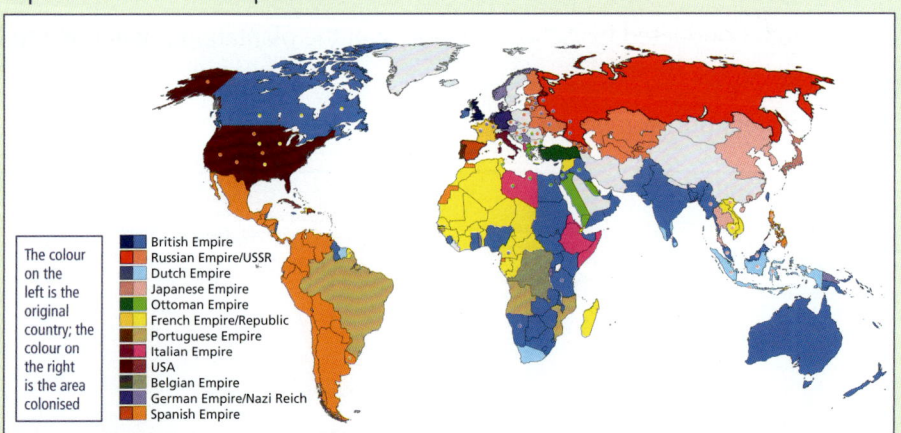

Fig. 10.34 Former colonial empires of the world during the era of imperialism

KEY THINKERS

NEOCOLONIALISM: TRADE, AID AND DEBT

Frank argued that new forms of colonialism – which he termed **neocolonialism** – have ensured that developing nations remain dependent on the west. Neocolonialism, in the form of MNCs and the international trade and aid systems, is responsible for the continued underdevelopment of some nations. The modern trade system has been shaped by the colonial legacy, with rules that favour developed countries. For example, companies from the developing world that export finished products are often unable to sell their products to wealthy markets in the developed world because countries in the developed world impose hefty **tariff** barriers. The EU and the US impose import tariffs on several products that are produced outside their borders.

At the same time, many large MNCs from the developed world outsource their manufacturing to developing nations to exploit the cheaper sources of labour and raw materials offered there. Out of sheer desperation for employment, developing countries are forced to accept the poor pay and conditions that these MNCs offer.

Profit-driven MNCs also attempt to create consumer markets in developing countries. This reduces the household income available to address bigger social issues, such as poverty, education and training.

In addition to this, the aid that is given to a developing country often comes with conditions attached: the donor country (the country providing the aid) may specify that the money must be spent on purchasing materials or services from the donor country. This is known as **tied aid**. An example of this was when the British government gave £234 million in aid towards the construction of a HEP dam in Malaysia in 1991 on the condition that the Malaysian government committed to an arms trade deal worth over £1 billion to the UK. In 2015, €1.1 billion of the EU's aid to developing countries was tied aid (CONCORD Aid Watch, 2016). The US ties more of its aid than any other donor in the world. The US provides roughly half of food aid globally at an estimated annual cost of US$2 billion. However, unlike many other major donors, virtually all American food

Fig. 10.35 The EU imposes trade barriers to protect its domestic manufacturers from having to compete with cheaper produce from developing countries

KEY TERMS

Neocolonialism refers to the modern-day practice of using capitalism, globalisation and cultural imperialism (the spread of ideas and values) to influence another country in lieu of direct military control. Left-wing critics argue that the US and other western powers are engaged in a neocolonial conquest of the rest of the world today.

A **tariff** is a tax or duty that must be paid on a good that is either being imported into or exported out of a country. Governments usually impose import tariffs to protect their local producers from foreign competition. For example, the EU imposes tariffs on certain agricultural imports to protect European farmers from competing with the cheaper prices of foreign agricultural produce when selling to the European market.

Tied aid refers to aid granted to developing countries on the condition that goods and services for the aid-financed projects are purchased directly from the donor country or from companies/countries decided by the country donating the aid.

KEY THINKERS

aid is 'tied' and must be bought from US suppliers and transported on US ships – even if there are cheaper alternative sources of food available in the developing countries to which the food is being sent. In effect, US aid is spent on supporting US farmers at the expense of poor farmers struggling to sell their produce in the developing world. In this way, tied aid ensures that poorer countries remain reliant on developed countries.

Although aid dependency has reduced in some developing countries in recent times, debt repayments still account for a significant portion of the national budgets of many developing countries. Since the global financial crisis of 2008, there has been a significant increase in lending from global institutions (e.g. IMF) and private investors (e.g. Credit Suisse bank) to the poorest countries. Annual lending to the governments of low-income countries has trebled, from US$6.1 billion in 2007 to US$20.5 billion by 2014. In October 2016 the World Bank and the IMF assessed 67 low- and middle-income countries in terms of repayment risks. Of the 67 countries assessed, 17 were at high risk of not being able to pay their debts, 34 were at medium risk, and some countries (e.g. Mozambique) were unable to make repayments.

In addition to repayments, some developing countries that take out loans are forced to implement structural adjustment policies attached to the loans. For example, the IMF often insists on the privatisation of valuable national assets and state resources, as well as the abolition of protectionist policies and tariffs that protect local farmers or industry. This puts local businesses at a disadvantage: they cannot compete with the large western-dominated funds and the MNCs that are now free to buy up assets in the developing country and flood the market with goods and services from the developed world.

QUESTIONS

1. What is dependency theory? Explain what the theory states. Do you agree with it?
2. Explain the different ways in which 'core nations' have gained an unfair advantage over 'peripheral nations' in the past.
3. What does the term 'neocolonialism' refer to?
4. How do modern-day international trade rules and the aid system exploit poorer countries and keep them dependent on wealthier countries? Refer to the examples given in the key thinkers box above.
5. How does debt contribute to the dependency of the developing world on the developed world?

ACTIVITY 10.5

Your teacher will assign your group the role of a country in a 'trading game'. You will manufacture and trade goods based on rules set by your teacher. The object of the game is to make as much money as possible for your country.

Case Study 2: Dependency Theory and Trade

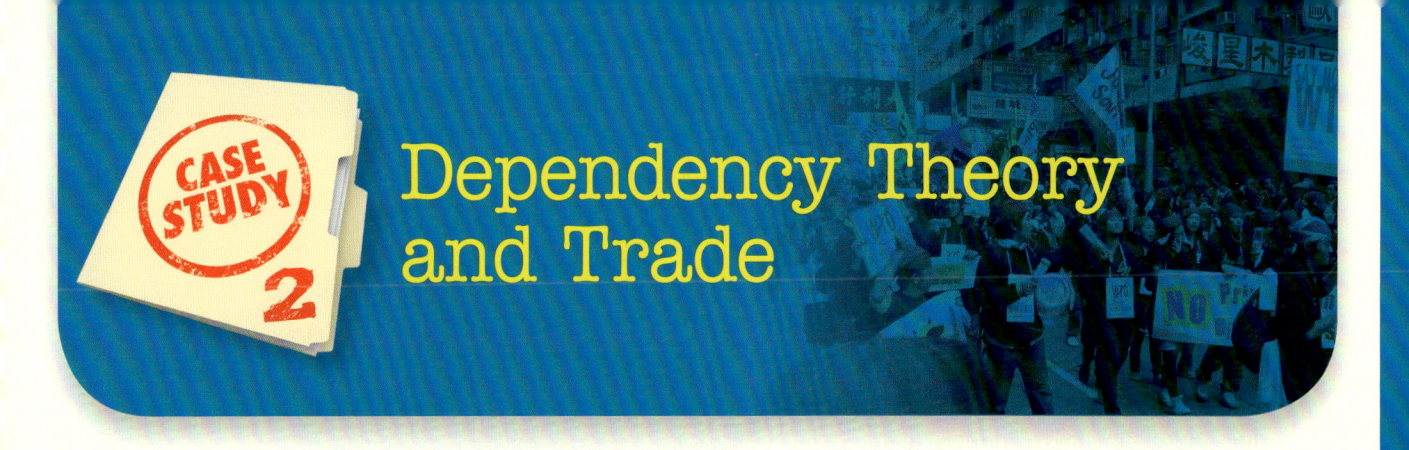

The international trade system is extremely unfair. The division of labour between developed and developing countries, and the rules for trading, place developing countries at a significant disadvantage.

Raw Materials

The economies of many developing countries are primarily dependent on the export of raw materials, such as crops and minerals in an unprocessed state (e.g. cocoa, coffee beans, cotton, iron ore, diamonds) to developed countries. Buyers in the developed world (mainly large **processors** and MNCs) keep the price for these unprocessed raw materials very low by bulk-buying and setting a low market price. As a result, the growers and producers of raw materials in the developing world are vulnerable to price changes in the international market. For example, cocoa prices dropped by 50 per cent between 1980 and 2012. This makes it difficult for developing countries that are dependent on one or two raw materials to plan and develop their economies.

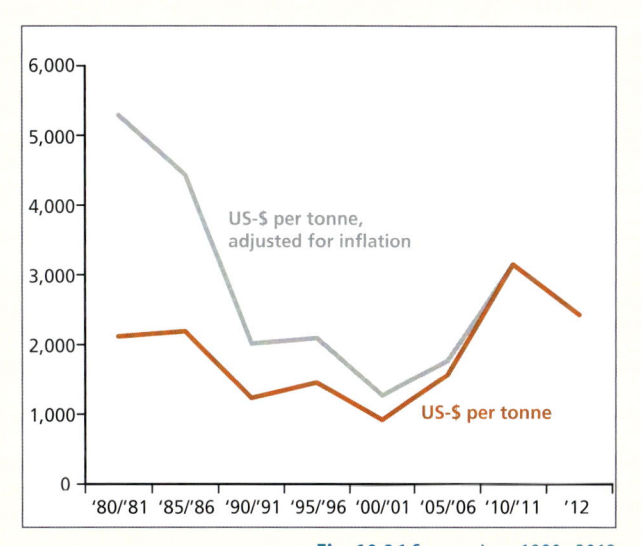

Fig. 10.36 Cocoa prices, 1980–2012

KEY TERM

A **processor** is a business engaged in processing agricultural products and preparing them for sale to the market.

Value Chain

The value chain of a product refers to its full 'life cycle': from sourcing the raw materials (e.g. cotton, cocoa), to production (e.g. textile industry or chocolate manufacturing), to consumption (e.g. clothing, chocolate). The item increases in value as it moves from source to consumption. Because of this, countries that are not involved in the production or consumption phases lose out. Unfortunately, most developing countries export unprocessed raw materials (e.g. cocoa) for a cheap price to the developed world.

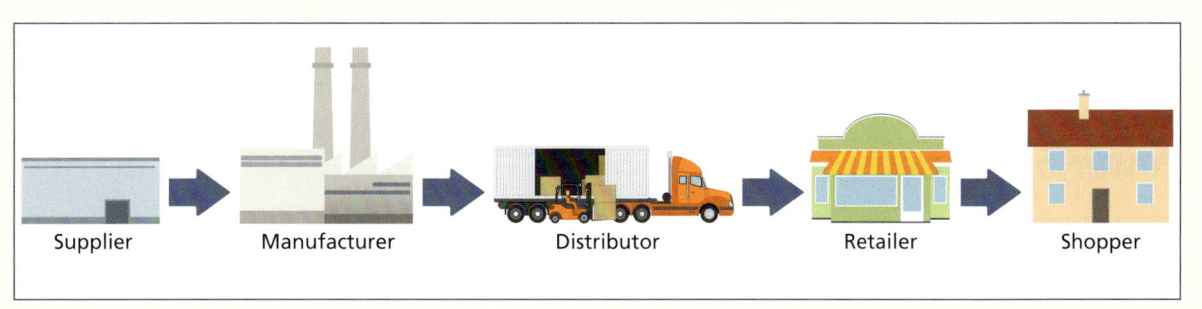

Supplier → Manufacturer → Distributor → Retailer → Shopper

Fig. 10.37 Value chain

GLOBAL DEVELOPMENT

CASE STUDY: Dependency Theory and Trade

Fig. 10.38 Share (%) in the value chain of chocolate production (Source: Cocoa Barometer, 2015).

- Chocolate manufacturer: 35.2%
- Retailer: 44.2%
- Processors and grinders: 7.6%
- Cocoa farmers (1980; 165): 2.1%
- Transportation and traders: 6.6%
- Taxes/Marketing board: 4.3%

The developed world processes these raw materials into more complex value-added finished products (e.g. chocolate) and often exports these products back to the same countries were the raw ingredients were initially sourced – but at a much higher price. While the value of chocolate has increased since the 1980s, the world market price for cocoa has halved. On average, cocoa farmers receive only 6 per cent of the price that we pay for a chocolate bar. Meanwhile, the chocolate manufacturer receives 35 per cent and the **retailer** receives 44 per cent.

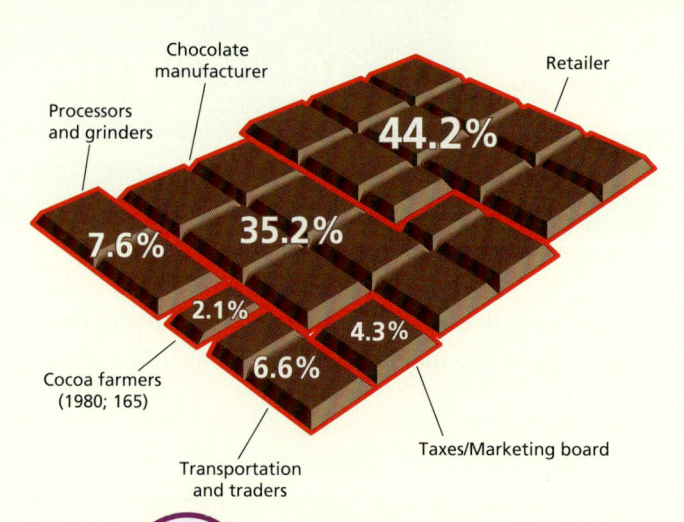

> **KEY TERM**
>
> A **retailer** is a person or business who sells goods to the public in relatively small quantities for personal consumption, rather than for resale.

Unfair Trading Rules

International trade has the potential to lift many poorer countries out of poverty. However, the rules are heavily stacked in favour of rich countries and companies. International trade is estimated to be US$ 10 million per minute, but poor countries benefit from only 0.4 per cent of this. The World Trade Organization is the forum where international trade rules are set. In 1994 the Global Agreement on Agriculture was finalised at the WTO. This agreement put a cap (limit) on the amount by which a country could support (subsidise) its domestic agricultural sector and exports. This was unfair for developing countries because, at that time, it was mainly developed countries that subsidised their agriculture sectors. Developing countries were either too poor or were not allowed to subsidise their agriculture because of the conditions in loans they had taken from the IMF and the World Bank. Today, developing countries must maintain the 1994 subsidy levels, which means that these countries cannot compete with developed countries for food and other exports. The global trade rules also prevent poorer countries from raising import taxes (tariffs) that would protect their domestic producers from foreign competition.

The Economic Partnership Agreements (EPAs) are trade agreements between the EU and countries in Africa, the Pacific and the Caribbean (ACP countries). Many of the EPAs contain conditions that disadvantage poorer countries, such as opening their markets to European imports and removing tariffs that protect producers in developing countries. In the past, up to 80 per cent of African products have been excluded from protection measures. Poorer countries are unable to compete with European products and companies. They cannot develop their own industries or create jobs, and so they cannot lift themselves out of poverty.

Power of MNCs

Powerful MNCs dominate world trade. Over 100,000 MNCs account for 70 per cent of international trade. The top 200 companies alone have a 28 per cent share of global trade. Apple is the world's most valuable company and it has more money than the individual GDPs of almost two-thirds of the world's countries. MNCs hold much power to influence governments to provide them with favourable trading

CASE STUDY: Dependency Theory and Trade

and operating conditions. For example, labour and environmental laws are often designed in a way that puts the interests of MNCs ahead of the interests of citizens and society.

Tax Justice

Many countries are pressured to lower taxes to entice MNCs in the hope of creating jobs and employment opportunities. This removes a potential source of much-needed income. Developing countries lose out because of tax avoidance. According to the UN, developing countries lose US$ 100 billion a year because of tax avoidance.

Fig. 10.39 Demonstration against unfair trade

QUESTIONS

1. What is a raw material? Give **three** examples of raw materials that come from the developing world.
2. Explain the term 'value chain'.
3. Which is the least valuable stage in the value chain?
4. Which **two** stages of the value chain are most valuable?
5. On which stage of the value chain are the economies of developing countries primarily based?
6. Explain how world trade is unfair and puts developing countries at a disadvantage. Refer to the chocolate trade in your answer.
7. Explain how organisations such as the World Trade Organization and the IMF contribute to unfair trade.
8. Ireland's corporation tax of 12.5 per cent has come in for criticism recently by the European Commission.
   (a) Give **one** advantage and **one** disadvantage of this low tax rate for Ireland.
   (b) How might Ireland's corporation tax rate have a negative impact on other countries in the world?

IN THE MEDIA

Fig. 10.40 Media views on unfair trade

Complete your next Reflective Journal entry (page 42)

GLOBAL DEVELOPMENT 401

ACTIVITY 10.6

Design a poster to show how underdevelopment and poverty in developing countries is caused by unfair trade. Present your group's poster to the class.

RESEARCH ASSIGNMENT 10.3

Examine the impact of unfair trade on the developing world in relation to one named commodity (other than chocolate) that you have researched. Write a summary report of your main findings.

See **RESEARCH TIPS** on page 33.

Tip:
Common commodities that are sold under unfair trading practices include cash crops such as coffee, tea, bananas, palm oil and cotton.

SKILLS BOOK LINK 10.3

Go to page 169 of your Skills Book to complete Skill Task 10.3 on the impact of unfair trade on the developing world.

Corruption

Corruption is often cited as an underlying cause of poverty and inequality. Corruption is the abuse of power and resources for private gain. It affects millions of people around the world. Corruption involves breaking laws that ensure citizens can enjoy rights (e.g. rights to health and education). Corruption also involves the abuse of power and resources (e.g. public funds). In developed and developing nations, corruption has the greatest effect on the poorest in society. In some countries, citizens must pay bribes to access public services which should be free, since they are human rights (e.g. primary education, treatment in hospitals, reporting crimes to the police).

Corruption affects all areas of society. It undermines the political and economic development of a country, democracy, the environment, and social wellbeing for citizens. Corruption usually leads to the theft of public resources. This can be done by public officials or private individuals at local, national and international levels. Corrupt practices have a devastating effect on poorer countries because corruption involves misusing resources that are already limited. There has been much research into the relationship between corruption and poverty.

What is the Cost of Corruption?

The cost of corruption can be be understood in four ways: political, economic, social and environmental.

Political Cost

Corruption is a major obstacle to democracy and the rule of law. In a democratic system, offices and institutions lose

Fig. 10.41 Corruption

POWER AND PEOPLE

their legitimacy when they are misused for private advantage. This is harmful in established democracies, but even more so in newly emerging ones. It is extremely challenging to develop accountable political leadership in a corrupt climate.

Economic Cost

Corruption depletes national wealth. Corrupt politicians invest scarce public resources in projects that will benefit themselves rather than communities. Corrupt politicians prioritise high-profile projects (e.g. dams, power plants, pipelines, refineries) over less spectacular but more urgent infrastructure projects (e.g. schools, hospitals, roads). Corruption prevents the development of fair markets and competition in a society, which in turn discourages investment.

Social Cost

Corruption corrodes the social fabric of society. It undermines people's trust in the political system, in its institutions and its leadership. A distrustful or apathetic public then becomes yet another hurdle in challenging corruption.

Environmental Cost

Environmental degradation is another consequence of corrupt systems. The lack (or non-enforcement) of environmental regulations and legislation means that precious natural resources are carelessly exploited, and entire ecological systems are ravaged. From mining, to logging, to carbon offsets, companies across the globe continue to pay bribes in return for unrestricted destruction.

WHAT THE RESEARCH SAYS!

CORRUPTION AND UNDERDEVELOPMENT

Corruption and Poverty in Nigeria

With a population of approximately 173 million people, Nigeria has the largest population in Africa. It is also Africa's largest exporter of oil and possesses the largest natural gas reserves on the continent. Nigeria has had one of the fastest-growing economies in Africa for many years. In 2015 Nigeria ranked 23rd in global GDP rates, just below Sweden. However, despite strong economic growth, Nigeria has high rates of poverty and inequality. In 2015, Nigeria had a HDI ranking of 151 (compared to Sweden in 14th place). In Nigeria, over 60 per cent of the population live below the poverty line.

Fig. 10.42 Nigeria

Nigeria is in the top ten countries with the highest rates of child mortality. Transparency International has published the Corruption Perception Index (CPI) since 1995. The CPI measures the perceived levels of corruption within the public sector in 176 countries worldwide. Nigeria scores high in the Corruption Perception Index (CPI) and low in the HDI. This shows that it has high levels of corruption and poverty.

In 2015 ActionAid International published a report on the role that corruption plays in Nigeria's poverty and underdevelopment.

Fig. 10.43 Anti-corruption demonstrators in Nigeria

Several different forms of corruption were identified by the research, including the misuse by government officials of public funds intended to provide important public services, bribes from private companies to government officials to gain contracts (especially in the oil and natural resource sector), and money laundering. All these practices led to a reduction in the availability of resources to tackle poverty in Nigeria. The report found that there was a direct relationship between poverty and corruption, pointing to several cases as evidence. The research showed that, in comparison with states where governors were lawful, the poverty levels were higher in several states where the state governors were found to be guilty of misusing and converting public funds into private use.

QUESTIONS

1. What does corruption have to do with poverty and underdevelopment?
2. 'A large inequality gap exists in Nigeria.' Give evidence from the research and data to support this statement.
3. What types of corruption were identified by ActionAid International?

Cross-Comparison of HDI and CPI Data

Sometimes comparing different data or indices on a country can provide us with interesting analysis.

HDI

Since 1990, global poverty has been measured annually by the UN Human Development Index (HDI). The HDI measures a country's performance against a set of standard indicators, including income levels, life expectancy, years of schooling, child mortality rates, and others. Each of the 188 countries are then ranked in the final index (see Fig. 10.44).

CPI

Transparency International has published the Corruption Perception Index (CPI) since 1995. The CPI measures the perceived levels of corruption within the public sector in 176 countries worldwide. Based on a mixture of public surveys and interviews with country experts from government, private sector, and civil society, the CPI ranks countries each year. Countries are scored on a scale ranging from 0 to 100, 0 being highly corrupt and 100 being very clean (see Fig. 10.45).

HDI rank VERY HIGH HUMAN DEVELOPMENT	Human Development Index (HDI) Value 2014	Life expectancy at birth (years) 2014	Expected years of schooling (years) 2014[a]	Mean years of schooling (years) 2014[a]	Gross national income (GNI) per capita (2011 PPP $) 2014	GNI per capita rank minus HDI rank 2014
1 Norway	0.944	81.6	17.5	12.6[b]	64,992	5
2 Australia	0.935	82.4	20.2[c]	13.0	42,261	17
3 Switzerland	0.930	83.0	15.8	12.8	56,431	6
4 Denmark	0.923	80.2	18.7[c]	12.7	44,025	11
5 Netherlands	0.922	81.6	17.9	11.9	45,435	9
6 Germany	0.916	80.9	16.5	13.1[d]	43,919	11
6 Ireland	0.916	80.9	18.6[c]	12.2[e]	39,568	16
8 United States	0.915	79.1	16.5	12.9	52,947	3
9 Canada	0.913	82.0	15.9	13.0	42,155	11
9 New Zealand	0.913	81.8	19.2[c]	12.5[b]	32,689	23
11 Singapore	0.912	83.0	15.4[f]	10.6[e]	76,628[g]	−7
12 Hong Kong, China (SAR)	0.910	84.0	15.6	11.2	53,959	−2
13 Liechtenstein	0.908	80.0[h]	15.0	11.8[i]	79,851[g,j]	−10
14 Sweden	0.907	82.2	15.8	12.1	45,636	−1
14 United Kingdom	0.907	80.7	16.2	13.1[d]	39,267	9
16 Iceland	0.899	82.6	19.0[c]	10.6[e]	35,182	12
17 Korea (Republic of)	0.898	81.9	16.9	11.9[e]	33,890	13
18 Israel	0.894	82.4	16.0	12.5	30,676	16
19 Luxembourg	0.892	81.7	13.9	11.7	58,711	−11
20 Japan	0.891	83.5	15.3	11.5[e]	36,927	7
21 Belgium	0.890	80.8	16.3	11.3[d]	41,187	0
22 France	0.888	82.8	16.0	11.1	38,056	4
23 Austria	0.885	81.4	15.7	10.8[d]	43,869	−5
24 Finland	0.883	80.8	17.1	10.3	38,695	0
25 Slovenia	0.880	80.4	16.8	11.9	27,852	12
26 Spain	0.876	82.6	17.3	9.6	32,045	7
27 Italy	0.873	83.1	16.0	10.1[d]	33,030	4
28 Czech Republic	0.870	78.6	16.4	12.3	26,660	10
29 Greece	0.865	80.9	17.6	10.3	24,524	14
30 Estonia	0.861	76.8	16.5	12.5[e]	25,214	12
31 Brunei Darussalam	0.856	78.8	14.5	8.8[e]	72,570[k]	−26
32 Cyprus	0.850	80.2	14.0	11.6	28,633	3
32 Qatar	0.850	78.2	13.8[l]	9.1	123,124	−31
34 Andorra	0.845	81.3[h]	13.5[f]	9.6[m]	43,978[n]	−18

Fig. 10.44 Human Development Index (HDI) data, 2014

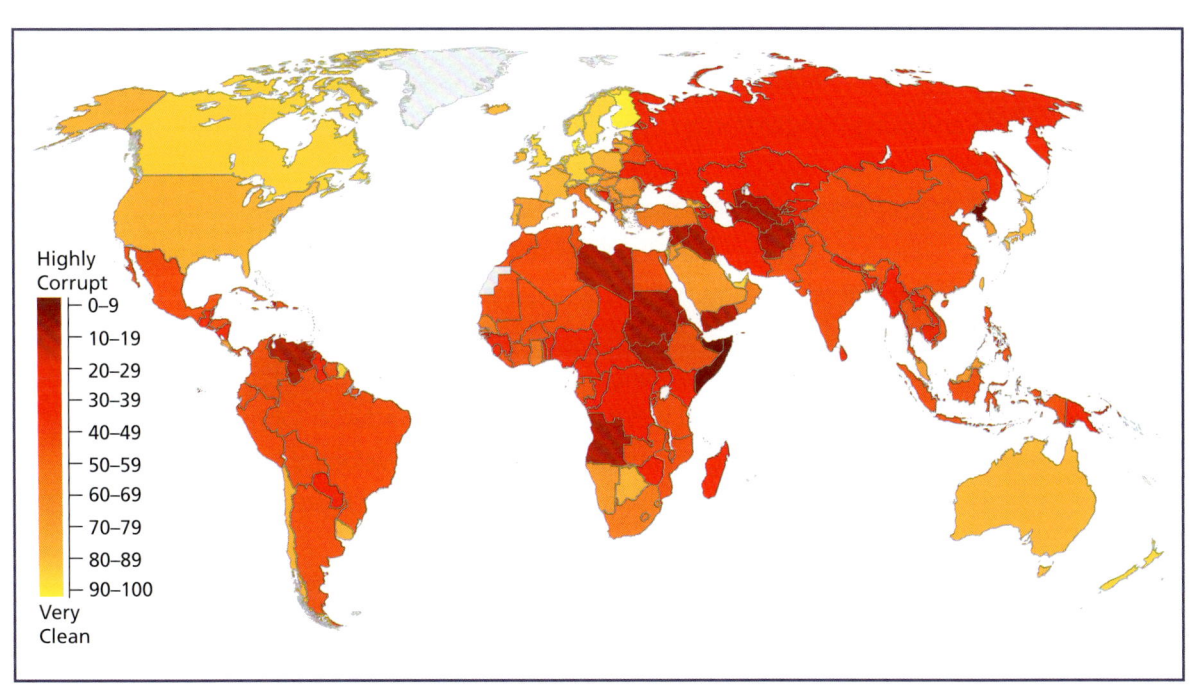

Fig. 10.45 Corruption Perception Index (CP1), 2016

SKILLS BOOK LINK 10.4

Go to pages 170–171 of your Skills Book to complete Skill Task 10.4 on HDI and the Corruption Perception Index.

See RESEARCH TIPS on page 33.

ACTIVITY 10.7

Your group will be assigned one developing country by your teacher. Examine the HDI score and CPI score for this country. Research the reasons for these scores. Create a profile of the country based on its level of development/underdevelopment and the extent of corruption in the country. Present the profile to your class.

ACTIVITY 10.8

Hold a classroom debate on the following motion:

'The west is to blame for poverty and underdevelopment in the developing world today.'

SUMMARY

- In recent decades, the world has followed an unsustainable model of development based on the reckless exploitation of natural resources, rapid industrialisation, urbanisation, environmental degradation, pollution and over-consumption.
- This model of development is unsustainable because it is compromising the ability of future generations to meet their needs.
- GDP and HDI are two methods used to measure a country's level of development.
- Whereas GDP is a narrow measure of economic development, HDI takes into account the quality of life and living standards in a country, by measuring health and education as well as income levels.
- Huge socio-economic inequality exists between the developed and developing worlds.
- According to modernisation theory, developing countries are underdeveloped because of a lack of knowledge and technology, native culture, and the traditional value systems that exist in these countries.
- Modernisation theory claims that developing countries must adopt a western, capitalist culture and will need more money and western technology in order to fully develop.
- Although industrialisation has brought employment to many developing countries, in many regions it has driven women into a position of powerlessness and poverty and has damaged the environment.
- Dependency theory is a critique of modernisation theory. It claims that the west is responsible for the underdevelopment of developing countries by imposing colonialism, neocolonialism and an unfair global trading system.
- Unfair trade, tied aid, debt and corruption are some of the main causes of inequality between the developed and developing world.

Fig. 10.46 Key Word cloud

REVISION QUESTIONS

1. Describe the **two** main methods used to measure a country's level of development.
2. Explain **three** reasons why the current model of global development is unsustainable.
3. Define the following terms: 'global warming', 'carbon footprint' and 'overpopulation'.
4. Describe **three** measures that **(a)** you could take and **(b)** the government could take to reduce our carbon footprint.
5. In what ways has inequality between the developing and developed world increased in recent decades?
6. According to modernisation theory, why are developing countries underdeveloped?
7. Explain the **five** stages of development according to Walt Whitman Rostow.
8. Give **one** criticism of modernisation theory.
9. Describe the negative impacts of industrialisation on women in the developing world.
10. Write an account of the main ideas of dependency theory. Refer to the following in your answer: Andre Gunder Frank, colonialism, neocolonialism, unfair trade, tied aid and debt.
11. In what different ways does corruption impact on the development of developing countries?
12. In your opinion, what are the biggest barriers to development in the world today? List the barriers and explain what might be done to overcome them.

DATA-BASED QUESTIONS

Complete the qualitative and quantitative research data-based questions exercise on pages 172–176 of your Skills Book.

EXAM FOCUS: Section B of LC Exam

REVISION EXERCISES

Complete the exercises on pages 177–178 of your Skills Book.

EXAM FOCUS — Section A of LC Exam

DISCURSIVE ESSAY TOPICS

1. Which theory – modernisation or dependency – best explains global development? Provide suitable evidence to support your argument.
2. Assess the strengths and weaknesses of any two mechanisms used to measure development.
3. 'Women in developing countries have not benefited equally from development processes.' Discuss.

EXAM FOCUS — Section C of LC Exam

Reflective Practice

Ensure that you have completed all the Reflective Journal entries for this chapter (page 42 of your Reflective Journal and Learning Portfolio) before moving on to the next chapter.

Complete the Learning Portfolio activities on pages 43–45 of your Reflective Journal and Learning Portfolio. This will help you to self-assess the extent to which you have achieved the learning intentions for this chapter, and will help you to monitor your progress.

CHAPTER 11
Sustainable Development

'Sustainable development is development that meets the needs of the present without compromising the ability of future generations to meet their own needs.'
Gro Harlem Brundtland

KEY TERMS

- Sustainable development
- Tax justice
- Fair trade
- Free market environmentalism (FME)
- The tragedy of the commons
- Eco-friendly vehicles
- The Green Revolution
- Genetically modified
- Planetary boundaries
- Ecological footprint
- Ecological deficit
- Global hectares

Introduction

The history of humankind has been characterised by breakthrough discoveries and innovations. From the earliest civilisations to the present day, the human race has engaged in a continual quest for progress and development. We have gained material benefits and improved living standards from this development, but it has come at a price. As we learned in Chapter 10, the traditional concept of development is based primarily on economic growth. This has led to a development that is unsustainable and unequal. In many parts of the world, economic development has taken place at the expense of the environment. The people in these regions have not benefited equally from this model of development.

In this chapter, we will explore the concept of **sustainable development** as an alternative approach. We will engage with arguments from the right and left of the political spectrum in relation to sustainable development and solutions to our environmental problems. In particular, we will focus on three key issues of modern sustainable development: climate change, **tax justice** and **fair trade**. Finally, we will look at examples of local actions that can be taken in support of sustainable development.

KEY TERMS

Sustainable development is development that meets the economic, social and environmental needs of our own generation without jeopardising the ability of future generations to do the same. Sustainable development means achieving economic growth, social justice and an adequate standard of living, within environmental limits.

Tax justice means that everyone (individuals and companies) pays their fair share of taxes.

Fair trade is an alternative to conventional trade, which ensures that farmers and workers are guaranteed a minimum price for their produce so that sustainable development is possible.

By the end of this chapter you will be able to:

- Define sustainable development.
- Evaluate the extent to which the world's environmental problems can be solved by technology and the free market.
- Explain how sustainable development in harmony with nature can be achieved through small-scale, self-reliant communities using renewable resources.
- Identify actions that can be taken to promote sustainable development.
- Describe the main causes of greenhouse gas emissions and climate change.
- Explain how your own energy usage contributes to climate change.
- Describe how climate change can impact on people in developing countries.
- Identify solutions to reduce greenhouse gas emissions and climate change.
- Explain the benefits of fair trade and purchasing goods that are ethically traded.
- Explain how your everyday purchases can either alleviate or contribute to environmental problems, global poverty and injustice.
- Assess the impact of tax injustice on the developing world.
- Describe examples of voluntary work and specific actions that you can take in your community to help achieve environmental and social justice.

By the end of this chapter you will have developed the following skills:

- Active listening skills by listening carefully, summarising accurately and responding critically to alternative viewpoints aired during class discussions and debate.
- Communication skills by putting forward and presenting your own evidence-based arguments on sustainable development.
- Dialogue skills by engaging in discussions and debates and allowing your opinions to be challenged and even changed in the light of better arguments.
- Research skills by sourcing and compiling suitable evidence for various research assignments on sustainable development.
- Critical and creative thinking skills in relation to the strengths, weaknesses and limitations of key pieces of research and important viewpoints on sustainable development issues.
- Teamwork skills by working effectively with others on different group tasks.
- Active citizenship skills by participating in an active citizenship project with the rest of your class.

ACTIVITY 11.1

Work with your partner to complete the following activity.

1. Your teacher will distribute images that relate to various aspects of sustainable development. Examine the images individually for a moment. *(Think)*

2. With your partner, examine the images and agree a definition for 'sustainable development'. *(Pair)*

3. Share your definition with the rest of the class. *(Share)*

What is Sustainable Development?

The model of development and economic growth the world has followed for many decades is producing negative effects on our environment and widening the gap between rich and poor. An alternative model of development is sustainable development. The concept was first described by the 1987 Brundtland Commission, also known as the UN World Commission on Environment and Development. The commission was established by the UN to research how development could take place without destroying the environment and depleting natural resources. The commission defined sustainable development as 'development that meets the needs of the present without compromising the ability of future generations to meet their own needs'.

Fig. 11.1 Sustainable development is an alternative form of development

Sustainable Development: Key Dates

1987

The term 'sustainable development' first entered global politics with the publication by the World Commission on Environment and Development of a report entitled *Our Common Future*. This report is also known as the Brundtland Report.

1992

The UN Conference on Environment and Development (UNCED), also known as the Earth Summit, was held in Rio de Janeiro, Brazil. The summit agreed on a declaration that established 27 principles to support sustainable development. The summit also agreed a plan of action, entitled Agenda 21, and recommended that all countries produce national strategies to take action on sustainable development. A special UN Commission on Sustainable Development was created.

2000

The UN Millennium Development Goals (MDGs) were established after the largest ever gathering of world leaders. A total of eight MDGs were agreed. They set targets to be achieved by 2015 to combat the following issues: poverty, hunger, disease, illiteracy, environmental degradation and discrimination against women.

2002

Ten years after the Rio Earth Summit, a second summit was held, in Johannesburg, South Africa. The summit aimed to review progress on global sustainable development. The Johannesburg summit looked at a broader range of issues, including poverty, water quality and availability, cleaner energy, health, women's rights and good governance. The lack of government progress on sustainable development since 1992 caused much frustration. The summit resulted in general agreements on the various issues. However, no targets or planned actions were identified.

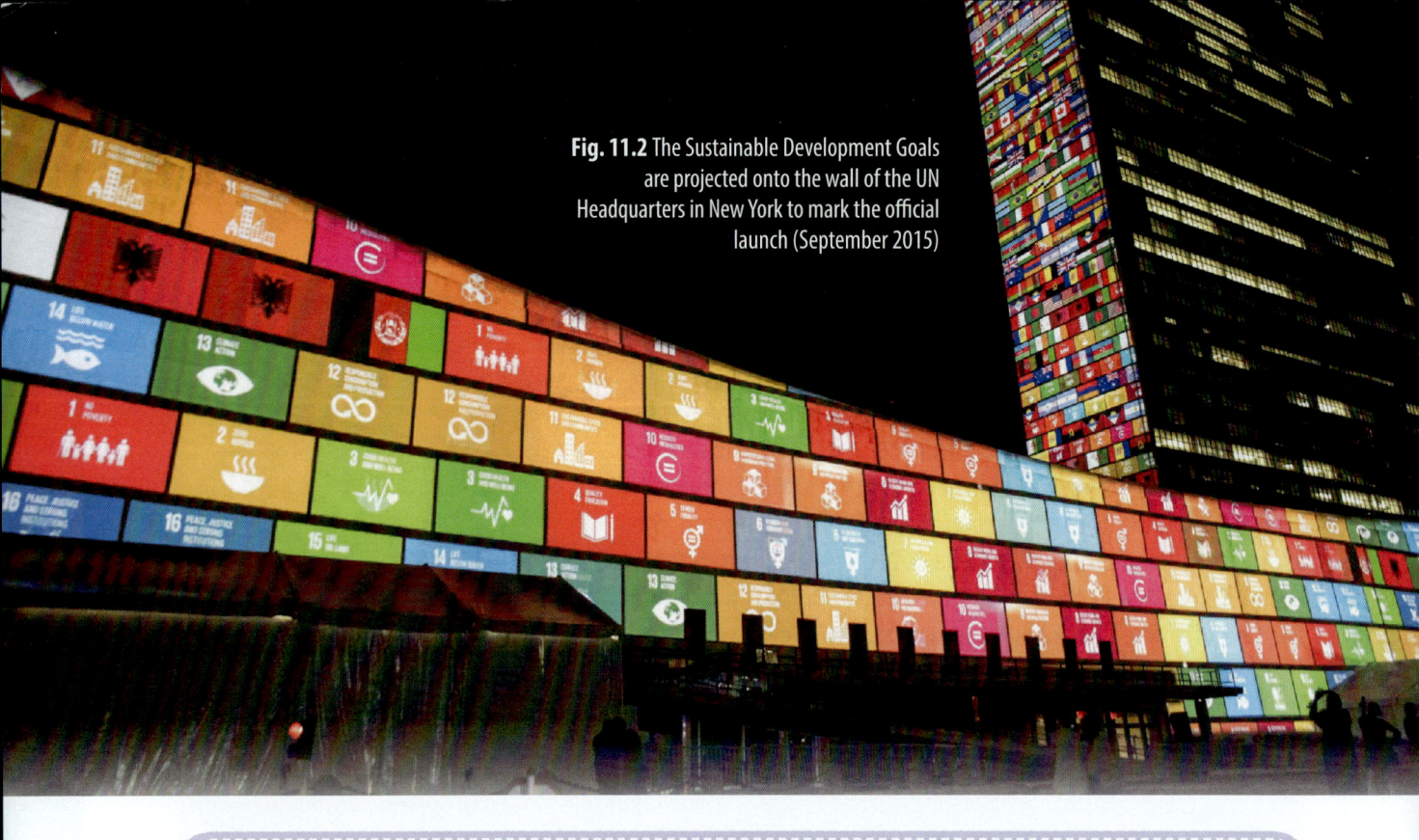

Fig. 11.2 The Sustainable Development Goals are projected onto the wall of the UN Headquarters in New York to mark the official launch (September 2015)

2012

The third international summit on sustainable development, Rio+20, was held in Rio de Janeiro, Brazil. The summit facilitated discussions on how countries could develop green economies (i.e. economies that reduce environmental risks). The summit also set forth a new framework for international cooperation on sustainable development. The main result of Rio+20 was a document entitled *The Future We Want*, which reaffirmed a global commitment to sustainable development, and support for the targets known as the Sustainable Development Goals (SDGs).

2015

The SDGs were adopted by 194 member states at the UN General Assembly. The SDGs replace the MDGs and consist of 17 goals and 169 targets, covering issues such as clean water (Goal 6), affordable and clean energy (Goal 7), decent work and economic growth (Goal 8), sustainable cities and communities (Goal 11), and climate action (Goal 13).

See page 306 for more information on the SDGs.

Sustainable development has three components: economic, social and environmental. Development is sustainable only when the three components are realised. The components are interconnected (see Fig. 11.3). Sustainable development acknowledges that the world can no longer deal with the economic, social or environmental aspects of development in isolation from one another. Environmental degradation and social problems are not the inevitable consequence of economic growth: they are the result of the *type* of development we have followed.

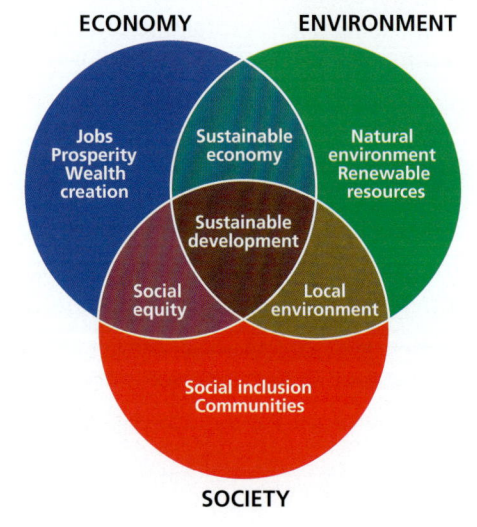

Fig. 11.3 The three pillars of sustainable development

POWER AND PEOPLE

Our modern consumption patterns and lifestyles use enormous amounts of energy and natural resources. This threatens the existence of the very environment that supports our survival. Sustainable development seeks to address and balance all our needs – social, material and economic – without endangering the environment. A healthy economy and society requires a healthy environment capable of providing sufficient food and resources, and clean air and water for its citizens. The overall goal of sustainable development is to improve the quality of life and living standards for everyone in the world – now, and for generations to come.

The Three Pillars of Sustainable Development

Social
Everyone in society has the right to access the basic social goods and services that enable them to lead healthy, fulfilling and productive lives. For example, education and training must be available, so that everyone has the chance to learn new skills and earn a decent living. Girls must have the same opportunities as boys to go to school and to get jobs. Women must have access to adequate healthcare and nutrition for themselves and their children. The elderly must receive the medical care and pensions they need to support themselves as they grow older.

Economic
Economics is a system of deciding how to allocate limited resources (e.g. food, money, bank loans, electricity, clothing) that will be used to meet the needs and wants of people in society. When a country's economy is healthy, resources are distributed fairly and everyone can, at a minimum, meet their basic needs.

Environmental
Developed and developing countries face environmental concerns. At the basic level, everyone needs clean air and safe drinking water. Economic growth has followed a path that involves damaging the environment. Industrial pollution and our lifestyle and consumption choices have greatly harmed and reduced the world's natural resources. Human activity (e.g. our reliance on fossil fuels such as coal and oil for our energy needs) has increased the amount of CO_2 in the Earth's atmosphere. This had led to negative climate change impacts. We have a responsibility to reverse these effects by promoting clean, renewable energy and other environmentally friendly practices in all societies.

How the Three Pillars Are Linked

Social Equity
Everyone should have equal access and opportunity to participate in, and benefit from, the economy. In return, the economy will benefit from the contributions of a more diverse range of innovative, creative and productive individuals. Social equity is about reducing poverty and inequality. Only then can a healthy economy develop to harness the potential of all groups in society.

Local Environment
A healthy environment produces positive social impacts. Without safe water, for example, people cannot lead healthy lives. Environmental damage and climate change impacts

(e.g. droughts and floods) increase hunger and health problems. In many rural communities in developing countries, women are worst affected by climate change and environmental degradation, since women provide the bulk of labour in agriculture. A healthy environment nurtures healthy lives and can provide the ingredients for a healthy economy, such as renewable and clean natural resources.

Sustainable Economy

This is also known as 'green economy'. It involves adopting an alternative approach to economic growth that does not focus only on GDP. A healthy economy should increase the wellbeing of everyone, while promoting and practising environmentally friendly approaches and a respect for the world's scarce natural resources. Agriculture and industry need to use natural resources (e.g. land, soil, forests, rivers, oceans, minerals) in a more efficient and responsible way. Clean and renewable energy sources (e.g. solar, wind, geothermal, biomass energy, hydroelectric power) should be adopted to reverse climate change.

Fig. 11.4 The three pillars of sustainable development are linked

The Relationship Between 'Local' and 'Global'

- Social concerns in one country can have impacts for other countries. Unequal access to education, a lack of job opportunities, poverty or conflict can lead people to migrate. This affects the country that the people leave – 'brain drain', the destruction of traditional familial support networks, etc. It also affects the country to which the people migrate – increasing demands on health and education systems, etc.

- Our economies are interdependent. Through trade, for example, economic decisions in one country will affect many other countries. From government policies on trade tariffs and subsidies, to consumer product choices, our local decisions have global impacts. Developing countries are often dependent on developed countries for goods or services. Developing countries often lack the technology or resources to produce consumer goods, and these countries can be impacted by unfair trade rules. At the same time, developed countries depend on developing populations as consumers of products.

- Environmental issues can be local or global. Increasingly, however, the local and global dimensions of the environment are connected. Industrial and human pollution of rivers and seas will have an impact that crosses national borders. Our consumer choices at the local level can have impacts on natural resource depletion in other countries. High levels of carbon emissions from certain countries are contributing to global warming. This impacts on the level of drought and desertification being experienced by countries in the Sahel region of Africa, for example. Climate change has been called the biggest global threat of our time. It can be resolved only if change occurs at all levels – individual, local, national and international.

QUESTIONS

1. What does sustainable development mean?
2. When and where did the concept first emerge?
3. In what year were the SDGs formally adopted by 194 countries of the UN?
4. Describe the **three** pillars of sustainable development.
5. Explain **one** way in which **two or more** of these pillars are interconnected.
6. We live in an interdependent world where actions in one country can have impacts on other regions of the world. Give **two** examples of how local actions can have global consequences.

SKILLS BOOK LINK 11.1

Go to pages 179–180 of your Skills Book to complete Skill Task 11.1 on sustainable development.

See RESEARCH TIPS on page 33.

SKILLS BOOK LINK 11.2

Go to pages 180–183 of your Skills Book to complete Skill Task 11.2 on *Sustainable Development Indicators Ireland*.

See RESEARCH TIPS on page 33.

Solutions to our Environmental Problems

There is a variety of perspectives on how we can address our environmental problems and move towards more sustainable societies. Arguments are offered from both sides of the left–right political spectrum: environmentalists and liberals on one side, and private business and conservatives on the other. Some believe that technology and the free market provide the solution, while others argue that we need to move towards simpler and more sustainable ways of living in harmony with nature.

Technology and the Free Market

Free market environmentalism (FME) proposes the following argument: the world's environmental problems will be best served by allowing the markets to freely come up with solutions. FME applies the general principles of the free market to the environment. From this perspective, the market and private sector actors (e.g. companies) are more successful than governments in resolving our environmental problems and responding to our environmental needs. This view contrasts with the most common modern approach, by which the government regulates the market to protect the environment. According to supporters of FME, our environmental problems arise because of the absence of clear property rights over different elements of our environment

Fig. 11.5 Technology will provide solutions to our environmental problems

Complete your next Reflective Journal entry (pages 46–47)

SUSTAINABLE DEVELOPMENT 415

(e.g. land, sea, air). The FME argument is based on the idea of the **tragedy of the commons**.

FME supporters argue that natural resources under private, rather than common, ownership receive better preservation and protection. Private owners of resources are far more likely to preserve and protect their privately owned asset to secure its market value. In the FME perspective, the environment is given a market value. Therefore, preservation of the environment is driven by economic interest. Pollution and destruction of the environment are less likely to happen because they reduce the market value of the resources.

> **KEY TERMS**
>
> **Free market environmentalism (FME)** is the theory that free markets rather than governments will be more successful in protecting our environment.
>
> **The tragedy of the commons** is the idea that resources (e.g. land) that are shared (held in common) will be overexploited or abused, because people acting in self-interest will use the resource to meet their needs without consideration for other people's needs.

Incentives to preserve and protect the environment should be provided. Individuals will undertake more of an activity if the benefits of that activity are increased or the costs reduced. Supporters of FME point to the successes of private wildlife conservation (e.g. hunting reserves, safari parks) and other environmental initiatives as evidence for their claims.

Tragedy of the Commons

The concept of the tragedy of the commons was first used by biologist Garrett Hardin in 1968. Hardin used the term to describe how shared environmental resources are over-exploited and eventually depleted. He used the example of a common grazing pasture to illustrate the idea. In this example, everyone with rights to the pasture grazes as many of their animals as possible, acting in self-interest for the greatest short-term personal gain. As a result, all the grass is used up and the shared resource is depleted. The argument rests on the premise that any resource that is shared will meet the same fate. Supporters of this idea point to examples, including: overfishing and the depletion of fish stocks, air pollution caused by traffic congestion on public roads, deforestation, and littering in our public parks and beaches.

Fig. 11.6 Common grazing pasture

QUESTIONS

1. What is FME?
2. Explain how the tragedy of the commons supports an FME approach to environmental conservation.
3. Can you think of any examples in your local area that contradict or support the idea of FME?
4. In your opinion, what are the strengths and weaknesses of FME?
5. Where on the left–right spectrum would you place the concept of FME? Give reasons for your answer.

Private Conservation Projects: Wildlife Ranches in South Africa

CASE STUDY 1

In 1991 the South African government passed a law – the Game Theft Act – which provided private individuals with certain ownership rights over wild animals (e.g. the white rhino) held in adequate enclosures. This law created a financial incentive for private individuals to begin to use wildlife (game) for commercial purposes. Many wildlife ranches were developed in South Africa. The idea was that private actors could play a prominent role in wildlife conservation. These private wildlife ranches are involved in a variety of commercial activities, including: eco-tourism (e.g. wildlife photographic tourism, birdwatching), breeding for private sale or auction, and hunting farms where people pay to kill the wildlife on the farms ('trophy hunting'). It is estimated that South Africa now has over 9,000 wildlife ranches, which house a total of 16–20 million wild animals. Wildlife ranching produces high annual turnovers. In 2014 the breeding and sale of wild animals in South Africa produced over €1.3 billion in revenue. Foreign hunters in South Africa spent an estimated €700 million in 2013 to kill 44,000 animals through trophy hunting.

Fig. 11.7 Wildlife ranch in South Africa

White Rhino Conservation: A Success Story?

In 1900 the southern white rhinoceros was the most endangered of the world's five rhino species: fewer than 20 rhinos remained in a single reserve in South Africa. By 2010, white rhino numbers had increased to more than 20,000, making the white rhino the most common rhino species on the planet. Most of the white rhino population (98.8 per cent) live in four countries: South Africa, Namibia, Zimbabwe and Kenya. In 2005 a team of geographers and biologists, led by Dr Nigel Leader-Williams, Director of Conservation Leadership in the University of Cambridge's Department of Geography, conducted a study on the impacts of the legalisation of hunting on the white rhino populations in South Africa. The research team found that the white rhino population had grown from under 100 to over 10,000 since the hunting

Fig. 11.8 White rhinos

SUSTAINABLE DEVELOPMENT 417

Case Study: Private Conservation Projects: Wildlife Ranches in South Africa

ban was dropped. Leader-Williams claimed that because hunting had made it profitable for landowners to introduce and breed white rhinos on their land, the market incentivised people to actively participate in conservation.

However, wildlife ranches – and particularly trophy hunting – face a number of criticisms.

- The free-market approach to wildlife conservation can further endanger certain species. Wildlife ranching is primarily driven by commercial interests and a monetary value is assigned to wild animals. White rhino trophy hunts have traditionally been sold to international hunting clients from the US and Europe for approximately US$20,000 each. This has created new threats to wild animals, such as poaching. Since 2008, the poaching of rhino for horn has increased significantly in South Africa each year. In 2014 alone, 1,215 rhino were poached. This increase in poaching is driven by the demand for rhino horn in Asian countries, particularly Vietnam. Rhino horn can be sold for up to US$65,000 per kg on the black market. Rhino horn is used in traditional Chinese medicine and, increasingly, as a status symbol to display someone's success and wealth. Wildlife NGOs such as the WWF have raised concerns that, at current rates, the wild rhino will be extinct within a decade.

Fig. 11.9 Rhino horn may be sold on the black market

- Ecologists and scientists argue that some of the breeding practices of wildlife ranches ignore important conservation principles, with devastating consequences. For example, cross-breeding of different species or in-breeding can cause genetic defects and low survival rates. Scientists also argue that systematically hunting the oldest members of an animal population, a common practice in trophy hunting, has negative effects on the gene pool of species. It can result in a reduction of the size of future generations, which will limit the ability of the species to survive. The killing of adult males in any species reduces the survival odds of young members of the species. The killing of females reduces future breeding rates.

- The economic benefits of wildlife ranching do not meet its social costs. Relative to the vast amount of land used for wildlife ranching, the economic results and job creation benefits are low. Local communities do not gain a fair share of the profits, and reinvestment in conservation projects is limited. In some cases, communities are removed from their land to make way for wildlife ranching projects.

Fig. 11.10 A 'trophy hunter'

POWER AND PEOPLE

CASE STUDY 2: Water Markets

Water Crisis in Australia

Clean, fresh water is one of the most valued precious natural resources of the twenty-first century. Global warming, widespread drought and increasingly polluted water systems present the world with challenges to meeting the global population's demand for clean, fresh water. Many parts of the world suffer from water scarcity. According to the 2015 UN World Water Development Report, the world will face a 40 per cent global water deficit by 2030, unless we find ways to conserve water.

Australia is the world's driest inhabited continent and it is prone to droughts. The Murray-Darling Basin in Australia is one of the world's driest river basins, with an evaporation rate of 90 per cent. The basin includes parts of the states of Queensland, New South Wales, Victoria and South Australia, and the Australian Capital Territory. The basin must meet the water needs of many different sectors.

- Community: Over 2 million people live in and around the basin, which provides water for over 3 million people.

- Agriculture: Over 40 per cent of Australia's agricultural production comes from the Murray-Darling Basin. It is Australia's most important agricultural region.

- Environment: The basin includes over 30,000 wetlands, upon which many species of wildlife and plant life are dependent.

Given the high water use of the basin, water management has been a critical issue. From the end of World War I up to the late 1970s, the Australian government invested heavily in the construction of mega-dams and hydroelectric projects to deal with water shortages and meet the water consumption needs of the domestic and agricultural sectors. The Australian government also facilitated water sharing between states,

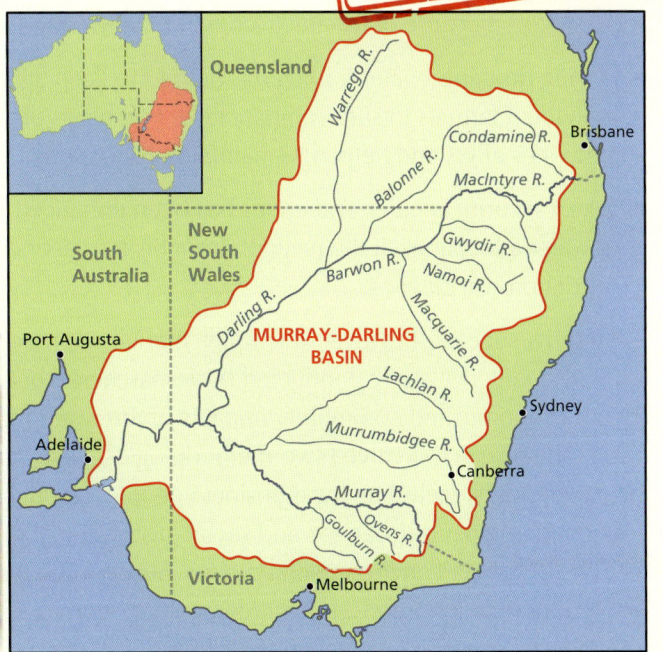

Fig. 11.11 Drought in the Murray-Darling Basin, southeast Australia

SUSTAINABLE DEVELOPMENT 419

Water Markets

CASE STUDY

since some states could have a surplus of water while other states had a scarcity. This approach worked for decades. However, there are increasing demands on water resources because of the rising population and the growth of the agricultural sector. There is also the growing problem of high salinity (level of salt in water) because of the reduced river flow in the basin. This places greater stress on the existing water management efforts. After several devastating droughts, including the major drought of 1967, it became clear that a new approach was required.

Trading Water Rights

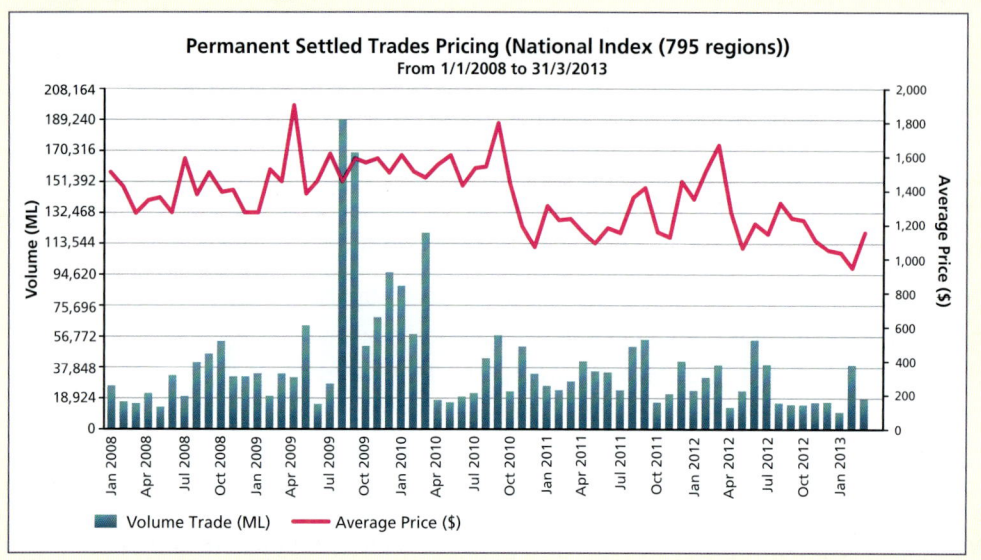

Fig. 11.12 Water prices in Australia

From the 1980s, Australia began to adopt a market-based approach to its water scarcity problems. The water market system involves establishing an annual cap (limit) on the amount of water that can be used without threatening the future supply of water. The annual amount of water that is permitted is then distributed among different users (e.g. farmers, companies) as entitlements. These entitlements can be traded – bought and sold – on a market. This is a free market approach, which places responsibility with private individuals. Water trading in Australia is particularly active during periods of drought. During periods of drought, a farmer who has a surplus of water (i.e. above his or her needs) can sell water rights to another user who needs water. The Australian water trading model has been presented as a global success story because of its effectiveness in the Murray-Darling Basin:

- During droughts, water trading has helped to keep agricultural production going and has helped individual farmers to survive financially. Purchases of additional water allocations kept almond trees and vines alive, and helped to maintain production.

- Water security in cities and towns has been enhanced: towns and cities can purchase large volumes of water allocations at the peak of droughts to meet demand and to limit the impact of water restrictions on citizens.

Despite its success, however, the water market approach in Australia has not been without its critics. A 2008 qualitative study conducted by researchers from the University of South Australia assessed the social, economic and community impacts of the water markets on a town located in the Murray-Darling basin. The research involved two methodologies. First, semi-structured interviews were conducted with 20 stakeholders, including local business people, health and human service workers, staff from the local council, participants in service and social groups, local indigenous people and farmers, and members of local irrigation and environmental groups. Second, the research team analysed available secondary data on local population trends, unemployment, economic activity, and public health. The study highlighted a number of negative impacts on the community:

Water Markets

- The water market has accelerated the trend of declining local farming populations. Many farmers face financial hardship, and selling water has become an attractive option. This results in lower levels of production and the closure of many small-scale farms.

- The logic of market-based solutions is to ensure higher economic returns. Water markets have resulted in the displacement of water through trading from traditional community-based agricultural activity, such as dairying or mixed farming, to high-value enterprises, such as horticulture and viticulture.

Two recent events also highlighted the weaknesses of the water market model. Without proper regulation, water for commercial purposes is often prioritised over environmental considerations. As water becomes a valuable commodity, it is captured more efficiently by users, and this results in less river flow. In 2012, the Australian government was forced to buy back water entitlements from farmers to redress environmental impacts, such as threats to the basin's wetlands. Also, in December 2016 the Australian government passed legislation to make it possible to clearly identify the holders of water entitlements, after concerns were raised about growing foreign ownership. In 2013, an estimated 13.7 per cent of all water entitlements on issue had some level of foreign ownership, compared to 8.5 per cent in 2010. There is growing concern that the entry of investment banks and other foreign investors could lead to increasing water prices, which would negatively impact local communities.

Privatisation of Water Services and User Fees

The water market in Australia is one of the world's most developed systems for trading water rights. However, across the world, the privatisation of water services is a developing trend. Since the 1990s the transfer of water service management from government to private companies has taken place in many countries. In 1989, under Margaret Thatcher's Conservative government, all water companies in England and Wales were privatised – these were the first countries to privatise water companies on a national scale. Since then, many other countries have followed the same model. International financial institutions, such as the World Bank and the IMF, placed conditions on loans to developing countries, requiring the privatisation of water services. This policy was based on the logic that the private sector would be more efficient in delivering water services, and that user fees would improve water conservation by reducing wasteful water consumption. Today, there are at least ten major corporations that control water services around the world. Three of these – RWE/Thames, Suez/ONDEO and Veolia – supply water to 300 million people in 100 countries. Despite this growing trend, there are several important criticisms of water privatisation:

Fig. 11.13 Citizens demonstrating against privatisation of water services

- One of the most common complaints about water privatisation is the increase in water tariffs (user fees), which can make safe water inaccessible to poorer members of society. Globally, for the typical household, privately owned water services cost 59 per cent more than public water services. In France, water fees increased by 150 per cent following privatisation.

CASE STUDY: Water Markets

- Water quality can suffer if profit-making is prioritised. Private companies can be unwilling to invest in hiring adequate staff to manage and maintain water systems. Many cities around the world are now returning water services to public management to make much-needed investments in water systems. A 2014 report by the Transnational Institute (TNI), Public Services International Research Unit and the Multinational Observatory suggests that in the last decade, 180 cities and communities in 35 countries, including Buenos Aires, Johannesburg, Paris, Accra, Berlin, La Paz, Maputo and Kuala Lumpur, have ended contracts with private companies and returned water service management to local government.

- Human rights advocates argue that access to clean drinking water is a human right and, therefore, governments – not private companies – should be responsible for ensuring that citizens have access to water.

Fig. 11.14 Human rights activists argue that access to clean drinking water is a human right

QUESTIONS

1. Explain how the South African government's Game Theft Act (1991) resulted in a positive environmental impact. Does this support the views put forward by the FME concept? Why/why not?
2. What was the positive impact of the government's decision to lift the hunting ban?
3. List **three** criticisms put forward against South Africa's FME approach to environmental conservation.
4. What **three** challenges are facing the world in meeting the demand for fresh water?
5. Who depends on the water in the Murray-Darling Basin in Australia?
6. Explain how the Australian government's water market trading system operates.
7. What are the benefits and disadvantages of this system?
8. In your opinion, should Irish water services be privatised? What are the pros and cons of privatising water services?
9. Is the privatisation of water services part of a left-wing or right-wing philosophy? Give reasons for your answer.

Technological Solutions to Environmental Problems

From the FME point of view, the private market is more likely to develop innovative and creative ways to solve environmental problems. Technology is viewed as a key to solving our environmental problems.

CASE STUDY 3: Eco-Friendly Vehicles

Around the world, fossil-fuelled vehicles (i.e. petrol, diesel) are responsible for a significant proportion of emissions of CO_2, the main greenhouse gas which is linked to climate change. Fossil-fuelled vehicles account for approximately 12 per cent of CO_2 emissions in the EU. The equivalent figures are 20 per cent in the US, 20 per cent in Ireland, and 10 per cent in China. Traditionally, fossil-fuelled vehicles were the only option available to consumers. However, technological advances in car manufacturing mean that we now have more environmentally friendly options with **eco-friendly vehicles**:

Fig. 11.15 Eco-friendly vehicles

> **KEY TERM**
>
> **Eco-friendly vehicles** are alternatives to fossil-fuelled vehicles. Eco-friendly vehicles include fuel-efficient, alternative-fuel, flexible-fuel, electric and hybrid-electric vehicles.

- Fuel-efficient cars use less fuel than other cars to travel the same distance. When less fuel is burned, less CO_2 is released into the atmosphere.

- Alternative-fuel vehicles run on fuels other than petrol or diesel. Burning natural gas produces less CO_2 than the burning of petrol or diesel. Burning hydrogen produces no CO_2 at all.

- Flexible-fuel vehicles can use a blend of up to 85 per cent ethanol (a fuel produced from corn, sugarcane, or other types of biomass) and 15 per cent petrol or diesel. These cars have been produced since the 1980s.

- Electric vehicles are powered by an electric motor instead of a traditional engine. Large batteries store energy to power the car, and the driver plugs in the car to refuel. Electric vehicles emit no direct pollution. Also, if sources such as wind and solar are used to generate the electricity that is used, the total CO_2 emission of an electric car can be very small.

- Hybrid-electric vehicles combine the benefits of traditional engines and electric motors. A hybrid car can travel up to twice as far on a litre of fuel as a typical petrol/diesel car.

Norway: Electric Vehicles

Since the late 1990s the Norwegian government has put policies in place to encourage drivers to switch to rechargeable electric vehicles to reduce the country's CO_2 emissions:

- Purchasers of electric vehicles in Norway are exempt from paying the usual VAT, which is extremely high on car purchases.

- Drivers of electric vehicles do not pay toll fees on the country's roads. They are entitled to free parking and the use of public bus lanes.

- The government has invested in an extensive network of electric stations to charge vehicles, making electric cars convenient for their drivers.

SUSTAINABLE DEVELOPMENT

CASE STUDY: Eco-Friendly Vehicles

The government's efforts have been highly successful: Norway now has the highest per capita use of electric cars in the world. During the first three months of 2016, approximately 25 per cent of all newly registered vehicles in the country were plug-in electric vehicles (PEVs) – a category that includes both pure electric and hybrid vehicles. The total market share is almost 30 per cent (see Fig. 11.17). By comparison, according to International Energy Agency (IEA) projections, electric vehicles will account for 8 per cent of total car sales in Ireland in the period 2016–20.

Fig. 11.16 Norway has the highest per capita use of electric cars in the world

Several other national governments are following the lead taken by Norway. Under the British government's Clean Air plan, all new petrol and diesel cars and vans will be banned on British roads from 2040. Similarly, the French government has announced its intention to ban all petrol and diesel cars by 2040. These initiatives will force car manufacturers to produce more economical and efficient environmentally friendly vehicles in the years ahead. Volvo has already announced that they will make fully electric or hybrid cars only, from 2019 onwards.

Despite their growing popularity, the use of electric cars as a solution to CO_2 reduction has not been without criticism:

- The manufacturing process for electric cars produces more CO_2 emissions than the process to make normal cars. The raw materials and energy it takes to manufacture the lithium-ion batteries can have a greater impact on the environment than conventional cars.

- The effectiveness of electric cars in reducing CO_2 emissions will also depend on how the electricity they use is *generated*. Many countries still generate electricity through fossil-fuelled power stations (e.g. coal). Almost all the power stations in China are fuelled by coal. This can greatly reduce the environmental advantage of electric cars.

Q1 2016 chart: # of PEVs registered (thousands) vs INS Automotive Plug-in Electric Vehicle Index Rank
- Rank 1: 10,927 – 29.5%
- Rank 2: 2,139 – 22.2%
- Rank 3: 7,992 – 1.6%
- Rank 4: 10,140 – 1.3%
- Rank 5: 26,332 – 0.8%
- Rank 6: 5,701 – 0.7%
- Rank 7: 8,800 – 0.7%
- Rank 8: 32,213 – 0.5%

China had a record year for PEV adoption in 2015 and that trend is continuing: China registered the largest number of PEVs in Q1 2016, yet ranks lowest on the Plug-in Electric Vehicle Index

#1 Norway once again leads the Plug-in Electric Vehicle Index ranking with almost 1 in every 3 vehicles registered in Norway in Q1 2016 being a PEV.

PEV market share in **France** (rank 3) is gaining ground on PEV market share in the **Netherlands** (rank 2). Attractive incentives are supporting adoption of PEVs in France, while a change in PHEV taxation in January 2016 inhibited the market in the Netherlands.

Germany, like in previous rankings, is in the lower half of the ranking system. In Q2 2016, a new subsidy directly supporting PEV sales was legislated in Germany for the first time. IHS Markit expects Germany to rise in the Plug-in electric Vehicle Index rankings in future editions.

Of all Q1 2016 PEVs registered in the eight countries analysed,

37% were PHEVs
63% were Evs

Plug-in Electric Vehicle (PEV) = Electric Vehicle (Evs) + Plug-in Hybrid Electric Vehicle (PHEVs)

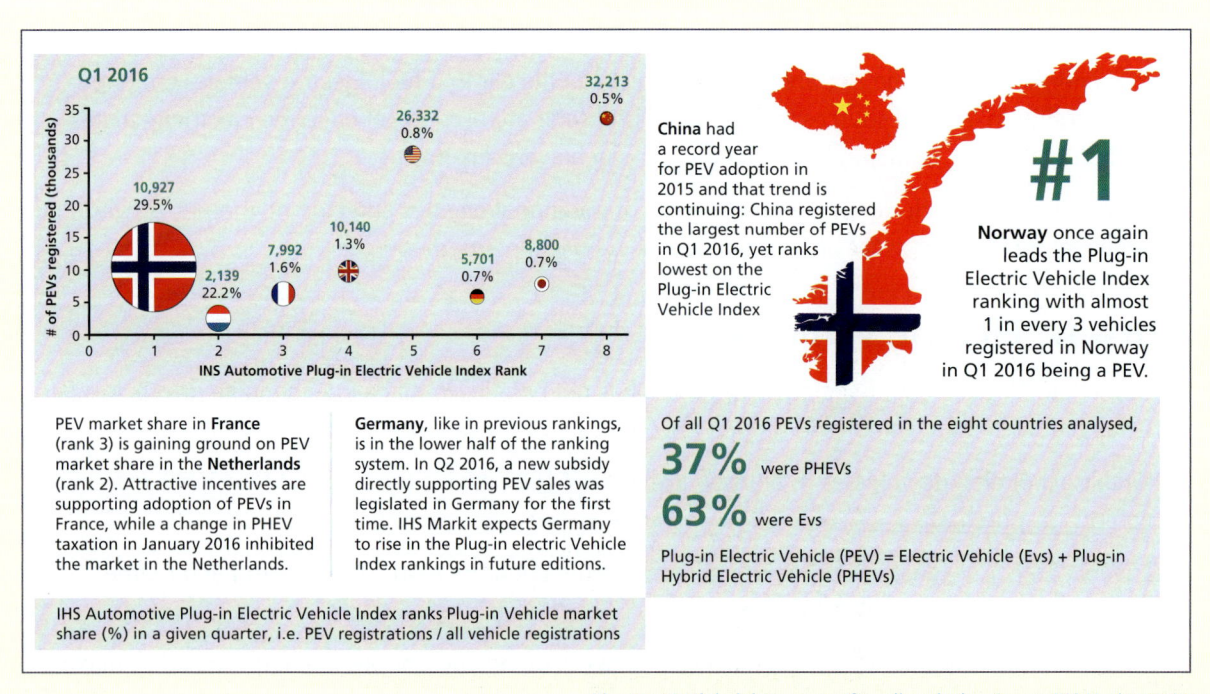

IHS Automotive Plug-in Electric Vehicle Index ranks Plug-in Vehicle market share (%) in a given quarter, i.e. PEV registrations / all vehicle registrations

Fig. 11.17 Global data on eco-friendly vehicles. Source IHS Markit, 2016

424 POWER AND PEOPLE

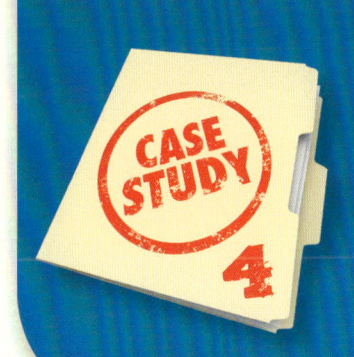

CASE STUDY 4: The Green Revolution

The Green Revolution is a term used to describe the dramatic increase in food production that took place in several developing countries during the 1960s because of scientific agricultural experimentation and the use of high-yielding or **genetically modified** variants of crops. The Green Revolution began in Mexico and quickly spread to other developing nations that aimed to achieve food security and agricultural self-sufficiency for their rapidly growing populations. The model was adopted by many Asian countries, including India.

Fig. 11.18 The use of irrigation was an important aspect of the Green Revolution

In 1943 the then British-controlled eastern region of India (including Bangladesh) suffered from a devastating famine (the Bengal Famine) which claimed over 3 million lives. Following independence in 1947, the Indian government made food security one of its top priorities. Even though there were increasing amounts of land under cultivation in India, food production was unable to keep pace with the country's rapidly growing population (which increased by 2 per cent per annum, and rose from 345 million in 1947 to 505 million in 1967). Faced with this food shortage crisis, a radical solution was needed. The Indian government turned to the Green Revolution in the late 1960s. The government introduced the practice of growing just a few varieties of high-yielding crops. The programme also increased the use of chemical fertilisers and irrigation practices.

Fig. 11.19 India introduced Green Revolution policies and practices in the late 1960s

KEY TERMS

The Green Revolution was a dramatic increase in food production in several developing countries during the 1960s. It was driven by scientific agricultural experimentation and the use of high-yielding or **genetically modified** variants of crops.

From the mid-1990s, genetically modified (GM) plant breeding was established under the Green Revolution. New varieties of

Fig. 11.20 Genetically modified plant breeding

SUSTAINABLE DEVELOPMENT   425

CASE STUDY: The Green Revolution

seeds – especially wheat and rice, but also millet and corn – were introduced to farms across India. These new 'miracle seeds' were modified to produce much higher yields, to be resistant to pests and to be immune to fungal, bacterial and viral diseases. As a result, wheat and rice production quadrupled. Tens of millions of extra tonnes of grain were produced each year and food production quickly caught up with domestic demand. Today, food production in India far exceeds domestic demand. The Green Revolution effectively transformed India from a famine-prone, food-deficient country to a self-sufficient, leading exporter of agricultural produce.

Despite its obvious agricultural and economic benefits to India, the Green Revolution has been criticised for its negative impact on the environment:

- The GM crops require regular spraying of chemical fertilisers to add additional nutrients to increase the yield. Pesticides and herbicides are also widely used to protect the crops from pests and diseases. These products contain chemicals that have been proven to cause environmental degradation and damage to human health.

- The high demand for oil-based fertilisers is unsustainable, as it depletes our finite global oil resources.

- Excessive use of fertilisers contributes to global warming. It causes the soil to emit high levels of nitrous oxide, a greenhouse gas with 300 times more heat-trapping power than CO_2. This can be seen in the states of Punjab and Haryana, where the Green Revolution has been most intensively implemented.

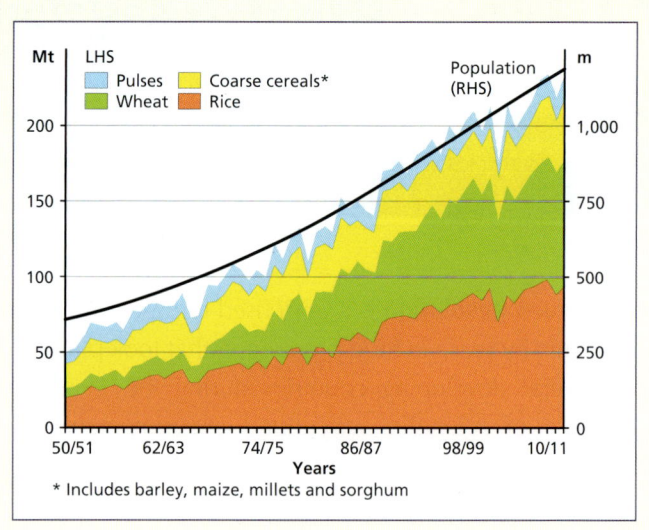

Fig. 11.21 India: crop production and population
*Includes barley, maize, millets and sorghum

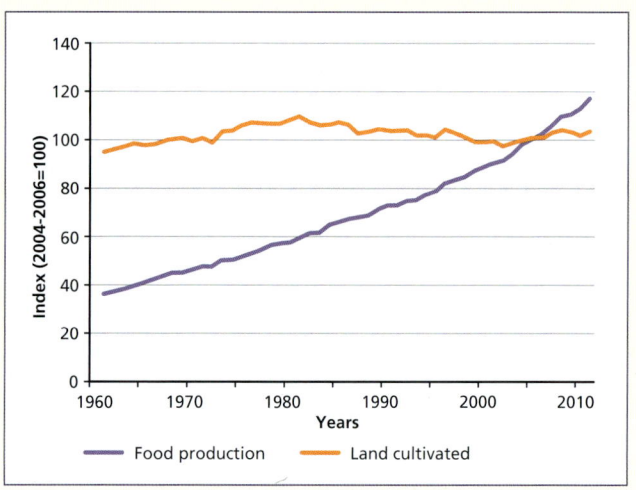

Fig. 11.22 The impact of the Green Revolution on agricultural yields in India

426 POWER AND PEOPLE

> **CASE STUDY**
> ## The Green Revolution

- Continuous and intensive use of fertilisers, pesticides and herbicides kills useful microorganisms, insects and earthworms – thus destroying natural soil-forming processes. This causes soil erosion and infertility, which leads to long-term dependency on expensive fertilisers.
- The overuse of pesticides and herbicides pollutes the soil and contaminates water sources surrounding the agricultural areas. In Punjab and Haryana, this has caused major pollution of drinking water.
- In Punjab, the widespread contamination of water by toxic pesticide chemicals has been linked to higher rates of cancer, renal failure, stillborn babies, birth defects and other life-threatening ailments.
- Research carried out by Punjabi University found a high rate of genetic damage among farmers, which was attributed to pesticide use.
- Many farmers in rural India are not trained in the proper usage and disposal techniques of chemical fertilisers. Many rural farmers do not use protective clothing and equipment when handling highly toxic chemicals. Pesticide containers are sometimes reused as kitchen storage containers. These practices contribute to the high risk of infection by carcinogenic toxins.
- GM crops are water-thirsty and require large-scale irrigation schemes. In India, this led to the construction of several dams and reservoirs. Malarial mosquitos and other bacteria breed in the warm, stagnant pools of water. This contributes to the spread of diseases such as bilharzia (which causes blindness).
- Large-scale irrigation schemes have also led to a rise in the salinity of the land.

The widespread use of GM crops has led to significant genetic erosion. The Green Revolution has decreased the 'biodiversity' of crops today. For example, it is estimated that before the Green Revolution, there were over 30,000 different varieties of rice in India. It is estimated that there are now only ten modified rice varieties in use today.

QUESTIONS

1. What measures did the Norwegian government take to promote the use of eco-friendly vehicles?
2. Explain how the use of electric cars can help the environment.
3. The positive impact of electric cars on the environment is open to debate. Give **two** criticisms put forward against the use of electric cars.
4. What was the Green Revolution?
5. What was the positive impact of the Green Revolution on India?
6. What are GM crops? Explain the positive and negative effects of using GM seeds.
7. How did the Green Revolution impact on the environment?

ACTIVITY 11.2

Hold a classroom debate on the following motion.

'Technology and the laws of the free market will solve our environmental problems.'

KEY THINKERS

TRADITIONAL KNOWLEDGE, BIODIVERSITY AND SUSTAINABLE LIVING

VANDANA SHIVA

Vandana Shiva is an Indian scholar and environmental activist. She is author of numerous books, including *Soil Not Oil: Environmental Justice in an Age of Climate Crisis* and *Staying Alive: Women, Ecology, and Development.* Born in the Himalayas in 1952, Shiva was heavily influenced by her father, a forest conservationist, and her mother, a farmer. She is now one of the world's foremost environmentalist and anti-GM activists and speaks out against the global seed industry and corporations such as Monsanto.

Shiva highlights the negative impact that the GM seed industry has had on local communities and the environment in India. According to Shiva, local and traditional agricultural practices and food systems have been destroyed by a growing corporate monopoly of agricultural inputs, such as seeds. For example, India used to grow over 1,500 varieties of cotton seeds. Today, almost all the cotton produced in India comes from one genetically modified seed. This seed is owned by one corporation – Monsanto, the world's biggest seed producer. Shiva works to protect the rights of farmers to their own seeds.

Fig. 11.23 The global seed industry includes powerful companies such as Monsanto

Corporations such as Monsanto have created property rights over seeds, by modifying and mutating them through genetic engineering. As a result, many of India's farmers (who are forced to purchase the seeds) have been pushed into debt. Small farming communities are collapsing and are being replaced with large-scale commercial agriculture projects. Shiva has linked high suicide rates within the male rural population with this situation.

Shiva argues that the GM food industry has caused significant environmental damage and rising food prices, which contributes to the world's hunger crisis. Shiva advocates instead for the promotion of small-scale organic farms as a sustainable solution to climate change and hunger. Shiva claims that ecological farms produce two to five times more food per acre than industrial alternatives. She also claims that urbanisation (migration from rural to urban locations) is being encouraged by corporate interests to push small-scale farmers off their land. Shiva argues that we need more people in rural areas to be involved in small-scale, self-reliant and ecological agriculture. We also need to make changes in cities. Every city should have its own 'food shed' – a surrounding area that provides enough organically produced food for local consumption needs – as well as gardens within cities. Food production should be part of town planning.

Fig. 11.24 Indian citizens demonstrating against the practices of the GM food industry

Fig. 11.25 The Nine Seeds movement protects the diversity of native or local seed variations

428   POWER AND PEOPLE

In 1987, Shiva established the Nine Seeds (Navdanya) movement in India to protect the diversity and existence of natural resources, particularly native or local seed variations. The movement is led by women and has established 122 community seed banks across 18 of India's 29 states. At the seed banks, natural seeds are saved and grown for a variety of crops indigenous to the local areas. Through organic methods, the seeds are supported to adapt to changing climate conditions, such as heavy rains and prolonged droughts. Through the seed banks, local farmers can obtain seeds and share them with each other. The Nine Seeds movement has also set up a system of schools, where over half a million farmers have received training on organic farming methods and sustainable agriculture. Farming techniques that use inputs provided naturally by the environment are promoted. Agriculture must respect and apply the laws of nature, such as natural water supplies and soil nutrients. The movement also manages India's largest fair trade organic network.

Shiva has fought cases against corporations attempting to patent (claim legal property rights) over indigenous plants and seeds. Shiva continues to support similar movements in Africa, Asia and Latin America and has served as an adviser to NGOs and to governments in India and abroad.

Fig. 11.26 The Nine Seeds movement has established 122 community seed banks in India

QUESTIONS

1. Who is Vandana Shiva?
2. How many varieties of cotton seeds existed in India before the introduction of GM seeds?
3. From where does almost all the cotton in India originate today?
4. Shiva claims that large corporations such as Monsanto are responsible for pushing small farmers into debt. Explain how this happens.
5. What does Shiva propose as an alternative to large-scale commercial farms?
6. What is the main benefit of ecological farms, according to Shiva?
7. What positive actions has the Nine Seeds movement taken to help local farming communities in India?

Development in Harmony with Nature

Since the Industrial Revolution, nature has been treated as a type of commodity to be used primarily for the benefit of humans, and technology has been viewed as the solution to our environmental problems. However, some argue that this human-centred approach to development has led to the abuse and overuse of the Earth's resources. We have transformed and manipulated the Earth. We have not addressed the problem of our unsustainable human consumption and production patterns, which have negatively affected the environment and the natural world. Instead, we have devised solutions to support the continuation of unsustainable lifestyles which are heavily dependent on the Earth's finite resources. This is destroying our planet. The alternative approach is to adopt a new world view to development – an approach which is Earth-centred. Humans must reconnect with nature and recognise that, in and of itself, the health of the Earth is valuable to our development. The Earth does not exist simply to meet our needs. The earth can regenerate, if we give it space and time

Fig. 11.27 Harmony with nature

SUSTAINABLE DEVELOPMENT

to do so. Economic, social and technological progress needs to take place in harmony with nature and with respect for our **planetary boundaries**. Since 2009, several countries working within the UN have put forth the idea that the Earth has rights itself, alongside our human rights. This approach contrasts with free market environmentalism, which views nature as property to be used for human and economic benefit.

KEY TERM

The concept of **planetary boundaries** was introduced in 2009 by a scientific team led by Johan Rockström from the Stockholm Resilience Centre and Will Steffen from the Australian National University. There are nine planetary boundaries, which we need to respect. We must avoid 'crossing' these boundaries if we are to ensure the continued survival and health of the Earth:

1. Stratospheric (ozone layer)
2. Biosphere (animal and plant life)
3. Chemical pollution
4. Climate change (levels of CO_2 in air)
5. Acidity of the ocean (rising levels of CO_2 in oceans)
6. Natural cycle of fresh water systems
7. Natural land systems (forests, grasslands, wetlands, etc.)
8. Levels of nitrogen and phosphorous in air and water
9. Natural hydrological system affected by aerosol usage (e.g. monsoons and cloud formation).

KEY THINKERS

FATHER SEÁN McDONAGH

An Irish Columban, Father Sean McDonagh is known around the world as an eco-theologian – a person who studies the relationship between religion and nature. Father McDonagh was a pioneer in the 1970s, writing about environmental issues before they became mainstream. He works to raise awareness on the connections between justice and peace issues, environmental sustainability and faith.

He is an outspoken critic of policies and practices that contribute to global poverty and the degradation of the environment, as well as our culture of consumerism, which is rapidly depleting the Earth of its natural resources. As a missionary priest in the Philippines in the 1970s and 1980s, Father McDonagh witnessed the devastating effects of deforestation and mining on local communities, including the T'boli people on the island of Mindanao. Since that time, Father McDonagh has played a key role in supporting the Catholic Church to take a more vocal stance on environmental justice issues.

He is the author of numerous articles and nine books, including *Climate Change: The Challenge to All of Us*, *Greening the Christian Millennium*, *Care for the Earth* and *Dying for Water*. He highlights the causes and consequences of issues such as global warming, genetically engineered food, water pollution, the nuclear industry and loss of biodiversity.

Father McDonagh made a significant contribution to the 2015 open letter from Pope Francis – the Encyclical *Laudato Si': On Care for Our Common Home* – which highlighted the moral and ethical dimensions of climate change and environmental damage from a Christian perspective and called on the Church to play its role in addressing these.

Father McDonagh's main arguments regarding sustainable development include the following.

- **Consumerism and consequent unsustainable lifestyles** were confined to Europe, the US and Australia until a few decades ago. Today, consumerism has taken a hold right around the world. Consumerism is practised by millions of people in Brazil, India, China and other emerging industrial economies. Aggressive advertising and planned obsolescence (the deliberate manufacturing of things to be functional only for a limited period of time) are probably the most important factors in spreading the culture of consumerism.

- **'Limits to growth' perspective:** Father McDonagh supports the view that there are limits to the Earth's capacity to cope with human activity in its current form, based on a focus on economic growth. The Earth is finite, and cannot sustain continuous depletion of resources and the irreversible destruction of ecosystems. Few people in government or in the economic disciplines have understood the importance of the Earth's limits. In fact, governments have played their part in developing a consumerist culture by promoting economic growth.

- **Growth in human population:** The global population is expected to grow to approximately 9 billion by the year 2050. Demand for food and other resources will double, which puts extra pressure on ecosystems that are already stressed and fragile. However, a fall in population levels will not, in itself, reduce the stress on the planet, unless it is accompanied by a drop in our consumption patterns.

- **Respect for other species:** If we are to protect other species from extinction, humans must show much greater generosity in sharing the global commons with them. Currently, most of our economic, political, religious and cultural systems believe that all the global space – on land, in the sea and the air – primarily belongs to humans.

- **Dependency on fossil fuels:** Industrialisation and development has been based on the easy availability of fossil fuels. We know that fossil fuel is finite and that we may have in fact achieved 'peak oil.'

- **Role of technology:** New technologies can sometimes help reduce the resources used in manufacturing goods, and can be renewable energy sources. However, one of the difficulties that offsets a reduction in the material used in manufacturing, is the *volume* of products being produced today. Without promoting necessary cultural changes in our consumption patterns and lifestyle, technology alone is unlikely to solve many of the environmental issues for our planet. In some cases, technology can have an adverse impact on sustainable development. The growth in robot and artificial intelligence technologies is reducing the number of jobs available to men and women, which impacts on their economic and social wellbeing.

- **Religion and sustainability:** Churches and religions can play a significant role in supporting the world to move away from consumerism towards a sustainable society. Each religious tradition has its own stories about the origins of the universe, the Earth and humankind. There is normally a wealth of wisdom in these traditions on how to live in a sustainable way.

Father McDonagh played a role in the drafting of the Encyclical *Laudato Si': On Care for our Common Home*. In this document, Pope Francis moved the Catholic Church from the periphery of global engagement with ecology right to the heart of the debate. The document had two central points. The first calls on all humans to respect, cherish and stop exploiting planet Earth – the home for all creation. The second point relates to how the poor and vulnerable are most affected by the deterioration of the environment and society.

QUESTIONS

1. What is an eco-theologian?
2. What did Father McDonagh witness during his time in the Philippines?
3. What is 'planned obsolescence'? How does it contribute to the culture of consumerism?
4. Father McDonagh supports the 'limits to growth' perspective. What is this?
5. Apart from a reduction in the world's population, what else does Father McDonagh claim we need to do to reduce stress on the planet?
6. Explain **one** positive and **one** negative impact that technology can have on the environment.
7. What influence has Father McDonagh had on the Catholic Church's position regarding sustainable development?
8. Which of Father McDonagh's arguments do you agree with most? Why?

Does Nature have Rights?

In April 2009, the UN General Assembly declared 22 April each year to be International Mother Earth Day. Bolivian President Evo Morales Ayma and the Bolivian delegation to the UN had taken the lead in developing the proposal, stating: 'Sixty years after adopting [the UDHR], Mother Earth is now, finally, having her rights recognised.' Since then, the UN General Assembly has adopted a total of five resolutions with respect to 'Harmony with Nature' to define a new relationship between humans and nature, and to develop the rights of the Earth. A resolution is a type of official statement from the members of the UN. While resolutions have no legally binding force on member states, they often have a significant and lasting impact and influence the future direction of policies and practices.

Fig. 11.28 Does nature have rights?

Universal Declaration of the Rights of Mother Earth

Bolivia continues to lead the push for the universal adoption and recognition of the Rights of Mother Earth. In 2010, the Universal Declaration of the Rights of Mother Earth was drafted after a three-day gathering in Bolivia known as the World People's Conference on Climate Change and the Rights of Mother Earth. Several countries, such as Bolivia, and environmental rights activists continue to demand that the declaration is adopted by the UN in the same way as the UDHR.

National Laws that Recognise the Rights of the Earth

Bolivia is among the few countries to have developed a national Mother Earth Law. The 2010 law gives equal rights to nature and demands that the country's economy and society move towards a more ecological model. The law established seven new rights for nature, including:

- The right to life and to exist
- The right to preserve the diversity of beings that comprise the Earth

- The right to continue vital cycles and processes free from human alteration
- The right to pure water and clean air
- The right to balance
- The right not to be polluted
- The right to not have cellular structure modified or genetically altered.

Fig. 11.29 Bolivia has developed a Mother Earth Law

Implementation of the law has been difficult, however, given Bolivia's heavy dependence on natural resources. In 2015, despite major protest from civil society and indigenous communities, the government approved initial plans to explore future fracking potential in several parts of the country. Fracking is a method of extracting gas or oil through the injection of highly pressured liquid (water and chemicals) deep underground. It has been criticised by environmental groups because of alleged pollution of water and soil.

ACTIVITY 11.3

Your teacher will assign your group a section of the Universal Declaration on the Rights of Mother Earth. Summarise the main points contained in the section and present it to the other groups in your class.

Ensuring that development takes place in harmony with nature requires a change in human behaviour and practice, and a move towards more sustainable ways of living. There are many initiatives which aim to put theory into practice, to promote sustainable living and a reduction in our **ecological footprint**.

KEY TERMS

The **ecological footprint** is the only metric that measures how much nature we have and how much nature we use. Established in 1990 by Mathis Wackernagel and William Rees at the University of British Columbia, ecological footprint measures the demand on, and the supply of, nature. According to the Global Footprint Network: 'It measures how fast we consume resources and generate waste compared to how fast nature can absorb our waste and generate new resources.'

Our ecological footprint relates to the resources we use and the waste we create, while our biocapacity is about the ability of our environment to recover and to renew natural resources. If a population's ecological footprint exceeds the zone's biocapacity, that zone has what is termed an **ecological deficit**. The demand for resources exceeds the environment's ability to recover and regenerate (e.g. overfishing, CO_2 emissions).

Both the ecological footprint and the biocapacity are expressed in units known as **global hectares**. The level of sustainability as measured by the Global Footprint Network is 1.78 gha. The average Irish person's EF is 5.6 gha. The ecological footprint is now widely used by governments, businesses, scientists and individuals as a way to monitor the use of ecological resources.

Visit the Global Footprint Network's interactive Ecological Footprint world map to see the ecological footprint of countries around the world: https://educateplus.ie/go/footprint

Case Study 5: Cloughjordan: Ireland's Ecovillage

Cloughjordan Ecovillage in Co. Tipperary is Ireland's only ecovillage. The idea for the village began in 1999 with the aim to establish a space for low-carbon living, i.e. a lifestyle that produces as few climate-changing carbon emissions as possible. Cloughjordan is now Ireland's largest renewable energy district. The community's ecological footprint is the lowest measured in Ireland. Based on a 2014 survey, Cloughjordan Ecovillage was estimated to have an ecological footprint of just 2 gha, the lowest recorded for an Irish settlement. This compares to an average ecological footprint of 4.3 gha for 79 settlements throughout the country.

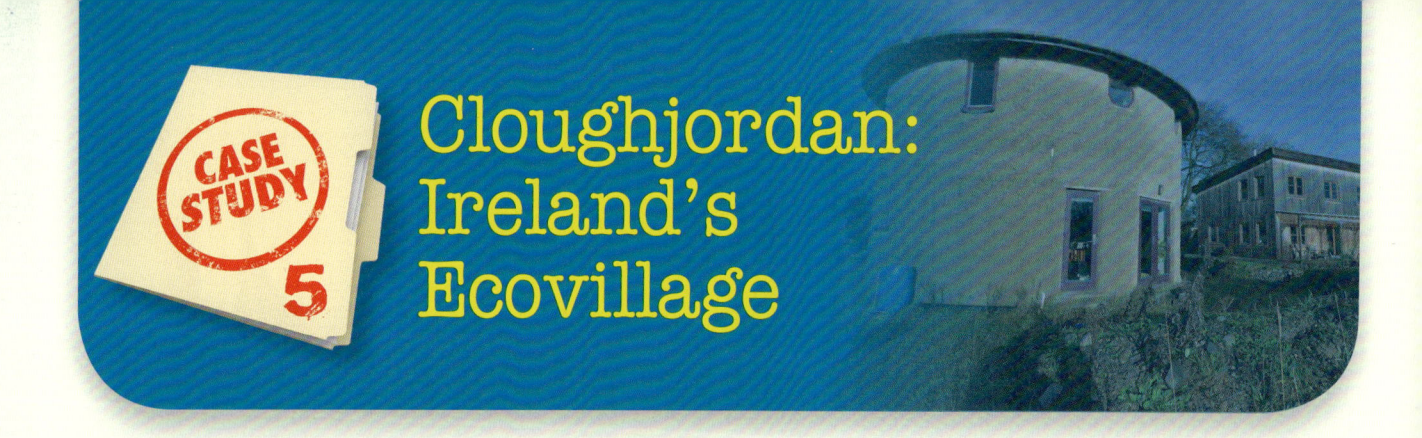

Fig. 11.30 Cloughjordan: Ireland's Ecovillage

What is an Ecovillage?

Cloughjordan is a member of the Global Ecovillage Network (GEN). The network defines an ecovillage as a community that works together in a participatory way to 'holistically integrate ecological, economic, social and cultural dimensions of sustainability in order to regenerate social and natural environments'. In 1998, the UN named ecovillages as among the top 100 best practices for sustainable living.

Cloughjordan Ecovillage is situated on a 67-acre (27-hectare) site behind the main street of the town of Cloughjordan in Co. Tipperary. The development of the ecovillage began in 2007 and it now has 55 green homes, 140 residents, an enterprise centre, a bakery, allotments for growing food, a hostel and a community farm. One-third of the site is devoted to woodland: 17,000 trees were planted in 2011, mainly native species such as oak, ash, Scots pine, birch, rowan, cherry, hazel and alder. An amphitheatre for outdoor arts events was built in 2016–17.

Fig. 11.31 Labyrinth at Cloughjordan

The members of the ecovillage developed an Ecological Charter: a document which outlines the basic principles that should be followed in the development and functioning of the village. The charter contains specific targets on energy supply and use, how to manage and use the land, water and solid waste, transport, and noise and light pollution.

Energy

Renewable energy supply is one of the key features of Cloughjordan Ecovillage. The entire heating and hot water for the ecovillage is supplied by a district heating system that uses no fossil fuels for its primary energy sources and emits no greenhouse gas emissions. A bank of solar panels to heat the water is planned. The fuel is provided from waste wood produced at a sawmill one hour from the ecovillage. The system

POWER AND PEOPLE

Case Study: Cloughjordan: Ireland's Ecovillage

supplies hot water to each house: residents do not need to install their own boilers, stoves, electric showers or electric water heating. The energy use of the inhabitants is monitored: houses are supplied with a monitor for heat and electricity use. Several houses are mounting PV (photovoltaic) panels to generate most of the electricity they use, and to share surplus with the national grid.

Land Management, Water and Waste

The development and maintenance of all land follows organic practices. Priority is given to indigenous plants to support wildlife. Corridors for the movement of wildlife are built into the design of common and private areas. Villagers are encouraged to compost organic matter and avoid using toxic or harmful substances. The community gets involved in regular communal work on shared areas of land.

- The ecological charter specifies a target for the use of potable water of 85 litres per person per day, which compares to a national average of 140 litres per person per day. Many homes harvest rainwater for outdoor uses.

Fig. 11.32 Woodchip District Heating System at Cloughjordan

Fig. 11.33 Woodchip District Heating System at Cloughjordan

Fig. 11.34 A composted toilet at Cloughjordan

- The village has a Sustainable Urban Drainage System (SUDS). Surface water from roads and roof-tops is piped to catchment basins, which naturally filter the water through the soil into the ground. These basins are designed to overflow into the nearby stream if heavy rain continues for many days. During heavy rains in winter 2015–16, while flooding occurred in other parts of the surrounding region, the ecovillage avoided flooding.

- Household waste is recycled as far as possible and organic waste composted. A composting site for the ecovillage has been developed. Members of the ecovillage recycle materials such as plastic, glass and paper among themselves for use in packaging or in cultivation. Waste that cannot be recycled within the ecovillage is currently collected by commercial waste disposal companies, although the ecovillage is planning its own natural waste treatment plant.

Sustainable Building

- The ecovillage has some of the highest standards of building energy ratings (BER) in Ireland. BER is a certificate given to each building based on its energy performance (i.e. how energy efficient it is in relation to water heating, ventilation and lighting). BER rating goes from A (most efficient) to G (least efficient).

Fig. 11.35 Rainwater harvesting system at Cloughjordan

CASE STUDY: Cloughjordan: Ireland's Ecovillage

Fig. 11.36 Sustainable building at Cloughjordan

Since 2008, all buildings in Ireland must have a BER certificate. Almost all the houses in the ecovillage have either an A or a B1 rating.

- Construction materials that are non-toxic and locally sourced are promoted by the ecovillage to reduce the environmental impact of both the transport and manufacture of building materials. The ecovillage has a variety of building types, including:

  - Timber-framed housing
  - Durisol blocks: blocks of chipped waste wood bonded with eco cement
  - Sheep's wool
  - Cellulose: shredded newspaper
  - Hemp-lime: lime is a traditional form of finish but the addition of hemp, a fibrous plant material, gives it strength and insulation
  - Cob: clay, sand and straw.

Natural slates or recycled plastic roof tiles and 'green roofs' are widely used.

Fig. 11.37 Sustainable building at Cloughjordan

Community Collaboration

- Transport: members are encouraged to reduce dependence on car travel and to make use of public transport (trains and buses). A car-sharing club has been established, allowing the households to share three cars and the costs of maintaining them. Bicycles are widely used by ecovillage residents for local travel.

- Noise and light pollution are kept to a minimum to limit disturbance to wildlife.

- Community-supported agriculture (CSA): Members of Cloughjordan Ecovillage have established Ireland's first member-owned and operated CSA farm in Ireland. It is one of the few CSAs in Ireland. Members pay a monthly fee (€64 for a household of typically two adults and two children) and can take what food they want from a central distribution point that is supplied twice a week, all year around. The consumption practices of the ecovillage are based on what food is available according to the season, the weather and the amounts planted.

- At the heart of sustainable living is the ability to generate sufficient income to live well. Several people who moved to Cloughjordan to live in or on the margins of the ecovillage have established businesses. These include an eco-hostel with 34 beds and a wood-fired bakery within the ecovillage itself, a bookshop and coffee shop on the main street, and Cloughjordan Catering Co-op which

Fig. 11.38 Community farm at Cloughjordan

Case Study: Cloughjordan: Ireland's Ecovillage

runs the Middle Country Café. A group of ecovillagers established a company called VINE (Village Internet Network Engineering) to provide internet and telephone services to ecovillage residents. Several organisations and businesses now have their main offices in the ecovillage, including entrepreneurs involved in low-energy and sustainable building techniques, and renewable energy. There is a Green Enterprise Centre which includes a Fabrication Laboratory (FabLab) called We Create, which offers 3-D laser cutting services: 3-D objects, such as jewellery, in a variety of materials (e.g. wood, metal, glass) are produced from a computer design by a special laser machine.

Fig. 11.39 Farm produce distribution point at Cloughjordan

- Community relations: There is a Process Group that facilitates community interactions. A Monthly Community Meeting allows any member to voice any issue that is troubling them, including issues of grievance and pain caused within the community.

Cloughjordan and its ecovillage have won a number of high-level awards. The ecovillage won the National Green Award for Ireland's greenest community three years in a row (2012–14) and won a gold medal at the 2013 International Awards for Liveable Communities (LivCom), also known as the Green Oscars, hosted by Xiamen in the People's Republic of China and supported by the UN Environmental Programme (UNEP). In 2012 the ecovillage was ranked by readers of *The Irish Times* in a national survey as one of the ten best places to live in Ireland. Cloughjordan Ecovillage was selected as one of the 23 most successful 'anticipatory experiences' in Europe of the transition to a low-carbon society, by a consortium of 14 research institutes funded by the European Commission to advise on future EU energy policy. In 2016 the Young Foundation in London identified Cloughjordan Ecovillage as one of Europe's most successful examples of social innovation.

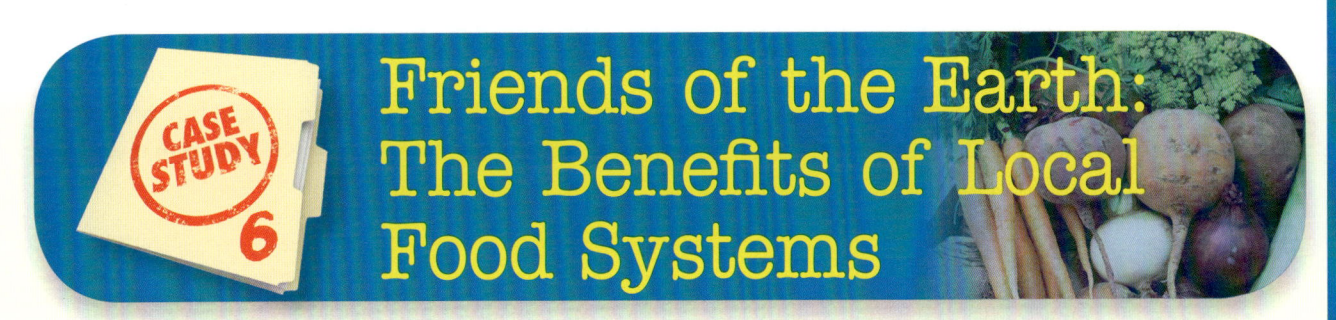

Case Study 6: Friends of the Earth: The Benefits of Local Food Systems

In 2015, Friends of the Earth (an environmental NGO) published a report entitled *Eating from the Farm*. The report highlighted the benefits of developing and supporting local food systems across Europe.

Friends of the Earth Europe

Fig. 11.40 A fruit and vegetable producer

SUSTAINABLE DEVELOPMENT 437

Friends of the Earth: The Benefits of Local Food Systems

Global Food System

The globalisation of food production has led to an industrial monopoly within the agricultural sector. A small number of companies now dominate the supply of seeds, agri-chemicals, processing, logistics and even food production. For example, in 2011 four retailers controlled 85 per cent of the German national food market; three retailers controlled 90 per cent of the food market in Portugal. Most of the EU's 12 million farms are family farms. However, it can be very difficult for these small-scale local farms to supply supermarkets, which favour non-seasonal produce (fruits and vegetables that are never out of season) and large-scale agriculture. National and EU policies (e.g. Common Agricultural Policy) and trade policies have focused on finding new global markets for EU agricultural products. Such policies have done less to support the initiatives that give farmers who produce sustainably the opportunity to sell their products locally through farmers' markets, farm shops, or to schools and other public institutions. Despite this, more and more communities across Europe are finding creative ways to take back control and develop local food systems that bring the producer and consumer closer together (e.g. farmers' markets, on-farm shops, and CSA projects). Local food systems have many important benefits: economic, social and environmental.

Fig. 11.41 A local food market

Economic

Research in the US has shown that local food supply chains generate 13 full-time jobs in agriculture for every US$1 million dollars in sales. By contrast, the large-scale agricultural sector generates just three full-time jobs per US$1 million dollars in sales. Local food supply chains created 68,000 jobs in the US in 2008. Another study in the US found that for every two jobs created in farmers' markets in Iowa, another one was indirectly created in the surrounding economy. In Europe, the New Economics Foundation (NEF), an independent think tank based in London, compared what happens when people buy produce at a supermarket compared to a local farmers' market or from a CSA programme. NEF found that when people buy their food locally, twice as much money stays in the community.

Social

Local food systems improve social relations by bringing the consumer and producer into direct contact with each other. Greater trust and connectedness is developed between consumers and producers. Farmers' markets and CSA projects create new spaces within communities for people to socialise.

Environmental

Shopping for locally grown food can have environmental benefits. This is the case when purchasing local products that are in season and based on organic methods of production which are in harmony with nature. Local food systems that involve a short food supply chain have less environmental impact. They often use fewer non-renewable resources for processing, transport and storage. Short food supply chains generally use less packaging than supermarkets, and less energy is used for storage because produce is fresh and seasonal. Local food systems rely on crops and products from animals that are adapted to the local environment and are part of the local ecosystems. This maintains biodiversity.

> **CASE STUDY**
>
> Friends of the Earth: The Benefits of Local Food Systems

CSA in Germany

In Germany, people have started to use CSA programmes (*Solidarische Landwirtschaft* or SoLaWi in German) as a way to obtain healthy and fresh local produce that benefits the local economy and environment.

The CSA concept is very simple. Groups of consumers finance work on a local farm. They sign a one-year contract and pay a fixed membership fee. In exchange, the farm provides the members with food. Once a week, the farm delivers fruit and vegetables (and occasionally animal products) to distribution centres that are close by. The exact deliveries depend on the season. The members help regularly on the farm and can take part in deciding what to plant.

Fig. 11.42 There are almost 100 CSA farms across Germany

There are currently almost 100 CSA farms across Germany. Consumers can find farms close to them through a website. The site provides a list of these farms and a short profile of each project, describing how they work, which produce they offer and their delivery area.

Organic Bazaars in Poland

In Warsaw, Poland, organic markets called 'bazaars' are bringing food producers and consumers closer together. Visitors to the organic bazaars can buy organic vegetables, fruit, dairy products, bread, cured meats, chickens, wine, tea and coffee. The market is exclusively for organic growers, and certificates are checked. Customers can drink fair trade coffee, take part in cooking workshops, and participate in innovative recycling schemes (e.g. exchanging used batteries and old computer hardware for flower seedlings or spruce trees in flowerpots).

Fig. 11.43 An organic bazaar in Poland

Organic Fruit and Vegetable Delivery Schemes

Local farmers are directly delivering organic produce to the homes of city dwellers in many European countries. In these schemes – commonly referred to as 'vegetable box schemes' – the consumer pays a weekly subscription to have fresh, seasonal, organic, locally produced fruits and vegetables delivered directly to their homes. The first organic box scheme, Farmaround, was established in London in 1994.

Fig. 11.44 A delivery from a vegetable box scheme

SUSTAINABLE DEVELOPMENT

QUESTIONS

1. What is an ecovillage?
2. What is an ecological charter?
3. Describe the sustainable and environmentally friendly aspects of Cloughjordan Ecovillage.
4. The success of Cloughjordan Ecovillage is dependent on the cooperation and collaboration of the local community. Explain the different ways in which the community of Cloughjordan cooperates and collaborates to promote sustainable environmental practices.
5. Who are the Friends of the Earth?
6. Why is the globalisation of food production a danger to local farmers and the environment?
7. What are the economic, social and environmental benefits of local community-supported agriculture?
8. Explain how CSA programmes operate in Germany.
9. Do you think that small-scale community projects such as those discussed above are associated with a left-wing or right-wing ideology? Explain your answer.

SKILLS BOOK LINK 11.3

Go to pages 183–184 of your Skills Book to complete Skill Task 11.3 by creating an ecological charter for your school.

RESEARCH ASSIGNMENT 11.1

'Development in harmony with nature requires a move away from big industries and urbanisation and towards small-scale, self-reliant communities using renewable resources.'

Imagine that you are the head of an environmental NGO seeking funding for a sustainable development project in a country of your choice. Create a funding proposal for the project. Include the following in your proposal:

- Statistics on the negative effects of large-scale industrialisation and urbanisation
- An explanation of the benefits of the alternative approach: small-scale, self-reliant communities using renewable resources
- A detailed description of the community project for which you are seeking funding
- A clear explanation of the positive economic, social and environmental benefits of your project.

Taking Action for a Sustainable Future

Sustainable development is about connecting the local and global. Although many of the world's development problems (poverty, inequality, conflict, climate change, etc.) have international dimensions, actions at local level can have significant impacts. Local actions can help or hinder development. Three sustainable development issues in particular – climate change, unfair trade and tax injustice – demonstrate this relationship between the local and global. Many successful sustainable development initiatives begin with taking action within our own communities.

Complete your next Reflective Journal entry (pages 46–47)

Case Study 7

Trócaire: Climate Change

Trócaire is an Irish Catholic overseas development agency that works in over 20 developing countries around the world to address the root causes of poverty. A major focus of Trócaire's work is to support communities to cope with the devastating effects of climate change.

Trócaire
Working for a just world.

Climate Change

Climate change is a significant change in weather trends and patterns (e.g. temperature, precipitation and wind) experienced by a region. While climate change can be caused by natural factors, the term 'climate change' is now generally used to describe the changes in our climate because of human activity. To understand climate change, we must understand the carbon cycle. Carbon dioxide (CO_2) enters the Earth's atmosphere from volcanoes, decaying plants, breathing humans and animals, and the surface of the sea. CO_2 leaves the Earth's atmosphere when it is used by plants during photosynthesis, absorbed into the sea or stored in soil and sediment. This cycle keeps everything alive on planet Earth.

CO_2 and the Greenhouse Effect

The CO_2 in the atmosphere traps heat from the sun. It is for this reason that CO_2 is called a greenhouse gas. CO_2 creates a blanket of warmth, known as the 'greenhouse effect' that keeps the Earth from freezing. The more CO_2 in the atmosphere, the warmer the Earth becomes. The level of CO_2 in the atmosphere over the last 8,000 years has been stable, creating suitable conditions for human beings to thrive.

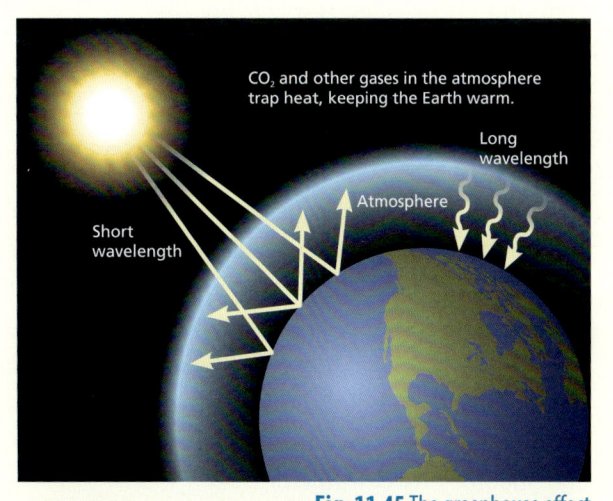

Fig. 11.45 The greenhouse effect

Human Activity and Increasing CO_2

About 200 years ago, humans began to dig up soil to extract fossil fuels. These fossil fuels (coal, oil and natural gas) are made from the remains of animals that died long before humans evolved. The energy stored inside them is used to fuel our factories and cars, and to create electricity. However, burning these fuels also releases more CO_2 into the air.

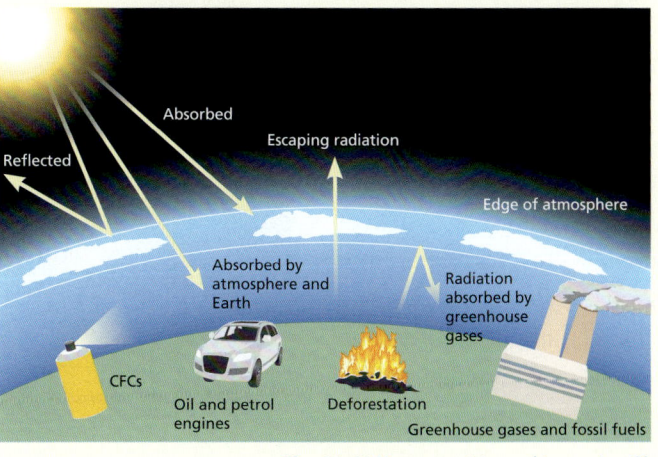

Fig. 11.46 Human activity and increasing CO_2

SUSTAINABLE DEVELOPMENT   441

CASE STUDY: Trócaire: Climate Change

In the past 200 years, forests have also been cleared for agriculture. This reduces the Earth's ability to remove CO_2 from the air. Every time we turn on the radio or television, or drive to the shops, we are contributing to the increase of CO_2 in our atmosphere. The more CO_2 in the air, the harder it becomes to ensure stability. The greenhouse effect is causing more heat to be trapped. Our world is getting hotter, and this is happening at an alarming speed. Each of the last three decades has been successively warmer at the Earth's surface than any preceding decade since 1850.

Ireland and Greenhouse Gas Emissions

Ireland is the second worst creator of carbon emissions in the EU per capita. Ireland made an agreement with the EU to reduce its carbon emissions by 20 per cent by 2020. However, Ireland's Environmental Protection Agency (EPA) estimated a likely *reduction* of 12 per cent by 2020, with an *increase* by the same amount (12 per cent) by 2030. In 2012, agriculture accounted for almost one-third of Ireland's carbon emissions. The energy and transport sectors are the next biggest contributors, at 20.5 per cent and 20 per cent respectively (see Fig. 11.47).

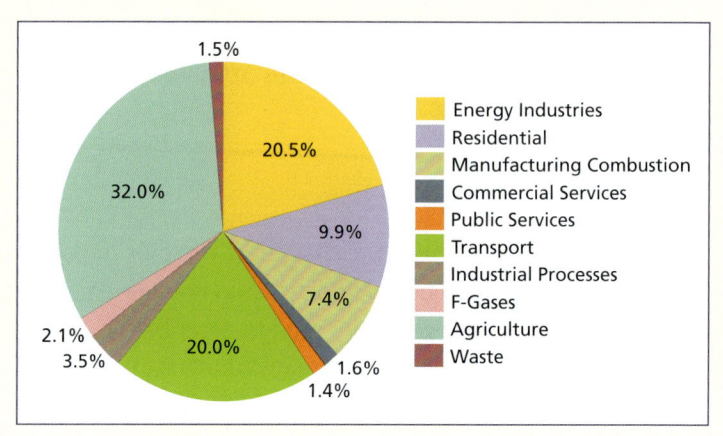

Fig. 11.47 Ireland's greenhouse gas emissions by sector for 2016

Impacts of Climate Change

Climate change is increasing the frequency and intensity of extreme weather events (e.g. storms and floods) as well as slower onset events (e.g. droughts). Climate change is causing sea levels to rise: the oceans expand because of higher temperatures, and increasing amounts of water from melting ice caps and glaciers flow into the oceans and seas. In Ireland, we have been experiencing more intense storms, rainfall and flooding. People in the Global South are experiencing the impacts of climate change even more than the people in Ireland. Two-thirds of the poorest people of the world live in rural areas and rely on farming for food and income. As a result of climate change, rainfall has become unpredictable. This makes it extremely difficult for farmers to grow their crops. In some cases, heavy rainfall washes away seeds; in other cases, the lack of rainfall prevents seeds from growing. Because of climate change, around 800 million people are currently at risk of hunger: about 12 per cent of our world's population.

Fig. 11.48 Taoiseach Enda Kenny visits flood-affected homes in the Midlands in December 2015

CASE STUDY: Trócaire: Climate Change

Actions on Climate Change: Ireland's Climate Action Law

Since 2008, Trócaire has been campaigning on climate justice issues, including the demand for a Climate Change Law in Ireland.

- **2010:** Trócaire campaigned with Stop Climate Chaos (SCC), a coalition of civil society organisations that campaign to ensure Ireland plays its role in stopping climate change. Trócaire held an event in Dublin where campaigners could directly lobby the Taoiseach, the Minister for the Environment, and their TDs for the government to prioritise a climate change bill and pass it into law.

- **2012:** Trócaire organised several public demonstrations outside the Dáil. Hundreds of campaigners attended the events and called for the government to prioritise the climate change bill.

- **2014:** A group of students from St Dominic's Secondary School in Ballyfermot, Dublin, submitted a petition with 7,313 signatures to the Taoiseach calling for the climate change legislation.

- **2015:** A second mass lobby event was organised by Trócaire and SCC in Dublin. Campaigners from Kerry, Mayo, Galway, Clare, Dublin and Leitrim met with their TDs to raise concerns about the draft climate change bill. The next day, many opposition TDs raised these issues during a Dáil debate on the bill. In June, Trócaire organised a climate change conference which included former Irish President Mary Robinson as one of the speakers.

- **2015:** On 3 December 2015, Ireland's Climate Bill (officially called the Climate Action and Low Carbon Development Bill) was finally passed and became law.

Fig. 11.49 Young citizens demonstrate for action on climate change

QUESTIONS

1. Explain the following terms: 'climate change', 'carbon cycle' and 'greenhouse effect'.
2. How do human activities contribute to the greenhouse effect and climate change?
3. Where does Ireland rank in the EU in terms of carbon emissions per capita?
4. List the top **three** sources of carbon emissions in Ireland.
5. What impact does climate change have on people living in the Global South (developing world)?
6. Describe any **three** measures that the Irish government could take to tackle the causes of climate change.

SKILLS BOOK LINK 11.4

Go to pages 184–185 of your Skills Book to complete Skill Task 11.4 on global warming.

RESEARCH ASSIGNMENT 11.2

Under the Climate Action and Low Carbon Development Act 2015, the Minister for the Environment is legally obliged to introduce a Low Carbon Transition Plan for Ireland every five years. Imagine that you are the Chief Environmental Adviser to the minister. Develop a Low Carbon Transition Plan for the minister's approval. Include the following in your plan:

- A brief analysis of the current levels of greenhouse gas emissions: examine Ireland's level of emissions compared to other countries
- A pie chart showing Ireland's current levels of greenhouse gas emissions by each economic sector: show the percentage of emissions from transport, agriculture, residential and other sectors
- Objectives of the plan: include specific goals and targets for reducing emissions over the next five years
- Strategies: provide a detailed breakdown of incentives and/or penalties that need to be introduced to reduce emissions for each sector (agriculture, industry, transport, residential, etc.).

- Visit the EPA's page on Ireland's greenhouse gas emissions at: https://educateplus.ie/go/emissions
- Visit the Union of Concerned Scientists page on reducing emissions at: https://educateplus.ie/go/reduce

CASE STUDY 8: ECO-UNESCO Young Environmentalist Awards 2016: Leap 2 the Future

ECO-UNESCO is Ireland's Environmental and Youth Organisation, which aims to raise awareness and promote actions for the protection and conservation of the environment. The Youth for Sustainable Development (YSD) Programme supports young people to develop their solutions for sustainable development at local and global levels. Young people undertake various 'local to global' action projects which are entered into ECO-UNESCO's Young Environmentalist Awards – a programme that recognises and rewards the work of young people who raise environmental awareness and improve their environment. Each year, young people from many secondary schools participate in the YSD programme and carry out a YEA project to address Ireland's contribution to climate change. In 2015, students from several secondary schools in Dublin participating in the YSD developed a project to contribute towards reducing Ireland's carbon emissions.

Fig. 11.50 ECO-UNESCO logo

POWER AND PEOPLE

ECO-UNESCO Young Environmentalist Awards 2016: Leap 2 the Future

Transport Sector and Carbon Emissions

According to the Environmental Protection Agency, Ireland's transport sector is the third largest contributor to our carbon emissions. In 2012 the transport sector accounted for 19 per cent of Ireland's emissions, and this is estimated to rise to 29 per cent by 2020. Private cars remain the preferred mode of transport in Ireland. According to the Department of Transport, in 2015, 75 per cent of all journeys were taken by car, 3.8 per cent by bus, and 1.5 per cent by rail/Dart/Luas. Cycling accounted for only 1.3 per cent of Ireland's transport. Cycling is the most sustainable form of transport. It provides social benefits (e.g. health) and it protects the environment from harmful carbon emissions.

Fig. 11.51 Young Environmentalist Awards

Leap 2 the Future

The Leap 2 the Future group aims to increase the use of the Dublin Bikes rental scheme by young people. As part of their initial research, the group examined the factors that contribute to low levels of usage among youth. Their research identified that many young people in Dublin could not access the bike scheme because it is compulsory to have a credit card with €150 credit available. The next step in the research was to identify and assess the possible solutions to address this problem. The group found that most young people in Dublin use public transport (e.g. buses, Luas, DART) and have a Leap Card (a type of travel credit card used for Dublin Bus, Luas and DART). The group came up with an interesting proposal. The Leap 2 the Future concept is to combine the Dublin Bikes rental scheme with the Leap Card. The group started a social media campaign and took their idea to the relevant decision-makers, meeting with local TDs and councillors. The project was officially approved in September 2016. Leap 2 the Future will ensure that infrared sensor technology, which can detect Leap Cards, will be available at the Dublin Bike stops. More young people will be able to access bicycles. This will increase the overall number of people in Dublin who use a sustainable mode of transport.

Fig. 11.52 Leap 2 the Future succeeded in making the Dublin Bike scheme more accessible to teenagers

The Leap 2 the Future group was rewarded for its exceptional efforts at the prestigious ECO-UNESCO Young Environmentalist Awards Final in both 2015 and in 2016, winning the Senior Transport Award in 2015 and the Special Achievement Growth Award 2016.

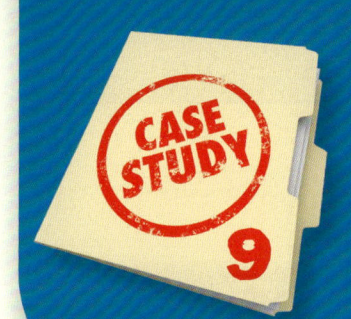

Case Study 9: An Taisce: Green-Schools

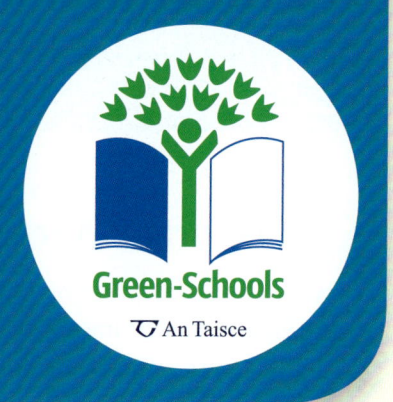

Green-Schools is an international environmental management and education programme of FEE (Foundation for Environmental Education), with 15 million students participating worldwide. The programme raises students' awareness of environmental and sustainable development issues through classroom study and action projects to make the day-to-day running of their school more environmentally friendly. Green-Schools is operated in Ireland by An Taisce, a charity that works to preserve and protect Ireland's natural and built heritage, and involves students, the wider community and local government.

Fig. 11.53 An Taisce Green-School

Green-Schools implement a seven-step process on the following themes:

- Litter and waste
- Energy
- Water
- Travel
- Biodiversity
- Global citizenship: litter and waste
- Global citizenship: energy
- Global citizenship: marine environment.

When a school completes a theme, it is awarded a Green Flag, which can be flown outside the school or displayed in the reception area. As of January 2017, there are 3,900 primary and secondary schools participating in the programme in Ireland.

St Mary's Secondary School, Mallow, Co. Cork

St Mary's Secondary School is an all-girls voluntary secondary school in Mallow with over 570 students. The pupils were awarded a flag for their 'litter and waste' work in May 2016, after they reduced the school's landfill waste by 33 per cent, improved recycling practices, and put an end to littering. The school undertook several important steps to achieve their success.

Step 1: Green-Schools Committee

A Green-Schools Committee was established and its members were drawn from elected candidates representing all year groups. The committee meet weekly to discuss litter and waste issues, and agree on actions they can take to improve the situation.

Step 2: Environmental Review

In September 2014, the committee conducted a survey with students and teachers at the school. Key findings from the survey included the following.

- Litter blackspots were identified in ranking order (from worst to least) in the canteen, locker areas and outside the school yard.

- 84 per cent of the student population felt that waste was a problem in the school.

CASE STUDY: An Taisce: Green-Schools

- Post-lunchtime was highlighted as a time when litter was particularly bad. Both students and teachers felt that there were not enough litter bins in the school.
- 65 per cent of the student population were unaware of which materials are recyclable.

Step 3: Action Plan

The committee developed an action plan to address some of the problems highlighted by the survey. The action plan focused on achieving five goals:

1. Reduce the school's landfill waste by 30 per cent in 8 months.
2. Increase recycling by 40 per cent in 8 months.
3. Increase cardboard recycling by 100 per cent in 8 months.
4. Educate the school community on litter and waste on a continuous basis.
5. Keep the school litter-free, targeting litter blackspots.

The action plan involved a special Green-Schools launch day, which was very successful in raising awareness and support among students and teachers for the five goals. One of their most successful actions was encouraging staff to reduce the amount of paper they used.

Step 4: Monitoring and Evaluation

The committee undertakes several important monitoring activities to ensure that the action plan is being successfully implemented.

- Litter is monitored by regular inspections of the known litter blackspots. The team reward students with a lollipop when they put their litter into the correct bin. If a litter blackspot is identified, the Green-Schools Team inform the Green-Schools coordinator. The coordinator visits the students who hang out in these areas during lunch break, and reminds them to be responsible and informed about recyclable and non-recyclable items.
- Data on the amount of school waste is regularly obtained from the waste disposal company. These figures are analysed during meetings.
- Bins are inspected every evening by committee members. While doing this task, the committee members check the recycling bins for non-recyclable items (e.g. food, tin foil, cling film) and check the general waste bin for recyclable items (e.g. plastic bottles). Non-recyclable items are removed from the recycling bins, and recyclable items are removed from the general waste bins. At weekly meetings, the findings from the previous week are discussed and a plan is made to target specific items that are being placed in the wrong bins. Plans include school announcements and poster campaigns.

Step 5: Curriculum Links

The school ensures that the topic of 'litter and waste' is covered where possible and appropriately in the syllabus of different subjects offered at the school. For example, the use of recycled materials was encouraged in Art classes, and students in English classes wrote a newspaper article entitled 'Future Generations Will be Furious at our Indifference to Protecting the Environment'.

Step 6: Informing and Involving

The Green-Schools programme can be successful only when the wider school community are well informed and engaged in the programme. Several activities ensure this.

- Waste figures are shared on the Green-Schools noticeboard and on the Green-Schools Committee Facebook page.

CASE STUDY: An Taisce: Green-Schools

- Posters are displayed close to waste bins to remind students which materials should be placed in which bins.
- Information regarding the latest work by the committee is posted in the school newsletter.
- The school community tweets about all school-related activities, including activities conducted by the Green-Schools Committee.
- The committee organised a Day of Action and National Spring Clean in conjunction with Mallow Tidy Towns.

Step 7: Green Code
In the final step of the Green-Schools programme, the school developed a statement on its commitment to environmentally friendly action. This statement is known as a Green Code.

QUESTIONS

1. What is ECO-UNESCO? How does the organisation contribute to sustainable development solutions?
2. Describe the specific steps taken by the Leap 2 the Future group to make their project a success.
3. What is the aim of Green-Schools?
4. Evaluate the strengths and weaknesses of the steps taken by the Green-Schools Committee at St Mary's. Can you think of any additional steps that could have been taken?

ACTIVE CITIZENSHIP: Ideas for Action

Task:
Design and carry out an action plan to reduce the ecological footprint of either **(a)** your school or **(b)** your local community.

Include the following in your plan:

- A description of the specific environmental issue or problem to be addressed
- An explanation of your proposed action to address the problem and your rationale for choosing this action over other alternatives
- Information about a person or organisation that has inspired your thinking on this plan
- An outline of the specific objectives of the plan
- A step-by-step strategy and timeline to achieve the objective
- A description of specific roles assigned to committees/individual students

After completing the campaign, evaluate the success of your action plan.

RESEARCH ASSIGNMENT 11.3

Write a speech to be delivered to students at your school on how their own energy use contributes to climate change. In the speech, explain how climate change is having a far greater negative impact on people in the developing world. Include suggestions on how students can reduce their energy consumption.

See **RESEARCH TIPS** on page 33.

Fairtrade

Fair trade is an alternative approach to conventional trade. The Fairtrade organisation was established in 1988. Representing 1.5 million farmers and workers in 74 countries, the movement provides some of the most disadvantaged farmers and workers in the developing world with a better deal in the sale of their produce. When we think about Fairtrade, we often think about products such as coffee or bananas. However, Fairtrade now encompasses many different products, including tea, sugar, chocolate, cocoa, confectionery, cosmetics, biscuits, fresh and dried fruit, ice cream, nuts, spices, fruit juice, honey, jams, rice, wine, oils, cotton and footballs.

Fig. 11.54 Fairtrade logo

International Certification

Fairtrade is an international certification. When a product carries the Fairtrade mark, this means that the product was produced according to certain international Fairtrade standards. These standards ensure that Fairtrade products are socially and economically fair and environmentally responsible. In 2015, Fairtrade products were sold in 127 countries worldwide.

Fairtrade Minimum Price

For most Fairtrade goods, there is a Fairtrade minimum price. This means that farmers and workers are guaranteed a minimum price for their produce. This reduces these people's vulnerability to fluctuation in market prices and provides them and their families with income security to meet their needs and plan for their futures. If the market price for their product is higher than the Fairtrade minimum price, the farmers and workers receive the market price. Fairtrade is the only certification scheme that offers such a safety net for farmers and workers.

Fairtrade Premium

As well as the Fairtrade minimum price, workers and farmers receive an additional sum of money called the Fairtrade premium. This money goes to a communal fund to be used as workers and farmers see fit, to improve their social, economic and environmental conditions. Premiums have been used to fund health and education initiatives in local communities, and to invest in cooperatives and organisations.

Fig. 11.55 Ellias Walekhwa, a Fairtrade grower in Uganda

SUSTAINABLE DEVELOPMENT

Fairtrade in Ireland

In 1996, Bewley's became the first Irish company to carry the Fairtrade brand in a coffee product. Since then, the Fairtrade movement in Ireland has grown. In 2013, Ireland ranked 7th in the Fairtrade International Sales Index. The Dáil became the first Fairtrade parliament in the world in 2008. Ireland has 48 Fairtrade towns, and an increasing number of Fairtrade schools and colleges. The Electric Picnic and BodyandSoul music festivals are also Fairtrade certified.

However, there is room for improvement. Research conducted by Globescan in 2013 showed that 82 per cent of people surveyed were aware of Fairtrade. However, only 8 per cent of bananas sold in Ireland during 2014 were Fairtrade, compared to 35 per cent in the UK and 60 per cent in Switzerland.

QUESTIONS

1. When was Fairtrade established?
2. How many farmers and workers operate under Fairtrade?
3. List **six** common Fairtrade products.
4. What does the Fairtrade international certification mean?
5. How do farmers benefit from Fairtrade?

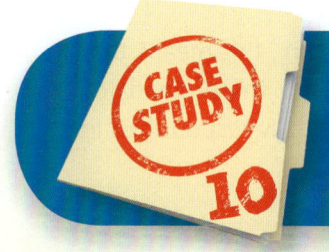

CASE STUDY 10: Fairtrade Town: Clonakilty, Co. Cork

In 2003 Clonakilty in Co. Cork became Ireland's first Fairtrade town. To become a Fairtrade town, several important criteria must be met:

- Fairtrade products (e.g. coffee, tea and chocolate) must be used by at least 10 of the town's businesses and organisations.
- The town council must pass an official motion supporting the Fairtrade campaign and encouraging people in the area to use Fairtrade products.

To achieve Fairtrade town status for Clonakilty, the local Fairtrade group in Cork took a variety of actions within the community over 12 months. The Fairtrade group:

- Held meetings with the local council
- Conducted a variety of talks in local churches and schools
- Visited local businesses.

As of November 2017, Ireland has a total of 48 officially recognised Fairtrade towns, cities and islands. In addition to the Fairtrade town initiative, schools, third-level colleges and festivals can also work towards obtaining the prestigious Fairtrade status.

Fig. 11.56 Ireland has 48 officially recognised Fairtrade towns, cities and islands

POWER AND PEOPLE

ACTIVE CITIZENSHIP: Ideas for Action

Task:
Design and carry out an action plan to make either **(a)** your school a Fairtrade school or **(b)** your local town a Fairtrade town.

A step-by-step guide from WorldWise Global Schools is available at: https://educateplus.ie/go/checklist

ACTIVITY 11.5

Hold a classroom debate on the following motion:

'Fairtrade is a much more effective way than aid to combat global poverty and inequality.'

RESEARCH ASSIGNMENT 11.4

Keep a diary of all the purchases you make over the next week. Research how the manufacturing of any two of these items may have had an impact on people in developing nations.

Tips:
Focus your research on the following questions:
- Where are the items produced?
- What are the pay and conditions like for the people who manufacture these items?
- Where does most of the profit go?

See **RESEARCH TIPS** on page 33.

Tax Justice: Debt and Development Coalition Ireland (DDCI)

Tax justice is an important part of sustainable development. It forms part of the targets for Goal 17 of the SDGs. Tax affects the quality of life of everyone. Tax revenue – collected by governments from individuals and companies – pays for important services (e.g. healthcare, education) in countries around the world. However, people living in the Global North and the Global South have very different experiences of taxation.

For people of the Global South, tax has become a matter of life and death. This is because southern governments often do not have enough funds to pay for basic services. They collect small amounts of tax revenue from their citizens and from companies working in their countries. This has led many southern governments to become highly dependent on loans and grants from richer nations and institutions in order to deliver basic services. It has recently become clear that southern countries are illegally losing a huge amount of tax revenue because of the ways in

Fig. 11.57 Citizens demonstrating for tax justice

SUSTAINABLE DEVELOPMENT 451

which the global tax system is used and abused. According to Christian Aid, countries of the Global South lose at least US$160 billion per year because of tax evasion by MNCs. Tax is not just about figures and percentages: it is about human rights.

Tax Justice: Key Facts

1. Southern countries lose an estimated US$160 billion every year in tax revenue because companies do not pay as much tax as they should.
2. One common way for companies to avoid tax is to exaggerate their costs of production. They can do this by, for example, claiming to have paid more for raw materials or machinery than their true value. This is called 'transfer mispricing'.
3. Major accountancy firms help to design schemes for companies to minimise the amount of tax they will pay a government. One of the biggest accountancy firms, KPMG, paid a fine of US$456 million in the US for 'designing, marketing and implementing illegal tax shelters'. This fine is bigger than the annual budget of the government of Burundi, a country of 9 million people (in 2008, Burundi's government had a budget of US$350 million).
4. Companies and wealthy individuals often place their money in what are called 'tax havens'. Tax havens include countries such as Switzerland, Bermuda and the Cayman Islands. These countries allow people to open bank accounts, even if they do not live in the country or conduct any business there. The details of the bank accounts are kept secret, and little or no tax is charged.
5. According to the Organisation for Economic Co-operation and Development (OECD), US$5–7 trillion is stashed in tax havens. Banking secrecy also facilitates corruption and organised crime.
6. The US$160 billion lost by southern countries every year is greater than all the aid they receive from wealthy countries. The tax income would provide them with enough resources to meet the SDGs.
7. Tax dodging would be much more difficult if MNCs had to file accounts showing how much tax they paid and how much profit they earned in each country.
8. The problems caused by tax havens could be minimised if every country agreed to share information with other countries about bank accounts held by their citizens. In this way, it would become clear if people or companies were using foreign bank accounts to avoid paying tax in the countries in which they have made their profits.

QUESTIONS

1. What has tax justice got to do with sustainable development?
2. According to Christian Aid, how much money does the Global South lose each year because of tax evasion by MNCs?
3. What is a 'tax haven'?
4. According to the OECD, how much money is currently stashed in tax havens?
5. What solutions can be put forward to help resolve this tax injustice?

ACTIVITY 11.6

Your teacher will assign your group an article or report related to tax injustice. Summarise the main findings of the report. Present your group's findings to another group.

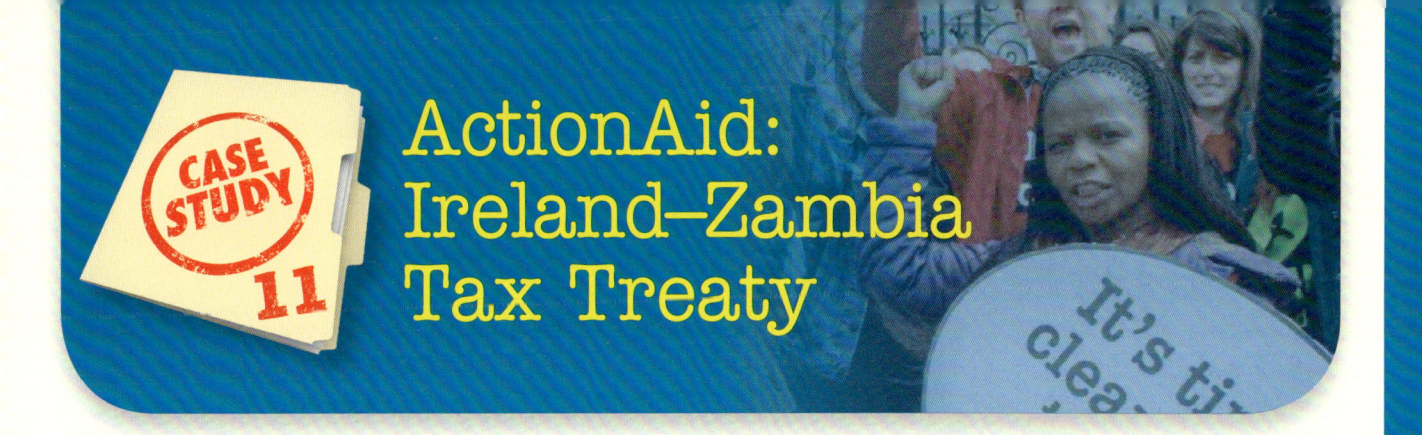

CASE STUDY 11: ActionAid: Ireland–Zambia Tax Treaty

ActionAid's Tax Power Campaign

Taxes are needed to pay teachers. Taxes are needed to train nurses. Taxes are needed to maintain roads, deliver medicine and provide clean water. Tax money pays for our public services and our human rights. Tax is the most important, sustainable and predictable source of public income for almost all countries. However, not everyone is paying their fair share. Tax evasion is the use of illegal methods to reduce the amount of tax a person or company pays. Tax avoidance is when a person or company exploits a weakness in the law to reduce the amount of tax they pay.

Fig. 11.58 ActionAid's Tax Power campaign

Every year, developing countries lose an estimated US$138 billion because of tax breaks for companies, and an additional US$200 billion because of companies avoiding taxes altogether. This is more than enough money to ensure that every child on the planet gets a quality education. In developed and developing countries, the tax revenues needed to cover the ongoing costs of public services are being undermined by the ability of some of the wealthiest taxpayers – including many MNCs – to effectively opt out of the corporate tax system. This happens because of a combination of tax avoidance schemes, and tax incentives awarded by governments. Tax dodging and avoidance are causes of poverty: developing countries lose far more money to unjust tax practices than they receive in aid each year.

Ireland and Tax Justice

In 2013, ActionAid released a report entitled *Sweet Nothings*. The report exposed how one of the world's largest food multinationals, the Associated British Foods (ABF) group, dodged an estimated US$10.4 million in taxes in Zambia between 2007 and 2012. The report concluded that a tax treaty between Ireland and Zambia enabled ABF to avoid paying fair taxes, which would have put 18,000 children in school in Zambia.

Fig. 11.59 ActionAid's *Sweet Nothings* report

ActionAid's investigation found that ABF's Zambian subsidiary company used an array of transactions that saw over one-third of the company's pre-tax profits – over US$13.8 million a year (Zambian Kwacha 62 billion) – paid out of Zambia, into and via sister companies in Ireland, Mauritius and the Netherlands. The effects of these transactions have been significant. While the main corporate tax rate in Zambia is 35 per cent, since 2007 ABF's Zambian

SUSTAINABLE DEVELOPMENT   453

CASE STUDY: ActionAid: Ireland–Zambia Tax Treaty

subsidiary has, overall, paid less than 0.5 per cent of its US$123 million pre-tax profits in corporate income tax.

The case of ABF is an example of how international tax legislation and loopholes coupled with tax competition in developing countries – an international 'race to the bottom' to attract foreign investors with huge tax breaks – can have a devastating effect on economies, public services and human rights.

ActionAid: Action for Tax Justice

ActionAid has campaigned on tax justice since 2011, with its Tax Power campaign.

- ActionAid provided stories to the Irish and UK media about the impact of tax avoidance on the lives of Zambian citizens. Citizens in Zambia shared stories of how tax money could improve their local school or hospital and called on ABF to pay their fair share of taxes in Zambia.

- ActionAid shared its report with the Irish and Zambian governments and asked them to take action to resolve the situation.

In 2015, a new tax agreement between Zambia and Ireland was renegotiated, which closed the loophole that had allowed tax avoidance to happen. This will make it more difficult for companies not to pay their fair share of the taxes which can be used to fund critical public services for Zambian citizens. In 2016, ActionAid published another report, *Mistreated*, which showed that Ireland still has several problematic tax treaties with developing countries.

Action Aid's campaign activities continue and there are a many ways to get involved:

- Host an ActionAid Ireland Tax Power exhibition in your school.

- Organise a talk to be delivered by ActionAid Ireland in your school.

Fig. 11.60 ActionAid campaigns for tax justice

- Meet, email or tweet your local TDs and MEP to raise your concerns.

- Go to ActionAid Ireland's Tax Justice campaign website to learn about the other actions you can take: https://educateplus.ie/go/tax-justice

IN THE MEDIA

Fig. 11.61 Ireland's tax justice responsibilities have been highlighted by the media

454 POWER AND PEOPLE

RESEARCH ASSIGNMENT 11.5

Write a speech to be delivered to a UN special summit on the topic of tax injustice. Include the following in your speech:

- A definition of tax injustice
- Up-to-date statistics on global tax injustice
- Information on the impact of tax injustice on the developing world
- Your proposals to create a fair and just global taxation system
- The steps the UN needs to take to achieve tax justice.

See **RESEARCH TIPS** on page 33.

✓ SUMMARY

- Sustainable development is development that meets the needs of the present without compromising the ability of future generations to meet their needs.
- Sustainable development is about addressing and balancing the economic, social and environmental needs of the world.
- The belief that our environmental problems can be solved by technology and the free market is a right-wing view.
- Supporters of a left-wing view would argue that the environment and the world's natural resources are not private property but are a matter of human rights. As with all human rights, the government is the primary dutybearer and, therefore, we need to regulate our use of natural resources.
- People of a left-wing view also believe that Mother Earth has rights that should be recognised and protected by international and national laws.
- Sustainable development in harmony with nature can be best achieved through small-scale, self-reliant communities that use clean and renewable resources.
- Human activities, such as the burning of fossil fuels, are the primary cause of climate change.
- Lower-income countries suffer more from the effects of climate change, through devastating droughts, floods and famines.
- Solutions to global warming include greater investment in public transport and the use of clean, renewable sources of energy (e.g. wind, solar, hydroelectric power).
- We can all contribute positively to stop climate change and to protect the environment, by reducing our energy usage and carbon/ecological footprint at home, at school and in our local communities.
- Fair trade can help to solve economic inequality between lower- and higher-income countries and regions.
- We can contribute towards social and economic justice by purchasing Fairtrade-approved and other ethical products.
- Tax injustice is one of the biggest causes of poverty. Every government must take responsibility for ensuring that everyone (individuals and companies) pays their fair share of taxes, which are vital to fund services such as education and health.

REVISION QUESTIONS

1. Explain clearly what sustainable development means.
2. List examples of how technology has been, or could be, used to solve our environmental problems.
3. What does a 'free market environmentalism' approach to environmental issues mean?
4. Explain **one** argument in favour of and **one** argument against an FME approach.
5. Describe the positive benefits of any small-scale, self-reliant, sustainable projects that you have studied.
6. What are the benefits of organic, small-scale farming, according to Vandana Shiva?
7. Explain the following terms: 'ecological footprint', 'ecological deficit', 'planetary boundaries' and 'ecovillage'.
8. Describe any **three** major contributors to greenhouse gas emissions.
9. What are the effects of climate change on the developing world?
10. Describe **three** actions to reduce carbon emissions that could be taken by each of the following: **(a)** your family, **(b)** your school and **(c)** the government.
11. What is Fairtrade? Explain the benefits of buying Fairtrade products.
12. Explain how tax injustice causes poverty.
13. List the actions that your class could take to promote: **(a)** fair trade **(b)** tax justice.

DATA-BASED QUESTIONS

Complete the qualitative and quantitative research data-based questions exercise on pages 185–188 of your Skills Book.

EXAM FOCUS — Section B of LC Exam

REVISION EXERCISES

Complete the revision exercises on pages 188–190 of your Skills Book.

EXAM FOCUS — Section A of LC Exam

DISCURSIVE ESSAY TOPICS

1. Critically assess the view that technology and the laws of the free market will solve our environmental problems. In your answer, refer to qualitative and quantitative evidence.
2. 'Development in harmony with nature requires a move away from big industries and urbanisation and towards small-scale, self-reliant communities using renewable resources.' Discuss this statement with reference to qualitative and quantitative evidence.
3. 'Sustainable development is development that meets the needs of the present without compromising the ability of future generations to meet their own needs.' Explore the meaning of this statement. In your answer:
   - Explain in your own words what the statement means, using examples from either a local or global context.
   - Suggest ways that individuals can live more sustainably.
   - Suggest actions that governments should take to support sustainable development.

EXAM FOCUS — Section C of LC Exam

Reflective Practice

Ensure that you have completed all the Reflective Journal entries for this chapter (pages 46–47 of your Reflective Journal and Learning Portfolio) before moving on to the next chapter.

Complete the Learning Portfolio activities on pages 47–49 of your Reflective Journal and Learning Portfolio. This will help you to self-assess the extent to which you have achieved the learning intentions for this chapter, and will help you to monitor your progress.

Global hectares
Fair trade
Climate change Genetically modified
Eco-friendly vehicles
Planetary boundaries Tax justice
Ecological footprint
Global hectares Climate change
Sustainable development Fair trade
Free market environmentalism
Tax justice Ecological deficit
The Green Revolution
Tragedy of the commons

Fig. 11.62 Key Word cloud

Appendix: Additional Information on Political and Social Thinkers

Émile Durkheim (1858–1917)

Émile Durkheim was a French sociologist in the late nineteenth/early twentieth century. He is considered to be the 'father of sociology'. Sociology is the academic and scientific study of societies. Durkheim believed that societies could, indeed should, be studied scientifically. He argued that sociology could provide an empirical (based on objective data) approach to the study of societies in a way that other traditions, such as philosophy, could not. Durkheim was interested in studying what he called the 'social facts' – structures, beliefs, values, norms and rules – of a society. Social facts are independent and external from the individual, but social facts influence each of us in how we think and act as a 'collective' (society). Examples of such collective rules and norms include: respecting one's elders; saying 'please' and 'thank you'; and avoiding certain behaviours considered to be rude or uncivilised in society. Durkheim was primarily concerned with what creates stability and integration in society. He developed his theories during a time of great political and social upheaval in France, which saw: the famous Dreyfus Affair; growing industrialisation; the rise of a militant working class; political power struggles between the Church, military and aristocracy; and tensions between the Church and secular segments of society for control of education in France. All these contextual changes were transforming the traditional ways of societal and collective bonding (i.e. family, Church and nationalism) and, in Durkheim's view, were giving rise to the age of the 'individual'.

Social integration – the level to which one feels connected to other people in one's community, group, or society – was a key focus of Durkheim's research. He named the lack of such social integration and societal regulation *'anomie'*. He demonstrated his theory in a famous study called *Suicide* (1897). Durkheim looked at data related to suicide rates across several countries to identify patterns and draw conclusions. He concluded that males (gender), single people (marital status) and Protestants (a religion with limited control and a looser community, compared with Catholicism or Judaism) were more likely to take their own lives. This was because they were more likely to suffer from *anomie* than other people in society. Durkheim argued that the wealthy were more susceptible to social disconnect than the poor. This is because the wealthy are more likely to have a strong sense of 'individualism' as opposed to 'community'. This formed the basis of Durkheim's critique of capitalism.

Durkheim's study on suicide is representative of his general understanding of society and social order, since he viewed the phenomenon of suicide as an indication of the breakdown of social integration.

He believed that too little social control (excessive individuation) or too much social control (excessive regulation) would lead to the state of *anomie*. In other words, *anomie* can come about either because of the *isolation from* **or** *the rejection of* social control. Sudden changes in a society – financial crashes, rapid economic growth, growing secularism in a traditionally religious country (or vice versa) – will lead to changes in societal norms, values and rules. This changes the degree of social control and, eventually, affects the level of social integration.

In *The Division of Labour in Society* (1893), Durkheim distinguished between two types of social integration present in pre-industrial (traditional) and industrialised (modern) societies. The first type, *mechanical solidarity*, is present in traditional societies, where people feel connected through common work, religion, education, family or other elements of lifestyle. A sense of 'group' solidarity is most common. With industrialisation, however, the age of the 'individual' emerges and *organic solidarity* comes to the fore. Connections between people become more complex in terms of interdependence. Although individuals may have different types of specialised work and different values, they depend on one another to be able to live in society. For example, a boat builder makes boats so that the fisherman can catch fish to feed the boat builder, and so on. Durkheim's *organic solidarity* is quite a 'functional' view of society.

Durkheim is famous for what is termed 'structural functionalism', which involves studying different social institutions and the roles they play in society. Society is like a body: it has various parts which are interdependent, functioning together as a whole. In society, the parts include the government, economy, laws, religion, education, etc. No one part can function without the others, and a change in one part will impact on the whole. For example, if our education system does not produce the talents and skills required by our economy or other aspects of our society (cultural, political), what impact will that have on society? Despite his functionalist approach to society, Durkheim did not believe that disorder in society was always a negative thing.

Durkheim's theory on *deviance* has contributed to how we think about social order and how it is maintained. He believed that deviance can actually contribute to social order because:

- Seeing someone punished for a deviant act reinforces society's norms and values with respect to what is acceptable or not.
- Deviance teaches society about what is right and wrong.
- Grave acts of deviance (e.g. terrorism) can bring society closer together.
- Certain acts, such as protest, can highlight problems or injustices in a society, which can eventually lead to positive change.

In later life, Durkheim began to focus on the *common set of beliefs* that hold society together, in addition to the cohesion achieved through functional interdependence. In his final work, *The Elementary Forms of the Religious Life* (1917), he discussed the role religion played in producing social cohesion and order. For Durkheim, religion plays an important role in society by providing a common set of social norms and beliefs, and authority figures. Religion was stronger in traditional societies than in modern societies.

Durkheim's main ideas can be viewed in his critique of capitalism. Durkheim was more positive than Marx on the effects of capitalism. However, given Durkheim's structural functionalist approach, he was fearful of the rise of individualism associated with *organic solidarity*. He was wary of the loosening of traditional bonds and forms of moral guidance, which had been provided by religion, for example. The greater importance of individual over collective needs could lead to a state of *anomie*. For these reasons, Durkheim argued that capitalism would not make us happier. It would make us more miserable and result in even higher suicide rates.

> ## Summary: Durkheim's views on society
>
> - Durkheim is famous for what is termed 'structural functionalism' – the study of different social institutions and the role they play in society. Society is considered like a body with various parts which are interdependent, functioning together as a whole; the government, economy, laws, religion, education, etc.
> - There are two types of social integration present in pre-industrial (traditional) and industrialised (modern) societies: 'mechanical solidarity' and 'organic solidarity'.
> - 'Mechanical solidarity' is present in traditional societies, where people feel connected due to sharing common work, religion, education, family or other forms of lifestyle. A sense of 'group' solidarity is most common.
> - 'Organic solidarity' is present in 'industrialised' societies. The age of the 'individual' emerges and connections between people become more complex, based on their different roles in society. Although individuals may have different types of specialised work and different values, they depend on one another to be able to live in society.
> - *Anomie* refers to a disconnect between the individual and community or society (social disintegration). Durkheim attributed anomie to capitalism and organic solidarity. He conducted a study of suicide which he considered a consequence of *anomie*.

Robert Nozick (1938–2002)

Robert Nozick was born in 1938 in New York. He studied philosophy at Princeton and Colombia in the United States, and later at Oxford in England, eventually lecturing at Harvard University. He was a libertarian (different from a liberal – see page 8) and is considered one of the greatest political philosophers of the twentieth century. As we learned in Chapter 5, Nozick is best known for a book entitled *Anarchy, State, and Utopia* (1974). He argued for minimal state. This is when a state/government limits its interventions so that it protects only the individual rights of life, liberty and property. Nozick's views were quite different from his contemporary, John Rawls, who argued that *more* state intervention is needed to ensure that there is equality in society. Nozick and Rawls were writing at a time of great upheaval in US politics and society.

Nozick shared some of John Locke's beliefs with respect to natural rights. Nozick believed in self-ownership and, in particular, ownership of the fruits of one's labour. Nozick applied this concept to the taxation system. He criticised the idea of wealth redistribution, which was put forward by egalitarian liberals such as Rawls. Nozick was not a supporter of the welfare state, viewing it as a 'theft' of legitimately earned wealth.

In Nozick's theory, a crucial point is *who* has ownership of resources. Nozick identified three ways in which an individual can be said to have a just *entitlement* to property and resources: *acquisition, transfer* and *rectification*. Similar to Locke, Nozick believed that if an individual invested (e.g. physical labour) in property not previously owned by another, he or she would have ownership rights (*acquisition*). The second type of entitlement, *transfer*, would occur in cases where an owner decides to sell or give the property rights to another. For this to be a legitimate transfer, however, the original owner would need to have obtained the property through just means (e.g. not from theft). The third type of entitlement is *rectification* and it involves correcting (making right) a previous acquisition or transfer that took place, which was not legitimate in the first place. Unlike egalitarian liberals, Nozick believed that wealth distribution is *just* if everyone in society has obtained their wealth and resources legitimately, based on his three principles. It is *just* even if it results in an unequal or unfair distribution. In Nozick's view, most economic decisions should be left to individuals and business actors – not governments or official institutions.

Nozick rejects the idea that government should play a role in ensuring equality. However, he does allow for communities and groups of different cultural, social, political, moral or religious viewpoints to establish their own rules on how they should live within a society – as long as they co-exist peacefully. This relates to multiculturalism (see Chapter 9).

Summary: Main elements of Nozick's theory

- The best form of government is based on the principle of minimal state, when a state/government limits its interventions so that it protects only the individual rights of life, liberty and property.
- Forced wealth redistribution systems, such as taxation, can be considered a type of theft.
- Fair distribution in society is achieved if individuals acquire their wealth and resources legitimately – through acquisition, transfer or rectification.
- Most economic decisions should be left to individuals and business actors, with limited government intervention.
- Communities of different viewpoints should be allowed to live by their own rules, if they can co-exist peacefully in a society.

Sylvia Walby

Sylvia Walby is a Distinguished Professor of Sociology and UNESCO Chair of Gender Research at Lancaster University. In 2008, Walby was awarded an OBE for her significant contribution to women's rights, equal opportunities and diversity. Like Kathleen Lynch, Walby uses her academic research to engage in political discussions to influence changes in policy and practice. Since the 1980s, Walby has contributed to the evolution of feminist theory. She has promoted a feminist perspective on many contemporary political and economic issues, such as the economic and financial crisis, multiculturalism and citizenship within the EU. She has developed an approach to measure gender inequality and has used this to look at how different social and economic policies (e.g. crime) affect, and are affected by, gender inequality.

For many people, Walby's greatest contribution to feminist theory is her book entitled *Theorizing Patriarchy* (1990), which was published during the so-called 'second wave' of feminism. At its simplest form, patriarchy is the system in society in which men are the primary power-holders, dominating all areas of society: political, social, economic, moral and cultural. Walby identified six key elements of the patriarchal structure which maintain gender inequality and the subordination of women.

Walby makes a distinction between private (in the household) patriarchy and public (wider society) patriarchy. She argues that we have moved from private to public in most western countries. Walby's model can be used as a lens when looking at many aspects of society and how power is distributed.

In *The Future of Feminism* (2011), Walby presents the argument for why gender needs to be 'mainstreamed' (integrated) in public policy development. She shows how public policies, laws and budgets affect men and women differently. For example, if a government cuts funding to childcare provision, will this impact on men and women equally? Walby herself has been at the forefront of promoting approaches and developing tools to 'mainstream' gender in relation to crime and sexual violence in the UK. She continues to study gender in terms of the policies and practices related to multiculturalism and citizenship within the EU.

> ### Summary: Key elements of the patriarchal structure in Walby's theory
>
> - In the sector of 'paid work', women often face discriminatory pay and treatment and are less often found in the higher professional levels (e.g. managerial).
> - The gender division of labour in the 'home' means that women assume a disproportionate level of responsibility for domestic duties and childcare, even if they are also working outside the home (within the 'paid work' sector).
> - The dominant culture as embodied in media, education, arts and religion produces and preserves patriarchal viewpoints of femininity. This often degrades women and can contribute to women's vulnerability to violence and poor treatment.
> - Despite some advancements (e.g. contraception, divorce), heterosexual relations (between men and women) are still structured by gender inequality.
> - Male violence against women is caused by, and contributes to, gender inequality.
> - Despite some gender equality reforms, the state and society are still structured to women's disadvantage.

Martha Nussbaum

Martha Nussbaum is an American philosopher and Professor of Law and Ethics at the University of Chicago. From the liberalist tradition, she has written extensively on social justice, equality and feminism, and has made significant contributions to how we now measure human development.

Since the 1980s, Nussbaum has worked alongside Bangladeshi economist Amartya Sen to influence international development policy and how countries measure 'development progress' (how we consider whether or not a country is 'developed'). Nussbaum criticised the traditional approach of simply measuring the macro-economic performance of a country with units of measurement such as income and Gross Domestic Product (GDP). Nussbaum attacked neo-liberal arguments that economic growth in a country will benefit everyone to some extent (the so-called 'trickle-down effect'). For Nussbaum, these approaches are unhelpful because they often mask gross inequalities and how poverty is actually experienced by the population. These approaches do not capture other important aspects of *quality of life*, such as health, education and political freedoms. For example, some countries with high levels of poverty and inequality (e.g. India and Brazil) also appeared in the top ten of the International Monetary Fund (IMF) GDP ranking in 2015. Nussbaum is critical of other utilitarian approaches that focus on measuring simple results or outcomes, such as increased healthcare, better education or higher income. Nussbaum questions the approach of measuring 'perceived level of happiness or satisfaction'. Nussbaum points out that people can adapt their mental state to accept even the most oppressive conditions as 'normal' or 'acceptable'.

In *The Quality of Life* (1993), Nussbaum and Sen began to put forward an alternative approach to measuring human development. The book focused on this central question: *What are people able to do and be?* This approach involves measuring the 'real' opportunities people have in shaping their own lives in terms of health, education, work and business, voting, political and social affiliations. This is called the *capabilities* approach or the *human development* approach. It places greater emphasis on human rights. It has influenced global development policy and can be seen in the annual Human Development Reports published by the United Nations, as well as the 'wellbeing' measurements now used by national statistics offices and government departments in most European countries.

With respect to the role of government, Nussbaum would share many of the ideas of Rousseau and Mill on promoting equality and social justice, and protecting freedoms. Nussbaum rejects concepts such as the minimal state (Nozick) and the view that the 'welfare state' model practised in most European countries is too 'maternalistic' (a type of 'nanny state'). Nussbaum's political ideology demonstrates the difference between positive freedoms (e.g. freedom *to* vote) and negative freedoms (e.g. freedom *from* violence). Nussbaum's capabilities approach is based on the idea that government policy should also focus on promoting the conditions necessary for people to enjoy positive freedoms and rights. These conditions not only include individual skills and capacities but also one's social, economic and political environment. For example, an individual from a lower socio-economic group may have the individual potential to be a great doctor, but what happens if the necessary Science subjects are not offered at his or her school? What if this person cannot afford the fees to attend university? What if this person does not have enough study time because of their part-time job to pay those fees? For Nussbaum, all these conditions affect an individual's capabilities, and all these conditions require government policy.

As we learned in Chapter 7, Nussbaum outlines ten 'universal fundamental political entitlements' which she considers as essential capabilities:

- Life: not dying prematurely
- Bodily health: including good health, nutrition and shelter
- Bodily integrity: including freedom of movement, freedom from violence, reproductive rights
- Freedom to imagine, think and reason
- Freedom to have and express our emotions
- Freedom to engage in critical reflection
- Freedom to have personal and social affiliations
- Ability to co-exist with nature and other species (i.e. animals)
- Ability to enjoy play, recreation and leisure
- Control over one's environment, both political (i.e. participation) and material (i.e. owning property).

Minimum thresholds or standards for each of these should be established. Then the government has a responsibility to ensure that everyone enjoys at least the minimum standard. Such an approach recognises that not everyone starts from the same 'rung in the ladder': there are inequalities in our societies (class, gender, disability and ethnicity). To achieve social justice, government policy needs to take account of the unequal conditions. Government needs to design policies and allocate resources accordingly.

In *Sex and Social Justice* (1999) Nussbaum extends her general theory of 'human justice' to feminism. She argues that women's rights and equality can be achieved through a liberal approach that places emphasis on a respect for human dignity, whereby all people have a right to be viewed as having equal worth. She states that liberalism 'must respect and promote the liberty of choice, and it must respect and promote the equal worth of persons as choosers'. Radical and socialist feminists have often criticised liberal feminism for what they consider to be its failure to address patriarchal structures in society and in particular the male dominance of the private sphere (home). While Nussbaum recognises the influence of patriarchy (as outlined by Walby) and the role played by 'unjust institutions and laws', she argues that the full application of her 'human justice' approach would address these. Nussbaum's analysis of the position of women in non-western cultures, and controversial issues such as the practice of genital mutilation, reflects important and long-standing tensions between the universality of human rights and respect for cultural beliefs and traditions (see Chapter 8).

Nussbaum has also made specific contributions to thinking on education. She proposes that we use education systems to cultivate humanity and global citizenship, rather than focusing on future professionals to contribute to our economies. Nussbaum looks to the arts and humanities (psychology, sociology, politics, philosophy, etc.) and points to important skills that can be learned here and incorporated in education systems at primary, secondary and third levels. These skills include the ability to think critically and to approach social and political problems beyond our self-interests. We can learn to think as 'global citizens', which will ultimately benefit society and democracy. You will have noticed how the Politics and Society course is based on these very ideas.

Summary: Main elements of Nussbaum's theory

- Traditional approaches to measuring a country's development (i.e. GDP or income) mask inequalities and do not capture the quality of life of its population.
- The *capabilities* approach involves measuring the real opportunities people have in shaping their own lives (health, education, work and business, voting, political and social affiliations).
- The capabilities approach has been used by the United Nations in its annual Human Development Reports, as well as approaches to measuring 'wellbeing' in many countries.
- Government policy should promote the conditions necessary for people to enjoy positive freedoms and rights.
- There are ten 'universal fundamental political entitlements' (as above).
- Women's rights and equality can be achieved through a liberal 'human justice' approach that places emphasis on a respect for human dignity, whereby all people have a right to be viewed as having equal worth.
- Education systems should aim to cultivate humanity and global citizenship, rather than simply producing future professionals to contribute to our economies.

Paulo Freire (1921–1997)

Paulo Freire was a Brazilian educator and social activist who developed important and influential ideas on the role of education in liberation. Freire was born to a middle-class family in 1920s Brazil. His family slipped into poverty following the Great Depression. Qualifying as a teacher, Freire devoted his life to educating the poor and illiterate communities of his home city of Recife. Freire criticised the traditional teaching method (*pedagogy*) of the time. He believed it dehumanised people and maintained the status quo of society. Through his writings and application of popular teaching methods, Freire was so successful in literacy education that his model was formally replicated by the government in every state of Brazil. However, following the 1964 military *coup d'état* in Brazil, Freire was briefly imprisoned. He lived in exile for 15 years, as his methods were considered subversive by the military regime. While in exile, Freire developed his ideas in several important books: *Education as the Practice of Freedom* (1967), *Pedagogy of the Oppressed* (1968) and *Education for Critical Consciousness* (1973).

As we learned in Chapter 2, Freire's main argument was that education is never 'neutral': it involves the active selection (and exclusion) of the types of knowledge that are imparted in society. Freire believed that traditional pedagogy maintains the status quo in society. The student is a passive actor receiving information and knowledge from the teacher, in a method of 'banking education': the teacher makes deposits of knowledge in the mind (bank) of the passive student. This dehumanises the student and leads to what Freire calls a 'culture of silence'. Students, and therefore citizens, do not develop the ability and skills to critically reflect on society and their lives. Instead, they passively accept all knowledge received through education, without question. Freire shared Marx's understanding of societal divisions and class conflict. He considered traditional approaches to education as serving the interests of the dominant class. However, he believed that just as education could play a role in maintaining oppressive relations in a society, education could also liberate.

Freire offered an alternative to the traditional approach of 'banking education'. He argued for 'problem-posing education'. In this model, critical inquiry, active dialogue, and mutually respectful learning between students and teachers in 'culture circles' (groups of 12–25 students) is a central approach. The classroom becomes a democratic space where the voices of students and teachers are equal. Students must question all representations of knowledge ('codifications') and deconstruct them through a process of 'decodification'. He strongly believed that education should have the active involvement of the student, with his or her own experiences and knowledge valued as an input in the process. Freire's model was based on a cycle whereby we critically reflect on an issue or subject, take action in relation to the issue, and critically reflect once more. Freire termed this process 'praxis'. Through 'praxis', Freire believed that students would develop a critical consciousness ('conscientisation') and have the skills and capacity to become better citizens who are able to contribute to society and address injustices. The approach has influenced modern teaching methodologies, social movements, and is the dominant teaching and training method used by international development agencies and non-governmental organisations in the developing world.

Summary: Main elements of Freire's theory

- Traditional approaches to education are based on a 'banking' methodology, whereby the teacher deposits knowledge in the minds of passive students.
- 'Banking education' maintains the status quo in society, and facilitates a 'culture of silence'.
- Freire's alternative approach is 'problem-posing education', which is based on active dialogue between students and teachers. The classroom is a democratic space.
- Dialogue is based on 'praxis': a cycle of critical reflection/action/critical reflection.
- 'Problem-posing education' will lead to 'conscientisation' – the development of a critical consciousness.

Index

A
ActionAid 393–5, 404, 453–4
Active citizenship 34, 173–4, 180–1, 233, 268, 448, 451
anarchy 73
Anderson, Benedict 321, 368
Angola 276–9
anthropology 11
anti-bullying contracts 46
Appiah, Kwame Anthony 360
Arendt, Hannah 2
Asian economic growth 392–3
asylum seekers 290, 291
autocracy 71–2
autonomy 37

B
Banking Inquiry 220
biodiversity 428–9
blasphemy 211
Bolivia 432, 433
Bowles, Sam 42, 43
Bretton Woods system 363–4
Brexit 131
Broadcasting Authority of Ireland (BAI) 193, 196, 211, 213, 214, 217, 218, 219
Buddhism 345–6
Bunreacht na hÉireann (1937) 97, 98, 162, 209, 210, 235, 241, 249
Burke, Edmund 75

C
capitalism 4, 23, 24, 35, 79
carbon footprint 379
Catalans 352–3
Central Statistics Office (CSO) 33, 80, 81, 147, 161
children
    corporal punishment and 284, 285, 286–7, 296, 309
    see also United Nations Convention on the Rights of the Child (UNCRC)
Children's and Young People's Constitutional Convention 177–8
citizen 69
citizen journalism 192, 199–200, 227–8, 229, 231
citizen voice 175–9
Citizens' Assembly 175
citizenship 34, 173–4, 180–1, 233
city councils 154, 172
civil religion 19
civil service 153–4
civil society 69, 85–6, 92, 158, 168
clash of civilisations 361
climate change 378, 379, 441–3, 455
Clonakilty, Co. Cork 450
Cloughjordan Ecovillage 434–7
colonialism 396
Comhairle na nÓg 175
Commission on Freedom of the Press 210
communism 5, 23, 24, 35
Competition and Consumer Protection Act 2014 225
conservatism 5, 8, 35
constituencies/constituents 106, 107–8
Constitutional Convention 175, 177–8, 211
consumers 382
corruption 402–4
Corruption Perception Index (CPI) 404, 405
cosmopolitanism 360
Council of Europe 128–30, 137, 171, 182, 292, 309
county councils 154, 172, 176, 179
Court of Justice of the EU 116
courts 98, 99, 116
CSA concept 438, 439
cultural appropriation 346
cultural assimilation 354
cultural convergence 340
cultural diffusion 340
cultural divergence 340
cultural diversity 312, 330
cultural iceberg 320
cultural imperialism 298
cultural integration 339, 354
culture 314–20, 343, 368
    dominant 315
    globalisation and 340
    high culture 343
    identity and 314, 338
    immigration and 344–5
    non-western 314, 360, 361
    popular 315, 343
    subcultures 315
    western 314, 360, 361

D
Dahl, Robert A. 50
Dáil Éireann 98, 102, 105–6, 107–8, 114, 120, 172
    see also Teachtaí Dála (TDs)
Dáil na nÓg 175–6
de Valera, Éamon 325, 329
Defamation Act 2009 211
deforestation 381
democracy 14, 72–3, 74
    deliberative 21, 173–4, 175
    direct 72, 74, 77, 92
    media and 208–9, 231
    parliamentary 114

representative 72, 74, 75–7
dependency theory 396–401, 406
developing countries 270, 299, 384
development 371, 373
   approaches to 302
   consumption growth 377–82
   dependency theory 396–401, 406
   evolution of the right to 303
   GDP and 373, 406
   Global Goals 306, 308
   global population growth 377
   HDI and 270, 273, 374–5, 404, 406
   international cooperation 305–6
   Irish Aid and 307
   MDGs 306
   modernisation theory and 386–9, 406
   overpopulation 382
   right to 302–3
   SDGs 306, 307, 308, 309
   UN Declaration on the Right to 303–4, 305
   unequal 383–5
   unsustainable 376, 406
   women and 390–1, 406
   see also sustainable development
dictatorship 72
discrimination 64–5, 256–7, 258–9
diversity, EU and 347–8, 349–51, 368
Durkheim, Émile 40, 43, 60, 322, 458

E
eco-friendly vehicles 423–4
eco-theologian 430–1
ECO-UNESCO Young Environmentalist Awards 444–5
ecological deficit 433
ecological footprint 433
Economic and Social Research Institute (ESRI) 33, 157
ecovillage 434–7
Educate Together, Ireland 57–8

education 41–4
   discrimination and 258–9
   feminist perspective 43–4
   functionalist perspective 43
   inequality and 42–3
   Irish national identity and 326–8
   Marxist perspective 42
   in Northern Ireland 334–7
   right to 249, 250–1, 254–5, 271
   right to, in Ireland 253
   state obligations and 252–3
Education Act, 1998 54, 56, 146
Education (Admission to Schools) Bill 2014 63
Electoral (Amendment) (Political Funding) Act 2012 134
electoral systems 132–3, 137
emoji language 342
Engels, Friedrich 5, 22, 35
Enlightenment 16
Equal Status Acts 256–7
equality 25–6, 81, 254–5, 263
equality of condition 255
Eriksen, Thomas Hylland 361
ethnic diversity 352–5
ethnic identity 355, 368
ethnicity 316–17, 349
   community and 357–8
   genocide and 356–7
EU Charter of Fundamental Rights 56
EU (European Union) 124
   bailout agreement (2010) 178
   diversity in 347–8, 349–51
   government in 124–31, 137, 138
   Ireland and 152
   languages 350
   migration 348–9
   UK and 131
EU legislation 170–1
EU treaties 152, 170, 182
Eurobarometer surveys 192
European Central Bank (ECB) 178
European Commission 130–1, 137, 171, 182, 192
European Convention on Human Rights (ECHR) 168, 209, 270, 293–4, 309

European Council 129, 137, 171
European Court of Human Rights 293, 295–6
   impacts in Ireland 297
European Parliament 125–8, 137, 171, 182
   MEPs and 125–6, 127–8
   political groups in 126

F
Fairtrade 449–50
Fairtrade town (Clonakilty) 450
fascism 7, 35
feminism 9, 35, 43–4, 66, 196, 231, 343
Fianna Fáil 87, 91
Fine Gael 8, 87, 91, 141
Fingal County Council 176
Foucault, Michel 61, 264
Foy, Lydia 167–8
France 353–5
Frank, Andre Gunder 396, 397
free market environmentalism (FME) 415–16, 422
Freire, Paulo 42, 464–5
Friedman, Milton 263
Friends of the Earth 437–9
functionalists 43, 195, 231, 343

G
Gellner, Ernest 321
gender 84, 92, 134, 147
Gender Equality Index 81
Gender Recognition Act 2015 167–9
Gender Recognition Advisory Group (GRAG) 168
Gender Recognition Bill 2014 163, 168, 169
General Agreement on Tariffs and Trade (GATT) 364
General Election (2002) 91
General Election (2011) 217–18
genetically modified (GM) crops 425–7, 428
Germany 439
Gini coefficient 127, 386
Gintis, Herb 42, 43
global development 300, 301, 371–406
   see also development; sustainable development

global economic decision-making 363–4
global emissions 380
global pop culture 341
global poverty 300, 301
global warming 378, 455
globalisation 312, 339–40, 363, 368, 371
   UNDP and 366–7
Good Friday Agreement (1998) 117, 121, 137
government
   head, selection of 115
   human rights obligations 247
   minority government 155, 182
   non-democratic country and 123–4
   selection of 96
   separation of powers and 97, 98
   types of 71–3
government in the EU 124–31, 137, 138
government institutions 94, 97–8
government of Ireland 136, 138
   Cabinet of Ministers and 113, 136
   checks and balances 97, 99
   coalition government 114
   committee system and 103, 136
   Constitution of Ireland and 97, 98
   departments 113
   executive 97, 98, 99, 113–14, 151
   judiciary 97, 98, 99
   legislature 97, 98, 99, 102–3, 104, 105–6
   separation of powers 97, 98, 100
   Taoiseach and 113, 114, 136
   see also Dáil Éireann; Oireachtas; Seanad Éireann
government in Northern Ireland 117–21, 137
Green Party 9, 91
green politics 9, 35
green revolution 425–7
Green-Schools 446–8

greenhouse gas emissions 441–2

H
Hammarberg, Thomas 167
Havel, Václav 60
heads of government, selection of 115
Health Insurance Act, 1994 172
Higgins, Michael D. 173
Hitler, Adolf 7, 72
Hobbes, Thomas 14–15, 36, 40, 52, 76, 96
homelessness 86
Human Development Index (HDI) 270, 373, 374–5, 404, 405
human rights 77, 234–6
   absolute 244
   Angola and 276–9
   conventions 274–5
   debates on 263–4, 298–9
   development, right to 302–3
   duty bearers 246, 247–8
   in Europe 292–6
   inalienable 243–4
   indivisible 244
   limited 244
   media and 237
   national institutions in Ireland 260
   principles 242–4
   qualified 244–5
   religion and 281–2
   responsibilities and 269–309
   rights holders 246
   Special Rapporteurs 274
   timeline 240–1
   types of 241–2
   Universal Periodic Review (UPR) 274–5
   see also European Convention on Human Rights (ECHR); United Nations Convention on the Rights of the Child (UNCRC); Universal Declaration of Human Rights (1948)
Huntington, Samuel 361

I
identity 368
   commemorations, role of 324–5

   cultural diversity 330
   culture and 314, 338
   education and 322, 326–8
   in a global age 359–61
   Irish national 323–8, 329, 368
   in modern Ireland 329–33
   national 321, 322
   national identities, Ireland and 321, 330
identity politics 361
ideology 1
immigration 344–5, 349, 354
Independent News and Media (INM) 225
Indonesia 115
inequality 25–6, 92, 384–5
   economic 80–1, 384
   education and 42–3, 147
   measurement 386
   school policies and 62–4
information and communication technology (ICT) 341, 385
International Civic and Citizenship Education Study (ICCS) 54
International Covenant on Civil and Political Rights (ICCPR) 77, 209
International Monetary Fund (IMF) 178, 363, 364, 365–6
Ireland–Zambia tax treaty 453–4
Irish Human Rights and Equality Commission (IHREC) 259, 261
Irish Times 220
Irish Water 172, 178

J
justice system 116

L
Labour Party (Irish) 91
laissez-faire 6–7
Law Society 172
law-making process 162, 167–9
   Acts and 162, 163
   bills, development and publication of 162–7, 182
   Dáil and 163–4, 166
   Green Papers and 162
   primary legislation 162–3

private members' bills 163, 164, 168
  Seanad and 164, 166
laws/legislation 141, 142, 143, 146, 150–1, 152
  EU legislation 170–1
  primary legislation 162–3
  secondary legislation 171–2
  statutory instruments 171, 172
learning methodologies
  debate 32
  group work 30–1
  jigsaw learning 31
  research activities 33
  research tips 33–4
  think–pair–share 30
libel 211
liberalism 4, 5, 6, 7
libertarianism 8, 35
Lincoln, Abraham 72
lobbying/lobbyists 158, 159–60
Locke, John 16–17, 40, 53, 76, 96, 149, 245, 263
Lukes, Steven 60
Lynch, Kathleen 25–6, 63, 64, 84, 149, 255

M

McDonagh, Seán, Fr 430–1
Madison, James 75
Maori 357–8
Marriage Equality referendum (2015) 179, 229
Marx, Karl 5, 12, 13, 22–3, 35, 40, 149
  class struggle and 64, 79, 84
  concept of alienation 42
  division of power 50
  human rights, power and 264
  main theories 24
  political representation 76
  selection of government 96
Marxism 5, 66, 195, 223, 231, 343
media 185–231
  agenda-setting theory 197, 198, 199–200
  BAI and 193, 196, 211, 213, 214, 217, 218, 219
  banking crisis and 220
  broadcast 187, 231

CNN effect 199
consolidation 224, 231
consumption patterns 189–90
content analysis 189
control of 213, 214, 215, 223, 224, 227–8, 231
democracy and 208–9, 231
digital 187, 188, 231
EU consumption 192
external influencers of 216
feminist perspective 196, 231
framing and 200–2
freedom of the press 208, 209, 226–7, 229, 231
functionalist perspective 195, 231
General Election (2011) and 217–18
Irish consumption patterns 193
Marxist perspective 195, 223, 231
mass media 185, 189
neo-Marxist perspective 223
ownership of 213, 215, 223, 224–7, 231
pluralism 223, 224, 225
policy-makers and 156
postmodernist perspective 223
power and influence of 197–8, 227, 231
print 187, 188, 231
propaganda and 201, 208, 226
public relations materials and 221–2
rights and responsibilities of 208–9
role in society 194–6, 231
social responsibility 208, 210, 211–12, 230
traditional 186, 188, 231
UK General Elections 227
US consumption 191–2
as watchdog 194
see also social media
Media Pluralism Monitor report 225
Medical Council 172
meditation 346

meritocracy 42, 43
migration 344, 348–9, 353–4
Mill, Harriet Taylor 21
Mill, John Stuart 20–1, 40, 96
Mills, C. Wright 50
minority government 155, 182
modernisation theory 386–9, 396, 406
monarchy 71, 115, 123–4
monoculturalism 312
Montesquieu, Baron de 76, 98
Moore, Wilbert E. 12
Mother Earth, rights and 432–3, 455
Mother Earth Day 432
multinational companies (MNCs) 390, 392, 397–8, 399, 400–1, 452–3
multiculturalism 312, 368
Murdoch, Rupert 226–7
Music Television (MTV) 341
Myanmar 392–3

N

nation 321
neo-liberalism 7
neo-Marxism 5, 223
neocolonialism 397
Nine Seeds movement 428, 429
Northern Ireland 117–21
  devolution and 117, 137
  discrimination, schools and 258–9
  education, segregated 334–7
  government in 117–21, 137, 138
  nationalist community 117
  power-sharing 117, 121, 137
  unionist community 117
Northern Ireland Assembly 118–19, 137
Northern Ireland Executive 119–20, 121
Northern Ireland Human Rights Commission (NIHRC) 259, 260
Nozick, Robert 150, 263, 460–1
Nussbaum, Martha 264, 462–4

O

Obama, Barack 159
Office of the Ombudsman 163
Oireachtas 136

INDEX **469**

committee system and 103
county councils and 154
policies, monitoring and 161
President and 98, 104, 105, 112
representatives 105–8
see also Dáil Éireann; Seanad Éireann
Oireachtas TV 104
oligarchy 72
Ombudsman for Children's Office (OCO) 261
orientalism 360
Oxfam 392, 393

P
Parnell, Charles Stewart 166
Parsons, Talcott 43
Pearse, Patrick 326–7
planetary boundaries 430
Plato 96
Pledge A Bed campaign 179
Poland 439
policies 141, 142, 145
civil society bodies and 158
decision-makers and 150–1
education policies 146
inequality and 147
influencers and 150, 151, 155
lobbyists and 159
media and 156
political parties and 155
public policy 143, 145, 182
research institutes and 157
think tanks and 157
universities and 157
policy-making 161
citizen participation and 173–4
citizen voice and 175–6
Green Papers and 161
political globalisation 363
political ideologies 4–9
political parties 70, 87, 88, 155
electoral manifesto and 143, 144
party political broadcasts (PPBs) 219
party whip system 99, 166
social divisions, Europe and 87–8
political representation 69, 70, 74–6, 92, 97–8
political science 11
political spectrum 1, 4, 35, 45
politics 2–3, 35
power 37, 50, 66
enforcement of rules 60–1
power struggles, social divisions and 84, 149
President of Ireland 98, 104, 105, 112, 136, 167, 182
processors 399
propaganda 201, 208, 226
Proportional Representation by a Single Transferable Vote (PR-STV) 21, 108–9, 133, 136
Public Participation Networks (PPNs) 176
public relations (PR) 216, 221–2

R
Raidió Teilifís Éireann (RTÉ) 211, 213, 217–18
Rawls, John 263
Reagan, Ronald 7
refugees 179, 290
Regulation of Lobbying Act 2015 159
religion 19, 281–2, 316, 337, 345–6, 350–1
religious fundamentalism 9, 35
retailers 400
Right2Water campaign 178
Robespierre, Maximilien 243
Rokkan, Stein 87–8
Rousseau, Jean-Jacques 18–19, 52, 76, 245, 263
rules 38, 41, 60–2
see also school rules
Rwanda 388–9

S
Said, Edward 360
Saudi Arabia 123–4
school rules 39, 41, 45–50, 60, 66
anti-bullying contracts and 46
Early School Leaving (ESL) and 46–7
impact of 62
mobile phone ban and 45
stakeholders and 48–9, 50
zero tolerance and 46–7
schools
admission policies 63, 258
corporal punishment and 286–7
decision-making and 51, 52–3, 66
discrimination and 257
policies, social inequality and 62–4
religion and 283
standing desks and 47
student councils and 53–5
Seanad Éireann 98, 102–3, 110–11, 136, 164, 166, 172
sectarian 336
segregationism 335
Sen, Amartya 263–4, 299
Shiva, Vandana 428–9
Simon Community 86
Single European Act (1986) 152
Sinn Féin 91
skills/key skills
being personally effective 27, 29, 36
communicating 28, 36
critical and creative thinking 29–30, 36
information processing 27–8, 36
working with others 29, 36
social class 12, 22, 23, 25, 80, 84, 92
social conflict theory 12, 13, 35, 66, 79, 196
social divisions
party systems and 87–8
power struggles and 84, 149
social media 179, 185, 191–2, 227–8, 229, 230, 342
social partnership 158
social status 84
social stratification 12, 35, 78
in Ireland 80–1
theories of 12–13, 78–9
Social Web for Inclusive and Transparent democracy (SOWIT) 176
socialism 5, 23, 24, 35
society 11–12, 35
cleavages in 87–8
groups in 77–8
the role of education in 41–4
sociology 11, 12, 13, 35, 66

South African wildlife ranches 417–18
sovereignty 363, 368
spin doctors 216
state 321
state agencies 153
student councils 53–5
student voice 55, 56, 57–9
supranational organisations 363
sustainable development 409–55
  biodiversity 428–9
  conservation projects 417–18
  eco-friendly vehicles 423–4
  environmental problems and 415–16
  free market environmentalism (FME) 415–16, 422
  green revolution 425–7
  harmony with nature 429–30
  local–global relationship 414
  MDGs 411, 412
  planetary boundaries 430
  SDGs and 412
  summits and 411, 412
  three pillars of 413–14
  tragedy of the commons 416
  water markets 419–22
symbolic interactionism 12, 13

T
Taisce, An 446–8
Tanzania 393–5
Taoiseach 113, 114, 136
tariffs 397
tax justice 409, 451–2, 453–4, 455
Teachtaí Dála (TDs) 106–8, 112, 114, 133, 134, 136
  party whip system and 99, 166
theocracy 73
Think-tank for Action on Social Change (TASC) 80–1, 157
tied aid 397–8, 406
trade
  dependency theory and 399–401, 406
  fair 409, 455
Fairtrade 449–50
Transgender Equality Network Ireland (TENI) 168
Trócaire 441–3

U
UN Declaration on the Right to Development 303–4, 305
UN General Comments 275
UN Treaty Bodies 274, 275
Union of Soviet Socialist Republics (USSR) 5–6
United Kingdom (UK) 115, 131, 133, 227
United Nations, periodic reports and 261
United Nations Convention on the Rights of the Child (UNCRC) 56, 175, 235, 249, 269, 270, 271–2, 309
  Article 6 and 275–8
  Article 14 and 281–2
  Article 19 and 284–6
  Article 31 and 288–90
  global implementation of 273
  summary of 272
United Nations Development Programme (UNDP) 366–7
United Nations Human Rights Council 274
United Nations Security Council 121
United States, selection of President 115
Universal Declaration of Human Rights (1948) 209, 235, 236, 238–9, 271
Uplift 179
utilitarianism 20, 21

V
veto 121
Voices of Youth Group 177
voting
  patterns 89–91
  PR-STV and 21, 108–9

W
Walby, Sylvia 64, 84, 149, 461–2
water 379–80
water charges, protests and 178, 201
water markets 419–22
Water Services (No.2) Bill 2013 178
water stress index 380
We The Citizens 175
Weber, Max 13, 50, 79, 84, 149
women
  Asian economic growth and 392–3
  development and 390–1
  land use and 394–5
World Bank 363, 364
World Trade Organization (WTO) 363, 364

X
xenophobia 7, 212

Y
yoga 346

Z
Zambia 453–4
Zappone, Katherine 168
Zionism 9

Acknowledgements

For permission to reproduce artwork, the authors and publisher acknowledge the following copyright holders:

© **ActionAid**: 453 (all), 454CR • © **Don Addis**: 197 • © **Advertising Archives**: 201BR (both) • © **Alamy**: 19, 21, 23TR, 32, 40C, 43CL, 43CL, 50CL, 60TL, 60CL, 61, 76BR, 84CL, 86BR, 98CR, 118, 120T, 121, 149TR, 154TR, 174C, 189 (Sky logo), 204TL, 204TR, 240CRT, 240BR, 241TR, 258CR, 275BC, 278, 281CL, 318BR, 321BL, 322, 323TL, 323TR, 323CR, 325, 334, 335T, 345BR, 354CR, 356CRT, 357BR, 358TC, 360CR, 361TL, 417TL, 422, 425CR, 428TL, 439BR, 459 • © **Anti-Austerity Alliance/People Before Profit**: 88 (table) • © **Associated Press**: 37CR, 72CR, 87, 202TR, 202CL, 202CR, 202BR, 364, 391TR, 418TR, 433, 442BR • © **Bigstock.com**: 117 • © **Broadcasting Authority of Ireland**: 214 • © **Can Stock Photo/Tawng**: 228 • © **Council of Europe**: 292CR, 293BR, 296 • © **CSO** (www.cso.ie): 81 • © **Dailyexpress.co.uk/N&S Syndication**: 201TR • © **Daily Star/N&S Syndication**: 204CR • **courtesy of the Department of Children and Youth Affairs**: 176TR • **courtesy of the Department of Education and Skills**: 146TR • **courtesy of the Department of the Taoiseach**: 146CR, 151BR, 168, 254 • **courtesy of the Disability Federation of Ireland**: 86TC • **courtesy of Principal Eileen Doherty and students of Gardiner Street School**: 317TR • **the logo of the Dublin Simon Community is used by kind permission of the organisation**: 86BL • © **ECO-UNESCO**: 444BR, 445TR • **courtesy of Educate Together**: 57BR • **courtesy of Equality Challenge Unit, 'Know Your Numbers: 2014'** (www.ecu.ac.uk/publications/know-numbers/): 147BL • © **EurActiv**: 401BR • © **European Court of Human Rights**: 295T, 295B • © **European People's Party**: 8C • © **European Union**: 129TL, 130TL • **courtesy of The Executive Office of Northern Ireland**: 97C, 120CR • © **Fairtrade**: 449 (both), 450 • © **Fianna Fáil**: 88 (table), 155BC • © **Fine Gael**: 88 (table), 155BR • **courtesy of Fingal County Council; graphic by Resonate**: 176B • © **Foundation for Economic Education**: 389BLB • © **Friends of the Earth**: 437BC • © **Friends of the Earth** (*Eating from the Farm: the social, environmental, and economic benefits of local food systems*): 437BR, 438, 439TR, 439CR • © **Getty Images**: 7CR, 9BR, 20, 40TR, 46BR, 71, 72TR, 89, 96TR, 96BL, 107BR, 128CL, 195 (photograph), 302, 323BL, 324CLT, 335BR, 340, 343TR, 353CL, 354TR, 356CRB, 363BR, 387TR, 390BR, 404, 419BL • © **Green Party**: 9TL, 88 (table) • © **Green Schools Ireland**: 446 (both) • **Flickr/Joelle Hatem/Creative Commons**: 236TL • **courtesy of the Houses of the Oireachtas**: 98TL, 100TC, 102TC, 102CL, 103, 104CR, 106CR, 141T, 161BR, 164CL, 164CR, 165, 166 • © **Immigrant Council of Ireland, 2014 'Count Us In' project (Naoise Culhane)**: 330TR • © **Independents 4 Change**: 88 (table) • **courtesy and with assistance of Irish Aid**: 307 (logo and all photograph) • © www.irishcentral.com: 107TC • **courtesy of Irish Congress of Trade Unions**: 86C • **courtesy of Irish Council for Civil Liberties (ICCL) and Children's Rights Alliance**: 56 • © *Irish Examiner*/www.examiner.ie: 4R, 62CR, 107TL, 107TR, 107CL, 145BR, 156CR, 157C, 237BR • **courtesy of Irish Human Rights and Equality Commission** (www.ihrec.ie): 259B • © *Irish Independent*: 4C, 7BRC, 90BCL, 145TL, 156BL, 201CR (both), 237TL, 389BLT, 454BR • **courtesy of** *Irish Medical Times*: 107CR • **courtesy of the Irish Refugee Council** (www.irishrefugeecouncil.ie): 86TL • © *Irish Tatler*/Harmonia: 343CRT • **courtesy of the Irish Wheelchair Association**: 86CL • © **iStockphoto.com**: 104T, 115T, 196TR, 258BR, 288, 293CL • © www.journal.ie: 90BR, 111BL, 156BR, 454BC • © **Stephano Kaniki Gogi/ActionAid**: 394TL • © **KaungHtet/Oxfam**: 393TR • © **Labour Party**: 88 (table) • © **Suzanne Lee**: 428BL, 428BR • **by permission Mike Luckovich and Creators Syndicate, Inc**: 160 • © **LWR/Jake Lyell**: 390BL • **courtesy of Kathleen Lynch**: 25, 64TL, 84CR, 149CR, 255 • © **Maxwell Photography**: 113 • © **John McElroy**: 282 • **courtesy of the Minister of Jobs, Enterprise and Innovation**: 97L • © **Mirrorpix**: 201TCB • **courtesy of the National Youth Council of Ireland**: 86TR • © **Nicholas Kristof/The New York Times/Redux/eyevine**: 279 • © **cartoon by Nicholson from** *The Australian* newspaper (www.nicholsoncartoons.com.au): 397 • **courtesy of the Northern Ireland Human Rights Commission**: 260 • **courtesy of the Ombudsman for Children**: 261 • **courtesy of Pearse Museum/OPW**: 327BL • © **Photocall Ireland**: 70TR, 133, 323CL, 330CR, 365 • © **Press Association**: 37CR • © **illustration by Richard Wilkinson**: 63 • © **RTÉ Archives**: 2, 217, 218, 274CR • © **RTÉ.ie**: 90BCR, 157BC • © **RTÉ**: 156TCL, 189 (logo), 213BL • © **Sinn Féin**: 88 (table), 155BL • © **Shutterstock Inc.**: 11, 31TR, 33, 37T, 45BR, 46TR, 47, 62BR, 65T, 69T, 69CR, 72BR, 73CR, 75TL, 94, 97R, 98TC, 98TR, 100CL, 100CR, 101, 115CRB, 115BR, 123CR, 125TR, 125CR, 129TR, 130BR, 131CR, 131BL, 131BR, 147TL, 147TR, 152TR, 152CR, 154CR, 156TL, 156TCR, 156CR, 163TR, 170CR, 170BR, 173, 180, 185, 187, 188 (all), 189 (all except RTÉ and Sky logos), 191BL, 191BR, 196CR, 199, 204CL, 209, 211, 212, 219, 220, 226B, 229, 230, 240TR, 244BR, 249, 259, 262, 273CL, 273BL, 273BR, 284, 286, 292BR, 303, 305, 312T, 315TR, 316CR, 316CL, 323CL, 339, 343CRT, 343BR, 344TR, 345TR, 345CRT, 346CR, 353TR, 371T, 374, 376, CR, 376CL, 376BL, 376BR, 376BC, 377CR, 388CRT, 389TR, 414 (all), 419CRT, 419CRB, 425TR, 426B, 428CR, 429BR • **Solo Syndication/MailOnline**: 204BL • **courtesy of St Louis High School**: 58 • **courtesy of Summerhill School**: 57CR • © *The Sunday Business Post*/www.businesspost.ie: 111TR, 145TR • © **TASC** (www.tasc.ie): 80 • © **TG4**: 213BR • © *The Irish Times*: 4L, 6BL, 7BL, 7BLC, 7BL, 26TC, 26TR, 62CL, 62C, 90BL, 106CR, 109, 111TL, 111BR, 145C, 145BL, 156TR, 157CL, 157BR, 167TR, 178BR, 195BR, 201 CL (both), 253, 283, 291TC, 291BR, 328, 389BC, 401BL, 401BCL, 401BRT, 434TR, 434CL, 435TR, 435CR, 435CL, 436TR, 436CL, 436BR, 437TR, 454BL • © *The Times*/News Syndication: 204BR, 227TL, 227TR, 237TR, 237BL • **courtesy of Trócaire**: 441TR, 443 • © **2017 UN**: 238, 269CRT, 274TR, 274BR, 275TR, 366BR • © **UN Photo/Cia Pak**: 412T • © **UN Photo/Mark Garten**: 357TR • **courtesy of Uplift**: 179 • **courtesy of US Coastguard**: 202TL • © **Jaap van't Veen** (www.flickr.com/photos/vtveen/403267754): 416 • © **Gary Varvel**: 200CRB • © *Village Magazine*: 26TL • **courtesy of Sylvia Walby/photograph supplied by Lancaster University**: 64TR, 84TR, 149CL, 462 • **Wikicommons**: 8L, 9CL, 14, 16TR, 17, 22, 23R, 40TL, 40TC, 40CL, 50BR, 52TL, 52TC, 52TR, 64TC, 75CL, 76TL, 76TR, 76CL, 76CR, 79, 84TL, 96TL, 96CL, 96CR, 102TL, 112, 115CRT, 123CL, 127BR, 149TL, 149TC, 153, 174CL, 174CL (both), 174CR (both), 240CRB, 243BL, 245(both), 327TR, 358TR, 361BL, 424TR, 430, 445BR, 463 • © **World Political Journal**: 389BR • **courtesy of Youth Work Ireland**: 54

The authors and publisher have made every effort to trace all copyright owners, but if any material has inadvertently been reproduced without permission, they would be happy to make the necessary arrangement at the earliest opportunity, and encourage owners of copyright material not acknowledged to make contact.

educate.ie

Redeeming Educate.ie ebooks

You are entitled to one complimentary ebook of this textbook.

To avail of this ebook, complete the following steps:

1. Visit Educate.ie and click the "**Redeem Ebooks**" button.
2. Select "**Sign in**" or "**Create Account**" ensuring you are using the correct email address*.
3. In your account, you will be asked to enter your redeem code. Enter this code ➔ and select "**Check Code**".

   Power + People Portfolio

   PP-BDD4CC

4. If the title is correct, select "**Yes, redeem my ebook**".**
5. Your title is now redeemed. To access your Educate.ie ebook app, select "**Ebook App**" or select "**Redeem Ebooks**" to redeem any further titles.

* ebook redeemable to one email address only.
** If the title is incorrect, select "**No, contact support**".

Free resources online

When you create an ebook account (see above), an account will also be created for you on **educateplus.ie** – our free Digital Resource site.

You can also go directly to **educateplus.ie**, if you wish, without redeeming an ebook and register an account there.

1. Visit **www.educateplus.ie**, and click 'Register', completing the online form.
2. Once logged in, select your textbook and access your resources using the same redeem code above.
3. Each time you log in, your resources will be in your dashboard.

If you need any help, please contact us at **support@educateplus.ie** and make sure to tell us what book you're using!